THOMAS CARTWRIGHT AND ELIZABETHAN PURITANISM 1535–1603

CAMBRIDGE
UNIVERSITY PRESS

LONDON: Fetter Lane

NEW YORK
The Macmillan Co.

BOMBAY, CALCUTTA and MADRAS
Macmillan and Co., Ltd.

TORONTO
The Macmillan Co. of Canada, Ltd.

TOKYO
Maruzen-Kabushiki-Kaisha

Mr. THO: CARTWRIGHT.

THOMAS CARTWRIGHT AND ELIZABETHAN PURITANISM

1535–1603

BY

THE REV. A. F. SCOTT PEARSON,

M.A., B.D., D.Th., F.R.Hist.S., F.S.A. (Scot.)

CAMBRIDGE

AT THE UNIVERSITY PRESS

MCMXXV

TO MY WIFE

PRINTED IN GREAT BRITAIN

PREFACE

IT has frequently been felt that a Life of Thomas Cartwright written in the light of modern historical research is long overdue. Knowing my interest in the subject several eminent scholars of the English Presbyterian Church urged me to undertake the task and now, after a few years of study at home and abroad, I present the results of my labours. My chief concern has been, not to fly in the face of tradition represented by such historians as Neal and Brook, but to test it by the touchstone of sixteenth century evidence, and to gather from contemporary sources the available data regarding the great Puritan. Most of the records consulted are preserved in London archives, *e.g.* at the Public Record Office, the British Museum, Somerset House, Dr Williams's Library, etc., but Cartwright's association with Geneva, Heidelberg, Antwerp and other cities on the Continent, and also with Cambridge, Warwick and Guernsey, has necessitated visits to most of these places. I believe that the extensive nature of the research involved has not been altogether incommensurate with the importance of the new information unearthed. I have been obliged to reject oft repeated assertions, such as that which ascribes to Cartwright the authorship of the *Second Admonition* and to rectify chronological inaccuracies of former biographers, *e.g.* in connection with his alleged visit to the Channel Islands in 1576. There are several portions of the accepted version of Cartwright's life that are extremely hazy and lacking in detail, *e.g.* those relating to his sojourn in Geneva, the eleven years of his exile, and his stay in Guernsey. To fill in these comparative blanks I have been able to collect a considerable amount of material. Of special interest is the new light obtained regarding the relations of Cartwright with the Brownists in

Zealand and his work at a later time as a Chaplain in Guernsey. My research has confirmed me in the opinion that Cartwright left an indelible mark upon the page of Elizabethan history and in particular that he occupies a place of supreme importance in the annals of Puritanism. It is impossible to disengage Cartwright's career from the movement with which he was associated. Accordingly I have sought to trace the development of the cause that was largely based upon his principles. His chief aim being the conversion of the Church of England into a Presbyterian body, the present work may be regarded as a contribution to the history of English Presbyterianism. The field that I have explored still calls for labourers and, in the hope that one piece of historical research may beget another, I have frequently pointed out problems of importance which students of history might usefully face. Among the subjects suggested for further investigation there is one that specially appeals to me as a minister of the Church of Scotland. It is the relationship that existed between the Elizabethan Puritans and the "sincere professors" in Scotland and in particular between the English and Scottish Presbyterian Hildebrands, Melville and Cartwright, and I hope that this subject will soon receive adequate treatment. When I state that Cartwright regarded the Church of Scotland as his ideal in practice I do not forget that the polity of the Scottish Church has passed through many changes and that at times it was not purely Presbyterian, but to the Puritan the Church of Scotland was a Church that aimed at being Free, National and Presbyterian, and at times this aim has been approximated and it has never been more fully realised, and that, as the Church of Scotland Act of 1921 bears witness, with full recognition of the State, than in the twentieth century.

Since the preparation of this work for the press two lectures have been published, which throw valuable light upon the connection between Elizabethan Puritanism and the Westminster Assembly. One, entitled *The Westminster Assembly—and After* (1925), by the Rev. J. Hay Colligan, furnishes a fresh study of seventeenth century Presbyterianism, its antecedents and developments; the other, a reprint of a Murtle Lecture, under the title *The English Authors of the Shorter Catechism* (1925), by Principal Sir Donald Macalister, emphasises the fact that the Westminster standards were chiefly the work of Englishmen and particularly of Cambridge men, and shows that "the tradition established by men like Cartwright two generations before had persisted and borne fruit." Both lectures point to the need, mentioned in the body of the present work, of the exhaustive treatment of the relationship between the movement led by Cartwright and the Westminster Assembly.

In the pursuit of my task I have received invaluable aid and counsel from many friends. I would acknowledge my special indebtedness to the late Mr E. G. Atkinson, F.R.Hist.S., the late Rev. Dr A. H. Drysdale, Dr Albert Peel, Mr Lockhart Campbell, M.A., Mr Thomas Kemp, Canon Toovey, Major Carey Curtis, the University Librarians at St Andrews, Glasgow, Cambridge, Leyden, Basel and Heidelberg, and the Librarian of the Church of Scotland Library, Edinburgh.

Grateful acknowledgment is also made of the contribution towards the cost of publication given by the Carnegie Trust for the Universities of Scotland.

A. F. SCOTT PEARSON

THE MANSE, WEST KILBRIDE
AYRSHIRE

CONTENTS

REFERENCES AND ABBREVIATIONS

A.C. = *Athenae Cantabrigienses*. C. H. and T. Cooper. 3 vols. 1858–1913.

Acts P.C. = *Acts of the Privy Council of England*. ed. J. R. Dasent. 1890–

A parte of a reg. = *A parte of a register, contayninge sundrie memorable matters, written by divers godly and learned in our time, which stande for and desire the reformation of our Church, in Discipline and Ceremonies, accordinge to the pure worde of God, and the Lawe of our Lande*. n.d.

A.R. = *Aërius Redivivus: or The History of the Presbyterians*. Peter Heylyn. 1670.

Arber, *Sketch* = *An Introductory Sketch to the Martin Marprelate Controversy*. E. Arber. 1879.

Baker = *History of the College of St John the Evangelist, Cambridge*. T. Baker, ed. Mayor. 2 vols. 1869.

Bancroft, *Survay* = *A Survay of the Pretended Holy Discipline*. R. Bancroft. 1593.

Bateson = *Records of the Borough of Leicester* (1509–1603). ed. Mary Bateson. 1905.

Bayne = *Book V of the Laws of Ecclesiastical Polity*. R. Hooker. ed. R. Bayne. 1902.

Birt = *The Elizabethan Religious Settlement*. H. N. Birt. 1907.

Black Book = *The Black Book of Warwick*. ed. Thomas Kemp. 1898.

Borgeaud = *Histoire de l'Université de Genève*. C. Borgeaud. 1900.

Briggs = *American Presbyterianism: its origin and early history*. C. A. Briggs. 1885.

Brook, *Lives* = *The Lives of the Puritans*. B. Brook. 3 vols. 1813.

Brook, *Mem.* = *Memoir of the Life and Writings of Thomas Cartwright*. B. Brook. 1845.

B.U.K. = *The Booke of the Universale Kirk of Scotland*. 3 vols. 1839–45.

Calderwood = *The History of the Kirk of Scotland*. D. Calderwood. 8 vols. 1842–9.

Clarke = *Lives of Sundry Modern Divines, Famous in their Generations for Learning and Piety and most of them great Sufferers in the Cause of Christ*. Appended to *A General Martyrologie*. Samuel Clarke. 1651.

Cooper, *Ann.* = *Annals of Cambridge*. C. H. Cooper. 4 vols. 1842–52.

D. & G. = *The Scottish Staple at Veere*. J. Davidson and A. Gray. 1909.

D'Ewes = *A Compleat Journal...of the House of Lords and House of Commons throughout the whole reign of Queen Elizabeth*. Simonds D'Ewes. 1693.

Dexter = *The Congregationalism of the last three hundred years, as seen in its literature.* H. M. Dexter. 1880.

Dixon = *History of the Church of England.* R. W. Dixon. 6 vols. 1891–1902.

D.N.B. = *Dictionary of National Biography.*

D.P. = *Daungerous Positions and Proceedings, published and practised within this Iland of Brytaine and under pretence of Reformation, and for the Presbiteriall Discipline.* R. Bancroft. 1593.

Drysdale = *History of the Presbyterians in England.* A. H. Drysdale. 1889.

E.E.D. = *The Early English Dissenters.* C. Burrage. 2 vols. 1912.

F. & P. = *A Full and Plaine Declaration of Ecclesiasticall Discipline owt off the word off God and off the declininge off the Churche of England from the same.* 1574.

Frere, *Hist.* = *The English Church in the Reigns of Elizabeth and James I.* W. H. Frere. 1904.

Froude = *The Reign of Elizabeth.* J. A. Froude. 5 vols. Everyman Lib.

Fuller, *C.H.* = *The Church History of Britain.* Thos Fuller. ed. J. Nichols. 3 vols. 1837.

Fuller, *Worthies* = *The History of the Worthies of England.* Thos Fuller. ed. P. A. Nuttall. 3 vols. 1840.

G.Bk = *Grace Book* Δ. *Containing the Records of the University of Cambridge for the years* 1542–1589. ed. John Venn. 1910.

Gee & Hardy = *Documents illustrative of English Church History.* H. Gee and W. J. Hardy. 1896.

Godly Letters = *Certaine godly and comfortable Letters, full of Christian consolation.* E. Dering. n.d.

Grindal Rem. = *The Remains of Edmund Grindal.* Parker Soc. 1843.

Grosart = *Memoir* of Cartwright prefixed to Cartwright's *Commentary on Colossians.* A. B. Grosart. 1864.

H. & W. = *Cambridge University Transactions during the Puritan Controversies of the* 16*th and* 17*th Centuries.* J. Heywood and T. Wright. 2 vols. 1854.

Hennessy = *Novum Repertorium Ecclesiasticum Parochiale Londinense.* G. Hennessy. 1898.

Heron = *A Short History of Puritanism.* J. Heron. 1908.

Hessels = *Ecclesiae Londino-Batavae Archivum.* Tomus II. ed. J. H. Hessels. 1889.

Kemp, *Warwick* = *A History of Warwick and its People.* Thomas Kemp. 1905.

Knox = *The Works of John Knox.* ed. D. Laing. 6 vols. 1895.

McCrie = *Life of Andrew Melville.* T. McCrie. 1899.

Martin = *Les Protestants Anglais réfugiés à Genève au temps de Calvin* 1550–1560. Charles Martin. 1915.

Matrikel = *Die Matrikel der Universität Heidelberg von* 1386 *bis* 1662. ed. G. Toepke. 3 vols. 1884–93.

Melville, *Diary* = *The Autobiography and Diary of James Melville.* 1842.

Mitchell = *Livre des Anglois.* ed. A. F. Mitchell. n.d.

Mullinger = *The University of Cambridge from the Royal Injunctions of* 1535 *to the accession of Charles the first.* J. B. Mullinger. 1884.

Mullinger, *St John's* = *St John's College, Cambridge.* J. B. Mullinger. 1901.

Neal = *The History of the Puritans.* Daniel Neal. 5 vols. 1822.

Nichols = *Progresses and Public Processions of Queen Elizabeth.* J. Nichols. 1788–1805.

Odgers = *The Old Nonconformity and the Theory of the Church.* J. E. Odgers. 1896.

Paget = *An Introduction to the Fifth Book of Hooker's Treatise of the Laws of Ecclesiastical Polity.* Francis Paget. 1907.

Parker Corresp. = *Correspondence of Matthew Parker.* Parker Soc. 1853.

Paule = *Life of Archbishop Whitgift.* G. Paule (1612) in C. Wordsworth's *Ecclesiastical Biography.* Vol. IV. 1818.

Peel = *The First Congregational Churches.* A. Peel. 1920.

Pierce, *Hist. Introd.* = *An Historical Introduction to the Marprelate Tracts.* W. Pierce. 1908.

Pierce, *John Penry* = *John Penry: his Life, Times and Writings.* W. Pierce. 1923.

Pierce, *Tracts* = *The Marprelate Tracts.* ed. W. Pierce. 1911.

P.M. = *The Presbyterian Movement in the reign of Queen Elizabeth as illustrated by the minute book of the Dedham Classis,* 1582–1589. ed. R. G. Usher. 1905.

Pollard, *Hist.* = *History of England from the accession of Edward VI to the death of Elizabeth.* A. F. Pollard. 1911.

Pur. Man. = *Puritan Manifestoes.* ed. W. H. Frere and C. E. Douglas. 1907.

R.E. = *Real-Encyklopädie.*

Rest = *The rest of the second replie of Thomas Cartvurihgt agaynst Master Doctor Vuhitgifts second ansvuer, touching the Church discipline.* 1577.

Sayle = *Early English Printed Books in the University Library, Cambridge.* C. Sayle. 4 vols. 1900–7.

Schickler = *Les Églises du Refuge en Angleterre.* Baron F. de Schickler. 3 vols. 1892.

Sec. Parte = *The Seconde Parte of a Register.* ed. A. Peel. 2 vols 1915.

2nd Rep. = *The second replie of Thomas Cartwright: agaynst Maister Doctor Whitgiftes second answer, touching the Churche Discipline.* 1575.

Soames = *Elizabethan Religious History.* H. Soames. 1839.

St. *Ann.* = *Annals of the Reformation...during Elizabeth's happy reign.* John Strype. 7 vols. 1824.

St. *Parker* = *Life and Acts of Matthew Parker*. John Strype. 3 vols. 1821.

St. *Whit.* = *Life and Acts of John Whitgift*. John Strype. 3 vols. 1822.

Survey = *A Survey of the Estate of the two Ilands Guernzey and Jarsey* in *A Full Relation of two Journeys: The One Into the Mainland of France. The Other Into some of the adjacent Ilands*. Peter Heylyn. 1656.

Sutcliffe, *Ans. to a Pet.* = *An Answere to a Certaine Libel supplicatorie...put forth under the name and title of a Petition directed to her Maiestie*. Matthew Sutcliffe. 1592.

Sutcliffe, *Exam.* = *An Examination of M. Thomas Cartwrights late Apologie*. Matthew Sutcliffe. 1596.

Sutcliffe, *Treatise* = *A Treatise of Ecclesiasticall Discipline*. Matthew Sutcliffe. 1591.

T. & S. = *A True and Short Declaration*. Robert Browne. ed. J. G. Rogers. 1888.

Transcript = *Transcript of the Registers of the Company of Stationers of London*. 1554–1640. ed. E. Arber. 5 vols. 1875–94. 1640–1708. ed. G. E. B. Eyre and C. R. Rivington. 3 vols. 1913–14.

Tupper = *History of Guernsey*. F. B. Tupper. 2nd ed. 1876.

Usher, *Reconstr.* = *The Reconstruction of the English Church*. R. G. Usher. 2 vols. 1910.

Venn, *Matrics* = *Book of Matriculations and Degrees...University of Cambridge from* 1544 *to* 1659. ed. John Venn and J. A. Venn. 1913.

Waddington, *Hist.* = *Congregational History*, 1567–1700. John Waddington. 1874.

Waddington, *Surrey* = *Surrey Congregational History*. John Waddington. 1866.

Wakeman = *An Introduction to the History of the Church of England*. H. O. Wakeman. 1908.

Wood = *Athenae Oxonienses* and *Fasti*. Anthony Wood. ed. P. Bliss. 4 vols. 1813–20.

W.W. = *The Works of John Whitgift*. Parker Soc. 3 vols. 1851–3.

Z.L. = *Zürich Letters*. Parker Soc. First Series, 1842. Second Series, 1845.

CHAPTER I

CARTWRIGHT'S ACADEMIC CAREER

Cartwright's early years—student at Cambridge—at Clare Hall—at St John's—Exilic Puritanism—Cartwright leaves the University in Mary's reign—his return to St John's—Fellow of Trinity—his oration before Elizabeth in 1564—the vestiarian controversy—Cartwright a Chaplain in Ireland—return to Cambridge—friend of Chevallier and Drusius—appointed Lady Margaret Divinity Professor in Cambridge—his lectures give rise to controversy—new University statutes promulgated—Cartwright deprived of his chair—withdraws to Geneva—his labours there as colleague of Beza—sojourn in Rouen—return to England in 1572.

THE traditional date of Thomas Cartwright's birth is 1535. Grosart deduced from the fact that he matriculated in November, 1547, that he was probably born in 1532. In the sixteenth century, however, students frequently entered the University at the age of twelve. Moreover, Cartwright's earliest biographer, Samuel Clarke, whose testimony is in many respects worthy of credence, asserts that he died in his 68th year. Accordingly we may regard the generally accepted date of his birth as probably correct. Till recently all that was known of his birthplace was that it was situated somewhere in Hertfordshire. This is the county specified by the scholars' register of St John's, Cambridge. But Urwick[1] has given good reasons for deciding upon Royston, in the hundred of Odsey, Herts, near the Cambridgeshire boundary, as the village in which he was born and brought up.

An important clue to the unravelling of Cartwright's pedigree is contained in his *Apologie* (1596), in which he supplies detailed information regarding his property at Whaddon, which, he explains in reply to the animadversions of Sutcliffe, he sold in order to enable him to purchase his manor at Saxmundham. "I solde," he writes (sig. C 4v), "of the inheritance my father and grandfather left, as faire a house for a farme, not only as is in that towne where it standeth, but in divers townes about, which had betweene eight or nine skoare acres of arable land belonging unto it,

[1] *Nonconformity in Herts* (1884), p. 800.

with commons, medow and pasture agreable to the Farmes in that countrey, by yeere more than three times worth the valew that either my father or I received for it, and yet we received betwene eight and nine pounds yearely of cleare rent discharged of all quitte rentes. That Mr Sutcliffe may the better enquire into it, the Farme is scituate in Waddon in the county of Cambridge, seaven miles from Cambridge, where I had also a coate with a close adioyning unto it, which I solde when I did sell th'other."

That there were Cartwrights associated both with Royston and Whaddon during the reign of Henry VIII and onwards is apparent from the Subsidy Rolls, pertinent extracts from which may be given thus:

Herts. 121/177. 37 Hen. VIII. (1545–6). Royston:
Thomas Cartwright. xxxvj li - vj s (rat. pro mense) - xxx s (rat. pro quinque mensibus)
Michaell Cartwright. xviij li - iij s - xv s.
Cambs. 82/176. 32 Hen. VIII. (1540–1). Whaddon:
Michael Cartwryght pro consimilibus (i.e. bonis et catallis) xs.
Cambs. 82/211. 37 Hen. VIII. (1545–6). Whaddon:
William Cartewryght. xiij li - xiij s.
Cambs. 82/234. 1 Eliz. (1558–9). Whaddon:
Thomas Cartewright in landes iiij li - x s - viij d.
Cambs. 82/248. 8 Eliz. (1565–6). Whaddon:
Mr Cartwright clerke in landes iiij li - v s - viij d.

The last mentioned "Mr" Cartwright appears to be the subject of our study. The first named Thomas Cartwright, however, seems to be the yeoman of Royston, whose will, made on the 28th of June, 1563, was proved on the 31st of March, 1564[1]. His bequests show that he was the owner of property both in Royston and Whaddon. He bequeathes, besides much of his possessions in Royston, two tenements and their appurtenances in Whaddon to John, his son, and Agnes, his daughter-in-law, and their heirs. He also mentions his son Michael, his deceased son William, his nephew William and his grandson, Edward, son of Michael. We cannot be sure whether the above Thomas was the grandfather and the above John and Agnes the parents of the

[1] *Som. Ho. Bk*, Stevenson, fol. 7.

famous Puritan, but at any rate it seems obvious that the latter belonged to the same family tree as they did and that the suggestion that his home was in Royston is well founded.

We fail to trace "the cultured and commanding lineaments of a 'blue blood' descent," which Grosart[1] saw in Cartwright's portrait. We can only regard him as a member of a respectable yeoman family. As such he would enjoy the privileges and amenities of an environment, that tends to breed men of piety and character. The proximity of his home to Cambridge University would stimulate the boy's intellectual ambition and induce his guardians to launch him, doubtless a lad of promise, upon a professional career. It was in the year of Edward VI's elevation to the throne that Cartwright set his foot upon the first rung of the ladder, by which he was to climb to distinction. On the 12th of November, 1547, he matriculated as a sizar at Clare Hall. It is noteworthy that neither Clarke nor Brook knew of his Clare Hall connection and relate that his academic course began in 1550 at St John's[2]. In the Hall made famous by the renowned Latimer material, disciplinary and educational provision was made for boys such as Cartwright, but at the time in question the statutory number of bible-clerks and scholars was not being supported[3]. As Latimer pointed out in his sermon on the 6th of April, 1549, the University was suffering from impoverishment. "There be none now," he said, "but great men's sons in Colleges, and their fathers look not to have them preachers," and he pleaded with his hearers to give of their means to the poor scholars of the University[4]. Cartwright seems to have been one of the exceptions to the rule of which the Bishop spoke.

Among the interesting events that took place during Cartwright's undergraduate days were the visitation of the University by a special commission appointed by the King and the arrival of the Continental Reformers, Fagius and Bucer.

[1] p. vii.

[2] The assertion of S. Brydges (*Restituta* (1814), I, p. 218) that Cartwright was educated at Jesus College, Cambridge, is contrary to fact.

[3] J. R. Wardale, *Clare Hall* (1899), pp. 9, 10, 186.

[4] Cooper, *Ann.* II, p. 26.

The visitation began in May and ended on the 4th of July, 1549. Ridley opened the proceedings on the 5th of May with a powerful sermon. On the 15th and 16th of the same month Cartwright's College received the visitors[1]. In all likelihood he would appear with the rest of the scholars before them. Again they came to Clare Hall on the 17th of June to undertake the disagreeable task of expelling the Master, Roland Swynburne, and one of the Fellows, Pulley[2]. In spite of the sentence of deprivation Swynburne appears to have remained in possession of the Mastership till April, 1552, when he was succeeded by Dr John Madew[3]. There seems to have been none of the Reformer in Swynburne. He reverted to Romanism after Mary's accession and was restored to the Mastership in 1553[4]. The visitors were empowered to unite two or more Colleges, to found a College of Civil Law, and endow the latter with the lands, etc., of the Colleges dissolved. Clare Hall was decided upon as one of the foundations to be thus utilised, but the plan was resisted by the Master and Fellows and came to nought[5].

In 1549 two distinguished alumni of Heidelberg, Paul Fagius (1504–49), a Hebraist of note, and Martin Bucer (1491–1551), the celebrated Reformer and apostle of moderation, arrived in England. Before long they were both installed as teachers in the University of Cambridge[6]. Soon after his appointment Fagius died (25 Nov. 1549), but Bucer lectured in Divinity till 1551[7]. The importance attached by their contemporaries to these two men may be deduced from the fact that their bodies were exhumed and burnt in Cambridge market-place in Mary's reign (Feb. 1556–7), and the subsequent attempt, soon after Elizabeth came to the throne, on the part of Cambridge University to make amends for the disgrace by doing honour in conspicuous fashion to their memory (July, 1660)[8]. Their short period of residence must have done much to kindle the interest of many members of the University in the Continental Reformation.

[1] Cooper, *Ann.* II, p. 28.
[2] *ibid.* p. 29.
[3] *ibid.* p. 63.
[4] *ibid.* p. 83.
[5] *ibid.* p. 33.
[6] *ibid.* p. 45.
[7] *A.C.* I, pp. 95, 101.
[8] Cooper, *Ann.* II, p. 161.

Lever in a sermon preached at Paul's Cross to the citizens of London in December, 1550, throws light upon the hard life of the students of Cambridge at this time. "There be dyvers ther," he says[1], "whych ryse dayly betwixte foure and fyve of the clocke in the mornynge, and from fyve untyll syxe of the clocke use common prayer wyth an exhortacion of gods worde in a commune chappell, and from sixe unto ten of the clocke use ever eyther pryvate study or commune lectures. At ten of the clocke they go to dynner, whereas they be contente wyth a penye pyece of byefe amongest iiii. havyng a fewe porage made of the brothe of the same byefe, wyth salte and otemell, and nothynge els. After thys slender dinner they be either teachynge or learnynge untyll v. of the clocke in the evenyng, whenas they have a supper not much better then theyr dyner. Immedyatelye after the whyche, they go eyther to reasonyng in problemes or unto some other studye, untyll it be nyne or tenne of the clocke, and there beyng wythout fyre are fayne to walk or runne up and downe halfe an houre, to gette a heate on their feete whan they go to bed." It is probable that Cartwright was among those who thus limited their time of repose to about five hours. Clarke[2] passes on the tradition that "he never used to sleep above five houres in a night, which custome he continued to his dying day." This statement, whether derived from hearsay or from a calculation based on the above-mentioned reference in Lever's sermon, has been fastened upon by later writers, who have made the most of it as a testimony to Cartwright's diligence. Doubt may be thrown upon his maintenance of this rigid rule if Clarke merely deduced it from his acquaintance with Lever's discourse. Grosart[3], while accepting the tradition, condemns the self-denying practice, and suggests that it ultimately proved detrimental to Cartwright's physical health.

On the 6th of November, 1550, Cartwright became a scholar of St John's College, Cambridge. His admission, third among those of that date, is recorded thus: *Ego Thomas Cartwright de comitatu Hartfordiae admissus sum in discipulum*

[1] *Sermons*, ed. Arber, p. 122. [2] p. 367. [3] p. vii.

pro fundatrice[1]. The Master of his new College was a Hertfordshire man, William Bill, who was also Vice-Chancellor of the University. He was succeeded in the Mastership by Thomas Lever (10 Dec. 1551–28 Sept. 1553).

It was no slight privilege for Cartwright to come under the stirring influence of Lever, an eloquent preacher and staunch Protestant, who unflinchingly adhered to his robust principles till the day of his death at Ware in July, 1577. Baker, in his *History of St John's*[2], pays a high tribute to him and holds that the cause of the Reformation flourished in the College during his Mastership, "as appeared best in the day of trial, when he with twenty-four of his fellows quitted their preferments to preserve their innocence."

Edward VI died on the 6th of July, 1553, and it was not long thereafter before professing Protestants were obliged to make momentous decisions. During the Marian regime some fled to the Continent, there to be built up in their faith; some remained in England, there to become martyrs; others, for prudential reasons, because of circumstances, or in weak compromise, maintained as far as they could the even tenor of their way at home.

English Puritanism passed through several distinct phases during the sixteenth century. Its roots were manifold. The Revival of Learning, the consequent new interest in the Greek New Testament, the various translations of the Scriptures into the vernacular, the lively heritage of Lollardism particularly in the eastern counties and in such towns as London, Northampton, Leicester and Norwich, and the direct influences of the Continental Reformation fostered the Puritan spirit. During Edward's reign such Reformers from abroad as Bucer, Fagius, Tremellius, Martyr, Alasco, and Knox from Scotland, by their learning and fervour furthered an advanced type of Protestantism. Such Bishops as Ridley and Hooper were advocates of a simple Reformed religion. Now the return of Roman Catholicism to England, by driving a large contingent of Protestants overseas, helped to create the party, who constituted the immediate precursors of the

[1] *First Reg. of College*, I, p. 200.

[2] I, p. 132.

Elizabethan Puritans. The division of the English exiles into Knoxians and Coxians is best illustrated by the history of the troubles at Frankfurt, while the development of exilic Puritanism is best exemplified by the story of the Reformers who settled in Geneva and organised an English Presbyterian Church there. Among the settlers in Geneva were Knox, Goodman, Whittingham, Gilby, Wiburn, Sampson, Humphrey, James Pilkington, Coverdale, etc.[1] It was from this company—the left wing of the Marian exiles—that there came the English Genevan Prayer Book and the translation of the Bible known as the Genevan version, two books which were afterwards highly esteemed by the Elizabethan Puritans, and it was the aims and principles of this group that animated the movement with which Cartwright was afterwards identified.

Cartwright, however, had no personal share in this exilic Puritanism. He was not, as has been stated[2], one of the exiles, and the tradition which, to exhibit his unyielding Protestantism, asserts that he left Cambridge along with Lever and others in 1553[3] is not trustworthy. It is evident that he did not withdraw from the University immediately after Mary's accession, as his name appears in the list of students who graduated B.A. in the academic year 1553-4. It is only recently that this fact has been definitely ascertained. In *Athenae Cantabrigienses*[4] it is suggested "that he proceeded B.A. in due course, although that degree does not appear to be recorded," and following up this suggestion C. H. Cooper in a letter to Grosart observed, "I suppose he went out B.A. at the end of January, 1550–1, a few months after he became a scholar of St John's, but it may have been January, 1551–2."[5] Thanks to the invaluable labours of Dr John Venn and his son, we have had light shed upon this point as upon many other obscurities connected with old alumni of Cambridge. In the *Grace Book* Δ[6] "Cartwryght" is thirty-fourth in *Numerus bacchalaureorum istius anni* (i.e.

[1] *v.* Martin, Mitchell.
[2] Mullinger, *St John's*, p. 58.
[3] Brook, *Mem.* p. 38; Grosart, p. vii.
[4] II, p. 360.
[5] Grosart, p. vi.
[6] ed. Venn, p. 93.

1553–4) *iuxta senioritatem*. Among his fellow graduates this year was his future antagonist John Whitgift, whose name is twentieth in the list. Although Cartwright did not leave Cambridge so soon as has been generally supposed, he did leave the University in Mary's reign, probably in 1556[1], and, according to Clarke[2], "betook himself to the service of a Counsellor, yet followed his studies very hard as taking more pleasure therein, then in the studie of the law." We have not yet discovered the name of the "counsellor," and we know nothing about his legal experience beyond what Clarke tells us. Fuller's conjecture[3] that his new occupation enabled him to fence the better when he entered the lists as a controversialist, and Heron's assertion[4] that he kept terms as a law student, are suppositions based upon the slightest foundation.

From Clarke[5] we learn that Cartwright's employer, some time after the accession of Elizabeth, commended his intellectual abilities to Dr James Pilkington, of St John's (admitted Master 20 July, 1559), and that the latter, after an interview in which he noted Cartwright's aptitude for learning, "with his master's consent," restored the budding scholar to his old College. Brook[6] states that in St John's Cartwright had as tutor the eminent Dudley Fenner. The judicious Grosart[7] has endorsed this untenable assertion. As was pointed out in *Athenae Cantabrigienses*[8], the statement is preposterous. Fenner did not matriculate till June, 1575, as a fellow-commoner in Peterhouse and he died in the late eighties before he was thirty years of age[9]. If he was born he was now a mere infant. Indeed, he was not publicly and officially associated with Cartwright till over twenty years later.

If, as is likely, Cartwright returned to St John's in 1559 it was less than a year afterwards that he was admitted a Fellow of the College on the Lady Margaret foundation (6 April, 1560)[10]. The entry runs: *Ego Thomas Cartwright Hertfordiensis admissus socius pro domina Fundatrice*. In the

[1] *v. infra*, p. 9.
[2] p. 367.
[3] Fuller, *Worthies*, p. 54.
[4] Heron, p. 111.
[5] p. 367.
[6] *Mem.* p. 40.
[7] p. viii.
[8] II, p. 72.
[9] *v. infra*, p. 274.
[10] *A.C.* II, p. 360.

same year, 28 June, he commenced M.A.[1] Of the Masters of Arts he stands twelfth in the Ordo Senioritatis. The Grace runs thus: *Conceditur...ut 9 termini post finalem eius determinationem in quibus lectiones ordinarias audivit licet non omnino secundum formam statuti cum tribus responsionibus et aliis exercitiis per regia statuta requisitis sufficiant ei ad incipiendum in artibus.* In order to account for the nine terms it seems that Cartwright must have been an Arts student in Cambridge from 1554 to 1556, as well as during the year 1559–60. This computation implies that he was not forward in making a display of his Protestantism during the reign of Mary, but the fact that he did interrupt his studies in order to serve with the aforementioned counsellor indicates that he did ultimately side with the Protestant party and determine not to pursue an academic career under the guise of a Papist.

In St John's College accounts for 1560 Cartwright gets three quarters of his stipend as Fellow; the next year he receives his full annual stipend as Fellow and ten shillings for the last quarter as Foundress Chaplain; in 1562 he receives stipend as Fellow for the first quarter and also a quarter's emoluments as Foundress Chaplain. Then his name disappears from the College accounts. There are several other references to Cartwright in the University records belonging to this period, which may be briefly given. An entry in the thick Black Book of St John's Treasury[2] runs thus: "2 Aug. 3 Eliz. (*i.e.* 1561) Letters of attorney to Tho. Cartwright and Jo. Willones to take possession of Rydgwell manor." This manor (of Thorington, Essex) was purchased *c.* 1522 by John Fisher, Bishop of Rochester and Hugh Ashton, Archdeacon of York, two of the executors of the Lady Margaret, foundress of St John's. Probably Cartwright as a Fellow and Willones, perhaps a lawyer, were appointed to collect arrears of rents and dues, the payment of which had been interrupted in the reign of Mary or merely formally to claim the ownership and take "seizin" of the manor in the name of the College. It is recorded that Cartwright became Junior Dean of his College on the 10th of January, 1561–2[3]. Shortly afterwards, 23rd

[1] *G. Bk*, p. 141. [2] f. 453 *b*. Baker, I, p. 387. [3] *A.C.* II, p. 360.

of January, 1561–2, he was elected one of the examiners for the B.A. for the academic year[1]. His fellow examiner was Richard Schacklock, B.A. (1555–6), M.A. (1559). Two "oppositores" or "examinatores questionistarum," commonly called "posers," were appointed annually at the same time as the proctors. It is probable that on their advice the "pater," one of the proctors, assigned the place of seniority according to merit[2].

In 1562 Cartwright became a Fellow of Trinity College[3], and it was as such that two years later he entered into the blaze of publicity in connection with Queen Elizabeth's visit to Cambridge. As his conduct on that occasion has given rise to conflicting interpretations, it merits detailed notice.

Clarke[4] does not say much about the occurrence beyond pointing out that Cartwright was one of the four "eminentest men" in the University chosen to keep a Philosophy Act before the Queen and that he performed his part "with extraordinary abilities, and to the great content and satisfaction both of the Queen and other auditors." Paule, on the other hand, attributes Cartwright's "first discontentment" to his treatment at the hands of Elizabeth at this time. Affirming that Thomas Preston (then of King's College and afterwards Master of Trinity Hall), one of the disputants, was both liked and rewarded by her Majesty for his comely gesture and pleasing pronunciation, and that Cartwright received neither reward nor commendation, Paule[5] proceeds to relate that Cartwright was grievously disappointed, that he uttered his no small grief to his intimate friends in Trinity, that the latter were also resentful because the honour of the disputation did not fall to their college, and that immediately after the royal neglect and not only *post* but also *propter hoc*, Cartwright began to "wade into divers opinions, as that of the discipline, and to kick against her ecclesiastical government." From that day Cartwright "grew highly conceited of himself for learning and holiness, and a great contemner

[1] *G. Bk*, p. 159. [2] *ibid.* p. x.
[3] *Admissions to Trinity*, Ball and Venn, II, p. 49.
[4] p. 367. [5] pp. 322 ff.

of others that were not of his mind." The last and chief alleged result of the incident was that Cartwright, in his chagrin and spleen, travelled to Geneva, where he fed his humour with the Presbyterian tenets prevailing there, and that in due course he returned to England determined to subvert the Episcopal government of the national Church and to abolish its accepted rites and ceremonies. This account, if true, would stigmatise Cartwright as a little-minded victim of pride and jealousy. It savours too much of bias to be accepted without inquiry.

Heylyn[1] bases his comments upon Paule, in parts almost to the extent of plagiarism. Let it here be noted, however, that Heylyn, who passes many an unfavourable verdict upon Cartwright, especially in *Aerius Redivivus*, is so inaccurate a recorder of facts and so partial an interpreter of history that he must be regarded as a thoroughly unreliable guide.

Fuller, approaching the subject in his own characteristic fashion, writes of it thus: "Cartwright disputed like a great, Preston like a genteel scholar, being a handsome man; and the queen, upon parity of deserts, always preferred properness of person in conferring her favours. Hereupon with her looks, words and deeds she favoured Preston, calling him her scholar, as appears by his epitaph in Trinity Hall chapel, which thus beginneth, *Conderis hoc tumulo, Thomas Prestone, scholarem quem dixit Princeps Elizabetha suum*." Fuller, however, proceeds to repeat Paule's account and then adds: "But Mr Cartwright's followers (who lay the foundation of his disaffection to the discipline established in his conscience, not carnal discontentment) credit not the relation. Adding moreover, that the queen did highly commend, though not reward him. But whatever was the cause, soon after he went beyond the seas, and after his travel returned a bitter enemy to the hierarchy."[2]

Strype, writing disinterestedly, breaks away from the Paule-Heylyn tradition and thus criticises it: "Reports have commonly been spread, that the cause of Cartwright's setting

[1] *A.R.* lib. VI, § 34.
[2] *Hist. Univ. Camb.* ed. Nichols (1840), p. 196.

himself so openly against the hierarchy as he did soon after (to the great disturbance of the peace of the English church) was from a disgust he took at this time; as though the queen showed more countenance to the other disputants than to him. But by the *Relation* of the queen's reception at Cambridge (now in the hands of a learned member of that university), there appears no clear ground for any such discontent. For the queen is said there to have approved them all; only that Preston pleased her most; and was made her scholar, with the settlement of a yearly honorary salary on him."[1] A marginal note gives "*Thomas Baker. soc. de. Johann*" as the learned member of the University referred to, *i.e.* the celebrated antiquary, transcriber of MSS. and author of the *History of St John's*.

Brook[2], in the spirit of a partisan, takes up the cudgels in Cartwright's behalf and repudiates the aspersion cast by biased critics upon his hero. He settles the matter by quoting Strype and accepts without questioning the latter's faith in the above-mentioned *Relation*.

Baker[3] bases his version of the royal visit in 1564 on certain manuscript accounts, which he styles *MS Bishop Cosin*, *MS D. Evans*.

J. Nichols, in his *Progresses and Public Processions of Queen Elizabeth*[4], prints an account of the Queen's visit and states that it is drawn from a sixteenth century manuscript which he purchased at Dr Askew's sale, 1786, and collated with a Baker transcript[5]. This source used by Nichols is entitled *Commentarii Hexaemeri Rerum Cantabrigiae actarum, cum Serenissima Regina Angliae etc Elizabeth in Academiam Cantab. adveneratr, An^o Domini*, 1564. *Collectore N. Robynsono.* Nicholas Robinson, who was the compiler of these memoranda, was an eyewitness of the happenings at Cambridge in August, 1564[6]. Besides his full and illuminating note-book there are two other informing contemporary writings, which shed light upon the memorable week, a narrative ascribed to one of the

[1] St. *Ann.* II, p. 107.
[2] *Mem.* pp. 41 ff.
[3] I, pp. 157 ff.
[4] ed. 1788–1805, III, pp. 27 ff.
[5] *Baker MSS.* X, p. 181 (*Harl. MSS.* 7037).
[6] *A.C.* I, p. 503.

esquire bedells of the University, Matthew Stokys[1], and a descriptive poem by a Fellow of King's College, Abraham Hartwell, entitled *Regina Literata: sive de serenissimae Dominae Elizabethae...in Academiam Cantabrigiensem Adventu etc.*[2]

In the calm clear light of these three documents we are able to give a dispassionate treatment of the events with which we are concerned. The philosophical disputation was arranged to begin on Monday, the 7th of August, at one o'clock. A large stage, constructed for the occasion, stretched from the "wall of the Belfrey head unto the Chancell" of St Mary's Church. The various dignitaries and members of faculties occupied their specially appointed places. Shortly after the University bell began to ring the Queen appeared. As she entered the Church all the graduates, kneeling, cried "*Vivat Regina.*" In due course the respondent, Thomas Byng, Fellow of Peterhouse, began his oration on the chosen subjects *Monarchia est optimus status Reipublicae* and *Frequens legum mutatio est periculosa.* After him, Cartwright, having obtained the Queen's leave, stood up to confute the arguments propounded in behalf of monarchy. Even although it was merely an academic discussion upon which he was entering, nevertheless it must have been a bold and trying task to attack monarchy in the presence of such an autocratic sovereign as Elizabeth. Robinson speaks highly of Cartwright's appearance, remarking upon his skill in words and the high quality of his subject matter[3]. Cartwright began straightway to analyse Byng's speech. He desired to get to the heart of the matter in hand and invade the very citadel of the respondent's reasons. If he were able to cut off the

[1] *Baker MSS.* x, p. 109; Nichols, I, pp. 14ff., *v. A.C.* II, p. 109; Cooper, *Ann.* II, p. 182.

[2] Published 1565. Nichols, vol. I; *A.C.* II, p. 383.

[3] *Surrexit* (*Principis primum obtenta venia, quam reliqui collegae impetrarunt etiam priusquam accingebantur ad causas*) *primo in loco, ad evertendam tam bene fundatam disciplinam Cartwrightus quidam, et rerum et verborum artifex ingeniosus, qui arcem primae defencionis viriliter invadens, et inde proreptans paulatim per singula quasi castella, visus est non nihil labefactasse universa: Nam omnino prosternere tam firmiter constitutam rempublicam tam subito tamque minimo apparatu, vix erat expectandum. Quamvis quo est et usu et animo, in hoc exercitationis genere, afflixit profecto paulo vehementius* (Nichols, III, p. 66).

head of the argument that had been developed it would fall to the ground, a lifeless corpse. Attacking the thesis that God's sovereignty supported an earthly monarchy, Cartwright affirmed that it smacked of insolence and intolerable conceit. Finite mortals should not be compared with the most wise, omnipresent and eternal King. Mere men required a fellowship of labour and counsel. The argument was an invalid syllogism from the major to the minor *affirmative*. He next combated the contention that the monarchical principle received weighty support from natural phenomena. If, by Nature, Byng meant God, he was but singing an old song—the deduction from the sovereignty of God already dealt with; if reference was made by the respondent to the mysterious inherent powers of Nature, Cartwright treated the notion with the uttermost scorn and, in words reminiscent of a passage in Cicero's *De Natura Deorum*[1], he pointed out that this kind of Nature produced freaks innumerable, the squint-eyed, the snub-nosed, the flap-eared, etc., who were cast into the world as into a theatre to be laughed at. But surely, he proceeded, the argument from Nature was one that told directly against the respondent's case. Everywhere it proclaimed the idea of community. After enlisting the service of Aristotle against the rule of an individual Cartwright went on to advocate that a commonwealth would be most wisely and beneficently governed when the monarch shared the government with others. In conclusion he controverted the quotation from Homer—"Ill fares the state where many masters rule; let one be lord, one king supreme"[2]—by observing that poets are authors not of facts but of fables, and that it was the Homeric Diomede, who took a companion with him when he was sent to reconnoitre the enemy's camp. If, however, Byng abode by Homer, Cartwright would pin his faith to the Homer of philosophers, Aristotle. Cartwright's Latin oration is given in full in Appendix I.

Hartwell reproduces one of Cartwright's favourite ideas in his poem, namely, that Nature does not give all her kisses to one of her numerous brood, that she does not love the

[1] *lib.* I, c. 29. [2] *Iliad* II, l. 204, Derby's transl. l. 231.

one and despise the many. This arrow of Cartwright's flies and after inflicting a wound falls to the ground. But, as the poet observes, although Cartwright's argument may be likened to a javelin that hurts, it cannot remove monarchies. Mere words cannot destroy the mighty, the very gods of the earth. As Hartwell's poem has not been used by any of Cartwright's biographers and is comparatively unknown, we give the section that deals with his oration in Appendix II.

The disputants who followed Cartwright were William Chaderton, Fellow of Christ's College, Thomas Preston and Bartholomew Clark, Fellows of King's[1]. Robinson is certain that all of them won the approval of Elizabeth, for she frequently intervened when the moderators wished to adhere rigidly to the time allowed for disputing. As this contemporary suggests, the belief that Preston specially distinguished himself may be a mere inference from the fact that shortly afterwards he was singled out for recognition by the Queen and named her scholar[2]. Stokys' account affords corroborative evidence that the four philosophical disputants made a favourable impression upon the Queen. "With whome," he says[3], "her Majestie was so much pleased, that she, by divers gestures, declared the same; and sundry times stayed the Proctors from taking them up. And, when they did cut them off, she seemed to be offended, saying, If she had the moderation, they should not have been so abridged."

It has not always been sufficiently noticed that Preston played a far more prominent part than Cartwright in the proceedings connected with the Queen's visit. For instance, he was one of the players in the tragedy of *Dido*, that was performed before Elizabeth on Monday night (7th August) in King's College. Evidently he was a man of literary gifts and histrionic ability, and these, made manifest in his speeches

[1] Nichols, III, pp. 68, 71, 74.

[2] *At vero*, says Robinson (*ibid.* III, p. 73), *quam aliorum animos in suam partem Preston inclinaverat verborum eloquentia vel hac conjectura colligitur, quod Reginalis sit paulo post a munificentissima Regina et appellatus et habitus. Probasse certe suos labores clementissimae principi omnes hos philosophos arbitramur, quod illis disputandi tempus sepe prorogarit, cum moderatores ad medicinam audiendam censuissent.*

[3] Nichols, I, B-E. p. 16; Cooper, *Ann.* II, p. 196.

and acting, would make their mark upon his royal auditor[1]. He was further privileged to deliver the valedictory oration to the Queen on the morning of her departure from Cambridge (Thursday, 10th August). She expressed her appreciation of his speech, and, as she was about to mount her horse, named him her scholar and offered him, Dr Baker and others her hand to kiss[2]. According to a shorter account drawn from an original manuscript by Nichols[3], Preston "made an Oracion before the Queenes Majestie in her lodging privately; which her Grace so well liked, that putting forth her hand for him to kisse, her Highness, as himself termed yt, dubbed hym her Scholar, and exhorted him to continue in his studie with diligence, saying, the whole body of the University might rejoyce that ever it nourished so profitable a member; and therewithal she gave him viii angels."

With the unvarnished facts before us we conclude that the conspicuous favour conferred by Elizabeth upon Preston was due to the excellence of his abilities displayed on several occasions and not merely for his oration in the philosophical disputation. His selection for particular royal attention was no more disparaging to Cartwright than to the other orators, who were chosen to feast the Queen's intellect. There are, besides, no grounds for the view that Cartwright was piqued. The slanderous charge that he was so embittered by her Majesty's neglect, that he forthwith launched out upon a revolutionary career is the fabrication of prejudiced minds, that turned an unsubstantiated surmise into a positive assertion. Suffice it to say that his choice as a disputant shows that he was held in high esteem in the University for his

[1] Preston is regarded as the author of *The Tragedy of Cambyses*. *A.C.* II, p. 248.

[2] *Inter tantos fremitus*, says Robinson (Nichols, III, p. 131), *Prestonus Collegii Regalis socius* (*quem antea diximus permulcisse complurimum animos singulari quadam dicendi praestantia*) *jam ad regii hospitii fores una paratus cum Bakero praeposito, aliisque nonnullis, Reginam polita ac suavi oratione ultimum salutavit*. After giving Preston's oration Robinson proceeds (*ibid*. p. 132): *Perplacuit illi hoc salutandi officium. Itaque in equum conscendens et huic* (*eum Regium ac suum scholarem appellitans*) *et hospiti Bakero, ac aliis quibusdam manum deosculandam offert*.

[3] III, p. 180.

intellectual qualities, and that his appearance would bring him before the notice, not only of Elizabeth, but also of such influential men as Cecil and Leicester, who accompanied her. It is also of interest to note that two members of the University, who were afterwards to be intimately associated with Cartwright, delivered orations before the Queen during her Cambridge visit, viz. Walter Travers, on Saturday, the 5th of August, and Edward Dering, four days later[1]. Paule[2], Heylyn[3], Soames[4] and others have expressed the opinion that Cartwright left England after his alleged humiliation at Cambridge and proceeded to Geneva, where he was infected with the anti-episcopal virus. Froude, changing the motive, says[5] that he continued in Cambridge "till the Vestment Controversy of 1564 sickened him," and then went over to Geneva, where he recovered his spirits in the Calvinistic atmosphere. There is abundant reason to regard this expatriation as considerably ante-dated. For some time after the royal visit to the University there are few traces of Cartwright, but the available data support the view that he did not go to Geneva until he relinquished his Professorship, and then from motives other than those mentioned above.

English Puritanism now entered into a new phase. Aware that there was considerable diversity in the Church in the observance of certain rites and ceremonies Elizabeth wrote (25 January, 1564–5) to Archbishop Parker reproaching him and the other Bishops for their inability to secure uniformity and enjoining them to put an end to nonconformity with all expedition[6]. The Bishops, as directed, sought to reduce the irregularities that abounded[7] and drew up a book of articles prescribing uniformity in apparel, etc. (March, 1564–5)[8], which was published a year afterwards and is generally known as Parker's *Advertisements*[9]. The Universities soon became centres of opposition to the new scheme. In Oxford Laurence

[1] Nichols, III, pp. 29, 89. [2] p. 324. [3] *A.R.* lib. VI, § 34.
[4] p. 143. [5] III, p. 213.
[6] Dixon, VI, p. 44; St. *Parker*, II, App. XXIV.
[7] Soames, p. 40; Paget, p. 25.
[8] Dixon, VI, pp. 49, 52; *Parker Corresp.* p. 233.
[9] Dixon, VI, p. 102; Gee and Hardy, p. 467.

Humphrey, President of Magdalen College, and Thomas Sampson, Dean of Christ Church, were the chief leaders of dissent[1]. In Cambridge St John's College in particular became the hot-bed of dissidence, one of the leading malcontents being William Fulke[2]. Beaumont, Master of Trinity, Whitgift, Lady Margaret Professor of Divinity, and others protested (26 November, 1565) to Cecil against the measures that were likely to lead to the deprivation of many of their best scholars[3]. But the Bishops pursued their policy of uniformity with rigour, *e.g.* those of the London clergy who refused obedience (26 March, 1566) were suspended[4]. The result of the scheme of coercion was the consolidation of dissent. The party emerged to which, according to Fuller, the name "Puritan" was now given[5]. They entered into a literary warfare in which they denounced the dregs of Rome that were being imposed upon them. Foreign divines, such as Beza, Bullinger, and Gualter, were inundated with letters from Puritans and their opponents[6]. Puritan emissaries, *e.g.* Percival Wiburn, George Wither and John Barthlett, presented and pleaded their cause in person at Geneva and Zürich[7]. Wither and Barthlett also addressed an intercessory memorial early in 1567 to the Elector Frederick III[8]. The Continental divines, aware of faults on both sides, advised mutual forbearance. The Church of Scotland, lamenting the dissensions caused by vain trifles, intervened (28 December,

[1] Dixon, VI, pp. 39, 55, 59.

[2] *ibid.* pp. 69, 70.

[3] *ibid.* VI, p. 68.

[4] *ibid.* VI, pp. 94, 96.

[5] Fuller (*C.H.* bk IX, s. 1, §§ 66, 67) says that the term was first applied in 1564. Heylyn took him to task for the assertion; Fuller's reply to Heylyn's *Animadversion* (*Appeal of Injured Innocence*, ed. Nichols (1840), p. 510) shows that the date, 1564, is but an approximate conjecture. Heylyn (*Ecclesia Restaurata*, ed. 1849, II, p. 421), basing his opinion on Genebrand, Gualter and Spondanus, states that the appellation was first given in 1565. Paul Hentzner in 1598 said that the Jesuit Sanders first applied it (W. B. Rye, *England as seen by Foreigners in the days of Elizabeth* (1865), p. 111; cf. Birt, p. 125 *n.*). Froude (*English Seamen* (1895), p. 6) found the earliest mention of the name in a document belonging to 1585, but it was certainly used long before that date. We have found it in prominent use from *c.* 1572 onwards.

[6] *v. Z.L. passim.*

[7] *ibid.* I, p. 187; II, p. 358, etc.

[8] *ibid.* II, p. 157.

1566) and pleaded for lenity to the nonconformists[1]. Besides leading to the appearance of a consolidated Puritan party, the new coercive measures resulted in the emergence of what we may call circumstantial Separatists, that is, dissenters who, although Genevan in principle, broke away from the Church of England in order to worship separately, unhampered by any of the obnoxious vestments or ceremonies. The latter, not true Congregationalists by conviction, were among the forerunners of such. Their best known meeting was discovered in Plumbers' Hall in June, 1567[2].

It is sometimes said[3] that Cartwright actively participated in the vestiarian controversy, and that at his instigation, towards the close of 1565, all the members of Trinity College, except three, appeared in chapel without their surplices, but this opinion seems to be due to a confusion of events. Near the end of 1565 disorders of this kind took place in St John's College[4], but the impression we receive from Whitgift's biographer, Paule[5], is that it was not till two years later that Cartwright, in the absence of Whitgift, then Master of Trinity College, preached so vehemently against the surplice, etc., that all the members of his College, with the exception of three, appeared at the evening service in chapel without their surplices. As Whitgift was not appointed Master of Trinity till the 4th of July, 1567, this occurrence, if we can be sure of Paule's testimony, must have taken place after that date. Seeing, according to the testimony of Chaderton and Grindal[6], Cartwright was a nonconformist in his apparel and always stubbornly refused the cap and such like ornaments, we should naturally expect to hear of his being at least in active sympathy with the vestiarian movement, but in default of definite evidence, there is little or nothing to say about his connection with it. As a matter of fact, his absence in Ireland while the vestment, or rather uniformity controversy was raging, would prevent him from taking a direct or leading part in it for a lengthy period.

1 *Troubles of Frankfort*, ed. Arber, p. 251.
2 *v.* Peel, pp. 6 ff.
3 *e.g. A.C.* II, p. 360.
4 Soames, p. 61; Dixon, VI, p. 72.
5 p. 324.
6 *v. infra* pp. 28, 30.

It was probably towards the end of 1565 or in the beginning of the following year that the scene of Cartwright's labours changed and he became domestic chaplain to Adam Loftus, Archbishop of Armagh. Clarke, Brook and Hanbury[1], etc., say nothing about this Irish appointment. Waddington[2] is misleading when he says that Cartwright accepted the chaplaincy on the completion of his studies, for, as we shall see, he afterwards resumed his academic career. Ireland was at this time an excellent resort for English dissenters, and there were now in that island many Puritan ministers, who were allowed to practise nonconformity with impunity. This we gather from the report given by Wither and Barthlett to Bullinger and Gualter in 1567, to which these Zürich divines allude in a letter to Bishops Grindal, Sandys and Parkhurst (26 August, 1567)[3]: *Addunt plures esse in Hibernia ecclesiarum ministros, qui non aliter sentiant aut faciant quam illi ipsi qui in Anglia sustinent persecutionem; illos autem episcopi sui beneficio et apud regiam majestatem interventu agere in summa tranquillitate.*

Cartwright's influence in Ireland seems to have been considerable. On none did he make a greater impression than Loftus himself, who in later years was suspected by the Queen of being a Puritan and a favourer of the then exiled Cartwright and Presbyterian doctrines. While defending himself against the imputations in a letter to Walsingham (16 March, 1576–7), Loftus did not hesitate to pay a high and affectionate tribute to his old friend. "Some little Inglinge," he writes[4], "hathe been given me (whether truly or no, god knoweth) that hir Matie hath been enformed that I am a puritane, and a favourer of Mr Cartwright and his doctrine. Truly Sir, I am utterly ignorant what the terme and accusation of a puritane meaneth. And as for Mr Cartwright, he was once my householde Chapleyne, and contynued in my house about twoo yeares, duringe which tyme, and before in the tyme of my acquayntance with him in

[1] *Life* of T.C. prefixed to ed. of Hooker's works (1830).
[2] *Hist.* p. 2.
[3] *Z.L.* II, Ep. LXIV.
[4] *S.P. Ireland, Eliz.* LVII, No. 36.

Cambridge, I have so conceyved of his life and learninge, that I must needes confesse I love and favour his person; for his doctryne, I have read his bookes, and the answers therunto; for my judgement and opynion wherein, as I dare not condemne all, so am I right hertily sory that he hath offended the state, wherein he never had ayde or comforte of me in any way. For when he was of my famylye, thes controversies were not then begonne. And since, as I have not once seen hym, so have I not heard often from hym. Well, I will not trouble you with any longe discourse of this matter, but will leave the judgement thereof to god almightye, who knowethe that the pureste of us all are impure and fowle, bothe in bodye and mynde," etc. When commending Cartwright to Cecil's favour in October, 1570[1], Loftus said that he had had "good experience of hym, for that he was a yere here with me," but in the above letter he says that Cartwright lived with him "about twoo yeares." It is difficult to reconcile these two statements, and we may take them as a sample of the inexactitude, of which sixteenth century writers were frequently guilty, when they reckoned duration of time.

Stirring events took place in Ireland during the period of Cartwright's chaplaincy. In 1565 the English Council prepared schemes for the pacification of the turbulent country, and in particular for the subjugation of the fiery Irish chieftain, Shan O'Neil, who was then at the zenith of his power. Sir Henry Sidney was entrusted with the administration, civil and military, and landed at Dublin in January, 1566[2]. His task was no light one, for the country had suffered from unwise and inefficient government, O'Neil's position in the north was not easy to reduce, the soldiers at the deputy's disposal were unreliable, and Elizabeth's reluctance to spend and the uncertainties of her obstructive and delaying policy were hard to surmount. It was not till September, 1566, that Sidney began active operations. The expedition was successful and Ireland was brought to a temporary peace and submission. The discomfited O'Neil was slain in a drunken brawl in June, 1567.

[1] *S.P. Ireland, Eliz.* xxx, No. 88.

[2] Froude, c. XI.

Just because they are face to face with the unalloyed and fanatical characteristics of Rome in Ireland, Protestants there are frequently more bitterly opposed to Roman Catholicism than their brethren in England. So it was in Cartwright's time and his Irish experience would tend to deepen his opposition to all that was Roman. If, as is likely, he came into contact with Christopher Goodman, the advanced and experienced Genevan, who served as a chaplain with Sidney, Cartwright would be brought under the influence of Puritanism of the extremest kind.

In the autumn of 1566 Loftus retired to England for the sake of his health[1]. On the 25th of November of that year he was admitted a Doctor of Theology of Cambridge. The *Grace Book*[2] states: *peregit omnia per magistrum Cartewright*. If Cartwright did not return to England with Loftus he must have come and resumed his studies shortly afterwards, for on the 31st of May, 1567, he obtained the degree of B.D.[3]

Before the year was at an end an attempt was made to bring Cartwright back to Ireland as successor to Loftus, who had been appointed to the Dublin see, in the Archbishopric of Armagh. The income was indeed moderate, about £20 a year[4], and the Cathedral of Armagh had been burnt to the ground by O'Neil in the previous year, but the prestige attached to the charge was considerable. In the opinion of Loftus there was none so eminently worthy of the post as the godly and learned Cartwright, and he warmly commended him to Cecil (5 December, 1567), whom he assured that Cartwright's appointment would greatly strengthen the poor Church in Ireland and give satisfaction to all the faithful Protestants, who deeply lamented his departure from the island. "I dubte not," writes Loftus to Cecil, "your honor consyderith that although the profyttes of that Busshopryke be very small, yet the place and auctorytie is verey great, and thearfore as a godly learnyd man in that Rowme myght profytt and do muche good, so an ungodly and ignorant man might hinder, and do muche harme. I have

[1] Shirley, *Original Letters* (1851), p. 269. [2] p. 205.
[3] *ibid.* [4] Shirley, *op. cit.* p. 279.

thought it my parte therfore, not only to put you in mynd hearof, but also to commend unto you one whom I knowe for his excellent learnynge and godly lyfe worthely mete for suche a place and dignitie. I meane one Mr Cartwryght, a bachelor of Dyvynitie, and fellowe of Trynytie Collage in Cambryge, who used hym self so godly (duringe his abode with me in Ireland) both in lyfe and docktryne that his absence from hence is no small greeff and Sorowe to all the godly and faythfull heare. Wold god the pore churche of Ireland myght obteyne thus muche of you (for suarly I wryte not in myne owne name, but in the name of all the faythfull heare) it myght thinke it selfe to have gotten no small treasure and benefytt, and contynually bound to be thankefull to god for your honor."[1] In spite of Loftus's praiseworthy endeavour Cartwright did not receive the appointment. Other honours and other tasks awaited him in England.

He had already been elected one of the twelve University preachers for the academic year 1567–8. He was appointed along with Edmund Chapman and Wm Wyckam on the 7th of November, 1567[2]. The other preachers for the year were (24 October) Robert Some, (28 November) Roger Goade, Jo. Grundye; (23 January) W. Sawnderson, Ludovic Wyllians, W. Tabor; (30 January) Jo. Bell, Jo. Lynsey; (3 February) Anth. Fourd. Cartwright now became famous for his eloquence in the pulpit. "When his turn came to preach at Saint Maries," says Clarke[3], "the Sextone was faigne to take down the windows by reason of the multitudes that came to heare him." This is the kind of happening that readily gives rise to legendary accretions and we are not surprised to read in Brook's *Memoir*[4] that the windows of the Church were actually taken down. Nevertheless, Cartwright seems to have had undoubted gifts as a preacher, which were much appreciated by many of his contemporaries. Clarke[5] refers to his coming to Cambridge "after long discontinuance," probably when Laurence Chaderton was

[1] *S.P. Ireland, Eliz.* XXII, No. 35.

[2] *G. Bk*, p. 216. The next Grace (9 July, 1568) dealing with Cartwright (*ibid.* p. 217) refers to his sermon *ad clerum*.

[3] p. 367. [4] p. 48. [5] p. 373.

Master of Emmanuel College (*i.e.* after 1584), and preaching on a week-day at St Mary's, "where there was a great confluence of all sorts to heare him; grave men ran like boys in the streets to get places in the Church. After sermon he dined at Master Chadertons, and many went to the house to see and hear him speak."

On the 29th of June, 1569, a petition was sent from Trinity College to Cecil for the regulation of the quota of scholars sent annually from Westminster School to Trinity. It was signed by Whitgift, and the following Fellows—Nicholas Shepherd, Thomas Cartwright, William Bingham, Robert West, Nicholas Browne, Edmund Chapman, John Cooke and Isaac Barrow. The petition dealt with a minor local grievance, which Strype discusses in full[1]. Its chief interest for us is that it is the last record of any co-operation between Whitgift and Cartwright before they appeared in public as the champions of two divergent and apparently irreconcileable ideals. Of the Fellows above-mentioned Chapman was the one who was to be most closely associated with Cartwright in the future.

Before proceeding to deal with Cartwright's appointment as a Professor, we shall consider briefly his connection with two foreigners, Anthony Rudolf Chevallier, the distinguished French Protestant scholar, Professor of Hebrew in Cambridge, and the young John Drusius, now living in exile with his father, Clement van der Drieschen. Chevallier came to England in the reign of Edward VI, as a guest of Cranmer. He went to Cambridge where he assisted Tremellius in the teaching of Hebrew. For a time he acted as French tutor to Princess Elizabeth. On the accession of Mary he proceeded to Switzerland. In 1557 he became pastor at Montreux. In 1559 he was appointed Professor of Hebrew in Strassburg, and shortly afterwards became Professor of the same subject in Geneva. After the Peace of Orleans he returned to France, but on the outbreak of civil war left his own country again and came to England, where he resumed the teaching of Hebrew in Cambridge. He left England in 1572 and was

[1] St. *Whit.* I, pp. 26 ff.

succeeded in Cambridge by Philip Bignon. Shortly after the massacre of St Bartholomew he died in Guernsey[1]. Drusius, after his sojourn in Cambridge, proceeded to Oxford, where for several years he taught Oriental languages. After the Peace of Ghent he returned to his own country and was called in 1577 to the Chair of Oriental Languages at Leyden, where he remained until he was appointed Professor of Hebrew at Franecker in 1585. Probably he met Cartwright when the latter, in his turn an exile, spent several years in the Netherlands. He died in 1616[2]. When Drusius came to Cambridge he took up residence in the house of Chevallier, and it was there that he received tuition from Cartwright. *In aedibus ejus* (says Curiander, the son-in-law and biographer of Drusius) *dum vivit, studiorum socium, aut potius ἐργοδιώκτην habuit Thomam Carthurigtum Theologiae Professorem Anglum, virum egregie doctum, & omnibus iis quae ad eam professionem requiruntur instructissimum*[3]. We learn from the same source that Cartwright's friendship with Drusius continued after the latter returned to the Continent. Curiander[4] includes Cartwright among the famous men, whose correspondence with Drusius was preserved by the latter's heirs: *Qui crebras ad Drusium literas dare solebant, quorumque epistolae ab haeredibus asservabuntur.*

Whitgift resigned the Regius Professorship in Divinity towards the end of 1569. William Chaderton was elected his successor[5]. Chaderton's appointment created a vacancy in the Lady Margaret Divinity Professorship, to which post Cartwright was now elected. This Chair was founded in the reign of Henry VII (1503) by the Lady Margaret, Countess of Richmond, the King's mother. The stipend, payable by the Abbot and convent of Westminster, amounted to 20 marks a year. A sum of £6. 13*s*. 4*d*. was also paid annually from the University Treasury to the Professor on condition

[1] *v*. F. Watson, "Notes and Materials on Religious Refugees in their relation to Education in England" (*Proc. Huguenot Soc*. IX, p. 318); Hessels, II, p. 371; *A.C*. I, p. 307.

[2] *v*. Watson, *op. cit*.; *R.E*., *sub nomine*.

[3] *Ioh. Drusii Vita* (1616), p. 4.

[4] *ibid*. p. 30.

[5] St. *Whit*. I, p. 29.

that he preached once a year at Burwell[1], but this payment was abolished during Cartwright's tenure of office and the money converted to the use of the University[2].

The new Professor began a series of lectures on the first two chapters of *Acts*. In these Cartwright dealt with questions of ecclesiastical polity as, according to his thinking, they arose directly from the exegesis of the text in hand. One can gather from his published works the line of thought that he adopted. In his first *Reply* to Whitgift he sought to prove from *Acts* i. that congregations should have a voice in the election of their ministers, that the latter must be fit to teach and be examined before their ordination, etc.[3] In his comment on *Acts* i. 15, in his *Confutation*, he points out that "Peter's supremacie in this place was no greater then is the speaker in the lower house or proclaimer in the convocation," thus regarding Peter as a kind of Presbyterian moderator, *primus inter pares*. Such deductions from the government of the primitive Church necessarily led to a comparison with the existing system in the Church of England. Ministers were not sufficiently examined; many of them were unable to preach; they were not elected by congregations but by Bishops, etc. Cartwright was unable to dissociate the functions of the interpreter and the advocate. As the former he read Presbyterianism in the constitution of the early Christian Church; as the latter he proclaimed that the Apostolic Church was the model for all time. He could not consistently approve of the, in his opinion, only allowable system, without condemning that which subverted it. The contrast between the ancient Church and the Church of England was apparent. Accordingly the exponent of Scripture and the advocate of the Presbyterianism revealed and commanded therein became the critic of the established Episcopate. If Cartwright was right the organisation of the Church of England must be radically altered and the existing hierarchy must go.

He has been censured for betraying his trust, for upholding

[1] Cooper, *Ann.* II, p. 229.
[2] *G. Bk*, p. 241.
[3] *W.W.* I, pp. 296–7, 300.

Presbyterianism and indulging in controversy on questions of ecclesiastical polity, when it was his duty as a Professor of Divinity to support the Church of England[1]. It is doubtful whether this point of ethics ever entered Cartwright's mind. He did not set himself up as a critic of the Church; primarily he was an expositor of Scripture. While it may be granted that there was a Genevan bias in his conscience, it cannot be affirmed that he was deliberately perfidious. Loyalty to the Word of God as he understood it was an obligation, with which loyalty to the Church as established could not for a moment be compared. If this sense of duty was based upon a false exegesis, he may be accused of a wrong judgment, but not of dishonourable dealing. He may have regarded his occupancy of the Chair as an excellent opportunity of pointing the Church in the direction of true reform. So he would fulfil his duty to the Church, not by acquiescing in its present state, but by the advocacy of its ideal. To resign his post would have been, in his eyes, a betrayal of the trust imposed upon him by God. Critics of to-day may think that his true position should have been in a nonconformist Chair, but such at the time was inconceivable. Cartwright's conscientious opinions landed him in a dilemma, which could be solved only by his eviction from office. The authorities of his time, who disagreed with his teaching, were bound to regard it as their duty to seek his downfall, not because he was an unprincipled renegade, but because his views were, in their opinion, mistaken and relatively to the Church of England as then constituted actually dangerous[2].

Cartwright's lectures soon produced a sensation in the University. By the force of his eloquence, the weight of his scholarship, and the outspoken nature of his doctrines, he attracted many hearers to his auditorium. He soon created a party of sympathisers and the University was threatened with dispeace and division. It is said that Whitgift replied from the pulpit to some of the most outstanding and objectionable of Cartwright's tenets[3]. Before long, the authorities,

[1] *A.C.* II, p. 360; Dixon, VI, p. 294; Paget, p. 37.

[2] *v.* Mullinger, p. 208.

[3] Paule, p. 326.

recognising that the chief question at issue was now one of polity and not merely of vestments, and that Cartwright's voice was regarded in a wide circle as authoritative, took action as they were in duty bound to do.

The first official complaint we meet with was addressed to Cecil by Wm Chaderton. In the course of his letter (11 June, 1570)[1] he says "one Mr Cartewrighte latelie chosen Into my place, reader of ye divinitie lector founded by ladie Margaret, who hathe allwaies stubbernelie refused ye cappe, and such like ornaments agreable to gods law, and ye Quenes Majesties Injunctions, dothe now In his daylie lectors teache suche doctrine as Is pernitious, and not tollerable in a christian commonwealthe: That is that in ye churche of Englande there is no lawfull and ordynarie callinge and chosinge or admittinge of ministers, nether anie ministerie: and that ye electyon of ministers and bishoppes at this daye is tyrannous: and *Archiepiscopi*, *decani*, *Archidiaconi* etc. be *officia et nomina Impietatis*." After complaining of Edmund Chapman, another Fellow of Trinity, and Robert Some, whom he calls an adherent of Cartwright and Chapman, Chaderton gravely draws Cecil's attention to the attempt "to overturne and overthrow all ecclesiasticall and civill governance that now is, and to ordeyn and institute a new founde pollicie," and beseeches the Chancellor "to take some order for reformation of suche disorders," either by means of ecclesiastical commissioners or through the Vice-Chancellor, who, in the writer's opinion, has not the situation sufficiently in hand.

John May, Vice-Chancellor of the University[2], after several communications with Cartwright concerning his teaching, procured from the latter the sum and substance of the obnoxious doctrines in six articles, which Cartwright drew up and subscribed with his own hand. These propositions, which were afterwards brought against him on the day of his deprivation, are very important. The gist of them is as follows: The names and offices of Archbishops and Bishops should be abolished. In their stead the offices of Bishops and Deacons,

[1] *S.P. Dom. Eliz.* LXXI, No. 11.

[2] *A.C.* II, p. 233.

as described in the New Testament should be established. The Bishop should have a purely spiritual function and the deacon should care for the poor. The government of the Church should not be entrusted to Chancellors of Bishops or Officials of Archdeacons, etc., but to the minister and the Presbytery of the Church. Each minister should be attached to a definite congregation. No one should, like a candidate, seek the office of a minister and none should be created ministers by the authority of Bishops, but should be elected by a Church. All should promote this reformation according to their several vocations, *i.e.* the magistrate by his authority, the minister by preaching, and all by their prayers[1].

Such are the chief formulated results of Cartwright's studies in *Acts*. The guiding principle running through them is that the Church should be modelled on that of Apostolic times and the inevitable consequence of this principle, according to Cartwright, should be the total abolition of diocesan Episcopacy and the establishment of Presbyterianism. There is no wonder, therefore, that the protagonists of the Church of England saw reason for quick and decisive action.

Grindal, lately elected to the Archbishopric of York, was well acquainted with the state of affairs in Cambridge. In a pointed letter to Cecil, written from St Paul's, London, on the 25th of June, 1570[2], he hurls the shafts of his ire at Cartwright as the chief ringleader of the University malcontents. He assures Cecil that the youth of Cambridge are thronging to Cartwright's daily lectures, in which the external government of the church is being attacked. The Vice-Chancellor and the heads are not dealing as roundly as they should with the case. Grindal suggests that Cecil should instruct Dr May and the heads to command Cartwright and his adherents to silence both in schools and pulpits, and that after examination the offenders should be reduced to conformity or duly punished by expulsion out of their colleges or out of the University as the cause should require. Mean-

[1] For the articles in Latin from the original document in the Cambridge Registry, *v.* Clarke, p. 368; St. *Whit.* III, p. 19; *Harl. MSS.* 7030, f. 197–8; and for copies with slight variants *S.P. Dom. Eliz.* LXXIV, Nos. 29 i, 30.

[2] *S.P. Dom. Eliz.* LXXI, No. 23; *Grindal Rem.* p. 323.

while, the Vice-Chancellor should not allow Cartwright to proceed D.D. at the ensuing Commencement, for he is not only guilty of the present singularity but is also not conformable in his apparel, and contemns many other laudable orders of the University. He encloses a summary of the "Positions written and delyvered by Mr Cartwright to the Vice-chauncelor of Cambrige."[1]

Immediately after these articles three notes are appended reflecting Cartwright's teaching as to the New Testament doctor, the right of the people to elect their minister, and the duty of the minister to preach to his own flock. According to this addendum Cartwright holds that "he himselfe being a reader of Divinitie is a Doctour exercisinge the office named Ephes. 4°, and therefore must onlie reade, and maye not preache."

Cecil was not long in giving his advice. Writing on the 26th of June he showed that he was in favour of repressing disorderly preaching and teaching, and promised his aid to the Vice-Chancellor and the heads in any endeavour they should make for the maintenance of the peace and order of the University. The date and contents of Cecil's letter are known from the reply sent to him by May and the heads on the 29th of June[2]. May gives an account of the troubles caused by Cartwright's supporters in a postscript which runs as follows:

"This day immediately upon the readinge of your honors letters in the regent house, suche insolent attempts were made for the preferment of Mr Cartwright to the degre of doctorship contrary as I take yt to your honors meanynge and to the good likynge of the auncient hedds of Colleges as the like hathe not heretofore byn seene, for every one of the auncient doctors there present, contrarye to our auncient custome, and to their great discredyt were denyd to be in the head for feare that they woulde stop Cartewrights grace upon your honors letters, and so none coulde be admytted to be in the same head for passinge of graces, but only suche

[1] *S.P. Dom. Eliz.* LXXI, No. 23 i; *Grindal Rem.* p. 323 *n.*
[2] *S.P. Dom. Eliz.* LXXI, No. 27.

as were knowen to favour Cartewrits cause, who neverthelesse was and is by my meanes stopped from his degre of doctorship. for wch my doinge I have sufferyd this day no smale troubles at his and his fauterers hands, and am like to sustayne more, unlesse by your honors authoritie I may be in my lawfull doinges assysted. Wherof I have no doubght, and thus most humbly I take my leave of your honor. postcribed in the presents of Mr Doctor Perne, D. Hawford, D. Harvy and D. Ithell."

Whitgift afterwards[1] referred contemptuously to Cartwright's anxious desire to secure the D.D. In his *Second Reply*[2] Cartwright rebuts the charge and makes the following interesting observations on the question: "Wherin beside that I moved nothing but yelded onely to the request off certein frindes: I had (before my grace propounded in the scholes) the advise off more than a dosen learned ministers. Who considering that I had the office off a Doctor in the universitie: were off opinion that (for the good they estemed might be done therby) I might swalow the fond and idle ceremonies which accompanie yt." Heylyn[3], of course, sees fit to regard the refusal of the D.D. as the reason why Cartwright and his adherents began to esteem all academic degrees unlawful![4]

The friends of Cartwright allowed but a few days to elapse after the eventful 29th of June before they drew up a Latin testimonial in his favour and forwarded it to Cecil. It was signed by eighteen members of the University and dated the 3rd of July. The memorialists are grieved to hear that Cartwright has incurred the Chancellor's displeasure. They so cherish him as a singular ornament of learning that they desire him to be reinstated in Cecil's favour. His character is beyond reproach. His profession of religion, free from Romish adulteration as well as the cult of novelty, against both of which he is a strong bulwark, is entirely scriptural. As to his learning, he is so proficient in Greek, Latin and

[1] *Defence of Answer*, p. 781.

[2] *Epistel*, sig.)()(*ii verso*.

[3] *A.R.* lib. VI, § 32.

[4] A doctorate is by mistake sometimes ascribed to Cartwright. G. Dyer, *History of the University and Colleges of Cambridge* (1814), I, p. 97.

Hebrew, that there is none his equal in the three together. His lectures are exceedingly popular, the multitudes who attend them being fascinated by his skilful interpretation, his felicity as a teacher, the importance of his subject-matter, his weighty judgments and his eloquence. He was never so highly esteemed in the University and he is particularly acceptable to the foreigners in exile, who regard him as on a level with Continental scholars of world-wide fame. He enjoys general goodwill at Cambridge; in fact, he is universally beloved. This comprehensive and beautiful testimonial, the original[1] of which is given in Appendix III, is signed not by mere striplings, but by men of worth and attainment. Most of them were at least Fellows of Colleges; many of them had been University preachers; one of them was Proctor for the year; one was Professor of Greek; and several of them afterwards won great distinction in the Church. Their names are William Pachet, Edmund Rockrey, Robert Tower, Robert Linford, Robert Soame, Bartholomew Dodington, John Swan, Osmund David, Richard Howland, Simon Bucke, Edmund Sherbroke, George Joy, Richard Greenham, Alan Par, Thomas Aldrich, Walter Alen, John Still and Robert Holland[2].

In a letter, dated the 9th of July, 1570, to Cecil, Cartwright defends himself against his enemies and lays before the Chancellor of the University a clear explanation of his position[3]. Lamenting that the breath of calumny has reached the Court and Cecil's ears, and regretting the need of vindicating himself, he protests that he is most averse from sedition and contention, that he has taught nothing that did not flow naturally from the context under treatment, and that he deliberately avoided the vestiarian controversy. He does not deny that he taught that the present ministry has declined from that of the ancient and apostolic Church, to the purity of which he desires that of the existing Church to be conformed. His advocacy of this reformation has been so

[1] Brook's version (*Mem.* p. 58) is faulty and misleading.

[2] For particulars of signatories *v.* Venn, *Matrics.*, *G. Bk*, *A.C.*, etc.

[3] App. IV.

quiet and modest, that none but the ignorant and malicious could find fault with it. He lays before Cecil a testimonial from some who heard his lectures. He does not doubt that, if the Vice-Chancellor had not refused him a *concio*, almost the whole University would have testified in his behalf. As he cannot include in a letter every particular of the lectures that have given offence, he is willing to substantiate what he propounded, if desired. He hopes that Cecil will not let him and the truth be overthrown by the hatred of his enemies.

The enclosed testimonial in Cartwright's favour (App. V) was drawn up by fifteen members of the University, who had attended his lectures. In the *Calendar of State Papers*[1] it is incorrectly stated that it was written by Aldrich, Par and fourteen others in their own defence. Lacking the weight and fulness of the testimonial of the 3rd of July, it consists of a few crisp and concise sentences, in which the writers furnish an effective vindication of their teacher. The rumour has reached them that Cartwright has fallen under Cecil's suspicion, because by his lectures he has fanned the flames of discord into a great conflagration, and that he has rashly plunged into a controversy concerning the ministry and the vestments. They certify that they have heard the lectures and that there was nothing in them of an inflammatory nature. Cartwright, indeed, never touched the vestiarian question, and although he suggested that the existing ministry should be reformed according to certain principles, he had done so with caution and moderation. Like the previous testimonial this one notes that Cartwright did not meddle with the vestiarian controversy. The fact is that he dealt with a matter that was to turn Puritanism into a new channel, the question of the ministry and of ecclesiastical government. No matter how innocent his intentions, his lectures marked a new point of departure in the history of Puritanism and both parties were conscious of the change. Of the signatories of the last-mentioned testimonial Tower, Some, Swan, Bucke, Howland, Aldrich, Par and Still appended their names to

[1] *Dom. Eliz.* LXXI, No. 33.

that of the 3rd of July. The other seven were Robert Willan, Richard Chambers, Christopher Kirkland, Thomas Barbar, Laurence Washington, William Tabor and John More.

A few days before his journey to the north, Grindal, in a letter to Cecil from Westminster, 27 July, 1570[1], urges the expulsion of the nonconformists from Cambridge if they do not renounce their factious assertions. He thinks, however, that even if Cartwright revokes his doctrines, he should never be permitted to lecture again in the University. He has conceived a definitely adverse opinion of the Puritan Professor, accusing him of having a busy head, stuffed full of singularities.

Cecil, having been, as we have seen, importunately besieged by both sides, now intervenes. On the 3rd of August he addresses a letter[2] to the Vice-Chancellor and the heads, in which he discusses the situation at Cambridge in the spirit of wise moderation. He observes that "the novelty is, ye late entry of Mr Cartwright...into some new observations of ye errors in ye ministry of ye Church, taxyng such ministeryes as namely Archbishopps and such lyke, as he fyndeth not expressly named in ye bookes of ye New Testament." As yet he is not sure of the degree of Cartwright's offence. He has received reports of the affair from Cartwright and his friends and also from his adversaries, and so far is inclined to the view that Cartwright has merely dealt with the questions at issue in academic fashion, and not as a turbulent innovator. "What mynd he had in ye moving of these matters by hym self in communication I perceave, the same not to be much reprehended, being as it semeth not of any arrogancy, or intention to move troubles, but as a reader of ye scriptures, to gyve notes, by waye of comparison betwixt ye ordre of ye ministry in ye tyme of ye Apostles, and ye present tymes now in this Church of England." Cecil, however, is aware of the danger that may arise from the promulgation of this teaching, and has accordingly thought good to use his authority as Chancellor "to charge Mr Cartwright

[1] *S.P. Dom. Eliz.* LXXI, No. 58; *Grindal Rem.* p. 304.
[2] *S.P. Dom. Eliz.* LXXIII, No. 4.

not to deale any furder in these kynd of questions in his redyngs or sermons, or any other wise, untill yt some furder ordre may be taken this Michelmas terme therin uppon some more commoditie of conference mete for such a matter, wherunto he hath accorded." While advising that the controversy should be held in abeyance, he is not desirous of commanding the University authorities in a matter, which, he modestly suggests, may be beyond his understanding, and states that he is willing to concur in any opinion or action which the Vice-Chancellor and heads may deem necessary and so continues: "for ye furder determination of these new Questions as well for common ordre as for ye truth of ye Controversy I shall gladly receave your adviscеs and opinions meaning therunto to conform my self for ye creditt I have in your wisdoms and gret lerninges and ye love yt I trust you beare to ye truth and common quietnes." While acknowledging Cartwright's apparent innocence and wishing to treat him fairly Cecil leaves the decision of the controversy to the Vice-Chancellor and the heads, and thus in effect leaves Cartwright at the mercy of his opponents.

Most of the heads were now away from home, but three of them, Hawford, Whitgift and Harvey, lost no time in sending an interim answer to Cecil's communication. They promise a full reply when the other heads return. "In the meane tyme," they write, 11 August, 1570[1], "we have thowght yt very convenient and necessarye to stay Mr Cartwright frome reading, bothe for the contagiusnes of the tyme, the absens of divers of hys auditors, and also lest hys admittans to reade agayne, being ones by the Vicechansler and heads inhybited (withowt some satisfaction) myght seme to gyve authoritye and creditt to hys new opinions." The trio state that Cartwright's views are untrue as well as dangerous and they beseech Cecil not to encourage "suche as wold be countyd authors of strange opinions and new devises." It is plain that they are uneasy. Cecil's letter contained passages testifying to Cartwright's irreprehensible motives that were sufficient to make them anxious, and doubtless they were

[1] *S.P. Dom. Eliz.* LXXIII, No. 11.

glad that he had expressed himself willing to conform to their official judgment.

On the same day that the three heads wrote to Cecil twenty-two members of the University also addressed an epistle to their Chancellor, but in a different strain[1]. They wrote as friends of Cartwright expressing their gratitude to Cecil for his favourable opinion of their esteemed Professor. They complain that Cartwright remains in silence, they miss his teaching, of which they have been long deprived, and beg that they may have the benefit of it again. They refer to their previous petition in Cartwright's behalf. Now they plead for themselves and the common good of the University. They endorse Cecil's kind judgment of Cartwright, but earnestly plead with him to go further in his vindication of their teacher and exercise his own authority. Probably they knew and were distressed by the knowledge that he was willing to agree with the ultimate verdict of the University heads. Fourteen of the appended names have already appeared in previous testimonials. The second Proctor for the year, Reuben Sherwood, now signs along with Aldrich. The seven other new signatories are Roger Browne, Robert Rhodes, Edmund Chapman, Hugo Boothe, John Knewstub, Thomas Leach and George Slater.

We gather from the number of names adhibited to the three testimonials sent to Cecil in July and August that Cartwright had a considerable following in the University. There were thirty-three subscribers in all. Five of them subscribed on the three occasions mentioned, twelve signed twice, and the rest once.

Cartwright also had well-wishers and admirers outside of Cambridge. Among these was his old friend, Adam Loftus, who wrote from Dublin[2] (26 October, 1570) beseeching Cecil to show his "honorable lovinge favor to my deare frend, Mr Cartwright, of Cambridge, a man bothe for his profounde learninge and sincere and godly life right worthy to be tendered and muche estemed." "I thinke," continues Loftus, "I nede not to commend hym any farther whose

[1] App. VI. [2] *S.P. Ireland, Eliz.* XXX, No. 88.

worthenes dothe abundantly commende hym selfe, and specially I nede not to commende hym to you, who (as I well remember) at my beinge with you did right worthely commend hym to me. I understand by some which are come hither from Cambridge, that he hathe been before you for certeyne questions and matters touchinge religyon, and I am enformed that he hathe tasted of your honorable favour, the whiche I moste hartely beseche you, and that for the churche of Christs sake, to contynew towardes hym. I havinge had good experience of hym, for that he was a yere here with me, do verely beleve that he will prove a rare and a singuler ornament to the churche and realme of England. As touchinge the matters that he maynteyneth, I do neyther fully know them, neyther do I mynde now to speke of them. But if peradventure he should be deceyved, he were with learninge and mekenes to be perswaded, and not with violence to be molested or greved."

Not content to let his cause be furthered merely by his friends Cartwright, in a Latin epistle written in Cambridge on the 18th of August, 1570, again makes a personal appeal to Cecil[1]. Among the evidences of the latter's good will he gives first place to the letters Cecil had addressed to him. He counts it a great honour that one of the highest rulers of the realm should write to such an insignificant person, *ad tantulum homuncionem*. After several such complimentary observations regarding Cecil's patronage Cartwright proceeds to bespeak the Chancellor's close examination of the discipline or system of government, which is necessary to Church and State. He considers the question at issue one that has concerned law-makers from the time of Moses and regards it as worthy of the attention of such an eminent statesman as Cecil. He enthusiastically promises that it will repay Cecil to devote himself to the cause of order and government, which is upheld by almost all pious men in England and in foreign nations and also has the approval of God. Cartwright plainly shows that the substance of his lectures was not merely academic, but that he ardently believes in the re-

[1] App. VII.

formation of Church government on apostolic lines. He is at pains to point out that his cause is not a novelty and hopes that Cecil will not hold with those who charge reformers with a desire to alter that which ought not to be changed or with a contempt of old laws. The cause he is defending, far from being a novelty, is 1570 years old. In conclusion, Cartwright refers to the unjust treatment he has received at the hands of the University authorities. Although he willingly accepted the conditions laid down by Cecil, that he should omit controversial matter from his lectures, the heads will not give him permission to read at all. So he commends his cause to his Chancellor and his God.

Cartwright's cause, however, was not prospering. Cecil, after hearing that the Vice-Chancellor and heads had suspended the Professor, evidently intimated that he concurred in the action taken. Whitgift, writing from Trinity College on the 19th of August, 1570[1], acknowledges receipt of Cecil's letter of acquiescence. "I have receavyd your letters," he says, "and have signifyed to the other which also writ unto youre honor your contentation with our doengs touching Mr Cartwright." He is not quite sure that the Chancellor is fully aware of the true nature of Cartwright's tenets and proceeds to furnish him with the substance of the disturbing doctrines and to impress upon him their dangerous character. Whitgift has held a private conference with Cartwright, and it was during this interview that the latter rehearsed the points in question, which Whitgift now passes on to Cecil: "I thingk your honor dothe nott fully understand Mr Cartwrights opinions, and therfore I have here sett down so many of them, as he hym self hathe utteryd to me in private conferens, the which he hath also openly taught." He then gives the substance of Cartwright's anti-Episcopal assertions, upon which divers others depend, "which wold brede a mere confusion, yf they showld tayke place."[2]

With this presentation of Cartwright's teaching before him Cecil could no longer cherish the mistaken belief that Cartwright was merely indulging in simple exegesis or an academic

[1] *S.P. Dom. Eliz.* LXXIII, No. 26. [2] St. *Whit.* III, p. 16.

comparison of the Apostolic with the existing Church. Whitgift made it plain that the suspended Professor had taught that the Church of England ought to be reformed according to what he considered the Apostolic model. Turning from the case of Cartwright Whitgift makes reference to the new University statutes, which were in course of preparation: "I towld your honor att my last being with you of certan things to be reformyd in the statutes and orders of this Universitye, and also of some things necessarilye to be addyd, for the better government of the same: your honor wyllyd me to confer with some other, and to draw a drawght, that your honor myght se them. Mr Vicechanslor, d. perne, d. Hawford, dr. Harvy, d. Ithell and I, have laboryd therein, and have allmost fynisshed the same. Bycause your honor ys trobled with other busynes, so yt yt wold be to muche for your self to pereuse them, yf yt wold please you to write youre letters to my l. of canterbury hys grace, or some other whom you thingk best, to tayke that paynes, and mayk report unto your honors, of them, we trust they wyll be thowght very necessary, and profyttable for the state of the universitye and good government of the same."

The new statutes passed the royal seal *Datum apud manerium nostrum de Reding* on the 25th of September, 1570. They are fully discussed by Cooper in his *Annals of Cambridge*[1], and are given *in extenso* by Heywood and Wright in their *Cambridge University Transactions during the Puritan Controversies*[2]. Widely unpopular and particularly obnoxious to the Puritans they were for several years the subject of bitter controversy in the University[3]. On the 6th of May, 1572, a notable protest against them was signed by 164 members of the University, among the signatories being Richard Bancroft, John Longworth, John Knewstub, Alan Par, Edmund Rockrey, Robert Willan, etc.[4] The chief feature of the change of constitution was the absolute power that was now given to the heads of houses, *e.g.* in the election of the *caput* and

[1] II, pp. 258 ff. [2] I, pp. 1–45.
[3] Cooper, *Ann.* II, p. 279; H. & W. I, p. 58; Mullinger, pp. 230 ff.
[4] H. & W. I, p. 61.

the Vice-Chancellor. Under the old ordinances the election of Cartwright to the Vice-Chancellorship was conceivable and, considering his influence and popularity with a large section of the University, probable. The new statutes entrusted the nomination of two candidates for that post to the heads. The rights of the regents and non-regents were withdrawn; these members of the University were now obliged to elect one of the nominees set before them[1]. The heads, being now antagonistic to Cartwright, were certain to appoint a Vice-Chancellor who shared their own inimical attitude to the reformer. Considering the position held by the Master of Trinity it was not surprising that the first Vice-Chancellor elected after the new statutes came into force, was Cartwright's doughty opponent, John Whitgift.

The new statutes made it easy for the heads to compel a Professor holding the views of Cartwright to renounce his tenets, or, on his refusal, to deprive him of his post and expel him from the University[2].

It is not allowable, however, for the historian to attribute motives without a plenitude of evidence. To assert with Brook (*Mem.* p. 66) that the statutes were procured by Whitgift and his colleagues in order to enable them to proceed against Cartwright with the utmost severity and to prevent his election as Vice-Chancellor, is to narrow the motives of these men unduly. It may be that they conscientiously believed that they were making provision for the better government of the University. Nevertheless, although we are not warranted in adjudging them Machiavellian monsters,

[1] c. XXXIV. *De electione procancellarii: Ille, ex duobus quos praefecti collegiorum nominaverint, et non alius, procancellarius erit, quem major pars regentium et nonregentium suffragiis suis elegerit.*

[2] c. XLV. *De concionibus: Prohibemus ne quisquam in concione aliqua, in loco communi tractando, in lectionibus publicis, seu aliter publice intra Universitatem nostram quicquam doceat, tractet, vel defendat contra religionem, seu ejusdem aliquam in regno nostro publica authoritate receptam et stabilitam: aut contra aliquem statum, authoritatem, dignitatem, seu gradum vel ecclesiasticum vel civilem hujus regni nostri Angliae vel Hiberniae: qui contra fecerit, errorem vel temeritatem suam concellarii jussu cum assensu majoris partis praefectorum collegiorum revocabit, et publice confitebitur. Quod si recusaverit, aut non humiliter, eo modo quo illi praescribitur, perfecerit, eadem authoritate a collegio suo perpetuo excludatur et Universitate exulabit.*

who sought to overturn the constitution of a University for the sake of private vengeance, the fact remains that the new ordinances were, *inter alia*, designed to stay certain excesses of the movement represented by Cartwright and that they claimed the Lady Margaret Professor as their first victim. It appeared even to contemporaries as if *post hoc* were *propter hoc*, and that the framers of the new laws were actuated by unworthy motives. Dering, in his bold outspoken fashion, rebuked the Chancellor for sending the unrighteous statutes to Cambridge[1] (18 November, 1570). He attacked the heads who had been concerned in their composition and alleged that Whitgift had been impelled to undertake the work by the force of personal feeling and plainly charged him with a "froward minde against Mr Cartwright."

On the 7th of November Whitgift, Perne, May, W. Chaderton, Harvey, Ithell, Byng and Shepherd thank Cecil "for the procuring of the late statutes."[2] Kelk in an appendix to the letter approves of the statutes, and condemns Cartwright's tenets, but adds "as fore mr cartwhrytt i have nether herd hym red nether conferd with hym and therfore i can say nothyng but by hersay." The writers affirm that the statutes have proved a great boon to the University, although "the younger sort for the restraynt of there Lybertye much murmur and gruge att them." They report that they intend to deprive Cartwright of his Chair, and certify their intention to Cecil that he may give his consent, and also to forestall untrue rumours that may come to his ears. They have done their utmost to persuade Cartwright to retract his assertions, "butt the more favorably he ys delt with, the more untractable we fynde hym." They enclose a copy of Cartwright's propositions[3], for which he has been forbidden to lecture, "which he hathe hym self sett downe and subscribyd with hys owne hand, wherunto also he ys fully bent to stand." Some of these are pronounced "to be untrew, dangerus and tendyng to the ruine bothe of learnyng and religion, as the 1. 2. 4. and 5. some untrewlye imaginyd, to mayk the common

[1] *Lansd. MSS.* XII, No. 86.

[2] *S.P. Dom. Eliz.* LXXIV, No. 29.

[3] *ibid.* No. 29 i.

sort beleve that to be, which ys nott, as the 3. and 6." Besides these six propositions Cecil was put in possession of other twenty, which are sometimes regarded as peculiarly Cartwright's. Cecil's endorsement of the list of all the six and twenty articles[1] expressly states that they are *Articuli propositi et divulgati per Cartrytum et alios*. The twenty should therefore be looked upon as tenets representative of the Puritanism of 1570 and not as *ipsissima verba* of Cartwright, although he probably believed in them all. Of these twenty propositions the following are typical[2]:

To reform the church it is necessary to reduce it to the Apostolic model. None should be allowed in the ministry unless they can teach. Only preachers should be allowed to conduct divine service or administer the sacraments. Only Canonical Scriptures should be read in public. Officiating at funerals is no more the function of a minister than of the other members of the Church. All Scripture should be regarded with equal reverence, and people should not stand at the reading of the gospel or bow at the name of Jesus. Sitting at Communion is preferable to kneeling or standing. Private administration of the Sacraments is not allowed. The cross in Baptism is superstitious.

On the 11th of December, 1570, Cartwright was duly deprived of his Professorship. He appeared before his judges —Vice-Chancellor Whitgift, Perne, Hawford, Kelk, May, Chaderton (Doctors of Divinity), Harvey, Ithel, Byng (Doctors of Law)—in the great chamber of the house of the Master of Trinity College (Whitgift's). The Vice-Chancellor begins the examination. He charges Cartwright with the six propositions, which the Puritan had written out and subscribed with his own hand. They are contrary to the established religion of the realm, but nevertheless Cartwright has openly taught them in his lectures and elsewhere, and has circulated them as matter that he would stand to. Most of the Doctors of the University have already pointed out his error before the late Vice-Chancellor, Dr May, by whom he

[1] *S.P. Dom. Eliz.* LXXIV, No. 30. 7 November, 1570.
[2] *v.* St. *Ann.* II, p. 381, for all of them in full.

was several times admonished to revoke his doctrine. On his refusal Cartwright was punished by the subtraction of his stipend. Now Whitgift requires an absolute answer. Will he abide by his tenets or revoke them? Cartwright acknowledges that, after divers communications with Dr May and several admonitions from the latter, he delivered to Dr May, then Vice-Chancellor, in writing and subscribed with his own hand, those articles with which Whitgift now charges him, but affirms that he did so on condition that he should know who his adversaries and judges would be and "that thys thing shoulde not be prejudicial to such order as Mr Secretary had taken with hym" (that he be allowed to lecture on non-controversial subjects). Whitgift brushes aside the conditions and bluntly asks Cartwright whether these subscribed articles are his own and whether he mindeth to defend or revoke them. Cartwright declares that they are his own, that he has openly taught them and that he is determined to maintain and defend them as truth. Whereupon Whitgift requires him better to consider with himself and withdraw for a space. On Cartwright's return Whitgift, perceiving that in spite of all admonitions he persists in his opinions, with the unanimous consent of the above-mentioned Doctors pronounces Cartwright removed from the Lady Margaret Professorship or lecture and declares the Chair vacant and further, in virtue of his office, the Vice-Chancellor inhibits the Puritan from preaching within the University and the jurisdiction of the same[1].

Thus Cartwright suffered for his principles. His unwavering allegiance to his convictions on this occasion elicits our admiration. He is sometimes sneered at as not having been made of the stuff of martyrs, but there is no cause to depreciate his conduct on this score in 1570. He was then deprived of his Chair because he was brave enough to follow the dictates of conscience before all else. His punishment did not include ejection from his Fellowship at Trinity,

[1] Strype (*Whit.* III, p. 17) gives a full account of the proceedings *e Regist. Academ. Cantabr.* *v.* account of the deprivation *desumpta ex Registro Acad. Cant.* by Baker, *Harl. MSS.* 7030, ff. 197–8.

which Soames and others say took place before his loss of the professorship and which, according to Brook[1], followed "soon after." This second deprivation belongs, as we shall see, to the year 1572 and on a different count. We may agree with Dixon[2] that the treatment meted out to Cartwright was merciful compared with the doom he would have met with in other countries, and that the authorities acted with leniency and without precipitation, giving him every opportunity to retract his opinions and so remain in office. It may be granted that from the point of view of his opponents his behaviour was dangerous, that he was playing into the hands of the unscrupulous, who would willingly see the Church destroyed that they might gather its spoils, and that his courageous stand in behalf of Presbyterianism was merely an exhibition of foolish obstinacy. But Cartwright has a right to his own point of view and many, eminent and wise, have endorsed it as superior to the other, and in their judgment he was willing to sacrifice his position and his undoubted prospects of promotion in University and Church rather than be disloyal to the voice of duty, truth and conscience. The chief result of his conduct was the resuscitation and reformulation of English Puritanism. He made the question of polity the distinctive and foremost note of the movement. By his stedfast spokesmanship and suffering he drew round him a band of Puritan enthusiasts. During his short career as a Professor he gave cohesion and a new stimulus to Puritanism, particularly in academic circles. On the other hand, however, he roused the vigilance of the Church authorities. Archbishop Parker himself was greatly perturbed by the free circulation of the view that Bishops should be abolished. He frankly expressed his grief on this point to the Queen[3] and to Cecil he wrote that he feared that the Precisians, as he called the Puritans, were nourishing some monster and that they would need to be stayed by coercion. He also stated that, as urged by Cecil, he had written to "him"—generally

[1] *Mem.* p. 74.
[2] VI, p. 296.
[3] 27 December, 1570. *Parker Corresp.* p. 371.

thought to be Cartwright—but apparently without success[1]. The most resolute and outstanding of the antagonists raised by Cartwright was Whitgift. The future Archbishop now stands in the forefront of the opposition to the rising tide of Puritanism and it is with him that the next document relative to Cartwright's professorial experience is connected.

Cartwright had been sincerely anxious that a public disputation should be held for the examination of the tenets in question. Whitgift had taken up the matter and invited him to a conference. The conditions laid down by Whitgift, namely, that the discussion should be conducted in private and in writing, did not satisfy Cartwright, who accordingly refused it. The rumour arose and spread that Cartwright had offered disputation and conference and that he could not obtain his request. This half-truth touched the honour of Whitgift to the quick and he caused a certificate to be drawn up, in which the subscribers (Whitgift, Perne, Hawford, W. Chaderton, May, Harvey, Ithell, Byng) testify that Cartwright "was offered Conference of divers, and namelye of Mr Dr Whitegifte; who offered that if the sayde Mr Cartwright woulde set down his assertions in writinge and his reasons unto them; he woulde answere the same in writinge allso." This Cartwright refused to do. Further, at the time of Cartwright's deprivation Whitgift did in the presence of the signatories, ask Cartwright whether he (Whitgift) had not several times offered him a conference: "To the which Mr Cartwright answered that he had bene so offred, and that he refused the same." At the foot of the document Matthew Stokys, notary public, who was present at the deprivation on the 11th of December, vouches for the truth of this last declaration: *et tunc et ibidem audivi Doctorem Whitgifte interrogantem Mrm Cartwright de praemissis allegatis, et Mrm Cartwright eadem confitentem. Ideo in fidem et testimonium praemissorum nomen meum requisitus subscripsi.* Further, it is affirmed in the body of the certificate that Cartwright never offered a disputation except on the condition "that he might knowe who shoulde be his adversaries and who shoulde be

[1] 21 January, 1570–1. *Parker Corresp.* p. 377.

his judges: meaninge such judges, as he him selfe coulde best like of." Even this kind of disputation was not denied him "but onelye he was required to obteyne license of the Q. Matie or the Counsell, because his assertions be repugnante to the state of the Commonwealth, which maye not be called into question by publique disputacion without license of the Prince or her Highnesse Counsell." This document[1] is entitled "Mr Cartwrights refusall to dispute with Mr Whitegifte before the Masters of Colledges" and is dated "18 Martii Anno Dn̄i. 1570," *i.e.* 1570–1, and was therefore not drawn up, as Dixon says[2], in Cartwright's presence on the day of his deprivation. It is a sufficient reply to the common bruit that Cartwright's challenge had not been accepted. It also explains the whole question of conference and shows that neither side would accept the other's terms. The matter cropped up later when Whitgift and Cartwright were engaged in their famous literary duel. When the latter in his *Reply*[3] suggests a public disputation Whitgift answers "I have sundry times, both privately and publicly, as I am able to prove by sufficient testimonies, and you cannot deny, offered you conference by writing of these matters; I have earnestly moved you unto it; and you have always refused it."[4] The reason for Cartwright's refusal is made clear enough in his *Second Reply* (1575)[5]: "For beside that I answered, that yt was meet the doctrine I had taught openly, should be defended openly: and beside that also I went to two off the universitie Doctors to be conferred with: I offered my self to his privat conference, which althowgh he had promised, yet under pretence that I was (as he said) uncorrigible, he would not performe. The truth is, he offered privat conference by writing: but having before experience off his unfaithfulnes many waies, I refused yt."

Not long after Cartwright was deprived of his Cambridge professorship we find him filling the rôle of an academic teacher in Geneva. Till recently the only warrant for thus

[1] *Petyt MSS.* (Inner Temple) 538, vol. XLVII, f. 39.
[2] VI, p. 293.
[3] *W.W.* II, p. 191.
[4] *ibid.* II, p. 192; III, p. 467.
[5] sig.)()(*ii verso.*

connecting him with the wellspring of sixteenth century Presbyterianism was thought to be a mere casual assertion in one of the Marprelate Tracts, viz. "Thomas Cartwright, who hath bene professour of divinitie both in Cambridge and in Geneva."[1] Even the *Dictionary of National Biography*[2] knows of no other authority and passes by the question. But the Genevan archives substantiate the words of Martin Marprelate and throw new light upon what has hitherto been a gap in the life of Cartwright. Scholars are greatly indebted to the painstaking Borgeaud for unearthing the important facts, which he has incorporated in his valuable history of Geneva University[3]. Unfortunately the register of the inhabitants of Geneva for the years 1560–72 is lost or we may have learned more of the Puritan in exile. The registers of the Council and the Company of Ministers supply the new information. The first mention in these of Cartwright's presence in Geneva is in June, 1571. It has been suggested that he may have accompanied Beza to the National Synod of the French Reformed Church held at La Rochelle in April, 1571, but the data to hand are insufficient to confirm the hypothesis[4]. It is now manifest however that Mullinger places Cartwright's departure to Geneva too late, viz. after September, 1571, when he states, in error, Cartwright was expelled from his Fellowship[5].

The Genevan ministers intimated to the Council that Cartwright had been asked by them to deliver lectures in theology twice a week, on Thursdays and Fridays, and that he was willing to do so. Their proposal came before the Council on the 28th of June and was approved: *Anglois ministre. Les ministres ayant fait advertir qu'il y a icy un Anglois, excellent théologien, lequel ils ont prié de faire quelques*

[1] *The Epitome*, sig. F. 2, ed. Pierce, p. 163.

[2] Art. "Cartwright."

[3] *Histoire de l'Université de Genève*, par Charles Borgeaud, Genève, 1900. Extracts from this work concerning Cartwright and Andrew Melville in Geneva are printed in *American Hist. Review*, v, pp. 284 ff., and separately, New York, 1899.

[4] *v.* "Early English Presbyterians" by Mrs W. W. D. Campbell in *Journal of Presb. Hist. Soc. of Eng.* II, No. 3, May 1922.

[5] Mullinger, *St John's*, p. 67, and *D.N.B.* art. "Cartwright."

leçons en théologie, le jeudi et le vendredi, ce qu'il leur a promis faire gratuitement, s'il est trouvé bon par Messieurs, arreste qu'on l'aprouve[1].

At this time the Genevan Academy was flourishing under the direction of the famous Beza, but a recurring plague was constantly threatening its prosperity. Writing to Peter Melius on the 18th of June, 1570, Beza observed: *Crescit haec nostra schola mirabiliter, sed, quod plane miserabile est, ex multarum aliarum ruinis. Pestis reliquiae, quanvis parvae, nonnihil tamen opus nostrum remorantur*[2]. In a letter of the same date to Christopher Thretius he wrote in a similar strain: *Crescit schola, sed ex aliarum multarum ruinis. Magnus pauperum etiam ministrorum et studiosorum numerus concurrit, ut pares huic oneri tam diu sustinendo non simus, quanvis Helveticae omnes Ecclesiae liberaliter nos iuverint....Pestis quartum iam annum nos exercet, nunc tamen admodum leviter, nec quisquam alicuius nominis nobis est ereptus*[3]. Evidently Beza would be glad of the co-operation of a man of Cartwright's attainments and academic experience to help him to cope with the work that was now increased by the large concourse of students. That he held the Englishman in high estimation is clear from the eulogy quoted by Clarke[4] from one of Beza's letters, in which he said that the sun did not shine upon a more learned man than Cartwright.

An entry in the journal of Sir Francis Walsingham, then acting as Elizabeth's ambassador in France, besides confirming Borgeaud's discovery, shows that Cartwright was not losing touch with his English friends. Walsingham was an active supporter of the reformer and frequently we come across traces of his sympathetic interest in Cartwright's career. According to his diary he received on the 3rd of July, 1571, letters from Geneva written by Portus and Cartwright: "Tewsday. 3. I went from Poissy to Paris to bed. Lettres receaved from Geneva from Mr Portus, Mr Cartwright."[5] Franciscus Portus, a native of Greece, was then

[1] *Reg. Conseil* (28 juin 1571). Borgeaud, p. 108.
[2] *Epist. Liber* I, 1575, p. 193. [3] *ibid.* p. 196. [4] p. 369.
[5] "Journal of Sir Francis Walsingham. Dec. 1570 to April 1583." *Camden Misc.* VI, 1870.

Professor of Greek in Geneva. One of his most distinguished pupils, Casaubon, referred to him thus: *Sincera pietas, virtus excellens, et singularis doctrina, bonis omnibus venerabilem reddebant*[1]. During his abode in Geneva Andrew Melville was an intimate friend of Portus, with whom, according to James Melville[2], he ventured to dispute concerning the pronunciation of the Greek language: "for the Greik pronuncit it after the comoun form, keiping the accents; the quhilk Mr Andro controllit be precepts and reasons, till the Greik wald grow angrie, and cry out, *Vos Scoti, vos barbari! docebetis nos Graecos pronunciationem linguae nostrae, scilicet!*"

In July, 1571, the plague at Geneva increased in virulence[3]. In the middle of the month Beza earnestly besought Bullinger to pray for the brethren of the Genevan Church. By September part of the school had to be closed down[4]. Even the ranks of the Professors were being thinned. Veyrat died, Portus was laid prostrate, and a pious and learned Englishman, who had given Beza great assistance, was beginning to languish: *Job Veyrat, professeur de philosophie est mort. Portus, qui est plus que sexagénaire, souffre de la fièvre. Un Anglais, homme pieux et savant, qui nous était d'un grand secours, commence à languir*[5]. Borgeaud suggests that the reference is to Cartwright, whom he commends for having helped Beza to keep the famous school of learning in life during these trying times[6]. The winter of 1571 brought an abatement of the pestilence and efforts to restore the school are recorded: *Scholam incipimus instaurare*[7], *Instaurandae scholae nostrae nunc toti incumbimus*[8]. But the calamitous visitation had prevented the usual influx of refugees and students. Even in the spring of 1572 Beza lamented to Knox that the city was not what he (Knox) had known it to be and deplored the empty benches in the school[9].

While Cartwright's labours were being much appreciated

[1] McCrie, p. 16 *n*.
[2] *Diary*, p. 42.
[3] Borgeaud, p. 119.
[4] Beza, *Epist*. p. 232.
[5] Beza to Bullinger, 19 September, 1571. Borgeaud, p. 119.
[6] Borgeaud, pp. 119, 316.
[7] 25 December, 1571. Beza, *Epist*. p. 317.
[8] 11 January, 1572, *ibid*. p. 312.
[9] 12 April, 1572, *ibid*. p. 314.

in Switzerland his presence was sorely missed by the Puritans in England. Some of them were urgent for his return and their desire was made known to the Genevan ministers by Chevallier in a communication, which was read at a meeting of the Company on Friday, the 18th of January, 1572: *Le vendredy* 18. *tous les Freres estans ensemble, lettres d'Angleterre escrites par M. Chevalier ont esté levées par lesquelles on rapelle M. Th. Carturit*[1]. Clarke[2] says that Cartwright was earnestly solicited to return "by letters from Master Dearing, Master Fulk, Master Wiburne, Master Leaver, and Master Fox." Chevallier would prove a fitting intermediary between the English Puritans and Geneva, because he had been a Professor of Hebrew there from 1559 to 1566, and would know many of the leading Genevans well. He had also been, as we have seen, a close associate of Cartwright when the latter was in Cambridge.

Keenly interested in the Presbyterian system Cartwright was anxious, before he returned home, to become thoroughly acquainted with the practical details of the much vaunted Genevan model. He and van Til, a Flemish minister, expressed the wish to Beza that they might be allowed to be present at a meeting of the local Consistory, that their experience might help them in the government of their own churches and that they might by first hand evidence be able to meet criticism of the Genevan system. Their desire was brought to the notice of the ministers by Beza; it commended itself to the brethren, who decided to ask the Council for their approval: *Le jeudi* 25*e* (24th) *M. de Bèze a proposé au Consistoire s'il trouveroit bon que M Carturit et M Van Til assistassent à quelques uns de nos consistoires, ce qu'ils desiroyent pour voir l'ordre qu'on y tient et y profiter et s'en servir, non seulement aux gouvernements de leurs Eglises, mais aussi pour respondre à ceux qui parlent de notre Consistoire autrement qu'il ne fault. La chose a esté trouvée bonne et a esté arresté que Messieurs seroient priés de l'approuver pour le consistoire prochain*[3]. The next day Cartwright, having been invited to

[1] *Reg. Comp.* (jan. 1572). Borgeaud, p. 108. [2] p. 369.
[3] *Reg. Comp.* (jan. 1572).

attend the meeting of ministers, was thanked by them for his services in the school. They commended the Church of Geneva to his prayers, as also to those of the brethren in England, with whom in the days of their exile a bond of friendship had been created, which the Genevan ministers wished to maintain. Cartwright reciprocated their good wishes, expressed his gratitude for the great kindness he had received in Geneva, and promised that he would do all he could for the Church to which he felt himself beholden for all time. The brethren further invited Cartwright and his English companions, who were in the city, to dine at the rectorial banquet in the house of M. Ch. Perrot on Tuesday, the 28th of January: *Le vendredi 26e* (really 25th) *M Carturit a esté apellé en nostre Compagnie et a esté remercié de la peine qu'il avoit prinse pour ceste Eschole laquelle nous désirons de recognoistre à nostre pouvoir et en général et en particulier, recommandant ceste Eglise à ses prières, comme aussi à celles des frères d'Angleterre, vers lesquels il alloit, lesquels comme on a veu icy volontiers et aimez, quand ils y estoient aultrefois retirez, aussi désirons nous ceste saincte amitié estre bien entretenue et que de nostre part nous serons tousjours très joyeux de leur faire service. M Carturit de sa part a remercié fort expressement les frères de l'honeur qu'il avait receu particulièrement d'eux, outre l'humanité et bon accueil qu'il avoit receu généralement en ceste cité, et s'est offert à ceste Eglise en tout ce qu'il pourroit, à laquelle il se sent à jamais obligé....Les frères l'ont prié et ses compagnons Anglois qui estoyent en ceste ville de souper avec eux mardy prochain au Banquet rectoral chez M Ch. Perrot*[1].

On Tuesday, the 29th of January, the Genevan Council recorded the circumstances connected with Cartwright's impending departure. In the preface of their minute they explained that he had retired to their city owing to the disfavour which he had incurred in England by publicly upholding in his lectures the ecclesiastical discipline as practised in Geneva. He appeared before the Council and thanked them for the hospitality he had received and particularly for

[1] *Reg. Comp.* (jan. 1572).

the honour of having been appointed colleague to Beza in the reading of divinity, in which capacity, according to the testimony of Beza, he had acquitted himself both faithfully and learnedly. It is interesting to learn that Beza acted as spokesman for Cartwright because the latter had not complete command of the French language. The Council decided to thank Cartwright for his services in the school and to offer him some recompense for his lectures. His request and that of van Til to have permission to be present in the Consistory was granted. The Council minute runs thus: *Thomas Carturit, anglois, docteur en théologie, s'estant retiré icy des quelques temps, pource qu'il estoyt mal voulu en Angleterre pour avoir publiquement en des leçons soustenu la discipline ecclesiastique comme elle est icy pratiquée, a comparu et a remercié Messieurs de l'honneur qu'ilz luy ont fait de l'avoir retenu en ceste ville, où il a encores été honoré de la charge de lire en théologie avec monsr de Bèze à son tour, où, par le raport de la Compagnie des ministres, tesmoigné par ledit M de Bèze qui a porté la parolle pour luy qui ne parle pas bon françois, il s'est porté fidellement et doctement. Et, veu qu'il est rapelé pour retourner en Angleterre, il n'a pas voulu partir sans remercier Messieurs et leur offrir service, supliant au reste luy donner permission d'assister une fois au consistoire affin de voir l'ordre qu'on y tient, pour en faire le raport par delà. Sur quoy a esté arresté de le remercier de l'honneur qu'il a fait à ceste eschole et luy offrir récompense de sa lecture, luy accordant au reste la réqueste qu'il a fait et semblablement aussi au sieur Van Til qui en a fait une de mesme, veu que ce qu'ils en font tend à bonne fin et qu'il ne procède pas de curiosité*[1].

Following upon the Council's permission Cartwright appeared in the Consistory on the last day of January: *Le jeudy dernier M Carturit assista en consistoire*[2]. As the Council recognised, it was not mere curiosity that induced the English Puritan to pry into their consistorial practices. He was seriously determined to transplant them into the Church of England.

Cartwright's stay in Geneva, although of less than a year's

[1] *Reg. Conseil* (29 jan. 1572). [2] *Reg. Comp.* (jan. 1572).

duration, is one of the most important and memorable episodes in his career. Till recently it has received little or no attention. So far as we are aware Cartwright came to Geneva in 1571 for the first time and not for the second as some, *e.g.* Soames[1], have said. Those who have stated that he proceeded to Antwerp after being deprived of his Cambridge Chair, *e.g.* Drysdale[2], have been obviously mistaken. It would be of the greatest interest to know who were his English companions in exile. Reference has been made to *ses compagnons Anglois qui estoyent en ceste ville.* We have made search in the Genevan archives for the names of Laurence Tomson, Walter and Robert Travers, who have been traditionally associated with Geneva, but so far we have not been able to trace them. Professor Borgeaud in a letter to the present writer states that the name "Anglois" was frequently applied to Scotsmen. This being so, there are at least two men, who immediately suggest themselves as probable and suitable companions of Cartwright in Geneva, namely, the venerable Henry Scrimgeour, who was professor of law at Geneva and a member of the Council, and his friend, the renowned Scottish reformer Andrew Melville. The latter was, not professor of Humanity in the Academy (*Schola Publica*) as has generally been held, but regent of the second class in the *Schola Privata*, to which post he was appointed on the 10th of November, 1569. Shortly before his departure for Scotland in April, 1574, Emile Portus, son of the beforementioned Professor of Greek, was elected to take charge of the second class in Melville's stead. Thus Melville abode in Geneva throughout the period of Cartwright's residence and doubtless the two likeminded protagonists of Presbyterianism became intimately acquainted in the city, to which they both owed so much and which was so greatly indebted to them. Above all, Cartwright came into intimate and vital contact at this time with Calvin's successor, Beza. He won the sincere esteem of the champion of French Protestantism, whose views on matters of Church government were essentially those held and afterwards published by Cartwright.

[1] p. 147. [2] p. 120.

His friendship with Beza[1] and his whole experience of Church life in Geneva would confirm the Puritan in his adherence to Presbyterianism, give him a thorough and practical knowledge of its principles and working, and make him more entitled than ever to be regarded as the leader of the disciplinarian movement at home.

Cartwright answered the call of the English Puritans without delay. Apparently he left Geneva early in February, 1572, but the time of his arrival in England is not definitely settled. The traditional chronology is very confused. It has frequently been asserted that he returned in November[2]. On the other hand some writers would have him back in time to take a hand in the *Admonition* to Parliament in the early part of the year. Clarke, for instance, places his return about the time when the *Admonition* was drawn up, but shows himself hazy about his dates by saying that Whitgift was then preferred to the Archbishopric of Canterbury and that Cartwright's ministry at Antwerp and Middelburg came before his return. That ministry, however, belongs to Cartwright's second sojourn on the Continent and not to the present period, and Whitgift's elevation did not take place till 1583.

We obtain unexpectedly new light from an old and frequently quoted *State Paper*, namely, a letter written on the 24th of March, 1571–2, by Edward Dering, in his characteristically bold and familiar style, to Burghley[3]. In this epistle Dering says that Cartwright has been invited to return home from Geneva by the letters of many honourable and good men and that he is at present in Rouen. He is tarrying there lest by a sudden and unexpected return he might offend Burghley and others, and subject his cause to the calumnies of his enemies. Prudence has suggested that due intimation

[1] Beza's friendly interest in Cartwright was long maintained, as may be seen in the letter from the Swiss Reformer to Travers (October, 1582), beginning thus: *Si quoties tui et C[artwrighti] nostri sum recordatus, mi frater, toties ad te scripsissem, jampridem esses literis meis obrutus. Nullus enim dies abit quin de vobis vestrisque rebus solicite cogitem, quod ita postulare non amicitia modo vetus nostra, sed etiam rerum ipsarum de quibus laboratis magnitudo videatur* (Fuller, *C.H.* bk IX, s. iv, § 19).

[2] *D.N.B.* art. "Cartwright"; Bayne, p. lxxix; Briggs, p. 42.

[3] *S.P. Dom. Eliz.* LXXXV, No. 75.

of his intended home-coming should be made to those in authority, that they might first indicate their pleasure or otherwise. Dering, voicing the prayers of many, accordingly beseeches Burghley to make Cartwright's return easy and safe. He merely asks his Lordship to signify in a word that it will not be displeasing to him. He further makes the recommendation that, seeing Chevallier has been recalled to his own country and has decided to go, Cartwright might be appointed to succeed him as Professor of Hebrew in Cambridge. Such an appointment would bring joy and blessing to the members of the University, increase the love of all towards Burghley, give incalculable support to the Church and fortify Burghley himself against his enemies. Then Dering proceeds, in surprisingly rude and blunt terms, to harangue Burghley on his lack of true religion. Evidently he fears that the latter has been carried away by the snares of the Bishops and Doctors. This letter has frequently been alluded to by historians but the details of the reference to Cartwright have never been set forth, particularly those indicating his temporary residence in France[1].

Cartwright was a much travelled man. He was indeed but one of the many Puritans forced by conscience to make a kind of Grand Tour. We have hitherto connected his exilic

[1] The apposite portion of the document runs thus: *Thomas Cartwrightus* (*ad nominis hujus memoriam noli quaeso excandescere*) *Cartwrightus* (*inquam*) *ille olim noster, literis multorum et honoratiss. hominum et optimorum virorum Geneva in patriam revocatus, nunc est Rotomagi, prudenti atque religioso consilio ibidem commoratus, ne repentino et inexpectato reditu vel te imprimis vel post te alios quos reveretur* (*quod nollet*) *offenderet. Vel causam suam optimam* (*quod vehementer exhorruit*) *inimicorum tot tantisque calumniis objiceret. Hoc est igitur quod petimus, ego calamo innumerabiles precibus, dignitatem tuam, ut ei facilem atque salutarem conficias reditum. Laborem nullum interponimus tuis maximis curis a rebus nostris hos utinam perferas et feliciter et diu, quos habes a rep. profecto maximos. Id solum rogamus, id contendimus, ut verbo uno significes, et Cartwrighti reditum tibi fore non ingratum, et ejus in hac rep. locum aliquem, tuo desiderio non repugnantem. Hanc gratiam tu si nobis feceris et ecclesiae dei, hoc de Cartwrighto tum deliberamus. Cevallerius revocatus ad patrios coetus quibus ita statuit inservire, ut nostram Cantabrigiensem academiam aliquando necessario relinquat. Cartwrightum ejus loco hebraica praelegentem si tu dederis academiae votum nostrum expleveris, patrocinii sui alumnos bearis, omnium in te amorem amplificaveris, ecclesiam* (*q. debes*) *iuveris, et tuam fidem adversus hostium impetus, qui olim* (*mihi crede*) *irruent, sartam tectam muniveris.*

days chiefly with Geneva, the Low Countries and the Channel Islands. But, as we shall see, we have to add many other places to the list of his foreign abodes and now we have a glimpse of him at Rouen. We may justifiably conjecture that in this French town he was the guest of Beza's friend Pierre Loiseleur de Villiers, sometimes known as Losellerius or Villerius. This interesting Frenchman played many parts in his day and had many points of contact with English Puritanism. Born about 1530, he studied at Orleans and Paris, and eventually, as a Protestant refugee, found an asylum in Geneva, where he was induced by Beza to enter the ministry. He afterwards became the pastor of the Reformed Church at Rouen. One of Beza's letters to him[1] is addressed: *Villerio, Rhotomagensis Ecclesiae fido Pastore, ac symmystae charissimo.* After the massacre of St Bartholomew he left his charge. In 1573 he published his edition of the Greek New Testament which was utilised by Laurence Tomson. We find him as one of the pastors of the French Church in London in 1574–5. His lectures in the metropolis attracted considerable attention[2]; he was even allowed to discourse in the Mercers' Chapel and St Dunstan's[3]; he corresponded with Burghley[4]. He afterwards became court preacher and private adviser to the Prince of Orange and played a prominent rôle in the affairs of the Low Countries. In 1578 he took part in the ordination of Travers in Antwerp and it is likely that Cartwright would meet him there and in Middelburg. In Rouen meanwhile Cartwright would find in Villiers a congenial and scholarly companion[5].

On the 3rd of April Burghley replied to Dering's "biting letter, pretended (as by the beginning of a few of your lines appeareth) for Mr Cartwright, whose name you reiterate, for that you will me not to be in heat at the memory of his name." He briefly answers the request concerning Cartwright thus: "As for so much as concerneth Mr Cartwright, I answer you,

[1] 24 February, 1570. *Epist.* No. 37.

[2] *Z.L.* II, p. 261.

[3] *Sec. Parte,* I, p. 188.

[4] *Cecil MSS. Hist. MSS. Comm.* Pt II, p. 116.

[5] For Villiers *v. Proc. Hug. Soc.* IX, p. 385; St. *Whit.* I, p. 477; Schickler, I, p. 229; Hessels, II, p. 622.

sine excandescentia (which is your term) that, *quo possum candore reditus ejus erit mihi gratus*: *eique optime cupio et opto*. But as for the reading of a public lecture in Cambridge, I can promise nothing of my self. For therein I know no power that I have. I know very well it is my duty to further all good learning and quietness in that university, that undecent contentions be excluded from thence." Burghley then goes on to deal at length with the disrespectful charges, which Dering had levelled at his personal piety[1].

Post haste, *e cubiculo mane*, Dering replied (5th April) and sought to mollify his Lordship and explain away his seeming rudeness. He repeats his advice that Burghley should follow his own counsels and warns him *ab iis qui sibi, non tibi blandiuntur*. Incidentally he expresses thanks for the message about Cartwright: *De Cartwrighto quod scribis, et laetor plurimum, et gratias ago, et quibus debeo officiis, utinam perpetuo referam*[2].

A document, dated the 6th of May, 1572, drawn up in opposition to the new statutes, was signed by 164 members of Cambridge University[3]. Among these were many of Cartwright's friends, but his name does not appear in the list of signatories. This omission suggests that he had not returned by the time that the protest was being prepared. In a postscript to an interesting letter written from Geneva on the 3rd of August Beza asks Jean Cousin, minister of the French Church in London to convey his greetings to Cartwright among others: *D. Carthuritum*, *Wiburnum*, *Sampsonem*, *Witinganum*, *Guilpinum et caeteros amicos rogo ut ex me salutes quam officiosissime*[4]. We shall afterwards consider a letter written by Cartwright to Burghley from Cambridge in the middle of October, 1572. With all the foregoing facts before us it is abundantly clear that the traditional date of Cartwright's return, viz. November, 1572, is wrong. The probability is that he came back to England soon after he heard that Burghley had no objection to his return and that he crossed the Channel about the middle or towards the end of April.

[1] St. *Ann.* IV, p. 483.
[2] *ibid.* p. 487.
[3] H. & W. I, p. 61.
[4] Hessels, II, p. 426.

CHAPTER II

THE ADVANCE OF PURITANISM

The *Admonition* of 1572—Cartwright loses his Fellowship—Whitgift's *Answer to the Admonition*—the Puritan ringleaders—the *Second Admonition*—the Presbytery of Wandsworth—the secret Puritan press—Cartwright's *Reply* to Whitgift—the literary duel between Cartwright and Whitgift—the Episcopal campaign against the Puritans in 1573—correspondence with Continental divines—the Puritan press unearthed—John Stroud, the Puritan printer—Edward Dering silenced—Cartwright and Michael Hicks—warrant for Cartwright's arrest.

During the spring of 1572 the Puritans in England were busily preparing for an advance. They set their hopes on the Parliament, which began on the 8th of May. A Bill introduced to further some of their ideals made some progress and caused considerable discussion, but on the 22nd of May Elizabeth intervened, stating through the Speaker that no more Bills concerning religion should be received in the House of Commons unless they had first been considered and liked by the ecclesiastical authorities[1]. According to Bancroft[2], Gilby, Sampson, Lever, Field, Wilcocks and others met in London and decided upon an *Admonition* to Parliament. It was not drawn up by this meeting as is sometimes stated[3]. This *Admonition*, although not formally presented to the House[4], was nominally addressed to it and according to Cartwright found favour with divers of the members[5]. Whitgift, who afterwards protested that these members did not consent to the manner of its publication[6], made much of the fact that the *Admonition* was propounded after Parliament was ended, or rather prorogued (30 June), and that, taking the form of a libel, and being seditiously spread abroad in corners and sent into the country, it was not in order[7]. To judge from Whitgift it would seem that the manifesto did not appear until after Parliament rose, but reckoning from the statement of Field on the 4th of

[1] D'Ewes, p. 213.
[2] *Survay*, p. 54.
[3] *D.N.B.* art. "Field."
[4] *W.W.* I, p. 80.
[5] *ibid.* III, p. 520.
[6] *ibid.* III, p. 521.
[7] *ibid.* I, pp. 39, 80; III, p. 521.

August[1] that he had been in Newgate for six weeks, it would appear that he was imprisoned for his share in the work before the end of June, and that accordingly the *Admonition* appeared before the parliamentary session was ended. Another Puritan document, *An Exhortation to the Byshops*, definitely states that the *Admonition* was put forth in the time of Parliament. The *Second Admonition* some months afterwards sought to meet the criticism that "it was not in fourme of lawe and imprinted."[2] Some writers, probably misled by the reprint of 1617, which says that the *Admonition* was addressed to the Parliament "begun anno 1570 and ended 1571," assign the work to 1571, but from internal evidence it is obvious that it belongs to 1572[3].

It has been said that Cartwright was the author of the *Admonition* or that he participated in its composition[4]. There is no evidence in support of such an assertion. The men imprisoned for writing it were John Field and Thomas Wilcocks and they confessed that they were the joint-authors[5]. Cartwright knew that the book was the work of divers persons and understood that the two writers wrote independently and that consequently there is a certain amount of repetition in it[6]. Whitgift refused to share this opinion, for both parts of the work were bound in one volume, under one title, were printed in the same type by one printer, and came out together and were never separate[7]. In *The Rest*[8] Cartwright replies that he said what he thought was true, and that Whitgift's arguments for collusion do not prove any communication between the authors "before their bookes were written or printed almoste." Cartwright also expressed his disapproval of certain quotations from Scripture wrongly used by the *Admonition*[9]. These observations indicate that Cartwright was not the author of the book and that he had no share in its composition.

1 *v. infra* p. 61.
2 *Pur. Man.* p. 88.
3 *ibid.* p. 20.
4 St. *Parker*, II, p. 110; Schickler, II, p. 448; Wakeman, p. 336.
5 *v. infra* p. 62.
6 *W.W.* II, p. 45.
7 *ibid.* II, p. 46.
8 p. 258.
9 *W.W.* I, p. 543; *Pur. Man.* p. 11.

The book is in two parts, the first entitled "An Admonition to the Parliament" and the second "A view of Popishe abuses yet remaining in the Englishe Church, for the which Godly Ministers have refused to subscribe." The first treatise, or Admonition proper, is a succinct and forcible document. In fresh crisp sentences it criticises the ministry of the Word, the observance of the Sacraments, and the exercise of discipline in the Church of England. The writer's chief aim is to point out the glaring contrast between the Apostolic Church and the Church established, and to advocate the abolition of diocesan Episcopacy and the erection of Presbyterianism. The second treatise covers much of the same ground, but its method is different. Its three sections deal with the subscription required to the Prayer Book, the apparel, and the Articles, but the main attack is upon the Prayer Book "culled & picked out of that popishe dunghil, the Portuise and Masse boke." The writer has little to say about the apparel or the articles of doctrine. The Puritans are ready to accept the latter and the former is of secondary consideration. The chief concern is "a true ministerie and regiment of the churche according to the word. Which thing once established the other melt away of them selves." The object of the Puritanism contained in the *Admonition* is thus to assimilate the English Church to Presbyterian standards. It is recognised that the chief enemies of the project will be the Archbishops, Bishops "and the rest of that proude generation, whose kingdome must downe holde they never so hard." It is also expected that these "Lordly Lords" will disapprove of these two treatises "bicause they principally concerne their persons and unjuste dealings."[1]

The *Admonition* and the ancillary writings, which were issued by the secret Puritan press in 1572, *i.e.* the two Exhortations to the Bishops, *Certaine Articles*, and the *Second Admonition*, have been recently reprinted by W. H. Frere and C. E. Douglas, by whom they are discussed in detail[2]. Although they followed up the pro-Presbyterian line of argument adopted by Cartwright in his lectures in

[1] *Pur. Man.* p. 5. [2] The reprints are entitled *Puritan Manifestoes* (1907).

Cambridge, these writings brought into prominence a note of bitterness and virulence that was to characterise a section of the Puritans for years to come, and they also made it clear that the Bishops were now regarded by that party as the chief and implacable foes of Puritanism.

Field and Wilcocks were imprisoned in Newgate, not on the 7th of July, as is usually stated[1], but to judge from Field's own reckoning—he wrote on the 4th of August to Gilby[2] saying "we have bin these six weekes close prisoners" —about a week or more before the end of June[3]. Eager to keep in touch with the Puritan movement the prisoners maintained a correspondence with the friends of the cause. In the above-mentioned letter Field exhorts the minister of Ashby-de-la-Zouch to promote the radical reform policy by conference or otherwise. He alludes to a recent Puritan conference and suggests the convening of another: "Of late ther was a conference, so yt might againe be renewed." Field knows that the Admonitioners and their supporters are being charged with heresy, Donatism, Anabaptism, etc., with being divided among themselves and with holding opinions that are accepted by no men of learning. He agrees with Gilby that a declaratory manifesto, in the form of a "Confession, Information and Petition" should be issued to meet the charges levelled against them[4]. Field is already beginning to fulfil the function of a Secretary or Clerk to the Puritan party. "The same I wryte to you," he says to Gilby, "I wryte to others." He and Wilcocks have now translated their book into Latin, probably intending thereby to reach the scholars of the Continent and enlist their sympathetic interest. The prisoners, however, have been advised not to publish their translation. They complain that during their six weeks of imprisonment none but their wives have been permitted to visit them. It would appear, therefore, that the

[1] Brook, *Lives*, I, p. 319; *Pur. Man.* p. xiii.

[2] *Baker MSS.* XXXII, Mm. I, 43, 442–4.

[3] *v. Sec. Parte*, I, pp. 87, 91.

[4] The Admonitioners' Confession, issued after Whitgift's *Answer* had appeared, is dated from Newgate, the 4th of December, 1572. *ibid.* I, p. 83.

visits of Wiburn, Cartwright, Dering, Humphrey, Lever, Crowley, Johnson, Brown and Fulke, said to have been made to the prisoners "according to the certificate given in of their names by the jailer of Newgate,"[1] could not have taken place before the 4th of August.

On the 3rd of September, 1572, Field and Wilcocks send a Latin petition to Burghley[2]. They solicit his intervention on the ground of the equity of their case, and also because of their wretched plight, the poverty of their wives and children, the desire of their friends and the grief of the faithful. On Thursday, the 11th of September, Pearson, Parker's Chaplain, held an interview with the two prisoners in Newgate. Wilcocks's account of the conversation is full of interest[3]. Pearson has been sent by Parker because the latter has received a letter from the wives of the Admonitioners accusing him of cruelty and injustice. Field tells the Chaplain that they have been unjustly imprisoned. The writing of a book such as theirs in the time of Parliament was no sufficient reason for their treatment. The trio then discuss some of the positions maintained by the Puritan faction, *e.g.* equality of ministers, the need of a "godlie seignorie" in every congregation, etc. Pearson complains of the tone of the *Admonition* and draws from Field the admission that he was chiefly responsible for "the bitternes of the stile." We learn from this prison talk that Wilcocks was but a young man, being only twenty-three years of age, and also that it was well known that the Puritans had wealthy supporters behind them. The latter fact is also borne out by Antonio de Guaras, who wrote on the 30th of August to the Duke of Alva about the new sectarians, who had been growing in numbers and influence for the last eight years[4]. He enclosed a book which they had printed, probably the *Admonition*, that his Excellency might be informed of their infernal propositions, and said that they had among their many adherents persons of high position.

[1] St. *Parker*, II, p. 240.
[2] *Lansd. MSS.* XV, No. 73; St. *Ann.* IV, Bk I, App. XIX.
[3] *Sec. Parte*, I, pp. 87–90.
[4] *Cal. S.P. Span. Eliz.* 1568–79, p. 409.

On the 2nd of October Field and Wilcocks were sentenced to a year's imprisonment. They and their wives frequently sought by petitions to Leicester, the Council, etc., to secure alleviation, if not release, but nothing was done to relieve them till the next spring. One of their complaints was that they had been illegally confined in Newgate for four months before their conviction[1].

Meanwhile the *Admonition* was passing through edition after edition. "Sir," wrote Parker to Burghley on the 25th of August, 1572[2], "for all the Devises that we can make to the Contrarie, yet sum good fellowes still labor to print owte the vaine admonition to the parliament. Since the first printing it hath been twise printed, and nowe with addicons wherof I send your honor one of them. We wrote lettres to the Maior and sum aldermen of London to laie in waite for the Charactes, printer and Corrector, but I feare they deceave us, they are not willing to disclose this matter."

Cartwright, whose name so far has not appeared in contemporary records in connection with the *Admonition*, reappears at Cambridge. Till this year (1572) he had held his Fellowship at Trinity College. Whitgift, the Master, had recently realised that Cartwright had not fulfilled his Fellowship oath which bound him to take his priest's orders within a stated time[3]. Cartwright was still only a deacon. Here was an opportunity for Whitgift to get rid of the obnoxious Puritan whose presence and influence in the University had filled it with contention. Writing from Trinity College, 21 September, 1572, Whitgift announces to Archbishop Parker that on the above ground he has deprived Cartwright of his Fellowship[4]. He believes that the latter is seeking to procure the support of some courtiers for his reinstatement, and accordingly begs Parker to lay the case, from Whitgift's point of view, before Burghley and Leicester if the Archbishop thinks this course expedient. The Master of Trinity is anxious to have Parker's approval and assistance; he fears the triumph of the Puritan party in the University; and

[1] *Sec. Parte,* I, p. 91.
[2] *Lansd. MSS.* xv, No. 38, f. 75.
[3] *v. infra* p. 65.
[4] App. VIII.

insists that, at any rate, Cartwright is flatly perjured and undoubtedly deserves the punishment he has received. It should be observed that Cartwright's deprivation of his Fellowship has been wrongly placed by some in 1570[1] and by others in 1571[2].

Having heard of Whitgift's charges Cartwright sent a long Latin epistle to Burghley[3]. This letter, dated from Cambridge the 17th of October, 1572, has been erroneously placed by many historians. This has been due in part to the fact that the year in the endorsement of the original is not decipherable. Apart, however, from the evidence of the contents, the address should help to determine the year. The letter is addressed thus: *Honoratissimo viro Domino Burleio Angliae thesaurario*, etc. Cecil was created Lord Burghley early in 1571, therefore it is wrong to date the letter 1570 as some do, and he became Lord High Treasurer in 1572, therefore the letter cannot belong, as others say, to 1571. At the outset of his communication Cartwright explains that, on his expulsion from Trinity College, he refrained from appealing to the Chancellor of the University because he was occupied with serious affairs of state. Now he lays his case before Burghley because he has heard that his adversaries have been making false charges against him. He is sure that Burghley will more readily hear a just defence than an unjust accusation. Fearing prolixity[4] he will not deal with the details of the matter in a letter; he would rather explain it to Burghley in person. Meanwhile, however, he is grieved to know that Whitgift, who has treated him as a matricide, now slanders him as a seditious schismatic. He protests that when deprived of his Fellowship and his chamber he quietly yielded and sought no revenge. Whitgift, fearing that, as long as Cartwright was a Fellow, his Mastership would be unsafe or uncomfortable, without consulting the senate, the cause unheard, arbitrarily pronounced the sentence of expulsion. All this Cartwright has meekly borne with, but he is amazed

[1] Soames, p. 145; Drysdale, p. 118.

[2] *D.N.B.*; Bayne, p. lxxxvii; Mullinger, p. 226.

[3] App. IX.

[4] Not "perplexity," as Brook states, *Mem.* p. 78.

that Whitgift is not satisfied with the harm he has done and now attempts to bring him into odium with Burghley. So he pleads with the latter to withhold his judgment until he hears Cartwright's side of the question, meanwhile assuring the Chancellor of his quiet behaviour and the injustice of the charges brought against him. His application, however, did not lead to his restoration, and before long we shall meet with Cartwright as the leader of the Puritan party, deeply engaged in bitter controversy with the Master, who had put an end to his academic career. The assertion that after protesting against the loss of his Fellowship he proceeded to Geneva is based upon a confusion of dates[1].

The question of Cartwright's failure to abide by the literal terms of his Fellowship oath and the consequent loss of his Fellowship crop up in the literary controversy between Whitgift and the Puritan. The former insists that he has merely executed those laws, which both he and Cartwright were obliged to honour[2]. Whitgift holds that the latter kept his Fellowship at least five years longer than was his right. If, he writes[3], "a man shall directly swear, either to do such a thing by such a time, or to leave his place, if by that time he neither do the thing by oath required, nor leave his place, but still usurp the same, at the least the space of five years, I think he ought to be displaced for perjury." The statute whose violation is alleged enjoins *ut socii qui magistri artium sunt, post septem annos in eo gradu plene confectos presbyteri ordinentur*[4]. Cartwright, having graduated M.A. in 1560 should thus have been ordained a priest in 1567. Whitgift regrets that he has been remiss in fulfilling the law: "The greatest injury that I acknowledge myself guilty of is unto the college, that I so long suffered you, contrary to your express oath, to usurp a place therein, to the great hindrance and disquieting thereof."[5] He thinks that he too would have been guilty of perjury if he had not deprived Cartwright, and is sure that the latter's malice is largely due to his own

[1] *D.N.B.*; *A.C.* II, p. 361.
[2] *W.W.* I, p. 507.
[3] *ibid.* III, p. 324.
[4] *Stat. Trin. Coll. Cant.* cap. xix; *v.* Mullinger, p. 623.
[5] *W.W.* III, p. 323.

performance of duty[1]. Whitgift also accuses the Puritan of violating his Fellowship oath in being disloyal to himself as Master of Trinity[2] and in reply to Cartwright's charge that he is a pluralist, says that he retained his livings "with a far better conscience than T.C. did one living (*i.e.* the Fellowship) for the space of certain years, and would have done still with all his heart if he might have been winked at, though it were expressly against his oath."[3] In reply to the charge of perjury Cartwright expresses his conviction that he fulfilled all the requirements of the College statutes concerned: "Yt ys a meer cavill. For the meaning off the statute off the howse, is to provide that men should not turne their studies to other professions off law etc: but that there should be to furnish the Colledge off a number off preachers, off which I was one, as sone as I entred. Nether was there any dutie of mynisterie, which the Colledg could require off me: that I was not inabled to doo according to the lawes of the churche off England, by vertue off that mynisterie, which I had received. So that the law yt self (as that whose meaning was fulfilled even with my entrie) did not require yt."[4] It appears that Cartwright was guilty merely of a technical offence, and not of a heinous crime.

After his expulsion from Trinity College he had no permanent abode for over a year. Whitgift accused him of spending this part of his life in idleness and as a parasite at other men's tables. But, as he produced his first *Reply* during this homeless period, Cartwright did not count his time ill or idly spent. He had certainly been made welcome in several private households, but in some of these he had sought to repay his hosts by acting as tutor to their children. In his *Second Reply*[5] he thus makes answer to Whitgift: "In the other part of my life, after he had thrust me out of the Colledge: he accuseth me for going up and downe doing no good, and living at other mens tables. That I was not idle, I suppose he knoweth to well: whether well occupied or no,

[1] *W.W.* III, p. 395.
[2] *ibid.* III, p. 396.
[3] *ibid.* I, p. 123.
[4] *2nd Rep.* 1575, sig.)( )(ii.
[5] sig.)( )(iii.

let it be iudged. I lived in deed at other mens tables, having no hous nor wife of myne own: but not without their desire, and with smal delight of mine, for feare of evil tonges. And althowgh I were not able to requite yt: yet towardes some I went abowte yt, instructing their children partely in the principles off religion, partly in other learning."

By September, 1572, Whitgift had finished, in rough draft, the confutation of the *Admonition*. He intimates this fact to Parker on the 21st of the month[1]. He has written out the first part in a fair hand and intends to send it to the Archbishop after the Bishop of Ely and Dr Perne or some others have perused it. The second part is still in draft, but will be completed shortly. He suggests that Toy should be entrusted with the printing and that Grafton, a chaplain of Parker's, should undertake the correction of the print. He also asks Parker's advice as to whom the work should be dedicated. Eleven days afterwards Whitgift is able to report progress to his Grace[2]. According to promise he has sent to Parker the first part of his answer, not to Cartwright's book, as the editor of Whitgift's Works, Parker Society, states[3], but to the *Admonition*. He asks the Archbishop to alter and correct it as he thinks fit. Bishop Cooper and Dr Perne have read and approved of the work. The second part is now almost written out fair. He thanks Parker for securing Toy as printer and proposes that the printing of the first part may be begun. He has asked Hanson of Trinity College to correct the proof sheets and again begs for Grafton's aid in the same direction. He expresses his anxious desire that no copies of part of the work should be published until the whole is complete, and once more asks advice as to the dedication[4].

The news soon spread that Whitgift's answer was almost ready for publication. Thomas Norton, writing from London (20th October) gravely counselled him that it was very impolitic to make any reply to the *Admonition*[5]. A few days later, in a letter to Norton, Whitgift carefully marshals his

[1] *v.* App. VIII.

[2] 2 October, *W.W.* III, p. 600.

[3] *ibid.*

[4] It was dedicated "To his loving Nurse, the Christian Church of England."

[5] St. *Whit.* I, p. 58.

arguments in favour of a confutation[1]. The *Admonition* is intolerable in its attempt to deface the whole ministry and constitution of the English Church; it evinces the very spirit and principles that lead inevitably to Anabaptism; it is now in every man's hand, and many think it unanswerable simply because it has not been answered; to be silent would be a breach of duty; Whitgift himself has been slandered by the Puritans and a defence is necessary. Whitgift considers that the matter would not, as Norton thinks, die of itself; the fact that the book has been reprinted again shows that it still grows in popularity; he is sure that the Papists would rejoice if the *Admonition* were unanswered, for it seeks to destroy what they abominate, the fundamental institutions of the Church of England; he absolves from all blame or responsibility his friend Dr Perne, who, in Norton's opinion, had unwisely egged on Whitgift to reply; he is convinced that the questions at issue are not of merely academic interest, and believes that a reply would greatly help to allay the factious spirit now manifest among the young men in the Universities. In conclusion, Whitgift points out that he did not undertake the task himself, but at the suggestion of leading clergy in the Church.

By the 21st of October Whitgift had brought his *Answer* to a conclusion, as is evident from his letter of that date to Parker[2]. From a contemporary Puritan letter[3] we learn that Whitgift's *Answer* was "put forth" before the 21st of November. Frere and Douglas[4] say that the work was not issued till February, 1573, but they seem to have confounded the publication of it with that of the *Defence of the Answer*, which was issued in February, 1573–4. The title of Whitgift's book is *An Answere to a certen Libel intituled An Admonition to the Parliament*... and was printed by Henry Bynneman for Humphrey Toy at London. It rebuts the pro-Presbyterian arguments of the Admonitioners and puts forward a clear and reasonable defence of the Establishment. Its main positions,

[1] 25 October, St. *Whit.* I, p. 61.
[2] *ibid.* I, p. 86.
[3] Tomson to Gilby, 21 November, 1572, *Baker MSS.* vol. XXXII, Mm. I, 43, f. 448.
[4] *Pur. Man.* p. xiv.

which are repeated in subsequent works of Whitgift, will be considered later.

The Puritan letter just referred to (21 November, 1572) was written from Leicester by Laurence Tomson to Anthony Gilby, and both the writer and his epistle are of particular importance. "There is another Admonition come forth," writes Tomson, "which I dogt not but you will like off, and M Hastings hath broght it you to read it. I pray you returne it, when you have done, unlesse uppon further occasion, you will take some paines about ye matter. Since the coming forth of yt Mr D Whitegift hath put forth an answere to the first, wherein he chargeth the autours of it and all that favoure it, with" Arianism, Puritanism, Rebellion, etc. Tomson was one of the most active promoters of Puritanism, but his career has hitherto been shrouded in obscurity. Only now and again have we been able to lift the veil of mystery that covers his elusive life. Born in 1539 in Northamptonshire, he was admitted a demy of Magdalen College, Oxford, in 1553. He took his B.A. on the 5th of June, 1559, and on the 20th of October, 1564, he commenced M.A. He became a Fellow of his College[1]. In 1566 he accompanied Sir Thomas Hoby, Elizabeth's ambassador, to France. In 1569 he resigned his Fellowship. We have not been able to ascertain at what date he became private secretary to Walsingham, but according to the State Papers he appears definitely as a politician of influence in 1575[2]. From that year onwards he seems to have acted as Walsingham's trusted secretary, and was frequently in attendance at Court. He was married before the 11th of October, 1579, on which date Nicholas Martin and N. Carey, in the name of the bailiff and jurats of Guernsey, wrote to Tomson concerning the complaints against their rule, and sent him a petticoat made in the island to himself and one to his wife[3]. He served as M.P. for Weymouth and Melcombe Regis between 1575 and 1587, and for Downton in 1588–9. His epitaph quoted by Wood[4] from the monu-

[1] *D.N.B.*; Wood, *Fasti*, I, pp. 156, 165.
[2] *S.P. Dom. Eliz.* CIII, Nos. 62, 65, etc.
[3] *ibid.* Add. XXVI, No. 24.
[4] *Athenae Oxon.* II, p. 44.

ment erected in the chancel of Chertsey Church, Surrey, refers to his accomplishments as a traveller, linguist and translator, and is worthy of being given in full: *Laurentio Tomsono honesta Tomsoniorum familia in agro Northamptoniensi oriundo, in collegio Magdal. Oxon. educato, peregrinatione Sueviae, Russiae, Daniae, Germaniae, Italiae, Galliae nobilitato; duodecim linguarum cognitione instructo; Theologiae, Juris civilis et municipalis nostri, totiusque literaturae politioris scientia claro; ingenii acumine, disputandi subtilitate, eloquendi suavitate et lepore, virtute omni pietateque insigni; linguae Hebraicae publica Genevae professione celebri; accurata Novi Testamenti Translatione notabili; In politicis apud Walsinghamum Elizabethae reginae scribam praecipuum diu multumque exercitato; post cujus mortem vitae privatae umbratilisque jucunditate annos XX continuos Lalamiae Middlesexiae perfuncto, et septuagenario placidissime religiosissimeque defuncto quarto calendas Aprilis an.* 1608*; Uxor Jana, et Jana filia ex quinque una superstes filiabus, amoris ergo posuerunt et pietatis.* This epitaph points to Tomson's connection with Geneva, but like most notices of him, fails to give a true estimate of the place he filled in the growth of Puritanism.

Tomson's translation of the New Testament, first published in 1576, is sometimes spoken of as the third Genevan version, those of 1557 and 1560 being regarded as the first and second respectively, but although identical in many respects with that of 1560 it is an independent work. Tomson's indebtedness to Beza and Villiers is made plain in the title which runs thus: *The new Testament of our Lord Iesus Christ, translated out of the Greeke by Theod. Beza. Whereunto are adjoyned briefe Summeries of doctrine upon the Evangelistes and Actes of the Apostles, together with the methode of the Epistles of the Apostles: by the said Theod. Beza. And also short expositions on the phrases and hard places, taken out of the large annotations of foresayd Author and Ioach. Camerarius, by P. Loseler Villerius. Englished by L. Tomson.* From 1599 the title-page has this addition: *together with the Annotations of Fr. Junius upon the Revelation of S. John. An epistle to the right honorable M. Francis Walsingham, Esquier and to the right worshipfull M. Francis Hastings* is followed by an address from Beza to French noblemen, dated March, 1565[1]. Tomson's Testament, like the Geneva Bible proper, was thoroughly Calvinistic and Puritan in point of view. It at once became popular, was frequently reprinted[2], and latterly, Dore says in 1587, it took the place of the Geneva Testament of 1560 in the so-called Breeches Bible[3]. It is the greatest monument to Tomson's Puritanism.

Probably Tomson, in his later University years, came under the influence of Laurence Humphrey, the noted Puritan president of Magdalen College, who, for his antipapal zeal, was dubbed "Papistomastix."[4] On the 22nd of March, 1568, Georgius Witherus, Laurentius Tomsonus, Georgius Allinus and Richardus Serger matriculated at Heidelberg University. They were registered as *nobiles Angli*[5]. In the Calvinistic atmosphere that prevailed in Heidelberg Tomson's Puritan convictions would be reinforced. We have not been able to ascertain the date of his abode in Geneva, to which his epitaph alludes, but there too his desire for further reformation would be confirmed. In 1572 he appears as one of the ringleaders of the Puritan party. We find him in close touch with Gilby, and obviously intimately associated with the publishing committee, who employed the secret press for the issue of the *Admonition* and cognate documents. Some of his letters to Gilby in 1572 and 1573 are preserved in the *Baker MSS.*[6] These show that Tomson was then residing in Leicester.

The town of Leicester was one of the centres of Puritanism. The leading family with which it was closely connected, the Hastings, were actively interested in the movement. Henry Hastings, third Earl of Huntingdon, Lord Lieutenant of the Counties of Leicester and Rutland, brother-in-law of Lord Leicester, and a possible successor to Elizabeth, was an outstanding patron of the Puritans[7]. He lived at Ashby-de-la-

[1] *v.* J. R. Dore, *Old Bibles* (1888), pp. 227, 230.

[2] *v. ibid.* pp. 228, 393.

[3] A. Edgar, *The Bibles of England* (1889), p. 162; W. J. Heaton, *The Puritan Bible* (1913), p. 143; Dore, p. 227.

[4] *A.C.* II, p. 80.

[5] *Matrikel*, II, p. 45.

[6] XXXII.

[7] *A.C.* II, p. 260.

Zouch, where, under his protection, Gilby exercised his ministry with impunity as an advanced exponent of Puritanism. Under the Hastings's influence a civic lectureship was founded in Leicester and the post was filled by Puritan preachers. The lectures were delivered twice a week and attendance on the part of householders was made compulsory by the corporation officials[1]. The preacher was appointed by the Borough but with the consent of the Earl[2]. In the Chamberlains' accounts there are frequent entries showing that gifts of courtesy were presented to preachers who, it seems, undertook the delivery of lectures. Among these occasional preachers were many Puritans. Those thus honoured by the Borough included Sampson, Gilby, Tymes, Key, Kynge, Beryn, Crane, Whittingham, Lever, Pachet, Culverwell, etc.[3]

The name of the noted nonconformist, Thomas Sampson[4], often appears in the civic records. As Master of Wigston Hospital he occupied a conspicuous and respected place in the life of Leicester and frequently received complimentary gifts from the corporation for his services[5]. It is almost certain that Tomson associated with him when in Leicester, and we may readily assume that Sampson would, through Tomson or otherwise, give the aid of his advice and maybe of his pen to the Puritan forward movement of 1572–3.

Another influential friend of the Puritans and evidently an associate of Tomson was Francis Hastings, a younger brother of the Earl of Huntingdon[6]. He represented Leicestershire in the Parliament of 1571 and in 1572 was appointed sheriff of the county. He was held in high esteem in the town of Leicester and was frequently honoured by gifts from the Town Council[7]. Apparently he and Sampson were friends[8]. Presumably he is the Mr Hastings referred to in Tomson's letter of the 21st November. The allusion points to his

[1] Bateson, pp. xxiii, li, 101, 118.

[2] *ibid.* pp. li, 226.

[3] *ibid. in loc.*

[4] *v. D.N.B.*; Wood, *Athenae Oxon.* I, p. 548; *A.C.* II, p. 43.

[5] Bateson, pp. 119, 133, 152, 172.

[6] *v. D.N.B.*; *A.C.* III, p. 27.

[7] Bateson, pp. 131, 133, 137, 146, 184.

[8] *ibid.* p. 195.

interest in the work of the Puritan press. He bore the copy of the *Second Admonition* that had been recently published to Gilby. With men like him and his brother, the Earl, behind them there is no wonder that the Puritans were making headway and that the Bishops were filled with apprehension.

A Second Admonition to the Parliament (November, 1572) is an interesting product of the secret Puritan press. It has been reprinted by Frere and Douglas[1]. Its chief purpose is to supplement the first. The author points out[2] that the first declared what was in need of reform; he now tells how the reformation is to be carried out, viz. by the erection of the Presbyterian system, the particulars of which he proceeds to set forth. He explains the functions of the Presbyterian courts, the Consistory (parochial), the Conference (modern Presbytery), the provincial, national and universal Councils or Synods. He constantly commends the example of the best Reformed Churches. He condemns the Roman Catholic elements in the English Church. The Book of Common Prayer in particular is denounced as a product of the vile Popish service book. Such abuses as pluralities and the bestowal of degrees upon men who are unfit to be teachers in the Church are sharply criticised. Throughout the book we note the author's bitter antipathy toward the Bishops. They are censured for their persecution of the so-called precisians; they are responsible for the manifold corruptions in the Church; they are its real enemies. In conclusion the writer desires those "that thinke I have bene too round with the bishops and that sort, to remember howe round they are with us, and how cruel." The author is a practical but hot-blooded man, who wields a facile pen. He reminds us of a Puritan who had seen Presbyterianism in practice. If he was the same as the writer of the Preface he was one of the secret Puritan publishing body[3]. As we read his flowing unparagraphic torrent of abuse, and note his fulness of knowledge and the constructive elements in his programme we

[1] *Pur. Man.* pp. 79 ff. [2] *ibid.* p. 90.
[3] *ibid.* p. 83.

think of such virile but acrimonious Puritans as Gilby and Goodman.

It is generally stated that Cartwright was the author of the *Second Admonition*[1], but we have no hesitation in breaking away from tradition on this point. His contemporaries (Whitgift, Bancroft, Sutcliffe, Hooker, Rogers, etc.), when alluding to it, are tacitly agreed in not ascribing it to him, and write as if they did not know who its author was, *e.g.* Whitgift frequently distinguishes Cartwright and the author of the *Second Admonition*: "Let both the Admonitions and your book,"[2] "either by the first or second Admonition or by this your work."[3] Cartwright himself makes a similar distinction. "It is unreasonable" he writes[4], "yow should charge them (*i.e.* authors of the first *Admonition*) with that which I write, or with that the second admonition writeth." Besides, the style is not that of Cartwright. Its unsparing violence has, however, served to lower Cartwright in the estimation of those, who believed that he wrote it[5].

Modern English Presbyterians regard the 20th November, 1572, as one of their historical landmarks, for it is generally held that on that date the first practical step in the organisation of English Presbyterianism was taken in the erection of the Presbytery of Wandsworth. The tercentenary of the event was duly observed in 1872, when it was decided that a memorial Church should be built at Wandsworth, which resolution was carried out, and at this new Presbyterian Church the 350th anniversary was celebrated in 1922. Looking at the foundation of this famous Presbytery in the light of modern historical research, we note in the first place that there is only one sixteenth century record of it extant. At the break up of the Puritan Presbyterian movement, *ca.* 1589–90, Bancroft accumulated many of the documents connected with the same, and among these numerous papers of John Field, who had acted for sixteen years as the organising

[1] *D.N.B.*; *Pur. Man.* p. xxiii; Paget, p. 85; F. J. Powicke, *Henry Barrow, Separatist* (1900), p. 186; etc.

[2] *W.W.* I, p. 93.

[3] *ibid.* I, p. 15; *v.* also pp. 30, 46, 54, 96, 100, 103, 109, 113, 118, 122, etc.

[4] *2nd Rep.* p. 152.

[5] Paget, p. 38; *v.* Bayne, pp. lxxix, lxxxviii.

secretary of the main body of Puritans. Bancroft utilised these materials in his *Dangerous Positions* (1593), and it is in that book[1] that the reference to Wandsworth occurs: "Whereupon, presently after the sayd Parliament (*vz.* the twentieth of November, 1572) there was a Presbytery erected at Wandesworth in Surrey (as it appeareth by a bill endorsed with Master Fields hand, thus: the order of Wandesworth). In which order the Elders names, eleven of them, are set downe: the manner of their election is declared: the approvers of them (one Smith of Micham and Crane of Roughamton) are mentioned: their offices and certaine generall rules (then given unto them to bee observed) were likewise agreed upon, and described." It should be noted that before dealing with Wandsworth, Bancroft discusses the *Second Admonition*, which, he says, came out towards the end of the Parliament of 1572. This statement is misleading, for Parliament ended on the 30th of June and that Admonition, as we have just seen, did not appear till November. We should also bear in mind that the above passage was written twenty years after the date of the Presbytery. Assuming, however, the accuracy of Bancroft's assertion that the said Presbytery was erected on the 20th of November, 1572, we may make several definite, though chiefly negative statements regarding it.

Field was not present on the 20th of November. He was still in prison. To say that the Presbytery was organised in order to "cooperate with John Field, the Lecturer of Wandsworth,"[2] is based upon an assumption, which is difficult to substantiate. Indeed, it has still to be proved that Field held office at Wandsworth at all. The writer of the article on Field in the *Dictionary of National Biography* wisely notes that his ministry there seems to be a mere inference from his presumed connection with the Presbytery. Waddington[3] makes a gratuitous assertion when he says "Wilcox and Field convened a few of their ministerial brethren" at Wandsworth, where they drew up their Presbyterian scheme[4]. Bancroft

[1] p. 67. [2] Drysdale, p. 144. [3] *Surrey*, p. 3.

[4] *v.* also Frere (*Hist.* p. 179) and Pollard (*Hist.* p. 365) for Field's supposed participation.

does not say that Field had anything to do with the Wandsworth meeting except that he endorsed the bill or paper, which contained a record of the appointment of the eleven elders, etc. We do not know when this paper came into Field's hands, or whether his endorsement contained the year as well as the day and the month, but we have abundant evidence that many documents connected with the Presbyterian movement were sent to him as a leading director and organiser of the cause, and not because he actively participated in the meetings from which such documents emanated.

On the same page, on which he deals with Wandsworth, Bancroft makes a distinction between those who met there and the London brethren. He observes that the latter were not so advanced by the year 1572 and wonders why. We are therefore not entitled to affirm, as many historians have done[1], that the Presbytery was attended by Standen, Jackson, Travers and other ministers.

The opinion held by Marsden[2], that a Presbyterian Church was actually built in 1572 at Wandsworth, and that among the founders were Field, Wilcocks, Travers, etc., is an interesting product of the imagination, but it is not history.

The order of Wandsworth is not, as McCrie says[3], identical with the *Directory of Church-government* of 1644. The latter is a translation of the Book of Discipline, which was compiled by the Elizabethan Presbyterians during the 'eighties[4].

The Wandsworth meeting could not have been a Presbytery in the modern sense. At that time the word Presbytery was generally applied to what we in Scotland now call a Kirk Session; for instance, Sandys writing to Bullinger, 15 August, 1573[5], gives as one of the tenets of the Puritans: *Habeat unaquaeque parochia suum proprium presbyterium.* These early English Presbyterians laid stress upon the congregational or parochial court, which was commonly spoken of as a Consistory, a senate of elders, or a Presbytery. When

[1] *e.g.* Brook, *Lives*, I, p. 34; Neal, I, p. 244.
[2] *History of the Early Puritans* (1860), p. 62.
[3] *Annals of English Presbytery* (1872), p. 131.
[4] *v. infra* p. 257.
[5] *Z.L.* I, Ep. CXIV.

in the 'eighties meetings representing several churches in a district came to be established they were called Conferences or *classes*, which correspond more exactly to modern Presbyteries. In the Channel Islands the Colloquy was the equivalent of our Presbytery. Fifty years ago Principal Lorimer did well to point out that in commemorating Wandsworth Presbytery we must disabuse our minds of the implications of modern ecclesiastical nomenclature[1]. Unquestionably Bancroft held that the Wandsworth meeting was a parochial or congregational Consistory. In the section of his book entitled *English Scottizing for Discipline by Practise*[2] he says: "Againe, concerning the Presbyteries (which the booke (*i.e.* the Puritan Book of Discipline) affirmeth should be in every parish) they want (in effect) nothing of all their whole platforme, if they could but once attaine unto the publike erecting up of those thrones. And how farre it is likely they have already prevailed therin, without staying any longer for her majesty, let these things following, whereof some have beene touched already, make it known unto you. Mention hath beene made of a Presbyterie set up at Wandesworth." Then he proceeds to enumerate other attempts at the erection of Consistories or particular church sessions. The Book of Discipline, from which he quotes, defines a Presbytery thus: *Praesbyterium in singulis ecclesijs constituendum est, quod est consessus et quasi senatus praesbyterorum*, which is translated in the *Directory* of 1644:—"Further in every particular Church there ought to be a Presbytery, which is a Consistory, and as it were a Senate of Elders." The elders are then defined as ministers and elders proper. It is clear, therefore, that Bancroft believed that a Consistory or session was erected at Wandsworth.

The *Second Admonition* gives a description of the Consistory or Presbytery that the Presbyterian Puritans desired to have established in every parish. This description appeared in print in the very year and month of the Wandsworth organisation and is therefore of the greatest interest. The Consistory

[1] *British and Foreign Evangelical Review*, Oct. 1872.
[2] *D.P.* p. 115.

or Presbytery, according to this Admonition[1] should comprise the ministers of a particular church and their assistants. "The assistants are they, whome the parish shall consent upon and chuse, for their good judgement in religion and godlinesse, which they know they be of, wherby they are mete for that office, using the advise of their ministers therin cheefely...and having made their choise, thereafter they shall publishe their agreement in their parishe, and after a sermon by their minister, at their appointment, and uppon their consent the minister may lay his handes uppon every of them, to testify to them their admission." It is evident that the opinion of the day was that the elders should be ordained and inducted by the minister or ministers of the congregation that elected them.

Why then is there no mention of the minister of Wandsworth Church? He was, not Field, but John Edwin, who afterwards was deprived for his nonconformity[2]. Probably he had Puritan leanings in 1572, but on this point we are not certain. Bancroft says, however, that Crane and Smith were "approvers" of the eleven elders. If this means that they admitted the elders to office we naturally wonder why the Vicar of Wandsworth did not perform this function. If the Presbytery had been a session attached to the parish Church it is not likely that he would have sought or required outsiders as "approvers." It seems therefore that the Wandsworth Presbytery was not the session of Wandsworth parish Church.

On the 12th of June, 1591, in the Star Chamber Cartwright affirmed that neither he nor any other to his knowledge had erected, practised, or put in use the authority or power of an eldership or Presbytery or any part thereof[3]. Not daring to call in question the veracity of the great Cartwright himself, the tenor of whose life forbids any such step, are we to conclude from his words that there was no such thing as a Wandsworth Consistory or Presbytery? Field's endorsement of the bill and Bancroft's use of the same forbid the con-

[1] *Pur. Man.* p. 118.
[2] *Sec. Parte,* I, p. 249.
[3] *v. infra* p. 334.

clusion. So we are forced to infer that Cartwright had no knowledge of the Wandsworth Presbytery, and this ignorance seems explicable only on the supposition that the said Presbytery did not occupy a position of conspicuous importance on the main line of Elizabethan Presbyterian history.

The name of Crane, presumably Nicholas, suggests a hypothesis, hitherto untried, but worthy of consideration. He was a Puritan preacher connected with a body of nonconformists, whose forerunners were unearthed in Plumbers' Hall, London, in June, 1567[1]. When these dissenters were examined by the ecclesiastical commissioners John Smith "the ancientest of them" pointed out that they desired to worship according to the book used by the English exiles at Geneva in the time of Mary, "which booke and order we nowe holde." By their advocacy of this book they have been claimed by some as pioneers of Presbyterianism; by their Separatism, maybe the result of circumstances rather than of conviction, they have been regarded by others as early exponents of Congregationalism. Many of them were imprisoned, but on their release they again resorted to private meetings, and most of their leaders were rearrested in the following year (4 March, 1567–8) "within the parishe of St Martens in the felde in the howse of James Tynne, gooldsmythe."[2] On the 22nd of April, 1569, twenty-four men and seven women were discharged from Bridewell and among them most of the original Plumbers' Hall leaders. Later in the year they sent a supplication to the Council to the effect that Grindal's promise to allow them to worship according to their conscience had not been fulfilled. At their request, they stated, he had appointed two preachers, Bonham and Crane, to keep a lecture. This allowance, however, did not last long. Bonham was committed to prison and Crane forbidden to preach in the London diocese[3]. The consequence was that their followers were driven to congregate in their own houses. Grindal wrote to the Council (4 January, 1569–70)[4] explaining

[1] *A parte of a reg.* pp. 23–27; *Grindal Rem.* pp. 201–16.
[2] These were not Papists, as Birt says (p. 530); *v.* Peel, p. 10.
[3] *Grindal Rem.* p. 316 *n.*
[4] *ibid.* p. 316.

and defending his action. He pointed out that Bonham and Crane and their followers had not kept their promise of conformity, and advised that the whole faction should be rigorously dealt with. Now we come to the point of the hypothesis. Crane, not allowed to preach in London, probably preached in the near neighbourhood of the city, but on the Surrey side of the Thames and took up his abode at Roehampton in the vicinity of Wandsworth. That his widow afterwards harboured the Marprelate press in this district (East Molesey) may indicate that he had resided in these parts. It is also probable that many of his followers came from London to enjoy his ministry, that they were joined by like-minded nonconformists in the country, and that Wandsworth was one of the centres, if not the only one, at which they met to worship in accordance with their beloved Genevan order. It is difficult to identify Smith of Mitcham. It is conceivable that he was the above-mentioned John Smith, but he may have been a Puritan preacher, whom we have not sufficient data to identify. If, Grindal having set his face against them, these people began to meet again in private conventicles in 1570, it would not be surprising to discover that by November, 1572, they had so developed their organisation and grown in boldness as to think of appointing elders. It is indeed possible that the Wandsworth Presbytery grew out of a meeting such as that held in Plumbers' Hall, and it is tempting to think that it may have been the direct descendant of the latter. If this hypothesis is correct the Presbytery must be regarded as the court of a secret and independent body containing Congregationalist as well as Presbyterian elements. Crane's own history shows that such an admixture was not impossible at the time. He was afterwards associated with Field, Wilcocks and others of the Cartwrightian party[1], while, on the other hand, shortly before his death he appears in connection with Greenwood, with whom and other "Brownestes" he was arrested at a conventicle in Henry Martin's house in October, 1587[2].

[1] *Sec. Parte*, I, pp. 70, 137; Peel, p. 12; *v. infra* p. 150.
[2] *v.* Peel; *A.C.* II, p. 39.

The above hypothesis must be modified if, as is possible, Bancroft antedates the Presbytery. He says that the London ministers although "nothing so forward" as the Wandsworthians had then their meetings in private houses, which were called Conferences according to the scheme outlined in the Admonitions, and considering the names of those given as members of these meetings, viz. Field, Wilcocks, Standen, Jackson, Bonham, Seintloe, Crane, and Edmundes, we are inclined to think that these Conferences took place after 1572. Most of these men did associate together about 1577[1] and probably Bancroft's "then" should apply to this date or even later. When the Dedham Conference was instituted a constitution was drawn up, which was called an "Order," and if Wandsworth Presbytery was erected five to ten years after the time stated it may have been such a Conference, an embryonic Presbytery in the modern sense, which Bancroft mistook for a parochial Consistory, but until fuller details are available it must be regarded as one of the many historical mysteries that still await an all-satisfying solution.

The Church authorities continued to keep a vigilant eye open for the secret Puritan press, but failed to unearth it. In November Parker told Burghley of the diligent search that had been made for it and the lack of success[2]. He complained at the same time of the high esteem in which the Puritans were held and of the widespread opinion that the Bishops were their persecutors. It seemed that the nonconformists who were slandering the Church dignitaries in infamous books and libels won the more applause the more they wrote. Soon, however, the rumour arose that the Puritan press was about to produce a more important work than any it had issued, namely, a reply to Whitgift's *Answer*. In December Cox wrote to Burghley[3] conveying the report that Norton was suspected as the author of this reply. This rumour was resented by Norton, who, regarding the continuance of the quarrel as largely due to the issue of obnoxious writings by the Puritans,

[1] *v. infra* p. 150.
[2] 22 Nov. 1572; *Lansd. MSS.* xv, No. 49.
[3] *ibid.* xv, No. 51; *Pur. Man.* p. xv.

repudiated the insinuation that he was cooperating with them[1]. The truth was that the man who was engaged with the refutation of Whitgift's *Answer* was Thomas Cartwright. Clarke[2] has handed down the interesting tradition that he was chosen by lot to undertake the task.

A few months after he was deprived of his Fellowship we have a fleeting glimpse of Cartwright in London at the house of a Mr Lonison, in all likelihood John Lonison, the master worker of the Mint. There, on the night of the 11th of December, 1572[3], Edward Dering asked a clergyman named Blage why he did not serve his cure himself. Blage excused himself on the ground that he was too busy with a book on the Lives of the Archbishops of Canterbury, probably Parker's *De Antiquitate Britannicae Ecclesiae*[4]. Dering, with a smile, observed that Blage might do well to be somewhat long in his life of Parker, as after him there would be no more Archbishops of Canterbury. Cartwright is said to have endorsed Dering's observation with the words *Accipio omen*. Both were expressing their hope that the Episcopal regime would soon come to an end and that the Presbyterian system would supplant it. The next year Dering's remarks, added to, distorted and turned into a dogmatic prophecy, were adduced as evidence of his disaffection. Almost twelve months after the event (26 Nov. 1573) he had to clear himself of the falsehoods connected with the utterance[5]. The chief interest of the trifling incident is that it reveals Cartwright consorting at the end of 1572 in the metropolis with one, who at that time enjoyed the reputation of being "the greatest learned man in England."[6] Dering's lectures on the Epistle to the Hebrews, then being delivered in London, were increasing his fame and influence. The 24th lecture had just been given (6 Dec. 1572) and was soon to be published as "a new yeares gift to the godly in London and elsewhere."[7] Intimacy with

[1] Norton to Parker, 16 Jan. 1572–3. St. *Parker*, II, p. 143.

[2] p. 369.

[3] *Petyt MSS*. 538. XXXVIII, f. 68.

[4] Dixon, V, p. 352; Soames, p. 208.

[5] *Cecil MSS. Hist. MSS. Comm.* II, pp. 63–4; St. *Parker*, II, p. 240; St. *Ann.* IV, p. 516.

[6] *Parker Corresp*. p. 410.

[7] *Godly Letters*, sig. A.

such a popular and virile Puritan would exercise a tonic effect upon Cartwright, who was now at work on his reply to Whitgift.

Field knew that a reply to Whitgift was in course of preparation and on the 28th of January, 1572–3, he wrote from Newgate to Gilby saying, "We hope that D. Whitgifts Booke will shortly be answered."[1] In the same epistle he intimates that he and Wilcocks are refraining from the production of any writings in favour of the Puritan cause lest their imprisonment be made perpetual. On the 1st of March, 1572–3, Tomson, referring among other things to Cartwright's *Reply*, writes to Gilby as follows: "As yet I heare nothinge of his Booke. I have written for it a weeke or two ago. If it comes to my handes (whereof I doubt not) you shall have it. For myne owen I can say nothinge but this, I thinke it shal not nede, when the first is owt which will be so full and ample, that the other and shorter may wel be spared: yet as it pleaseth them in whose handes it is, I am content. I trust I have written a trueth, and nothing but trueth. If it be otherwise, I am very wel content to be redressed, errare nolo. The sharpnes is not much, as I take it. I do but turne uppon his owne, and that you see, without any further bitternes. The Lord did so direct me, but if it be thoght to much, I do willingly amend it. I cannot tell what we shold do with that Boke of M Fulkes, nether wold I wishe Mr Goodman to let it go. For if it shold chance to be put forth by them, it might hurt the cause. You know there are certaine thinges in it, not agreed uppon, and those of weight. Let such thinges be prevented."[2] From this letter it appears that Tomson lived at some distance from the press that was producing Cartwright's *Reply*, and that although he was an interested party he had nothing to do with the actual printing. On his own confession Tomson's style could be sharp and bitter. Fulke's book, to which he refers, was not published till 1584, and then by Waldegrave under the title *A Briefe and Plaine Declaration*, with the running headline *A Learned Discourse of*

[1] *Baker MSS*. XXXII. Mm. 1. 43, f. 444.
[2] *ibid*. ff. 447–8.

Ecclesiasticall Government. Fenner in *A Defence of the godlie Ministers* (1587)[1] refers to it thus: "This Treatise was written divers years past, by a learned and deepe Divine, who hath bin after Master Jewell and M. Nowell, the chiefest Defendor by writings, both in our tongue and in Latin, of the trueth against the papistes: and was nowe only revised and published by us. Both because we had it in reverent regarde for the learning of the man acknowleged of both partes: & because we thought it would appeare to be most voyde of percialitie, whiche was not written upon the occasion of these late grievances. Nowe what lesse duetie of thankfulnesse could wee performe to this learned mans labours, then to give it the tytle of a learned Discours."[2] Fenner here alludes to Fulke's early Puritanism, his later adherence to a more moderate and conservative position, and his numerous and learned writings against Roman Catholicism[3]. As the *Learned Discourse* had a direct and important connection with the Marprelate controversy we may observe that there are several other points of contact between the literary activities of the Puritans in 1572–3 and the notorious Tracts of 1588–9, and we are confident that consideration of such questions as the following would repay detailed study: the similarity in style of the products of the earlier and the later secret presses, Field's connection with both, the probability that literary materials were amassed from 1572–3 onwards by some central Puritan person or body, and that some of these were used, maybe in revised form, in the 'eighties, etc.

The mention of Goodman in Tomson's letter is also very suggestive. We are naturally inclined to assume that this must be Christopher, Knox's old colleague and friend, a man with a long experience of Presbyterianism both in Geneva and Scotland, one who was probably intimate with Cartwright in Ireland, one "whose lyfe and learning" according to a Scottish testimony[4] "the verie wicked can not bot praise," "a man" according to Jewel[5] "of irritable temper and too pertinacious in any thing that he has once undertaken." His

[1] p. 56. [2] *v. infra* pp. 273, 275. [3] *v. A.C.* II, p. 57.
[4] *Knox*, VI, p. 573. [5] *Z.L.* I, Ep. VII.

whereabouts at this time might throw light upon the locality of the press that produced Cartwright's first book, for he seems to have acted as its chief director. But the accounts of his life, after telling of his return to Chester in August, 1571, leave a gap that extends to 1580, and we are left to wonder[1].

The Puritan press maintained its secrecy well. The authorities hunted for it long but in vain. That it was located at Wandsworth[2] is an assumption based upon a confused association of ideas. In March, 1573, a suspicion arose that it lay somewhere to the north, probably in Northamptonshire. At Greenwich, on the 31st of the month, the Privy Council decided to act in the light of the current rumour and sent "A letter to Sir John Spencer and Sir Robert Lane, knightes, to make inquerye for a booke likely to be printed in the countie of Northampton, an aunswer against Whitegiftes booke, to committ the principal doers to prison, to send up some of the bookes and to advertise what they finde."[3]

That there was ground for suspecting Northamptonshire is evident from the plaintive appeal sent by the Bishop of Peterborough to Burghley on the 13th of April. "Vouchsafe," he wrote[4], "to looke upon theis sheires of Northampton and Rutland...and ayde me with your counsaile....Those whom men doe call puritans and their fautours...are growen apparentlie to neglecte, if theie doe not abhorre, the devine service sett owte by publique aucthoritie. So that in the towne of Overton where Mr Carleton dwelleth there is no devyne service upon most Sondayes and hollidaies accordinge to the booke of commen prayer, but in steede thereof ij sermons be preached most commenlie by one Mr Standen and one Mr Kinge, men for their opinions not licensed by me to preache at this daie. When they are determined to receyve the communion theie repaire to Whiston, where it is theire joye to have manie owte of divers parishes, principallie owt of Northampton towne and Overton aforesaid with other townes thereabowte, theare to receive the sacramentes with preachers and ministers to their owne likinge,

[1] *D.N.B.*; Wood, *Athenae Oxon.* I, p. 721; *Knox*, VI, p. 699.

[2] Sayle, No. 5896.

[3] *Acts P.C.* VIII, p. 93.

[4] *Lansd. MSS.* XVII, No. 27; *Pur. Man.* p. xvii.

and contrarie to forme prescribed by the publique order of the realme.... To their purposes they have drawen divers yonge ministers, to whome it is plausible to have absolute authoritie in their parishes. In their waies theie be verie bolde and stowte, like men that seme not to be withowt greate frendes." If the scheme that was set on foot in Northampton and neighbourhood in 1571[1] was carried into effect it is not surprising that the county should have turned into a nursery of Puritanism. According to that scheme the town of Northampton was to become a veritable Geneva, and ministers and people round about were to be brought under the sway of the Discipline, the Exercises, the Sermonising and the Sabbatarianism that were characteristic of Calvinism. It is also a notable fact that in 1588–9 the Marprelate press was harboured for a time in Northamptonshire[2] and we wonder whether Cartwright's *Reply* was printed under the auspices of a man of influence in that county who was one of the "greate frendes" of the Puritans both in 1573 and in 1588–9.

Wherever it was printed Cartwright's long expected *Reply* appeared and by the end of April was in circulation. "As yet," wrote Sandys to Burghley on the 30th of April, 1573[3], "I could never come by that boke although it is Current amongst many." It is entitled *A Replye to An Answere made of M Doctor Whitgifte Agaynste the Admonition to the Parliament by T.C*" (n.d.). We read of the difficult circumstances in which it was produced in the interesting foreword of the printer. "It falleth out (gentle Reader)," he writes, "that I neyther having wealth to furnishe the Print wyth sufficient varietie of letters, have bene compelled (as a poore man doth one instrument to divers purposes) so to use one letter for three or foure tongues. And being for wante of long training up in thys mysterie, not so skilful to spie a faulte, so soone as it is made, have lefte oute, or ever I was aware, divers quotations in the margent, displaced other some, and com-

[1] St. *Ann.* III, p. 133.
[2] Pierce, *Hist. Introd.* pp. 156 ff.; Arber, *Sketch*, p. 77.
[3] *Lansd. MSS.* XVII, No. 30, f. 61; *Pur. Man.* p. 152.

mitted some other faultes in the texte. Whereof also the cause hathe bene, not onely that I was sometimes, for wante of healpe, driven bothe to worke at the presse, to sette, and to correcte: but also that I wanted the commoditie that other Prynters commonly have, of being neare, eyther unto the author, or to some that is made privie unto hys booke. Whych maye the better appeare, for that after the author came unto me, whych was when the halfe of the booke was Printed, the faultes neither are so many, nor so greate as before. In consideration whereof, I will humbly desire thee (gentle Reader) the rather to beare wyth me, considering that that whych I doe in thys Arte, I doe not in respecte of any gaine, but only for the desire I have to advaunce the glory of God: and considering also that I have procured the groser faultes, and those wherein there is any daunger of misleading the reader, to be amended wyth the penne" (unsigned). A second edition of the *Reply* was printed before the 11th of June and, in spite of the Royal Proclamation issued on that date against it, shortly afterwards published with a new address from the printer to the reader. This address is signed by "J. S," *i.e.* John Stroud the Puritan printer, who was soon to suffer for his labours[1]. "Some perhaps will marvel," says Stroud, "at the newe impression of thys boke...notwythstanding our most gracious Princes late published proclamation, procured rather by the Byshops then willingly sought for by her maiestie....But cease to muse, good christian reader, whosoever thou art: and learne to know that no lawes, were they never so hard and severe, can put out the force of Gods spirite in hys children....For the profite therefore of the godly and their instruction have we hazarded our selves, and as it were cast our selves into such daungers and troubles as shalbe layed upon us if we come into the hands of the persecuting Bishops...."[2]

In this *Reply* Cartwright came forward as the champion of the Admonitions, and by the weight of his learning and

[1] *v. infra* p. 110.

[2] For full reprint of Stroud's preface *v. Sec. Parte*, I, p. 112 *n.*, where it is stated in error that the second edition of Cartwright's *Reply* was printed in 1574.

prestige, and the facility of his pen, made their arguments more specious and, from the point of view of the Established Church, more dangerous. The severe attack on his *Answer* roused Whitgift to instant activity. Within a year he published his *Defence of the Answer*, which elicited from Cartwright a *Second Reply* in two parts (1575 and 1577). Walton is obviously wrong in stating, in his *Life of Hooker*, that Whitgift had the last word in this controversy. It was with the second part of Cartwright's *Second Reply* (1577) that the literary duel came to an end. At this point it is convenient to summarise the arguments put forward by Cartwright in this memorable conflict. Chief attention will be given to his first *Reply*, which was generally known among his contemporaries as "Cartwright's Book"; his *Second Reply*, although it elaborates, does not add anything material to the chief lines of argument. The most accessible reproduction of the first *Reply* is that reprinted by the Parker Society in *Whitgift's Works*[1].

While Whitgift in both his books labours the analogy between the Puritans and the Anabaptists, Cartwright points out that the latter are detested as much by his party as by Whitgift and that the Puritans seek no separation from the Church but merely its further reformation. According to Cartwright the Commonwealth and the Church stand in the same relationship as the twins of Hippocrates, which prospered or languished together, and he affirms that therefore the State would benefit by the reform of the Church. Inasmuch, however, as he holds that conscience is the basis of Puritan nonconformity and that the things for which he and his associates stand, are of such importance that if every hair of their heads were a life it should be given in defence of the cause, Whitgift is surely justified in his fear that, like the Anabaptists, the Puritans will produce dispeace and disorder in the realm. It should be noted that Cartwright, like his

[1] Reference to Cartwright's trilogy will accordingly be given thus: *W.W.* for the first Reply, *2nd Rep.* for the second (1575), and *Rest* for *The Rest of the Second Replie* (1577), which three references correspond to Hooker's lib. i, lib. ii and lib. iii. *v.* W. Beloe, *Anecdotes of Literature and Scarce Books* (1807), I, p. 21.

fellow reformers, frequently repudiates the name "Puritan," which is now used to designate the party he represents, and it is interesting to observe that he repels the charge that this party manifest a peculiar straitness of life. They introduce no monachism or anchorism; they eat and drink and are apparelled like other men, and use those recreations that other men do[1].

Whitgift classes Puritans with Papists in their opposition to the Church of England, but Cartwright notes that their opposition is not animated by the same principles. The Papists mislike the Prayer Book because it swerves from the mass-book; the Puritans mislike it because it has too much in common with the same. The Puritans would not only unhorse the Pope but would also take away the stirrups so that he should never get into the saddle again. They would have up both stump and root[2]. In their attitude to Rome Whitgift and Cartwright represent different principles.

The main contention of Cartwright is that the Church of England should be reformed according to the model of the Apostolic Church, and this to his mind was undoubtedly Presbyterian. Whitgift therefore pronounces Cartwright's whole programme as based upon two rotten pillars, viz. that the Church should have the same government as that which prevailed in the Apostolic age, and that nothing that has been abused by Rome should be retained in it[3]. He holds on the other hand that Scripture leaves much to the discretion of the Church in the matter of its external polity and that those things, that are of value in themselves, should, if thought fit, be kept in the Church even though they have been wrongly used by Rome.

Cartwright does not hold, as is commonly supposed, that nothing can be in the Church unless it is expressly commanded in Scripture. He certainly states that the Word of God contains the direction of all things pertaining to the Church, yea, to any part of man's life[4]. He denies, however, that it is his belief that no ceremony or order may be in the Church unless the same is expressed in Scripture, but he is of opinion that

[1] *W.W.* I, p. 110.
[2] *ibid.* I, p. 120.
[3] *ibid.* I, p. 6.
[4] *ibid.* I, p. 190.

men are bound to follow the general rules of Scripture which he proceeds to set down. Whitgift says, "Hold you here and we shall soon agree."[1] The disputants are at one in believing that the Bible does not express particularly everything that is to be done in the Church and that certain appointments, that may vary with time and circumstance, depend upon the Church's judgment[2]. Cartwright's general rules are that none be offended, that all be done decently and in order, to the glory of God and the edification of men, for which rules he furnishes the appropriate texts. By these rules such matters as are not specified in Scripture, *e.g.* the hour of worship, are determined. Theoretically it is not the authority of Scripture that is in dispute. It is only when Cartwright and Whitgift proceed to expound and apply Scripture that their opinions clash. The former is convinced that God who made provision for the tabernacle and the temple even to the pins, snuffers and besoms, was sure to lay down in His Word the essentials and ornaments of His Church, and that in Scripture He does enjoin Presbyterianism as the only government of the Church; the latter, on the other hand, finds no particular polity commanded in Scripture at all. Whitgift holds that the Bible contains all that is necessary to salvation, and so rejects the sacrifice of the mass and such like, but he cannot see eye to eye with Cartwright when the Puritan affirms that Presbyterian discipline is an essential part of the Gospel[3].

This divergence is marked in the consideration of the judicial laws of the Old Testament. Cartwright holds that all Scripture is equally binding and that therefore the death penalties announced in the Old Testament for blasphemy, murder, adultery and heresy are valid still and ought to be put into force[4]. Whitgift counts himself not so Jewish as to think that Christians are bound either to the ceremonial or the judicial laws[5]. Cartwright admits that the ceremonial law has been abrogated, but insists that the marrow and substance of the judicial laws, because of the equity inherent in them,

[1] *W.W.* I, p. 194.
[2] *ibid.* I, pp. 191, 195.
[3] *ibid.* I, pp. 180, 364.
[4] *ibid.* I, p. 264; *2nd Rep.* p. 101.
[5] *ibid.* I, p. 265.

have never been annulled[1]. Of course, he is of opinion that the civil magistrate should execute the prescribed capital punishment, and incidentally says that the only reasonable excuse for the presence of Bishops in the House of Lords is that they should there aid the civil government to carry out such laws of God[2]. He is taken to task by Whitgift for holding an extreme view of the pronouncement in Zechariah, c. xiii, concerning the punishment of false prophets[3]. Whitgift believes that under the Gospel there is less severity than under the old dispensation and that repentance will blot out punishment. Cartwright, however, is sure that God is more severe under the Gospel and concludes "off that place off Zecharie... that the same severitie off punishmente that was used against false Prophets then, owghte to be used now under the gospell, againste false teachers, comparing one parson and circomstance withe another." He that hath fallen away from God and seeks to draw others away should be handled according to the law prescribed in Deut. c. xiii. "If this be bloudie and extreme," he proceeds, "I am contente to be so counted with the holie goste....And althowghe in other cases off Idolatrie, uppon repentance liffe is given...yet in this case of willing sliding backe, and moving others to the same, and other some cases, whiche are expressed in the lawe as off open and horrible blasphemie off the name of God: I denie that uppon repentance, ther owghte to followe any pardon off death, whiche the Judiciall lawe dothe require."[4] Green in his *Short History of the English People*[5] fastens upon this passage as if it contained the quintessence of Cartwright's teaching and accordingly represents him as combining the despotism of a Hildebrand with the cruelty of a Torquemada. "Never," says Green, "had the doctrine of persecution been urged with such a blind and reckless ferocity" and in support of this unjust and crushing verdict he furnishes a misleading and incomplete excerpt from the above passage. The extract, wrung from its context, gives colourable ground for Green's assertion that no leader of a religious party ever deserved

[1] *2nd Rep*. p. 94. [2] *ibid*. pp. 102, 104. [3] *W.W*. I, p. 331.
[4] *2nd Rep*. p. 115. [5] c. VIII, sect. 1.

less of after sympathy than Cartwright. There is no doubt that this sweeping judgment of Green has influenced succeeding historians and has tended to perpetuate a false and unfavourable impression of Cartwright's personality and message. We certainly do not endorse the Puritan's "bloody" tenet, but we can understand it in its setting. It represents an enthusiastic devotee of Scripture, whose conscience obliged him to accept as perpetually binding a literal interpretation of the Old Testament judicial laws. Undoubtedly, if Cartwright had had power to execute these laws he would have regarded it as his duty to put such false prophets as Roman Catholic priests to death—of course through the agency of the civil authorities—not because he was a cruel bloodthirsty man, but because he considered himself the willing servant of a God Who had declared His will in unmistakeable terms. His intolerance was equivalent to obedience to God's behest and the end of it was, not the slaughter of men, but the furtherance of God's glory. This he makes clear when he says: "He that killethe a man, and takethe awaie his corporall liffe owghte to die: it followethe much more, that he whiche takethe awaie the liffe off the sowle, should die. And iff yt be meete to mainteine the liffe off man, by the punishment off death: howe shoulde the honor off God, whiche is more precious then all mens lives, be withe smaller punishmente established?"[1] He further argues that the breaches of the second table of the Ten Commandments are due to the transgression of the first, and that the magistrates ought therefore to enforce penalties for breach of the first lest the Commonwealth should be endangered by non-observance of the second. Cartwright is but an example of the godly man in the sixteenth century whose lack of toleration sprang from conviction, whose readiness to persecute and inflict the death penalty was inspired by the loftiest motives and by a deep sense of duty. In his opinion the dire duty to put to death was expressly commanded by God Himself in His infallible Word. To refrain from the enormity was to disobey God. If therefore we differ from him let us not, like Green, regard

[1] *2nd Rep*. p. 117.

him as an inhuman monster, but as a sincere and conscientious religious man, whose convictions were misdirected by an excusably wrong view of Scripture.

Cartwright criticises the Book of Common Prayer on the ground that it is taken in large measure from the Church of Antichrist. His principle is that religion should, as far as possible, differ in form and fashion from that of idolaters, especially Papists[1]. As a stick bent in one direction should be bent in the other to straighten it, so the best way to banish popery from the Church is to reform it on purely anti-Roman lines. Feeling the force of Whitgift's contention expressed in the proverb *Abusus non tollit usum*, Cartwright denies that it is one of his principles, that it is not lawful to use the same ceremonies which the Papists used, but adds "thei are not to be used, when as good or better may be established."[2] Although he claims that what is good in popery belongs to the Church, nevertheless his general rule is that "Church ceremonies owght to be unlike the Antichristian."[3] As a true and typical Puritan he denounces the use of homilies, the Apocrypha, the ring in marriage, the term priest, the ceremony of confirmation, the observation of holy days, curtseying at the name of Jesus, prayer for the dead, etc.[4] The administration of the Sacraments should always be accompanied by preaching and should never be performed in private or by unordained persons. The very essence of the Sacraments depends on their being administered by a minister[5]. Cartwright complains that the authorised prayers are too often mere shreds and that too many of them are merely directed against the incommodities of this life[6]. He also objects to the over-repetition of the *Gloria Patri*, and the use of the *Benedictus*, *Magnificat*, and *Nunc Dimittis* as ordinary and daily prayers. In short, the Prayer Book has too much in common with Rome and too little with the usage of other

[1] *W.W.* II, p. 440.

[2] *Rest*, p. 171.

[3] *ibid.* p. 171, headline.

[4] *W.W.* II, pp. 438 ff.; III, pp. 340 ff.; *Rest*, pp. 116 ff.

[5] *W.W.* II, p. 525. Cartwright is quoted as an authority on this question in the seventeenth century (*A Letter of many Ministers in Old England*, p. 87).

[6] *W.W.* II, p. 478.

Protestant Churches. When condemning the use of funeral sermons Cartwright reveals his acquaintance with some who had been members of the English Church in Geneva during Mary's reign. Although the Genevan Prayer Book allowed such sermons "yet," he says, "(as I have heard of those which were there present) it was not so used."[1] When arguing against kneeling at Communion he alludes to the Black Rubric, which has been ascribed to Knox, and asks, "how came it to pass that in King Edwards days there was a protestation added in the book of prayer to clear that gesture from adoration?"[2] Whitgift replies that the Rubric was added "to satisfy (if it might be) such quarrellers as you are, and to take away all occasion of cavilling, not for any great fear of adoration."[3] Cartwright, however, prefers sitting, not because it is absolutely necessary, but because it comes nearest to the usage of the Last Supper and because kneeling is beset with Romish dangers[4]. For the Book of Common Prayer Cartwright would substitute a book after the Genevan model.

The chief weight of Cartwright's criticism, as Whitgift recognises, is directed against diocesan Episcopacy[5]. He considers that the only allowable Bishops are Presbyters and that they are all equal. While discussing this Presbyterian parity he points out that Calvin, having been frequently chosen Moderator in Geneva, "misliked that that small preheminence shoulde so long remaine with one, as which in time might breed inconvenience: likewise that I hearde my selfe off Maister Beza, which misliked off yt for the same cause."[6] For the Archbishop Cartwright can find no justification at all. He is the head of the popish hierarchy, which came out of the bottomless pit of hell; his office is not even mentioned in Scripture; and his title is only proper to our Saviour[7]. While declaiming against a monarchical episcopate Cartwright affirms that Whitgift's arguments tell in favour of the papacy and denies that the Church is obliged to accommodate itself to

[1] *W.W.* III, p. 378. [2] *ibid.* III, p. 90. [3] *ibid.* III, p. 91.
[4] *ibid.* III, pp. 96–7. [5] *ibid.* II, p 81.
[6] *2nd Rep.* p. 631. [7] *W.W.* II, pp. 81 ff.

the form of government maintained by the Commonwealth. He incidentally remarks that it is not absolutely necessary that there should be one over all in a Commonwealth and Whitgift in his *Defence* pertinently observes "Note this suspicious speech of the kind of government."[1]

We can readily believe that Elizabeth would not look with kindly eyes upon a man, who dared to utter such an opinion and to advise her duly to consider the abuses said by the first *Admonition* to prevail in the services of the royal chapel[2]. But the whole system advocated by Cartwright was in many points at variance with the claims of the Tudor autocrat. Unwilling to yield the civil magistrate more authority than the Word of God permits Cartwright proclaims that, although the godly magistrate is head of the State, Christ alone is Head of the Church, of which the magistrate can be but a member[3]. Like other members of the Church the civil ruler must be amenable to its discipline: "That Princes should be excepted from ecclesiastical discipline, and namely from excommunication, I utterly mislike."[4] It is the ruler's duty to reverence the Church and to see that God's laws respecting religion are observed. Cartwright repudiates the Roman Catholic view of the relationship between Church and State and does not claim the exemption of ministers from the civil jurisdiction of the magistrate[5], but he insists that in spiritual affairs the Church must be autonomous. Cartwright is thus the advocate of a Free Presbyterian National Church similar to that which exists in Scotland. He acknowledges the debt the Church of England owes to Elizabeth for leading it out of the spiritual Egypt of popery; he professes the utmost loyalty to the Queen; and he points out that he merely desires a "further reformation."[6] Knowing that the opposition to his scheme is due to the authorised policy of uniformity he naively states, "We also desire an uniform order."[7] But it is a Presbyterian uniformity for which he pleads and there lies the chief point at issue.

[1] *W.W.* II, p. 263.
[2] *ibid.* III, p. 393.
[3] *ibid.* I, p. 390; III, p. 198.
[4] *Rest*, p. 65.
[5] *W.W.* III, p. 311.
[6] *ibid.* III, p. 314.
[7] *ibid.* III, p. 324.

Cartwright is convinced that Scripture prescribes the Presbyterian form of government and that the Apostolic Church is a model for all ages. The only allowable ministers therefore are those called Presbyters or Bishops in the New Testament. It is plain to Cartwright that they must be elected with the consent of the people. To prove this point he provides Scriptural evidence, particularly from the *Acts of the Apostles*. That congregations should have an interest in the election of their pastors is also supported by reason and the usage of the Reformed Churches[1]. When dealing with the question of ecclesiastical franchise Cartwright is careful to distinguish Church and Parish and maintains that "when there is a Christian magistrate, he owght to provide, that those which are not off the churche, thrust not in them selves into such affaires."[2] He is not, however, an advocate of pure congregationalism. Ministers are to be tried and examined by Presbyters before their appointment to a charge and after their election they are to be ordained by the same officials. Cartwright also expressly says that if a congregation fails to elect a fit minister the Presbyterial courts concerned must intervene and that if they fail the magistrate is to annul the election and command another[3]. He holds that the New Testament evangelists, apostles and prophets, who had no fixed congregations, were extraordinary ministers specially called by God and that the ordinary and perpetual ministers are tied to a particular Church. Whitgift denies that a spiritual shepherd may not have the general care of other shepherds and many flocks, holds that there is nothing in Scripture to prove that every preacher should have a flock, and twits Cartwright with having no flock of his own[4].

The combatants indulge in personal aspersions when they come to the question of non-residence. Cartwright criticises Whitgift for having a mastership of a college in one corner of the land (Trinity, Cambridge), a deanery in another (Lincoln) and a prebend in a third (Ely)[5]. Whitgift retorts that Cartwright and others do no good at all in any place, but only range

[1] *W.W.* I, p. 455; *2nd Rep.* p. 224.
[2] *2nd Rep.* p. 146.
[3] *W.W.* I, pp. 375, 419; *2nd Rep.* p. 147.
[4] *W.W.* I, p. 479.
[5] *ibid.* I, p. 506.

up and down, living at other men's tables and disturbing the Church. He is persuaded that the minister who preaches in his cure but one sermon in a year offends God less than the Puritans who have forsaken their calling[1]. Cartwright replies that the Puritans have been driven from their posts and are now being unjustly blamed for leaving them. Non-residence was an undoubted grievance and modern critics of the Puritans generally agree with them in their denunciation of this evil. The hungry sheep looked up and were not fed.

Cartwright also denounces the occupation of civil offices by ministers. Their efficiency as pastors and preachers is thereby impaired[2]. He advocates frequent preaching and condemns those ministers "which make the word of God novel and dainties, and as M. Latimer pleasantly said, strawberries coming only at certain times of the year."[3] He is of opinion that the widespread lack of preaching could be cured by exercises or prophesyings[4]. He also thinks that ministers should supplement their preaching with catechising[5].

The office of catechist belongs properly to the doctor[6]. Concerning this official Cartwright does not seem to have made up his mind. He believes that Scripture distinctly prescribes a teaching office and that it is different from the pastoral, but he is not sure whether one minister may not perform both functions. Knowing the difficulty of procuring even one efficient minister for each congregation he evidently regards it as practically impossible to have both a pastor and a doctor in every Church, and accordingly contends that, failing a doctor, the pastor may undertake such work as the catechising in his stead[7]. In this connection it may be noted that Cartwright objects to the conferring of academic degrees, such as B.D. and D.D., upon ministers who are unlearned or incapable of teaching, not, as Whitgift suggests, because he desires the abolition of schools and universities and resents the repulse he suffered when he desired the D.D. for himself but because such degrees are frequently bestowed upon men

[1] *W.W.* I, p. 517.
[2] *ibid.* III, pp. 432 ff.
[3] *ibid.* III, p. 5; *v.* Latimer's *Sermons*, Parker Soc. p. 62.
[4] *2nd Rep.* sig.)( )( )(, iii *verso*.
[5] *ibid.*
[6] *ibid.* p. 634.
[7] *ibid.* pp. 296, 517.

of no scholarship and because a doctorate should be given only to those who hold the office of a doctor[1].

Next in importance to the ministers in Cartwright's scheme are the governing elders or seniors, whose office is to help the pastor or bishop in the government of a Church and particularly in the admonishing of the erring by the administration of ecclesiastical censures[2]. Cartwright interprets the text, I Tim. v. 17, as meaning that there are two kinds of elders or presbyters, "the one which doth govern and teach, the other which governeth only"[3]; he discovers allusions to the governing elders in I Cor. xii and Rom. xii and is sure that it was such officials who were appointed by Paul and Barnabas. Whitgift disagrees with these interpretations and argues that, though there may have been lay elders in the primitive Church, it is not meet or even possible to have them in every congregation now and that the Christian magistrate has the authority the seniors may have exercised in the Apostolic age[4]. In the scriptural injunction, "Tell the Church," the Church, according to Cartwright, means the pastor and elders, its representative governors, whereas Whitgift regards the command more generally as signifying any who are lawfully appointed to govern the Church[5].

The deacon, according to Cartwright, is not a minister but an office-bearer, who has charge over the poor. Cartwright suggests that the existing collectors should become deacons[6]. Of deaconesses or widows he does not speak with his usual dogmatic confidence. He observes that there was greater need of them in the early Church because of the "multitude of strangers through the persecution, and by the great heat of those east countries, whereupon the washing and suppling of their feet was required; yet, forsomuch as there are poor which are sick in every church, I do not see how a better and more convenient order can be devised....If such may be gotten, we ought also to keep that order of widows in the church still. I know that there be learned men which think

[1] *W.W.* III, pp. 470, 511.
[2] *ibid.* III, pp. 150, 167.
[3] *ibid.* III, p. 150.
[4] *ibid.* III, pp. 175–8.
[5] *ibid.* III, p. 168.
[6] *Rest*, p. 114.

otherwise, but I stand upon the authority of Gods word."[1] He further says, "The perpetuity of that commandment touching widows remaineth in that sort it was given, that is, upon condition."[2]

It is obvious that the quarrel is no longer purely vestiarian. Cartwright points this out and notes that the Continental Churches have been misinformed[3]. He thinks that the minister should wear the obnoxious apparel rather than leave the ministry[4]. Nevertheless, he is of opinion that the cap, tippet and surplice, especially the last, are unmeet attire for ministers of the Gospel, not because there is any pollution in the things themselves, nor only because Papists have superstitiously used them, but because having been abused as notes and marks of popish abominations they are hurtful monuments of idolatry, grieving the godly who hold everything connected with Antichrist in detestation, tending to draw weak brethren back to Rome, and confirming stubborn Papists in the opinion that the Protestant religion cannot stand by itself and in the hope that their other trumpery and baggage will come again[5]. He concedes that the magistrate may command a distinctive clerical garb but observes that it does not follow that popish apparel should therefore be adopted[6]. Cartwright, however, regards the whole controversy about garments as secondary. The issue is higher and more momentous.

The chief emphasis is placed upon discipline. Hence Cartwright and his associates commonly came to be known as Disciplinarians. Besides private admonition and reprehension Cartwright includes in his definition of discipline (i) the election, abdication and deposition of ecclesiastical officers, (ii) the excommunication of offenders and the absolution of the repentant, (iii) the decision of all matters touching corrupt manners and perverse doctrine. Like Whitgift we may be inclined to object that this definition is too wide and that it comprises the whole system of ecclesiastical polity

[1] *W.W.* III, p. 292.
[2] *ibid.* III, p. 173 *n.*
[3] *ibid.* II, p. 1.
[4] *2nd Rep.* p. 403.
[5] *W.W.* II, pp. 1, 3, 6, 8.
[6] *ibid.* II, p. 17.

or government[1]. Cartwright indeed expressly says "The word discipline is used in good autors for the whole maner of government,"[2] and this comprehensive meaning of discipline must be kept in mind if we are to appreciate aright the contentions of the Puritans. Cartwright insists that all parts of discipline are in the hands of the eldership, *i.e.* ministers and elders. The Church also has an interest in excommunication, etc., but its decisions are made through its representative officials. "Harder and difficulter causes" should be referred from particular Church sessions or presbyteries to synods, which should represent shires, dioceses, provinces and nations respectively in a pyramidal hierarchy of courts. These courts having the management of discipline in the wide sense, those of the Bishops and Archbishops, *e.g.* the court of faculties, the courts of chancellors, commissaries, etc., must be abolished. The latter are relics of Antichrist. Besides dealing with ecclesiastical affairs that belong to the jurisdiction of the eldership, they meddle in civil affairs and thus interfere with the office of the magistrate[3]. Regarding the officers of these courts Cartwright forcibly states: "Most of them are either papists or bribers or drunkards (I know what I write) or epicures."[4]

Not only does Cartwright put forward Presbyterianism as the scheme of ecclesiastical polity enjoined by Scripture, but he is convinced that it will cure a multitude of evils rampant in Church and State. Sectarians, such as Anabaptists, are rife because the ministers are not efficient, discipline is lacking because there are no elders to assist the pastors, drunkenness, blasphemy and immorality are common because there is no eldership to watch and admonish offenders, and rogues and beggars abound because the office of deacons has not been established. He eulogises Geneva as a city that has been purified and exalted by the adoption of the discipline.

Such are the salient points in Cartwright's triplex reply. The polemical circumstances that inspired his writing conspired to prevent him from setting forth the claims of

[1] *W.W.* III, p. 221.
[2] *Rest*, p. 78.
[3] *W.W.* III, pp. 229, 263–7.
[4] *ibid.* III, p. 268.

Presbyterianism in a simple and systematic manner, and prompted him at times to deviate from the path of straightforward exposition to indulge, like his opponent, in acrimonious insults. In his first reply he appears as the champion of the Admonitioners, in the other two he defends himself against Whitgift's *Defence*. He frankly confesses that he was much handicapped by lack of books when writing his first *Reply* and acknowledges his great debt to Flaccus Illyricus's work "that he intituleth *The Catalogue of the Witnesses of Truth*, of whom I confess myself to have been much holpen in this matter of the choice of the church touching the minister....For, lacking opportunities divers ways, I was contented somewhat to use the collection." Whitgift's marginal note is "Not only much, but almost altogether."[1] Cartwright's future critics frequently sought to depreciate the value of his work by alluding to his dependence upon secondary sources, *e.g.* Sutcliffe[2] calls Illyricus "as true a quoter of textes almost, as ever was Th. Cartwr. his scholler.' Cartwright on the other hand pointed out that if all the quotations were taken out of Whitgift's *Answer to the Admonition*, as wind out of a bladder, the result would be instead of a book of two shillings a mere pamphlet of two pence[3]. It may be noted that in his first *Reply* Cartwright answers a little work in Latin "which is called the Book of the Doctors, which goeth from hand to hand."[4] This book is not, as the editor of Whitgift's works suggests[5], a reply to the *Explicatio* of 1574, but was issued before the latter.

In the spring of 1573 the authors of the first *Admonition* received more favourable consideration. Probably due to the influence of their patrons, to whom both they and their wives had explained their distressful state[6], their case came before the Privy Council on the 20th of March, 1573, and before the month was at an end they were released from the close confinement of Newgate[7]. Although they had promised some measure of conformity they were not yet allowed full freedom

[1] *W.W.* I, p. 448; cf. I, pp. 399, 419, 439, 449.

[2] *Ans. to a Pet.*, p. 7.

[3] *W.W.* I, p. 239.

[4] *ibid.* II, p. 112.

[5] *ibid.* II, p. 106.

[6] *Sec. Parte*, I, p. 91.

[7] *Acts P.C.* VIII, pp. 90, 93.

and were quartered upon Archdeacon Mullins. Should their behaviour continue to prove satisfactory they had the hope of a royal pardon. But they hankered after further liberty and both they and noblemen who befriended them petitioned the Bishop of London for a complete deliverance. Field and Wilcocks proved a source of nuisance to Mullins as so many of their Puritan brethren resorted to them and for the Archdeacon's sake Sandys thought of transferring them to the house of some merchant of their faction[1]. In July, however, we find that they are still billeted in Mullins's house[2]. Towards the end of the year, after at least fifteen months' imprisonment, and after humble suit to Leicester and to the Council as a body they received their final discharge[3]. In December we find Wilcocks at Coventry, from which town on the 21st of that month he addressed a letter to Gilby[4]. Field became a preacher in the Church of St Mary Aldermary, where for four years he "labored painfullie" "preching purely the word of God and catechising" until he was suspended. His wellwishers in the congregation petitioned Leicester to procure his restoration but in vain[5].

Cartwright's first *Reply* was not long published before it was decided that Whitgift should set forth an answer to it. On the 19th of May, 1573, Laurence Tomson, writing to Gilby from the town of Leicester, transmitted the latest rumours from London as follows[6]: "I heard from London this last weke, that hir Maiestie had read our Brother his Booke twise over, and hath caused the enemie of the trueth to staye from answeringe. This is given forth in London, of the trueth of it I am not certaine." The note sent by Parker to Burghley on the 5th of June[7] appears to corroborate the report that Elizabeth was of opinion that the Church dignitaries should let the controversy die and that Whitgift should stay the answer he had already begun. Parker, how-

[1] Sandys to Burghley, 30 April, 1573. *Pur. Man.* p. 152.
[2] Sandys to Burghley, 2 July, 1573. *ibid.* p. 154.
[3] *v. Sec. Parte*, I, p. 91.
[4] *Baker MSS.* XXXII, Mm. I, 43, f. 441.
[5] *D.N.B.*; *Sec. Parte*, I, p. 135; Brook, *Lives*, I, p. 322.
[6] *Baker MSS.* XXXII, Mm. I, 43, f. 448. [7] *Parker Corresp.* p. 427.

ever, was of another mind. He was persuaded that silence would do great hurt to "hir maiesties governance" by encouraging and emboldening the Puritans. Anxious for the Queen's "saftye and estimation" he advised Burghley to take proceedings against the revolutionaries. At the same time he forwarded a letter, dated the 4th of June[1], which he had received from Whitgift, which shows that the latter was already far advanced in the task of vindicating himself as well as the *status quo* in Church and State against the attack of Cartwright.

That Parker was greatly annoyed by Cartwright's *Reply* is made evident by the document[2], undated but probably belonging to 1573, which he drew up for Burghley, wherein he pointed out that Cartwright's animadversions against the extravagant prelates could not apply to him. In his anxiety to clear himself personally he submitted an abstract of his expenditure, showing how great were the demands upon his ecclesiastical income and how little he profited by it. The Archbishop's personal grievance would reinforce his belief in the policy of literary retaliation. We are not surprised therefore that he gave his warm sympathetic support to Whitgift's new undertaking. In his letter of the 4th of June to Parker Whitgift unfolds his plans with regard to the composition of his *Defence*, a large portion of which he has already written. "The boke wyll be something bygg," for he intends to include in it his *Answer to the Admonition*, Cartwright's *Reply* and his own *Defence*. He hopes, however, to have it finished by next Parliament. In sweeping terms Whitgift proceeds to condemn Cartwright's *Reply* as the unscholarly production of a highly overrated man: "Yet ys yt so stuffed with grosse oversightes, false allegations of authors, misconstrueinges and expoundinges both of scriptures and doctors, lack of skyll in logyke, and fonde reasons, that he that shale thorowly peruse yt, wyll thingk the author thereof to have read hymself very litle, and not to be the man yt he ys reported to be."

Cartwright's *Reply* brought the alarm of the ecclesiastical

[1] St. *Parker*, II, p. 253. [2] *Parker Corresp.* p. 453.

and civil authorities with regard to the Puritan movement to a head. For long the primate had sincerely dreaded it[1]. In May he warned Burghley[2] that if it was not forcibly repressed England would witness a democratic rising of the kind that had disturbed Germany nearly fifty years before, an attempt to establish Munzer's commonwealth, in which the lower orders of society would assert their rights and seek to abolish all class privileges and those feudal survivals that savoured of bondage. The other Bishops were equally timorous. Some were inclined to regard Puritanism as a recrudescence of Anabaptism[3]. Cox, writing to Gualter[4], set forth the disturbing nature of the Puritan demands. In June, however, he wrote to Gualter expressing the hope that the Queen and some of her chief ministers would soon effectively suppress the attempted revival of ancient Presbyterianism[5].

Proof that the Episcopal hopes were far from baseless was given in the Royal Proclamation, 11 June, 1573[6], in which religious dissent in general was denounced and the products of the Puritan press in particular were condemned. Aiming a direct blow at the latter, one of the chief sources of non-conformist influence, the Queen commanded, upon pain of penalty, the suppression of the first *Admonition*, Cartwright's *Reply* to Whitgift's *Answer* (the words "one other in defence of the sayde *Admonition*" apparently refer to Cartwright's work) and any other books written in the same strain as these, and she enjoined that all copies of the said writings should be handed over to the authorities within twenty days.

Immediately after the expiry of the specified time limit Sandys wrote to Burghley[7] complaining that, although there were plenty of the prohibited books in London, none had been brought to him. He also thought that the Privy Councillors had not received many. In his judgment this ominous fact implied that to a large extent the people had already

[1] *v.* Parker to Burghley, 12 March, 1572–3; *Parker Corresp.* p. 418.
[2] *ibid.* p. 424
[3] Horn to Bullinger, 10 Jan. 1572–3. *Z.L.* 1, Ep. cv.
[4] 4 Feb. 1572–3. *ibid.* 1, Ep. CVII.
[5] 12 June, 1573. *ibid.* 1, Ep. CIX.
[6] *Pur. Man.* p. 153.
[7] 2 July, 1573. *ibid.* p. 154.

been infused with the spirit of boldness and disobedience characteristic of the new writers. A month later the Bishop's consternation was greater than ever, as appears in an illuminating and important letter that he sent to Burghley and Leicester[1]. In this epistle Sandys paints the prospect of the Church in the gloomiest colours. Puritanism is increasing so rapidly that he has the utmost difficulty in securing for Paul's Cross the services of ministers who are not tainted with the new Presbyterian notions. Even those who could be trusted to preach discreetly in 1572 have become inoculated with the virus of dissent. He instances Crick, Chaplain to the Bishop of Norwich, hitherto noted for his learning and sobriety, who recently at the Cross spitefully inveighed against the present constitution of the Church of England and advocated the platform contained in Cartwright's book. He also mentions Wake of Christ Church, Oxford, who made a good appearance the previous year at the Cross. On Sunday last, the 2nd of August, at the same place, he revealed his Puritan-Presbyterian leanings, railed at the existing state of the Church and upheld all that Cartwright had asserted in his *Reply*. Measures have certainly been taken to secure Crick's arrest, but these have not yet fructified. Wake hurriedly left on Monday for Oxford and is now beyond the Bishop's jurisdiction. Sandys is baffled and exasperated. His letter bears testimony to the great authority that Cartwright now exercises as the exponent of a system of Church government in accordance with the Apostolic type. The *Reply* to Whitgift has become the standard work on the subject and many men of weight and learning have accepted its teaching and are bold enough to expound the same in public. Indeed, the Bishop acknowledges that most of the best preachers have now been drawn to the ranks of the Puritans. Further, he is certain that a conspiracy is breeding in his diocese, the purpose of which is to form a band of subscribers sworn to defend Cartwright's *Reply* even unto death. He refers to Squire, Master of Balliol College, for proof that a Presbyterian Covenant is a grave and menacing

[1] 5 Aug. 1573. *Lansd. MSS.* XVII, No. 43, ff. 96–7. *v.* St. *Whit.* III, p. 32.

fact. Squire himself had been approached with a view to his participation in the said Covenant, but had refused his consent.

What then is the first step to be taken? Sandys suggests that such Puritan leaders as Field and Wilcocks, who are still under surveillance, and Cartwright, who is lying hid in London, should be removed far from the city. "The people resorte unto them as in poperie they were wonte to runne on pilgrimage; yf theese idolles, who are honoured for Saintes and greatlie enriched with giftes, were removed from hence, their honour would fall into the dust, they would be taken for blockes as they be." Deeply grieved because some aldermen and wealthy citizens of London are giving the Puritans "greate and stowte countinannces," Sandys proposes that the Queen should send such influential supporters a sharp letter of reproof. As the French ministers are also aiding and abetting the malcontents he thinks that these foreigners should be prohibited by Elizabeth or the Privy Council from intermeddling in English religious affairs and that they should be commanded not to allow the admission of any English subjects to their communion. It is evident at any rate that the Royal Proclamation has been of no avail. Not one book has been brought in. Some other remedy for the intolerable situation must be found. The Bishop himself is heartily wearied of the tumultuous enterprises of the new-fangled fellows. Despairingly he confesses that Episcopal authority and prestige have been undermined by them and with passionate earnestness he pleads with Burghley and Leicester to intervene and save the realm and the Church from the dangers that threaten.

The same note of distress is sounded by Sandys in his letters to Continental divines. On the 15th of August in an epistle to Bullinger[1] he bewails the wretched state of his beloved Church. He throws the blame upon a band of foolish young men who are seeking an ecclesiastical revolution. He is not surprised that the Puritans are popular, for the populace are fond of change. That they enjoy the support

[1] *Z.L.* I, Ep. CXIV.

of certain noblemen must be because the latter are looking for gain: *Populus mutationes amat, et libertatem quaerit: nobilitas vero utilitatem.* Sandys proceeds to provide a short summary of the tenets of the Presbyterian party, in which outline we can detect echoes of Cartwright's *Reply*. Sandys then invites the opinion of Bullinger and his brethren respecting the controversy, which, he thinks, should be left to the arbitration of these exponents of Reformed doctrine. He points out that meanwhile the Puritans are claiming that they have all the Reformed Churches on their side.

Puritanism had travelled far since the vestiarian quarrels of the 'sixties and was now recognised as a complex movement, the chief feature of which was an avowed endeavour to presbyterianise the Church of England. We feel that the interested Leicester was in all likelihood drawing the proverbial red herring across the path when he commanded Sir John Wolley to obtain through Sturmius the verdict of Beza, Gualter and others upon the question, whether ministers should be compelled to use certain habits, especially such as had been used in the Roman Church[1]. We meet with a better statement, although a prejudiced one, of the facts of the situation in the letters written by the Bishops to the leaders of the Continental Protestant Churches. These letters of explanation and vindication throw valuable light upon the Puritan movement. Writing to Gualter on the 20th of July, 1573[2], James Pilkington, Bishop of Durham, acknowledges that the quarrel is concerned not merely with vestments but also with matters of polity, discipline, etc. He notes that only in point of doctrine there is no difference. In many quarters the Bishops are being blamed for the disorders but Pilkington observes that they can make no accommodating changes without the sanction of the Queen and the alteration of the existing laws. He devoutly wishes that both parties might learn of Gualter's own spirit of moderation and be willing to agree to some diversity of rites and regulations. The Puritans, however, are in his opinion intolerant

[1] Wolley to Sturmius, 24 July, 1573. *Z.L.* II, Ep. XCI.
[2] *ibid.* I, Ep. CX.

of any ecclesiastical scheme that is not a complete replica of the Apostolic model. Grindal in his letter to Bullinger, 31 July, 1573[1], also lays stress on the wider nature of the new movement as compared with the vestiarian conflict. He regards the Puritans as undoubted Presbyterians. They believe in the equality of ministers and consequently attack the existing hierarchical distinctions. They advocate the erection in every town or parish of a consistory composed of the minister and seniors. He believes however that the late Royal Proclamation will hurt and retard the movement. Like Sandys he looks upon it as a young men's affair and thinks that their supporters are animated by the hope of ecclesiastical spoil. He rejoices that such men as Humphrey and Sampson, who took an active interest in the vestment controversy, are apparently keeping aloof from the dominant faction.

With such views presented to them by the Episcopal party what opinion did the foreign divines hold with regard to the new developments in English Puritanism? We may consider the carefully expressed judgment of Gualter of Zürich. He was already implicated in the controversy. A letter of his to Bishop Parkhurst had, without his leave or knowledge, been printed by the Admonitioners. After hearing the Bishops' case he had allowed another letter, in which he appeared to revoke his former criticism, to be printed along with Whitgift's *Answer to the Admonition*. In February Cox sent him a brief résumé of the Puritan aims. On the 26th of August, 1573, Gualter replies at length[2]. When discussing the hierarchical system of the Church of England, to which he gives but lukewarm support, he does not hesitate to bring forward the widely accredited charge that the Bishops are guilty of unnecessary and harsh proceedings against godly nonconformists and offers Cox some strong words of advice on the subject of tolerance. He produces scriptural precedents for and against the election of ministers by the people. He points out that he himself was elected thirty years before by the people, but that popular election does not now prevail in

[1] *Z.L.* I, Ep. CXII. [2] *ibid.* II, Ep. XCIV.

the city or canton of Zürich. He thinks it wise to tolerate those ecclesiastical customs and forms of government that cannot be altered without peril or disturbance. He is in favour of set forms of prayer as long as ministers may subjoin at the close of the sermon prayers suited to the subject of their discourse. He is entirely in sympathy with the Puritan demand for the conjunction of preaching with the administration of the sacraments. He is also inclined to agree with them in their dislike of funeral sermons. On the other questions, *e.g.* equality of ministers, confirmation, etc., he takes the side of the Bishops. It is noteworthy that Gualter, who feared that Presbyterianism tended towards tyranny[1], thus strongly sympathised with many of the leading principles and tenets of the English Puritan-Presbyterians. We do not wonder, therefore, that the latter believed and affirmed that the Reformed Churches were on their side, especially when we bear in mind that many of these, *e.g.* in France, Geneva, Heidelberg, etc., were of a distinctively Presbyterian type.

Now we return to the consideration of the anti-Puritan campaign in England. From the Bishops' point of view the month of August, 1573, brought them the firstfruits of success. On the 28th of that month the exultant Bishop of London (Sandys) intimated to Burghley that he had ferreted out a Puritan printing press in the country[2]. The printer, Lacy, and his confederates had been arrested. They had been engaged on another edition of Cartwright's *Reply* and had printed a thousand copies. Doubtless the press is the one, located at Hampstead, which was seized by John Harrison, one of the wardens of the Stationers' Company and a pursuivant on the 26th of August. Interesting particulars concerning the capture are to be found in the Registers of the said Company, *e.g.* "Item. laide owte the xxvjth of Auguste, 1573, for my (*i.e.* Harrison's) Jorney to Hempsteade with the pursevaunt. xixs.

Item to the Carter yat brought the presse xs.

Item to ye Constable of Hempsteade for bringing up ye men viijs vjd.

[1] *Z.L.* II, Ep. XCVI.

[2] *Pur. Man.* p. 155.

Item for nailes to naile upp the chestes xijd.
Item to the pursevaunt for his paines xxxs."[1]

From the same Registers we learn that the type was handed over to Bynneman: "Item. Recevyd of master Bynneman for wearinge the lettre that came from Hempsted ...xvs."[2] Bynneman used the captured type for the printing of Cartwright's *Reply* incorporated in Whitgift's *Defence of the Answer*. We are left in the dark as to the county to which the Hampstead specified belongs, whether Middlesex, Essex, Herts, Sussex or Berkshire. H. R. Plomer[3], who assumes that Lacy and Asplyn, who worked on the Hampstead press, were assistants of Stroud, is of opinion that the town indicated was probably Hemel Hempstead or Hampstead, Essex.

Another stroke of good fortune for the Bishops was the apprehension of the printer, John Stroud. By profession he was a minister but he had not served in a Church since 1568 when he was deprived for nonconformity[4]. The edition of Cartwright's *Reply*, characterised by his signed Preface, was printed before the Royal Proclamation of June, 1573, but notwithstanding the same it was published soon afterwards, as he confessed on the 25th of November, when he was examined at the Guildhall by the Bishop of London, Dean Gabriel Goodman and others of the ecclesiastical commission: "First, beinge asked of Mr Cartw. bookes where the rest were that were printed, he said he had delivered 34 of them to the B. of Lond. in one bundell, more he said he had, but his wife had burned them, as she told him. And for the rest, they were dispersed abroad, he knew not where, for they never came to his hands, for he was an 100 miles of. Then, being asked how he durst be so bold as to Imprinte them the second tyme, seeing the queenes proclamation was againste them, he answered that if they had bene to print after the proclamation was come out, he would not have printed them, but they were printed before, and herein he confessed himself to have offended the lawe....Lond. What,

[1] *Transcript*, ed. Arber, I, p. 467. [2] *ibid.* I, p. 470. *v.* also I, p. 471.
[3] *Short History of English Printing* (1915), pp. 111–2.
[4] *Sec. Parte*, I, pp. 113, 118.

are those bookes of Mr Cartwrits good, godly, and lawfull or not, and wilt thou defend them to be true? Strowde. As there is no booke without his faults (Gods booke onely excepted) so will I not affirme that his booke is altogeather without falts, but to defend that I will not; he is of age to defend it himself. And as for the booke, I thinke your L. will not utterly condemne it. L. I confesse there is something in it godly, for it is a very evell booke that hath no good thinge in it, but I saye the booke is wicked, and is the cause of errour and dissention in the church."[1] This examination does not disclose the location of Stroud's press. It may have been "an 100 miles of" from London rather than at Yalding, as W. Tarbutt[2] affirms, and it is a notable fact that a hundred miles to the north of London lay those parts of Warwickshire, Leicestershire and Northamptonshire, which constituted a hotbed of Puritanism, that had already come under the suspicion of the authorities.

According to his own account Stroud's ordeal in the Guildhall ended thus: "L. (*Bishop of London*). Well then, thou wilt condescend and agree to these three things?

1. that thou hast offended the lawe in printing Cartw. books.
2. that Cartw. booke is nether godly nor lawfull.
3. that thou doest not condemne the booke of common prayer, but wilt receave the Sacram. of the L. Supper accordinge to the order prescribed.

S. I say as I said before. If I had condemned the booke... I would not have resorted to the church as I have done.

Garett. But wilt thou subscribe, say yea or nay?

S. I will."[3]

Stroud's future conduct shows that he continued to be an ardent Puritan-Presbyterian propagandist. In the following year he seems to have acted as a tutor and a preacher in Yalding and neighbourhood, but at the beginning of 1575 he fell into trouble again[4], and that through his connection

[1] *Sec. Parte*, I, pp. 112–3.

[2] *Annals of Cranbrook Church* (1870–5), p. 10. [3] *Sec. Parte*, I, p. 114.

[4] *ibid.* I, pp. 108 ff. This section in Peel's Calendar, dated 1573–6, definitely belongs to 1575. "The first of May, beinge Sundaye" decides for 1575.

with another book devoted to the exposition of Presbyterianism, viz. *Ecclesiasticae Disciplinae...Explicatio* (1574). "Upon the 20 of Januarye" (*i.e.* 1575), writes Stroud[1], "I haveinge occasion to come to Rochester...I came into the chamber of the saide doctor Nevesonn...and...founde there Mr Chansler, Mr Geninges, parson of S. without Temple Barre, and also parson of Chenocke and vicare of Zeal, the vicare of Detford, Johnsonne, the Bishopps baylye, with divers others, for yt was a court daye. And...after he had enquired my name and dwellinge place, he sate him downe in his chaire, and haveinge a booke in his hand of *Ecclesiastica disciplina*, asked me if I knew the same, to whom I answered I knew not everie booke by the forrell; then he opened the booke, and asked me if I then knew it; I turneinge me backe, and seeinge Mr Genings somwhat blushe, began to suspect (for that Mr Genings had about the moneth of November at the request of a frend of mine had one of the above named bookes) and said, If it be the booke that I, beinge desired by a frend of mine, did lend Mr Genings, it is called *ecclesiastica disciplina*, and it is my booke. There is in it, saith he, treson, rebellion, and heresie; wherefore I must committ you to the bayle, and you must go to prison." According to this valuable testimony of Stroud the *Explicatio* was in circulation in England by November, 1574. He proceeds to relate that the Bishop of Rochester wrote on Friday, the 21st of January, 1574–5, "to Mr Robinson, the Register, to this effect, that he should commaunde me that I should cease as well from teachinge of children as also from prechinge within the parishe of Yaldinge or elswhere, that I should depart the dioces within one moneth or 40 dayes at the farthest, and also that Mr Robinson should send the same commandement to the churchwardens of Yaldinge, that they should see yt done, the which letter came...upon Saturdaye...so I was delivered out of prison, and shortly after the copye of theffect therof came to Yaldinge."[2] In spite of an appeal to the Archbishop of Canterbury and his promise that Stroud should remain at liberty for the next six months the printing

[1] *Sec. Parte*, I, p. 108. [2] *ibid.* I, p. 109.

preacher and the Yalding Church office-bearers were cited to appear in February at Rochester[1]. In April Stroud appeared again at Rochester court and, after his refusal to answer the queries that were put to him, was duly excommunicated[2]. It appears that Stroud now changed his abode and became a resident in Cranbrook[3], the vicar of which was Richard Fletcher, grandfather of the poets, Phineas, Giles and John. Soon after his arrival in Cranbrook Stroud became the centre of a bitter controversy, in which the vicar's son, Richard, father of the celebrated dramatist, John Fletcher, took a prominent part[4]. It is evident from the large number of contemporary documents contained in the *Seconde Parte of a Register*, which deal with Stroud's troubles, that this outspoken and zealous Puritan won the sympathy as well as the material support of many ministers and laymen in Kent, and that he was regarded by the authorities as a dangerous propagandist and probably a distributor of revolutionary Presbyterian literature[5]. Brook's account of Stroud[6], which, like most of Brook's work, requires considerable correction, is based upon the above-named *Register*. According to Tarbutt[7] the printing preacher died of the plague on the 16th of October, 1582.

Besides Lacy and Stroud, other smaller fry of the printing fraternity were dealt with, *e.g.* Thomas Asplyn, son of a London cooper, one of Day's former apprentices. Arber's assertion[8] that Asplyn was arrested for working at the secret production of the *Second Admonition* is a deduction from Parker's statement that he was "a printer to Cartwrightes boke" and is misleading, for "Cartwright's Book" meant in the years 1573 and 1574 none other than Cartwright's *Reply* to Whitgift's *Answer to the Admonition*. Asplyn was arrested, probably along with Lacy, examined, set at liberty and again apprehended and imprisoned after his attempt to kill Day. "Sir," wrote Parker to Burghley on the 13th of November, 1573[9], "this mornyng cam the warden of the printers,

[1] *Sec. Parte*, I, pp. 109–10. [2] *ibid.* I, p. 111. [3] *ibid.* I, p. 115.
[4] *ibid.* I, pp. 116 ff. [5] *ibid.* I, pp. 108–20. [6] *Lives*, I, p. 296.
[7] *op. cit.* p. 12. [8] *Transcript*, I, p. 466.
[9] *Lansd. MSS.* XVII, No. 56.

harrison, and brought me one other boke in quayers, and told me that one asplyn, a printer to Cartwrightes boke, was after examination suffred agayn to go a brode, and taken in to service into master Dayes house, and purposed to kyl hym, and his wif &c and being asked what he ment, he answered 'The Spryte moved hym'."

Asplyn's case serves to remind us that several times during Elizabeth's reign crazy individuals of Asplyn's type, who were more or less identified with the Puritans, sought, often under the supposed guidance of the Holy Spirit, to achieve their reforms by means of assassination. One of the most notorious of such ill-advised attempts took place on the 11th of October, 1573, when Peter Birchet, a student of Middle Temple, who was a religious fanatic, intending to kill Christopher Hatton, whom he regarded as an enemy to true religion, mistook his man and wounded Sir John Hawkins, a naval officer, instead[1]. The mad assassin, after killing one of his keepers in the Tower, was hanged on the 12th of November in the Strand at the place where he had stabbed Hawkins. This affair would certainly tend to bring great odium upon Puritanism. Maybe it hastened the decision of the Queen and Council to take action. Soames says[2], "To the fear of assassination, engendered in Elizabeth and her advisers by this fatal ebullition of insanity, may be, probably, attributed an order for the apprehension of Cartwright." Martin Hume[3] affirms that the incident "led to the arrest of Mr Cartwright." This hypothesis, however, is, in view of the complex variety of anti-Puritan forces at work, too simple wholly to account for the issue of the warrant against Cartwright. In any case the affair could only have led to the attempt to arrest him, for, as we shall see, he was not actually apprehended. Of course, only the most prejudiced historians would lay the guilt of such madmen as Asplyn and Birchet upon the general body or the leaders of the Puritans, who

[1] *Lansd. MSS.* xvii, No. 88; H. Nicolas, *Memoirs of Sir Christopher Hatton* (1847), p. 31; Soames, p. 195.

[2] p. 198.

[3] *The Great Lord Burghley* (1898), p. 291.

were in no wise responsible for the doings of fanatical individuals, who nominally adhered to their cause.

One of the most prominent supporters of Cartwright's *Reply* to be silenced by the authorities in 1573 was Edward Dering. We have already noted Cartwright's association with him. For his outspoken criticism of the Church he was ordered to cease the reading of his public lectures at St Paul's, but in June he was allowed by the Privy Council to resume the same on condition of good behaviour[1]. On the 6th of July Parker and Sandys, writing to one of the Ecclesiastical Commissioners lamenting the favour shown to the Puritans by those of the populace who were desirous of liberty and by some of great calling who sought to gain by other men's losses, refer to Dering's case[2]. They enclose certain articles taken out of Cartwright's *Reply* and propounded by the Council to Dering, along with the latter's answers. In his answers Dering shows that he believes that we are "Tyed by Gods worde to the order and use of the Apostles and primitive Church."[3] While confessing that the Church of England is in many points imperfect he deprecates separation from the same[4]. As a Presbyterian he states that "there ought to be Elders as at the first"[5] and supports the equality of ministers[6]. He expresses the current Puritan opinions with regard to the patrimony of the Church, preaching, a prescript form of service, baptism of papists' infants, non-residence, etc. Like Cartwright he insists upon Christ and not the Prince being the Head of the Church and advocates the observance of the judicial laws of Moses. The articles and answers (twenty in all) are given in full in *A parte of a register*[7] and are summarised by Brook[8] and Strype[9]. The Bishops feared that the Councillors were going to ignore the desire of the ecclesiastics for a rigorous repressive policy and to deal too leniently with Dering. They wished to have him

1 *Acts P.C.* VIII, p. 120.
2 *Petyt MSS.* XLVII, f. 518; *Parker Corresp.* p. 434.
3 art. 3.
4 art. 4.
5 art. 6.
6 art. 7
7 pp. 73 ff.
8 *Lives*, I, pp. 201 ff.
9 *Ann.* III, pp. 415 ff.

silenced altogether. Before the end of July they had their way and Dering was enjoined by the Council to discontinue his lecturing[1]. Sandys, resenting a widely accepted report that he was responsible for Dering's deprivation, makes his position clear in a long plaintive letter to Burghley on the 28th of August[2]. "No man hath lived in worse times," writes the disheartened Bishop, "no man more wronged then I." In face of the Puritan opposition he finds his office intolerable. Dering in particular is proving a thorn in the flesh. "Evill have I bene abused by these arrogant spirites many ways, and specially by Mr Deringe." One chief count against the obnoxious Puritans is that they are supporters of Cartwright's book, *i.e.* the first *Reply*. The Bishop mentions, besides Dering, Wiburn and Johnson as favourers of it[3].

Dering, an avowed advocate of plain speech, sent an exposition of his principles to Burghley on the 1st of November[4]. Holding that the Church is essentially a spiritual institution he inveighs against the assumption by Bishops of civil powers and the lordship that is involved in prelacy. He expresses himself in favour of the primitive Episcopate, Presbyterian parity, the attachment of a minister to one cure only, etc. He points out the diversity between the prevailing diocesan Episcopacy and the primitive system. He also is convinced that all Reformed Churches are on the side of the Puritans.

Towards the end of November Dering defended himself in a written statement against various charges, among them being that to which we have already alluded, viz. his alleged prophecy that Parker would be the last Archbishop of Canterbury[5]. A testimonial, dated the 26th of November and signed by witnesses, certified that this accusation was false[6]. On the 16th of December, in his answers to four articles sent to him for subscription, Dering freely criticised the Book of Common Prayer, etc., and showed that he still

[1] 22 July, 1573. *Acts P.C.* VIII, p. 133.
[2] *Lansd. MSS.* XVII, No. 45, f. 100.
[3] *v.* St. *Parker,* II, p. 239.
[4] St. *Ann.* III, pp. 400–13.
[5] St. *Ann.* IV, pp. 511–7.
[6] *Cecil MSS. Hist. MSS. Comm.* Pt II, p. 64.

stubbornly adhered to his Puritan position[1]. He was greatly grieved, however, when on the 18th of December he was forbidden to preach altogether and that by express command of the Queen: "D.W. on Friday last as I was about to Preach, forbad me in her Maiesties name, so I stand now forbidden, not by the Bb. but by our Princesse."[2] Crushed and disappointed, Dering gradually became the victim of a fatal malady, of which he often complained in his *Godly Letters* to certain female friends, *e.g.* Mrs Barret, who had a house at Bray, and Mrs Henry Killigrew, who resided at Hendon. Among his correspondents were several other pious and wealthy ladies, who doubtless warmly supported the Puritan cause, *e.g.* Mrs H., Lady G. and Lady M.[3] He died in his prime at the priory of Thobie, Essex, on the 26th of June, 1576[4].

Thus, one by one, the Puritans fell into the clutches of the Bishops, but measures directed against individuals, such as Stroud and Dering, left the general movement untouched. A definite step in the direction of a comprehensive coercive policy was taken by Elizabeth through her Council on the 8th of November, when letters were issued to the Bishops enjoining them to proceed against all nonconformists in their dioceses[5]. For the sake of uniformity the Puritan movement must be suppressed. In furtherance of the Queen's desire and the Council's order Parker instructed the Bishops in his province to cause an inquisition to be made throughout their dioceses and to report the names of all who refused to conform before Christmas[6]. Grindal acted likewise in the province of York[7]. In his letter to Parker he evinced a particularly lively interest in the inquisition in London and marked out as worthy of special attention such men as Penny, Wiburn and Johnson, who were content to hold the livings of the

[1] *A parte of a reg.* pp. 80–5.
[2] *Godly Letters*, sig. A 4. [3] *v. ibid.* [4] *A.C.* I, p. 356.
[5] *Acts P.C.* VIII, p. 140; Soames, p. 194; Frere, *Hist.* p. 185.
[6] Parker to Sandys, 24 Nov. 1573. *Petyt MSS.* XLVII, f. 508; *Parker Corresp.* p. 451.
[7] Grindal to Parker, 9 Dec. 1573. *Petyt MSS.* XLVII, f. 26; *Grindal Rem.* p. 347.

very Church they condemned. Penny, for instance, was prebendary of Newington[1], Johnson was said to hold fou prebends[2], and Wiburn, who had been (till 1566) vicar o. St Sepulchre's, Holborn, was still a prebendary of Westminster[3].

A few days before Christmas (21 Dec. 1573) Wilcocks, now in Coventry, sent the latest news from London to Gilby, with whom he had lately been consorting[4]. His letter is entirely occupied with the results of the inquisition in the metropolis. Brother Fuller and others have been imprisoned in the Counter, Brother White and others have been committed to Newgate, Brother Johnson and others have been laid in the Gatehouse at Westminster. Some of those supposed to belong to the Puritan party, like Wager, have conformed and many of the common people have fallen back.

Now that the hunt was keen and the net was closer how was Cartwright faring? He was the recognised leader of the Puritan-Presbyterians and his *Reply* had been accepted as the best exposition of their principles. Wonder has sometimes been expressed that he gave no name to a sect, but in 1573 the Elizabethan Presbyterians came near to being known as Cartwrightians, for then they were commonly called supporters or favourers of Cartwright's book. To unearth and arrest the writer of the *Reply* was, therefore, naturally one of the chief objects of Episcopal zeal.

We have frequently come across traces of Cartwright in London. There he drew around him many of his fellow-enthusiasts; there he was regally entertained by some of the bountiful Puritan sympathisers; there when the winter inquisition began he was supposed to be lying hid. On the 9th of December Grindal passed on to Parker the rumour that he was lodging in Cheapside at the house of Martin, the goldsmith, whose wife was suspected of having been the stationer for the first edition of the *Reply*[5]. Strype[6] supposes

1 Hennessy, p. 41.
2 *Parker Corresp.* p. 45.
3 Hennessy, pp. 383, 444.
4 *Baker MSS.* XXXII, Mm. 1, 43, f. 441; Brook, *Lives*, II, p. 191.
5 *Grindal Rem.* p. 347.
6 *Parker*, II, p. 241.

that Martin was he who was connected with the Mint and afterwards became Mayor of London, but misquotes Grindal's letter when he says "that his wife was the stationer for all the first impressions of her husband's book." It is Mrs Martin to whom Grindal alludes. Cartwright was not yet married.

On the 9th of December Cartwright wrote a letter of thanks[1] to Michael Hicks, who had generously contributed to his upkeep and had also recently given him money apparently to provide for his impending flight. Hicks, who became one of Cartwright's lifelong friends, was a man of piety, wealth and social influence, and affords a good example of the laymen who gave sympathetic and material assistance to the clerical advocates of Puritanism. He was the eldest son of Robert Hicks, the mercer, whose shop, "The White Bear," was situated at "Soper's Lane End," Cheapside[2]. Probably therefore Grindal's surmise that Cartwright was lodging in Cheapside was correct. Michael himself was reared in that district. About the end of his fifteenth year—he was born on the 21st of October, 1543[3]—he entered Trinity College, Cambridge, as a pensioner (Michaelmas, 1559)[4]. Probably it was at the University that he came to know Cartwright, but we learn from the latter's letter that till 1573 their acquaintance had been but slight. On the 20th of March, 1564–5, Hicks was admitted to Lincoln's Inn and was eventually called to the Bar[5]. His father, Robert, died in 1557; his mother, Juliana, died in 1592 (her second husband, Anthony Penn, died *ca.* 1572). His youngest brother, Baptist, after arriving at years of maturity, carried on the business at "The White Bear" and became an eminently successful merchant and financier; he was knighted (24 July, 1603) by King James, and raised to the peerage as Viscount Campden by Charles I in 1628[6]. It is uncertain

[1] App. x.

[2] Mrs W. Hicks Beach, *A Cotswold Family: Hicks and Hicks Beach* (1909), p. 50.

[3] *ibid.* p. 59.

[4] He took no degrees (Venn, *Matrics.*). His tutor, Mr Blithe, was Fellow and Junior Dean in 1560 (Hicks Beach, *op. cit.* p. 106).

[5] *ibid.* p. 106.

[6] *ibid.* pp. 64 ff., 83 ff.

when Hicks first entered Burghley's service, in which he proved himself "a man of slow dispatch and of slender understanding." His rare devotion to the great statesman prevented his dismissal and was rewarded by his being promoted to be one of the permanent and trusted secretaries of the Lord High Treasurer. After Burghley's death (1598) Hicks acted as secretary to his son Robert. He was knighted in 1604. Among his friends and debtors he included Francis Bacon. On the death of Lady Anne Bacon, Francis invited Hicks to his mother's funeral, promising a good sermon on the occasion by Mr Fenton, the preacher of Gray's Inn. He knew Michael's religious tastes. When over fifty years of age (*ca.* 1594–5) Hicks married Elizabeth, widow of Henry Parvish, a London merchant, owner of the manor of Ruckholt, in the parish of Low Leyton, Essex. On the 15th of August, 1612, Hicks died at Ruckholt, which had become his home[1]. It is worthy of note that the Burghley Papers passed out of the hands of the Hicks family about 1682, when they were sold by Sir Michael's great-grandson (Sir William) to a London stationer, Richard Chiswell, who disposed of them to John Strype, Vicar of Low Leyton. After Strype's death they were sold to James Webb, and through him they came to Lord Lansdowne, after whom they are known as the Lansdowne MSS.[2]

Such was the man to whom, likely along with others, Cartwright was indebted for the provision of lodgings in London and for means to enable him to flee from the city when danger was nigh. It was only two days after his letter to Hicks was written that a warrant for Cartwright's arrest was issued by the ecclesiastical commissioners[3]. It was signed by the Bishop, the Mayor and the Recorder of London, the Dean of St Paul's, the Dean of Westminster (Gabriel and not Christopher Goodman as Soames[4] suggests), the Master of the Rolls, the Master of Requests, the Attorney General, the Solicitor General, etc., and was addressed to all mayors, sheriffs, bailiffs, constables and other such officers

[1] Hicks Beach, *op. cit.* pp. 102 ff.

[2] *ibid.* p. 64.

[3] App. XI.

[4] p. 199 *n.*

of the Crown, requiring them in the Queen's name to procure the apprehension of Thomas Cartwright, student in divinity, and to bring him before the ecclesiastical commissioners in London in order that he might be tried by them for his unlawful dealings and demeanours in civil and religious matters.

Cartwright's liberty was now at stake. The alternatives before him were prison or exile. Knowing well that he could still further the Presbyterian cause by the use of his pen in a strange land he chose exile and fled, not, as some say, to the Channel Islands[1], and not, as others say, to Antwerp[2], but to Germany.

[1] Odgers, p. 23. [2] Heron, p. 116.

CHAPTER III

PURITANISM FROM 1574 TO 1577

Puritanism in 1574—the Nedeham conspiracy—Whitgift's *Defence of the Answer*—Cartwright at Heidelberg and Basel—the production of Puritan books on the Continent—the *Explicatio* of 1574—*A Brieff Discours*—Cartwright's *Second Reply*, 1575—*The Rest of the Second Reply*, 1577—Cartwright's correspondence with the Puritans in England—the Exercises—Presbyterianism in the Channel Islands.

THE year 1574 was one of apparent retrogression for the Puritan cause. As Cox explained to Gualter[1], this was largely due to the Queen and her strict enforcement of uniformity. The duty of carrying out her injunctions to this end had, through her Council, been laid upon the Bishops, who had performed their task in the winter inquisition with unwonted energy and thoroughness, and now, as the Bishop of Ely laments, they were being charged for their pains with responsibility for a cruel and unwarranted persecution. On the 12th of July, after thanking Gualter for his letter of the 16th of March, in which the Swiss divine condemned the tyrannical tendencies inherent in Presbyterianism, Cox again refers to the severe castigation that had reduced the Puritans to silence and adds as another reason for their overthrow the publication of a learned refutation of their tenets, viz., Whitgift's *Defence of the Answer*, which book had appeared in the spring: *Severiori castigatione jampridem compescuntur, et doctissima refutatione convincuntur*[2]. The editor of the Zürich Letters is wrong in identifying this refutation with Whitgift's answer to the first *Admonition*[3]. To Bullinger Cox has the same tale to tell[4], but he fears that, although the Puritans are terror-stricken and crushed by the exercise of royal authority and by Whitgift's learning, they are nourishing some monster in secret: *Puri nostri fratres partim ferula nostrae Reginae territi delitescunt, partim docti cujusdam libello doctissimo refutati silent. Interim quid monstri secreto alant*

[1] 3 Feb. 1573–4; *Z.L.* I, Ep. CXV.
[2] *ibid.* I, Ep. CXX.
[3] *ibid.* I, p. 306 *n.*
[4] 20 July, 1574; *ibid.* I, Ep. CXXI.

nescitur. Sandys, commenting upon the quiescence of the nonconformists, informs Bullinger and Gualter in August that many of the supporters of the new discipline have lost their enthusiasm and that the noblemen, who were behind the movement, have been disillusioned[1].

The inquisition or, as Cox called it, the castigation, that began in the winter of 1573, certainly did much to suppress Puritanism. We have already noticed some of its effects. One leader after another was put to silence. It was not only in London that the policy of eradication was pursued. In Northamptonshire, for example, on the 29th of January, 1573–4, the Puritan ministers, Arthur Wake, Eusebius Paget, Thurston Mosley, George Gildred and William Dawson, after refusal to subscribe a *forma promissionis* were deprived of their parishes (Great Billing, Owld, Hardingston, Collingtrough, Westonfavell) by Bishop Scambler's Chancellor. These men were "learned prechers, speakers in the exercise and godly" and four of them were graduates, and to the grief of the Puritans their charges were filled "by outlandishe men, such as cold scarse be understande."[2] Several of the cases of eviction received considerable notice, notably that of Robert Johnson, one of Cartwright's contemporaries at Cambridge, for some time Chaplain in the household of the Bacons at Gorhambury, at one period preacher at Northampton and latterly in St Clement's, London[3]. In a bold and critical letter from the Gatehouse to Sandys, "Superintendent of popish corruptions in the Dioces of London," Johnson bitterly denounced the Bishops' method of dealing with Puritan reformers[4]. "Popishe logike of slaunders and imprisonment" he wrote "will not prevayle. The silogismes of the Fleete, and Enthimema of the Gatehouse, An induction of Newgate, A Sorites of the Whyte Lyon, and example of the Kings benche, will not serve." It was not long, however, before the Bishops' logic brought his life to a conclusion. On the 20th of February, after seven weeks in prison, he was examined by the High Commission in Westminster Hall

[1] *Z.L.* I, Epp. CXXIII, CXXIV.
[2] *Sec. Parte*, I, pp. 121–3.
[3] *v. A.C.* I, p. 323.
[4] 2 Feb. 1573–4. *A parte of a reg.* pp. 101–5.

and condemned to a year's imprisonment[1]. On the 16th of May the Privy Council, having heard that Johnson "was very sore sicke and like to dye unles he might enjoye more open eyer," advised Sandys that the prisoner should be released on bail[2]. It appears, however, that the lenient decision of the Council came too late and that Johnson died soon afterwards "in the Gate." He was a Puritan of the Presbyterian type, whose death was directly due to the persecution and the imprisonment, which he himself had so outspokenly condemned. "Although there bee no death offered for these causes," he had written to Sandys[3], "yet there is persecution ynough, and to much for them, whylest some are imprisoned, and by that meanes loose not onely their libertie, but are in daunger of their lives, whylest they are compelled to remayne in filthy and uncleane places, more unhosome (*sic*) then dunghilles, more stinking than swyne styes."

The Privy Council also used their moderating influence in connection with Bonham and Standen, who had been committed to prison for nonconformity[4]. On the 9th of May the Councillors, who had received supplications from these two Puritans, send a letter to the Archbishop of Canterbury and the rest of the ecclesiastical commissioners straightly informing them that the Council do not "like that men shold be so long deteyned without having the cause examined, and therefore desire them to proceade in suche cases more spedelye hereafter, and to examine the said complainantes cause; and incase any be so sicke that they cannot well there continew, to suffer them to be bailed till their cause be ended."[5] At the end of June the Council again consider the same case and decide to send "A letter to the Archebisshop of Caunterburie signifieng that for good consideracions her Majesties plesure was that Barham (*sic*) and Staunden, being by his Lordship

[1] *A parte of a reg*. pp. 105–11. [2] *Acts P.C.* VIII, p. 239.
[3] *A parte of a reg*. p. 101.
[4] Standen, who played a more conspicuous part than Bonham in the Puritan movement, was one of the leaders in Northamptonshire in 1573; he appears again in 1577 as a friend and ally of such men as Field, Wilcocks, Penny, Wake, Crane, Gawton, etc. *v. Sec. Parte*, II, p. 70; *A.C.* II, p. 12; Brook, *Lives*, I, pp. 174, 317; Peel, pp. 11, 12.
[5] *Acts P.C.* VIII, p. 235.

committed for the breache of thorders established for Uniformitie in Religion, shold be set at libertie upon warninge to conforme themselfes according to the lawe in the ministerie, or els to absteine to intermeddle in the same."[1] The action of the Council would redound to the credit of the merciful Queen and reflect upon the cruelty of the Bishops. Maybe these gentle measures were due to the interest of individual Councillors, such as the Earls of Leicester and Warwick, in the Puritan movement or to their special intercession in behalf of prisoners who were well known to them. Standen, for instance, had been a Chaplain with the Earl of Warwick a few years before. But the chief reason for their release seems to have been the exposure of the bogus conspiracy concocted by Humphrey Nedeham and his accomplice Undertree, with which Bonham and Standen were supposed to have been concerned.

Parker, writing to Burghley immediately after the receipt of the Council's letter for the enlargement of the two prisoners, evinced a laudable desire that amends might be made to the Puritans who had wrongfully been brought under suspicion by the counterfeit letters of the lewd scrivener, Undertree, and hoped that this varlet might be hanged[2]. The Archbishop had been grossly deceived. Having seen some of the forged letters circulated by Undertree and regarding them as authentic documents, which proved that the Puritans were hatching a secret and dangerous plot against the Church and the State, he had written warmly to Burghley about the deep, devilish and traitorous dissimulation[3]. It seems that the cautious Burghley was also for a time hoodwinked[4]. An official list of the persons implicated by the letters was drawn up and proceedings were about to be set on foot against them when the whole affair was discovered to be a hollow mockery[5]. This list is of considerable interest. It records the names and alleged abodes of persons regarded as being ringleaders and accomplices in the plot, *e.g.* Field and Wilcocks (no abode given), Bonham and Standen (in prison), Cartwright and

[1] *Acts P.C.* VIII, p. 259. [2] *Lansd. MSS.* XIX, No. 11; *Parker Corresp.* p. 464.
[3] 19 June, 1574. *Lansd. MSS.* XIX, No. 6; *Parker Corresp.* p. 461.
[4] *v.* analysis of the letters in *Cecil MSS. Hist. MSS. Comm.* Pt IV, p. 48.
[5] *ibid.* Pt II, p. 75.

John Browne (at Newport, Isle of Wight), Stroud (at Ninon's, the clothworker's house by the Three Cranes), Croker (in St Catherine's), Penny (over against Leaden Hall), Ripley (in Fenchurch St), Harley (in the Middle Temple), Lowther (in the Inner Temple), Richard Martin, the goldsmith (at the Mint in Milk St), Bodley (near the Three Cranes), Ninon (between the Three Cranes and the Hythe), Laurence (Mayor of Bedford), Lynford (in Bedford), Bradburn, a hatmaker (in Bermondsey St), Swaldon or Waldon (by the Old Swan in Thames St), Butler (with Ripley), Dyer (in Bedford), Westerman and William Clark (in St Albans), etc.

After much delay and shifting on the part of Undertree he was at length, towards the end of June, laid hold of, examined and exposed[1]. It was discovered that the alleged plot was chiefly the work of Humphrey Nedeham[2], who was promptly imprisoned in the Tower, where he languished for a considerable time[3]. At the beginning of July, 1574, his case came before the Privy Council[4]. In November the Council went the length of proposing that Nedeham should be brought to the rack in order that they might find out "who set him on."[5] During the next few months the letters counterfeited by him continued to engage the attention of his examiners, who were enjoined by the Council "in aunswer of theirs declaring the wante of some letters that had passed betwixt the Lord Archbishop of Caunterbury, Wendsley and him and Undertree to and fro" to request Parker to supply what was lacking "seing such personadges touched and the matter of such importaunce."[6] Not only did the correspondence pretend to disclose the whereabouts of Cartwright and his associates, but also to reveal the complicity of the Earl of Bedford and the Duchess of Suffolk in a secret design to publish another of Cartwright's books. In one document Nedeham is described as "committed for practisinge of sedicious libelles and letters against the Earle of Bedford."[7]

[1] *Parker Corresp.* pp. 463–4.

[2] Cartwright suggests that he had been suborned by others, *v.* App. XXII.

[3] We find him still in the Tower in Nov. 1575. *Acts P.C.* IX, p. 53.

[4] *ibid.* VIII, p. 261.

[5] *ibid.* VIII, p. 319.

[6] 10 Dec. 1574, *ibid.* VIII, p. 322; 12 Feb. 1574–5, VIII, p. 340.

[7] 27 Nov. 1575, *ibid.* IX, p. 53.

In the State Record Office, London, most of the letters are gathered together in a bundle[1] the cover of which is endorsed by Burghley thus: "A lewd practise of on Nedeham, under Collor to apprehend Mr Cartwright he gott mony of ye Archbish. of Canterbury." In a second endorsement Burghley refers to the correspondence as the work of "Nedeham, yt counterfetted all ye lettres included, to abuse D. Parker, Archb. of Cantyrbury, wt opinion yt Mr Cartwrytt was in England." The letters are 45 in number, but No. 44 is missing. The dates of the epistles range from the 29th of March to the 18th of June, 1574. Some have been erroneously dated 1590[2] and Brook places several of them indefinitely after Cartwright's return from exile[3]. The only letter of the series purporting to have been written by Cartwright[4] is ostensibly addressed to John Browne from Sandwich, 15 April (1574) and runs as follows: "The cause of my writing unto you at this time is to desire you and my brother Pennye to send me word how all things goeth with you: and I desire you to go to my lord of Bedford, and desire him that he will lend me 10 l., and also to thank his honour and let him understand that I received 8 l. from him. And forasmuch as you write to me as concerning our book, I would fain it were at my brother Bradborns, and so I pray you let my lord understand: for the which I pray you to carry all things thither when you do think good: and also to desire my brother Pennye to lend my brother Undertree an horse to go thither whither I have appointed him, and that with speed. And my brother Denbye shall come to you, when you do write me answer. And I pray you let my lord understand that the letters which I told him of be come to my hands, but I lack money to pay for them. Wherefore I desire you to make as much haste to him as you can, and also to send it to me as soon as you can: and then my brother Undertree shall bring you them (*sic*) letters. And I pray you look well to all things, and to make speed of all things that I have written to you. And as far as I know, I shall be with you the 24th day of

[1] *S.P. Dom. Eliz.* XCIII, No. 4.

[2] *e.g. Calendar, Lansd. MSS.* LXIV, Nos. 23–9.

[3] *Mem.* p. 250.

[4] 4th letter in *S.P. Dom. Eliz.* XCIII, No. 4.

this month, and also my brother Denbye." Some of the letters are addressed to Cartwright, presumably by John Browne, the Duchess of Suffolk's Chaplain. Throughout the correspondence it is insinuated that Cartwright is still in England, now in Sandwich, now in Southampton. Circumstantial details are given as to the establishment of a secret press at which a new book of Cartwright's is to be printed, and the Earl of Bedford is represented as supporting the project financially and otherwise. Mention is also made of the conspirators' design to procure the downfall of their enemies, of whom the Bishop of Winchester is regarded as one of the chief. The base purpose of the forgers, however, is apparent in such requests as this: "I pray your grace lend me 20s for all that I have is in their hands, and I will be true in all things."

In the course of a letter to Burghley in 1590[1] Cartwright, while vindicating himself against the false accusations that sullied his good name, refers to the Nedeham affair as a complete imposture: "Your L. hath bene acquainted ere this with the shamefull surmises of one Nedham against me, and with his subornation by men whose note and profession is best knowen to your L. which had the sifting of that matter. I dout not but yow remember thend, and that beside the forge of his own head, and others as evill disposed as he, there was not so much as a shadow of that he charged upon me; being the man whome (to my knowledg) to this day I never saw."

The fictitious correspondence, which set the Elizabethan authorities upon a wild goose chase and kept them on tenterhooks for several months, has also deluded modern historians. The letters, regarded as genuine by the uncritical Benjamin Brook, roused him to serious and needless reflection. "Having already smarted under resistless power," he writes of Cartwright[2], "he used greater caution in future. He made arrangements for publishing one of his books, probably a new edition of one of his Replies to Whitgift; but, the press being closed against all such productions, he was under the necessity of proceeding with the utmost possible circumspection. During

[1] *v.* App. XXII. [2] *Mem.* p. 250.

these arrangements, he held correspondence with many persons favourable to his design, from whom he received strong assurances of kindness, with handsome donations towards the expense. Among those who espoused the cause, who patronised the publication, and who sent him pecuniary assistance, was the excellent Earl of Bedford, whose repeated benevolent acts ought not to be forgotten." The verdict, however, of Parker, Burghley and Cartwright himself was, as we have seen, that the correspondence was counterfeit. Cartwright was in Heidelberg at the time when, according to the letters, he was supposed to be in England. These facts, along with an examination of the documents themselves, sufficiently entitle us to look upon the whole affair, not as a horrible conspiracy, but, apart from its mercenary and possibly malicious purpose, as one of the few incidents in ecclesiastical history that partake of the nature of a hoax.

Whitgift's book, reckoned as one of the causes of the eclipse of Puritanism in 1574, appeared in February under the title *The Defense of the Aunswere to the Admonition against the Replie of T.C. by Iohn Whitgijt, Doctor of Divinitie*[1]. On the 5th of February, 1573–4, Whitgift sent Burghley a copy of the work and in a covering letter of that date to his Lordship expressed the hope that the book would do good in exposing the manifold untruths, false quotations, abuse of Scripture and weak reasoning contained in Cartwright's *Reply*[2]. The *Defence* is divided into Tractates, which deal in order with the subjects in controversy. The arguments of Cartwright are examined and rebutted in a manner at once lucid and impressive. The Scylla of Rome and the Charybdis of Geneva are both avoided by the champion of Canterbury. At times the author departs from the subject in hand to deal out blows *ad hominem*, which are of special interest to the biographer of Cartwright. Whitgift complains of the latter's spiteful and

[1] Printed for Humphrey Toy by Henry Binneman, who also printed for Toy in 1574 *A defense of the Ecclesiasticall Regiment in Englande defaced by T.C. in his Replie agaynst D. Whitgifte.* Sayle (No. 1478) records that a MS. note in the Cambridge copy of this work runs "Writt. by the L. Henry Howard."

[2] *Lansd. MSS*, XVIII, 26; *W.W.* III, p. 601.

slanderous manner of writing, which, he is convinced, is due to the just treatment Cartwright received at his hands in Cambridge[1]. Cartwright has always been inclined to be hostile "even sithence our first acquaintance, but especially sithence the time wherein, upon just occasions, I began to stir you."[2] As Master of Trinity Whitgift complains that Cartwright by his open hostility has violated the oath, which he took on admission as a Fellow of Trinity, viz., *me huic collegio fidelem et benevolum futurum...atque etiam magistro ejusdem, non solum dum in eo vixero, sed etiam postea, pro virili, cum opus sit, benevolentiam et opem praestiturum*[3]. Cartwright in his next *Reply* vindicates himself against this charge thus: "Yf I owe you fidelitie, I owe yt more unto the lorde: yf good will, the trwth must be preferred: yf the master of Trinitie Colledg be a frend, the trwth is more: yf yow a brother, the trwth owght to be brother, sister, mother, and al."[4]

We have noticed that contemporaries attributed the apparent collapse of Puritanism in 1574 to the exercise of royal and episcopal authority and the issue of Whitgift's *Defence*. The flight of Cartwright to Germany and the transference of Puritan press work to the Continent also contributed to the temporary lull in England.

Cartwright chose as the first place in which to spend his exile the renowned and beautiful University town of Heidelberg. Those who formed a kind of central Puritan propaganda committee were acquainted with his intentions and movements. They knew that his design was to proceed to Heidelberg. "Doctor Whitgiftes Boke is not yet come out," wrote Wilcocks to Gilby from his house in Colman St, near Swan Alley, on the 2nd of February, 1573–4[5], "but we loke for it daylie. I suppose that when we see it, we shall find that true, that hath bin sayd longe agoe, *nihil est dictum nunc, quod non sit dictum prius*. Our brother Cartwright is escaped, God be praysed, and departed this land since my cominge up to London, and I hope, is by this tyme in Heidelberge....His

[1] *W.W.* I, p. 14. [2] *ibid.* I, p. 107.

[3] *Liber Statut. Coll. Trin.* cap. XII, *De Sociorum Electione.*

[4] *2nd Rep.* sig.)( )(, *iii verso.*

[5] *Baker MSS.* XXXII, Mm. I, 43, ff. 439–40.

earnest desire is, that you and all the godlie should remember him in your earnest and hartie prayers with God and therefore I the more boldlie and willinglie make mention of him." As Wilcocks was in Coventry on the 21st of December, 1573[1], this letter shows that Cartwright tarried in hiding in England about a fortnight at least after the warrant for his arrest was issued. On the 4th of April Laurence Tomson reported to Gilby that news had been received from Cartwright and that he was well[2]: "We have heard of late from our Brother Tom. Cart. who God be thanked is wel, and theruppon we have taken such advise as God gave us."

Shortly after his arrival in the Palatinate Cartwright enrolled as a student of Heidelberg University. So far this important fact has been overlooked by his biographers or it has been unknown to them. The date of his matriculation is the 25th of January, 1574[3]. The Roll shows that another Englishman, Richard Smith, matriculated on the same day as Cartwright, the entry being as follows:

No. 8 Thomas Cartirrightus } Angli
„ 9 Richardus Smithus }

Doubtless some of Cartwright's friends, who had studied at Heidelberg University, had drawn his attention to its claims. Thomas van Til, his Genevan acquaintance, was a student at Heidelberg in 1567, and after leaving Geneva in 1572 returned to his old University[4]. The Puritan, George Wither, matriculated there on the 22nd of March, 1568, and obtained the Heidelberg degree of Doctor of Theology along with Zanchy on the 21st of June of the same year[5]. The remarkable Laurence Tomson was also an alumnus of Heidelberg, having been admitted on the same day as Wither[6]. Other Englishmen who were students at this University in the years immediately prior to Cartwright's flight were: Wilhelmus Barlo (3 July, 1567), Georgius Allinus, Richardus Serger (22 March, 1568), Guillelmus Rowe, Samuel Corwelwel (8 Nov. 1572). During his stay in Heidelberg three Englishmen were enrolled: Robertus Writhus, Eduardus Barfuth, Ricardus Couts (31 Jan.

[1] *v. supra* p. 118.
[2] *Baker MSS.* XXXII, Mm. 1, 43, f.. 448.
[3] *Matrikel*, II, p. 69.
[4] *ibid.* II, pp. 44, 63.
[5] *ibid.* II, pp. 45, 601.
[6] *ibid.* II, p. 45.

1575)[1]. It is reasonable to suppose that some of these men, maybe Tomson, commended the famous University town on the Neckar to Cartwright as a fitting home for a Puritan fugitive.

The merits of Heidelberg University, however, would require no special commendation. In the time of the Elector Frederick III it was one of the most flourishing Universities in Europe. It was now even more celebrated than Geneva for its instruction in arts and theology and drew, as Geneva in its heyday had done, a large number of foreign students to its classrooms. *Haec, sicut et aliae multae scientiae, et Theologia accuratissima olim proposita Heydelbergae fuerunt*, wrote Daniel Dedieu from Frankfurt to Godfried Wingius on the 17th of April, 1579[2], *cum vivente adhuc Domino Principe Frederico Academia illa floreret....Si quis ergo eo tempore Heydelbergensem scholam celebriorem Genevensi in liberalibus artibus, in ipsaque Theologia dixisset, verum dixisset, nec tamen videretur idcirco Genevensem contemnere*. The theological faculty was particularly distinguished. Among the professors were men of world-wide fame, *e.g.* Tremellius, Ursinus and Zanchius. Such eminent scholars as Boquin, Olevian (who had collaborated with Ursinus in the compilation of the famous Heidelberg Catechism) and Francis Junius (later Professor in Leyden) also resided in Heidelberg at this time. These men were able and enthusiastic exponents of the Calvinistic principles, which, under the influence of the Elector, had supplanted Lutheranism. The sympathies of Frederick were entirely with reformers whose aims were of the Genevan type. He was on friendly terms with the Protestants of France and the Low Countries. Religious refugees from these countries flocked to the Palatinate and received a ready welcome. Even to the detested Anabaptists he showed a spirit of broad toleration. *Viele zerstreute Glieder dieser Sekte fanden in der Pfalz freundliche Aufnahme; in Frankenthal entstand eine ganz niederländische Kolonie aus diesen Leuten, zu denen sich später auch vertriebene Reformierte aus Frankreich und den Niederlanden gesellten*[3].

[1] *Matrikel*, II, pp. 43, 45, 64.
[2] Hessels, II, p. 631.
[3] *R.E.*, Herzog. art. "Friedrich III."

By the time of Cartwright's arrival Presbyterianism with its rigorous disciplinary system was firmly established in Heidelberg. Strangely enough, it was the English Puritan, George Wither, who was one of the chief agents in the consolidation of the Presbyterian movement in the Palatinate. In his thesis for the D.Th. in June 1568 he laid stress upon the necessity of ecclesiastical discipline and the right of the Church to excommunicate. The public disputation held in connection with his thesis gave rise to a momentous controversy[1]. Wither's position was warmly supported by such theologians as Olevian and Ursinus, but it was sharply assailed by the Professor of Medicine, Thomas Erastus, and others. Erastus, whose aim was to prove that excommunication is not a divine ordinance and that the offences of professing Christians should be punished by the magistrate and not by the administration of ecclesiastical discipline, particularly of excommunication, wrote an important book on the subject entitled *Explicatio gravissimae questionis utrum excommunicatio ...mandato nitatur divino, an excogitata sit ab hominibus*, which was published posthumously in 1589. *Dicam planius*, he says[2], *oppugno tantum Iudicium de moribus, quod hodie Ecclesiasticum nominant, distinctum a Iudicio politici magistratus. Nempe duas jurisdictiones sive duo discriminata de moribus Iudicia publica et externa nego in una Repub. esse oportere cui pius magistratus a Deo praepositus est*, and in his Preface he refers to Wither and the origin of the controversy thus: *Accidit deinde ut Anglus quidam, qui propter rem vestiariam ex Anglia ferebatur excessisse, Doctoris titulo cuperet insigniri, et de adiaphoris ac vestibus disputationem proponeret. Hanc Theologi admittere noluerunt, ne scilicet Anglos offenderent....Quare inter alias hanc thesim proposuit, oportere in quavis recte instituta Ecclesia hanc servari procurationem, in qua ministri cum suo delecto ad eam rem Presbyterio ius teneant, quosvis peccantes, etiam Principes, excommunicandi*. Hooker alludes to the same matter in the Preface to his *Ecclesiastical Polity*[3], but does not identify Wither as the disputant concerned: "To one of those churches

[1] J. F. Hautz, *Geschichte der Universität Heidelberg* (1862–4), II, p. 79.
[2] p. 258.
[3] II, § 9.

which lived in most peaceable sort, and abounded as well with men for their learning in other professions singular, as also with divines whose equals were not elsewhere to be found, a church ordered by Gualter's discipline, and not by that which Geneva adoreth; unto this church, the church of Heidelburg, there cometh one who craving leave to dispute publicly defendeth with open disdain of their government, that 'to a minister with his eldership power is given by the law of God to excommunicate whomsoever, yea even kings and princes themselves.' Here were the seeds sown of that controversy which sprang up between Beza and Erastus.... Beza most truly maintaineth the necessity of excommunication, Erastus as truly the non-necessity of lay-elders to be the ministers thereof." Erastianism in its modern sense is, of course, a development of the original question at issue, but it is of great interest to note its historic connection with Heidelberg and one of the Elizabethan nonconformists[1].

The Elector Frederick took the part of the rigid disciplinarians and in July, 1570, formally established a Presbyterian system based on the Genevan model in Heidelberg[2]. Soon the town was to become notorious for its Church's despotic exercise of power. The Zürich divines, especially Gualter, warned the English Bishops against the tyranny that was supposed to be inherent in Presbyterianism, and on several occasions cited the case of Heidelberg, where the principles, to which Cartwright and his party adhered, were in full operation. In the eyes of Gualter the excessive severity of the Heidelberg system of ecclesiastical government was enough to put the very Papists to shame. *Vehementer metuo*, he wrote to Cox, 16 March, 1574[3], *ne sub presbyterio oligarchiae affectatio lateat, quae tandem in monarchiam, imo in apertam tyrannidem, degeneret. Neque hoc frustra metuo. Novi enim (et unum e multis attingam) urbem non obscuram, in qua post introductam illam disciplinae formam intra trienii spatium tyrannidis exempla sunt edita, quorum Romanenses puderet*[4]. As an *exemplum* we may mention the case of the minister, Sylvan,

[1] *v. Enc. Brit.* art "Erastus"; R. Lee, *The Theses of Erastus* (1844).
[2] Hautz, *op. cit.* p. 80. [3] *Z.L.* II, Ep. C. [4] *v. ibid*, Epp. XCVI, CIV.

who was beheaded for heresy, viz., Arianism, in the Market Place of Heidelberg[1]. Till the death of Frederick (26 Oct. 1576) the Genevan régime held sway. Then, on the accession of Ludwig VI, a decided Lutheran, a reversal of policy was effected, and those divines who had ruled for so long in the spirit of the Old Testament and the Roman inquisition had to vacate their posts and depart from Heidelberg. It seems that this seat of aggressive Presbyterianism was Cartwright's headquarters till towards the end of 1576, when he took part in the general Calvinistic exodus. He migrated to Basel and became a matriculated student of the University there. The exact date of his admission is not given in the matriculation roll, but his name appears towards the end of the register for the year 1576, when Felix Platter was rector, thus: *Thomas Cartrytus Anglus, vi solidi viii denarii*[2]. Apparently, therefore, he settled in Basel late in that year, and not in 1577 as has been suggested[3]. Of his activities in Basel we know nothing definite, but we have discovered certain interesting particulars concerning his Heidelberg period (1574–6).

Cartwright's first important task in Heidelberg was to prepare for publication a notable Latin book, the authorship of which was ascribed in the sixteenth century to Walter Travers. Whitgift, writing to Burghley in 1584, said: "Mr Travers...is to no man better known, I think than to myself; I did elect him fellow of Trinity College, being before rejected by Dr Beaumont for his intolerable stomach; whereof I had also afterwards such experience that I was forced by due punishment so to weary him, till he was fain to travel and depart from the College to Geneva; otherwise he should have been expelled for want of conformity towards the orders

[1] L. Häusser, *Geschichte der rheinischen Pfalz* (1845), p. 50.

[2] For a list of Englishmen and Scotsmen who studied at Basel in the 16th century *v. The University of Basle. General Information for foreign students* (n.d.), pp. 42 ff. Among Cartwright's predecessors were Christopher Goodman (1554); Francis Walsingham, Anthony Gilby, Roger Kelk, Thomas Bentham, Laurence Humphrey (1555); John Fox, Francis Knollys, James Pilkington (1556); Robert Horn (1558); Laurence Bodley, John Davidson (1575); and after him came Thomas Bodley (1578), Francis Hastings (1579), etc.

[3] Venn, *Alumni Cantabrigienses, sub nom.*

of the house and for his pertinancy....The book *De Disciplina Ecclesiastica*, by common opinion, hath been reputed of his penning since the first publishing of it; and by divers arguments I am moved to make no doubt thereof."[1] Since the sixteenth century the work has generally been attributed to Travers, but it is noteworthy that one copy sold at Sotheby's (Napier Sale) in March, 1886, contained a note running thus: *Laurentius Tompsonus, Oxoniensis, Theologus doctissimus, est hujus libri author*, 1574[2]. The full title of this book is *Ecclesiasticae Disciplinae, et Anglicanae Ecclesiae ab illa aberrationis, plena e verbo Dei, & dilucida explicatio*. It is frequently referred to by its running headline, *De Disciplina Ecclesiastica*. According to the title-page, the book was ostensibly printed at La Rochelle, but in several original copies examined *Rupellae* has been scored out as if the owners knew or suspected that the book was printed elsewhere. The printer's name is given as "Adamus de Monte." The vigilant pursuivants employed by the Bishops and the London Company of Stationers were making it dangerous or impossible to have the book printed in England. Besides, the book was in Latin and nearly all the English printers at this time were reputed to be ignorant of Latin: *Sed negligentia typographi, Latini sermonis ignari, uti sunt plerique omnes qui hic agunt*...[3].

The Preface of the *Explicatio* is usually ascribed to Cartwright, and luckily we are able to prove by his own words that this ascription is correct. In a letter to Christopher Hatton *ca.* 1580[4], after suggesting that his views in regard to Church reform may be obtained by a perusal of his own writings, Cartwright says, "Yf yt may seeme to longe, lett the triall be by *the ecclesiastical discipline* in latten, whiche, as it handleth the same matter, so by a preface sett before itt, I have testified my agreament therewith."[5] This Preface seems to have been written in Heidelberg shortly after his matriculation there.

[1] Bayne, p. xci; Sutcliffe also regards Travers as the author, *Treatise*, pp. 102, 197.

[2] Odgers, p. 39; Paget, p. 70 *n*.

[3] Corranus to Bullinger, July, 1574. *Z.L.* II, Ep. CI.

[4] *v.* App. XIV.

[5] *v.* Sutcliffe, *op. cit.* p. 5: "The discourse of Ecclesiastical discipline commended by T. Cartw."

It is dated the 2nd of February, 1574: *Quarto Nonas Februarii anno salutis humanae* 1574. As in it Cartwright says that the book had been entrusted to his care, *apud me depositum*, it appears that the opportunity of Cartwright's flight was taken to procure the publication of the work at a Continental press and that he brought the manuscript from England with him or that the book was already passing through the press when Cartwright settled in Heidelberg and that he was asked to complete it by adding a Preface. If Tomson was the author it is almost certain that he entrusted the book to Cartwright before the latter departed from England; if Travers was the author the question of how the book came into Cartwright's hands depends upon the whereabouts of Travers at this time. Was he already on the Continent? In any case it seems to be beyond dispute that it was in Heidelberg that Cartwright wrote the Preface. If the date of it is questioned on the ground that it should be 1574–5 in conformity with the English style, according to which the year began on the 25th of March[1], it may be pointed out that the first of January was frequently regarded as the beginning of the year by Englishmen residing abroad in the sixteenth century, *e.g.* the date of the first edition of the Genevan Prayer Book is 10th Feb. 1556, not 1556–7[2]. But there is no adequate ground for doubt on this point. The *Explicatio* was published in 1574. On the 9th of August of that year Bishop Sandys, writing to Gualter, makes mention of it[3]. After commenting on the languishing state of the Puritan movement, he points out that the author of the disturbing innovations is next to Beza a certain young Englishman, Thomas Cartwright, who is now said to be residing in Heidelberg, where he has written a Latin book in defence of the new discipline: *Auctor istarum novarum rerum, et post Bezam primus inventor, est adolescens Anglicanus nomine Thomas Cartwrightus, quem aiunt jam haerere Heidelbergae. Inde jampridem scripsit librum Latine in defensionem novae*

[1] Bayne (p. xcii) says that the *Explicatio* was published in 1574–5. *D.N.B.* art. "Travers," also suggests 1574–5. Usher (*P.M.* p. xxxii), who has been followed by Frere and Douglas (*Pur. Man.* p. xx) dates the book 1573.

[2] Martin, p. 79; cf. *Knox*, IV, p. 147.

[3] *Z.L.* I, Ep. CXXIV.

istius disciplinae, quam nobis obtrudere voluit. The Bishop has not yet seen the treatise, but he has heard that printed copies have already arrived in England and promises to send one to Gualter as soon as he can procure it. Evidently the reference is to the *Explicatio*, the authorship of which Sandys erroneously attributes to Cartwright. Even the testimony of contemporaries may err! We have also seen that Stroud had the book in November, 1574[1]. Grindal, writing to Parker on the 4th of March, 1574–5[2], suggests that Aylmer is a fit man to answer the book, but thinks that neither he nor Dean Nowell will take the pains. Some think that Still should undertake it. Grindal wishes that the refutation were done. Parker in a letter to Grindal, 17 March, 1574–5[3], mentions that although Aylmer has declined to refute *De Disciplina*, there is an answer already prepared, but that it is of indifferent quality[4]. It is obvious that Mullinger[5] is wrong in saying that the book was for long unknown to the ecclesiastical authorities in England.

We are practically certain that, although *Rupellae* appears on its title-page, *Ecclesiasticae Disciplinae...Explicatio* was not published at La Rochelle, and that "Adamus de Monte" is a pseudonym. In 1573 the same printer issued at Orange a book by "Eusebius Philadelphus" entitled *Dialogus quo multa exponuntur quae Lutheranis et Hugonotis Gallis acciderunt.* This is one of a series of writings inspired by the massacre of St Bartholomew and published by a secret press. The author of the *Dialogus* is generally supposed to have been Nicholas Barnaud[6] who is said to have fled to Geneva after the massacre. It is also recorded that the anti-royalist and anti-Roman sentiments contained in this and subsequent writings were not relished even by Protestants, who feared the results of the bitter attack, and that once a man named Lafin, meeting Barnaud in a street of Basel, boxed his ears for his imprudence[7]. A French edition of the *Dialogus*, *Dialogue auquel sont*

[1] *v. supra* p. 112. [2] *Grindal Rem.* p. 353.
[3] *Petyt MSS.* XLVII, f. 22; *Parker Corresp.* p. 474.
[4] St. *Parker*, II, p. 399. [5] p. 292.
[6] *Biographie Universelle*, Paris (1843). *Dictionnaire de Géographie*, Paris (1870), *sub* "Orange."
[7] *Manuel du Librairie*, Paris (1863), *sub* "Philadelphe."

traitees plusieurs choses... was issued in Basel, also in 1573. The foreword to the Reader in the Latin edition is dated, *Basilaeae die 7 mensis quinti ab infausto & funesto die proditionis* (7 Jan. 1573), but the French edition contains the subscription: *acheve d'imprimer le 12e iour du 6e mois d'apres la iournee de la trahison.* The references to Basel make the investigator wonder whether Adamus de Monte was a printer in that town. To make confusion worse confounded, however, the *Dialogue* was augmented and another added to it, and both appeared in Latin and in French, in 1574, as the work of Eusebius Philadelphus at the pseudonymous press of James James, Edinburgh. Some have evidently been led or misled by this clue to score out *Rupellae* on the title-page of the *Explicatio* and substitute *Edinburgi.* H. G. Aldis[1], and Dickson and Edmond[2] are agreed that the press of James James was not located in Scotland and that the printer's name and location are fictitious[3]. A careful examination of such books and kindred writings (*e.g.* Prisbach's *Responsio*, and *Epistola Ioannis Monlucii...*), supplemented by researches in Switzerland, has not enabled the present writer to come to a definite conclusion regarding the identity or abode of the mysterious Adamus. He certainly printed both the abovenamed *Dialogus* and the *Explicatio*, but whether in Basel, or Geneva, or elsewhere is a question still to be decided by bibliographical experts. We may suggest, however, that whether or not Adamus de Monte was connected with John le Preux of Geneva, who employed the same Roman type and the same device of the printer's shop as are used in the *Explicatio*, or with John Operinus, the friend and employer of John Fox, and the publisher of several works by English Reformers, the whole problem of the relationship between English Puritanism and Switzerland, so ably dealt with in fragmentary fashion by Theodor Vetter[4], should be thoroughly explored.

[1] *A List of Books Printed in Scotland before* 1700 (1904), p. 115.

[2] *Annals of Scottish Printing* (1890), p. 512.

[3] *v.* R. B. McKerrow, *Dictionary of Printers*, 1557–1640 (1910), *Printers' and Publishers' Devices in England and Scotland*, 1485–1640 (1913).

[4] *Literarische Beziehungen zwischen England und der Schweiz im Reformationszeitalter*, Zürich (1901).

The identification of the printer of the *Explicatio* might be easier if we knew all about Cartwright's whereabouts in 1574. He was at Heidelberg when the Preface was written and may have engaged a printer for the book through the Frankfurt Fair in the spring, but it is possible that he paid a visit during the year to old haunts and associates in Switzerland. We have come across a copy of one letter which purports to have been written by him in Geneva to the father of Walter Travers, and it is dated 1574[1]. As it is only a copy we have to allow for its manipulation and corruption by transcriber and transmitter, but so far we have found no reason to throw doubt on its date and place of origin. It has been preserved in the Towneley collection as a notable specimen of a consolatory letter. It was composed shortly after the death of Robert, a brother of Walter Travers, who had been studying at a foreign University, presumably that of Geneva. In a long and pious exhortation Cartwright seeks to comfort the stricken parents. He laments the young man's death, for he had hoped to reap great benefit from his sweet and loving company. There are many of the godly who share the parents' sorrow. Walter is much upset by the loss of his brother: "He could hardly be brought to receive comforte." It appears that Walter is not a robust man himself: "I wisshed him to come home because his thinne nature will hardly devour and overcome the difficulties of travell, but I coulde not perswade him." It is evident that the "head" and the "neck" of English Puritanism were at this time intimate associates in exile. The chief clue contained in the letter as to their abode is found in the passage, which states that the young Englishman "was buried in the Land of Conoran very comlye accompanied with the studentes and professors in the Universitie." Borgeaud, Martin and the present writer have discussed the implications of the epistle, but with no satisfying result. We cannot find any trace of Cartwright's stay in Geneva in 1574; no record of Travers' abode there can be discovered; but as "Conoran" may well be a copyist's transcript of Cornavin, which was and still is a suburb of

[1] App. XII.

Geneva, it is likely that Cartwright refers to the cemetery of the Church of St Gervais situated outside the old town, and this identification would prove that Cartwright, Travers, and the latter's brother were in Geneva at the same time.

The *Explicatio*, probably because of its title *Ecclesiasticae Disciplinae etc.* or its headline *De Disciplina Ecclesiastica*, and because it was frequently called *The Book of Discipline* even by contemporaries, has been confused[1] with a later work, *Disciplina Ecclesiae etc.*, which was the Puritan Book of Discipline *par excellence* and is best known by the title of its translation *A Directory of Church-government* (1644). The book was translated into English (it is generally supposed to have been by Cartwright[2]), and published in 1574 with the title *A Full and Plaine Declaration of Ecclesiasticall Discipline owt off the word off God etc.* This translation has been frequently but erroneously identified with the English version of the above named Puritan Book of Discipline[3]. It undoubtedly came from the same press as Cartwright's *Second Reply* (1575), and *A Brieff Discours* (1575). These books do not mention their printer, and the task of locating their press still requires fulfilment. Geneva, Zürich, Frankfurt and Middelburg have been suggested. Sayle[4] thinks that they were printed by Christopher Froschauer, Junr, at Zürich, and McKerrow[5] is inclined to follow him. Froschauer seems to have acted as an intermediary between English Reformers and their Zürich friends, particularly on his visits to Frankfurt Fair, where he met English merchants[6], and it is possible that Cartwright negotiated there with him for the publication of his own work and the writings in his custody. As R. Steele points out, however[7], the history of these and other books printed in the Zürich or Marburg type has yet to be written.

[1] *e.g.* by Mullinger (p. 632) and Frere (*Hist.* p. 196).

[2] Bancroft (*Survay*, p. 237) speaks of the "Translator in Cambridge." Was he Laurence Chaderton or did Bancroft confuse the translator of the *Explicatio* with the translator of the Book of Discipline? *v. infra* p. 259.

[3] *e.g.* Mullinger, p. 633.

[4] pp. 1414–5.

[5] *Dictionary of Printers*, p. 110.

[6] *Z.L.* I, p. 224; II, pp. 180, 243, 294, 305.

[7] *Notes on English Books Printed Abroad*, 1525–48, *Bibliog. Soc. Trans.* vol. XI, p. 213.

A Full and Plaine Declaration was reprinted in 1580 (Geneva) and 1617 (n.p.). It was probably the book issued by the Cambridge press in 1584 and suppressed. Whitgift referring to this edition said that it was "the same which Travers ys supposed to have sett forth in Laten, without anie addition or retraction."[1]

The *Explicatio* or its translation was at once received as an authoritative pronouncement by the Puritans and continued to serve them as a clear and comparatively dispassionate exposition of Presbyterianism. Interesting evidence of its early appearance in Scotland is given by a copy of the Latin edition, preserved in the Library[2] of St Andrews University, which, to judge from the note on the title-page, *A.M.d.d.* 1575 *id. decēb*, and the fact that the copy belonged to Arbuthnot, Principal of King's College, Aberdeen, appears to have been brought home by Melville and given to his friend, Arbuthnot. In his prefatial Epistle to the Pious Reader Cartwright observes that Elizabeth is delighted with books written in Latin and hopes that she will read the *Explicatio* and come to a just understanding of the position, which the Puritans in England were seeking to advance. So far she had been influenced by unfair criticisms of their platform. "Nowe whereas Her Maiesty, accordinge to the excellent learninge and amongest women without all comparison, whiche she hathe, is delighted with thinges that are written in latin: wee have conceived great hope, that this cause which hytherto she hath tasted here and there, out off the false rumores off those which deale iniustly with us, as it were out of the channels, shall more fully be drawen out of our owne bookes, as it were out off the founteines." Cartwright refers to the fact that his *Reply* had taken the form of an attack upon an importunate adversary and regrets that because of the personal recriminations in it he has created offence. This work, being devoid of any arguments *ad hominem*, should not offend the daintiest mind. In commending it as a jewel of great excellence, he speaks of its having been committed to his custody, and of his part in bringing it to light, thus showing

[1] St. *Whit.* I, p. 299; Paget, p. 71. [2] *B.N.* 8. 141.

that he was responsible for the publication of at least the Latin edition. He considers the author a notable workman "althoughe I saw him differinge from me in the interpretation off a place or two."

The object of the book is to uphold the "Necessitye off Disciplyne." The author defines ecclesiastical discipline as "the pollicie off the Churche off Christe ordeyned and appointed off God for the good administracion and government off the same."[1] Diocesan Episcopacy is rejected as unscriptural. The true Bishop is the minister of one Church. Of Bishops there are two kinds, doctors and pastors. The former are "Bishoppes who are occupied in the simple teachinge and expoundinge off the holy doctrine and trew religion."[2] Pastors apply the Scriptures, administer the Sacraments, and care for the spiritual welfare of their flocks[3]. The other chief office-bearers of the Church should be deacons. They are of two kinds, the deacons proper, whose office is to look after the poor, and the elders or governors, who rule over the Church along with the minister in the Consistory. In the Latin version the Consistory is called *Ecclesiasticus Senatus* or πρεσβυτέριον, and the elders *senatores*, the use of which terms afterwards provoked the mockery of Bancroft[4]. The great importance attached to the Consistory is noteworthy. The governors should, especially in grave matters, consult the congregation. Passing beyond the consideration of particular Churches, the writer deals with the governing bodies of a group of Churches, namely, the Conferences and Synods[5], but does not examine these in detail, as an account of them may be found in "lerned writinges of some off our daies which have lately writen touching this matter."[6] It has been stated that government by Presbyteries (in the modern sense) was not a necessary part of the Puritan Discipline, and that in the treatise attributed to Travers they are not even mentioned[7]. Odgers[8] says "As far as I have read, my impression coincides with

[1] *F. & P.* p. 6. [2] p. 138. [3] p. 147. [4] *Survay*, pp. 88, 95.
[5] p. 178. *Colloquia* and *synodi* in Latin edition, p. 137 *b*.
[6] p. 179.
[7] J. Hunt, *Religious Thought in England* (1870), I, p. 214. [8] p. 38.

that of Mr Hunt, that there is no mention of the presbyterian government of associated churches; there is no presbytery but the parochial consistory." This opinion is entirely wrong. As is apparent from our references given above, modern Presbyteries, although briefly dealt with in the *Explicatio* or *Declaration*, are there regarded as part of the complete Presbyterian system, but they are discussed under the name of *colloquia* or Conferences. After discussing them the author returns to the subject of the Consistory[1]. The jurisdiction of this indispensable court is meanwhile usurped by the Diocesan Bishops, who are duly warned of their crime in preventing the establishment of the Presbyterian system.

A Brieff discours off the troubles begonne at Franckford in Germany Anno Domini 1554... (1575 n.p.) is a book of considerable note[2]. On the authority of McCrie the authorship has been ascribed to William Whittingham. Nearly half of the book[3] deals with the troubles in Frankfurt from the 13th of January to the 30th of September, 1557, and was not written by Whittingham but by one of the Frankfurt Church, who remained behind after the radical reformers had left it. "This Controversy, which you have now heard, from the 13th of January hitherto," says the author or rather compiler of the book, "I find written by the hands of such as are both learned and of credit; but yet, I must needs say, by those that were parties in this broil."[4] The compiler appears to have been one of the Marian exiles who settled in Geneva. He has preserved his materials for twenty years (since 1554), but cannot keep them secret any longer, because the Episcopal party are blaming the Puritans for the present dissensions in the Church and ought to be exposed[5]. He has therefore "thought good, by a short and Brief Discourse, to let you see the very Original and Beginning of all this miserable Contention."[6] His aim is to show that the controversy raging in 1573–4 was but a continuation of the strife

[1] *F. & P.* p. 180.

[2] Reprinted 1642 (London), in vol. II of *The Phenix*, 1707–8 (London), by Petheram, 1846 (London), and by Arber, 1908 (London). *v. Knox*, IV, p. 8.

[3] pp. 97–215 in Arber's edition.

[4] *ibid.* p. 215.

[5] *ibid.* p. 234.

[6] *ibid.* p. 22.

between nonconformist and conformist exiles in the Frankfurt Church and that in both instances the enemies of the Puritans should be held responsible. For the light it sheds upon the life of the English exiles between 1554 and 1557, particularly their experiences at Frankfurt and the secession to Geneva and elsewhere, the book is invaluable. It furnishes much detailed first-hand evidence. But its connection with the Puritan movement in England has not been fully recognised. One object of the publication was to further the movement that was developing under the influence of the *Admonitions* and Cartwright's *Reply* and to place that movement in a proper perspective; it was evidently issued by the same publishing coterie, who were responsible for the production of these Puritan writings, and, what is more important, it was set forth as an instalment of a series of records, which were intended to deal with the history of the "old Grudge; which, as it seemeth, was never yet thoroughly healed: as will more and more appear, as this Discourse shall be, from time to time, continued, till it be brought even to this present time," *i.e. ca.* 1574[1]. This statement bears witness to the fact that the Puritans were already keeping a register for propaganda purposes and in view of the publication at a later date of *A first parte of a register* and the compilation of *The Seconde* we note again that the continuity between the literary activity of the Puritans in the 'seventies and that in the 'eighties is worthy of close examination.

The same unnamed Continental press that produced *A Brieff discours* issued, also in 1575, *The second replie of Thomas Cartwright: agaynst Maister Doctor Whitgiftes second answer, touching the Churche Discipline*. This is a long verbose answer to Whitgift's *Defence*[2] and adds nothing material to the contents of the first *Reply*. There is indeed some truth in Whitaker's criticism, which was sent to Whitgift to dissuade him from attempting a rejoinder: *Quem Cartwrightus nuper emisit libellum ejus magnam partem perlegi. Ne vivam, si quid unquam viderim dissolutius, ac pene puerilius...ut de*

[1] p. 231 in Arber's edition.
[2] pp. xxx + 666 + xiii; p. DCLXVI being wrongly printed DLXVI.

Ambrosio dixit Hieronimus, verbis ludit, sententiis dormitat, et plane indignus est, qui a quopiam docto refutetur[1]. Its main contents have already been considered.

In a Preface "To the Reader" Cartwright excuses the late appearance of his answer on the ground of his frequent sickness and lack of books. He brought only a few books with him, and in order to deal with Whitgift's quotations he has been obliged to seek in other men's libraries: "The cause off the slownes of answer hath bene in part my often sicknes and want off bookes off all Sortes: a few onely excepted, which I brought with me, and those for the most part English: so that for every place almost cited off the D. I was constreined to seek in other mens libraries, and after I had used the book, to cary it home againe." Besides, he has found his printer slow: "Ad hereunto: the slacknes off the print. For althowgh yt had bene my singuler advantage, both for polishing and better ordering off thinges, to have put nothing under the pres, before the whole book had bene finished: yet beginning to print, after I had made an end off one treatise, and begon an other, yt was notwithstanding scarce able to overtake me." He proceeds to explain why he has divided the *Second Reply* into two parts: "Amongest the causes, why I set forth one part, before the whole was ended: one ys, for that this former part rose to a iust volume. An other, that if any thing have escaped which may be hurtfull unto the trwth: I might (being advertised) amend yt in the later part: wheroff I desire the Godly reader, with as convenient speed as he can, to gyve me understanding." Further, he has postponed his full treatment of the apparel. This subject was exceedingly controversial and Cartwright desired to consult with the Heidelberg divines as well as the Puritans at home before he gave his final verdict: "The treatise off the apparel I have passed by, the causes wherof (assigned by me) if they shall not be approved, by those to whose iudgement I submit my selfe: upon signification off their minde in that behalf, I will resume yt again in that place where I shall handle the convenience and inconvenience off the ceremonies off the church unto

[1] Bancroft, *Survay*, p. 303; Paule, p. 331.

which place I wish I had reserved the most part off that Tractat, which in my book ys the first." After telling the gentle reader that he is now in good health Cartwright makes the following request: "If thow take any profit off my labors, remember me in thy praiers unto the lord for his assistance in the rest off my life, and namely for that which remaineth of answer unto the D(octors) book."

Sometimes the authorship of a little book entitled *An Examination off M. Doctor Whitgiftes Censures* has been ascribed to Cartwright[1], but the following interesting extract from one of his prefaces to the first portion of his *Second Reply* makes it manifest that he had no part in its production: "After I had ended my book[2], and was entred upon the preface I received a treatise called *An Examination off M. Doctor Whitgiftes Censures, Conteined in two Tables, set before his book intituled the Defence of the Answer to the Admoni.* Wherof as I was glad for the truthes sake which shall receive strenght by yt so I was sory, that I received yt no sooner, for that it might both have eased me off muche labor, and have served me for a good direction in those places, which might seem to require a larger defence, then the shortnes yt foloweth, would receive. And as those off the churche which acknowledg this trwth, so I especially, for whose support (I take) yt was written, hartely thanck the autor and desire the reader to use yt for a supply, where my answer doeth not satisfy him."[3]

The rest of the second replie of Thomas Cartvurihgt (*sic*) *agaynst Master Doctor Vuhitgifts second ansvuer, touching the Church discipline* was not published till 1577. Cartwright meant to answer Whitgift's *Defence of the Answer* on the question of the baptism of infants of Papists in *The Rest*, "Howbeyt, the trwth is, until I came to the place of the printing, where I had not his book with me: I forgot yt,"[4] which declaration indicates that this book was not written in the same place as it was printed. It was probably composed in Heidelberg, but the place of its publication remains a

[1] *A.C.* II, p. 364.
[2] *i.e.* *2nd Rep.* 1575.
[3] *ibid.* sig.)( )( )( )(, iii verso.
[4] *Rest*, p. 142.

mystery. The type[1] and the format are entirely different from those of the *Second Reply*. Zürich[2], Paris[3], or even Scotland[4] has been suggested as the seat of the press, but Cartwright's residence in Basel (1576–7) and his removal to the Netherlands (1577) point to one or other of these places.

Cartwright had *The Rest* ready about a year before he published it, and in his Preface to the Reader he explains and excuses the delay in its appearance: "According unto my promes, yow have here the residw of my reply, unto the Doctor's answer. Of the late appearing whereof, yt wil not be uneasy to conjecture: yf boeth the distance whereby I am removed from yow, and the alterations in the place where I remayned, be remembred. In me verely, the cause was not: which more then a year agoe, had brought yt in a maner, to the redines which yt was in, when yt began to be printed." He is well aware of the displeasure, which his writings have brought upon him in England, but he is still determined to uphold at all costs the cause he has at heart: "I see not, how I could perswade my self, to have to the quantitie of a grain of mustard seed, of trw love towards hym (God): yf unto the trwth laboring and travailing in this point, I should deny my simple help. And verily, yt were a deintynes and delicacy untollerable, yf I should afourd, the los of a little ease and commoditie unto that, whereunto my life yt self, yf yt had bene asked, was dw: if I should grudg to dwel in another korner of the world for that cawse, for the which, I owght to be ready, altogether to depart owt of yt: finally, yf I should think much, to witnes with a little ink and paper that, which numbres, in other places, have alredy witnessed with their blood."

As promised, Cartwright deals in *The Rest* with the burning question of the duty of the minister with regard to the 'popish' apparel. He sums up his verdict thus[5]: "As towching that point, whether the Minister should wear yt, althowgh yt be inconvenient; the truth is, that I dare not be autor to any, to forsake his pastoral charge for the incon-

[1] Note the use of the wrong fount for *w*; *v.* J. Ames, *Typographical Antiquities*, vol. III (1790), p. 1647.

[2] *B.M. Catalogue.*

[3] Sayle, No. 6762.

[4] Kippis, *Biographia Britannica*, p. 285.

[5] pp. 262–4.

venience thereof: considering that this charge being an absolute commandement of the lord, owght not to be laid aside for a simple inconvenience of uncomelines of a thing, which in the (*sic*) own nature is indifferent....When it (the surplice) is laid in the skoles, with the preaching of the word of god, which is so necessary for hym that is called thereunto, that a wo hangeth on his head, if he doe not preach yt....For my part, I see no better way, then with admonition of the weak that they be not offended, and prayer to god to strengthen them thereunto, to kepe on the cours of feeding the flok committed unto him....Althowgh I can remember nothing in ether of my bookes[1], contrary unto this judgment: yet if there be any thing that may be drawen against yt, yt is meet that yt fal, that the truth may have the upperhand." These latter words bear upon the suspicion prevalent among some of the Puritans that Cartwright was now relinquishing his position as stated in his former books.

Evidently the question of the minister's duty in a Church, that enjoined the wearing of apparel and the observance of certain ceremonies, seriously exercised the mind of Cartwright at this time. After much deliberation he came to the decision that the minister's primary duty was to remain at his post as a preacher of the Gospel. He should not for secondary matters, such as apparel or ceremonies, secede from the Church. In coming to this conclusion Cartwright incurred the disapproval of some of the more radical Puritans in England. Several of these "Brethren," apparently in 1576, sent the following question to Cartwright: "Whether the Ministerie bee for certaine ceremonies that are of the dregges of Poperie (namelie the Cope, the surplesse, the crosse in Baptisme, and other like) laid uppon them under pretence of Church pollicie onlie, and not with any opinion of worship or religion to be forsaken or not?"[2] Cartwright replied as follows: "I thinke it is not to be forsaken: for as concerning the offending of certaine weake brethren, whose minds

[1] *i.e.* first and second replies. Note that the *Second Admonition* is not acknowledged as his work.

[2] *A parte of a reg.* p. 401 (English); *Sec. Parte*, I, p. 136 (Latin).

thereby are not only much grieved, but also by withdrawing themselves thereupon from sermons, they sinne against their owne salvation, being the point of most waight in this cause... I thinke it absurd that the commandement of the holy Ghost, and namely which doth greatlie concerne the safetie of the brethren should depend upon the becke and pleasure of men. ...Since therfore things indifferent are of their nature in our owne power, but the preaching of the Gospell is of necessitie upon them that are called thereto, and since the Apostle doth condemne the offending of weake brethren upon this only respect, that we do lesse regard it then our own commoditie, and since the office of preaching falleth not within the compasse of this doctrine of Paul concerning offences: thereupon it also followeth, that in respect of offences the Ministerie is not to be forsaken....I denie it to be lawful, either by scribing or subscribing to allow them [popish ceremonies], as fit and agreeable to the doctrine of the Gospel, yea and I affirme that the discommoditie of them is to be taught in due and convenient time. Touchinge the matter of these popishe ceremonies I have drawen out into few words the principal poincts of the whole treatise, which either I have written in this matter before, or shal nowe in this later parte[1] where this tractate is handled. Therof I have had the judgement of the professors and ministers in Heidelberge, which approved it[2]. I would if you have so much leasure as to let me understand the brethrens judgment in time, howe thei like of this, and if thei do not to send me their reasons which lead them to thincke otherwise."[3]

The above question and Cartwright's answer appended were sent to a group of representative Puritans, viz., John Field, Thomas Wilcocks, Thomas Penny, Nicholas Standen, Arthur Wake, Henry Salisbury, Nicholas Crane, Giles Seintloe, Richard Gawton and George Gildred, who, as requested, passed judgment on Cartwright's opinion[4]. The ten

[1] *i.e. Rest.* [2] *v.* Preface to *2nd Rep. supra* p. 146.

[3] *Sec. Parte*, 1, pp. 136–7, partly Latin and partly English; *A parte of a reg.* pp. 401–2, English trans. as above; concluding paragraph of T. C.'s answer is omitted in *A parte*.

[4] *A parte of a reg.* pp. 402–8; cf. *Sec. Parte*, 1, p. 137.

stalwarts, who had suffered deprivation for their nonconformity, express their uncompromising opinion that "the filthie corruptions" must not be tolerated by Christ's ministers. After giving fourteen reasons for their opinion, they pronounce an adverse verdict on Cartwright's reply to the original question[1]. A copy of their judgment was sent from London on the 25th of Ma. (March?), 1577, along with a letter to Cartwright[2]. The letter was signed by nine of the Puritans above mentioned and Nathaniel Baxter in place of Wake. Wake was now Chaplain at Mont Orgueil, Jersey. As he was there by June, 1576, the judgment in which he participated must have been signed by him before that date or during a visit to the mainland after it. Probably the absence of his signature to the letter was due to his being in Jersey on 25 Ma. 1577. "Brother Cartwright," they wrote, "we your brethren, who have hereunto set our name, have upon some good grounds thoght it meete to write these few lines unto you....We send you inclosed...in such sort as we did sett the same down to the bretheren that requested the same of us, praying you to consider therof, as apperteyneth to a cause so grave and weighty. We for our own parts stand resolved that what we have don touching this matter of ceremonies, as the crosse, etc., is most agreable to Gods Word and the testimonie of a good conscience grounded theron, which minde we hope you are of, not withstanding whatsoever you have written privately, as desirous, perhaps, to understand other mens minds. Your first boke extant to the view of the godlie[3] is (as we are persuaded), [*as with*] us here, so with your self, farre more authentical than any schrole or paper of yours whatsoever. And ground there is, why it shold be so with both, because the Churches with you (as you your self write) have approved [*and*] allowed the summe thereof[4]; to goe backe from which what were it els but to fight against your self [*and*] tread under feete the judgement of the Church and brethern. And therefore in our minds it were a great

[1] *A parte of a reg.* pp. 406–8. Gilby's letter to Cartwright on the same subject and in the same vein as the judgment of the ten is in *Sec. Parte*, I, p. 139 ff.

[2] *Sec. Parte*, I, pp. 137–9. [3] *i.e.* the *Reply* of 1573. [4] *v. supra* p. 150.

[*deal*] better not to write any whit at all touching this point than in your writings to set your selfe against your selfe, and against the Church and brethern also....The same good opinion we have also conceaved of you, nothing at al doubting but that he who hitherto hath made you a glorious witnesse to his truth will strengthen you stil to run forward in that course. And yet we thinke it meete, that in respect both of our own dulnes to good things, [*and the*] naughtines of the daies which are come upon us, every one, yea, the quickest amongst us, shold be pricked forward, and at no hand to go backward in the causes of God, seeing the world is so backeward in religion and earnest and readie in things wicked and ungodlie. But because we deale with you whom both for learning [*and*] godlines we verie much love and reverence in the lord, and touching whom we hope that a little [*said will*] suffice in this behalf, we are the more spare herein, and so for this time commend you unto God and the word of his grace...."

The criticism in this letter failed to produce any alteration of Cartwright's opinion. He denied in *The Rest* which was published after the receipt of the letter, and therefore after the 25th of March (?), 1577, that he was contradicting assertions made in his previous books[1]. Waddington[2] in error quotes this communication to prove that Cartwright's withdrawal to Warwick was not approved by the more zealous Puritans! Brook also misses the point of the letter, of which he gives an abridged and garbled version[3]. He thinks it important chiefly because it would bring comfort to the heart of the exile by showing him "that he was not forgotten, but highly esteemed and honoured by his brethren at home, who, far separated, were not debarred from holding a friendly correspondence with him." Certainly the correspondence shows that after three years' absence Cartwright was still much loved and reverenced by the Puritans at home, but it also indicates that they were now apprehensively aware of his being an advocate of compromise in what he deemed the unessential features of the controversy. They feared that the Puritan party might divide into two camps, moderate and

[1] *v. supra* p. 151. [2] *Hist.* p. 16. [3] *Mem.* pp. 220–1.

radical, and to a certain extent their fears were justified. Meanwhile Cartwright laid stress upon the duty of a Christian minister to remain at his post, while the critics of his judgment emphasised the intolerable nature of the popish corruptions. The difference was largely one of emphasis; both Cartwright and the home radicals were desirous of a further reformation of the Church along Presbyterian lines; he was willing to accept what was possible in an intolerant age, while they were resolved to achieve their goal without any appearance of compromise. The rift between the exiled chief and an influential section of the Puritans in England had begun. Their growing manifestation of revolt and dissent did not please Cartwright, to whom schism and secession were loathsome. He preferred to bear witness to the need of patient reformation within the Church. Nevertheless, even among the radical Presbyterians, who differed from him on the question of vestments and ceremonies, Cartwright continued to be regarded as an authoritative exponent of the general principles of Presbyterianism.

Cartwright's association with the Heidelberg divines apparently inclined him to the less radically revolutionary attitude that he now adopted. Indeed, his judgment regarding vestments and ceremonies was practically identical with theirs. Zanchy, in a long and able letter addressed to Queen Elizabeth[1], roundly condemned the popish apparel and about the same time, in an epistle to Jewel[2], he plainly indicated that the view of the Heidelberg theological Professors concerning the minister's duty, when Romish ceremonies were enjoined, was that now advocated by Cartwright: *Numquam enim propter res sua natura adiaphoras deserenda set vocatio legitima et necessaria.*

Among Cartwright's other correspondents at this time was a pious "Mrs D. B." Two copies of his letters to her, dated from Heidelberg the 24th of October, 1575, and the 18th of February, 1576, are extant[3]. In these he offers sympathy and consolation to one in spiritual distress. They are long, diffuse

[1] 10 Sept. 1571, *Z.L.* II, p. 339.

[2] 2 Sept. 1571, from Heidelberg and signed "H. Zanchius, Suo et collegarum nomine," *Z.L.* II, Ep. LXXV.

[3] *MSS.* C.C.C. Oxford. CCXCIV, ff. 163–170, 171–183.

and tedious, but they evince a sincere and tender desire to minister to the soul of an afflicted woman, who had befriended him before he left England. She seems to have belonged to a body of strict religious professors and Cartwright even questions whether he is worthy to have any part or fellowship with her and "the rest of that Company." Was she a Separatist? It appears that other godly Puritans were ministering to her in her trouble. According to the second of the above-mentioned letters, one of these was Edmund Chapman, who wrote to Cartwright between October, 1575, and February, 1576, telling him that Mrs B. had been shaken by a "fearefull tempest," which had plunged her into fresh despair. We gather from Cartwright's epistles to her that she was a zealous Christian, who liberally helped the godly preachers. It also appears that she was young and that her husband was still alive. Was she Dering's friend, Mrs Barret[1], or was she a Mrs Buckley, whose name appears in another letter of the Oxford collection?[2]

During the years of Cartwright's connection with Heidelberg and Basel rumours of sects constantly engaged the attention of the authorities at home[3]. Nonconformists of the Separatist type, who had affinities with the Puritans and were sometimes rightly and sometimes wrongly identified with them, continued to meet in their private conventicles, *e.g.* in the beginning of 1575 the Privy Council and the Bishop of London dealt with a company of "precise persons discovered to have used conventicles in Fewter Lane."[4] The disturbances in the Low Countries had driven many foreign Anabaptists and adherents of the Family of Love to seek refuge in England. These sectarians, who were detested equally by Anglicans and by Puritans[5], received particularly rigorous treatment[6] of which we may draw a notable illustration from

[1] *v. supra* p. 117. [2] *MSS.* C.C.C., CCXCIV, ff. 184–200.

[3] *Grindal Rem.* p. 353; *Parker Corresp.* p. 474.

[4] *Acts P.C.* VIII, pp. 334, 338; cf. *ibid.* pp. 320, 338, 388.

[5] *W.W.* I, p. 76 ff.; *v.* illuminating controversy between the Puritan, William White, and an English Anabaptist, 'S.B.,' in Dr Peel's *A Conscientious Objector of* 1575.

[6] B. Evans, *Early English Baptists* (1862), I, p. 151 ff.; *Acts P.C.* VIII, pp. 369, 370, 389, 398, 402; *Parker Corresp.* p. 479.

Stowe[1]: "1575. On Easter Day, which was the 3 of Aprill, about 9 of the clocke in the forenoone, was disclosed a congregation of Anabaptists Dutchmen, in a house without the barres of Aldgate at London, whereof 27 were taken and sent to pryson, and foure of them bearing fagots recanted at Pauls Crosse on the 15 of May....The 21 of May, being Whitsun-even, one man and 10 women, Anabaptists Dutch, were in the Consistory of Paules condemned to bee burnt in Smithfield, but after great paines taken with them, onely one woman was converted, the other were banished the land.... The 22 of July, 2 Dutchmen Anabaptists were burnt in Smithfield, who died in great horror with roaring and crying."

During these years (1574–7) the Puritan movement proper remained at an apparently low ebb. Cox was still of opinion that the faction was kept quiet by the menacing hand of the vigilant and determined government[2]. He feared, however, that under the cloak of silence the Puritans were brewing some mischief[3]. Isolated instances of the suspension or deprivation of Puritan ministers occur, *e.g.* Gawton and Harvey[4]. In some districts we meet with concerted Puritan activity, *e.g.* as we have already seen, Field, Wilcocks, Penny, Crane, etc., appear in league in London in 1576–7, and on the 25th of September, 1576, John More, Richard Crick, Thomas Roberts, George Leeds, Richard Dowe and William Hart, ministers of Norwich diocese, petitioned against conformity to the ceremonies[5]. On the whole, however, a superficial observer might readily affirm that during this period the forces of Puritanism had been submerged. One of the chief reasons for this state of apparent quiescence seems to have been the use now made by the Puritans of the widespread exercises or prophesyings, by means of which they were able to associate, to nourish and propagate their ambitions, and prepare for future triumph.

1 *Annales* (1631), p. 679.
2 Cox to Bullinger, 25 Jan. 1574–5, *Z.L.* I, Ep. CXXV.
3 1576, *Z.L.* I, Ep. CXXVIII.
4 *A parte of a reg.* pp. 393–400; St. *Ann.* IV, pp. 59, 61.
5 *Sec. Parte*, I, p. 143 ff. Five of them, J. M., R. C., T. R., G. L., R. D. along with Vincent Goodwin and John Mapes, made a qualified submission (21 Aug. 1578) in order to be restored to preaching.

These meetings, ostensibly based upon the prophesyings of the Apostolic Church, were sanctioned by several of the Bishops, because they were calculated to deepen the acquaintance of the clergy with the Scriptures and increase the number of preachers[1]. The sets of rules determining the procedure of the exercises were commonly called "Orders."[2] These regulations were frequently ignored or infringed. At times factions arose and the established laws and customs were criticised. Grindal, who was particularly enthusiastic in his advocacy of the exercises, published orders for the reformation of the abuses connected with them[3]. In these orders he noted that divers ministers, who had been deprived for their nonconformity, had intruded themselves into the exercises and there disseminated their obnoxious opinions. Such were to be prohibited from taking part in the meetings. The Queen was aware of unlawful assemblies that went under the name of exercises and of the abuses connected with those that were formally recognised. Besides, the increase in the number and efficiency of preachers, such as the exercises were alleged to produce, did not win the royal favour. Accordingly she decided that the exercises should be suppressed altogether[4]. She asked Grindal to carry out her decision, but so highly did the Archbishop value the exercises that he was willing to become a nonconformist for their sake, and in a letter (Dec. 1576), justly celebrated for its exhibition of noble courage, he explained to Elizabeth the nature of the meetings, emphasised their worth, pointed out that the abuses, such as she detested, were to be redressed, and humbly declined to enjoin their abolition[5]. Elizabeth therefore took the matter into her own hands and issued a command to the Bishops (May, 1577) to suppress them, and Grindal, for his nonconformity, suffered sequestration as well as the Queen's displeasure[6].

Undoubtedly Elizabeth's action was another blow to

[1] Soames, p. 223.

[2] *Sec. Parte*, I, p. 133; St. *Ann.* III, p. 472; J. Browne, *History of Congregationalism in Norfolk and Suffolk* (1877), pp. 18–20.

[3] *Grindal Rem.* p. 373.

[4] *ibid.* p. 375; Soames, p. 225.

[5] *Grindal Rem.* p. 376.

[6] *ibid.* p. 467; Soames, p. 226.

Puritanism. After the inquisition of 1573–4 the exercises were among the best practical agencies for the spread of Puritan principles. Under cover of a legitimate conference the zealots were enabled to advance their cause quietly and inconspicuously. There is also good evidence that the Puritans did make use of their opportunity. It is stated that the Northamptonshire ringleaders, Wake, Paget, Mosley, Gildred and Dawson, who were deprived in 1574, were speakers in the exercise and that three of them were moderators of the same[1]. The Norwich Puritans complained in 1576 that "there be alreadie 19 or 20 godlie Exercises of preching and Catechizing putt downe in this Cittie by the displaceing" of the nonconforming ministers[2]. These exercises, with their moderators and their mild form of disciplinary jurisdiction, were really embryonic Presbyteries of the modern type. That the Puritan-Presbyterians of this period realised the value of these meetings will again be evident when we consider their attempt, not long after the suppression of the exercises, to resuscitate them under the name of Conferences or *classes*, but this time in secret and under the direction of ministers, who aimed at the establishment of Presbyterianism in the Church of England.

Although the efforts of the Puritans to presbyterianise the Church had so far been effectually frustrated, "yet," to say with Heylyn[3], "was it questionlesse some comfort to their souls, that their device, however it succeeded ill in England, had spred it self abroad in Guernzey and in Jarsey, where it had now possession of the whole Islands." The Protestantism introduced into the islands in the reigns of Henry VIII and Edward VI and practically obliterated in that of Mary reasserted itself shortly after the accession of Elizabeth. Chiefly under the influence of the Governors and the Huguenot ministers, who sought refuge in the isles, the forces of the

[1] *Sec. Parte*, I, p. 121. [2] *ibid.* I, p. 145.

[3] Heylyn, *A Full Relation of two journeys* (1656), p. 337. Bk VI is entitled *A Second Journey: containing A Survey of the Estate of the two Ilands Guernzey and Jarsey. With the Isles appending...*, and its running headline is *A Survey of the Estate of Guernzey and Jarsey.* Hereafter quoted as *Survey*.

reformed faith developed. William Beauvoir, who had been a deacon in the English Church at Geneva and there had been associated with Knox, Lever, Goodman, Whittingham, Wiburn, etc.[1] was largely instrumental in bringing the Genevan Discipline to his island home, Guernsey. At his request for a suitable minister to supervise the beginnings of a Presbyterian Church in that island Calvin commended Nicholas Baudouin, under whose direction the first Consistory (kirk-session) was established in St Pierre Port[2]. Similar work was done at St Helier in Jersey by another French minister, William Morise[3]. Francis Chamberlain, Governor of Guernsey, and Amias Poulet, Lieutenant of Jersey, countenanced the movement and acted as members of the Consistories. So far had Presbyterianism proceeded in the Channel Islands by the year 1563. The first joint-meeting of the Consistories was held in Guernsey in June, 1564[4]. On the 7th of August, 1565, the Queen, through her Council, sanctioned the new Presbyterian organisation but definitely confined it to St Pierre Port and St Helier[5]. The rural parishes were still formally obliged to continue the Anglican service and usages[6], but it appears from a letter of Adrian Saravia to Cecil (26 Feb. 1565–6) that Protestantism of the Anglican or Reformed type was not popular in the country districts of Guernsey[7]. Saravia considered the islanders worse than Turks in their irreligion and lawlessness. By an order of the Privy Council (16 March, 1568–9) the islands, which had hitherto been in the diocese of Coutances, were transferred to the see of Winchester[8]. A letter written by Nicholas Berny in the name of the Guernsey Presbyterian Church (*Gerenesiensis ecclesiae nomine*) on the 13th of December, 1575, to Horn, Bishop of Winchester, throws considerable light upon the advance made by Presbyterianism

[1] Martin, pp. 332–5; W. B. was in Geneva before 13 Oct. 1555 and was a deacon from 1556 to 1558.

[2] Drysdale, p. 168; Tupper, p. 154; G. E. Lee, *Discipline Ecclésiastique des Iles de la Manche* (1885), p. v.

[3] Drysdale, p. 168.

[4] *ibid.* p. 169; Tupper, p. 154; Schickler, II, p. 372.

[5] Drysdale, p. 169; Tupper, p. 152.

[6] *ibid.* [7] Tupper, p. 155. [8] *ibid.* p. 154.

in Guernsey at that date[1]. There are now several Consistories in the island. The appellations for the Consistory are of interest, viz. *presbyterium*, *ecclesiasticus senatus*, *ecclesiae synedrium*. The Guernsey Church, however, has passed beyond the consistorial stage, and reference is made to the calling of a Colloquy (Presbytery in the modern sense): *Omnes hujus insulae verbi Dei administri cum suarum ecclesiarum quibusdam senioribus et nonnullis piis magistratibus in colloquium convocantur*. Anti-Presbyterian dissent is already being put down with a strong hand, but the case of a contumacious individual, who refuses to acknowledge the Presbyterian Church and to submit to its discipline, is referred to the Bishop of Winchester. Thus a request is made by a Presbyterian Church to an Anglican Bishop for assistance in the exercise of ecclesiastical discipline, and shortly afterwards the Bishop readily offers his aid through the Governor of the island, Thomas Leighton[2].

The progress of the Presbyterian Churches in the islands reached a culminating point at a Synod, which met on the 28th of June, 1576, at St Pierre Port and was attended by the Governors of Jersey and Guernsey and other magistrates, the ministers and the Governors' Chaplains. At this important Synod the Church of the Channel Islands, in the presence and with the consent of the Governors, adopted its first Form of Discipline, which seems to have been largely based upon the Discipline of the Reformed Church of France and was thoroughly Presbyterian in character. There are extant two copies of the Form of 1576, one in the Bibliothèque de l'Arsenal, Paris[3], and the other (mutilated) in the British Museum[4]. Baron F. de Schickler prints the document in full in his excellent and most useful book, *Les Églises du Refuge en Angleterre*[5]. In his certificate appended to the B.M. copy Nicholas Berny gives some interesting and valuable particulars concerning the new Presbyterian constitution: *Ceste presente Police a esté collationnée à l'original par moy sousigné commis pour scribe au Synode tenu à Guernezé le* 28, 29 *et*

[1] *Z.L.* II, Ep. CVI. [2] *ibid.* I, Ep. CXXX. [3] *MSS.* 3847, No. 16.
[4] *Cotton MSS. Calig.* E. vi. 324. [5] III, pp. 311–356.

30e jours de Juing auquel Synode elle a esté receué et signée au derniers fueillets des seings de Messrs les Gouverneurs Amies Poulet, Thomas Leigthon (sic), Helier de Cartereth, Philippes de Cartereth, G. Beauvoir, H. Beauvoir, N. Saumares, N. Martin, N. Trohardy, N. Careye, Jean Delacourt, Persival Wiborn, Art. Wak, Pierres Henry, N. Berny greffier, N. Baudouin, Jean Quesnel, Edouart Herault, Maturin Loumeau S. Alix, N. le Duc, Jacques Godard,...et plusieurs autres tant Ministres qu'Anciens des Isles de Guernezé, Gerzé, et Serk, lequel original est demouré entre les mains de Mr le Gouverneur de Guernezé, laquelle copie pour servir comme de raison estant collationnée fidelement par moy, comme dit est, ès presences de Mr Simon, Mr du Gravier, et Mr Trefoy, j'ay signée de mon seing cy mis le 6e jour de Juillet 1576 *et delivrée à M. Nicolas Baudouin. N. Berny*[1].

The Governors who signed the Form of Discipline were Poulet and Leighton. Shortly after the Synod Poulet was appointed ambassador to France[2]. In October, 1585, he became keeper of Mary, Queen of Scots[3]. Leighton, appointed Governor of Guernsey in 1570[4], held the post throughout the reign of Elizabeth. He made the growth of the island Church his special care, as may be shown by the interest he took in the new school at St Pierre Port, which he hoped would prove a nursery of native ministers[5]. The sympathies of both Poulet and Leighton were with the Puritan party. They also belonged to Leicester's faction. This latter relationship did not escape mention in the scurrilous and brutally frank libel, commonly known as *Leycesters Commonwealth*, which appeared *ca.* 1584[6]: "The two Ilands of Gersey and Gernsey are in the possession of two friends and most obliged dependents. The one, by reason hee is

[1] Lee, *op. cit.* p. vi.
[2] *Acts P.C.* IX, p. 194.
[3] *v. Letter-Books of Sir Amias Poulet*, ed. Morris (1874).
[4] *S.P. Dom. Eliz. Add.* XVIII, No. 70.
[5] *ibid. Add.* XIX, No. 26.
[6] ed. Burgoyne, p. 78. This book has been issued under various titles: *The Copie of a Leter wryten by a Master of Arte of Cambrige...* (*ca.* 1584), *Leycesters Commonwealth* (1641), *Secret Memoirs of Robert Dudley, Earl of Leicester* (1706), *The perfect picture of a Favourite* (1708), *History of Queen Elizabeth, Amy Robsart and the Earl of Leicester* (ed. Burgoyne, 1904).

exceedingly addicted to the Puritane proceedings: the other, as now being joyned unto him by the marriage of Mistres Besse his wives Sister, both Daughters to Sir Francis, or (at least) to my Lady Knooles, and so become a rivale, companion and brother, who was before (though trusty) yet but his servant."

The first ministerial signatures to the Discipline of 1576 are those of Percival Wiburn and Arthur Wake. They were now stationed as chaplains at Castle Cornet and Mont Orgueil respectively, and were to fulfil their duties there and take an active share in the work of the growing Presbyterian Church of the islands for some considerable time. Both were ardent members of the Puritan party. Wiburn, a native of Kent, was a particularly conspicuous figure in the history of Elizabethan Puritanism, and his career is well worthy of investigation[1]. A graduate of Cambridge and a Fellow of St John's College, he went, in the reign of Mary, to Geneva and became a member of the English Church there (May, 1557). Shortly after the conclusion of his academic course, which he resumed on the accession of Elizabeth, he received rapid promotion in the Church, *e.g.* he became a Prebendary of Westminster (16 Nov. 1561) and Vicar of St Sepulchre's, Holborn (8 Mar. 1563–4)[2]. During the vestiarian strife he took his stand with the Puritans and for his nonconformity was deprived of his charge in Holborn in July, 1566[3]. In the same year he went to the Continent as one of the Puritan emissaries and received particular kindness at the hands of Beza, whom he visited along with Kingsmill and Warcup[4]. In the following year his conflict with the Bishops in England was renewed[5] but he stedfastly adhered to the cause which he had espoused and came to be regarded as a redoubtable adversary both by Anglicans and Papists. Reference is made to him in some rare and little known controversial verses composed by Thomas Knell, Junr., in 1570 and entitled *An Answer at large to a most hereticall, trayterous, and*

[1] *v. A.C.* II, p. 449; Baker I, pp. 286, 291, 325.
[2] Hennessy, pp. 383, 444.
[3] *ibid.* p. 383.
[4] Hessels, II, p. 618.
[5] Dixon, VI, pp. 134, 154.

Papisticall Byll, in English verse, which was cast abrode in the streetes of Northamton, and brought before the Judges at the last Assises there[1]. It should be noted in connection with Wiburn's residence in Northamptonshire at this time that his son, Nathaniel, is stated to have been born at Whiston in that county[2]. Regarding Wake, who was evicted from his Northamptonshire charge in 1574, there are two unpublished documents, which are important and illuminating. From one[3] we learn that the writer's "brother, Mr Arthure Wake, Mr of Arte, ys nowe and hathe ben this twelvemonith in Jersey with Mr Paulet captayne there and intendith there to contynue and there wilbe meanes made to the Quenes Matie for him that he maye inioye his livinge notwithstanding his absence." The writer continues "yf they had the byll made he wolde have a copie and wolde take advise for the sure making in lawe. My cosin Nicasius or Mr Wyndebanke made one this last somer for one Mr Wyburne who lykewise ys in Jersey (*sic*)." The accompanying document[4], apparently a letter from the Earl of Leicester to the Bishop of Lincoln, strikingly illustrates the Earl's use of his power in the interest of his Puritan friends: "After my most hartye commendac̄ons to your good L. I am gyven tunderstand that you have of late molestyde my very loving frende Mr Arthure Wake in seeking to remove him from the possession of a certen hospitall which he hathe in Northampton. What cause there ys to induce you so to do I knowe not; but I presume so moche of his gret honesty as there ys no cause gyven by him towarde you. Wherefore these are to praye you in anye wyse from hensforthe to forbeare anye further to deale therein and to suffer him quietly to enioy the same without anye your further let by anye meanes, as you intende to have me favorable in anye your requests hereafter, and as you will gyve me cause to contynue your frende and thinke well of you."

If the first Form of Discipline owed anything to the English Puritans, it would be to Wiburn and Wake and not, as has so

[1] Printed at London, 1570, by John Awdelye, and reprinted, 1881, at Northampton by Taylor.

[2] Baker, I, p. 291.

[3] *S.P. Dom Eliz. Add.* XXIV, No. 52 ii. n.d. [4] *ibid.* XXIV, No. 52, i.

often been affirmed, to Cartwright and Snape. It has been widely accepted[1] that the latter were called to the Channel Islands in 1576 to help in the establishment of Presbyterianism there and that their labours resulted in the production of the Discipline of that year, but this tradition, in our opinion, is a tissue of inaccuracies and should now be discarded. The matter is worthy of detailed examination. First, let us consider the statements of historians, whose sympathies are with the Puritans. Neal, giving Heylyn as his authority, says[2]: "Mr Cartwright and Snape were invited to assist the ministers in framing a proper discipline for their churches: this fell out happily for Cartwright, who being forced to abandon his native country, made this the place of his retreat. The two divines being arrived, one was made titular pastor of Mount Orgueil, in the isle of Jersey; and the other of Castle Cornet, in Guernsey. The representatives of the several churches being assembled at St Peter's Port in Guernsey, they communicated to them a draught of discipline, which was debated, and accommodated to the use of those islands, and finally settled the year following," and then Neal gives the title of the Form of 1597! Brook, also following in the wake of Heylyn, elaborates and embroiders the tradition[3]: "Mr Cartwright, in a state of exile, engaged in various important avocations, especially in the care of the churches, showing great solicitude for their purity and prosperity. For the advancement of this object, he was invited to the islands of Jersey and Guernsey, where he remained some time.... Mr Cartwright was unexpectedly invited, with Mr Edmund Snape, another persecuted minister, to assist in framing their ecclesiastical discipline....The two divines having arrived in Guernsey, an assembly of the ministers and elders of Jersey, Guernsey, Sark, and Alderney, was convened at Port St Pierre, when, the governors being present, a form of discipline was presented, and agreed to be adopted by those islands."

[1] *A.C.* II, p. 361; *D.N.B.* art. "Cartwright"; Drysdale, p. 171; Grosart, p. xiv; Pierce, *John Penry*, p. 149; R. M. Serjeantson, *History of the Church of St Peter, Northampton* (1904), p. 25; D. Macalister, *English Authors of the Shorter Catechism* (1925), p. 9.

[2] I, p. 271.

[3] *Mem.* pp. 217–19.

After giving the title of the 1597 Discipline and stating that it was published in 1577, Brook proceeds "Mr Snape, on this important mission, preached at Mountorguil in Jersey; but, the conferences having terminated, he returned to England....Mr Cartwright, in addition to the special object of his mission, preached at Castle-Cornet in Guernsey; and, on the final organization of the churches, he returned to Antwerp and resumed the charge of his beloved flock." Drysdale[1] implicitly follows Neal.

The historian responsible for the origination of this account of Cartwright's activity in 1576 was Peter Heylyn. The narrative in his *Survey*[2] runs thus: "Not content with that allowance her Majesty had given unto it in the towns of St Peters and St Hillaries; the Governours having first got these Isles to be dissevered from the Diocese of Constance (*sic*), permit it [the Presbyterian polity and discipline] unto all the other Parishes. The better to establish it, the great supporters of the cause in England, Snape and Cartwright, are sent for to the Islands; the one of them being made the tributary Pastor of the Castle of Cornet, the other of that of Mont-orguel. Thus qualified forsooth they conveene the Churches of each Island, and in a Synod held in Guernzey, anno 1576, the whole body of the Discipline is drawn into a forme. Which forme of Discipline I here present unto your Lordship, faithfully translated according to an authentick copy, given unto me by Mr Painsec Curate of our Ladies Church of Chastell in the Isle of Guernzey." Forthwith[3] Heylyn provides the translation, which is that of the second Form of Discipline adopted in 1597! In his *Aërius Redivivus*[4] Heylyn repeats his prejudiced and unauthenticated tale: "It was thought fit that Snape and Cartwright, the great Supporters of the cause in England, should be sent unto them to put their Churches in a posture, and settle the Discipline amongst them in such form and manner as it was practised in Geneva, and amongst the French. Which fell out happily for Cartwright, as his case stood; who being worsted in the

[1] p. 171. [2] p. 337. [3] *ibid.* pp. 338–363.
[4] lib. VII, § 8.

last Encounter betwixt him and Whitgift, had now a handsome opportunity to go off with credit; not as if worsted in the fight, but rather called away to another tryal. Upon this Invitation they set sail for the Islands, and take the charge thereof upon them; the one of them being made the titular Pastor of the Castle of Mount Orgueil, in the Isle of Jersey; and the other of Castle Cornet, in the Rode of Guernsey. Thus qualified they convene the Churches of each Island, communicate unto them a rude Draught of the Holy Discipline; which afterwards was polished, and accommodated to the use of those Islands: but not agreed upon and exercised until the year next following; as appears by the Title of it"; and then Heylyn proceeds to give a translation of the title of the 1597 Form of Discipline. Where, however, the title of the original says that the Discipline was revised and confirmed at a Synod "tenu à Guernezé les 11, 12, 13, 14, 15 et 17 jours d'Octobre l'an 1597," Heylyn translates "holden in Jersey the 11, 12, 13, 14, 15 and 17 days of October 1577" and these two mistakes "Jersey" and "1577" have been slavishly copied by succeeding historians[1]. We therefore break away from the tradition that Cartwright was in Guernsey in 1576 and that he participated in the production of the Discipline of that year. As we have seen, he fled, not, as Heylyn says, after Whitgift's *Defence* appeared, but before its publication, and proceeded to Heidelberg, which he made the headquarters of his retreat from 1574 to 1576 and then repaired to Basel. The posts supposed to have been occupied by him and Snape at Castle Cornet and Mont Orgueil in 1576 were then held by Wiburn and Wake. It is true that Cartwright and Snape did minister at these places, but not till about twenty years afterwards[2]. They also played a prominent part in the drawing up of the second Form of Discipline in 1597, but it was Wiburn and Wake who signed the first. Historians have not always distinguished the two Forms of Discipline and have consequently confused events and personages connected

[1] Neal, I, p. 271; Falle, *Account of the Island of Jersey* (1837), p. 197; Brook, *Mem.* p. 218; Drysdale, p. 171, etc.

[2] *v. infra* pp. 373 ff.

with them. This confusion and the resultant blunder in the accounts of Cartwright's life are largely due to the errors and inexactitudes of the seventeenth century historian, Peter Heylyn. The latest survey of early Presbyterianism in the Channel Islands[1] is of great value, but the writer vitiates her work by confounding the Discipline of 1576 with that of 1597. It is a case of Heylyn Redivivus.

[1] *Journal of Presb. Hist. Soc. of Eng.* May 1923, II, No. 4, p. 181 ff., by Mrs W. W. D. Campbell.

CHAPTER IV

CARTWRIGHT IN THE NETHERLANDS

Cartwright migrates from Basel to the Netherlands—factor at Middelburg—the English Church at Antwerp—Travers appointed its minister—the Puritan interests of Davison, Killigrew, Tomson, etc.—the marriage of Cartwright—he succeeds Travers at Antwerp—Spenser's allusion to Cartwright in the *Shepheardes Calender*—Cartwright called to Leyden and St Andrews—his removal to Zealand—his Confutation of the Rhemish New Testament—his dealings with the Brownists in Zealand—his return to England.

BROOK, finding the materials for his life of Cartwright during the years 1574–85 far from copious, fills in the blanks without due regard to chronological order in his diffuse and seriously imaginative fashion. He assumes that the fugitive, after the alleged and unsubstantiated visit to Guernsey, passed the rest of the period as a minister in Antwerp and Middelburg[1]. "It appears," says Brook[2], who believed that Cartwright had already spent about two years (1570–2) as pastor in these towns "that he went again to Antwerp, and a second time became preacher to the English merchants." Heylyn[3], who is followed by Neal[4], states that after visiting Guernsey Cartwright "put himself into the Factory of Antwerp, and was soon chosen for their Preacher." Clarke[5] places Cartwright's settlement in Antwerp shortly before the appearance of the first *Admonition*. W. Steven[6], who has been followed by Grosart[7] and Drysdale[8], says: "We are not aware that divine service had been statedly performed in the English language at Antwerp, since the year 1571, when the well known Thomas Cartwright, Professor of Divinity at Cambridge, was here, and left it for Middleburgh."

There thus exists the utmost confusion as to the date of Cartwright's settlement in the Low Countries. Our con-

[1] Brook, *Mem.* p. 216. [2] *Lives*, II, p. 146.
[3] *A.R.* lib. VII, § 23. [4] I, p. 289. [5] p. 369.
[6] *History of the Scottish Church, Rotterdam* (1832), pp. 283, 315.
[7] p. xiv. [8] pp. 255, 259.

tention is that it did not take place before 1577. As we have already observed, Cartwright, when on the Continent in 1571–2, abode in Geneva, and when he returned to exile, he resided in Heidelberg and latterly in Basel. Although his sojourn at Heidelberg and Basel may have been broken by visits to other places, there is no trace of his going to the Channel Islands or of his ministry at Antwerp during this period (1574–7). In a Preface of *The Rest* he clearly indicates that he had not engaged in the practical work of the ministry since his second exile began: "Yt is not the least part of my comfort, that in this vacation from the ministery the lord hath not suffered me to be altogether idle: but imployed me if not in griffing and setting, which are the master-workes, yet in hedging and ditching abowt the Orchyard of his church." This declaration supports our view that he could not have been minister in Antwerp at any rate before 1577.

Documentary research, however, reveals Cartwright first of all in the Low Countries at Middelburg in September, 1577, not as a minister but as a factor of the Merchant Adventurers. It is indeed probable that Heylyn, when he says that Cartwright "put himself into the Factory of Antwerp," refers to "the office of factory," which the Puritan held[1]. Robert Beale, writing to Walsingham from Antwerp on the 8th of September, 1577[2], about the loss he has incurred at the hands of pirates, says that he has appointed "one Thomas Cartwright a factor for the Merchant Adventurers to folowe the cause; who dwelleth in Middelburge" and encloses a letter he recceived from Cartwright by which Walsingham may "understand of ther preparacion and what accompt soche disordered persons make of her majestyes subsidy, especially nowe in the absence of the prince who ys at St Getrudensberg." In January of the following year, Beale, in the course of his return journey from Germany, complains to Davison, then in Brussels, that no restitution had been made. "I hear from Zealand," he writes from Antwerp on 25 Jan. 1578[3], "that the party [Cartwright]

[1] *v.* D. & G. p. 183.

[2] *S.P. Eliz. German States*, I, No. 17.

[3] *S.P. Eliz. Holl. and Fland.* V, No. 27.

whom I charged to follow this suit dare not, for threatening and danger, proceed in it any further, which in these days of pretended amity, seems to me very strange."

At first sight it may seem surprising that a Puritan, who had been a Cambridge Professor and a ringleader in ecclesiastical controversy, should settle for a time in Middelburg as a factor to English merchants. On enquiry, however, into the nature of the post we find that Cartwright was the very man for it. Many of the merchants were among the first to become inoculated with Protestant doctrines. They exercised an incalculable influence as mediators between the Continental Reformation and that in Britain. Through them the anti-Romanist ideas and literature filtered into London and the Eastern counties. Through their association with the exponents of the reform movement on the Continent many of them became the staunchest protagonists of Protestantism, and it was a notorious fact that wealthy merchants were among the most generous supporters of Puritanism. The factors resident at their seats of trade occupied a position of considerable trust. As representatives of the owners of goods it was their duty, not to buy and sell, but to supervise transactions and to remit the proceeds of sales. In such a country as the Netherlands, where the struggle between Romanism and Protestantism was being carried on with relentless and bloody bitterness, the British merchants were eager to be represented by men of their own religious persuasion. In view of the defalcations of which factors were frequently guilty and of their temptation to engage in trade on their own account, it was desirable to secure the services of one whose religious convictions would bind him honourably to the terms of his commission. In face of the loyalty to Rome and Spain that induced Roman Catholic factors to play their Protestant creditors false and indulge in misappropriations at the expense of heretical merchants, it was expedient that the latter should appoint commissioners of unimpeachable Protestant principles. In corroboration of these statements we may refer to the experience of the Scottish Staple in the Low Countries, in whose behalf the Convention of Scottish

Burghs decided in June, 1582, that none should be factors, who did not profess the Reformed religion: "Becaus thair is dyveris and sindry merchantis of this realme greitumlie hurtt, and utheris alluterlie wrakkit and hereit, be the playing of bankeroutt of sundry factouris within the contrie of Flanderis, Thairfoir it is statute and ordanit that at na tyme heirefter na maner of persoun be admitted, sufferitt, or permitted to use or exerce the office of factory in the pairtis of Flanderis, ather in Zeland, Holland, or Brabant, be the Conservatour bot sic as ar professouris of the trew religioun of Jesus Christ."[1] Cartwright was a man of ability, distinction and piety, whose well-known and resolute championship of English Puritanism would readily commend him as a suitable and trustworthy agent. Besides, the amenities of the office would help to ameliorate the lot of one, whose exile would be viewed with compassion by many of the merchants, who had espoused the very principles for which Cartwright was suffering. It is also probable that William Davison, Elizabeth's ambassador in the Low Countries, who was one of Cartwright's influential well-wishers, helped to secure the appointment for the Puritan.

The details of Davison's life till 1576 are peculiarly meagre. His biographer, Harris Nicolas, has to confess that nothing is known of his ancestry or the time and place of his birth, but suggests that he was of Scottish extraction[2]. His marriage with Catherine Spelman of Norfolk connected him with Burghley, Leicester, Cheke and the Byngs of Wrotham[3]. Elizabeth's dishonourable treatment of him as Secretary of State in connection with the procurement of the death warrant of Mary, Queen of Scots, and the sufferings he endured as Elizabeth's scapegoat have singled him out as the cynosure of the just and the pitiful. Like his friend and fellow diplomat, Henry Killigrew, whom Bannatyne called "a good and godly Protestant"[4], Davison was sympathetically interested in the growth of the Reformed religion. In the spring of 1576 he was sent by Elizabeth on a special mission to the Netherlands

[1] D. & G. p. 392.
[2] *Life of William Davison* (1823), p. 212.
[3] *ibid.* p. 4.
[4] *Knox*, VI, p. 633.

and early in August, 1577, he proceeded to the same country in the rôle of English ambassador.

Davison's interest in Puritanism soon revealed itself in connection with the Church of the English Merchant Adventurers at Antwerp. In October, 1577[1], the merchants gave expression to their urgent desire for a chaplain to resume services at the English House, their headquarters in Antwerp. Davison broached the subject to Laurence Tomson, Walsingham's Puritan secretary, through a messenger, John Furrier. Writing from Hampton Court, on the 15th of December, 1577[2], Tomson acknowledges receipt of Davison's request to provide some honest, godly and learned man to be minister of the English family and company in Antwerp, heartily favours the proposal and commends the ambassador's interest in the religious welfare of his "little commonwealth of Israel." William Charke, who had been approached by the merchants, had already consulted Tomson and the latter now advises Davison to write to Charke and promises to second the effort to persuade him to accept the post, but, failing Charke, he intimates that he has in mind a Scotsman of the same name as the ambassador. This Scottish preacher was evidently John Davidson, an alumnus of St Andrews, now living in exile from his native land. He matriculated in Basel the year before Cartwright; in October, 1579, he was dealt with by the English Privy Council for uttering "certen lewde and disordered speches to her Majesties discontentacion"[3]; he afterwards became noted for his opposition to Bancroft.

Fully three weeks later, 9 January, 1577–8[4], Tomson again writes from Hampton Court to Davison and reports the progress of his negotiations for a chaplain. "I have," he says, "since your last letter broke with Mr Charke in ye matter, whome I finde in yt good minde to be bestowed amongest yow for ye enlarginge of Christs Kingdome, as I hoped for and yow greatly desired: if yow can procure amonge ye companie of our nation there theire good likinge, and yow and

[1] *Cal. S.P. For.* 1577–8, No. 394.
[2] *S.P. Eliz. Holl. and Fland.* IV, No. 38.
[3] *Acts P.C.* XI, p. 289.
[4] *S.P. Dom. Eliz. Add.* XXIII, No. 3. Calendared as 1572–3.

they please to signifie ye same unto him by a letter signed with your and their handes testifyinge the great desire they have to be instructed in the matters of God, and to yt ende have made choice of him, as of whome they conceive so wel for many good respects, as they do not better of any, I thinke he wil make himself readie to repayre over to yow and them in such sort and order, as yow shall finde and appoint for him. To which purpose they may write to their companie here for order to be taken for his transportation, and yow yourself may deale with such as yow shal best thinke off may further the same, to desire and crave their best assistance and furtherance to so good a purpose. I thinke ther shall not nede any special licence from her Maiestie for his goinge over, wherein notwithstandinge yow may, if yow please in your privat letter, move my Mr, I doubt not but his honor wil give it ye best furtherance he can, both by way of Counsail, and other wyse, if necessitie shal so require." Charke, however, did not receive the appointment. He afterwards became preacher at Lincoln's Inn[1].

The redoubtable Walter Travers had also been approached. On the 8th of January, 1577–8[2], Killigrew sends Davison a letter regarding the charge and encloses one from Travers. "I think," writes Killigrew, "yt wold be hard to procure hem lycens here to goe to that charge and therefore he must com over as one of yours unto your Lordship. When he is there you may conferr with hem etc. but my opynion is that he first be Receaved to Read a letter (i.e. lecture) ther in the Inglysch howse which yow must obtayne at the prynces hand that he may so doe. and seing the lyke permyssion hathe not hetherto bin allowed to our nation there this cuming at your espetiall sewt from the prynce who may desire that suche ordre as is there intended to be kept in seremonis may for examples sake or for avoyding contention in these begynnings be also used by Mr Travers among our nation. I speake thus that in case after he have ben there a whyle setled any of ours shold myslyk that kind of ordre and compleyne. yt might serve for aunswer to our Counsell that you were glad

[1] St. *Ann.* v, p. 79.

[2] *S.P. Dom. Eliz. Add.* xxv, No. 68.

first to obtayne to have one to Read to our nation the word of God in our owne tong which before was never yelded unto there and so thought not best to urge them with myche formalytye or many particulars which yf you wold desire all our seremonius ordres must neads have byn don and consequently doubt of the sequell. you se how I am occupyed about a nedlesse matter unto you. I have spoken with Mr secretary Walsingham and doe perceave by hem that hardly wyll any Lycens be obtayned for any suche man as Mr Travers is to goe to that service, therefore I suppose he must first be gotten into possession by suche or som lyke mean as I have before descrybed. now I leave the Reast to your selfe and till I may heare agayne from you assuring you that I shall doe my best to content your desire in this matter."

It is evident that Davison and his friends were anxious to establish in Antwerp an English Church on Reformed lines, and that in order to secure the appointment of such a pronounced Presbyterian as Travers it was necessary, as Killigrew pointed out, for them to indulge in finesse. That Killigrew was hand in glove with the Puritan Presbyterians in connection with the Antwerp venture is clear. In a communication to Davison written on the 22nd of February, 1577–8[1], he shows that John Field, the organising secretary of the Presbyterian enthusiasts, was being consulted in the matter and proclaims the bent of his own mind as being at one with the aims of "suche as by mallice are called by the nic name of puritaynes." Largely through his mediation and generosity the arrangements for the election of Travers were successfully completed. In March Killigrew announces to Davison[2] that the acceptance of the appointment depends now upon the terms of the letter expected by Travers from the ambassador. "I did looke," he says[3], "to have Receaved an aunswer from you to Mr Travers lettres and so did he also, which I pray you to sende with all speed convenient. for the marchants lettres doe Reffer all the matter to your lordship and he is desirous to have your awne lettre. in this meane tyme he is gon into the Contry to take leave of his

[1] *ibid.* xxv, No. 74. [2] *ibid.* xxv, Nos. 78, 79. [3] *ibid.* xxv, No. 79.

mother and other frynds. You must in your lettre be ernest with hem and inlarge the good that may follow of his travayle there. I think vearyly yf you wright your selfe he wyll com and for the maner of his cumming over yt must be undre your name for other wyse there wyll no passport be gotten for hem. and for the charges of his iornay yt wold lykwyse be considered I have promysed to fornysh hem with so myche money as shall serve his turne thether. yf any of your men be here agaynst the 15 or xxth of this next yt wold doe well for his better cumming thether." "I looke now dayly for Mr Travers," Killigrew reports to Davison on the 12th of April, 1578[1], "and yf he com in tyme I wyll send hem over with your servant now here. I kepe your lettre tell his Retorne from his mother." Towards the end of the month Travers arrived in Antwerp. He brought with him a letter of commendation from Thomas Randolph, another Puritan diplomat, who had recently returned from Scotland. Randolph had an intimate knowledge of Scottish Presbyterianism. He knew Knox and other Scottish reformers personally. He had cherished the ideal of a united Protestant Church in England and Scotland. He has recorded his impressions of the "great decencie and verie good order" of the Scottish communion service. During his residence in Scotland he was greatly influenced by the power and eloquence of the Presbyterian preachers[2]. Now in his letter to Davison (23 April, 1578, from London[3]) he extols the ambassador's godly purpose in providing such an excellent minister as Travers for the Antwerp Church and laments that such preachers as he are forced to seek suitable employment abroad when the need of them at home is so clamant. He promises every assistance to Davison and his new pastor.

Some of the State Papers written after the arrival of Travers in the Low Countries make mention of him, *e.g.* Killigrew to Davison, 23 Aug. 1578[4], and 1 Nov. 1578[5]. A few days after Travers left England reference is made to him by

[1] *S.P. Dom. Eliz. Add.* xxv, No. 86.
[2] *Knox*, vi, pp. 110, 116, 119, 122, 129, etc.
[3] *S.P. Eliz. Holland and Fland.* vi, No. 29.
[4] not 1577 as in *Cal.*
[5] *S.P. For. Eliz.*

Cartwright's brother-in-law, John Stubbe, in a letter to Davison on 30 April, 1578, from London[1], which shows not only that Stubbe is cognisant of Travers's departure to Antwerp, but also that he, weaving pious phrases into the subject matter of his epistle, is writing as a Puritan to a Puritan. The leading patrons of Puritanism were evidently known to one another.

It is obvious that Davison and his friends were working for the establishment of a Presbyterian Puritan Church among the Antwerp merchants. John Brown[2] says that the Church was formed by the English "and Scottish Merchant Adventurers," but we have not met with any warrant for the introduction of the Scots. Walsingham was already acquainted with the ambassador's designs, but when the merchants in London brought the matter to his notice he thought good to advise a policy of caution. Writing on the 8th of May, 1578, to Davison[3], he says that the London merchants have told him of the intended alteration of the exercise of common prayer in the English House at Antwerp, contrary or at least not agreeable to the received order of the Church of England. They have informed him that Davison is the principal "furtherer" of the proposed change. He points out that, should the Queen come to hear of it, the royal displeasure would be meted out to the company of adventurers for yielding to such an innovation and to Davison for giving it his support. Accordingly, Walsingham cannot but advise the ambassador to take no further step in the matter and to suppress the new order, before he comes over, if it has been established. He acknowledges that personally he does not mislike the scheme, but he is desirous that it should be approved by public authority. Travers already knows his opinion. Walsingham fears that the cause of further reformation will suffer if its adherents do not walk warily. He thinks that policy carries more weight than zeal in such times and that patience and prayer will advance their aims better than the bold proceedings intended at Antwerp.

[1] *S.P. Dom. Eliz. Add.* xxv, No. 91. [2] *Pilgrim Fathers* (1895), p. 56.
[3] *S.P. Eliz. Holl. and Fland.* vi, No. 54.

The advice of the Secretary of State came too late. The Thursday on which he wrote his words of grave caution was the day of Travers's Presbyterian ordination in Antwerp. The 14th of May is generally given as the date of this important event[1], but that is due to a misreading of the Presbyterial certificate signed on the Wednesday after Travers had been ordained and received by the whole congregation. This certificate faithfully transcribed by Fuller[2] from the original furnishes us with the exact date of the foundation of the English Presbyterian Church in Antwerp, viz., the 8th of May, 1578, if we reckon the beginning of the new organisation as synchronous with the ordination of Travers, or the 12th of May, if we judge by the unanimous election of the new minister on the part of the congregation.

Travers's Presbyterian ordination became a notable bone of contention at a later period, when he became the rival of the illustrious Hooker for the Mastership of the Temple. The hue and cry raised regarding the validity or irregularity of the orders of the Presbyterian Dean of Durham, William Whittingham, and cut short by the Dean's death in June, 1579, became clamant again, and Travers was obliged to vindicate his status as a Presbyterian minister against the growing party in the Church of England, who resented the occupation of positions of trust in their Church by ministers not ordained by diocesan Bishops[3]. In a list of reasons set forth by Travers in 1586 against his reordination[4] he points out that the question at issue was not raised before Whittingham's case and that in spite of all objections the Dean of Durham continued in his ministry till his death. Whitgift, whose annotations accompany the list, replies that if Whittingham had lived he would have been deprived and denies that there is a parallel between the two cases, Whittingham having been ordained in the time of persecution, whereas Travers, refusing to be ordained at home, went abroad in

[1] *D.N.B.* art. "Travers"; Neal I, p. 189.

[2] *C.H.* bk IX, *sub anno* 1591.

[3] *Troubles at Frankfort*, ed. Arber (1908), pp. 14 ff.; St. *Ann.* IV, p. 167; Soames, p. 230; *v. infra* pp. 253–4.

[4] *Lansd. MSS.* L, No. 80; St. *Whit.* III, pp. 182 ff.

the time of peace, thereby condemning the orders of the Church of England. Travers holds that the universal practice of Christendom proves that the ministers lawfully made in any true Church ought to be acknowledged as such in any other. Whitgift, on the other hand, excepts those Churches that allow of Presbytery and practise it and says: "As wel may Mr Cartwright and his adherents now make Ministers at Warwick, to serve in this Church of England, as he and Villiers might have don at Antwerp." Travers affirms that many Scotsmen and others, made ministers abroad, have been allowed to execute their ministry in the Church of England and do so still. Whitgift knows none such but says that their case would be different from his. Travers also says that his ordination was recognised by Archbishop Grindal, who was content that he should preach in England and that the Bishop of London made no objection to his preaching at the Temple during a space of nearly six years[1].

Heylyn, beginning with the unwarranted premises that Cartwright had recently come from Guernsey to Antwerp, where he was chosen preacher to the English merchants, continues the confusion of his narrative[2]: "The news whereof brings Travers to him; who receives Ordination (if I may so call it) by the Presbytery of that City, and thereupon is made his Partner in that charge." The fact is that Travers was made the sole and the first Presbyterian minister of the Church in question. Heylyn further asserts[3] that the fashion now set in among many of the Puritans of going to the Low Countries to be ordained according to the Presbyterian form: "Some of which following the example of Cartwright himself, renounced the Orders which they had from the hands of the Bishops, and took a new Vocation from these Presbyters; as Fennor (*sic*), Arton (*sic*), etc., and others there admitted to the rank of Ministers, which never were ordained in England; as Hart, Guisin, etc., not to say anything of such

[1] *v. Lansd. MSS.* XL, No. 90, Travers to Burghley, his reasons why, having been ordained abroad, he ought not to be re-ordained, 1586; Travers's supplication to the Council is given in Hooker's *Works*, ed. Hanbury (1830), III, pp. 335–52.

[2] *A.R.* lib. VII, § 23.

[3] *ibid.*

as were elected to be Elders or Deacons in those Foreign Consistories, that they might serve the Churches in the same capacity at their coming home." Brook[1] faithfully repudiates the statement concerning Cartwright's renunciation of his orders and also the conjecture[2] that he assisted at the ordination of Travers and forthwith seeks to throw light on the matter by making the unsupported assumption that Cartwright was "pastor to the English congregation at Antwerp at the time of Mr Travers' ordination, who afterward assisted him in the ministry, which might probably give occasion to the misstatements" of such historians as Heylyn and Strype. So far, however, we have found no mention in contemporary documents of Cartwright in connection with the Antwerp Church and we have come across no trace of his participation in its establishment on Puritan lines. Apparently he was still the merchants' factor at Middelburg.

The erroneous opinion, supported by Heylyn, Neal, Brook, etc., that Travers came to Antwerp to assist Cartwright in the ministry there has been perpetuated even to this day[3]. The reverse is nearer the truth, for as we shall see Cartwright soon appears in Antwerp first as Travers's *locum tenens* and ultimately as his permanent successor. As to the frequently made allegation that Cartwright received Presbyterian ordination in the Low Countries we have his own testimony in June, 1591, before the court of the Star Chamber, that since his first ordination and calling by an English archbishop he had not been called to the function of the ministry by any ministers[4]. In a letter to Lord Gray, 15 Jan. 1591–2[5], he again denies that he repudiated his Anglican ordination and points out that he adhered to it "against some excepting unto it as no ministery."

The only known item of information regarding Cartwright in 1578 refers to his marriage. Being now placed in circumstances that justified him in taking unto himself a wife, he chose as helpmate Alice, the sister of one of the staunchest

[1] *Mem.* p. 216. [2] St. *Whit.* I, p. 477.

[3] Heron, p. 134; *v.* Mrs W. W. D. Campbell in *Journal of Presb. Hist. Soc. of Eng.* II, No. 3, p. 131.

[4] *v. infra* p. 334. [5] App. XXXI.

and most outspoken Puritans, John Stubbe. The marriage seems to have taken place about the beginning of 1578, not in 1577 as Brook says[1]. We learn the news from a letter written by Stubbe from Buxton on the 17th of March, 1577–8, to his old friend, Michael Hicks, at Lincoln's Inn. Stubbe, one of Cartwright's contemporaries at Cambridge, and an intimate of Hicks, Cartwright's benefactor, was a lawyer of considerable means[2]. A man of personal piety and an upholder of Puritan principles, he was a warm admirer of Cartwright, as his letter to Hicks indicates. "I am glad," he writes[3], "that I shall once be out of youre debt for a letter, and yet I shold not have beene soarie to have ought you yet an other letter, but yt may be your business are greater then in times past. I wishe then for your advancement and good perhappes yt is but your earnest studies, and yet since the most earnest studie is the deepest otiun, me thinkes you shold find som leisure for to speake to soe old a frend. We have noe newes heere but that Mr Cartwright hath maried my sister which many speake. And if with you also yt be publykely knowen, and any mislyke myne act in providing soe for my sister, tell him on my behalf that I contented me self with such an housband for hir, whose lyvelihood was learnyng, who shold endow his wyf with wisedom and who might leave to his children the rich porcion of Godliness by Christian carefull education. and if this apologie will not defend me, let him not mervail if I esteemyng these thinges as precious stones, while he rather chuseth the worldlie commended thinges, richess favour etc, which I deeme less worth then a barlie corne. Commend me hartely to your mother (now Mrs Anthony Penn), to Mr Blythe (Hicks's tutor in Cambridge) when you see him and desyre him to defend me when he seeth cause. Commend me to our good maisters of the Barre and felowship of Lincolnes Inne, Mr Spenser Mr Branthut and whoe you will ells. ffarewell as me self. The Lord Jesus ever keepe you his. at Buxton. 17 Marcij, 1577[–8]. By your own loving frend John Stubbe."

[1] *Mem.* p. 219.
[2] *v. infra* p. 306.
[3] *Lansd. MSS.* xxv, No. 66, f. 135.

Not long after Travers's settlement in Antwerp Lord Cobham and Sir Francis Walsingham came to the Low Countries to make a bid for the restoration of peace. Rumours of their coming reached Davison long before their arrival. The puritanical Killigrew, who frequently corresponded with him and often sent compliments to Villiers and Travers through him, kept the ambassador informed as to the prospects of the special mission[1]. On the 28th of June, 1578, Cobham and Walsingham with their suite arrived in Antwerp, which was their headquarters for the next three months. During this period they were attended by Laurence Tomson, and for part of it by Henry Killigrew[2]. Walsingham, Davison, Killigrew and Tomson were all imbued with strong Reformed principles and their presence was bound to strengthen the position of the Church of Travers. It is also likely that Cartwright, whose residence was not far from Antwerp, would come into touch with these pillars of Protestantism at this time.

After the departure of the special mission (end of Sept. 1578) the Governor of the Merchant Adventurers sought to stay the course which the Antwerp Church was taking under Travers's direction. He, Nicholas Loddington, even put Travers to silence for his lack of conformity to the usages of the Church of England. This action of the Governor brought the Puritan forces of Walsingham, Tomson and Davison into the field against him. Walsingham intimates to Davison on 11 Oct. 1578 that he has written to Loddington and encloses a copy of his letter[3]. Tomson, expatiating more freely than his master on the subject, points out in a letter to Davison on 11 Oct. 1578, that Cobham and Walsingham made no alteration in the form of the "exercise" when they attended it, advises the ambassador to use his authority in behalf of

[1] *S.P. Dom. Eliz. Add.* xxv, Nos. 98, 99. Killigrew was also in direct communication with Travers in whose work he was deeply interested: "I receaved a lettre from Mr Travers which I shall aunswer at more leysure being glad of his good aryvyall there" (*ibid.* xxv, No. 99), "I desire to know where monsieur de Plessis is and how monsieur de Vylliers and his familie doe, and how Mr Travers dothe there, no doubt among many traversis no new thing to the chylderne of god" (*ibid.* xxv, No. 117).

[2] *Cal. S.P. For. Eliz.* 1578–9, Nos. 38, 48, 58, 59, 125; *v. Cotton MSS. Galba, C,* VI.

[3] *S.P. Eliz. Holl. and Fland.* IX, No. 59.

the *status quo*, and reminds him of the talk which they with Killigrew had had in the garden in Antwerp about the affairs of the Church[1]. Meanwhile the Governor should be humoured and a special request should be made to the States through Prince William of Orange to confirm the present Reformed character of the Church. On the 19th of October Davison writes to Walsingham informing him that the Governor had arbitrarily changed the venue of the services from the common court house to a private room allotted to the ambassador and that on the Sunday after Walsingham's departure he had interrupted the service because the Book of Common Prayer was not being used and had read that Book himself to carry on the service[2]. To avoid like interruption again Travers intimated after the sermon that those who desired to hear the preaching should resort to Davison's lodging. Loddington shut the doors of the place where the services were wont to be held and tried to prohibit them altogether. Davison then charged the Governor with his misdemeanours only to be answered with insolence. But after hearing from Walsingham Loddington calmed down and offered any room in the English House. The Governor, however, is going to England next week and Davison fears that he will play some underhand part. Writing to Loddington on the 25th of October Walsingham acknowledges receipt of the Governor's letter of the 19th of that month[3]. He is glad to hear that the difference between Loddington and Travers has been compounded. Averring that he does not mislike the former's anxiety to have the Prayer Book used, Walsingham assures him that the latter is also an upholder of the same. Travers had testified, when Walsingham was in Antwerp, his willingness to show himself conformable to the Book and in other disputable matters, and accordingly it was thought fit that he should continue the order into which he had entered. While commending Loddington's zealous loyalty to the established religion Walsingham promises that Davison will see to it that the Church is carried on as it ought to be. The next day,

[1] *S.P. Eliz. Holl. and Fland.* IX, No. 60. [2] *ibid.* IX, No. 67.
[3] *ibid.* IX, No. 81.

26 Oct. 1578, Walsingham advises Davison and his minister to act warily lest Loddington misreport their doings[1]. The Book of Common Prayer should be used. Travers should make some show of conformity to it and arrange that the person who was wont to read the lessons should begin with the Confession and read some Psalms till the time of the full assembly and the beginning of the sermon. Walsingham had talked with Travers and had found him willing to do this. Now the Secretary intimates that he has commissioned his servant, Tomson, to write at length to Travers about the whole matter. On the 5th of November Davison informs Walsingham that his last letter to the Governor came too late as Loddington departed for England "last week," but reports that Walsingham's "well-handling" of their adversary produced satisfactory results and that Travers goes peaceably forward in his good work[2].

In spite of opposition and the constant danger of exposure to the Queen's indignation the Antwerp Church continued to retain its Presbyterian character. On the 12th of November, 1578, we find Travers writing to Davison, then at Bruges, suggesting that a deacon should be elected to look after the poor[3] and under the date 21 May, 1579, the following entry appears in the extant extracts taken from the Church register: "Upon Mr Davisons occasion to depart for England were chosen more Elders of the Church, viz., Hugh Ratcliffe, George Gilpin, Leonard Elliott, Nicholas Stockbridge and Thomas Hill." The extracts referred to are contained in the Boswell Papers in the British Museum[4] and are entitled "Extracts out of ye Registre book of ye English Congregacion at Antwerpe Ao Xti 1579.80.81.82." They are misread by Burrage when he states[5] that they place the appointment of Travers to the ministry of the Antwerp Church in 1579. That, as we have seen, belongs to the previous year. The departure of Davison to which allusion is made, took place before the end of May, 1579[6]. In the same month, probably in order to

[1] *S.P. Eliz. Holl. and Fland.* IX, No. 82. [2] *ibid.* X, No. 9.
[3] *ibid.* X, No. 26. [4] *Add. MSS.* 6394, ff. 113–4.
[5] *E.E.D.* I, p. 137. [6] *Cal. S.P. For. Eliz.* 1578–9, Nos. 648, 669, etc.

evade the interference of officials of the company of Adventurers, who were hostile to any appearance of Presbyterian nonconformity, the services were transferred by leave of Archduke Matthias from the English House to a place built by the Genoese near the Church of St Francis[1]. Here Travers continued to minister till July, 1580, when, without resigning his pastorate, he returned to England for an indefinite period. He bore with him a letter from Villiers, who testified to Davison that Travers had so acquitted himself in his office that he was in good odour both with the English and the Netherlanders[2]. Villiers earnestly hoped that Travers would not long remain away from his charge.

The work of the Antwerp Church was carried on during Travers's absence by a *locum tenens*, who was none other than Thomas Cartwright. If there was great danger of rousing the Queen's displeasure because of the Presbyterian character of the Church and the selection of the "neck" of the Puritan movement as its minister, there would be cause for still greater indignation on her part if it became known to her that the "head" of the Puritans occupied the post. Cartwright's brother-in-law, Stubbe, had but recently inflamed Elizabeth's anger against the set to which they both belonged by the pamphlet *The Discoverie of a Gaping Gulph*, in which Stubbe, intolerant of Roman Catholicism, bitterly inveighed against the proposed marriage of the Queen with the Duke of Anjou. The book was published in August, 1579, and on the 3rd of November Stubbe and his bookseller Page were punished by having their right hands struck off. It is recorded that Stubbe, immediately after he had lost his right hand, waved his hat with his left and cried "God save the Queen." He afterwards dubbed himself Scaeva[3]. Strype[4] suggests that Cartwright was asked his opinion of the intended marriage and that he wrote a short answer decidedly in the negative to the question: "Whether it be lawful for a protestant to marry with a papist?" The answer given by Strype is in

[1] *Extracts*, f. 114.
[2] 2 July, 1580. *Cal. S.P. For. Eliz.* 1579–80, No. 349.
[3] Froude, c. XXVI; Soames, p. 236, etc.
[4] *Ann.* IV, p. 469.

harmony with Cartwright's known views, but we cannot say whether it was actually written by him. Heylyn[1] assumes, without authority, that Cartwright was in all likelihood privy to the production of the anti-Romanist libel of Stubbe, who is stated with Heylynian perversity to have married one of the sisters of Cartwright! Nevertheless there was sufficient cause for the fear, such as was expressed by Villiers[2] that Stubbe's book would involve others in trouble, and doubtless Elizabeth's adverse opinion of Cartwright would only be exacerbated by the work of his brother-in-law. We are not surprised, therefore, that the new Governor of the Merchant Adventurers, Christopher Hoddesdon, was exceedingly uneasy when he found Cartwright conducting services in the Antwerp Church in 1580. About the end of the year he wrote to Burghley for advice[3]. The merchants had pleaded with Travers to return or send a suitable substitute. Travers, however, had ultimately decided to relinquish his post altogether and the ministers, who had been approached, had refused to accept it as long as Cartwright held it. Hoddesdon had tried to persuade Cartwright to retire, but in vain. Besides, the Puritan leader was held in high esteem in Antwerp. Hoddesdon was accordingly at a loss to know what to do. He did not wish to incur the Queen's displeasure by countenancing Cartwright and at the same time he was unwilling to disturb the Antwerp Church by an attempt to remove him from the ministry there. To escape from the dilemma he seriously contemplated resignation from his governorship. His letter to Burghley runs as follows: "Right honorable my very good Lorde Having contrary to my expectation founde Mr Cartwrite at my coming over in the ministery of our church here, and fearing such displeasure as might growe both to my self and the company by retayning one against whom I doubted her Maiestie to be offended I endevored by all meanes so to remedie the danger herof, as

[1] *A.R.* lib. VI, § 27.

[2] *S.P. For. Eliz.* 17 Oct., 20 Nov., 28 Nov., 1579.

[3] Dec. 1580; *S.P. Eliz. Holl. and Fland.* XIII, No. 90. Cf. his letter to Walsingham, evidently written about the same time, 24 Dec., 1580; *ibid.* XIII, No. 85.

our church might neverthelesse be sufficiently provided for. And therupon after conference with the rest of our company about this mater it was thought convenient to write to Mr Travis beinge then in Englande and lately before elected for our preacher, that either he should repaire with expedition to his charge here, or else send hether some fitt man to supply the roome. Wherupon he procured one Smith to come over unto us who being sundrey tymes requested by the company to take the function upon him refused notwithstanding (I knowe not for what cause) to do the same. So that we were enforced the second tyme to write very earnestly for Mr Travis his retourne with expresse order sett downe in our generall courte, that if he came not hether nowe by Christmas at the furthest, then his stipende which we allowed him should forthwith surcease, thincking by this meanes to have hastened him forwarde: But he being resolved to remayne still in Englande hath made full answere, that he can by no meanes repaire again unto us. I have in like sorte dealt by lettres with divers other learned men about their coming over, but none will medle with the place so longe as Mr Cartwrite continueth in the same; for which cause I moved him to intermitt and abstaine from preaching any more in our church, considering he was neither chosen nor entertained by our company: wherunto he alledged that forasmuch as he receyved no allowance at our handes we had the lesse to do to restraine him from preaching, and that he thought our church here was as free for him in that respect as for any other minister, which his allegation I finde to be of such force that as the tyme and condition of things presently standeth I can not greatly impugne it, especially for that he is very well thought of by the preachers and learned of this towne." We learn from the *Extracts out of ye Registre book*[1] the date of Travers's letter of resignation and the fact that in this epistle he recommended Cartwright as his successor: "A letter was receaved from Mr Travers excusing his not returning out of England and commending Mr Cartwright to be Minister here in his place, etc. dated 17 Decem" (1580).

[1] f. 113 *verso*.

From the supplication of Travers to the Council[1] we gather further particulars regarding the duties and the remuneration of the minister of the Antwerp Church: "But my cause is yet more easy, who reaped no benefit of my Ministry by Law, receiving only a benevolence and Voluntary Contribution; and the Ministry I dealt with being Preaching only, which every Deacon here may do being licensed."

On the 25th of February, 1580–1, Governor Hoddesdon again reviews the situation in a letter to Walsingham[2]. "Right honorable," he writes from Antwerp, "Upon the warning which was geven me secretly in England, I declared unto the Company at my arrivall here, what danger (as I thought) might ensue by enterteyning Mr Cartwrite, which mater being opened to them in a generall Courte they resolved for preventing the worst, to write very earnestly for Mr Travis his repayre, but understanding his determination to continue still in Englande, they immediatly by their seconde lettres requested his helpe in the provision of some other. Wheruppon he sent hether such a one to supplie his place, as would neither preach nor take the ministery upon him. through which meanes divers of the Assistents seing the Company deluded in this sorte have since their retourne into Englande dealt with sundrey learned men about their coming hether, but none will medle with the charge save onely one Keltrige, whom by reason of his youth, I iudge not so fitt as is requisite for this place, and therfore have dispatched away Thomas Longston to make choise of an other, humbly beseching your honor to graunte him your favorable advise for his better direction in this behalf. And so I cease presently to be further troublesome, praying thalmightie to blesse your honorable estate with longe continuance of helth and daily encrease of all prosperous successe." All negotiations apparently broke down and Cartwright carried on his ministry in the English Church in Antwerp until the merchants removed to Middelburg and continued to be their minister in the latter place till the spring of 1585. "The space of five years," says

[1] Hooker's *Works*, ed. Hanbury, III, p. 341.
[2] *S.P. Eliz. Holl. and Fland.* XIV, No. 33.

Cartwright[1], "I preached at Antwerpe and Middelborough," and in a letter to Burghley[2] he lays weight upon the fact that he spent five years of his exile as minister of a Church, which be it noted represented and was a part of the Church of England abroad: *Quinque iam annos peregre a patria agens, eos prope omnes in ecclesiae Anglicanae, quae in transmarinis partibus haeret, ministerio consumsi.* Although he had his enemies in Antwerp he was also surrounded by a band of enthusiastic admirers, one of whom, Cholmeley, a correspondent of Field and evidently a wholehearted disciplinarian, compared his relationship to Cartwright with that of the first disciples to the Lord. *Sicut*, wrote Cholmeley to Field from Antwerp in 1582[3], *discipuli olim presto habuerunt ipsum Dominum: ita magistrum Cartwrightum dominum meum habeo presentem.*

The compiler of the *Extracts*, which cease with the year 1582, states[4] that "The Cong^ion^ of Merchants Adventu^rs^: removed from Antwerpe to Middelborough Ao Dni 1582 or in the beginning of 1583. Mr Th. Cartwright being their Minister having succeeded Mr Travers." With the aid of certain State Papers we are able to determine the date of the transference of the merchants' headquarters as October, 1582. In August and September they occasionally declared their purpose to remove to Zealand because they mistrusted their goods and persons in Antwerp, now rendered unsafe and unprofitable as a trading centre by the Spanish campaign[5]. The citizens of Antwerp were as loath to part with the merchants as those of Middelburg were eager to welcome them[6]. The former moved the Duke of Anjou to intercede with Elizabeth for the retention of the English traders in Antwerp. The Duke attributed the proposed change to some Spanish inducement[7]. His petition, however, was unavailing and by the middle of October the merchants had agreed with the town of Middelburg for the establishment of their seat

[1] *Apol.* 1596, sig. C 2 *verso*.
[2] App. XV.
[3] Bancroft, *Survay*, p. 377.
[4] f. 113.
[5] *Cecil MSS. Hist. MSS. Comm.* Pt XIII, Add. p. 204; *Cal. S.P. For. Eliz.* 1582, Nos. 302, 303, 338, 388.
[6] *ibid.* Nos. 361, 377.
[7] *S.P. Eliz. Holl. and Fland.* XVII, No. 45.

of trade in that place and before the end of the month most of them had already taken up residence there[1]. Assuming that Cartwright left for Middelburg about the same time as the merchants we are forced to break with tradition as to the length of his Antwerp ministry and limit it to a period of two years at the most, the terminal dates being July, 1580, and October, 1582.

When Cartwright was in the Low Countries Edmund Spenser published his *Shepheardes Calender* (1579–80) and in his July eclogue introduced as the opponent of the English Bishops represented by Morrell (Aylmer) a Puritan minister under the name of Thomalin. We agree with J. J. Higginson[2] that the latter was a prominent Puritan, whose Christian name was Thomas, and we are inclined to identify him with Cartwright. Higginson prefers Wilcocks because he came into conflict with Aylmer in 1577, whereas Cartwright did not suffer at Aylmer's hands till 1585 and was abroad when the *Calender* was written, but in our opinion it is not necessary to assume that Thomalin had been actually persecuted by Morrell and Cartwright's absence from England is no sufficient reason for setting him aside. Without question Cartwright, although in exile, was generally regarded as the most representative Puritan of the time and particularly so by a Cambridge man like Spenser. His latest reply to Whitgift (1577) had recently come to England and kept him in the forefront as the outstanding opponent of the Bishops. The arguments of Thomalin—his contrast of the pure Apostolic Church with the present corrupt Episcopate, his denunciation of the idleness, wealth, lordship, etc., of the Bishops—are all reflected in Cartwright's works. Spenser was a student at Cambridge when Cartwright was Professor there and would be intimately acquainted with the controversy carried on by Cartwright and the sufferings he endured for his advocacy of Puritan ideals. It appears indeed that Spenser, probably under Cartwright's influence, warmly sympathised

[1] *S.P. Eliz. Holl. and Fland.* XVII, Nos. 49, 65; *S.P. Eliz. Ger. Emp.* I, No. 42.

[2] *Spenser's Shepherd's Calender in Relation to Contemporary Affairs* (1912), p. 199.

with the aims of Puritanism and gave expression to his own criticism of ecclesiastical abuses through such characters as Piers and Thomalin[1]. Gabriel Harvey, knowing Spenser's interest in the controversy that disturbed the peace of his old University for so long, wrote to him on the 7th of April, 1580, about the state of affairs in Cambridge, saying "No more adoe aboute Cappes and Surplesses: Maister Cartwright nighe forgotten."[2] It is also of peculiar interest that the printer of the first edition of the *Calender* was Hugh Singleton, who, a few months before, had printed the libellous *Gaping Gulph* of Cartwright's brother-in-law, John Stubbe. Higginson[3], unable to fit Thomalin of the March eclogue into his Wilcocks hypothesis, is disinclined to identify him with any historical personage and is content to observe that Spenser here alludes to some contemporary love-affair. The comment of E. K. on this eclogue is: "In the person of Thomalin is meant some secrete freend, who scorned Love and his knights so long, till at length him selfe was entangled, and unawares wounded etc."[4] This allusion suits our suggestion that Thomalin is Cartwright, for the latter married Alice, the sister of Stubbe, shortly before the 17th of March, 1577–8, when he was about forty-two years of age.

An important and hitherto unknown letter of Cartwright's apparently belongs to this period[5]. It is addressed from Antwerp to William Davison on the 2nd of July (1580?)[6]. The letter is significant. It shows that Puritan exiles were frequently maintained by their wealthy patrons, that Davison was one of these benefactors, to whom Cartwright himself was personally obliged, and that Davison was sincerely interested in the Puritan movement. Cartwright extenuates his dependence upon others on the ground that he is brought by the Lord's cause to some more need than otherwise he should

[1] *v.* Winstanley on "Spenser and Puritanism" in *Mod. Lang. Quarterly*, III, 1900.

[2] *Works* of G. Harvey, ed. A. B. Grosart (Huth Library, 1884), I, p. 71.

[3] *op. cit.* p. 198. [4] *ibid.* p. 197. [5] App. XIII.

[6] The endorsement which gives the year as "86" is evidently not contemporary and as, so far as we know, Cartwright was not in Antwerp in 1586 it seems to date the document four to six years too late.

have been, "keeping therein company with th'appostle and ye lord hymself, which were mainteined at others charges." All he has been able to give his patrons, Davison among others, in return for their weighty gold is "the light wares of paper and yncke." He knows that his letters are highly esteemed: "my letters (hou light soever) are, by acceptation and an overweening of me, laid in the balance with the gould yt self." He himself does not underrate the value of his own writings, but he thinks that they can be of little importance to Davison. He has left order with his wife, who apparently is not now residing with him in Antwerp, "that she should not be lighthanded in receiving that alwayes that might be offered." "Ones she is come over with a gilt cup and cover to yt," for which Cartwright offers thanks. He regrets that he never met Davison's wife. As the *Extracts*[1] state that divers children of Davison and of Matthias, Governor in Antwerp, were christened in the English Church there, we infer that Cartwright did not officiate at the baptisms and was then in Middelburg.

When in Antwerp Cartwright received two calls to University Chairs, one in Leyden and the other in St Andrews. The invitation to Leyden has escaped the notice of students of Puritanism, although it has long been known that Cartwright was an intimate friend of some of the Leyden Professors and that he sojourned in their city for some time. Polyander in his Preface (dated Leyden, 10 Jan. 1617) to Cartwright's *Commentarii...in Proverbia Salomonis* gives a short account of the author, which really constitutes the earliest biography of the Puritan leader. After referring to his pastorate in Antwerp and Middelburg Polyander concludes his interesting *vita* thus: *In hac nostra quoque Academia aliquamdiu cum Theologis nostris agendi causa subsistens, Clariss. V. Iunio & Trelcatio patre familiariter usus est. Postea Angliam repetens, apud Gargesenienses gravissimi ac vigilantissimi Ecclesiastae officio defunctus est. Tandem senio & lucubrationibus confectus, venia prius a Gargeseniensibus impetrata Warnicum* (sic) *reversus est, ut reliquam vitae suae particulam fideli popularium*

[1] f. 113.

suorum institutioni consecraret. Following up this clue to Cartwright's connection with Leyden we have sought to find out the time of his visit to his friends there, but so far we can merely state that it must be placed in the period, 1592–1602, when Junius held his Dutch Professorship. In the course of our search, however, we have made the interesting discovery that Cartwright was offered a chair of Divinity in Leyden in 1580. The *Acta Senatus* of the University contain several allusions to the call. The whole matter is summed up under the date, 16 July, 1580, thus: *Vocatus publice ad professionem Theologiae Thomas Carterwichtus Anglus; respondit ambigue et postea recidit.* There are, however, two letters in the *Acta*[1] which furnish new and important information regarding Cartwright. They are addressed by him to the two men through whom the call was presented to him, namely the curator of the University and the consul of the City of Leyden: *Clarissimis viris et mihi summe observandis Dominis Jano Dousae a Nortwick Lugdunensis Academiae Curatori et Joanni Honts Leidensis civitatis Consuli.* The first letter is dated 10 *Calend. Sextilis*, i.e. Saturday, the 23rd of July, 1580. It was written immediately after Cartwright had received the news of his call. In it he points out that the request for an answer the next day and his engagement to preach then at the English Church do not allow sufficient time for mature deliberation: *Litterae vestrae (clarissimi viri et Domini mihi plurimum observandi)* 10 *Calens Sextilis a prandio redditae sunt, simul et a nuncio vestro insequentis diei hora ad meam responsionem duodecima dicta est. Quod mihi, his praesertim eodem ipso die in Anglicana ecclesia pro concione dicturo: tum ad meum in vos gratiarum actionis officium, tum ad maturiorem de re tota deliberationem parum commode cecidit.* He expresses his warm gratitude for the honour of the invitation and says that he is willing to accept it if the services of a better man cannot be secured. But he cannot at present give an absolute promise: *Quanquam ne hoc quidem pure et praecise polliceri possum.* In the first place, he is bound by

[1] I, p. 96ff. Printed in *Bronnen tot de Geschiedenis der Leidsche Universiteit* (1913–) ed. P. C. Molhuysen.

a prior compact. Having been asked by the senate of the English Church in Antwerp to take the place of their minister, *i.e.* Travers, for about two months, he has promised to do so and as a man of honour he must abide by his word; the Leyden call, however, is urgent and if it is possible for Travers to return earlier than arranged or to send another *locum tenens* from England, Cartwright may yet see his way to accept the call before the end of the two months: *Primum enim cum nihil de hac muneris ad me delatione resciscerem, rogatus ab ecclesiae Anglicanae senatu, ut ministro in Angliam iam profecturo vicariam duos circiter menses operam prestarem: eam in me provinciam suscepi. Ex quo videtis, me solenni promisso, quominus vestrae festinationi respondeam, praepediri. Quamquam si plurimum hoc vestrae scholae interesse sentirem: darem operam ut aut minister citius constituto rediret, aut alium qui suas partes abiret ex Anglia submitteret.* There is another serious consideration. He has heard of the dissension concerning discipline that is troubling the Leyden Church and, as the University and the Church are like the twins of Hippocrates, he fears that the University may become affected. It appears that his real dread in this connection is that as a true Disciplinarian he would be drawn into the fray and that his academic usefulness would suffer, and, although he does not mention the fact, that his hope of being restored to Elizabeth's favour would be utterly blighted: *fructum quem ex ministerio meo sector, perexiguum prospicio, si manum, non prius hac lite sopita, admoverem. Sicut autem contentionis omne genus reformido, ita se tanta re et tam ecclesiae necessaria litem hanc exerceri, me certe presente gravissime ferrem.* He will not haggle about the salary. He merely asks sufficient for the maintenance of himself and his little family and the upkeep of his library: *De Salario in annum solvendo cum vobis tam praestantibus viris non licitabor. Equidem ex schola vestra rem facere non cupio: modo suppetant quibus meam et familiolae vitam honeste tollerare possim et nonnullum in tuenda bibliotheca sumptum facere, satis erit. Ea vero mihi suppeditari non tam mea quam scholae interesse, vestra prudentia novit: cuius ad rationes imprimis pertinere scitis, ut a presentis vitae curis liberrimus sim. Hanc rem igitur vobis qui ista melius novisse potestis, permittam.* Cartwright repeats that if the difficulties mentioned are obviated he is willing to accept the call, but regrets that he has not had time to consult the Antwerp ministers, and in particular his friendly counsellor, Villiers, about the matter: *Atque hijs exceptionibus si vocetis, venio, si iubeatis pareo. Ministros ecclesiae Antwerpiensis et cum primis D Villerium primum scilicet meum ad hanc rem suasorem, libenter si per tempus licuisset consuluissem.*

Cartwright's next letter to the Leyden officials was written on the 1st of August, 1580, 5° *Nonas Sextiles.* He regrets that he cannot yet give them a satisfactory answer. He has laid the matter before the senate of the Antwerp English Church. They are evidently pleased that he should seriously consider the call but not that he should leave them immediately: *Senatus me quidem rogare, ut animum meum ad illam professionem adijcerem: sed an illud e vestigio facerem a me rogatus, authorem se mihi esse non posse respondebat.* He is therefore confirmed in his former opinion that his present duty is to carry out his engagement as *locum tenens*: *Quod responsum ut me in superiori sententia confirmavit: ita ad vicariam operam ad quam fidem meam obstrinxi, accommodatum esse videtur.* A speedy decision has been made more difficult by the fact that Travers has left London and gone to the north of England to arrange some domestic affairs and cannot quickly be communicated with: *Litteris enim acceptis certior factus sum, pastorem, Londino relicto, in Aquilonares Angliae partes erciscundae familiae causa concessisse.* Cartwright shows that he is not responsible for the delay. He has written to London to arrange for Travers's return or the appointment of another minister in his place. He is still willing to go to Leyden, but he now adds as a condition of his acceptance of the Chair the stipulation that he shall be recognised as free to leave it should he be called to a permanent ministerial charge in England. His heart's desire apparently is to serve in the Church in which he has been reared: *Unum illud libenter apposuerim, ut si me Anglicana ecclesia, in qua et natus et educatus sum, ad constans et perpetuum ministerium revocaverit: eam mihi per vos repetere liceat: cum hac cautione, si tempus quo de successore prospiciatur, commodum et opportunum praestitutum fuerit.* That the authorities in Leyden were sincerely anxious to have Cartwright as one of their Professors is further attested by the fact that the Rector of the University himself (J. Lipsius) proceeded to Antwerp and there conferred with the Puritan in person. But the claims of the Antwerp Church were greater than those of the rising Dutch University and the Rector's mission proved in vain: *Antwerpiam Rector ivit, rei suae causa*[1], *Rediit Rector; exposuit se coram Antwerpiae cum Carterwichto egisse; frustra*[2].

Fuller[3] puts Cartwright's call to a position on the staff of St Mary's College, the Divinity Hall of St Andrews University, *sub anno* 1591 and the author of the article on Travers in the *D. N. B.* accepts that year as probable. Paget[4] says in error that "Andrew Melville tried hard to get him to Glasgow," but he is evidently following Mullinger[5], who conveys the impression that Melville used his best efforts to induce Cartwright and Travers to assist him, *ca.* 1574, as Principal at Glasgow[6]. It is certain, however, that the call to the Scottish Professorship belongs to Cartwright's Antwerp period (1580–2) and appears to have been given shortly after Leyden University tried to secure his services.

It was provided in the scheme for the reformation of St Andrews University[7] that the New College, St Mary's, should be converted into an exclusively theological seminary. This part of the project was chiefly due to the efforts of Thomas Smeton and Andrew Melville, who desired to counteract the influence of the recently established Jesuit seminaries on the Continent[8]. By the General Assembly that met in Edinburgh in October, 1580, Andrew Melville was "sear against his will, decernit and ordeanit to transport him selff from Glasgow to St Androis, to begine the wark of Theologie ther, with sic as he thought meit to tak with

[1] 26 Aug. 1580; *Acta Senatus.* [2] 3 Sept. 1580; *ibid.*
[3] *C.H.* bk IX. [4] p. 36. [5] p. 366.
[6] *D.N.B.*, art. "Cartwright," has 1584; *A.C.* II, p. 361, *ca.* 1582.
[7] Ratified by Parliament, Nov. 1579, *Acts Scot. Parl.* III, pp. 178–82; McCrie, cc. 4 and 5.
[8] Melville, *Diary*, p. 76.

him for that effect, conform to the leat reformation of that Universitie, and the New Collage thairof, giffen in be the Kirk and past in Parliament."[1] In November, 1580, Melville left Glasgow and in the following month took up his abode in St Andrews as the Principal of St Mary's College[2]. The staff of the new theological faculty actually consisted, not of five as was intended, but of three Professors, Melville himself, James his nephew, and John Robertson[3]. Two of the proposed five Chairs were offered to Travers and Cartwright, who declined to accept the honour. The invitation was sent to the Puritans, probably in 1580, in the name of the minister of Glasgow and the chief officials of Glasgow University[4]. The signatories are as follows: James Boyd, Chancellor of Glasgow University; Andrew Hay, Rector (1569–86); Thomas Smeton, Dean (1578–80); Andrew Melville, Principal (1574–80); and David Wems, minister of Glasgow. To Smeton and Melville at any rate the Puritan leaders were likely to be well known. Smeton travelled and studied on the Continent, was acquainted with Walsingham, and after the massacre of St Bartholomew came to England "whar he remeaned scholmaister at Colchester till his coming to Scotland."[5] Cartwright, as we have seen, lectured in Geneva when Melville taught there, and his capability and worth as a Professor would be known to the Scotsman. It is indeed probable that the call to St Andrews was presented to the leaders of English Puritanism chiefly through Melville's influence.

The invitation, which in the original Latin is printed by Fuller[6] shows that the trials of Cartwright and Travers and their brave adherence to principle were well known to their Scottish brethren. The Puritans are applauded for their steadfast promulgation of the discipline of the Lord's Church among their fellow-countrymen: *in asserenda apud populares vestros ecclesiae suae disciplina*. It is lamented that the two able exponents of Presbyterianism should, because of their

[1] Melville, *Diary*, p. 83; *B.U.K.* II, pp. 466, 471.
[2] Melville, *Diary*, p. 84. [3] *ibid.*
[4] Fuller, *C.H.* bk IX, sect. VII, §§ 51–2.
[5] Melville, *Diary*, p. 73. [6] *C.H.*

enemies, have to hide their light under a bushel. They should be engaged in public teaching and preaching. Their friends in Scotland have often prayed that their services might be utilised in that land and now an opportunity has come. Then reference is made to St Andrews University. All the faculties are in a sufficiently healthy state save that of theology. Since the Reformation chief attention has been given to the instruction of the people, but now that there is a danger of a dearth of preachers greater attention to the training of candidates for the ministry is necessary. The General Assembly has taken up the question and with the king and nobles has decided to remedy the deficiencies. Accordingly Parliament has decreed that a college, now St Mary's, St Andrews, should be consecrated entirely to theological study and that none should be admitted to the ministry till after the completion of a prescribed course of study pursued during a period of four years under five Professors, three of whom will be supplied by the home Church, while Cartwright and Travers are invited to be the other two: *Ex hoc numero adhuc desunt Thomas Cartwrightus et Gualterus Traversus: reliquos nobis domi ecclesia nostra suppeditabit*. There awaits them a harvest worthy of their learning and piety. The king, the nobles, the godly, the ministers of the Church of Christ, and Christ Himself invite them and it is hoped that the Puritans will accept the call without delay.

Fuller says that the invitation was refused because Cartwright and Travers "were loath to leave, and their friends loath to be left by them, conceiving their pains might as well be bestowed in their native country." This may be true of Travers but not of Cartwright, who was labouring in the Antwerp Church when the call came. In the Dedication to King James prefixed to his *Metaphrasis et Homiliae in.. Ecclesiastes*[1] Cartwright refers to the invitation: *me olim ante annos viginti ad theologicam professionem in una Academiarum tuarum vocare dignatus sis*. He would gladly have accepted the offer, but was prevented from doing so by the claims upon him of the Antwerp Church, which he was then serving as

[1] Published posthumously in 1604.

minister: *nisi pastoritio vinculo, quo Anglantuerpianae Ecclesiae tum adstrictus eram, praepeditus fuissem*[1].

While Cartwright held a place of distinction and was regarded with honour in the academic world, he failed to enjoy the favour of his own sovereign. Her displeasure was a burden that he never could endure, especially seeing he was inspired by the warmest feelings of loyalty towards her. But there were persons, hostile to the tenets that he taught, who sought to construe them as dangerously revolutionary and anti-monarchical. Such persons gained the ear of Elizabeth at this time. Cartwright's feelings in these circumstances are well reflected in an extant copy of a letter written by him to Christopher Hatton, the date of which it is difficult to determine[2]. It is found in a collection of letters, none of which apparently relate to Hatton after his appointment to the Lord Chancellorship in 1587[3]. Nicolas[4] is unable to assign it to its proper place but suggests 1582. Cartwright's reference to the restraint of his liberty "these sixe yeares" (not five years as Brook[5] states) may be taken as an allusion to the time that has elapsed since the warrant for his arrest was issued and would thus place the epistle *ca.* 1580, or it may apply to the six years after his return to England in 1585 and thus belong to *ca.* 1590–1. In any case the letter's chief significance is that it contains Cartwright's *Apologia* and profession of fealty and may appropriately be dealt with at this point. "I am charged," he writes, "with thinges, which not only I did never write, butt which never entered so much as in to my thoughte. As to geve the attempte of the overthrowe of all good goverment in the Comon wealth, to myslike of magistrates, and especially of monarkes, to like of equalitie

[1] Henry Jacob, in his Epistle to King James set before his *Reasons... proving a necessitie of reforming our Churches in England* (1604), while referring to the King's "godly & tender commiseration towards us," alludes to the above acknowledgement of Cartwright thus: "As it is with all humble thankfulnes acknowledged (to your immortall honor) by a Reverend Father (margin: *M. Cartwr. Epist. to the King before his Homil. on Eccles.*) one that heertofore tasted therof, and now lately sleepeth in the Lord."

[2] App. XIV.

[3] Nicolas, *Memoirs of Sir Christopher Hatton* (1847), p. vii.

[4] p. 301.

[5] *Mem.* p. 320.

of all estates, and of a hedles rulynge of the unrulie multitude. In the Churche, to perswade the same disorder of setting no difference betwene the people and their gouvernors: in their gouvernors to leave no degrees. To geve to the Mynisters in their severall charges, an absolute power of doinge what them liketh best, without controllement of either Civill or Ecclesiasticall authoritie: and for the present estate of our Churche, that I carry suche an opynione of yt, as in the myslike therof, I disswade the Ministers from their Charges, and the people from heering the worde...." Such charges he rebuts and refers Hatton for a statement of his true opinions to his own writings and also to the *Explicatio* of 1574, with the principles of which he is in agreement, as he has testified in the Preface that he set before it. "So shall I be suer to be eased," he proceeds, "of the slanderous surmyse of my disloyaltie to her maiesties estate, and to the common wealthe: likewise of my love to puritanisme, and Church confusione: the contrary of booth which, I doe most ernestlie protest." With earnest insistence he pleads that the Queen's mind may be disabused of suspicion concerning his loyalty to her and of the unfavourable opinion she now entertains regarding him.

Cartwright was not able to win the good will of Elizabeth. She resented his tenure of the Antwerp charge and declared her desire that he should be removed. Walsingham, following her wishes, intimated to Cartwright that he must leave Antwerp and his post there. At the same time, the Secretary, whose personal sympathies were with the exile and the Puritan cause, made Cartwright a generous offer. He invited him to undertake the confutation of the seditious works that were being published by the English Jesuits and in particular of the translation of the New Testament that had recently been issued by the English Roman Catholics at Rheims, promised the necessary financial assistance, and hinted that the work, which might be dedicated to Elizabeth or to Burghley, would help to reinstate him in favour with the authorities at home. The invitation has been wrongly dated 1583 by Cooper, Brook, Strype and others[1], who follow

[1] *A.C.* II, p. 361, Brook, *Mem.* p. 259, St. *Whit.* I, p. 482.

the publisher of the *Confutation*[1], who conjectures, but incorrectly, that Walsingham's overture was made "about the yeare 1583, as appeareth by the date of Cartwrights letters in answer of the foresaid motion, which testifie also of the receit of that hundred pound." Walsingham's letter, however, is dated "From the Court at Grenwiche this vth of Julye, 1582"[2] and runs thus: "Sr. I have heretofore written to our good freind Mr Longston to acquaint you with hir Mats pleasure for your removing from thence, who taketh your being there offensively, by what occasions I know not, neither may we inquire of those matters but only content ourselves in dewtifull sortes to stand to hir H. pleasure uppon this occasion. it hath bin earnestly desiered by some that you would bestowe your time in answeringe such books of the Jesuites of our nacion as dayly are cast abroad, not all or every one of them, but such as your owne opinion and by advise of the learned from hence shalbe thought meate to be answered. The testament they would have first begonn. withall the order to be this in your travaile, that as you have donn and finished any worke to send it over hither to be seane and allowed by the best learned of both the Universities and yt you dedicate them to ye L. Treasurer if not to her Matie ioyning to the L. Treasorer whom you best lyke and this way is thought best to make an overture for your further favor. For your paines you shalbe allowed one hundred pound by ye yere, which I will see you payde in such order and sort as you shall dyrect me, if you please you shall have it alwaies with the half yere before hand. Appoint you what place for your residence you will, it wilbe well lyked of so yt it be for your safetie and health. And if you will have any companie to you to helpe you, you shall have whome you will, and as many as you will, and they lykewise shall have good allowance made them. I pray you retourne me your answere by this bearer, yt in both parts I may give answere according to deuty, both for hir Mats satisfaccion and for this good worke last mentioned. And so wishinge you increase of all blessings from above, with my hearty com-

[1] sig. A 2.

[2] *S.P. Dom. Eliz.* CLIV, No. 48.

mendaccions, I leave you to the grace of God." Clarke[1] transmits the story that Elizabeth had previously requested Beza to answer the Rhemists' Testament and that he modestly refused "and returned answer that she had one in her own Kingdome, far abler then himself to undertake such a task, and upon further enquiry declared that it was Master Thomas Cartwright." J. Peirce in his *Vindication* hints that Elizabeth furnished the money that Walsingham sent to Cartwright. Petheram, on the other hand, says[2]: "But if she had done so, the Archbishop would hardly have interfered in opposition to her will." It should be noted, however, that Whitgift did not oppose the undertaking at the beginning, but prohibited its completion and publication when the nature of it became known about four years afterwards.

In spite of Elizabeth's attitude to him or because she was persuaded to connive at his ministry among the merchants Cartwright remained in Antwerp till the autumn of 1582 and only removed to Zealand when the Adventurers saw fit to do so also. The new literary enterprise, which Walsingham and the influential Puritan patrons, whom he represented, solicited him to undertake, immediately engaged Cartwright's attention and during the following years we find him at work on the refutation of the Rhemists' translation of the New Testament, the most important of the recent Romanist writings aimed at the subversion of English Protestantism. This book was issued in the spring of 1582 at Rheims, to which the English College, established in 1568 at Douay chiefly under the influence of William Allen (afterwards Cardinal) for the purpose of educating young Roman Catholics from England and of providing a body of missionary priests, whose goal should be to win their native land back to Romanism, was transferred ten years after its foundation. George Martin was the chief translator. Richard Bristow was the author of the numerous annotations, which accompanied the translation and constituted a commentary of a highly polemical and decidedly anti-Protestant type. This version of the New Testament was incorporated in the so-called

[1] p. 271. [2] Marprelate's *Epistle*, ed. J. Petheram (1842), p. 75.

Douay Bible, published, 1609–10, at Douay, to which town the College had returned in 1593[1].

The Rhemists' Testament being one of the weightiest products of the Counter-Reformation, it was a high compliment to Cartwright's scholarship and ability that so many of his contemporaries singled him out for the distinguished task of demolishing the latest bulwark of Romanism. Besides the political and diplomatic patrons, who were behind Walsingham's invitation, there were many ministers who provoked him to battle. Roger Goad, William Whitaker, Thomas Crook, John Ireton, William Fulke, John Field, Nicholas Crane, Giles Seintloe, Richard Gardener, William Charke and others, unnamed by the publisher because they were still living when the *Confutation* was printed, directly urged him to wield anew the controversial pen, not this time against a brother minister, but against the inveterate enemies of the Reformed Church[2]. The rank and file of the Puritan ministers also discussed the matter in their Conferences and sought to stir him up "to this holie busynes."[3] Their satisfaction as to Cartwright's eminent suitability for the task, their eagerness that he should immediately take it in hand, and their hope that by so doing he might be restored to favour and be allowed to return to England are well expressed in the letter sent to him by members of the Dedham *Classis*[4] on the 19th of April, 1583. This letter is addressed to Middelburg and is signed by Chapman, Crick, and six others. Cartwright replied to it and to another of the same kind from the Suffolk Puritans thus: "To tell you the truth, my reverend and loving brethren, havinge bene diversly and earnestlie delte with in the same suite that you write me of, I yelded my weake shulders unto soe heavy a burden, wherfore although I knowe what interest yow have even to command me in the thinges

[1] *v.* Carleton, *The Part of Rheims in the making of the English Bible* (1902).

[2] *Confut.* sig. A 3–A 4.

[3] *e.g.* ministers of London, Suffolk and Essex; *ibid.* sig. A 2. The minute book of the Dedham *Classis* mentions the matter on 4th Feb. 1582–3, thus: "A motion also was now made for to write to Mr Cartwright to undertake the answeringe of the Rhemish Testamt but it was deferred." (*P.M.* p. 29.)

[4] *Gurney MSS.* f. 248 b; *P.M.* p. 78.

which I can conveniently doe yet havinge geven my promise before your request, I wante some parte of the comforte which I shuld have receyved if your demand had prevented my promise, for I shuld by soe much more have undertaken the worke with greate assurance, as by a fuller consent of the godlie lerned brethren, I mighte have heard the lord more plainly and more distinctly speaking unto me....ffrom Middelborough the 5 of May the morrow after the receipt of your loving letters."[1]

In fulfilment of his promise Cartwright worked steadily at his refutation, in Middelburg and afterwards in Warwick, in spite of the great discouragements and hindrances, that according to the publisher of the *Confutation* moved him "ofttimes to lay pen aside, as appeareth by the letters of 1586 to an Earle and privie Councellor of great note in answer of his letter to encourage him in the work and to understand the forwardnes thereof."[2] In this very year, however, it appears that he was forbidden by Archbishop Whitgift to proceed any further, the reason for the inhibition being that it was feared by the ecclesiastical authorities that his reply to the Romanists would tell against many of the semi-Roman usages of the Church of England and bolster up the Presbyterian Puritanism, with which Whitgift and his colleagues were at feud[3]. By this year Cartwright had finished a rough draft of his whole counterblast, and his answer to the Preface of the Rhemish Testament seems to have reached practically its final form.

The Puritans were as anxious to have the work published as the Church dignitaries were to suppress it. In November, 1586, Dr Chapman moved in the Dedham *Classis* that in their letter to the godly brethren in London for the furtherance of the Discipline the Essex Puritans "shuld put them in mynd of Mr Cartwrights booke of the Confutation of the Rhemish Testament, and to further yt unto the presse."[4]

[1] Addressed to his "most loving and reverend brethren the mynisters of Suffolke and Essex to be directed unto them by the handes of Mr D. Chapman and Mr Knewstub." *Gurney MSS*. f. 248 b. *P.M.* p. 80.

[2] *Confut.* sig. A 2 *verso*. It is signified by the publisher that the Earl was Burghley.

[3] St. *Whit.* I, p. 482.

[4] 7 Nov. 1586; *P.M.* p. 59.

When it came to be known that the publication of the *Confutation* had been prohibited the Puritans were deeply disappointed. Martin Marprelate voiced their grievance in *The Epistle* (*ca*. Oct. 1588) and declared that the publishing of the work was a necessary condition of peace between the Martinists and the Bishops[1]. Waldegrave withdrew from his connection with the Marprelate Press after he had printed the tract, *Hay any Worke for Cooper*, at Coventry in March, 1589. According to the deposition of the Northampton book-binder, Henry Sharpe, Waldegrave gave up his post as Martinist printer partly because all the preachers he had conferred with disapproved of the tracts "but chiefly for that he had now gotten the thing he had long desired," and this thing was none other than a copy of a part of Cartwright's *Confutation*, which Waldegrave now meant to print in some secret corner of Devonshire[2]. It is probable that during his residence in Coventry Waldegrave became acquainted with Cartwright's adverse views on the question of the Marprelate tracts, for Cartwright was then Master of Leicester Hospital, in Warwick, and thus a comparatively near neighbour; but we do not know how the printer managed to secure a copy of a portion of the much coveted *Confutation*. We learn, however, from the author himself that a part of his work had been sent to Walsingham, and that some, into whose hands Cartwright did not wish it to fall, had obtained possession of it, and that he, by means of letters and the intervention of friends in England and Scotland, had with great difficulty been able to frustrate the printing of the same.

Defending himself against the slanderous charges of Sutcliffe in his *Apologie* (1596) Cartwright says: "That my silence in the cause of Discipline is not altogeather either of th'inhabilitie or fears, Mr Sutcliffe would so willingly fasten, or rather force upon me, let this be for an Argument, that where I was set on worke by the right honorable Sir Francis Walsingham for th'aunswere of th'annotations of the Iesuites upon the new testament, & had traveled therin to a rude and first draught of a great part thereof: understanding from some

[1] *v. infra* pp. 280–1. [2] *v. infra* p. 279.

in authoritie that I might not deale with it, I did not onely not set any thing out my selfe, but also earnestly laboured by letters and friendes heere and in Scotland both the hinderaunce of printing some partes therof, which beeing brought to Sir Francis, afterwarde (much against my will) came into the handes of divers to whom I would never have let them come."[1] This declaration thus shows that through the prohibition of the printing of his *Confutation* Cartwright became convinced of the inexpediency or futility of publishing any writing of a pro-Presbyterian nature. It not only throws light upon the motives that explain the silence of his later years, but also upon Cartwright's attitude to the ex-Martinist printer's attempt to publish the prohibited work. It is practically certain that a portion of the *Confutation* which had been sent to Walsingham was that which fell into the hands of Waldegrave, and that the latter sought first to print it in England and afterwards in Scotland, where he eventually settled. It was not till 1602 that this important part of the *Confutation* was published by Waldegrave at Edinburgh under the title Σὺν θεῷ ἐν Χριστῷ: *The answere to the preface of the rhemish Testament. By T. Cartwright.*

That Cartwright endeavoured to eliminate controversial matter and, in particular, arguments in favour of Presbyterianism from the *Confutation* is plain. The correspondence that followed Burghley's request to see the answer to the Preface of the Rhemish Testament bears interesting testimony to Cartwright's anxiety to give Whitgift and the Bishops no cause for offence. Writing from Warwick on the 5th of August 1590 to the Lord High Treasurer Cartwright says: "According unto your Lordships good pleasure, as soone as I could both get it written, and finde a fit messenger: I have sent your h. the copie of my aunswer unto the praeface of the Remish Testament. wherein that there is some small difference, betweene this copie, and that his Grace of Canterbury hath;

[1] Cartwright's *Apol.* (1596), sig. C 2. Job Throkmorton, who edited the *Apologie*, makes this marginal note: "And if he stayed the publishing of that whereunto he was once alowed by authoritie, it is not in al likelihood to be thought that he would hastely publish anie thing of him self, howsoever he might be perswaded of the truth of it."

the cause is, that sithence that time, reading yt over agayn, I made (as I may yet further as long as yt remayneth a nurceling at home with me) some small alteration. Howbeit as touching the matters of the discipline praesentlie in controversie: there is as much here as there, that is to say nothing at all. for as I esteemed yt dutie to defend the truth thereof, when the Jesuites expresly expugn yt, and see not how I could in good conscience leave a blanck, where they have made a blot: yet in the care I have of not provoking, and of covering our disagreement in that behalf; I never come to anie of those poynts, but where they call me. And there I answer with as much brevitie, and as great generalitie as I can, without anie application unto our church, or any the governers in the same. And in this sort, I confesse I had drawn a rude draft of an answer, even to the Apocalypse some four years agoe, untill I understood from the Archbisshop, that I was no further to deal in yt. Wherein I doe not so much lament the churches losse in the want of my poor labors, that cannot much inrich yt: as I am greived that some things which came to other handes (after they were in Mr Secretary Walsinghams) have bene in danger to be imperfectlie and mangledly set forth, to a disadvantage of the truth: which yet hetherto partlie by my importunate labor to them that have the copies, and partly in that they could not get the rest out of my hand, hath bine stayed."[1]

It was not till 1618 that Cartwright's whole work was published at Leyden under the title *A Confutation of the Rhemists Translation, Glosses and Annotations on the New Testament, so farre as they containe manifest Impieties, Heresies, Idolatries, Superstitions, Prophanesse, Treasons, Slanders, Absurdities, Falsehoods and other evills. By Occasion whereof the true Sence, Scope, and Doctrine of the Scriptures, and humane Authors, by them abused, is now given. Written long since by order from the chiefe instruments of the late Queene and State, and at the speciall request and encouragement of many godly-learned Preachers of England, as the ensuing Epistles shew. By that Reverend, Learned, and Iudicious*

[1] *Lansd. MSS.* LXIV, No. 17, f. 57.

Divine, Thomas Cartwright, sometime Divinitie Reader of Cambridge. The volume gives the Rhemish translation of St Matthew's Gospel, at the end of which the following notice appears: "The Publisher to the Reader. Understanding that D. Fulke upon this subiect is reprinting in the former manner, I thought it needlesse to proceed with the Rhemists Text[1], since also the Author dealeth onely against their Annotations: and their Translation is so absurd, troublesome, and fruitelesse; and also since it is not likely, that many will desire the same, but such as neither will nor neede, bee without D. Fulkes answer, which may more boldly beare the charge then this." The reference is to the third edition of Fulke's *Confutation*, which, it should be noted, is an independent work and not, as has been said[2], a completion of Cartwright's unfinished treatise[3].

In his preface to the reader the publisher gives a short account of the origin and progress of Cartwright's work and is careful to point out that Fulke's reply was originally of an interim character and was not designed to oust that which Cartwright had undertaken. He also informs us that excerpts from Fulke's book were used to supply the deficiencies in Cartwright's manuscript: "The onely griefe is, that the copy is not perfected, further then the 15. of Revelation. Beside the small defects by Mice, through 30 yeares neglect, which we have supplied out of D. Fulk."[4]

In his answer to the Rhemish Preface Cartwright, while he disapproves of the Roman Catholic translation in many points, pronounces the opinion that the accompanying commentary is more vicious and dangerous than the version itself. The very words of the Holy Spirit have been "twitched aside with the wrench and wrest of their Annotations."[5]

[1] Carleton (*op. cit.* p. 22) is therefore wrong in saying that Cartwright's *Confutation* printed the Rhemish N.T. "at full length."

[2] Mullinger, *St John's*, p. 63.

[3] Issued in 1589 Fulke's work was reprinted in 1601, 1617, 1633. *Vide* Carleton (*op. cit.* p. 25) who thinks it likely that it was due to Fulke's *Confutation*, which printed both the Bishops' and the Rhemish N.T., that the latter exercised a great influence on the A.V.

[4] *Confut.* sig. A 2 *verso*. A manuscript copy of the *Confutation* is in *Lambeth MSS.* vol. ccccliii.

[5] sig. C 4 *verso*.

He considers, however, that the translation is very deficient in being merely a rendering of the Vulgate and is at great pains to uphold "the royall value of the originall Greeke."[1] In his introductory disquisition on the canonicity of Scripture he displays considerable ability as he rebuts the Rhemish contention that the Church's witness is the chief guarantee of Scriptural authority[2].

Throughout the *Confutation* Cartwright manifests a decided animus against Popish doctrines and usages. He denies the primacy of the Pope[3] and expressly declares him to be Antichrist[4]. He regards the Council of Trent as a mere conventicle[5] or a conspiracy of which "wee make no account."[6] He argues against Purgatory[7] and the immaculate conception of the Virgin[8], and condemns Mariolatry[9], the invocation of saints[10], the veneration of relics[11], pilgrimages[12], monasticism[13], celibacy[14], auricular confession[15], etc. With regard to the Sacraments two only are recognised[16], the private administration of them is disallowed[17], Baptismal regeneration is repudiated[18], and at considerable length the Roman doctrine of the Mass is refuted[19]. The Protestant doctrine of justification by faith receives full treatment[20].

Many of Cartwright's counter-annotations are capable of being construed as criticisms of Anglo-Catholic teaching. He argues against the Lenten fast[21], the altar[22], apostolic succession[23] and disapproves of the very name of priest[24]. His philosophy of history is diametrically opposed to that maintained by Anglo-Catholicism inasmuch as he regards the primitive Church as the only pure model and the Roman Church "for the space of 980 yeares, or thereabout, Antichristian."[25] His objection to ministers holding civil offices[26] and his attitude to the "chopping and hacking of the

[1] sig. E 4 *verso*. [2] sig. f. [3] pp. 47, 205, 489.
[4] p. 522. [5] sig. D 2. [6] p. 182.
[7] pp. 231, 718. [8] p. 144. [9] p. 144.
[10] pp. 85, 108. [11] p. 44. [12] p. 137.
[13] pp. 9, 16, 197. [14] pp. 38, 108, 547. [15] p. 194.
[16] p. 476. [17] p. 142. [18] pp. 14, 311.
[19] pp. 27, 85, 125 ff., 199, 612, 637, 714. [20] pp. 147, 482, 489, 658.
[21] p. 17. [22] p. 26. [23] p. 492.
[24] p. 662. [25] pp. 521, 576, 592, 692. [26] pp. 101, 582.

Scripture"[1] and to the short shreds of collects patched together in the Roman service[2] are reminiscent of the Admonitions of 1572 and could be looked upon as criticisms levelled at current practices of the Church of England. His opinion that the exercises or prophesyings had been provided by the Lord "for the more plentifull nourishment of the faithfull in all times" was not likely to commend itself to Elizabeth or the Church dignitaries so soon after an Archbishop had suffered the Queen's displeasure for countenancing them.

In spite of Cartwright's declared anxiety to reduce the exhibition of his Presbyterian leanings to a minimum the *Confutation* frequently expresses the principles of the party, of which he was the most distinguished leader. The true Church is "the companie of the elect"[3]; the visible Church, liable to err, should take as standard that of the Apostolic age when the Bishops "which are Pastors and Elders"[4] were "tied as it were to the stake or glebe of one particular Church."[5] These Bishops "in the ordinarie functions of their particular Churches are the highest officers of the Ecclesiasticall Presbyterie."[6] They should be able to teach and preach[7]. Indeed, Cartwright thinks that preaching is their principal service[8]. Originally there were two kinds of governors in the Church, "one that governed and taught, the other which governed onely."[9] Cartwright divides the Church officials into two classes, Bishops and Deacons, the former including pastors and doctors, the latter non-preaching elders and deacons[10]. Non-preaching elders "should bee assistant unto the Bishops."[11] All the elders, of both kinds, in their corporate capacity, constitute "a Senate or an Eldership."[12] *Dic Ecclesiae* is interpreted as referring to them[13]. Replying to the charge of the Jesuits that the heretics condemned University degrees Cartwright says that their accusation is manifestly confuted by the practice of the Reformed Churches "where are both Maisters of Art and

[1] p. 2. [2] p. 29. [3] p. 495.
[4] p. 291. [5] p. 536. [6] p. 537.
[7] p. 574. [8] p. 29. [9] p. 293.
[10] p. 498. [11] p. 528. [12] p. 663. [13] p. 92.

Doctors of Law and Physick, yea of Divinity also: albeit they bee not with so full consent of all the godly...the Doctorship of the Church is of Christs own institution... Heereupon they thinke it not so meete, that hee which is by office a Pastour, should seek to have the name of a Doctor; nor that hee which already, according to the Apostles rule, hath obtained the office of a Doctor, should seeke for the name of his office from some other fountaine."[1] The equality of ministers is duly affirmed[2]. It is pointed out that governing elders and deacons "meddle not with the ministry of the word"[3] and have no right to administer the Sacraments[4]. "By Deacons hee [Paul] understandeth all those officers of the Church which were not occupied in teaching, as it appeareth manifestly in that hee requireth no gift of teaching in them. Wherefore as by the Bishop is understood Pastors and Doctors: so by Deacons are comprehended the Elders that governe onely, and teach not, and those that have care of the poore and sicke of the Church, which are called by the common name of Deacons."[5] The employment of the word 'Deacon' in two senses, a wider and a narrower, has to be carefully noted. The interests of the congregation as such are conserved by Cartwright. Each particular Church has ineradicable rights in "the election and deposition of her ministers, the excommunication and absolution of her repentant or unrepentant Citizens."[6] In the last resort the officials are only the representatives of the congregation.

Presbyterianism being thus imbedded piecemeal in Cartwright's work it would appear to the Church of England authorities not only as a confutation of the Rhemists, but also as a new and more insidious edition of his refutation of the position held by Whitgift. The Archbishop, therefore, need not be charged with tyrannical intolerance[7] for suppressing a book, which, from his point of view, was dangerous, revolutionary and likely to support the very movement against which he was fighting so vigorously. To countenance it was to prepare a rod for his own back and to supply a buttress

[1] p. 112. [2] pp. 111, 677. [3] p. 492. [4] p. 272.
[5] p. 552. [6] pp. 291, 383, 528. [7] Brook, *Mem.* p. 263.

for a party, the overthrow of which was deemed by him a paramount duty. The erudition and exegetical skill exhibited by Cartwright are worthy of admiration and his exposure of Romanist principles and practices is weighty, but Brook[1] seems to be unaware of the fact that the volume in parts does greatly favour the Genevan discipline and is guilty of the prejudice of a partisan when he attributes the prohibition of its publication by Whitgift to the "haughty and troublesome humour of this domineering archprelate."[2] Fuller[3], adopting another attitude, says "Distasteful passages (shooting at Rome, but glancing at Canterbury), if any such were found in his book, might be expunged; whilst it was pity so good fruit should be blasted in the bud for some bad leaves about it." One could not reasonably expect a work, no matter how learned and able, which contained the pro-Presbyterian elements that are certainly to be found in Cartwright's *Confutation*, to receive the official sanction of a Church, which distrusted and dreaded Presbyterianism, particularly in an age when a rigid uniformity was regarded as an ideal and intolerance as a virtue.

It is worthy of note that the *Confutation* was issued by the shortlived Pilgrim Fathers' press at Leyden about two years before the 'Mayflower' sailed for America. This press, financed by the wealthy Thomas Brewer, was carried on by the famous Elder Brewster and had a brief but eventful history. Established in 1616 it published several books that could not openly be printed in Britain. Probably the first of its productions was Cartwright's Latin commentary on Proverbs, which appeared early in 1617. Two notorious writings *Perth Assembly* and *De regimine Ecclesiae Scoticanae* appeared in 1619, brought the wrath of King James upon Brewer and Brewster, and led to the suppression of their printing establishment[4]. It is interesting to learn from Governor Bradford's memoir of William Brewster that the latter was for several years the trusted and familiar servant

[1] Brook, *Mem.* p. 265. [2] *ibid.* p. 264. [3] *C.H.* bk IX, sect. vi.

[4] E. Arber, *Story of the Pilgrim Fathers* (1897), pp. 195 ff., 237; W. H. Burgess, *John Robinson* (1920), pp. 164 ff.; J. Brown, *Pilgrim Fathers* (1895), pp. 127, 160 ff.; R. G. Usher, *The Pilgrims* (1918), p. 37.

of "that religious and godly Gentleman," William Davison, Cartwright's friend and supporter. Davison, says Bradford[1], "found him [Brewster] so discreet and faithful, as he trusted him above all other that were about him, and only employed him in matters of greatest trust and secrecy. He esteemed him rather as a son than a servant, and for his wisdom and godliness, in private he would converse with him more like a familiar than a master. He attended his master when he was sent in ambassage by the Queen into the Low Countries (in the Earl of Leicester's time) as for other weighty affairs of State, so to receive possession of the cautionary towns; and in token and sign thereof the keys of Flushing being delivered to him in her Majesty's name, he kept them some time, and committed them to his servant, who kept them under his pillow on which he slept the first night. And, at his return, the states honored him with a gold chain, and his master committed it to him, and commanded him to wear it when they arrived in England, as they rode through the country, until they came to the Court." Apparently Brewster, who would almost certainly meet Cartwright at Flushing in 1585, shared his old master's esteem for the Puritan and by printing the *Confutation* was doubtless fulfilling the desire of its original promoters, with whose views he would become intimately acquainted during his attendance on Davison in the years 1585–7[2].

In 1582, before Cartwright left Antwerp, both he and the Merchant Adventurers were brought into touch with the Brownist movement, the leaders of which, Robert Browne and Robert Harrison, had recently come from Norwich to Middelburg with a small company of their followers[3]. Shortly after his arrival in Zealand Browne's treatises, in which he enunciated the classical tenets of Separatism, were published by the Middelburg printer, Richard Schilders. By August, 1582, the Prince of Orange, Villiers, Audley Danett and others were seriously considering the problem raised by the settle-

[1] A. Young, *Chronicles of the Pilgrim Fathers* (1841), p. 463.
[2] *ibid.* p. 463; Brown, *op. cit.* pp. 55 ff.; Arber, *op. cit.* p. 189.
[3] Dexter, p. 72; C. Burrage, *True Story of Robert Browne* (1906), pp. 15 ff.

ment in the Low Countries of a community, whose views were frankly hostile to those of Elizabeth and the Church of England[1]. The Deputy and assistants of the Adventurers wrote to Burghley and Walsingham about the matter. Their letter to the latter is dated the 22nd August, 1582, and is signed by Richard Godard[2]. They sent to Walsingham a copy of Browne's book, evidently *A Treatise of Reformation without Tarying* and *A Booke which sheweth*, which seem to have been issued as one volume. They reported that the author was now exercising a ministry in a corner at Middelburg and had deluded certain of Elizabeth's subjects to follow him thither. Copies of his book had been brought to Antwerp by William Pagett, sometime a brewer's clerk in London, who had publicly offered them for sale to the merchants on the English Bourse. Cartwright, their minister, having been requested to examine the book, declared it to be erroneous in certain points of doctrine. He condemned the general scope of the work, but the Epistle in particular, as tending neither to the peace nor the edification of the Church. Accordingly, the Company caused Pagett to be apprehended and resolved to send him and the books to England. But this was beyond the Company's jurisdiction. Even the magistrates of Antwerp had no power to expel Pagett out of Brabant, but they forbade the circulation of the books and allowed the merchants to take Pagett's remaining copies from him. The merchants sharply admonished Pagett and were sure that no more books would be brought to Antwerp. They were also taking measures for the suppression of the writings in Zealand[3].

J. Dover Wilson who, in a valuable paper read to the Bibliographical Society in October, 1910[4], speaks of the need of a "bibliographical Napoleon who will attack the whole subject of English books printed abroad in the sixteenth

[1] Danett to Walsingham, 19 Aug. 1582. *S.P. Eliz. Holl. and Fland.* XVI, No. 113.

[2] *ibid.* XVI, No. 117.

[3] A royal proclamation was issued in June, 1583, commanding that the books of Browne and Harrison should be delivered up to be burnt or utterly defaced (*Transcript*, ed. Arber, I, p. 502).

[4] Printed in *Transactions*, vol. XI, 1912.

century," has prepared the way for this effort in one important field. His paper, entitled "Richard Schilders and the English Puritans" deals in an illuminating and exhaustive manner with Robert Browne's printer. Schilders, or Painter, as he sometimes called himself, came to London in 1567 probably as one of the refugees from the Netherlands. On the 3rd of May, 1568, he was admitted a member of the Stationers' Company[1]. In 1571 he was employed by Thomas East evidently as the owner of a press of his own. On the 24th of November, 1578, he was appointed journeyman compositor to Thomas Dawson[2]. Not later than 1580 he settled in Middelburg, which had been wrested from the Spaniards, and from that year till his death (1634) he was printer to the States of Zealand. A long list of English books printed by Schilders is given by Wilson. Many of these are religious works composed by English Puritans, *e.g.* Fenner, Throkmorton, etc., and among them is Cartwright's *Apologie* of 1596.

The "Epistle" to which Cartwright took greatest exception is apparently the *Treatise of Reformation*, for the title of Browne's twofold work is *A Booke which sheweth...Also there goeth a Treatise before of Reformation without tarying for anie*, *and of the wickednesse of those Preachers*, *which will not reforme themselves and their charge*, *because*, *they will tarie till the magistrate commaunde and compell them*[3]. In this treatise Browne aims a direct blow at the party and policy represented by Cartwright. The latter and his followers desired to presbyterianise the Church of England but with the help of the civil magistrate and by constitutional means. Browne argues that the magistrates have no ecclesiastical authority at all and stands forth as an advocate of liberty of conscience and of spiritual independence. "The Lords people," he says, "is of the willing sorte." "It is the conscience and not the power of man that will drive us to seeke the Lordes Kingdome." "To compell religion, to plant churches by power and to force a submission to Ecclesiastical govern-

[1] *Transcript*, ed. Arber, I, p. 366. [2] *ibid.* II, p. 882.
[3] ed. J. G. Crippen (1903).

ment by lawes & penalties belongeth not" to the magistrates. "The outwarde power and civil forcings, let us leave to the Magistrates: but let the Church rule in spiritual wise and not in worldlie maner."[1] Browne's principles were thus in some respects more enlightened than Cartwright's. In theory at least he held a more advanced view of religious toleration. His view of the relation between Church and State was also diametrically opposed to that of Cartwright. The whole treatise was indeed a condemnation of the latter's position with regard to the competence of the civil rulers to reform or control the Church and naturally earned the Puritan's warmest disapproval.

Further proof of Cartwright's hostile attitude to Browne's book is contained in an important letter addressed by one of the Merchant Adventurers on the 2nd of September, 1582, to Walsingham[2]. From this epistle we learn that over a thousand copies of the obnoxious work had been printed and that a large consignment of these had already been sent to England. The Prince of Orange had adopted a decidedly antagonistic attitude to the book and was endeavouring to suppress it. The Brownists, an ill-conditioned company numbering between thirty and forty, were suffering from the climate. The exiles were shown much friendliness by the inhabitants of Middelburg, many of whom attended the services, which were held in Browne's house and not, as has been stated[3], in the Vischmarkt Kerk. The apposite portion of the letter, which throws invaluable contemporary light upon both Cartwright and the Brownists, is as follows: "Yt may please your honor, beinge at Flushinge I wrote unto you by Monsr de Bee, a gentleman of Monsr Marchemonts traine, since which time beinge at Middelbourge, I found of Brownes boks to be sold openly: there have bene printed of them above one thousand, and many sent into England: after I had staied a daye there, about Mr Nores busines, I understode by the Treasorar, one of the Councell of the

[1] *Treatise*, ed. Crippen, pp. 18, 20, 25, etc.

[2] Danett to Walsingham from Antwerp. *S.P. Eliz. Holl. and Fland.* XVII, No. 3.

[3] *Bibliog. Soc. Trans.* XI, p. 76.

State there, that the prince of Orange had written for the suppressinge of the books, which ar alredy sent into England as the Treasorar saithe, for in Middelbourge he saithe there ar none to be found. Browne was alsoe sought but not found and yet I thinke not out of the towne; there is an assembly there of some thirty or fourty persons, which ar in very poore estate, and for the moste parte visited with sickenes, not well aggreinge with the aire in those parts. They geve out of them selves that they ar in all respects duetifully affected unto the Q. Matye, that there booke hathe beene seene and allowed by the Ministers of Middelbourge and namely by Mr Cartwright abidinge at Antwarp, with whom I have talked and find him so farre from approvinge the same, that he dothe utterly mislike the epistle, touchinge the reformation withoute attendinge the Magistrate, and some other points of the doctrine therein contained, wherein he saithe Mr Browne hathe absurdly erred. Yt shold appere that the Ministers and people in Middelbourge ar not ill affected unto Browne and his followers, beinge perswaded that there voluntary exile is for matter of relligion and for there conscience, and many of the towne understandinge englishe, doe oftentimes repaire to there praiers and assemblies, which ar kepte in Brownes house which he hathe hired in the towne..."

It has often been affirmed that when Browne and his followers came to Middelburg they first joined Cartwright's congregation. Heylyn says that Browne, not able to abide any longer in a Church so impure and filthy as the Church of England "puts himself over into Zealand, and joyns with Cartwrights new Church in the City of Middleborough."[1] Burrage, who says[2] that Browne deliberately chose Middelburg because of Cartwright's presence there, corrects himself in a later book[3], where he, after a study of the *Extracts* from the Register of the Antwerp Congregation[4], suggests that Cartwright probably arrived in Middelburg after Browne, who came about the beginning of 1581–2. We have now abundant evidence to show that the Brownists were already

[1] *A.R.* lib. VII, § 29.
[2] *op. cit.* p. 17.
[3] *E.E.D.* I, p. 137.
[4] *Add. MSS.* 6394, f. 113.

settled in Middelburg when the English Church under Cartwright was established there.

For fully a year after Cartwright's arrival he would have Browne and Harrison as fellow townsmen, but there is no record as to the relationship that existed between them. It has been conjectured that after Browne's departure for Scotland towards the end of 1583 Harrison and his followers united with Cartwright's congregation for a short time[1]. The conjecture is based on the following passage from Cartwright's letter to Harrison[2]: "Your first page had raysed me unto some hope for the reunitinge of your selfe, with the rest of your company unto us, from whome you have thought good to sunder your selves." It appears to us that Cartwright merely expresses the hope that the Separatists would join the Church of England with which his particular Church was identified, and that "us" means the general body of the English Church from which they had seceded. We must bear in mind that Cartwright regarded himself as being employed at that time in the ministry of the English Church[3]. He did not consider himself a Seceder, and, as we shall see, his aim was now to prove to the Separatists that secession was unjustified. Browne also points out that Cartwright's letter to Harrison was "for joyning with the English churches," not merely with the English Church at Middelburg. Union with the latter would have followed the more comprehensive one, and was doubtless under practical consideration.

According to Burrage[4] Browne left Zealand for Scotland in the late autumn of 1583, after several months of dissension, and before leaving wrote his autobiographical work, *A True and Short Declaration*. We learn from this book that Harrison was not such a rabid Separatist as himself. He admired such Puritan ministers as Roberts, More and Dering[5]. Browne, on the other hand, could not abide their conformity; he has in his *True and Short Declaration* nothing but bitter reproaches for the conforming Puritans: "They sai thei mowrne and prai for amendment & behould thei are fed of the rich

[1] Dexter, p. 76; Burrage, *True Story of Robert Browne*, p. 17.
[2] p. 86. [3] *v.* App. xv. [4] *op. cit.* pp. 26–7. [5] *T. & S.* p. 9.

and upheld bie great men."[1] Harrison and Browne in their discussions could not agree on the question of the dumb or reading ministry. "Herein they agreed not, because R.H. said that faith might be bred & first wrought, in some onelie bie reading the Scriptures; and R.B. said, no, for though it might be nourished and increased bie such reading, yet the first worcking thereof is by hearing the word preached."[2] The basis accepted by Browne's company included in writing the following resolution: "That we are to forsake & denie all ungodlines and wicked felloweship and to refuse all ungodlie communion with wicked persons."[3] They were ultra-Puritanical and thus covenanted to have no connection with even the Cartwrightian or Presbyterian Puritans. But they proved a disunited body in Middelburg. In a section of his autobiography[4] Browne tells "of the Breach and Division which fell amongst the companie in Middelburg." Even Harrison turned against him: "There were sundrie meetings procured against R.B. by R.H. and his Partakers for certain tales and slanders." Eventually Harrison and his associates condemned Browne "as an unlawful pastor," forbade him to keep exercises, and demanded a confession of his faults before they would join with him again. He prohibited the use of his chamber for their meetings; "Soe afterward thei held their meetings in another place: where again thei condemned R.B." Browne[5] charges Harrison with malice and a "troublesome mind" and says "he had divers partakers that clave fast unto him, because he taught them that thei might Lawfully Return Into England, and there have their dwellinge. This Doctrine thei liked Because thei were wearied of the hardnes of that contrie." Again and again Browne was condemned by this party. Some of the charges were trifling, some imbued with the spirit of backbiting, but eventually he was charged with being a heretic because "he saied thei did sinn which had a ffull purpos to dwel still in England," and because he had "saied (which he never did) that some might be of the outward church of God while they resorted

[1] *ibid.* p. 12. [2] *ibid.* p. 9. [3] *ibid.* p. 12.
[4] *ibid.* p. 21. [5] *ibid.* p. 23.

to that false worship & idol service then used in England, & ioined with others therein, but nowe blamed them which held such doctrine." A party of the Brownists, headed by Harrison, were in sympathy with the Puritan point of view, that the Church of England though not perfect was yet a Church and membership in it allowable. We are not surprised, therefore, that Harrison entered into a friendly discussion with Cartwright of the question of Separation from the Church of England in general, and of the feasibility of a union of the Harrisonian Brownists with Cartwright's Middelburg Church in particular, although we are surprised to find Harrison theoretically a more uncompromising Separatist than according to Browne's *Declaration* one would expect.

After receiving Harrison's letter Cartwright offered "the choyce for the first conference, whether you would have it in writing or by speech of mouth." "I attended," says Cartwright, "some dayes for your answere of that matter: which because it was not returned, I esteemed that you held you still to the request of your letters, which was to receave some thing from me by writing." Cartwright therefore proceeds to write his answer to Harrison's letter. He appears to be busy but in order to reply cuts out time from his "weightiest and most necessary busines." The first page of the letter had inspired Cartwright to hope that Harrison would return to the Anglican fold and join his Church. The second page shattered his hope. Harrison is "not unwilling to come unto us," but the chief obstacle appears to be "the receaving without publique repentaunce of those which come from the Churches of England." These Churches are not held by Harrison to be "lawfull assemblies of the Churche of Christ." "Your feare," says Cartwright, "is least in uniting your selves with such you shoulde be unequally yoked, and made fellowe members of some other body then of that whereof Christ Iesus is the head." He accordingly sets out to prove that the ordinary assemblies of the Church of England are Churches of Christ. Christ is owned as their head; the true faith is professed therein; and the Spirit of God has sanctified many of their members. If it be objected that all who profess the Gospel in the English Church do not believe it, the same can be said against all other Reformed Churches. After affirming that "the trueth of the church standeth not in the nomber," Cartwright pronounces the amazing opinion that one truly faithful member of a Church is sufficient to make it a Church of God. Browne in his *Answere*[1] considers this rank "poyson" and holds that many ill-doers make it no Church. If it be objected that most of the English Churches are "dumped with dumbe ministers" and are therefore to be reckoned no Churches, Cartwright argues that these congregations may have received the true faith through some former minister or otherwise. Further, if preaching ministers are necessary in a true Church, "then at every vacation of the ministry and whensoever by death the Lorde shoulde put out one of his lightes, it shoulde followe that that assembly by the fall of their minister into the grave shoulde from the hyest heaven fall into the grave of hell." Browne afterwards replied[2] that a preaching minister is not necessary to a Church, but that two or three agreeing together in the truth and keeping separate from the wicked in their meetings constitute a Church. To the objection that the Churches of England are not Churches of Christ because they lack "his commaunded discipline" Cartwright replies that the Christian Churches in Europe acknowledge the Church of England as a Church of Christ, which fact ought at least "to staye all sodayne and hasty iudgments unto the contrary." Cartwright now comes to Harrison's two chief reasons for not recognising the English Churches. "And first of all to the reason of the discipline, for the want wherof you give them all without exception the blacke stone of condemnation from being the churches of christ." Cartwright distinguishes between the *esse* and the *bene esse* of a Church and employs the analogy of a man, who if he have his vital parts is still a man although his legs are off and his eyes out. The Churches of Germany that hold wrong views of the Sacrament of Communion are nevertheless Churches of Christ. So the Church of England, although the discipline

[1] p. 6. [2] *Answere*, pp. 11, 13.

of Christ is not yet established in it, may be the Church of God. "To say it is none of the Church of God, because it hath not received this discipline, me thinkes is all one with this as if a man woulde say, it is no citie because it hath no wall, or that it is no vineyarde because it hath neither hedge nor dyke." Harrison's second particular reason for not joining with the Church of England is the existence of a dumb ministry. Cartwright has already dealt with the conclusion "that the assemblies where they be are none of the churches of god." There remains Harrison's inference that the Sacraments administered by dumb ministers are null and void and therefore not to be received at their hands. "First," says Cartwright, "I agree with you that their ministerie is unlawful," but "that they are no ministers of god so far as to receive the good thinges they offer unto us, that I suppose I may not well yeelde unto." Being allowed by the Churches of God, "they ought untill remedie may be founde of so great disorder to be heard and received as farre as they can give us any thing that is of christ." Christ allowed the Scribes to be heard and commanded the leper to go to the priest. Accordingly Cartwright argues "that he may bee holden for a minister which hath the Churches calling albeit he be not able to doe the principall charge of that ministerie." He may be a minister although not a good one. Browne[1] calls this distinction a "fopperye." Finally, Cartwright deals with "that which is obiected of communicating with their impietie, in taking any thing at their handes." A son does not partake of the guilt "of his fathers murther, because he receiveth of his fathers gifte some parte of his owne landes and moveables." The dumb minister only dispenses the gifts of the Lord. In refusing the Sacraments offered by him "we put the Lorde awaye from us." We "may communicate with a minister that is an adulterer without being partaker of his adulterie. Even so also may I communicate with a dumbe minister, and yet neverthelesse be free from his impietie."

Cartwright, having finished his argument, says that he is willing to "hearken unto any (much more unto you whom

[1] *Answere*, p. 56.

the Lord in mercie hath bestowed good graces upon) shewing better thinges." He cherishes a high esteem for Harrison and has not been carrying on a controversy with him in the same spirit that animated his duel with Whitgift. He is willing to have a personal conference with the Separatist, but "I must" he says "thorough businesse be inforced to reserve it to conference by word of mouth, sometimes after dinner." There is no evidence however to show that Harrison was persuaded to join forces with Cartwright. The differences between them were too great. Cartwright was willing to compromise and to wait for a favourable opportunity to advance the cause of reformation, while Harrison would have all or nothing and at once. Both desired a pure scriptural Church, but they did not agree in their method of attaining their ideal. It is likely that Harrison would willingly have united with Cartwright if the latter's Church had been an independent Presbyterian organisation, but it was a branch of the Church of England and there was the rub. The Puritan was willing to serve in the Church of England in spite of its corruptions and labour and hope for its reform; the Separatist could only think to flee from the corruptions and set up a new sect. Cartwright's letter to Harrison is invaluable as a reasoned exposition of the attitude of an Elizabethan Puritan to the State Church on the one hand and to radical Dissent on the other.

Five or six weeks after Cartwright wrote this letter it or a copy of it fell into the hands of Browne, who immediately penned a reply entitled *An answere to master Cartwright His letter for ioyning with the English Churches whereunto the true copie of his sayde letter is annexed*[1]. Burrage[2] says that Browne came back to Zealand about the end of 1584 or the beginning of 1585, and soon after the 8th of February, 1584–5, returned to England, probably bearing his answer to Cartwright with him. Cartwright's letter to Harrison would therefore be written towards the end of 1584 and Browne's *Answere*, which was printed in London, would

[1] Cartwright's letter occupies the last eleven pages, *i.e.* pp. 86–96.
[2] *op. cit.* p. 31.

appear early in 1585. "You have in this booke," says Browne in his Epistle to the Reader, "an answere to an answere written unto Master Harrison at Middleborough by Master Cartwright upon occasion of controversie betweene them concerning the true spouse of Christ or his ordinarie visible Churches in Englande." Browne[1] says that he never saw Harrison's letter. Cartwright's letter, however, "is in many mens handes, and was seene (sent?) abroade unsealed and open, as if he cared not who shoulde read it, wherefore I may the more boldely answere it, and the rather because the matter thereof is publike and pertaining to the Church of God. It came but lately to my handes, and was written as they tell me more then five or sixe weekes agoe."[2] Browne regards the Puritan's epistle as an attempt to prove the Separatists enemies to Church and State and deems an immediate answer necessary "for so much as we have so small respite of time."[3] He gives a direct denial to Cartwright's affirmations. As the Scribes were not to be heard unless they taught truth, so dumb ministers are not to be heard unless they give us something of Christ. But they are not of Christ and are therefore not to be regarded as ministers at all. The Church of Christ must be pure, therefore separation from the wicked is imperative. The Christian's duty with regard to the Church of England is to leave it.

Cartwright's experience of Brownism confirmed him in his loyalty to the Church of his native land. It turned the critic into a protagonist. This does not mean that he renounced his ardent hope that the English Church might become Presbyterian, but that in face of those who condemned it outright he came forward as a champion of the Establishment and proclaimed the doctrine that the proper way in which to achieve a further reformation of it was to accept things as they were and labour for improvement by gradual and constitutional means from within the Church.

The disputation with the Brownists reveals not only the division of Elizabethan Congregationalists into extremists and moderates, represented by Browne and Harrison re-

[1] *Answere*, p. 5. [2] *ibid.* p. 1. [3] *ibid.* p. 1.

spectively, but also the complete severance of the former from their Presbyterian antecedents. Brownism was cradled in a Presbyterian atmosphere. When a student at Cambridge Browne himself probably came under the influence of Cartwright's ideas. Even Dexter[1], who is sometimes guilty of misrepresenting Puritan Presbyterianism, says that Browne was essentially the master of his own thinking "with the exception of the participation which he had in that general reforming of the Cambridge mind which was largely due to Cartwright." Browne's friendship with Greenham of Dry Drayton, "whoe of all others he hard sai was most forwarde,"[2] points in the same direction. Many of Cartwright's principles were merely carried out by Browne to what he considered their logical conclusion. Ultimately, however, probably after he came under Anabaptist influences in Norwich, the gulf between Browne and the Presbyterians was complete. Harrison represented more faithfully the genealogical connection with Puritan Presbyterianism.

We have remarked upon Cartwright's literary activity during his residence in the Low Countries. This reveals him chiefly as an ardent anti-Romanist and a convinced anti-Separatist. Positively he was a true Disciplinarian and at the same time, as far as his convictions allowed, a loyal minister of the Church of England. He was afterwards (1590) accused by the High Commission of carrying on in the Netherlands a purely Presbyterian Church, at whose services he refrained from using the English Prayer Book and in connection with which he superintended a fully developed Consistory[3]. Sutcliffe, when referring to the love of discipline evinced by the Presbyterian Puritans—"excommunications flie out upon everie light grudge among them"—finds an illustration in Cartwright's ministry at Middelburg. "It is said," writes Sutcliffe[4], "that Th. Cart. at Middleburg, would have excommunicated a certaine marchant, that dealt sharpelie with his prentise a brother, that had defrauded him of great summes." On the other hand, in answer to the charge that

[1] p. 103. [2] *T. & S.* p. 2. [3] Fuller, *C.H.* bk IX, sect. vii, § 27.
[4] *Treatise*, p. 182.

he was not in favour of prescribed forms of prayer, Cartwright adduces his usual practice at Antwerp and Middelburg, saying: "In the space of five yeres I preached at Antwerpe and Middelborough I did every sunday read the praier out of the booke" (*i.e.* the Book of Common Prayer)[1]. Apparently he sought to be Presbyterian and Conformist simultaneously.

When in Zealand Cartwright composed a letter of particular interest, dated the 23rd of March, 1583 (? 4), that has not received attention at the hands of former biographers. It is an answer to a request, apparently from Arthur Hildersham[2], for advice as to the study of divinity. It sheds new light upon Cartwright as a Biblical student and reveals the extent of his acquaintance with theological literature and the discriminating mind that he applied to it. The copy we have examined is contained in a volume of MSS. in Corpus Christi College, Oxford[3]. Cartwright makes it clear that he was loath to comply with the request, modestly saying that his lot is now to instruct the simple and unlearned and not to be a teacher of teachers and confessing that he would not have composed his reply "if Mr...had not in your behalf pressed it out." He thinks so little of his answer that he begs the enquirer to keep it secret or else "let it smell of the fyre." In the first instance he commends the daily study of the Bible, "for whithersoever you goe out of the paradise of the Holy Scriptures, you shall in the best grownds meet with thornes and thistles, of which you are in danger of pricking, if you carry not the forest bill of the Lords Word wherewith to stubbe them and crabb them up." He thinks an equal study of both Testaments is desirable, the Old being the foundation of the other and "of greater capacity of doctrine" for the decision of all manner of controversies, while the New is supremely valuable for the light it sheds on those points "which are of greatest strife in Christian Religion." Among the books of the Old Testament that require "special attendance" because of their necessary

[1] *Apologie*, sig. C 2 *v.*, C 3.
[2] *v.* title of the letter in MS. No. 295, Trinity College, Dublin.
[3] CCXCIV, ff. 137–46.

or general use he specifies the Pentateuch, particularly Deuteronomy "the fountaine of the rest of the Scripture, and wherewith all the Prophets after Moses unto the last Apostles themselves watered theyr Garden," the book of Joshua, which contains "the topographie almost of the whole Bible," and the "Stories," which "bring a singular light unto the Prophets by comparison of the State and Government of every time with the exhortations and rebukings of the Prophets that prophesied in the same." He notes that some books of the Bible need careful study because they are difficult to understand, *e.g.* Daniel, Ezekiel, Zechariah and the Apocalypse, which are "hard for the matter they handle," the poetical books, wherein the verse "hath caused some cloud," Hosea, which carries a smack of the writer's old age in the shortness of his speech, Ecclesiastes, which was written in Solomon's latter days, the Psalms, Proverbs, and the Epistle to the Romans, which are rendered less easy to comprehend by the large element of doctrine in them. Even the most difficult books, however, are not "like the proud and coy Dames which contemne their sutors," but yield their secrets to intensive and constant application.

Passing on to the interpreters of the Bible Cartwright advises his correspondent not to suffer his ear "to be nailed to the dore of any private mans interpretation, considering that that privilege belongeth onely to the Holy men of God, ...his Publike Notaries, and Recorders of his good pleasure towards us, whom he did sit by, and as it were continually hold their hands whiles they were in writing." Cartwright counsels the study of the moderns before the ancients and of the new writers, as he calls them, the "Patrons of the truth are to be read before the Adversaries." Ecclesiastical history should first be read and he commends particularly as an introduction to the "Stories" a very profitable treatise by John Phrygius. He then lays down directions as to Commentaries. He prefers the "Greek Writers, who as they were inferiour unto the Latines in the soundnesse of certeine Doctrines, so seem they much more religious and simple in commenting upon the Scripture." Of the Greek Fathers he holds "Chrysostom to have the name of all, who, besides his interpretation, was another Apollos, and furnished the Pulpit better then any I can remember to have read." Of modern interpreters he puts Calvin first and remarks upon his adherence to the meaning of the text. He admires Oecolampadius for his excellent learning and Peter Martyr for his "singular and much reading," but points out that the latter's expositions are Commonplaces rather than Commentaries. Dealing with systematic theology or Commonplaces he sums up his views thus: "Here you are not ignorant what place is given to Mr Calvins Institutions, to Mr Beza his Confession: Amongst the Adversaries, after the Master of the Sentences, and Aquinas, Hosius, Canisius, seem to carry the bell." He now advises a study of the Councils and Canons, observing that the older they are the further they are from corruption. As to theological works not yet dealt with he points out the pre-eminence of the learning of the Greek Fathers, commending Gregory of Nazianzus in particular for his profound knowledge. Of the Latin Doctors he names Tertullian, "howsoever toward the latter end he fayned himself," Cyprian, who "for his singular piety hath been allwaies reverend, and ought so much the more to be amiable, as he (with the whole of the Africk Ministery both before and after) kept more steps of the Apostolick Discipline then the other Bishops did," Hilary, whose "Bookes of the Trinity are well written," Ambrose, Augustine, and Jerome, whose "epistles (especially those which are not baseborne) seem to be amongst the floure of their workes." Augustine's *De Civitate Dei* is singled out for praise as a work of learning, while a warning is given that Jerome "with his heat is oftentimes lifted out of his hinges...and therefore is to be taken heed of, especially when he hath an adversarie." As to the new writers, apart from their Commentaries and Commonplaces, he mentions Luther, who "both for his worthy service in the work of the Gospel, and also for the pregnancy of his wit, should not be passed by," but notes that the writings of other famous men of the age, *e.g.* Bucer, need not be read if the student confines his attention to Calvin, who "hath in a manner taken that which is fittest in them."

During his Middelburg years Cartwright was kept acquainted with the doings of the Puritans in England and particularly with the critical events that followed the elevation of Whitgift to the Archbishopric of Canterbury in 1583. Whitgift's vigorous policy of uniformity gravely menaced the whole Puritan movement. It led immediately to the division of the Puritans into two parties, those who were determined at all costs not to conform to the demands of the new regime, and those who were willing to compromise. Among the moderates was Edmund Chapman of Dedham, who on the 4th of November, 1584, wrote to Cartwright lamenting that he was not at hand to give counsel to his brethren and beseeching him to write at length as to the best means that should be adopted for the procurement of peace[1]. A wise leader was urgently required to keep the Puritans from falling into two irreconcileable wings, to prevent their total suppression and to guide them in the course they ought to pursue in relation to the intolerance of the Bishops. The perilous position of his fellow religionists was sufficient to constitute a call to Cartwright to come over and help them.

As it happened he was now anxious for other reasons to come to England. His physical constitution was not robust. It had been undermined by his long study, his labours in plague-stricken Geneva and the rigours of exile. Like the Brownists he found the climate of Zealand telling upon his health. One of his successors, Matthew Holmes, writing from Middelburg, 30 Oct. 1596, to the Earl of Essex, complains that, although he is well entertained by the merchants, the air is so pestilent that he has been sick twice and looked for no life and accordingly desires to return to the ministry in England[2]. By the beginning of 1585 Cartwright was suffering from a complete breakdown in health and was advised by his medical attendants to leave the Low Countries altogether and repair to England. Under this imperative necessity he applied to the Privy Council for leave to return and, apparently before the leave was granted, he sailed for home.

It has been stated that Cartwright returned to England

[1] *P.M.* p. 81.

[2] *Cecil MSS. Hist. MSS. Comm.* Pt VI, p. 460.

because of material want[1]. In his *Apologie*[2], when dealing at length with his finances, he speaks of the time of his exile as that of his greatest necessity, and in his letter to Davison he tells of his dependence upon the generosity of his patrons. One of his successors at Middelburg, Johnson, had, according to Governor Bradford[3], "great and certain maintenance" allowed him by the English merchants, which Bradford reckoned at £200 per annum. Travers received as salary "only a benevolence and voluntary contribution" and in 1580, while in Antwerp, Cartwright received no official allowance at the hands of the merchants' Company[4]. We are not sure what the sources of Cartwright's income during this period were, and whether he was given, besides an honorarium from individual merchants and well-wishers for his ministerial services, a salary for acting as factor. We have to bear in mind, however, that he was receiving a considerable sum of money to help him with his literary work. But we have his own declaration to the effect that his post in Zealand was more lucrative than that to which he was afterwards called. In June, 1590, he wrote to Burghley[5]: "The living my L. of Lecester toke me from, to bring me to this [Warwick Hospital], was (for profit) much better in regard of the charges that this place casteth upon me which th'other did not." Clarke[6] relates what has the appearance of a reliable tradition, viz., that "when he understood that the Merchants, by whom he was maintained, through their great losses decayed in their estates, he returned his salarie to them again." We may conclude that Cartwright, if not living in affluence, does not appear to have been in pecuniary straits and was not forced by penury to leave the Low Countries.

Cartwright's ministry in the Middelburg Church lasted for about two-and-a-half years, from *ca.* October, 1582, till April, 1585. Besides the work of his pastorate, his literary labours, etc., he seems to have acted as a diplomatic intermediary, for we find Stephen le Sieur writing to Walsingham

[1] Waddington, *Hist.* p. 15. [2] sig. D 2 *verso.*
[3] A. Young, *Chronicles of the Pilgrim Fathers* (1841), p. 424.
[4] *v. supra* pp. 185–6. [5] *v.* App. XIX. [6] p. 369.

on 1 March, 1583–4, asking that his letters may be directed to one "Thomas Cartwrit" at Flushing, who would forward them[1]. He was succeeded as chaplain to the merchants at Middelburg by Dudley Fenner (? –1587), Francis Johnson (1589–91), Matthew Holmes (? –1596), Henry Jacob (*ca.* 1599), Hugh Broughton (? –1611), John Forbes (? –1621), etc. The divine service of the merchants, according to Steven[2], was held in the Gasthuis Kerk.

On his arrival in England Cartwright supplemented his petition to the Council with a private appeal to Burghley. In this letter, written in Latin and dated the 17th of April, 1585[3], Cartwright reminds the Lord High Treasurer of his connection with Cambridge University, of which Burghley was still Chancellor, and also claims consideration on the ground that he has spent the last five years in the service of the Church of England. But the chief ground of his appeal is his state of health. Immediately after his arrival he finds that he is still suspected of sedition and disloyalty and that, as if he were a flagrant evildoer, the pursuivants are already on his track. Accordingly, he beseeches Burghley to win Elizabeth's favour for him.

The fear expressed by Cartwright was well grounded. Aylmer, Bishop of London, served a warrant for his apprehension in the Queen's name and committed him to prison. Great multitudes visited the returned exile in prison, much to the annoyance both of Cartwright and the authorities[4]. Their visits amounted to a demonstration of welcome and appreciation. In face of the favour that Cartwright enjoyed among some of her courtiers Elizabeth, ostensibly annoyed by Aylmer's action, repudiated it and visited her temporary displeasure upon the officious prelate. The latter now became one of Burghley's petitioners and, while he sought to explain and justify his conduct, implored his Lordship to appease the royal anger. "I understand," he wrote on the 22nd of June, 1585[5], "my selfe to be in some disgrace with her

[1] *S.P. Eliz. Holl. and Fland.* XXI, No. 39.
[2] *History of the Scottish Church, Rotterdam* (1832), p. 316.
[3] App. XV. [4] *v.* App. XXIX. [5] *Lansd. MSS.* XLV, No. 44.

maiestie about M. Cartwrite because I sent word to your LL: by the clerke of the counsell that I committed him by her maiesties commanndement. Alas my L. in what a dilemma stande I, that yf I had not served that warrant I should have had all your displeasures which I was not able to beare, and usinge it for my shilde (beinge not forbidden by her maiestie) I am blamed for not takinge uppon me a matter, wherin she her selfe would not be seene. Well I leave it to god, and to your wisdome to consider in what a daungerous place of service I am, but god whome I serve, and in whose handes the hartes of princes are as the rivers of waters: can and will turne all to the best, and stirre up such honorable frendes as you are to appease her Highnes indignation."

Cartwright could not have endured imprisonment for several months, as has been stated[1], for he was free on the 17th of April and we find him rejoicing in his liberation by the beginning of June. On the 2nd of June he warmly thanks Burghley for procuring his liberty[2]. He expresses his gratitude for the favourable *testimonium*... *quod in clarissimo regni senatus consessu de me dixisti*. He is especially gratified by the honourable mention made of his services to the Church of England overseas. This gratification was due to his anxiety to impress upon the anti-Presbyterians the fact of his devotion to the welfare of the Church, which his opponents thought he was seeking to destroy.

In December, 1583, Whitgift, while addressing a deputation of nonconformists, declared that he was willing to befriend Cartwright should he come home and live peaceably: "And for Mr Cartwrite and my self, we mighte both have bene better occupied, especially the man that first began, yet of my self I doubt, because I have defended the booke which so manye martyrs have sealed with their bloude. But since this diversitie hath bene in the church, religion hath gon backwarde, and popery hath so encreased that now it seemeth it will not be satisfied but by the Princes bloude, whom God longe preserve. It hath bene reported that I should repent me of my workes against Mr Cartwrighte, but I protest I

[1] Brook, *Mem.* p. 232.

[2] App. XVI.

do it not, nor never will, yet I love the man, and if he would returne and live in the peace of the church, he should not find a better friend than my self."[1] As good as his word the Archbishop, in 1585, showed all kindness and courtesy to Cartwright. The latter spoke very highly to Leicester of his usage at Whitgift's hands.

Always eager to maintain the integrity of the Church of England, Cartwright was, after his recent encounter with the Separatists, more earnest than ever in his desire to preserve its unity. He had not changed his principles and still cherished his constant ambition to presbyterianise the Establishment, but his characteristic of loyalty to the Church was now emphasised both by friend and foe. On the ground of this devotion Leicester sought to impress upon Whitgift the desirability of granting Cartwright a licence to preach. In the Earl's opinion such a concession would greatly further the Church's cause and help to bring the body of nonconformists to obedience. Leicester's letter to Whitgift, written from the Court on the 14th of July, 1585, is transcribed from the original by Fuller[2].

Whitgift knew that his old antagonist now professed an unwonted degree of allegiance to the Church and promised to uphold, both privately and publicly, the estimation and peace of the same[3]. On the other hand, he was aware that Cartwright, while regretting the manner in which the Replies had been written, still believed in the views therein expressed. He was consequently chary about granting the request for a licence to preach. In view of the strenuous campaign against nonconformity which Whitgift was directing and the esteem in which Cartwright was held by the Puritans, it is not surprising that Whitgift considered it his bounden duty to refrain from further approbation of Cartwright until he had more than a mere promise of partial conformity. The Archbishop carefully explained his attitude to the Puritan in his reply to Leicester on the 17th of July 1585[4].

[1] 5 Dec. 1583. *Sec. Parte*, I, p. 216.
[2] *C.H.* bk IX, sect. vi, § 29.
[3] *ibid.* bk IX, sect. vii, § 27, articles 7, 8.
[4] *ibid.* bk IX, sect. vi, § 29.

Leicester's campaign in the Netherlands was soon to open, and Cartwright seems to have been chosen by his influential friends, maybe because of his intimate knowledge of the country, to take a part in the initial stages of Elizabeth's venture in the interest of the victims of Spanish force and cruelty. Following upon Elizabeth's treaty with the United Provinces (10 Aug. 1585), it was agreed that her troops should hold Brill, Flushing, and the fort of Rammekers, for the purpose of securing the Scheldt and the estuary of the old Rhine. Davison, who had been engaged in a special mission to the Low Countries in 1584 (Nov. 1584 to May, 1585), was again sent over at the end of August, 1585[1]. On the 30th of September Brill was occupied by the English, Davison formally receiving the keys of the town. On the 19th of October Flushing was taken over by Davison pending the arrival of the Governor, Philip Sidney, who arrived on the 18th of November. Leicester himself did not reach Flushing till the 10th of December, and two days later went to Middelburg, which he left on the 17th of December[2]. These details are given because they concern the movements of Cartwright's friends, with whom he was likely to associate at this time. On the 15th of October he wrote to Walsingham from Flushing. His letter shows that he was now acting as a forwarding agent between M. Bertrand Combes and Walsingham. Combes, a Frenchman, had served as an intelligence officer with the late Prince of Orange, and had been commended to Davison by Count Adolf of Neuenaar (Comte de Moeurs). He proved a faithful servant of England[3]. Cartwright had been at the Hague, where he received from Combes the communication now accompanying his letter. The latter runs thus: "Right honorable, beinge by a gentleman named Mounsr Combes requyred to convey safely unto your honor all such letters as he should send me for your honor, As also safely to send to him into Germany such letters as from your honor shalbe dyrected unto him, by such conveyans as he hath appoynted me, And most desyrous

[1] *Cal. S.P. For.* 1584–5.
[2] *ibid.* 1585–6.
[3] *ibid.* 1585–6, pp. 195, 267.

to employ eny servyce for your honor, have promysed him faythfully and dilligently to accomplysh his request, And beinge on Satterday last in the Haaghe in Holland, he delyvered me for your honor this enclosed, which I send by Mr Bornet servant to Mr Davydson Embassador for his Majesty in thes partyes. Thus cessinge I most humbly commytt your honor unto Allmighty god. From Flushinge this 15th of Octobr stilo veter."[1]

A few weeks later, 6th Nov. O.S., Cartwright again transmits important papers to Walsingham, his covering letter running as follows: "Right honorable, I received yesternight late a Packett from the Graeve of Newenaer, and therin this enclosed, with ordre to se the same safely conveyed to your honor, wherein (as his honor wryteth me) there is a packett for her Matie. And for the safe Conveyance thereof I have delyvered yt herein closed to Liewtenant Powele, who hath promysed safely and spedely to se the same effected, Thus resting to do your honor all dewtifull service, I most humbly commytt the same to Allmighty god. Flushing 16th November, 1585. stilo novo."[2]

These are the last letters known to us written by Cartwright in the Netherlands[3]. Shortly afterwards he came back to England again. We are not sure of the date of his return. He may have come with Davison in February, 1585–6. But it was evidently not long before he was installed as Master of the Leicester Hospital in Warwick.

[1] *S.P. Eliz. Holl.* IV, p. 42. [2] *ibid.* V, p. 15.

[3] It is possible that the Thomas Cartwright we have met with in Flushing was not the same person as the Puritan, but because proof is lacking and the autograph letters concerned do not lead to a decisive conclusion, we have identified him with the subject of our study.

CHAPTER V

PROGRESS AND DOWNFALL

Progress of Puritanism from 1577 onwards—the Conference movement—Whitgift's articles—Puritan consolidation—the influence of the Scottish exiles—the Puritan appeal to Parliament—the Puritan Book of Discipline—the heyday and fall of the Puritan meetings—the Marprelate Tracts—the death of Field and Leicester—the suppression of the Puritan movement—Puritan literature—Cartwright and Marprelate.

DURING the years of Cartwright's sojourn in the Low Countries (1577–85) English Puritanism continued to make slow but measurable progress. The Bishops were aware of its disturbing influence. On the 27th of June, 1577, Aylmer suggested to Burghley that such men as Charke, Chapman, Field and Wilcocks should be transferred to Lancashire, Staffordshire, Shropshire and other barbarous counties to draw the people from gross ignorance and Popery[1]. Thus the Puritans would be utilised and got rid of. The novel practical experiment, however, was not put into effect. The Privy Council was kept in touch with isolated instances of nonconformity throughout the country. Their Acts contain numerous references to the spread of the Family of Love and other sectaries[2]. More serious were the reported gatherings of Puritans in Northamptonshire, *e.g.* Peter Wentworth was summoned before the Council in connection with secret meetings held in his house at Lillingston, to which "great resortes of sondrie persons" came from surrounding parishes "to receive the Sacramentes after an other sorte."[3] Vice-Chamberlain Hatton, whose house was near Northampton, and others were ordered to enquire into the alleged disorders. The Queen had been informed that certain ministers, evidently Puritans, were evading their duty and relieving their conscience by undertaking preaching only

[1] *Lansd. MSS.* xxv, No. 30. Cf. proposal to transport Puritans to Ulster. *S.P. Eliz. Dom. Add.* xxi, No. 121.

[2] *Acts P.C.* x, p. 426; xi, pp. 74, 77 (Conventicles in Gloucester Diocese), xi, pp. 138, 444 (Familists in Suffolk and Exeter Diocese).

[3] *ibid.* xi, p. 132 (20 May 1579), *v.* pp. 133, 219.

while they secured the services of others for the administration of the Sacraments. There were thus springing up two classes of ministers, reading ministers willing to celebrate and preachers who would not celebrate the Sacraments. The Council accordingly sent a general letter, dated 10th January, 1579–80, to all Bishops enjoining them to see that ministers did not disjoin their preaching and sacramental functions[1]. At this time the Council as a rule looked with a kindly eye upon the Puritan ministers, dealt leniently with their irregularities and on occasions even bestowed more favour upon them than upon the Bishops. For instance, having heard that the Bishop of Norwich was going to restrain two Norwich Puritan ministers, More and Roberts, from preaching, the Council sent instructions (5th April, 1580) to the Bishop to deal charitably with them[2]. The Bishops naturally felt sore at being hampered and thwarted by the Councillors in their effort to stamp out nonconformity. For their literal devotion to duty they received neither thanks nor support. They frequently complained of this[3] and on the 26th of May, 1579, Aylmer frankly told Burghley that he was the man who most discouraged him. By blaming the Bishops for their severity and finding excuses for nonconforming preachers he was emboldening the Puritans and hindering the Bishops in their labours for the peace and unity of the Church[4].

There was sufficient reason for this strange state of affairs. If the Puritans were fortunate at this period in having an Archbishop, who sympathised with many of their aims, they were more fortunate in the enjoyment of a spell of leniency and connivance on the part of the civil authorities, which was due to the latter being preoccupied with a rigorous anti-Roman policy. A series of events—the Northern rebellion of 1569, the issue of the Papal Bull in 1570, the recurring conspiracies connected with the Queen of Scots, the advent of the Jesuit missionaries, etc.—had accentuated the Roman

[1] *Acts P.C.* XI, p. 367.
[2] *ibid.* XI, p. 437.
[3] *Parker Corresp.* pp. 344, 367, 369.
[4] *Lansd. MSS.* XXVIII, No. 72.

danger. Cuthbert Mayne, the proto-martyr of Douay, arrived in 1576 and was executed the following year. He was followed by a stream of Roman Catholic enthusiasts, whose object was to seduce the Queen's subjects from their allegiance, to consolidate their co-religionists in England, to foment rebellion and prepare the way for the downfall of Elizabeth, the triumph of Mary and the dominion of the Pope and the Spaniards. Spain and Rome were working in concert; both took part in the invasion of Ireland in 1579. The mission of Parsons and Campion began in the summer of 1580 and took the form of a political campaign rather than a religious crusade. National peace and security were thus at stake. A Royal Proclamation was issued in July, 1580, against the Jesuits and their supporters; Parliament in 1581 issued stringent enactments against Romanists, whose faith now practically became equivalent to treason. The Puritans were among the most ardent of English anti-Romanists; Field, Charke and others distinguished themselves, in writing and disputation, as antagonists of the Jesuits. Parsons and other Jesuits pointed out that the Puritans were among the Papists' most determined enemies[1], and the Queen of Scots referred to the designs of the Puritans against herself[2]. It was therefore politic for the secular authorities not to repress such useful enthusiasts. Besides, to weaken the Protestant front by crushing Puritanism and thereby creating dissension in Church and State would have been insane and disastrous. The anti-Roman policy of the government thus befriended the cause of Presbyterian development and prevented the Bishops from having their own way with nonconformity until the Roman danger passed away, that is, till the defeat of the Spanish Armada.

In these circumstances we are not surprised to find that the Puritans began to resuscitate the exercises or meetings of a similar kind under the name of Conferences. Some of them suggested that these assemblies, open only to ministers,

[1] Froude, *English Seamen* (1895), pp. 6, 120.

[2] *S.P. Mary Qu. of Scots*, XVII, No. 84. The place of the Puritans in the opposition to Romanism in general and the Scottish Queen in particular is an important subject that is worthy of special examination.

should be held monthly at the deaneries as "a speciall remedie to redresse the fearfull sinne of the great ignorance of the ministerie of this age."[1] The scheme of such reformers was to graft a nascent Presbyterianism on to an Episcopal Church. This aim being meanwhile impracticable many of the Puritans carried on such Conferences without official recognition in secret. Bancroft, when dealing with the doings of the Puritans during the period, 1572–83, says: "They had then their meetings of Ministers, tearmed brethren, in private houses in London: as namely of Field, Wilcox, Standen, Iackson, Bonham, Seintloe (*sic*), Crane, and Edmonds, which meetings were called conferences, according to the plot in the first and second admonitions mentioned."[2] These Conferences, in the opinion of the Second Admonitioner[3], were equivalent not merely to the exercises, but also to the modern Presbytery—a court of a Presbyterian Church standing midway between the Kirk Session (then called a Consistory) and the Provincial Synod. We have already noticed that most of the men mentioned by Bancroft were as a body in correspondence with Cartwright in 1577 and that there were kindred bodies in other parts of the country, with which the Londoners were in intimate touch, in the same year. At this date, therefore, there were already several associations, which virtually formed self-constituted and embryonic assemblies of a Presbyterian Church of England, which it was their aim eventually to establish.

"In these London-meetings, at the first," writes Bancroft[4], "little was debated, but against subscription, the attyre, and booke of common prayer. Marry after (saith hee[5]) that Charke, Travers, Barber, Gardner, Cheston, and lastly Crooke and Egerton, joined themselves into that brotherhood, then the handling of the Discipline began to be rife." They now resolved "That for the better bringing in of the said forme of Discipline they should not onely (as well publikely

[1] *Sec. Parte*, I, p. 153.
[2] *D.P.* p. 43, *i.e.* p. 67.
[3] *Pur. Man.* pp. 96, 107–8.
[4] *D.P.* p. 43.
[5] *i.e.* Thomas Edmundes, then of the Presbyterian faction, from whose depositions before the Eccl. Commissioners and in the Star Chamber Bancroft gleaned the information given.

as privately) teach it, but by little and little, as much as possibly they might, draw the same into practise, though they concealed the names, either of Presbytery, Elder, Deacon, making little account of the name for the time, so that their offices might be secretly established."[1] Travers returned from Antwerp in 1580 and soon after his homecoming became a lecturer at the Temple. His experience of Presbyterianism abroad and his status as an ordained Presbyterian minister would greatly strengthen the metropolitan brotherhood with which he identified himself. He had served a Church which although nominally Anglican was virtually Presbyterian and, if he did not initiate, he would heartily concur in the insinuating advance policy now adopted by the London Presbyterians.

The forward movement was also manifesting itself outside of London. Bancroft refers to a notable gathering of Puritans at Cockfield, where John Knewstub was minister, on the 8th of May, 1582: "There was an assembly of three score Ministers, appointed out of Essex, Cambridge-shiere, and Norfolke, to meet the eighth of May 1582. at Cockefield, (Master Knewstubs towne) there to conferre of the common booke, what might be tollerated, and what necessarily to be refused in every point of it: apparel, matter, form, dayes," etc.[2] Heylyn's chronology is at fault when he says[3] that the meeting at "Corkvil" was due to the great influence of Cartwright after his return from the Continent. Cartwright was still in Antwerp at the time. Within two months, at the time of Commencement, another meeting was held in Cambridge[4]. As Fuller[5] points out: "The year (1582) proved very active, especially in the practices of presbyterians, who now found so much favour, as almost amounted to a connivance at their discipline. For, whilst the severity of the state was at this time intended to the height against Jesuits, some lenity, of course, by the very rules of opposition, fell

[1] *D.P.* p. 44.

[2] *ibid.* Bancroft's authority is a letter from Pig to Field, 16 May, 1582.

[3] *A.R.* lib. VII, § 25.

[4] *D.P.* p. 45.

[5] *C.H.* bk IX, sect. iv, § 18.

to the share of the nonconformists, even on the score of their notorious enmity to the Jesuitical party."

Fortunately we are in possession of the minute book of one of the Conferences that were established in the year 1582, namely that of Dedham and district[1]. This book, which covers the years 1582–89, furnishes invaluable information regarding the development of the Conferences during the 'eighties. It records the progress of what was virtually a Presbyterian association and throws light upon the general Puritan movement with which it was affiliated. The constitution of the Dedham Conference was drawn up in October, 1582, and illustrates the nature of the assemblies that were now spreading[2]. It had all the appearance of an exercise, but differed from the earlier Elizabethan exercises in that it had no official recognition and was obliged to meet privately. It is noteworthy that at first it was called merely a "meeting," "assembly" or "Conference," not a "*classis*" or "Presbytery," although it was really the nucleus of the latter. Its history shows very clearly the part played by the exercises or Conferences in the progress of Presbyterianism and how, step by step, the definitely articulated organisation of the latter grew out of such meetings.

During the year 1583 the members of the Dedham Conference discussed such subjects as the Sabbath, divorce, baptism and the Prayer Book[3]. Their nonconformist character is apparent in their repeated consideration of the question: "how far a pastor might goe in reading the book of common praier."[4] That theirs was the Puritanism, which is generally charged with being hostile to the joys of this world, may be gathered from their attempt "to staie the playes of Maietree."[5] As we have seen they discussed early in the year the invitation made to Cartwright to undertake the confutation of the Rhemish Testament and in April eight of the brethren wrote urging him to take the task in hand[6]. The Conferences were

[1] *The Presbyterian Movement...illustrated by the Minute Book of the Dedham Classis*, ed. R. G. Usher (*Cam. Soc.* 3rd ser. vol. VIII), 1905. Quoted as *P.M.*

[2] *ibid.* pp. 26 ff. The first regular meeting took place on 3 Dec. 1582.

[3] *ibid.* pp. 28 ff. [4] *ibid.* pp. 28, 31. [5] *ibid.* p. 29. [6] *v. supra* p. 201.

already in touch with one another and were preparing the way for a Presbyterian confederation. The Dedham minute book shows that the Essex ministers consulted their brethren, evidently members of other Conferences, in Cambridge, London, Norwich and Suffolk, *e.g.* on the 24th of June it was agreed "that Mr D. Chapman, Mr Stocton and Mr Morse crave the iudgmentes of some godly men in Cambridge tutching the question of the Sabboth"[1] and on the 7th of October: "The thinges moved were these: first that it were good the Archb. shuld be written unto to be favourable to ye Church and to discipline. the answer was, that letters shuld be sent to other brethren about it, and yt D. Chapman shuld write to London and Norwich and Mr Sandes to Cambridge about it, and to the brethren in Suffolk, and that Mr D. Withers shuld be written unto."[2]

Whitgift, immediately after his confirmation as Archbishop of Canterbury, prepared a set of articles, which were designed to secure uniformity in the Church of England[3]. Approved by the Queen, they were sent to the Bishops (19 Oct. 1583) to be put into execution. The whole series of articles was unfavourably received by the Puritans[4]. In opposition to that dealing with Popish recusants they urged that the best way to spread true religion was to "encourage the number of true, painfull, watchfull, and zealous prechers." They feared that the article concerning the censorship of books was aimed at Cartwright's "awnsering of the Jesuits Testament, allreadie by report in some good forwardnes." They upheld the use of the Geneva Bible as against the Bishops' Bible now exclusively authorised. They pointed out that there would not be a desire for the conventicles, which were forbidden in another article, if parishes were duly furnished with "a sufficient, able, preching ministerie"; they also opposed this article on the ground that it affected deprived ministers forced to sustain themselves as chaplains and tutors in private houses, as well as the valuable Con-

[1] *P.M.* p. 30. [2] *ibid.* p. 31.

[3] St. *Whit.* I, p. 229; Frere, *Hist.* p. 224; G. W. Prothero, *Select Statutes 1558–1625*, Elizabethan section VIII, § 16; Gee and Hardy, p. 481.

[4] *Sec. Parte*, I, pp. 172 ff.

ferences privately held by ministers since the suppression of the public exercises. They naturally objected to the new request for uniformity of apparel. The greatest discussion, however, was caused by three articles, subscription to which was made obligatory on the part of all who exercised any ecclesiastical function. These in effect run thus:

1. That her Majesty under God has and ought to have the sovereignty and rule over all persons born within her realms and that no foreign power, prelate, state or potentate has any jurisdiction or authority within the said realms.

2. That the Book of Common Prayer and of ordering Bishops, etc. contains nothing contrary to the Word of God and that the same may lawfully be used and that the subscriber will use the said book and none other.

3. That the subscriber allows the book of Articles of Religion agreed upon in the Convocation of 1562–3 and that he believes all the Articles therein contained to be agreeable to the Word of God.

The Puritans found no fault with the first of these three articles, except that it was superfluous, every ordained minister having already taken his oath of allegiance. They disallowed altogether subscription to the second, the Book of Common Prayer being in their opinion not entirely conformable to the Word of God. The third was deemed acceptable in terms of the statute[1] which, according to the Puritan interpretation, required subscription to the doctrinal Articles only. The second of these three articles was the crucial one. It created a violent storm of opposition in the ranks of the Puritans and led to widespread suspensions and depositions.

In November, 1583, several of the ministers in the diocese of Chichester refused to subscribe the three articles. Having been suspended they sent a deputation to interview Whitgift in London[2]. In the course of their "lardge speach" with the Archbishop on the 5th of December, the latter said to them: "Because you are the first that have bene thus farr proceeded againste in this case, you shalbe made an example to all

[1] 13 Eliz. c. 12. [2] *Sec. Parte*, 1, pp. 209 ff.

others in this busines." "I see," said he, "whence you have the most of your doubtes; yonge men and unlearned have done more harm in translateinge then ever they will do good; it had bene good they had not bene borne." Then he referred to his controversy with Cartwright, evidently holding the writings of the latter responsible for much of the hostility to the demand for subscription[1]. As was common with the adversaries of the Puritans he spoke slightingly of their youthfulness: "You are unlearned, and but boyes in comparison of us, who have studied divinity before you for the most were borne." Eventually the ministers gave a modified subscription, Whitgift's satisfaction with which shows that he was at this point willing to be lenient and capable of compromise. The qualified submission, however, was ill taken at Court, and doubtless this fact stiffened Whitgift's attitude to non-subscribers in the future[2]. During the year 1584 many ministers were suspended or deprived for their refusal to subscribe[3]. They were charged with being Puritans whose object was "to erect a new popedome in everie parish, in advauncing of their new presbiterie."[4] They protested that they were "neither Puritans nor Brownists, nor of the Family of Love, nor sectaries of any sort," and that their chief desire was to bring the Church into conformity with the Word of God[5]. "The question betweene us," said John Edwin, the non-subscribing Vicar of Wandsworth (30 April, 1584), "is whether in the booke of common prayer be any thinge repugnant to the worde of God."[6]

The new demand for subscription served to unify the forces of the Puritans and to make their voice more articulate. "Sir," wrote Field to Chapman on "the 19 of this 11th moneth 1583,"[7] "though our entercourse of writinge hath faynted of late, yet methinkes there is good occasion given that yt shuld be agayne renewed, for the trials being many that are laid upon us it shuld provoke us to stirre up one another that we might stand fast...Our new Archbishopp,

[1] *v. supra* p. 230.
[2] *Sec. Parte*, 1, p. 219.
[3] *ibid.* 1, pp. 221 ff.
[4] *ibid.* 1, pp. 231, 233.
[5] *ibid.* 1, p. 234.
[6] *ibid.* 1, p. 251.
[7] *P.M.* p. 96.

now he is in, sheweth himself as he was wonte to be...he is egerly set to overthrowe and wast his poore Church. use what meanes you can by writing, consultinge and speakinge with those whom yt concerneth and who may doe good. It wilbe to late to deale afterwarde. The peace of the Church is at an end, if he be not curbed. you are wise to consider by advise and by iogning together now to strengthen your handes in this worke. The Lord directe both you and us that we may fighte a good fighte and fynish with joy." "By the meanes," wrote Chapman to Field[1], "of to much straungnes (as yt seemeth to me) we are distracted into a miserable variety of Answers to these Articles, which I feare one day wilbe cast as dunge upon our faces...let us growe to a more generall conference for unity both in affection and iudgment if yt may be, that we may see and feele more comforte in ourselves and in our brethren. Such a holy meetinge is longed for of many. write what you thinke good herin." Besides feeling the need of consolidation the Puritan ministers and their sympathisers aired their grievances and cried out for redress. Supplications were addressed to Whitgift, Burghley, and the Privy Council[2]. The suppliants protested against subscription especially to the second of the three articles and claimed the liberty of ministers who desired the further reformation of the Church to remain in office. The Clerk of the Council, Robert Beale, a Puritan lawyer with a bitter anti-Roman bias, worked hard to procure favour for the nonconformists, wrote against the articles and brought himself into bad odour with the Archbishop by his efforts[3]. Sir Francis Knollys humbly besought Whitgift to stay the crusade against the non-subscribers, particularly on the ground that the Popish danger could only be thoroughly met by the preaching of such zealous ministers as those who were being ousted from office[4]. Like other prominent statesmen he regarded the Puritans as a bulwark against the

[1] n.d. *P.M.* p. 95.

[2] *Sec. Parte*, I, pp. 223 ff.; Fuller, *C.H.* bk IX, sect. V; St. *Whit.* I, pp. 249 ff.

[3] St. *Whit.* I, pp. 283 ff.; III, pp. 87 ff.

[4] 8 June, 1584; *ibid.* III, p. 103.

threatening invasion of Romanism. In July, 1584, Burghley himself wrote to Whitgift severely criticising the harsh measures employed against dissenting ministers—especially the list of twenty-four articles drawn up in May, to be executed *ex officio mero*—and complaining that the Archbishop's proceedings savoured too much of the Romish inquisition[1]. Whitgift in his reply pointed out that in order to satisfy Burghley and others he was now dealing with ministers, not because they would not subscribe, but because they did not conform to the laws of the Church, and maintained that the course he was pursuing was purely in the interest of the established religion and the unity of the Church and not, as some supposed, for personal reasons, viz., for the better maintenance of his book against Cartwright[2]. On the 20th of September, 1584, Burghley, Warwick, Leicester, Hatton, Walsingham and other Councillors, lamenting the eviction of so many good preachers and the consequent dearth of religious instruction in many parishes, earnestly solicited Whitgift and Aylmer to stay their ruthless campaign[3]. Parliamentary supporters of the Puritans pleaded, in a petition to the House of Lords for the reformation of the Church, for the restoration of the suspended and deprived ministers and proposed that exercises or Conferences should be allowed in the archdeaconries of the various dioceses, but the Lords refused to entertain the proposals[4]. Supplications to Convocation and conferences between Church dignitaries and Puritan representatives were also of no avail[5].

In order to look at the momentous crisis from the viewpoint of the Conferences we shall now consider the conflict between Whitgift and the Puritans as it is reflected in the minutes of the Dedham Conference for 1584. In January the Essex ministers were already contemplating the course they "might take for going before the Bishop."[6] On the 2nd of March: "It was thoughte good if anie of the brethren

[1] St. *Whit.* III, p. 104.
[2] *ibid.* III, pp. 107 ff.; *W.W.* III, p. 602.
[3] St. *Whit.* I, p. 328.
[4] Feb., 1584–5; *ibid.* I, pp. 347 ff.; III, p. 118; D'Ewes, p. 357.
[5] *Sec. Parte*, I, pp. 275, 296.
[6] *P.M.* p. 33.

were called to subscribe to require tyme to deliberate."[1] On the 6th of April Chapman, who was particularly anxious for the unification of the Puritan forces, "moved that the Bs proceeding did admonish the ministers to have a generall meeting to conferre what might be done" and his proposal was sympathetically received by the Conference: "It was thought good every one shuld stirre up his friend to consider of it."[2] A month afterwards, 4th of May, "It was thought good a generall meetinge of lerned brethren shuld be procured for better advise and consent about the cause of subscriptions."[3] On the 1st of June it was agreed that a deputy should consult the London brethren about the proposed General Conference: "ffor the generall meeting moved before it was thought good yt Mr Newman shuld goe to London and understand the brethrens mynd and certify us of it."[4] It was arranged that the said Conference should meet on the 30th of August. It was evidently attended by representatives from Norfolk, Suffolk, Essex, Kent and London, and it is important to notice that one of the chief subjects discussed at it was: "Whether yt were not fytt that a generall supplication were presented to her Majesty with a full draughte of the discipline we desire."[5]

When any of their members suffered suspension or deprivation the Dedham Conference considered the matter of temporary supply[6]. It is noteworthy that some of the ministers, although they had lost their charges because of their refusal to subscribe, still continued to attend the meetings of the Conference, *e.g.* Dowe, Tilney, Sandes and Crick were suspended in January, 1583–4[7]. In June it was decided that the congregations affected should make supplication in behalf of the pastors who had been taken from them[8]. In July Mr Dow moved "what course he shuld take for Stratford one having gott the presentation" and was advised "to ask counsell and to gett his parish to iogne with him."[9] In the same month cases of other non-subscribers were discussed,

[1] *P.M.* p. 34.
[2] *ibid.* p. 35.
[3] *ibid.* p. 35.
[4] *ibid.* p. 35.
[5] *ibid.* p. 94.
[6] 4 May, 1584; *ibid.* p. 35.
[7] *Sec. Parte*, I, p. 243.
[8] *P.M.* p. 36.
[9] *ibid.* p. 36.

e.g. "Mr Tilney moved whether he shuld goe to the court, he was at his 3 admonicion. it was thought good he shuld not goe. Mr Negus was advised to tarry with his parish if the godlie desired it and wold mainteyne him."[1] We thus see the Puritans ousted from their offices; we observe that conforming clergy are appointed in some instances to take their places; but of most interest is the endeavour of the Puritan ministers to win the support of the laity and to move the members of their congregations to make supplication in their behalf. In view of the fact that some of the lay petitions were initiated by the ministers Usher says "it will now be difficult to contend that these documents represent a spontaneous or widespread feeling in the ministers' favour among their congregations."[2] Doubtless the Puritan movement at this time was not supported by the rank and file of the laity. There are however instances on record of popular attachment to evicted Puritan ministers[3]. This attachment may not always imply acceptance of the Presbyterian tenets held by the preachers, but it seems sufficiently genuine to entitle us to regard Usher's assertion as too sweeping.

In order to strengthen their case the Essex Puritans drew up a Survey of the clergy of their district. The matter was broached by Crick on the 1st of July, when "it was thought good that enquiry should be made of the number of mynisters nere us which are both insufficient in lerninge and notoriouslye offensyve in liffe."[4] This work of surveying was taken up by the Puritans in most of the counties where they had a following and was designed to reveal the dire need of reforming an institution, which tolerated an exceedingly large number of non-preaching, non-resident and even scandalously unworthy ministers, while it sought to repress many of its most earnest and efficient representatives. Surveys taken by the Puritans, 1584–6, in the counties of Cornwall, Lincoln, Oxford, Berks, Bucks, Middlesex, Surrey, Norfolk, Essex, Warwick, and Rutland are contained in the *Seconde Parte of a Register*[5]. These Surveys constituted an argument in the form of

[1] *P.M.* p. 37. [2] *ibid.* p. 36 n. [3] *Sec. Parte*, I, pp. xiv ff.
[4] *P.M.* p. 36. [5] II, pp. 88 ff.

schedules against the existing state of the Church and an eloquent plea in favour of the downtrodden Puritans. The latter, regarding them as an instrument that might lead to the redress of their grievances, brought them before the notice of the civil rulers, as is apparent from the title of the general Survey of 1586: "How miserable the state of our Church is for want of a godlie learned ministerie thorow out this Realme, maie appeare by this brief of divers Countries and shires, gathered trulie out of the surveis made the last parliament and partlie this, 2 of November, 1586."[1] The Essex schedule was sent to the Privy Council before the 20th of September, 1584, and so impressed the Councillors that they, on that date, wrote an urgent letter to Whitgift and Aylmer, pointing out the evil of depriving the Puritans, who were so useful for the instruction of the people against Popery and of retaining in office so many ministers, who were totally inefficient[2].

On the 3rd of August, 1584, the question of the oath, which was now being administered in some cases along with the articles, came before the Dedham Conference: "Mr Lewis told us that the Archb. offred Articles to some and an othe: and therfore moved the brethren to shew what course shuld be taken. it was answered we shuld heare something by the brethren to whom the othe was offred."[3] At the same time it was reported that "the iudgment of the lawyers is that the othe offred by the Bishops is not to be allowed."

We have already noticed that Chapman, in a letter to Cartwright, November, 1584, expressed his "dislike of both parties for their hotte and violent manner of proceedinge." In August he had made his views known to his brethren in the Dedham Conference: "Mr Chapman moved whether it were thought good that a reconciliation shuld be offred to the Bs: that since we professe one god and preache one doctrine we may iogne together with better consent to build up the Churche." The majority, however, were opposed to compromise and the proposal was rejected[4]. Here we see

[1] *Sec. Parte*, II, p. 89.
[2] St. *Whit.* I, pp. 328 ff.
[3] *P.M.* p. 37.
[4] *ibid.* p. 37.

signs, not only of the breach between the Bishops and the Puritan party, but also of a split within the latter itself.

It is abundantly demonstrated by the Dedham minute book that individual Puritans were confirmed in their non-conformity by the Conference, from which, when they were dealt with by the Bishops, they sought advice and guidance, *e.g.* Newman was advised on the 7th of September, 1584, not to yield to subscription[1]. But the Conference was careful not to come to rash and rebellious conclusions with regard to its suspended members, who, in spite of their inhibition, were eager to preach, *e.g.* "Mr Negus alleged the B. had proceeded with him against law, and therefore he thought he might preach agayne. it was said unto him, that he might aske advise of some wise and discreet lawyers tutching that point and if it be not against law then to proceed."[2]

As the opening of Parliament[3] approached the Essex Puritans made preparation to bring their cause before it. At their meeting on the 2nd of December it was moved "whether it were not convenient that a fast shuld be against Parliament that was at hand" and "it was thought necessary that ther shuld be one and every man to stirre up his people to earnest prayer for the good of the Churche." It was further "agreed upon at this tyme that in every cuntrey some shuld be chosen so farre as we could procure it that some of the best creditt and most forward for the gosple shuld goe up to London to solicite the cause of the Churche."[4] On the 2nd of December a member of the Conference urged his brethren to stir up any gentlemen of worth and godliness to be zealous for the reformation[5]. On the 4th of January, 1584–5, "Mr Dcw moved this, whether it were not needfull that ther shuld be praier and fastinge agayne bycause of the assembly of parliament," and the Conference, accepting the proposal, resolved "that the brethren of London shuld be written unto, to know when they appoint to have theirs, that we might ioigne with

[1] *P.M.* p. 38. [2] 5 Oct. 1584; *ibid.* p. 39.
[3] 23 Nov. 1584—29 March, 1585.
[4] *ibid.* p. 40. [5] *ibid.* p. 40.

them, and that some shuld contynue to solicite the cause of the Church there."[1]

The sitting of Parliament focussed the attention of the Puritans on London, emphasised the leading position held by the metropolitan brethren, and served to unite the Conferences still more closely. Bancroft says[2]: "At the time of the Parliament last mentioned (1584–5), I finde, that there was a nationall Synod held likewise in London by these brethren: according to their former decisions and Synodical Discipline. This appeareth by three letters," viz., one, dated 26 Jan. 1584–5, from eleven Essex ministers arranging for a fast on the same day as that chosen by the London brethren, the second, dated 2 Feb. 1584–5, from nine of the Essex ministers intimating that they had elected two deputies to co-operate with the London Puritans, and the third, dated 29 Nov. 1584, from Gellibrand of Oxford to Field, apologising for absence "from that holy assembly without leave." We have to bear in mind that the London Conference would, like the provincial Conferences, hold regular meetings, probably monthly. When Parliament met, it was easy and natural for the London brethren, by themselves or along with representatives from the other Conferences, to serve as a central committee, with John Field as secretary. The London meetings at this period are properly designated Conferences, or, when attended by provincial deputies, General Conferences. It is to one of these meetings, of which there were in all likelihood several during the winter of 1584–5, that Gellibrand refers. With regard to the one in February Bancroft's notice of it may be supplemented by an entry in the Dedham minute book, 1 Feb. 1584–5: "Mr D Chapman moved..to seeke by what means the great cause of the Church that is now in hand might be delt in and good done in it, and for to procure some good, it was concluded that Mr Knewstub for Suffolk and Mr Gifford and Mr Wright of Essex shuld be moved to deale for the church and letters to be written to them to that

[1] *P.M.* p. 41; cf. *D.P.* p. 75, where reference is made to a letter, dated 26 Jan. 1584–5, from eleven ministers of Essex to Field, "wherin they desire to be certified, whether the brethren meant to be exercised in prayer and fasting, and upon what day."

[2] *D.P.* p. 75.

ende."[1] The meeting which these deputies attended would constitute a General Conference, which, while partaking of the nature of a National Synod, was not, as Bancroft asserts, definitely and officially convened as such. Bancroft is also misleading in stating that the London Synod of this time was based upon the *Synodical Discipline*, for the latter as outlined in the Book of Discipline did not precede but followed such representative assemblies.

During the critical events of the year 1584, the Puritans in London and elsewhere were supported and inspired by the Scottish Presbyterians who had been forced to flee from their native land. Among the exiles was the redoubtable protagonist of Presbyterianism, Andrew Melville. He and his fellow refugees would help the English brethren to frame a counter policy to meet the measures of Whitgift, and as experienced advocates of the Genevan system of Church government their influence would naturally tend to reinforce the Presbyterian elements in English Puritanism. We know that the London Puritans conferred with the Scotsmen, and that Melville, Lawson and others "visited the Universities of Oxford and Cambridge, and conferrit with the most godlie and lernit ther, retourning againe till London."[2] Bancroft quotes from a letter written by Gellibrand to Field in July, which tells of the meeting of the Puritans with the ministers of the Church of Scotland in Oxford: "Here have beene a good company of godly brethren this Act. Master Fen, Wilcox, Axton: the Scottish ministers, and we have had some meeting and conference to our great comfort that are here. One point I would wish to be throughly debated among you and them, concerning the proceeding of the Minister in his dutie, without the assistance or tarrying for the Magistrate."[3] The latter part of this letter is reminiscent of Robert Browne and shows that some of the Puritans were at least discussing their relationship to the civil authorities and wondering whether they could realise their aims only by asserting their absolute spiritual independence. Their chief hope seemed to lie in Parliament, but hitherto, chiefly because of Elizabeth,

[1] *P.M.* p. 42. [2] Melville, *Diary*, p. 219. [3] *D.P.* p. 74.

it had proved a broken reed, and they were naturally tempted to adopt a plank in the platform of the Brownists. Melville was now in England simply because he would not tarry for the magistrate and declined to recognise his absolute jurisdiction, and probably the above words reflect his influence. But constitutional counsels prevailed. The Puritans would try again to gain their ends through their many friends in Parliament. Indeed, success by any other means was practically inconceivable.

The Puritan party was strongly represented in the Parliament of 1584–5. Petitions in favour of suspended and evicted ministers and for the supply of sufficient men to serve vacant cures were sympathetically entertained in the House of Commons. The latter as a whole even sent a general petition to the House of Lords for the further reformation of the Church, *e.g.* for the restoration of deprived ministers, for the discontinuance of the oath *ex officio*, the revival of the exercises, the abolition of non-residence and other abuses. The answer of the Upper House through Burghley and Whitgift was delivered to the Commons by Sir Francis Knollys on the 25th of February, 1584–5, and showed that there was little hope of any effective redress being obtained[1]. On the 14th of December Dr Turner put the House of Commons "in remembrance of a Bill and Book heretofore offered by him, which had been digested and framed by certain Godly and Learned Ministers" but it was not even read[2]. The Bill and Book were, according to Bancroft[3], none other than a draft of the Presbyterian programme, and a new edition of the Genevan Prayer Book. But the presentation of all these documents and appeals was in vain. Parliament could not change the ecclesiastical *status quo* and the Puritans were left to pursue their nonconforming ways in a state of mingled hope and despair. It was at this stage that some of them expressed to Cartwright, who was still in Holland, their need of his helpful presence.

It has been said that the Puritans endeavoured to get

[1] D'Ewes, pp. 339, 340, 344, 349, 354, 357.
[2] *ibid.* p. 339.
[3] *Survay*, p. 66.

Presbyterianism imposed upon the country by Parliament without consulting the Church[1], but this statement is not correct. An appeal was now delivered by four representative preachers to Convocation for reformation along Presbyterian lines. Their petition, however, "was not suffered to be read in the Convocation house, but was suppressed."[2]

During the year 1585, in spite of the suspension of such leading and outspoken Presbyterians as Field and Fenner[3], the Conference movement continued to thrive. A General Conference was held at Cambridge in July. Two representatives from Dedham Conference, Newman and Sandes, were appointed on the 28th of June and reported to their brethren on the 2nd of August[4]. To judge from the Dedham minutes the Conferences were gradually winning authority and developing at least the appearance of a claim to jurisdiction. They were manifesting the same process of evolution that had transformed the Conferences or Exercises of the Church of Scotland into Presbyteries.

As we have seen, a proposal was made in 1584 that a draft of discipline should be made. Such a draft was drawn up, and offered along with the Puritan Prayer Book to the Parliament of 1584–5. It was now thought expedient that a complete outline of the system of ecclesiastical government desired by the Puritans should be prepared, in order that the aims of the party might be authoritatively and definitely known and that there might be uniformity in its demands. The outcome was the production of the Book of Discipline, *Disciplina Ecclesiae sacra*, etc. The Book grew, and although Cartwright probably had to do with the later stages of its growth, it was not he, but his friend Travers, who was chiefly responsible for the preparation of it at this stage. It is indeed likely that Andrew Melville and the other Scottish ministers commended the idea of a Book of Discipline and, drawing from the experience of their own Second Book of Discipline, furnished helpful advice for its compilation. Travers, however, was the man to whom the task was en-

[1] Wakeman, p. 348.
[2] *Sec. Parte*, I, p. 296; II, p. 85.
[3] *ibid.* I, pp. 283, 296.
[4] *P.M.* pp. 50–1.

trusted. On the 3rd of July, 1585, Field wrote to Travers urging him to hasten his work: "I would wish, that the Discipline were read over with as much speed as could be, and that some good directions were given, for the brethren abroad, who are earnest to enter some good course for the furtherance of the Lords cause...I find many abroad very willing to joyne with the best, to put in practice that which shall be agreed upon by the brethren. If it might please the brethren therefore, that those of the like instructions (which we had) with a perfect copie of the Discipline, might be sent, I would wholly imploy my selfe in that service."[1] On the 9th of November, 1585, Gellibrand wrote to Field: "I pray you hasten the forme of Discipline and send it," and on the 30th of January the same writer repeated his request: "I pray you remember the forme of Discipline, which M Travers promised to make perfect, and send it me when it is finished. We will put it in practice, and trie mens minds therein, as we may."[2]

The great delay in the completion of the draft of discipline was, maybe, in part due to the vicissitudes through which its author was passing. Some months after the death[3] of Canon Richard Alvey, Master of the Temple, Travers, who had assisted him as Lecturer for about four years, was discharged from his office[4]. He failed to secure the Mastership, which was given by the Queen to Richard Hooker. For some time after Hooker's appointment Travers continued to lecture in the Temple Church, which became the scene of a remarkable controversy. Travers tried to persuade Hooker to introduce Presbyterianism into the Temple, but in vain. The one preached Genevan doctrine; the other was a staunch upholder of the Establishment. Ultimately Travers was prohibited by Whitgift and others of the High Commission from exercising any ministerial function in the Temple or elsewhere, one of the chief grounds of the inhibition being that he was not properly ordained. Many excellent accounts of the controversy and its consequences

[1] *D.P.* p. 76. [2] *ibid.* p. 76. [3] Aug. 1584.
[4] Feb. 1584–5; F. A. Inderwick, *The Inner Temple, 1505–1603* (1896), p. 333.

have been given, *e.g.* by Walton, Hanbury, Paget, Inderwick, Bayne, etc. Although marked down by the authorities Travers had many well-wishers both in London and in the country. In the records of the town of Leicester we come across a letter[1] from the municipal officials to the Earl of Huntingdon reporting the death of Johnson, their preacher, and asking for the appointment of Travers, now without a cure, as his successor. He did not however obtain the appointment[2]. It was during this time of storm and anxiety that Travers was occupied with the composition of the Book of Discipline.

During the autumn of 1586 the Puritans were actively engaged in preparations for the presenting of their case to the approaching Parliament[3]. Numerous petitions were drawn up and sent to the Queen, the Council, and the Bishops, as well as to Parliament and individual members of the Houses. These flowed in from counties, townships, corporations, etc.[4] The burden of the supplications was that the country required a preaching ministry, that faithful pastors who had been deprived should be restored, that Church reform was urgent. The Puritan Surveys showing the dearth of sufficient ministers in many shires and lists of godly preachers, who had been ousted from their charges, were also presented to Parliament[5]. The remedy requested was the establishment of Presbyterianism[6]. Many Puritans, says Bancroft, "were sent to attend at the Parliament, from the most parts of England. And one resolution was, that some twenty or thirty of them should have come in their gownes, with all gravitie, to the Parliament-house doore, and there have desired by petition a disputation."[7] On the 7th of November, 1586, Dr Chapman moved in the Dedham Conference "that a letter might be written to the godlie brethren in London, who though they were forward in furthering of discipline, yet a letter wold encourage them to be more zealous, and we shuld be moved the rather to write bicause some of them

[1] 12 April, 1586.
[2] Bateson, p. 226.
[3] 29 Oct. 1586—23 March, 1586–7.
[4] *Sec. Parte* II, pp. 174 ff.
[5] *ibid.* II, pp. 70 ff., 261.
[6] *ibid.* II, pp. 98 ff.
[7] *D.P.* p. 81.

are of mynd to aske a full reformation and to accept of none if they had not all, but the iudgment of the brethren was that some reformation might be accepted of if it were graunted. Secondlie he required that in the letter they shuld put them in mynd of Mr Cartwrights booke of the Confutation of the Rhemish Testament, and to further yt unto the presse."[1] This Parliament, however, was preoccupied with "the great Cause touching the Scottish Queen," who for her complicity in Babington's conspiracy was eventually executed on the 8th of February, 1586–7. A few weeks after this tragedy, viz., on the 27th of February, it looked as if the Puritans were at last to have their innings in Parliament. On that day Mr Cope introduced a Bill and Book into the House of Commons. The Bill contained a petition "that all laws now in force touching Ecclesiastical Government should be void" and that the Prayer Book now offered should be adopted in place of the Book of Common Prayer[2]. In spite of Speaker Puckering's warning that the Queen had commanded the House not to meddle in religious matters the members were eager to have the Bill and Book read. Time however was wasted in discussion and neither came to a reading. Elizabeth sent for the documents and suppressed them. Wentworth, for his advocacy of the liberty of the House, and Lewkenor, Hurlston, and Bainbrigg, for their pleading in behalf of the Bill and Book, were committed to the Tower[3].

The 'Bill' was a petition in favour of the conversion of the Church of England into a Presbyterian organisation. A copy of it is contained in the *Seconde Parte of a Register*[4]. Although a Presbyterian document it is not identical with the Book of Discipline, with which Bancroft confused it[5]. Indeed we have found no evidence that the Book of Discipline was ever presented to Parliament. The 'Book' was substantially the same as that which had been offered to the House of Commons in December, 1584. It was a modification of the Geneva Prayer Book or Book of Common Order,

[1] *P.M.* p. 59.
[2] D'Ewes, p. 410.
[3] *ibid.* pp. 411–2. *v.* "Peter Wentworth" by J. E. Neale in *Eng. Hist. Rev.* XXXIX (1924).
[4] II, pp. 212 ff.
[5] *Survay*, p. 66.

sometimes known as Knox's Liturgy[1]. It is referred to in one of the Puritan papers (1586?) thus: "The Geneva Liturgie as yt hath bene corrected is to be communicated with the conferences and the booke to be preferred here at the parliament and used in the partes abroade if the brethren there shall thinke good."[2] This Prayer Book of the Puritans has sometimes been confused with their Book of Discipline[3]. Three times it was presented to Parliament: "It is saide, as it had bin twise before, so this last Parliament, nowe the thirde time, to have bin presented to that high and honorable Court."[4] "Of the principall printed copies of that which was written and presented, he (*Bridges*) nameth three, whiche should be printed in three sundrie Countries, Englande, Scotlande, and the lowe Countries, a matter of as much untrueth, as the rest of his replies."[5] This book was essentially a Presbyterian document. It provided directions for the appointment of pastors, doctors, elders and deacons, recognised the weekly assembly or exercise as part of the system of a truly reformed Church, and implied that the true Church ought to be governed by local elderships, lesser and greater Conferences. The desire of the Puritans for its recognition is sufficient to show that they were dissatisfied with the Book of Common Prayer and diocesan Episcopacy, and were anxious to presbyterianise the English Church.

The effort of the Puritans to further their cause in Parliament was thus cut short by Elizabeth. "Tarrying for the magistrate" had proved an inglorious failure. So they set about establishing their platform quietly and systematically by other means. Before the Parliamentary session was finished the Puritan leaders at a meeting in London decided that the whole movement should be organised along certain definite lines. "At the tyme of the laste Parliament," wrote the members of Braintree Conference to those of Dedham,

[1] The edition printed by Waldegrave is reprinted in *Fragmenta Liturgica*, vol. I, ed. P. Hall (1848); cf. reprint of Schilders' 1586 edition in *Reliquiae Liturgicae*, vol. I (1847).

[2] *P.M.* p. 93.

[3] P. Lorimer, Introduction to the *Directory* of 1644 (1872), p. 3.

[4] Travers, *Defence of the Ecclesiasticall Discipline* (1588), p. 23.

[5] *ibid.* p. 113.

"order was taken by consent of many of our godlie brethren and fellow labourers assembled at London that all the mynisters which favoured and soughte the reformation of our church should sorte themselves together, etc."[1] It appears that the Puritans had now a manual in hand, which was calculated to provide the necessary regulations for the organisation desired. This was Travers's Book of Discipline, which seems to have been adopted by a General Conference in 1586[2]. The Book is a compendious directory of Presbyterian Church Government. It is divided into two parts, one entitled *Disciplina Ecclesiae sacra Dei verbo descripta*, and the other *Disciplina Synodica ex ecclesiarum quae eam ex verbo Dei instaurarunt usu Synodis atque libris de eadem re scriptis collecta, et ad certa quaedam capita redacta*. It is well known in the English translation, *A Directory of Church-government...Found in the study of the most accomplished Divine, Mr Thomas Cartwright, after his decease*... (1644), reprinted in facsimile in 1872[3]. The Latin original has been printed from different manuscript copies as an Appendix by Bishop Paget in his *Introduction* to the fifth Book of Hooker's *Ecclesiastical Polity* (1907) and by the present writer in *Der Älteste Englische Presbyterianismus* (1912). The date and identity of the book have puzzled historians and many modern writers seem to be unaware of the existence of its Latin original. It is therefore hoped that this Book of Discipline, which played such an important part in the history of the Elizabethan Puritans, may before long be issued with annotations as a separate publication.

During 1587 individual Puritans continued to suffer for their nonconformity and the flow of supplications in their behalf was maintained[4]. Field was still busy collecting information regarding the oppressions of the Bishops, *e.g.* an account of Giles Wigginton's troubles was sent to Field at the latter's request[5]. But the chief subject of interest was the Book of Discipline. Copies were sent through Field to

[1] *P.M.* p. 98.
[2] *ibid.* p. 92.
[3] ed. P. Lorimer. Also, as an Appendix, in Neal and Briggs.
[4] *P.M.* pp. 61, 64; *Sec. Parte*, II, p. 231.
[5] May, 1587; *Sec. Parte*, II, p. 238.

the Conferences in the country in 1587[1]. On the 8th of March, 1586–7, the Book is mentioned in the Dedham minutes for the first time: "Mr Tay moved that the booke of discipline set downe by the brethren might be vewed and their iudgments given of it," and the last reference occurs on the 8th of August, 1587: "The dealing with the booke of discipline was deferred till the next meetinge bicause Mr Tay was now absent."[2] It is clear that some of the Conferences had difficulty in coming to a decision regarding the Book, *e.g.* Dedham Conference was asked by another in June, 1587, to lend assistance "for the concludinge of the matter of discipline."[3]

On the 8th of September, 1587, an important General Conference (*conventus*) was held in or near Cambridge. There it was decided that the Puritan meetings—Conferences (*colloquia*) and Synods (*conventus*)—should be based upon the new Book of Discipline: *Ratio habendi colloquia et conventus sumenda ex synodica disciplina*[4]. Meanwhile, however, certain questions respecting the Book were referred to the next General Conference: *Ad quaestiones de sacra disciplina et synodica, I. An conveniat cum verbo Dei*, 2. *Quousque cum pace ecclesiae uti liceat, nondum responsum est a plerisque. Quod curandum in proximum conventum*. It appears that some of the General Conferences were unable to accept the Book as it stood and that others had not expressed their opinion of it: *Responsio ad dubitationes certorum conventuum de disciplina, dilata est, donec reliqui conventus suam de tota disciplina sententiam significarint*. The Book was the chief topic of the day and the Puritan leaders were now pressing for the general recognition of it as the authoritative standard of their party. With this end in view it was now agreed that the Book (called *libri* because of the two sections *sacra* and *synodica disciplina*) should be printed and circulated through the Synods: *Curandum de libris disciplinae imprimendis, et per conventus dispergendis*. The Book however was never printed by the Elizabethan Puritans. It was also proposed

[1] *D.P.* p. 76.
[2] *P.M.* pp. 63, 65, 66.
[3] *ibid.* p. 65.
[4] *i.e.* Pt II of the Book of Discipline.

that Cartwright's books on ecclesiastical discipline should be translated and Laurence Chaderton and Edward Gellibrand were enjoined to attend to this matter: *De libris D:*[1] *Cartwright de Disciplina, rogandus ipse primum ut vertantur; D: Chatterton et D: Gellibrand procurent.* This may be another reference to the Book of Discipline. If so, it indicates that Cartwright had completed the task begun by Travers and was regarded by his fellow Puritans as the author of the Book. In this case the desired translation is probably that published in 1644. We cannot be sure whether Cartwright translated the Book or whether it was the joint task of Chaderton and Gellibrand. There is no evidence, however, that the English version was circulated among the Elizabethan Puritans as Kennedy[2] suggests. Even Bancroft does not appear to have known an English version and in *D. P.* gives his own translation of extracts from the Book. The *Confutation of the Rhemists Translation* still occupied the minds of the Puritans and it was now decided that Fen should write to Lord Leicester and Dudley Fenner about it: *De libro responsorio ad Remensis Testamenti translationem, scribendum a D: Fenn ad Comitem Lecestrensem et ad D: Fennerum.* The next meeting of a General Conference or *conventus* should be called by the Warwick Conference or *classis*, of which Cartwright was the leader *ex sententia classium ejusdem Comitatus modo intra tempus semestre et non ante trimestre*[3].

By 1587 the Puritan movement, moulded by the influence of the Book of Discipline, was thus assuming the definite features of a Presbyterian organisation. The nomenclature of the Book was adopted and Conferences now came to be known as *classes* and the other assemblies *conventus*, *synodi*, etc. The development is fully illustrated by Bancroft in his account of the Northamptonshire *classes*, which met in the vicinity of Northampton, Daventry and Kettering respec-

[1] Not *de* as in St. *Ann.*

[2] W. P. M. Kennedy, *Studies in Tudor History* (1916), p. 261.

[3] The decisions of this Cambridge Synod are given in *Harl. MSS.* 7029, ff. 127–8 and have been printed by Strype (*Ann.* VI, p. 477). In the collection of *Harleian MSS.* they follow a copy of the Book of Discipline itself in Latin (*Harl. MSS.* 7029, ff. 115–26).

17–2

tively[1]. Among the members of the Northampton *classis* were Snape, Penry, Sibthorpe, Edwards, Littleton, Bradshaw, Lark, Fleshware, Spicer, etc.; Daventry *classis* consisted of Barebon, Rogers, King, Smart, Sharp, Prowdloe, Elliston, etc.; those who attended Kettering *classis* were Stone, Williamson, Fawsbrook, Patinson, Massey, etc. These *classes* generally met in private houses about every three weeks. Representatives of the three *classes* (two from each) usually met at Northampton every six or eight weeks as a County *conventus*. Snape, who was the Clerk of the Northampton *classis*, was also a leading spirit in the larger meeting. It was through him that the correspondence with the brethren of other Conferences, *e.g.* in Oxford, Cambridge and London, was carried on. This and other information regarding the Northamptonshire Puritans came to the knowledge of Bancroft through the depositions of Johnson, a member of the Northampton *classis*.

One of the most important assemblies of the year 1588 was the Warwickshire Synod, the Acts of which, in Daniel Wight's handwriting, were entitled *Acta conventus Classium Warwic. die decimo quarti* (probably 10th April) 1588[2]. We gather from Cartwright's answers in the Star Chamber (12 June, 1591) that this Synod did not meet in the town of Warwick but near it. Bancroft suggests that it met in Coventry[3]. The questions referred to it by the Cambridge Synod of the previous year were laid before it: *Quaestiones a fratribus ex Synodo Cantabrigiensi anno superiore delatae, ea quae sequitur formula sunt explicatae*[4]. These questions, which Bancroft translates from the Latin, deal with private Baptism, the sign of the cross, the reading of homilies, the recognition of the Bishops' authority, the expediency of soliciting the people to practise the Discipline, etc. It is wrong to regard these questions as resolutions or decrees. This Cartwright pointed out in the Star Chamber in 1591. The Warwickshire assembly, however, approved of the Book of Discipline as "a draught of Discipline, essential and necessary for all times: and certaine articles (being

[1] *D.P.* pp. 77 ff. [2] *D.P.* p. 86. [3] *ibid.* [4] *ibid.*

devised in approbation, and for the manner of the use of that book) were then brought forth, treated of, and subscribed unto (as Master Nutter and Master Clevely, two that were then present, have deposed) by Master Cartwright, Master Fenne, Master Wight, etc., who promised to guid themselves by the said discipline, and according to it, as it is set downe in the said articles."[1] Cartwright, Fen, Lord and Wight afterwards confessed in the Star Chamber that they subscribed above three years before the information was exhibited against them there. A copy of the articles of subscription is contained in the *Harleian MSS.*[2] The twelve signatories in this copy are Jo. Oxenbridge, Humphrey Fen, Edwarde Gelibrande, Hercules Cleveley, Leonard Fetherston, John Ashbye, Thomas Cartwright, Mathewe Hulme, Antonye Nutter, Daniell Wighte, Edwarde Lorde, Edmunde Littleton. Most of these were ministers in Warwickshire, but Gellibrand was from Oxford, Nutter from Fenny Drayton, co. Leicester, and Littleton from Deane, co. Bedford.

These articles are of two kinds, declaratory and promissory. In the first the subscribers declare their approval of the Presbyterian system set forth in the Book of Discipline, with certain reservations concerning parts of the Book, about which the Puritans never reached an unanimous agreement. In the second they promise, as far as is compatible with the laws of the land and the peace of the Church, to be guided by the Book and "for more especiall declaration of some points more important and necessary" they promise to put into operation certain definite portions of the Book, which are mainly concerned with the conduct of divine service and the holding of the various prescribed meetings. The qualified nature of the subscription was explicitly pointed out by Cartwright in the Star Chamber (June, 1591), when he said "that he did agree to put two points only, as he remembreth, of the said book of discipline in execution, viz., the one to

[1] *D.P.* p. 87.

[2] 6849, f. 222. Printed in *D.P.* p. 98. (Under Maister Wights hand); in Brook, *Lives* I, p. 405 (from *Harl. MSS.* 6849). A copy of the articles of subscription, with slight variations and evidently earlier (1586?), is given in *P.M.* p. 92.

follow the order of preaching put down in the book of discipline, and the other to observe the order of meeting expressed also in the same book, as far forth as the same might stand with the peace of the Church now established in England and the laws of the land, and no otherwise or further."[1] The subscribers of the Book of Discipline, aware of the limited and provisional character of their approval, accordingly make express mention of their intention to use all lawful means, *e.g.* suit to the Queen, the Council and Parliament, to secure that change in the constitution of Church and State, which was necessary before their Presbyterian scheme could be legitimately realised. It was the failure to fulfil this condition that made the Puritan design impracticable. The Queen and the Bishops prevented them from obtaining the sanctions they required.

It is difficult to give the exact date of the articles of subscription. They were certainly drawn up, probably in London, after the Book of Discipline, which they presuppose. About the same time the 'Decrees' were issued. Bancroft gives a translation of these from the Latin version in Wight's handwriting[2]. Their chief goal is the establishment of the hierarchy of meetings, beginning with the *classis*, laid down in the Synodical Discipline, *i.e.* the second part of the Book of Discipline. But there is an element of compromise or adaptation in the Decrees. While safeguarding the rights of the Church and its assemblies in the election of ministers they allow ordination by Bishops, for the sake of peace, and suggest that churchwardens and collectors may be transformed into elders and deacons. A section of the Puritans were willing to have the Presbyterian system grafted upon the existing Episcopal constitution at least in the initial stages of the further reformation. In one of the Decrees comitial assemblies are urgently requested to make collections for deprived brethren, Scottish ministers and others. Bancroft was led to place the document in the year 1583 because of the reference to the Scottish ministers, who, he supposed, were those then in exile, but there were ministers

[1] *v. infra* p. 333. [2] *D.P.* p. 46.

from Scotland in England several years later, *e.g.* Melville and others did not return home till 1585 and gifts were presented to Scottish preachers by the Borough of Leicester in 1586–7 and 1589–90[1].

At Stourbridge Fair time, *i.e.* September, in 1589 a General Conference, said to have been attended by Cartwright, Snape, Stone, etc., was held "in Saint Johns Colledge in Cambridge. Where (saith M. Barber) they did correct, alter, and amend divers imperfections contained in the booke called *Disciplina ecclesiae sacra verbo Dei descripta*: and (as master Stone affirmeth) did not onely perfect the said forme of Discipline, but also did then and there (as he remembreth) voluntarily agree amongst themselves, that so many as would should subscribe to the said booke of Discipline after that time."[2] The Master of St John's, Whitaker, and most of the Fellows were indignant at the report that a Presbytery had been erected in their College and complained to Burghley about the slander[3]. In December, 1595, on the death of Whitaker, complaints were again preferred against Henry Alvey and the party who wished him to succeed to the Mastership that "In our masters absence they suffered a conventicle of Mr Cartwright and his complices to be gathered in oure Colledge Anno 1589: Mr Alvey keepinge our masters lodginge where they then mett."[4] This Cambridge meeting is the last General Conference of which we have definite knowledge[5]. The Book discussed in it was now doomed to remain a documentary monument of a lost cause. The final struggle between the Bishops and the Presbyterians had begun and in the downfall of the latter the Book of Discipline was perforce laid aside.

By 1588 many of the Puritans had reached the conclusion that all their efforts for reform were fruitless as long as the Bishops would not relinquish their present uncompromising position. The Dedham minutes of this year show that the feeling of the brethren was hardening against their ecclesi-

[1] Bateson, pp. 241, 264.

[2] *D.P.* p. 89.

[3] *Lansd. MSS.* LXIII, Nos. 91–3, 95.

[4] *ibid.* LXXIX, No. 61.

[5] Bancroft refers to a Synod held a month after Michaelmas, 1589, at Ipswich, but gives no details. *D.P.* p. 89.

astical overlords: "Mr Tay moved in his exercise that the brethren wold consider whether the Bs were anie longer to be tolerated or noe: not delt in" (31 March), "Mr Sandes moved whether the course of the Bs were such and of such moment, that they were not to be thought of as brethren, and soe to be delt withall in our publike and in our private speeches and praiers: it was debated of but not concluded" (2 June). The members of Dedham Conference were embittered by their own experience; their secretary had recently been suspended and others of their number were now threatened with deprivation for refusal to wear the surplice[1]. Before the year came to an end the smouldering embers of antipathy in the hearts of the Presbyterian radicals burst into a lurid flame in the famous antiepiscopal Marprelate Tracts.

By the autumn of 1589 the Martinists were effectually silenced. The press itself was unearthed in August and the printers arrested. The Wigstons, Hales and Knightly, who had harboured the press were imprisoned and in due course heavily fined. Now freed from the menace of Romanism by the defeat of the Armada the authorities were determined to crush the whole movement of which Martin Marprelate was an extreme representative. Chiefly through the detective activity of Richard Bancroft a mass of incriminating evidence relating to the meetings and the Book of Discipline was obtained. According to the testimonial written by Whitgift in favour of Bancroft in 1597, when the latter was appointed Bishop of London, this zealous Chaplain was credited with the discomfiture of Marprelate, the unmasking of Puritanism, and the provision of materials, drawn from the Presbyterian archives and the intercepted correspondence of the Puritans, upon which the Bill and Articles afterwards exhibited against Cartwright and his accomplices in the Star Chamber were based[2]. One by one the Conferences were dissolved. The last recorded meeting of that of Dedham took place on the 2nd

[1] *P.M.* pp. 69–70.

[2] *Baker MSS.* M. m. 1. 47, f 333; *Petyt MSS.* 538. XXXVIII, f. 155; St. *Whit.* II, p. 386. For Bancroft's part in the detection of Elizabethan Presbyterianism and in the reconstruction of the English Church *v.* Usher, *Reconstr.* I, pp. 42, 68 etc.

of June, 1589. The Clerk, Parker, makes an entry in the minute book regarding the cessation of "this blessed meeting." "Yt ended," he writes, "by the malice of Satan, some cause of it was compleints against us preferred to the B. of London, for which cause I was called up to London and examyned of it; but the chiefest cause was the death of some of the brethren and their departure from us to other places."[1]

Among the chief pillars of Puritanism recently removed by death were John Field and the Earl of Leicester. Field died in March 1587–8 and was buried on the 26th of the month at St Giles, Cripplegate. He "was a great and chiefe man amongst the brethren of London, and one to whome the managing of the discipline (for the outward practise of it) was especially (by the rest) committed. So as all the letters, that were directed from the brethren of other places to have this or that referred to the London assemblies, were for the most part directed unto him."[2] We have noticed that during his sixteen years of propagandism he acted as the recognised general secretary to the whole body of Puritans. He collected innumerable papers relating to the movement, many of which now fell into the hands of Bancroft. One portion of his collection, saved by the Puritans, was shortly afterwards published as *A parte of a register*; another portion left in manuscript has been recently printed and edited as *The Seconde Parte of a Register*[3]. These registers are invaluable for the student of Elizabethan Dissent. Field took special pains to gather materials concerning the oppressive measures taken by the Bishops against the godly brethren and some of these evidently came into the possession of, and were utilised by, those who issued the Marprelate Tracts. Henry Sharpe deposed that on asking who composed the first Tract he was told by Penry "that some such notes were found in Master Feilds study, that Master Feild upon his deathbed willed they should be burnt, and repented for collecting them."[4] Sutcliffe was of opinion that Field, Udall, Penry and Throkmorton all concurred in the making of Martin[5]. Although

[1] *P.M.* p. 74. [2] Bancroft, *Survay*, p. 369. [3] ed. A. Peel (1915).
[4] Arber, *Sketch*, p. 94, cf. p. 128. [5] *ibid.* p. 175.

Field was certainly not Martin he provided a documentary quarry which the latter turned to good account. Field was a practical idealist, to him was due much of the success of the consolidation and organisation of Elizabethan Presbyterianism, and it was well that he passed away before the child of his dreams was laid in the dust[1].

Leicester was a pillar of another sort. He died on the 4th of September, 1588, at Cornbury Park, Oxfordshire. His body was brought to Warwick and buried in the Beauchamp Chapel there. Among the courtiers of Elizabeth he was the outstanding champion of Puritanism. The unique favour he enjoyed at Court and the widespread influence that he and his party exercised gave immeasurable strength to the ultra-Protestants. Even though Leicester's aims may have been based on selfish ambition or guided by patriotic and political motives, and not like those of the Puritan ministers on personal piety and loyalty to Scripture, nevertheless his outlook largely coincided with theirs[2]. Whether during Elizabeth's marriage negotiations, in face of Romanist plots or the dangers connected with the Queen of Scots, or with regard to the plight of the Low Countries, Leicester and the Puritans generally saw eye to eye. Some of the most influential statesmen of the age belonged to Leicester's party and like him gave their countenance to the Puritans. Their relationship to him and to the Puritans is worthy of a special dissertation, and some aspects of their policy, for instance, the influence of what we may call political Puritanism upon the activities of the Elizabethan seamen or the fate of Mary, Queen of Scots, deserve to be thoroughly worked out. We have already mentioned *Leycesters Commonwealth*, one of the most outrageous libels of the sixteenth century. It pointed out the high and important positions occupied, presumably for

[1] Field's will, dated 16 Feb. 1587–8, proved 1 June, 1588, is in Somerset House, 38, *Rutland*. He bequeathed all his goods to his wife Joan.

[2] For an interesting tradition handed down through Travers and Archbishop Usher regarding Leicester's approval of Cartwright's teaching because it harmonised with and was calculated to further the Earl's design to alienate the lands and revenues of the Bishops, *vide* extracts from Plume's pocketbook in *Essex Review*, XII, XIII.

sinister purposes, by adherents of Leicester's party; it attributed to the Earl the most selfish and unscrupulous motives; it tore his character into shreds. Its estimates have been too widely accepted as true and Leicester's fame has come down to posterity besmirched. Historians, otherwise trustworthy, have inclined to depreciate his merits and bestow the honours upon Burghley, forgetting that it was Leicester's policy as opposed to that of Burghley, *e.g.* in fostering a breach with Spain, in encouraging such adventurers as Drake, in urging on the execution of the Scottish Queen, etc., that brought lustre and triumph to the reign of Elizabeth. We look forward to Frederick Chamberlin's promised biography of Leicester for the redemption of his life from "three centuries of continuous vilification."[1] Puritans at any rate have good cause to cherish his memory for the support he gave to their fathers in the faith. If Field could organise, Leicester could patronise, and the successes of the Puritans depended to a large extent upon their enjoyment of the Earl's favour. His death and the passing of the Romanist and Spanish dangers now put their enemies in a position to crush their domestic foe and they proceeded to do so with ruthless efficiency.

The course of action pursued by the Bishops and the consequences of the same are well illustrated by the case of Edmund Snape. As one of the ringleaders he was arrested and required to answer certain interrogatories submitted to him by the High Commissioners. He refused to answer the questions before he had seen them. "Having perused them, he was further off," says Bancroft, "then he was before: and writt to his friends, what was the summe of them: to the intent they might be forewarned, and so (as he sayd) become better armed. Which course taken by him was not without the great providence of God. For thereby their whole plot, and all in effect, that was laid to their charges, was discovered. His letters were intercepted, wherein he writeth after this sort: 'Reverend and beloved, this day Aprill the 7 (1590)

[1] *v.* Introd. to *The Private Character of Queen Elizabeth* by F. Chamberlin (1921).

I have been againe before the Commissioners. After much adoe, I obtained to see and peruse the Articles against me (but briefly and in their presence onely), they are many (36. 37. besides those under mine owne hand) and very large, some twelve, some twenty lines long, consisting of many branches. As far as I could (for the time) conceive and remember, they may be referred to these two heads: some concerning my selfe, together with others, and some touching my selfe alone. The former sort are touching Classes and Synodes: wherein there are mentioned particular places: (London, Oxford, Cambridge), times (Act, Commencement, Sturbridge fayre, Tearme), persons (Cartwright, Perkins, Travers, Charke, Egerton, Barebon, Stone, Snape, Knewstub, Allen, Dike and divers others) and some things dealt in and agreed upon, etc. By all which, besides many other things specified, it is most evident, that they have manifest and certaine knowledge, not onely of generals, but also of specials and particulars.'"[1]

On the 11th of April Snape wrote to Barebon informing him that the Northamptonshire Conferences were unmasked. He suspected that one of their associates, John Johnson, had turned Queen's evidence. To his warning he added the suggestion that Cartwright should at once be made acquainted with the gravity of the situation. "Beloved," wrote Snape, "I have twise appeared before the high Commissioners, the first time the issue was prison; the second, close prison. This is my state now: the causes of both, and the proceedings in both, you shall receive of Master Knightlye, the former more large in a Dialogue, the latter more briefly in a Letter: both unperfect, both unperused: read them, and returne them with what speed you may, for I have now no coppy of them: let them be wisely kept, lest they breed more anger. I have procured another coppy to be sent to Master Stone, that in both places you might be forewarned and forearmed. Touching the conferences, those of our Countrey are yet more particularly discovered: persons (besides those there named) Kinge, of Coleworth, Prowdloe, of Weedon etc.

[1] *D.P.* p. 91.

Spicer, of Cogenho, Edwardes, of Cortenhall etc. places: Sharpes house at Fawsely: Snapes chamber at Northampton etc. Si quis conjecturae sit locus: I would judge Iohn Iohnson to have beene the man: because (to my remembrance) persons and things of his time being mentioned, hee onely is not named. Whosoever and howsoever, wee see the Lord calleth us to be more resolute. They will not, they cannot be any longer concealed: now whether it be better and more safe, that one man with the consent of the rest, should boldly, freely and wisely confesse and lay open etc. or that some weake (or wicked) man should without consent and in evill sort acknowledge etc. Iudge you: the thing they ayme at is a conventicle. It must come to tryall. In the cause of murther etc. it is wont to be enquired, whether the party fled upon it: consider and apply to this matter, and the Lord give us wisdome in all things. It were good you sent to T.C. with speed."[1]

A Lansdowne MS.[2] which belonged to "Mr Leakes in the Old Baily," furnishes a list of the charges formulated by the Commissioners against the Puritans in general and those of Northamptonshire in particular[3]. They had met in *classes* and Synods. Their Synods generally met at London, Cambridge (at Commencement and Stourbridge Fair), and Oxford (during the Act), because at these places and times they could assemble with least suspicion. The Synods considered what had been propounded at the *classes* and the decrees of the Synods were authoritative. A Synod was held at Cambridge last Stourbridge Fair. Among those who met at such Synods were Whitaker, Cartwright, Knewstubs, Travers, Charke, Egerton, Greenham, Ward, Fludd, Chaderton, Perkins, Dike, Snape etc. In the said Synods it has been decreed that those who cannot preach are no ministers, that every minister should endeavour to establish the Presbyterian government, that an oath binding a man to reveal anything penal to himself or his brethren is not to

[1] *D.P.* p. 92. [2] LXIV, f. 51.

[3] 16 July, 1590. This MS. was printed as *A Paper on Puritans in Northamptonshire* by Taylor & Son, Northampton, 1878; *v.* St. *Whit.* II, pp. 6 ff.

be taken etc. The determinations of the Synods have been put into execution by the *classes*. The ministers of the Northamptonshire *classes* are Snape, Stone (Warkton), Edwards (Courtenhall), Spicer (Cogenho), Atkins (Higham), Fletcher (Abington), Lark (Wellingborough), Prowdlove (Weedon), King (Coleworth), Barebon etc. They have met at the Bull, Northampton, in Sharp's house, and in Snape's chamber. Snape had said that the Northamptonshire *classes* had decreed that the dumb ministry is no ministry at all and that the Presbyterian government should be taught in their several charges. He had in his possession forbidden books, e.g. *A Defence of the Ecclesiasticall Discipline* against Bridges. He had refused to baptise a child called Richard because the name was not scriptural. "Beeinge or pretending to be Curate of St Peters" Snape had not conducted divine worship there in accordance with the Book of Common Prayer. He did not recognise his Episcopal ordination and was chosen by the congregation of St Peter's before he would minister to them. Lark was approved as a minister by a *classis* (Snape and others) and then willed for safe standing to go to a Bishop, as to a civil magistrate for certification. Hocknell not receiving entire commendation of the Northampton *classis*, which examined him for approval, quarrelled with them. Such were the charges brought against the Puritans in 1590. These were soon to be amplified and other advocates of the cause, among them Cartwright, brought to prison.

From 1586 onwards, Cartwright, then resident in Warwick Hospital, took a prominent part in the direction of the Presbyterian movement. He attended many of the Conferences in London, in Warwickshire and elsewhere and was regarded throughout as one of their chief leaders. His place in the movement will be brought out more particularly when we deal with the proceedings of the High Commission and the trial in Star Chamber. Meanwhile we may refer to items in the correspondence, which was used by Bancroft, to show that the latter's verdict, that Cartwright was "the Patriarche' of the Puritans and "their chiefest counsaylor," is justified[1].

[1] *Survay*, p. 375.

"If," says Bancroft, "hee bee in prison, prayers are made for his deliverance: if hee bee delivered, great thankes are publickely given unto God for the same...When great matters are to bee handled: he must needs be one in every place: Coventry, Cambridge, London etc."[1] In 1585 Chapman wrote to Field after Cartwright's return: "Salute our most reverend brother Maister Cartwright, for whome prayers are made with us."[2] 'M. R.' wrote to Field after Cartwright regained his freedom in 1585: "As soone as I knewe of Maister Cartwrightes delivery, I sent for Maister Travers, and we had psalmes of thankesgiving and prayers to the same purpose and a sermon: his text being the 20 of Ieremie. 10.11.12.13.14. verses."[3] In 1586 Gellibrand of Oxford wrote: "Wee want bookes, whereby wee may come to the knowledge of the truth. I meane T. C. bookes," and again[4]: "I would gladly knowe when I might come to see T. C."[5] Far(mer?) wrote to Lit(tleton?) in 1586: "I thanke god I have satisfied in part my longing with conference with M. Cartwright: of whom I thinke as she did of Solomon."[6] Cartwright's oracular authority was eagerly sought not only on questions of polity, but even with regard to the style of coiffure adopted by women. Should women set out their hair on wires? Should they be allowed to come to Church with their hair thus arranged? Such questions disturbed the Puritan conscience at this time and appeal is made to Cartwright for the resolution of a problem that is almost a vestiarian one. "Move Maister Cartwright," wrote Pig to Field in 1586[7], "and some other our reverend brethren to deliver their iudgements, whether all layinge out of hayre bee forbidden unto all women: especially at their repayre to the publique meetings of the Church."[8] Cartwright's opinion that a minister should not forsake his charge for the sake of obnoxious vestments, etc., made him suspect in the eyes of the uncompromising

[1] *Survay*, p. 375. [2] *ibid.* p. 375. [3] *ibid.* p. 375. [4] n.d.
[5] *ibid.* p. 375. [6] *ibid.* p. 375. [7] *ibid.* p. 368.
[8] For proposal to refer a difficult matrimonial affair in 1589 to Cartwright, Travers, etc., *v.* MSS. of Sir A. A. Hood, *Hist. MSS. Comm.* Rep. VI (1877), p. 346 *a*.

Puritans. So we come across such a letter as this[1]: "I heare some whispering allready (yet among them that favour the cause) that he (*T. C.*) hath councelled the brethren rather to use those corruptions then to leave their charges. I wish and hope it be not so: not onely least men should iudge the man to be inconstant, but especially for that these times be such, that in them such yealding will doe no good."

Elizabethan Presbyterianism with which Cartwright was thus so closely identified had practically collapsed by 1590. Legally it was now to be put on a long and tedious trial. Before, however, we deal with this trial we shall consider some of the literary associations of Puritanism during the 'eighties and also Cartwright's connection with Warwick from 1586 to 1590.

In considering the nonconformist literature of this period we shall not attempt to complete the valuable and extensive bibliography of Dexter (in his *Congregationalism of the Last Three Hundred Years*). Much has been done to this end in recent Transactions of the Congregational Historical Society, but the work has not yet been exhaustively performed. Our aim is illustrative. We desire to throw light upon Cartwright and the movement with which he was associated by a brief consideration of the writings that were issued by its representatives and their opponents from the beginning of the Whitgiftian regime. The Puritan Prayer Book and the Book of Discipline have already been mentioned. Probably early in 1584 *An Abstracte of Certain Acts of parlement etc.* was produced in order to discredit the jurisdiction of the Bishops by references to ecclesiastical laws which had become obsolete. Dr Cosin, Dean of the Arches, replied in 1584 and in turn was answered by Fenner in *A Counter Poyson*. Copcot replied to Fenner at Paul's Cross in a sermon that was afterwards printed and the Puritan vindicated himself in 1586 in *A Defence of the Reasons of the Counter Poyson*. Thus the pens of both sides were engaged in a boomerang warfare. The most important of the productions of 1584 was published in London by Robert Waldegrave, viz., *A Briefe and Plaine*

[1] Hart to Field, n.d., *Survay*, p. 376.

Declaration, which from the running headline inserted by the publishers, came to be known as the *Learned Discourse*. It has frequently been confused with the English translation of the *Explicatio*, *A Full and Plaine Declaration* (1574), a totally distinct work[1]. It condemns current abuses, *e.g.* non-residence, pluralities, and advocates as a remedy the Presbyterian system, which it exhibits in a clear and pointed exposition. This well-known and popular work had been written by Fulke, before he left the Puritan party, and had been preserved by Field for twelve years[2]. It was not surreptitiously published by Fulke, as Pierce suggests[3], but without his knowledge and doubtless against his will. Sutcliffe, when objecting to a Puritan for quoting Fulke as if he were a sympathetic authority, says[4]: "Neither hath the libeller," *i.e.* the author of *A Petition*, "any reason to build his fancies upon M. Fulkes opinions, for in the confutation of the notes of the Rhemish Testament, he doth defend the governement of the Church of England as now it is: & albeit he was sometime of other mind, yet did he afterward retract his former sayings. And when Iohn Field contrary to his mind did publish the pamphlet called *the learned discourse*, hee was offended with him, and if he had lived, would have confuted the same himselfe." As Pierce points out[5] the *Learned Discourse* was the groundwork of the Marprelate controversy. Dr John Bridges, Dean of Sarum, preached against it in 1584 at Paul's Cross and afterwards in 1587 answered it in a diffuse and wearisome tome of over 1400 pages entitled *A Defence of the Government Established*. This volume called forth two notable replies, one by Fenner, *A Defence of the godlie Ministers* (1587) and the other by Travers, *A Defence of the Ecclesiasticall Discipline* (1588).

Fenner was one of the most remarkable of the young men who supported Puritanism. Waldegrave in his Dedication of *Certain Godly and Learned Treatises* (1592) to Lord James Lindsay (the Dedication is dated, Edinburgh, 24 Dec. 1591)

[1] Dexter; *D.N.B.* art. 'Bridges,' etc.
[2] *v. supra* pp. 83–4.
[3] Pierce, *Tracts*, p. xiv.
[4] *Ans. to a Pet.* p. 41.
[5] *Hist. Introd.* p. 311.

pays tribute to the precocious and stalwart Puritan thus: "Amongst the number of those, whome in the Lords great mercies wee inioyed, and lost for our unthankfulnesse, M. Dudley Fenner was one, whome the Church of God in this age could have hardliest spared. He ended his testimonie in this life, being under thirtie yeares of age; but yet of that growth in the knowledge of God, that fewe (if ever anie of his yeares) have left behind them the like monuments of great knowledge and learning, in the true and sound feare of God, as hee hath done." Fenner matriculated at Peterhouse, Cambridge, 15 June, 1575, but took no degrees. Early in 1583 he came to Cranbrook, where Stroud had been, to assist Richard Fletcher, the Vicar. His children 'More Fruit' and 'Faint Not' were baptized at Cranbrook on the 22nd of December, 1583, and the 6th of June, 1585, respectively[1]. The father of children with such names was bound to be a resolute Puritan[2]. On the 12th of June, 1585, he was suspended for refusal to subscribe Whitgift's three articles[3]. Towards the end of the year he published his *Sacra Theologia* (his epistle to the reader is dated *Londoni. Octobris 14. 1585*), to which Cartwright prefixed a letter of commendation addressed *Ornatissimo et Clarissimo Fratri et in ministerio collegae, Domino Dudleio Fennero* and dated *3 nonas Septemb. An. 1585*. In his epistle Cartwright speaks of the work as providing a view as from Nebo's height of the axioms, laws, etc., of celestial Canaan. He has had great pleasure in reading the book that has been handed to him for perusal. It strengthens the bond between him and Fenner, who had already served as Cartwright's colleague in the Church at Antwerp: *me tibi jam ante ex conjuncto in ecclesia Anglantuerpiana ministerio plurimum devinctum*. Some confusion has arisen regarding Fenner's *Sacra Theologia*. Brook[4] states that it is preserved in manuscript in Dr Williams's Library, but an examination of the volume there[5] shows that it is not the original work but a well written copy of an English version

[1] Tarbutt, *Annals of Cranbrook Church* (1870–5), pp. 14–15.
[2] *v.* C. W. Bardsley, *Curiosities of Puritan Nomenclature* (1880), p. 124.
[3] *Sec. Parte*, I, p. 296. [4] *Mem.* p. 222. [5] *Ref.* No. 1632.

entitled *Sacred Theologie* (*or Divinitie*) *or The Truthe which is accordinge to Godlines*[1]. Cartwright's epistle of five pages is addressed, "To his most adorned and deerest Brother and Colleague in the Ministerye," and is wrongly dated "ye 3d nones of September. Ano. 1583." The error in date has been followed by Brook[2] and Cooper[3].

Fenner was a voluminous writer. Most of his works were printed by Schilders in Middelburg[4], and among them *A Defence of the godlie Ministers, against the slaunders of D. Bridges, contayned in his answere to the Preface before the Discourse of Ecclesiasticall governement*... (1587). According to the reprint in *A parte of a register*[5] the book was written by Fenner "a moneth before his death." It is a defence not of the whole *Learned Discourse* but of the Preface, for which the publishers were responsible. Fenner, who knew the inner working of the Puritan Publication Committee, gives an interesting account[6] of the issue of Fulke's book and an explanation of its apparently vain sub-title. He writes as an ardent admirer of Cartwright whose Replies, he thinks, have been wisely left unanswered. He identifies himself with the Puritan party in England, to some of whose doings he makes important references. "In the time of the first Session of Parliament holden in Anno 1585," he writes[7], "wee offered in most humble maner, fayre and legiblie written, unto the Convocation house our reasons why we refused to subscribe unto the second article," and he shows how the appeal was treated with contempt: "After this petition was presented by us, by the hands of a godlie and reverend D. of Divinitie, a member at that time of that house: it was caried up to the upper house of the Convocation, where the spirituall Lordes sate: From whom no answere was brought unto us untill this day."[8] Fenner regards as authoritative expositions of Puritan principles[9] "the bookes of Maister

[1] According to Black's note in the Catalogue of MSS. in Dr Williams's Library, there are other MS. copies of the work, *e.g.* in the British Museum, *Harl. MSS.* 6879, and in the Lambeth Library, *MSS.* 465.
[2] *Mem.* p. 221.
[3] *A.C.* II, p. 74.
[4] Dover Wilson gives a list in *Bibliog. Soc. Trans.* XI.
[5] p. 387.
[6] *v. supra* p. 84.
[7] *op. cit.* p. 78.
[8] *ibid.* p. 80.
[9] *ibid.* p. 120.

Car. the treatise intituled Ecclesiasticall Discipline, The discourse of Discipline, The Sermon upon the 12 to the Rom." He makes manifest his fondness for pithiness and clear cut logic (marks of the first Marprelate Tracts), and the general Puritan desire for a conference, when he beseeches Bridges "to reason pithelie and Syllogisticallie out of Gods worde, to performe his promise, in ioyning in such maner of conference, as him self at last yeeldeth to be good, so the iudgement be committed to her Maiestie, or their Honors."[1] When he expounds Presbyterianism Fenner is clear and restrained, but when he deals with the Bishops his hostility breaks out. His *Defence* is given out as the forerunner of another work: "Wee shall have occasion to speake of it [*the Eldershippe*] more largelie in the Defence of the Discourse it selfe."[2] Do we have here a reference to the first Marprelate Tracts?

The other reply to Bridges is entitled *A Defence of the Ecclesiasticall Discipline ordayned of God to be used in his Church. Against a Replie of Maister Bridges to a brief and plain Declaration of it which was printed in* 1584... This work was attributed to Travers by Bancroft[3] and Sutcliffe[4]. It is also a thoroughly Presbyterian document. It is well written and sets forth the usual Puritan arguments in favour of the reformation of the Church on a Scriptural basis. The author regards Beza as "the best interpretour of the New Testament."[5] In his Preface he repeats the tale of the preservation of the *Learned Discourse* in manuscript for many years till 1584. He expresses his high estimation of the Scottish Books of Discipline[6] and replies to Bridges' observations on the differences between the usages of the Church of Scotland and those set forth in the Puritan Prayer Book[7]. He holds Cartwright in honour and defends him against the strictures of Bridges: "We acknowledge and reverence [*T. C.*] as his rare giftes of knowledge and zeale and his learned workes, and constant suffring in this cause, and at this time his continuall travell in preaching the gospell, doe worthilie

[1] Fenner, *Defence*, p. 150.
[2] *ibid.* p. 109.
[3] *Survay*, p. 372.
[4] *Ans. to a Pet.* p. 145.
[5] Travers, *Defence*, p. 86.
[6] *ibid.* p. 22.
[7] *ibid.* pp. 113–4.

deserve: for which cause hee was worthy other respect then the replier here doth give him."[1]

The press from which this *Defence* was issued is also thought to have been that of Schilders[2]. The Puritans were sorely handicapped by the recent restrictions of the liberty of the press and had to print their books abroad or, at the risk of incurring heavy penalties, use a secret press at home. The late decree of the Council in the Star Chamber (23 June, 1586) allowed printing only in London and at the Universities, set up a strict censorship of books, and empowered the Company of Stationers to seize illicit presses, and prescribed severe punishment for breach of the law[3]. The operation of such measures may be seen in the case of Udall's book *Diotrephes*[4]. This was printed by Waldegrave, whose press, along with copies of the work, was seized in April, 1588. Waldegrave, however, saved some of his type and the Puritan printing went on. About August he issued Udall's *Demonstration* at East Molesey and shortly afterwards, October, 1588, the first Marprelate Tract was produced by the same press.

Udall's works were based upon the same foundations as those of Fenner. The writings of Cartwright and Travers are expressly held up by him as standard authorities. None of the compositions of these venerable leaders, however, give more lucidly and concisely the essential features of the Elizabethan Presbyterian platform, so far as the single congregation is concerned, than Udall's *Demonstration*[5] does. This fact should be kept in mind by the student of Marprelate. The first of his Tracts were issued by the very press that was the handmaiden of Presbyterianism and we would expect the Tracts to run in the same Presbyterian channels. A short examination of them proves that the continuity of thought and aim was maintained.

The Marprelate controversy now demands our attention. The writings of Martin and his allies, the replies of the Anti-Martinists, the story of the secret press and of its

[1] Travers, *Defence*, p. 32. [2] *v.* Dover Wilson, *op. cit.*
[3] Arber, *Sketch*, p. 50. [4] Reprint ed. Arber (1879). [5] ed. Arber (1880).

eventful wanderings from E. Molesey *via* Fawsley, Norton, Coventry, Wolston, to Newton Lane, near Manchester, the capture of the press (Aug. 1589), the arrest of printers and abettors, the examination of the accused and their punishment—all have been faithfully dealt with by Pierce, Arber, and Bonnard, who have left us little to do in this part of the Elizabethan field of research[1]. But it is an interesting and mystifying corner of the vineyard and we linger over one or two aspects of the controversy, which raged for about a year at a crucial juncture in the history of the Puritans. It contained two distinct elements, the one grave and the other gay. The former was animated by the principles of the Puritan Presbyterian party, by the ideals of Cartwright himself; the latter was mingled with gall and represented the quintessential ire, bathed in wit and irony, of the Puritans against the Bishops. Heron says[2]: "It is clearly established that the Presbyterians or Puritans proper had no part in the Tracts." This statement is misleading. The writings were certainly produced by a section of the Puritan party and they advocated, though in a questionable manner, the platform of the party as a whole. Marprelate repeats the usual arguments in favour of Presbyterianism as the Scriptural form of Church Government and denounces the abuses, *e.g.* non-residence, a dumb ministry, the sign of the cross in Baptism, customarily condemned by the Puritans. Undoubtedly the Tracts did not win the favour of such moderate men as Cartwright, but that was because of the manner and form in which they were composed, and we are sure that they hurt the cause of Puritanism and hastened the fast ebbing tide. The authorities took advantage of the literary outburst to put down with a heavy hand the movement they were designed to further.

Marprelate's chief printer was at first Robert Waldegrave, a man who occupied an important place in the history of English and afterwards of Scottish Presbyterianism. He was as ardent in his Puritanism as he was efficient in his printing.

[1] *v.* Pierce, *Hist. Introd.*; Pierce, *Tracts*; Arber, *Sketch*; G. Bonnard, *La Controverse de Martin Marprelate* (1916).

[2] p. 140.

It is probable that it was through the influence of Cartwright that he relinquished his post (after printing *Hay any Worke for Cooper* at Coventry, March, 1589). During a walk with Henry Sharpe in the fields near Wolston during Easter week he gave the chief reasons for his retiral. He had consulted with some of the leading Puritan ministers and their objections had prevailed with him: "All the Preachers that I have conferred withall do mislike yt." Marprelate evinced a vital interest in Cartwright's *Confutation* and his desire to print it was evidently shared by his printer, who said "that he had now gotten the thing he had long desired," viz., a part of this *Confutation* (as Penry afterwards informed the deponent, Sharpe) and that "he wolde go print yt in Devonshire."[1] At the time in question Waldegrave was residing in close proximity to Warwick and would most certainly come to know Cartwright's attitude to the Tracts and probably met the Puritan leader. Accordingly we hold it likely that Cartwright was one of the ministers who dissuaded the printer from further participation in the Marprelate enterprise.

Martin himself is still shrouded in mystery, in spite of many efforts to establish his identity. Field, Udall, Penry, Wigginton, Barrow, Throkmorton and others have been suspected. In considering the problem of authorship we should differentiate between the primary and secondary Tracts. With the latter Penry and Throkmorton had much to do, but their complicity does not identify them with Martin. It is even doubtful whether Martin acted single-handed in the earlier effusions. He certainly utilised the collections of others. The first two Tracts of Martin Marprelate are ostensibly sequels to the Defences of Fenner and Travers. The titles of *The Epistle* and *The Epitome* begin with the same sentence, "Oh read over D. John Bridges for it is a worthy worke." Did Fenner, who knew in 1587 that a vindication of the *Learned Discourse* against Bridges' attack was to be issued, have anything to do with the project of Martin? We also wonder whether Laurence Tomson—a Northamptonshire man, an alumnus of Oxford, a learned layman, an

[1] Arber, *Sketch*, p. 99.

earnest Puritan, who lived at Laleham a few miles from E. Molesey, and who was an intimate friend of Mrs Crane[1] and had been connected with the Puritan press since 1572—was involved in the controversy. Now we pass to a consideration of Cartwright's connection with it.

The references in the Tracts to Cartwright are numerous. Martin, who belonged to the left wing of the Cartwrightian school, frequently pays homage to the Puritan leader. He finds pleasure in taunting Whitgift with his failure to answer Cartwright's last Reply. He is convinced that the former was worsted in the literary combat that began in 1573: "His grace will cary to his grave I warrant you the blowes which M. Cartwright gave him in this cause."[2] "It is a shame for your grace Iohn of Cant. that Cartwrights bookes have bene now a dozen yeares almost unanswered. You firste provoked him to write and you first have received the foyle. If you can answer those books, why do you suffer the puritans to insult and reioyce at your silence. If you cannot, why are you an Archb. He hath prooved the calling to be unlawfull and Antichristian. You dare not stand to the defence of it."[3] "You shall not deale with my worshipp as Iohn with his Canterburinesse did with Thomas Cartwright, whiche Iohn left the cause you [*Bridges*] defend in the plaine field, and for shame threw downe his weapons with a desperate purpose to runne away and leave the cause, as he like a coward hath done: For this dozen yeares we never saw any thing of his in printe for the defence of his cause, and poore M. Cartwright doth content himselfe with the victorie, which the other will not (though in deed he hath by his silence) seeme to grant."[4] One of Martin's particular suits is that permission be granted for the publication of Cartwright's *Confutation of the Rhemists Translation*: "My 2 suit is a most earnest request unto you, that are the hinderers of the publishing of the confutation of the Rhemish Testament by M. Cartwright, [*that it*] may be published. A resonable

[1] In a letter to her, 26 Feb. 1585–6, he subscribes himself "your most obedient sonne." *Sec. Parte*, II, p. 48.

[2] *The Epistle* (printed at E. Molesey, Oct. 1588), Pierce, *Tracts*, p. 18.

[3] *ibid.* p. 21.

[4] *ibid.* p. 43.

request, the granting whereof, I dare assure you, would be most acceptable unto all that feare God, and newes of wofull sequell unto the papists. For shall I tell you what I heard once from the mouth of a man of great learning and deepe iudgement, who saw some part of Master Cartwrights answere to the sayde Rhemish and trayterous Raffodie? His iudgment was this. That M. Cartwright had dealt so soundly against the papists, that for the answering and confuting of the adversary, that one worke woulde be sufficient alone. He farther added, that ye adversary was confuted by strange and unknown reasons, that would set them at their wits end, when they see themselves assayled with such weapons, whereof they never once drempt that they should be stroken at. And wil your grace or any els that are the hinderers of the publishing of this worke, still bereave the Church of so worthie a Iewell: nay, so strong an armour against the enemie. If you deny me this request, I will not threaten you, but my brother Bridges and Iohn Whitgiftes bookes shall smoke for this gear. Ile have my peniworths of them for it."[1] So impressed is Martin with the worth of the *Confutation* that he explicitly lays down as one of the necessary conditions of peace between himself and the Bishops "that they suffer M. Cartwrightes answere to the Rhemish Testament to be published."[2]

In the second Tract[3] Martin refers only twice to Cartwright: "Master Canterburie hath proved that which Master Cartwright confuted," "Thomas Cartwright who hath bene professour of divinitie both in Cambridge and in Geneva."[4] Marprelate has already heard (*i.e.* by November, 1588) that the Puritan leaders—and probably Cartwright among them—have expressed their disapproval of the new method of attacking the Episcopate displayed in *The Epistle*: "The Puritans are angrie with me, I meane the puritane preachers. And why? Because I am to open. Because I iest."[5]

[1] *The Epistle*, Pierce, *Tracts*, p. 63. [2] *ibid.* p. 80.

[3] *The Epitome* (printed by Waldegrave at Fawsley House, Northamptonshire, Nov. 1588).

[4] Pierce, *Tracts*, pp. 135, 163. [5] *ibid.* p. 118.

In the next primary Tract[1] there are frequent allusions to Cartwright. This Tract is to a large extent a reply to Bishop Thomas Cooper's *Admonition to the People of England*, in which Cooper meets the criticism directed by *The Epistle* against Whitgift for not answering Cartwright's books thus: "Hee (*Whitgift*) never thought them so necessarie to be answered, as the factious authors of the Libel pretend. And of that opinion are not a fewe wise and learned men, that beare good will unto the party, and with all their hearts wishe, that God woulde direct him to use his good giftes to the peace and quietnesse of the Church. There is sufficient written already to satisfie an indifferent reader. Hee that with indifferent minde shall reade the answere of the one, and the replie of the other, shall see great difference in learning betweene them."[2] As a self-constituted champion of Cartwright's superiority to Whitgift Martin again affirms that the Puritan emerged as victor from the duel that ended with his *Second Reply*: "The which Iohn [*Whitgift*] although he hath bin greatly favoured by the said Thomas [*Cartwright*], in that Thomas hath now these many yeares let him alone and said nothing unto him, for not answering his books, yet is not ashamed to make a secrete comparison betweene himselfe and Thomas Cartwright. As who [*should*] say, Iohn of Lambehith were as learned as Thomas Cartwright."[3] "Ye puritans T. C. did set Iohn of Cant. at a *nonplus*."[4] "He that readeth his graces [*Whitgift's*] answere, and M. Cartwrights reply, shal see which is the better lerned of the two... And T. C. [*Thomas Cooper*] you your selves grant T. Cartwright to be learned, so did I never thinke Iohn Whitgift to bee, what comparison cann you make betwene them? But Thomas Cartwright, shall I say, that thou madest this booke against me [*An Admonition to the People*] because T. C. is sett to it, wel take heed of it, if I find it to be thy doing, I will so besoop thee, as thou never bangedst Iohn Whitgift better in thy life...If I had thy learning Thomas Cartwright,

[1] *Hay any Worke for Cooper* (printed by Waldegrave at White Friars, Coventry, March, 1589).

[2] Cooper's *Admonition to the People of England*, ed. Arber (1882), p. 32.

[3] *Hay any Worke*, Pierce, *Tracts*, p. 215. [4] *ibid.* p. 216.

I would make them all [*The Bishops*] to smoak."[1] The well-known initials, 'T. C.' which were common to Cartwright and Bishop Cooper, tempted Martin to make a distinction at the expense of the latter: "But Thomas Cartwright, thou art T. C. so is Tom Cooper too. The distinction then, betweene you both, shall be this: he shalbe profane T. C. because he calleth Christ Iesus, by whom the government by Pastors, Doctors, Elders and Deacons was commanded, to be he knowes not whom: and thou shalt be simple T. C.... Once preaching at Canter. he [*Cooper*] was disposed to note out T. C. I meane simple T. C. in his sermon, his part he placed after this sort. He noted 4 great Hidraes of the gospell in his sermon. I. Carnal security. 2. Heathenish gentility. 3. Obstinat papistrie. 4. saith he, when I looke in his forehead, I finde T. C. written therein, which I cannot otherwise interpret, then thankles curiositie, thanklesse for the benefits already received, and more curious than needs in vain and needles questions. The old student did not know himselfe to be T. C. when he thus spake, and this is yt thankles curiosity yt hath answered Martin."[2]

In *Hay any Worke* Martin reverts to the fact that he is disliked by some of the Puritans and seeks to vindicate his use of banter and invective in the cause of Presbyterianism: "I saw the cause of Christ's government, and of the Bishops' antichristian dealing to be hidden. The most part of men could not be gotten to read anything written in the defence of the one, and against the other. I bethought me, therefore, of a way whereby men might be drawn to do both."[3] He insists that his purpose was to do good, viz. to advocate the scriptural form of Church government and to expose the Bishops, who, in his opinion, were the chief enemies of Church and State.

The difference between Martin and the Puritans was one of method and degree. "Those whom foolishly men call Puritans," says Martin[4], "like of the matter I have handled,

[1] *Hay any Worke*, Pierce, *Tracts*, pp. 266–7.
[2] *ibid.* pp. 268, 281. [3] *ibid.* p. 245; cf. pp. 238–9.
[4] *Theses Martinianae*, Pierce, *Tracts*, p. 304.

but the form they cannot brook." Cartwright and others disliked the satirical and abusive means adopted and if he himself had been guilty of bitterness in controversy he objected to the unheard of pitch of scurrility that marked the Tracts. But it is evident that the main purpose of the writings was the same as that cherished by Cartwright. His principles run through the jesting and at times his very words are echoed, *e.g.* Martin says, "The government of the church of Christ is no popular government, but it is monarchical in regard of our Head, Christ; aristocratical in the eldership; and democratical in the people. Such is the civil government of our Kingdom; monarchical in her Majesty's person; aristocratical in the Higher House of Parliament, or rather at the Council table; democratical in the body of the Commons of the lower House of Parliament,"[1] the source of which passage is evidently in Cartwright's first *Reply*[2].

In the secondary Tracts, which presumably are not wholly the work of Martin Marprelate himself, Cartwright is mentioned several times[3], but there is nothing important or illuminating in the references. Suffice it to point out that he is always spoken of with the same admiration as is paid to him in the primary writings and is regarded as the most prominent authoritative exponent of Puritan Presbyterian principles. In the interesting auxiliary pamphlet *A Dialogue Wherin is plainly laide open*[4] "Puritane" holds that Cartwright refuted Whitgift: "He that looks in both their works with a single eie cannot but confesse M. Cartwright to have confuted him by unanswerable evidences: or els why would he not have answered M. Cartwrights workes, nowe a dozen yeares extant and more," and says[5]: "I wil tel you what a noble man professing the Gospel saide, he demaunded of the olde Lorde Henry Howard (the Earle of Arundels uncle nowe living, being a professed papist) what he thought of Whitgifts answere to Cartwright, who answered, *There was no comparison to be made betweene them*, *for Whitgift* (saith

[1] *Hay any Worke*, *ibid.* p. 252. [2] *W.W.* I, p. 390.
[3] Pierce, *Tracts*, pp. 319, 376, 403.
[4] sig. A 3 *verso.* [5] sig. C 4 *verso.*

he) *is not worthy to cary Cartwrights books after him for learning*: marke heere the opinion of a papist, you knowe a deadly adversarie to Master Cartwright."

The estimation in which Cartwright was openly held by the Martinists made him a target for the scathing abuse of the littérateurs employed by the ecclesiastical dignitaries to beat Martin at his own game. The Anti-Martinist tract *An Almond for a Parrat*[1] supplies an interesting and typical revelation of the Anti-Martinist attitude to Cartwright. The author is of the opinion that Martin has borrowed his chief weapon from the armoury of "the aged champion of Warwicke."[2] Breathing out vengeance upon the Martinists he writes, "I am eagerly bent to revenge, and not one of them shall escape, no not T. C. himselfe as full as he is of his miracles."[3] Regarding Cartwright as the *fons et origo* of Martinism the author thinks fit to give a brief but prejudiced account of the Puritan's revolt from the Church: "T. C. in Cambridge first invented this violent innovation, when as his mounting ambition went through every kinde of Ambitus to compasse the office of the Vicechauncelourship. But after he saw himselfe disfavoured in his first insolence, and that the suffrages of the university would not discend to his dissentious indignityes, his seditious discontent devised the meanes to discredite that government, which he through his il behaviour might not aspire to. Then began his inveterat malice to undermine the foundations of our societies and reduce our Colledges to the schooles of the Prophets, to discard all degrees of art as antichristian, to condemne all decency in the ministery as diabbolicall, and exclude all ecclesiasticall superiority forth the Church as Apocrypha. No sooner had these new fangled positions entred the tables of young students, but Singularity the eldest childe of heresy, consulted with malecontented melancholy, how to bring this misbegotten scisme to a monarchy. To which purpose hipocriticall zeale was addrest as a pursuivant into all places of Suff. Norff. Essex and Midlesex, with expresse com-

[1] By Thomas Nash? early in 1590.

[2] *An Almond for a Parrat*, ed. Petheram (1846), pp. 15, 26. [3] *ibid.* p. 16.

mandement from the sinod of Saints, to proclaime T. C. supreme head of the Church."[1] Martin's defence of Cartwright's learning and pre-eminence as a controversialist is treated with derision: "Put case his reading be gret and his malice more, that he hath plodded through cart loads of paper, and bin the death of ten thousand pound of candels, yet as Gregory saith 'perit omne quod agitur, si non humilitate custodiatur.'... If T. C. hath made thee his atturney, to urge the not answering of his bookes, then I praie thee bee my Mercurie this once, and tell him thus much from Mar-Martine, that he hath undone more Printers with his pybald pamphlets, then his dish-clout discipline will sette up agayne this seaven yeeres. Much inkehorne stuffe hath hee uttered in a iarring stile, and intruded a greate deal of trashe to our eares by a daintie figure of *idem per idem*, but for anie new peece of arte he hath shewed in those idle editions, other than that his famous adversary hath before time confuted, he may wel enough bequeth it to Dunce or Dorbel, whence his blundering capacity is lineally descended. What maister T.C. you think that no man dare touch you, because you have plaid the scurvie scolde anie time these twentie yeeres, but Ile so hamper your holynes for all the offences of your youth, as all geering puritans shall have small cause to insult and reioyce at my silence."[2]

Martin made much of Cartwright's *Confutation* and the desirability of its publication. The Anti-Martinist in seeking to discredit the work incidentally furnishes us with an interesting piece of information regarding its composition. We learn that Cartwright, while engaged on the book in Middelburg, had a band of zealous collaborators in Cambridge, who, maybe under the leadership of Laurence Chaderton, the first Master of Emmanuel College (founded in 1584 by Sir Walter Mildmay) met every week, evidently to study in particular the detailed evidence of the Fathers and the Councils with regard to certain positions upheld by the Rhemists, and regularly sent their findings to Cartwright overseas. The

[1] *An Almond for a Parrat*, ed. Petheram (1846), pp. 29–30.
[2] *ibid.* pp. 31–3.

apposite passage is as follows: "[Cartwright] will have the helpe of his fellow Brethren, if he hath any thing to write against Bishops, Were not al the elected in Cambridge assembled about the shaping of the confutation of the Remish Testament? O so devoutly they met every Friday at Saint Laurence his monastery, wher the counsails and fathers were distributed amongst several companies, and every one of the reformed society sent there combined quotations weeke by weeke in a Capcase, to my brother Thomas, yet wandring beyond sea, such a Chaos of common places, no apothegmatical Lycosthenes ever conceited. Bishops were the smallest bugs that were aimed at in this extraordinary benevolence, God shield, the court have escapt their collections. Some thing it would prove in the end if it wer published, that is pouldred with the brains of so many Puritan springols, and polluted with the pains of such an infinite number of Asses."[1]

Some of the Anti-Martinists did not hesitate to blacken the personal character of Cartwright, much to the latter's annoyance, *e.g.* "Martin sweares I am some gamester," says the author of *Pappe with an Hatchet*[2], "Why, is not gaming lawful? I know where there is more play in the compasse of an Hospitall, than in the circuite of Westchester. One hath been an old stabber at passage: the One that I meane thrust a knife into ones thigh at Cambridge, the quarrel was about cater-tray, and ever since he hath quarrelled about cater-caps."

It is beyond doubt that Cartwright had no hand in the production of the Marprelate Tracts. He viewed them from the first with disfavour. By the time they appeared he was pronouncedly in favour of a moderate policy, which was diametrically opposed to the virulent radicalism of the Tracts. We would not expect him to countenance the *modus operandi* adopted by Marprelate and we have his own explicit repudiation of any connection or sympathy with him. In a letter to Burghley[3] he says that he had not "so much as a finger in the bookes under martins name." He complains that the

[1] *An Almond for a Parrat*, ed. Petheram (1846), p. 43.
[2] ed. Petheram (1844), p. 15. For Cartwright's disclaimer, *v.* App. XXI.
[3] 4 Oct. 1590; *v.* App. XXI.

Anti-Martinists have levelled their shafts of ridicule and abuse at him not only as an unlearned man, but also as a dicer, a man of violence and of bibulous habits: "yet," he continues, "am I hable to make good profe, that from the first beginning of martin unto this date, I have continually upon any occasion testified both my mislike and sorow for such kinde of disordered proceding."

Shortly after this letter was written the official suspicions with regard to Cartwright's relationship to Marprelate were set forth in two of the thirty-one articles preferred against him by the Ecclesiastical Commissioners[1]. One charges him with having had knowledge of "the penners, printers, or some of the dispersers of the several libels" (*i.e.* the Tracts and cognate writings) without divulging the same to the authorities. The other contains the accusation that when asked his opinion of such books he answered in effect that the Bishops deserved the treatment meted out to them in these writings.

Matthew Sutcliffe afterwards trumped up this hearsay report in his general vilification of Cartwright and the latter in his *Apologie* of 1596 replies as follows to his malevolent critic: "Let it be iudged what christian love it is to committe such things to print upon a bare report. And if the reporters had bene named as in other cases where he doth call out the persons by their names, the trueth might have the better appeared: For me I am able to produce witnesses, that the first time that ever I heard of Martin Marprelate, I testified my great misliking and grief, for so naughtie, and so disorderly a course as that was. And therefore where fol. 51 pa. 1 he asketh when I will condemne th' unlawfull and uncivill practise of Martin and Penry? I aske again what office or charge I have to publishe condemnation upon every unlawfull and uncivill writing that cometh abroad? And yet I have witnesses, that even publikely when I was alowed to preach, I condemned all dealing in that kinde."[2]

It is noteworthy that the Ecclesiastical Commissioners in 1590 did not impute to Cartwright any direct and responsible

[1] Fuller, *C.H.* bk IX, sect. vii, § 27, arts. 23, 24. [2] *Apologie*, sig. C 2.

connection with Marprelate and that their allegation respecting his approval of the contents of the Tracts was based merely on hearsay. Indeed, it appears that they failed to observe that Cartwright's opinion was misreported. He did not hesitate to commend some of the Puritan writings issued immediately before Martin took the field. As he says in a letter to Burghley[1]: "I esteme (Martin set apart) some dutifully and learnedlie written, which they or sum of them (perhaps) may iudg libels." Some such expressed opinion was confusedly and erroneously made to imply approval of Marprelate.

In view of these statements no credence can be attached to such a verdict as Timperley's[2], that Cartwright approved of the Tracts, knew the writers, and was frequently consulted by them, and it is impossible to hold with Maskell, the prejudiced Anglo-Catholic historian[3], that the Puritan leaders did not express their disapproval of the Tracts when they appeared, but only after they were faced with the terrors of the High Commission, the Tower and the rack. Maskell indeed suggests[4] that the work of Marprelate was "an experiment which the Puritan leaders, Cartwright and Travers and the rest, were willing enough to try. Doubtless, being wise in their own generation, when they fancied it about to fail, they neglected not the providing some ground to retreat upon, by a timely disconnecting of it with themselves." For this view there is not the slightest shred of evidence, at any rate so far as Cartwright is concerned.

[1] 4 Nov. 1590; *v.* App. XXIII.
[2] C. H. Timperley, *Dictionary of Printers* (1839), p. 403.
[3] W. Maskell, *History of the Martin Marprelate Controversy* (1845), p. 102.
[4] *ibid.* p. 103.

CHAPTER VI

FROM WARWICK TO THE FLEET

Cartwright in Warwick—Master of the Leicester Hospital—his Warwickshire associations—death of his brother-in-law, John Stubbe—correspondence with Mrs Stubbe—effect of Leicester's death—Cartwright's trial by the High Commission—imprisoned in the Fleet—the Copinger-Hacket conspiracy—Cartwright's correspondence with Bancroft—his trial in the Star Chamber—the Church of Scotland and the Puritans—the intervention of King James—Cartwright's correspondence with Burghley, Lady Russell, etc.—petitions of the Puritan prisoners—their release in 1592.

LORD LEICESTER'S HOSPITAL, with which Cartwright was intimately connected—with one or two intervals—from 1586 till the day of his death, is one of the most picturesque places of historic note in Warwick. A fourteenth century building, it originally belonged to the Guilds of the Holy Trinity and St George[1]. After the dissolution of the Guilds in the reign of Henry VIII it passed into the hands of the corporation, who used it partly as a burgers' hall and partly as a school. Its further fortunes were largely decided by a Bill, passed by the Parliament of 1571 (2 April–29 May), which gave licence to the Earl of Leicester to found a Hospital. The Bill was read for the first and second time on Monday, 21 May, 1571 and a third time on the following day[2], not in spring, 1572, as Kemp states[3]. In the words of John Fisher, who with Edward Aglionby represented Warwick in this Parliament, "It had pleased him [Leicester] to be sutor not only to the quenes ma^tye^ but also to the whole parliament to have licence & warraunt to erect & found an hospitall either in the towne of Warwik or Kenelworth and to give towards the mayntence therof lands tenements hereditaments & possessions to the yerely value of twoo hundreth pounds by the yere which should have perpetuytie for ever and that the lands tenements possessions & hereditaments so to be by him given should be assured by auctorytie

[1] Kemp, *Warwick*, pp. 177 ff.
[2] *Black Book*, p. xxviii.
[3] *Warwick*, p. 180.

of the said parliament A thing both notable & to be thankfully acceptid of by all the whole countrey which his sute it pleasid her heighnes most favorably to heare & likid also the whole state of parliament."[1] While on a visit to Warwick at Michaelmas, 1571, Leicester came into St Mary's churchyard and "viewed where he might build a convenient house for to make an hospitall for certen poor pep[l]. But not liking of that place for divers causes J[hn] Butler being bothe his servant & one of the principall burgesses said unto his Lordship that the towne wold bestowe on his hon[r] towards the said hospitall not only a place to sett the same uppon but also a chapell & some building there if his Lordship thought the place convenient for that purpose which chapell & other things being alredy made woold save him v[c] mks in his purse which the said Lord hearing desired to see the place presently whereunto the said John Butler brought his Lordship without knowleig of bailief or any other. And being come to the said place which is the burgers hall the said Earle allighted and went into the same & so into the chapell & viewing the same liked well thereof insomuch that his Lordship apointed one Spicer being his surveyor of his woorks, to survey the same with spede & to signifie him of his opinion."[2] Leicester, acting on his surveyor's report, intimated through John Butler, to the Bailiff of Warwick that he required all the premises connected with the burgess hall for his hospital. Accordingly, at a meeting of the Bailiff and the principal burgesses on Saturday, 27 Oct. 1571, "it was agred by all that the whole house chapell & other things there should be given frely to my L without any mony taking therefore" on condition that in return Leicester should help to make provision for a new burgess hall, school and schoolhouse[3]. In their letter of 5 November, 1571[4], the Warwick magistrates "willingly offer & most freely give unto your honor [Leicester] our house callid the Burgers hall with the chappell & all houses & buildings therof towards the furtheraunce

[1] *Black Book*, p. 28. [2] *ibid.* p. 38.

[3] *ibid.* p. 39. Buildings and land were granted for the new hall and school by Leicester and Ambrose, the Earl of Warwick, by deed dated 8th April, 1576, *ibid.* p. 224. [4] *ibid.* p. 41.

of the same your most godly determynacion," which letter was delivered to his Lordship by John Fisher "in Leycester house in London the ixth day of the same moneth."[1] Shortly afterwards Fisher had an interview with Leicester at Greenwich, where the Court then was, and the Earl agreed to accept the site offered for his Hospital and expressed his desire that the Corporation should draw up a deed of conveyance forthwith[2]. The Bailiff and principal burgesses met on the 26th of December and "agreid that the Dede made to the Earle of Leycester of the gift of the burgers hall &c should be sealid and sent upp to his L for his neweyers gift" and on the same day the deed was duly sealed[3].

The Hospital, detailed descriptions of which are given by the local historian, Thomas Kemp[4] and by Nathaniel Hawthorne[5], has undergone little change since Cartwright's time. The date of foundation, 1571, has been given a conspicuous place on that part of the building which faces the High Street. On the North side of the inner quadrangle stands the Master's house, and the Chapel, in which the Master and brethren meet for divine service daily, is built over the West or Hongyn Gate that adjoins the Hospital. Within this beautiful sanctuary hangs a printed abstract of Cartwright's last will and testament as a memorial of the distinguished Puritan Presbyterian, who once ministered there.

It is generally stated that Cartwright was the first Master of the Hospital, but a counterclaim to this distinction has been made in several quarters in favour of Ralph Griffin, who is frequently mentioned and designated "the preacher" in the Warwick municipal records from 1570 onwards[6]. Ex-Mayor Kemp places Griffin's name first on the list of Masters[7]. In the Hospital log-book[8] (in the present Master's possession) Samuel Jemmat, writing as Master in 1686, states that Cartwright was the first of his predecessors in office, but a correcting pencil-note by W. Haynes points out that Griffin

[1] *Black Book*, p. 44.
[2] *ibid.* pp. 44 ff.
[3] *ibid.* p. 62.
[4] *Warwick*, pp. 181 ff.
[5] *Our Old Home*, c. III.
[6] *Black Book*, p. 174.
[7] *Warwick*, p. 186.
[8] p. 140.

"Professor of Divinity" was the first Master according to the deed of incorporation. F. L. Colville, in his *Worthies of Warwickshire*[1] says that Cartwright followed Dr Griffin, who had been promoted to the Deanery of Lincoln. Griffin's alleged tenure of office is, however, somewhat hazy and requires further investigation.

Although the Hospital was founded in 1571 its "Ordinances, Statutes and Rules" were not completed till the 26th of November, 1585, on the eve of Leicester's expedition to Holland and shortly before Cartwright's settlement in Warwick. The parchment roll on which the ordinances are written is kept in the muniment room below the Hospital Chapel. A modernised copy of these statutes was printed in 1840 at Warwick for the use of the foundation.

It is worthy of note that according to these Statutes Cartwright would be called upon to take the oath of supremacy before his installation as Master, that he had to reside in the Hospital, and for a prolonged absence required permission from the Bishop of Worcester and the Recorders of Warwick and Coventry or any two of them, and that provision is made for the visitation of the Hospital after Leicester's death by the Bishop, Dean and Archdeacon of Worcester. But of special interest is the type of service specified in article No. XXX. A note on the article signed by Leicester himself shows that he was aware of its unusual and important character: "This article for prayer to be referred to the Master, to be such as he shall find most necessary and meet for private Prayer within the House, being agreeable to the Book of Common Prayer, and according to the Word of God." The service in chapel was adapted to that of the English Church at the same time as it allowed scope for the tastes and judgments of a Puritan.

Cartwright had now the prospect of living comfortably during the rest of his days in what Hawthorne calls "one of the jolliest old domiciles in England." His post was exempt from the ordinary jurisdiction of the prelates. The Mastership was conferred upon him for life. "I have," he wrote to

[1] (1870), p. 95.

Burghley[1], "a patent of yt for life." His assured income was also considerable, viz., £100, for in addition to his stipend of £50 he received from Leicester by letters patent an annuity of £50 for life. "Th' Erle of Lecester," he informed Burghley[2], "over and above th'ordinary stipend of the master gave me by Letters patentes other 50li during my life." Compared with his fellow ministers he was in a position of affluence; for instance, the Vicars of St Mary's and St Nicholas's, Warwick, had as stipends £20 and 20 marks respectively[3]; but, as we shall see, he was not left long in the undisturbed enjoyment of his large income.

The first known mention of Cartwright in Warwick municipal records occurs in *The Book* of John Fisher, town clerk and deputy recorder of Warwick, which gives "A note of the names of such communicants as dwellid in St Mary parish in Warwik at Ester anno domini 1586 and in the xxviijt yere of the reigne of our souereigne Ladye Quene Elisabeth."[4] This document shows that Cartwright was safely installed as Master of the Hospital by the 3rd of April, on which day Easter fell in 1586. In the list of communicants, 1291 in all, he and his wife are entered along with fifteen other inmates of the Hospital. This list of the Hospital communicants has been omitted from Kemp's edition of Fisher's *Book*, but has been separately printed and a copy of it now hangs on the south wall of St Mary's Church. Besides the twelve brethren and the two female domestic servants there occurs the name of another man, who, as Mr Kemp has suggested to the present writer, may have been the Hospital porter. Cartwright's children, being too young to be communicants, are not mentioned.

Another entry in Fisher's *Book*[5] reveals Cartwright's active interest in the affairs of Warwick. He was evidently anxious that the relief of the poor of St Mary's parish, who were at the time surprisingly numerous, should be put upon a systematic and equitable basis. The entry runs thus: "Uppon

[1] 12 Oct. 1590; *v.* App. XXII. [2] 23 June, 1590; *v.* App. XIX.
[3] *Sec. Parte*, II, p. 165.
[4] *The Book of John Fisher*, 1580–1588, ed. Kemp (n.d.), p. 193.
[5] p. 165, dated ix and x Maij, 1586, Ao xxix^{o} (*sic*) Eliz.

many exclamacions & complayntes made and sett furth by Mr Cartwright & Mr dafferne towching the disorder of Beggers A view and survey of the poore was made by the said Mr dafferne & the constables & Willm hopkyns who found as hereafter ensueth." Then follows a detailed list of the beggars, inquiry into whose circumstances had been carefully made, and of the persons liable to pay poor rates. Some of the beggars were pronounced capable of working for their livelihood and others were ordered to repair to their own native towns.

In the first year of his residence at Warwick Cartwright, as we have seen, was forbidden by Whitgift to proceed with his *Confutation of the Rhemists Translation*, which he had almost completed. He was precluded by authority from the publication of this writing because he was known to adhere to his Presbyterian tenets, some of which were supposed and rightly so to be incorporated in his anti-Roman work. That his Presbyterian convictions were as strong as ever was soon made evident by the active share he took in the brisk forward movement, that was now being carried on by his fellow Puritans[1].

It was probably in autumn, 1586, that Cartwright created a great sensation in Warwick and district by his behaviour in connection with the sudden and tragic death of Henry Chaplin. This man appears to have been one of the principal burgesses of Warwick and in the *Black Book of Warwick* is spoken of as "lately decessed" on the 7th October, 1586[2]. Clarke[3] gives a plain and unvarnished account of the incident thus: "There was one Master Chaplin, a woollen Draper in Warwick, who made a Profession of Religion, but many times brake out into scandalous practices; Master Cartwright on a time walking with him in his garden dealt plainly and faithfully with him, rebuking him for his miscarriages, and shewing him the dishonour that he brought to God and the Gospel thereby; this so wrought upon Chaplin, that he presently sunk down, and being carried home, died within

[1] *v. supra* p. 270.

[2] *Black Book*, pp. 379, 385; *v. Book of John Fisher*, p. 63.

[3] p. 373.

a few houres after." Sutcliffe afterwards recounted the incident as an instance of the miracle-mongering, which the followers of Cartwright imputed to him, and because of which he was accounted by them a saint. The Sutcliffian version runs thus: "One Chaplin of Warwike being taken sicke in the hall of the hospitall, where M. Cartwright contrary to lawes of hospitalitie had revelled at him, and threatened Gods judgement against him for his supposed drunkennesse; he not long after the mans death going up into the pulpit, and taking the historie of Ananias and Saphira, Act. 5, for his text, did there say, that Chaplin was stricken, as was Ananias and Saphira"[1] and Sutcliffe proceeds to say that Cartwright denounced Chaplin as unworthy of Christian burial and takes the Puritan to task for arrogating to himself the wonder-working powers of a Saint Peter. Other instances of Cartwright's alleged miracles are of a similar kind: "One Browne died after that M. Cartwr. had denounced Gods iudgement against him for denying that he had begot his mayd with child: and yet his wife and others say, the poore man was impotent and unable to doe it," "One Harris being threatened with Gods wrath by M. Cartwr. not long after languished and died."[2] The incidents reveal Cartwright as the Puritan who hates sin, rebukes the sinner, and seeks to inspire the latter with a fear of God's punishment. It is possible that by striking terror into the heart of a guilty man like Chaplin his words hastened a physical collapse, but it is likely that the death of those rebuked was merely connected, after the event, by reports begotten of imagination and credulity with the condemnation uttered by a man reputed by many to be in possession of extraordinary spiritual power. As the stories were retailed they would gather legendary accretions, turn coincidences into results, and exalt Cartwright to the level of a miracle-monger. Cartwright, however, utterly repudiated the allegations. "Being (as I feele my self)" he wrote in his *Apologie*[3], "short of th'ordinary works

[1] Sutcliffe, *Exam.* p. 38 *verso.* "Testified by divers honest men in Warwike."
[2] *ibid.* p. 39.
[3] sig. B 4 *verso.*

of my calling both in generall duties of christianitie, and in the particuler way of the governement of mine owne familie: woe should be unto me if I should vainly boast of miraculous works, which my self have especially written against in condemning extraordinary callings whereof miracles are the seales: yet Mr D Sutcliffe seemeth to insinuate thus much (I say insinuate) for that the brethren he brandeth to have them in estimation (I doubt not) he meaneth to be men so favouring me as they would bee loth to doo it if they thought it would not stande with my good liking. Now let the towne wherein I dwell be examined, whether any voice tending hereunto did ever come from me. And as I thinke, none can be produced that will glory in this follie: so my desire is, that when this Legend shall come forth, there may be for the credite of him that setteth it out, the names of the reporters, and likewise of the brethren layed downe that are guiltie of the dotage he speaketh of, that thereby they may be cleared, or otherwise passe condemnation of the follie he chargeth them with."

When in Warwick Cartwright would be brought into more or less intimate association with many persons of interest and note connected with the affairs of Warwickshire or the Puritan cause. The Earls of Leicester and Warwick were of course among his most distinguished supporters and in virtue of his Mastership in the Hospital he was practically one of Leicester's trusted and favoured servants. The Recorder of Warwick, when Cartwright came to the town, was Edward Aglionby, who retired because of old age in 1587, and was succeeded by James Dyer (29 Sept. 1587). Dyer was followed by John Puckering, Sergeant at Law, owner of the Priory at Warwick (30 April, 1590)[1]. Puckering, who afterwards became Lord Keeper of the Great Seal, was one of the men in high official position with whom Cartwright was on terms of intimacy and who befriended him when his good fortune forsook him.

The Vicars of the parish in which Cartwright resided (St Mary's) were Martin Delaine (admitted 11 Aug. 1573),

[1] *Black Book*, pp. 332–4.

Leonard Fetherston (12 June, 1589), Andrew Bourdman (11 Jan. 1590), and Thomas Hall (*ca.* 1594)[1]. The Puritan Survey of 1586[2] characterises the first two thus: Delaine—"Learned in the tongues, yet the people profit not," Fetherston (in 1586 minister of Ichington)—"No allowed precher, but dilligent in his cure and honest." The latter would be a congenial associate for Cartwright as, according to Bancroft[3], he took part in the Puritan Conferences and signed the Book of Discipline. Probably when Fetherston was Vicar, Cartwright would be frequently invited to preach in St Mary's. Bourdman, however, was of another stamp. He was entirely opposed to the Puritans and openly took his stand against the teaching of Cartwright. Reference is evidently made by Cartwright to Bourdman's antagonism when, writing to Puckering (20 May, 1590), he expresses the hope that the Church of Warwick may be served by ministers, who though "differing in judgment from us may notwithstanding boeth in some good skill and care proceed in thedification of the Church without bitterness of spirit against other poore men which are other wise mynded." It was apparently during Bourdman's tenure of office that special preachers came to Warwick to defend the Church of England against the strictures of Cartwright and used the occasion to inveigh against the latter. "There hath bene directed to the place of my abode," wrote Cartwright to Burghley (4 Oct. 1590), "twise or thrise men that have made whole sermons invective against me." According to the charge sheet of the High Commissioners (1590) Cartwright became so arrogant that he could not brook the discourses preached by Bourdman and others in defence of the English Church and took upon himself to confute these in sundry sermons[4].

The Vicar of St Nicholas's, when Cartwright became Master, was Humphrey Waring, whose qualifications are thus summarised by the aforementioned Survey[5]: "Some knowledge, little discretion, he precheth sometimes, but negligentlie, he is thought to be unsound in some points of Christian Religion,

[1] Kemp, *Warwick*, p. 140.
[2] *Sec. Parte*, II, pp. 165, 174.
[3] *D.P.* p. 88.
[4] Fuller, *C.H.*, bk IX, sect. vii, § 27.
[5] *Sec. Parte*, II, p. 165.

loveth the alehouse well, and verie much subject to the vice of goodfelowshippe." Waring was succeeded by Hercules Morrell (Dec. 1593)[1], who as minister of Hatton in 1586 was registered by the Puritan detectives as no preacher "yet honest and zealous, and daily profiting and expounding to the people."[2]

That Cartwright did not confine his preaching to the Hospital is certain. Several interesting details regarding his services in the two Parish Churches of Warwick have been handed down by his biographer, Samuel Clarke. Clarke, although inaccurate in some of his statements, *e.g.*, that the Rhemish New Testament was published after Cartwright came to Warwick, supplies traditional elements in the life-story of the Puritan that are worthy of credence. His father, Hugh Clarke, was invited by Roger Wigston to succeed Edward Lord as minister at Wolston in 1590 and was pastor there till 1634. Samuel was born in that parish in 1599 and afterwards, for five years, was assistant to the Vicar of St Mary's, Warwick[3]. He had therefore excellent opportunities of learning authoritative accounts of Cartwright's life in Warwick. He says that Cartwright's "imployment was to pray with the poor men twice a day, to catechise twice a week, and to preach once on the Lord's day at the Parish Church," *i.e.*, St Mary's. It does not appear from the Hospital Statutes that the last item was part of Cartwright's duty, but that he exceeded his duty is apparent from the further explicit account, which has all the marks of verisimilitude. "He was a man of a very laborious and indefatigable spirit," says Clarke[4], "it was his meat and drink to be doing the will of his heavenly father; so that besides all his pains in writing, and in the Hospital, he preached every Sabbath day in the morning about seven o'clock in the lower parish of Warwick (*i.e.* St Nicholas's) and, when he could be suffered, in the upper parish (*i.e.* St Mary's) in the afternoon. Besides which, he preached a Lecture on Saturdays in the afternoon in the upper Church, in which he went over a great part of the *Proverbs* and *Ecclesiastes* with singular judgement and profit;

[1] *Black Book*, p. 399.
[2] *Sec. Parte*, II, p. 169.
[3] Colville, *op. cit.* pp. 112–22.
[4] p. 370.

and this he did of his owne free will, without demanding or receiving one penny for his pains. And whereas he was sometimes suspended by the Bishops from preaching in the Churches, his manner was at those times to preach in the Hospital, whither many resorted to hear him, though they were sure to be brought into the Bishops Courts for the same." It should be noted that much of this activity probably belongs to Cartwright's later days in Warwick.

In the articles directed against Cartwright by the High Commission in 1590 ample reference is made to his relations with the Warwick Churches in the years 1586 to 1590[1]. In these it is pointed out that "being to be placed in Warwick" he promised that if he might be allowed to preach he would not condemn the Church of England as established, but would endeavour to secure the peace of the same, but that, although no licence to preach had been granted, he has preached and in his sermons inveighed against the government and practices of the Church. In these articles he is further charged with having so indiscreetly and offensively criticised certain Church usages that some of his fellow parishioners "had conspired to have mischieved him with stones in the open streets." He is also accused of aiding and abetting a faction of malcontents in Warwick in their opposition to the Book of Common Prayer. He has persuaded his own wife to refuse to be churched after child-birth and "some other women also of that town, by such permission and example, did use the like contempt." He refused to kneel at a Communion in Warwick: "he sate or stood upon his feet, and divers others, induced by his persuasions and example, both then and at other times did the like." For such irregularities he was convened before the Bishop of Worcester, in whose Consistory he impugned the lawfulness of the Prayer Book. For his contempt he was suspended from preaching *et ab omni functione ministerii* by the Bishop. Cartwright appealed against the suspension but did not prosecute within a year, and accordingly, the cause being remitted to the Bishop, he was again declared suspended. "Nevertheless, in contempt

[1] Fuller, *C.H.* bk IX, sect. vii, § 27.

of the authority ecclesiastical, he hath preached at Warwick, Coventry and elsewhere since the said time." He is also stated to have exercised discipline in St Mary's Church on one of his own men servants, without having received authority to do so. Although some of the affirmations in these articles may contain exaggerations they are to be taken as more than mere *ex parte* assertions. They show Cartwright as the foster father of Puritanism in Warwick, participating with other Puritan preachers in the self-appointed fasts of a growing nonconformist party, and exercising such a notorious influence as to create dissension in the town and compel the Church authorities to take action.

An interesting tradition regarding Cartwright's appearance before the Bishop of Worcester is preserved in one of the *Baker MSS.*[1] According to this account Cartwright came bravely to the Consistory accompanied by some of his supporters. Freake seems to have dreaded the examination, and his prebendaries, Goldsborough and Lewis, for fear, it is suggested, of offending Leicester, unworthily left him to perform his task alone. Dr Longworth, an old fellow-student of Cartwright's, unexpectedly arrived upon the scene, greatly to the comfort of the Bishop. When charged with disturbing the peace of the Church, Cartwright answered that he took the Word of God for his warrant and the example of the Reformed Churches for his guide. Longworth reminded him of their time in Cambridge when they were both Fellows of St John's, accused him of having been always noted for his factious disposition, and warned him that his propagation of Genevan principles was likely to bring upon him the penalty, which the Papists incurred for alienation of the Queen's subjects from their allegiance. Longworth defiantly proposed to answer Cartwright's doctrines before any University in Christendom. It is said that Cartwright "having no great stomach to have any thing to do with this our Longworth" quietly stole away[2].

[1] XXVIII, ff. 443–5; App. XVII.

[2] Brook confuses this Longworth with Richard Longworth, who had been Master of St John's and died in 1579; Brook, *Mem.* p. 293; *A.C.* I, p. 399.

In the near neighbourhood of Warwick there lived several ministers, who were closely associated with Cartwright in the Puritan forward movement. The Survey of Warwickshire, 1586[1], enumerates 186 incumbents of whom "48 are of verie suspected life and religion, offensive to the gospell manie waies"; 120 are declared dumbe, and resident ministers able to preach number only 29. Among the preachers were most of Cartwright's Puritan associates. Humphrey Fen, a graduate of Cambridge, was Vicar of Holy Trinity, Coventry, from 1577 to 1590. He was suspended for refusal to subscribe Whitgift's articles—"suspended," says the Survey[2], these "10 monethes for not subscribing, and the cure ever since neglected." Cartwright sometimes officiated for Fen and gave the folks of Coventry the benefit of his Puritan doctrine. "On tuesday," wrote Far(mer?) to Little(ton?) in 1586[3], "M. Cartwright kept M. Fens lecture; text psalme 122. 4. unto the ende: takinge thrones as Tremellius doth, and urginge the discipline, the want wherof hee affirmed to bee the cause, that some friendes forsooke our church etc." Edward Lord was minister of Wolston till 1590. One of his letters to Fen shows how deeply involved Cartwright was with these ministers in the affairs of the Conference movement in Warwickshire. "I had lately," writes Lord in 1589[4], "some speech with Maister Cartwright concerning our next meeting, who advised me to put you in mind of some thinges etc. Hee saith that at your late being together at Wroxall, you determined our nexte meetinge to bee at Warwicke at the quarter sessions that twesday, for the humbling of our selves: and the day following to consult of other matters. His request is that you will give notice thereof unto the brethren of our conference, and also that by your meanes, there may bee some of us appointed to exercise in private that day. If this his request cannot conveniently bee performed, then I take it necessary that you write so with some speede to M. Cartwright, that hee may provide a remedie else where." Lord and Fen were subsequently fellow-prisoners with Cartwright

[1] *Sec. Parte*, II, p. 97.
[2] *ibid.* II, p. 169.
[3] Bancroft, *Survay*, p. 377.
[4] *ibid.* p. 376.

in the Fleet. At a later date Lord acted as Cartwright's Deputy in Warwick Hospital. Daniel Wight, an Oxford graduate, was minister at Stretton. He acted as Clerk to the Warwickshire *classes* and his documents were seized by the authorities and frequently quoted by Bancroft in his *Dangerous Positions*. He was also imprisoned in the Fleet. John Oxenbridge, of Southam and afterwards of Coventry; Matthew Hulme or Holmes, of Levington Hastings, and later Chaplain at Middelburg; Hercules Cleveley, of Wroxall and John Ashbie, of Cotone, were also members of the meetings in which Cartwright took part. All of the above ministers, with Cartwright, Gellibrand, Nutter and Littleton, subscribed the Book of Discipline about the same time[1].

Among the leading Warwickshire laymen, whose sympathies were with the Puritans, were John Hales, of White Friars, Coventry, Roger Wigston, of Wolston Priory, and Job Throkmorton, of Haseley, all of whom, and especially Throkmorton, were deeply involved in the Marprelate episode. With the last, whose residence was quite near Warwick, Cartwright was on particularly friendly terms. Job, the eldest son of Clement Throkmorton, graduated B.A. at Oxford (13 Feb. 1565–6), inherited Haseley Manor on the death of his father in 1573, entered Parliament as member for East Retford (1572) and afterwards represented Warwick (1586). He had distinguished social connections, his father being cousin of Katherine Parr, and his mother a daughter of Sir Edward Neville. His cousin Bess was one of Elizabeth's maids of honour. He married Dorothy, daughter of Thomas Vernon, of Houndhill. Interesting evidence of Throkmorton's Puritan zeal is found in the *Black Book of Warwick*[2]. He was evidently anxious to take part in the organised appeal of the Puritans to Parliament (1586–7) and to this end canvassed hard for his election as one of the representatives of Warwick. A section of the magistrates were not at all desirous of having him as their member. He did not fulfil the necessary condition of being a burgess and they suspected that his chief desire was not to represent the town, but to sit in "the

[1] *v. supra* p. 261. [2] pp. 386 ff.

Parliament where peradventure some freends of yours may have some causes in handeling." They also viewed him with disfavour because of his "familiarity with Richard Brooke," ringleader of a band of malcontents (Puritans?) in Warwick. After much debate Throkmorton ultimately took the burgess oath and was duly elected. During the first year of his residence in Warwick Cartwright is known to have preached at Haseley. Bancroft[1] quotes a letter from Farmer to Little(ton), 1586, which runs thus: "M. May and I ridde with M. Cartwright to M. Throgmortons, two miles out of Warwicke: where hee preached: more he sayde then ever he did in his life before." At a later date, according to a charge preferred against him by the High Commissioners[2], Cartwright preached at the baptism of one of Throkmorton's children, and on that occasion condemned the Episcopal system of Church Government and advocated the establishment of Presbyterian courts "seeking to prove and establish such elderships out of that word in one of the Psalms, where thrones are mentioned." The reference is apparently to Psalm 122, 5: "For there are set thrones of judgment, the thrones of the house of David," one of Cartwright's favourite texts, on which he had already preached at Coventry. Throkmorton afterwards visited Cartwright in the Fleet, was implicated in the Copinger-Hacket affair, published a Defence of himself against the slanders of Sutcliffe, and in 1596 edited Cartwright's *Apologie*. We come across him associating with Lady Margaret Hoby and her friends in London at the end of 1600[3]. It is said that he latterly removed from Haseley to Canons Ashby in order to benefit by the ministry of John Dod[4].

An attempt has been made to connect Cartwright's name with that of Shakespeare. Dr Thomas Carter in his *Shakespeare, Puritan and Recusant*[5] suggests that Shakespeare's father and other prominent inhabitants of Stratford might have been seen Sunday after Sunday wending their way along

[1] *Survay*, p. 377.
[2] Fuller, *C.H.* bk IX, sect. vii, § 27.
[3] *Trans. of R. Hist. Soc.* II, p. 171.
[4] *v. D.N.B.*; Colville, *op. cit.* p. 752.
[5] (1897), p. 168.

the pleasant country lanes in the direction of Warwick to listen to Cartwright's eloquence. Carter's book contains a short superficial survey of Elizabethan Puritanism, to which is attached the writer's case for the Puritanism of John Shakespeare. Cartwright is simply dragged into the book because he lived in the neighbourhood of Stratford. We should, however, bear in mind the dates of Cartwright's residence in Warwick, viz. 1586–1590, 1592–1594–5, 1601–1603, and note that Shakespeare's connection with Stratford during most of these years was not close[1]. It is indeed likely that Cartwright was known to the Shakespeares and occasionally drew Stratford Puritans to Warwick, but that is as far as we can go. The preacher of Stratford, Barton, is mentioned in the Puritan Survey (1586). The note there attached to his name runs: "learned, zealous, and godlie, and fit for the ministerie; a happie age if our Church were fraight with manie such."[2] Such an approved man would have been a congenial companion to Cartwright, but we have no evidence of their friendship. In connection with Cartwright's social relationships Clarke[3] sums up as follows: "His carriage and deportment was such, that there was not a Nobleman or Gentleman of quality in all the country that looked Heavenward, or was of any account for religion and learning, but they sought to enjoy his company and found much pleasure and content therein, for his conversation was such, that scarce a word came from his mouth that was not of some good use and concernment."

At this point we may take note of the death of Cartwright's brother-in-law, John Stubbe, in connection with the execution of whose will grave charges were afterwards preferred against Cartwright. Stubbe before leaving England for France with the troops under the command of Lord Willoughby hastily drew up his last will and testament (25 Sept. 1589), "Being dryven," he says, "to do this in haste uppon my suddayne jorney into France with the most honorable generall of the forces of her Majestie to ayde the moste christian King againste his Rebells." Shortly afterwards the

[1] *v.* Sidney Lee, *Life of Shakespeare*. [2] *Sec. Parte*, II, p. 166. [3] p. 370.

redoubtable Scaeva died, probably in the spring of 1590[1]. His will was proved in the prerogative court of Canterbury on the 27th of June, 1590. The will certainly does not name Cartwright, but in the course of it Stubbe writes: "I praye my kynnesfolke and friendes not to thinke much thoughe I remember them not by name with any Legaceys. I am in haste and will adde some schedule yf God permitt." The executors appointed are his wife, Anne, and his son-in-law, Francis Scharnbourn. References are made in the will to Stubbe's son, his mother, who was still alive, and his brother Edmund. An interesting name among the witnesses is that of Edmund Copinger. He anxiously provides that his debts should be paid out of the sale of his lands and properties, which we learn were numerous and chiefly in Norfolk, *e.g.* at Thelveton[2], Dickleborough, Shymplinge, Skole, Osmondston, Buxton, Frense, Frettenham, Horstead, Stratton, Hamford. Most of his possessions are left to his "faithfull and right well deserving wife." Among the trustees appointed to look after her interests are "his deerlie beloved and worthilye trusted Friends and Allies" Sir Robert Jermyn and Charles Seckford, his "good cosin" Sampson Leonard, and his "deere friende" Richard Catlyne[3].

Sutcliffe in 1592[4] accused Cartwright of gross inconsistency in that, although he was a minister, he refused not the execution of Stubbe's will. Throkmorton in his *Defence* of 1594[5], took up the cudgels for Cartwright, saying: [Sutcliffe] "chargeth him with th' execution of his brother Stubbes his will (*margin:* He is not so much as once named in his will), a thing that I have heard him say he never dealt in in any sorte in al his life. And I doo the rather beleeve it, in that in one of his bookes he bringeth testimonie (as I remember) out of one of th'auncient Fathers, that it is either unmete or unlawfull for a Minister of the worde, to be so much as an Executor, much

[1] Certainly not in 1591, as is stated in *A.C.* II, p. 112.

[2] The will runs: "I John Stubbe Sceva of Thelveton in Norfolk, gentleman, do..."

[3] The will is at Somerset House; *Book Drury*, f. 40. For life of Stubbe, *v. A.C.* II.

[4] *Ans. to a Pet.* p. 8.

[5] sig. E *verso*.

lesse that he should be encombred with anie civill office." Cartwright gives a fuller reply to the charge in his *Apologie*[1]: "I was not so much as named in my brothers will, and to put of Mr Sutcliffes shift of answere he hath made to excuse him self in his latter booke, that by the woord of last will he would understand any conveiance lately made before his death, wherein trust was committed unto me; I answere, that my brother Stubbes did never either long before or soone after his death put me in trust with anie of his worldly estate either by woord or writing. Neither is there (as Mr Sutcliffe surmiseth) any unkindnesse of my Brothers towardes me, in not putting me in trust which would not that way be employed, or my unkindnesse towards him, who trusted him with my whole estate that way. And that my Brothers wife and kindred rested not satisfied with my dealing: either is an untrueth of Mr Sutcliffes report, or a most causelesse complaint of their behaulf. For where in regard of my wifes portion of twoo hundred pound, I had an annuity in fee-simple, for default of payment whereof after his death (besides th'annuity and arrierages) I had a lease of a hundred yeres graunted me of certeine pastures to the yearely valew of six pound by estimation for a pepercorne only I was content, to th'end that the landes might be sold for the satisfying of my brothers creditours, freely and for naught to release my interest in that lease, which the law, for want of paiement of th'annuitie, did evidently cast upon me: also to yeeld up mine annuitie for the same summe of mony I had payed to my Brother, without both which my Brothers lande would have found no convenient sale for the paiement of his creditors untill this day. And of my dealing herein I take witnesse of Sir Robert Iermin of Suffolke, Mr Atkins and Mr Tindall of Lincolnes Inne: who were (in deed) the men my brother trusted with his worldly estate: and who (in my iudgement) acquited the trust my brother reposed in them accordingly."

Cartwright's sister-in-law, Mrs Anne Stubbe, was as interested as her husband in the reformation of the Church.

[1] sig. C 3.

She belonged to a zealous company of Separatists, with whose views she was in complete sympathy. She entered into a long discussion on the principles of Separatism, both by word of mouth and in writing, with Cartwright, which the latter brought to a close at the end of August, 1590. A synopsis of the earlier part of their friendly debate is given by Waddington[1]; the last stage is represented by a lengthy letter written by Cartwright from Warwick on the 30th of August, 1590[2]. "Sister," Cartwright begins, "notwithstandinge my buisines press me much, and I might for the multitude of them, although not utterly have denyed, yett delayed unto you this duity of aunswer, yett my desire to do you good hath prevailed with me; the rather for that the day of my trouble approchinge, I knowe not whether if nowe I lett it passe I should after recover the opportunity to aunswer to your lettre." "Your grounde," he writes, "that you maie not communicate with us in the worship of God, ys for that we are none of the Church." Identifying himself with the Church of England Cartwright argues that although it is not a perfect Church, it is not, therefore, no Church at all. To Mrs Stubbe's second reason that the Church of England is not the true Church, because it does not have the authority of Christ or the keys of God's Kingdom, Cartwright answers, that it has both although it may not use them as it should. "Your thirde argument," he says, "that we are not the Churche of Christ is for that we have no free eleccon of the mynisters of the church." "Howe much more," he replies, "are you none of Christes churche, which have no mynisters at all and therefore no eleccon att all." Cartwright holds that none of Mrs Stubbe's company are even fit for the ministry. To her argument in favour of the election of ministers by the whole congregation, he objects that pure Congregationalism is unworkable, and shows that one member or a

[1] *Hist.* pp. 19 ff.

[2] *Harl. MSS.* 7581, ff. 50 *b*–56 *b*. Dexter (p. xx) reproduces the signature of this MS. as Cartwright's autograph. By mistake he numbers the vol. 7851 and evidently was unaware that the letter is a transcript of the original. For Mrs Stubbe's letter and Cartwright's reply *v.* also *C.C.C. Oxon. MSS.* CCXCIV, ff. 357–72.

minority can prevent the rest from exercising authority. If Paul and Barnabas disagreed regarding Mark mere "novices in the graces of God" will more readily fail in unanimity. Cartwright rehearses some of the arguments already used by him in his letter to Harrison, *e.g.* the *esse* of a Church may exist in an imperfect Church, even as a mutilated man is still a man as long as he retains the essential parts of his body, or the Churches of God have given the hands of fellowship to the English Church and therefore the latter is a Church of God. "Thus, Sister," he concludes, "have I in love and in desire to do you good, written some aunswer to your lettre, which I would with greater labor have done, had not my daily buisines taken up some parte of my travaill that way, and my cousins soddaine departure into the Cuntry caused me to hasten myne aunswer more then otherwise I would or should have done, if the conveyannces of lettres from hence to you ward were not so seldome with any assurannce and safety....And albeit I care not who of your frendes and favourers in this cause examine myne answer, yet would I crave thus much att your hand, that it maie have the first reading in your chamber by your self...."

After giving extracts from the above letter Brook[1] writes: "Mr Cartwright, however, did not stop here; but, having entered into this dispute, he engaged in further controversy with the Brownists" and proceeds to discuss *A Reproofe of Certeine Schismatical Persons*, which he ascribes to Cartwright, and then his letter to Harrison, which, as we have seen, was written some years before. Other writers[2] regard the above correspondence as an indication that in 1590 Cartwright saw fit to sever himself distinctly from the Brownists. But there is no difference between his attitude to Separatism in 1590 and that adopted at the beginning of the Brownist movement. This discussion with his sister-in-law is indeed a repetition in miniature of that between Cartwright and Harrison in Middelburg. Cartwright was never a believer in Disestablishment or sheer Congregationalism; his opinions regarding these were brought into prominence by the emerg-

[1] *Mem.* p. 303. [2] *e.g. D.N.B.* art. "Cartwright."

ence of Brownism and they never changed. The fact that Mrs Stubbe was associating with other Separatists in Norfolk in 1590 probably indicates that Browne's influence in that county was still active, although he himself was now reconciled to the Church of England.

Further illustration of Cartwright's attitude to Brownism and to the Establishment may be gleaned from an undated manuscript entitled "Resolutions of Doubtes, touching a mans entrie into ye Ministerye"[1] in which are given Cartwright's answers to the scruples of a conscientious objector regarding the question of election and ordination. Cartwright endeavours to salve the conscience of the doubter by pointing out that he may have the essence of true election by winning the approval of the majority of the faithful in his congregation and the substance of ordination at the hands of a Bishop, not as a diocesan Bishop, but as a minister of the Gospel, and that he may be as self-consistent as a minister of the Church as he now is as a member of the same. To the objection that the Church of England is in many respects anti-Christian he replies that it is not altogether so and holds that if it were the Puritans must logically be obliged to follow the Brownists: "If yt were meerly and absolutly Antichristian I see not how yt could be avoyded but that we must with ye Brownistes confesse that we have noe church at all in ye Land."

Leading representatives of the party that sought a Presbyterian reformation frequently disclaimed any sympathy with the Separatist point of view[2]. Even Marprelate, when maintaining that no Puritan regards tithes as unlawful, says that he "doth account no Brownist to be a Puritan."[3] This attitude to Separatism coincides with and reflects that of Cartwright. Historical writers have not always been fair to the latter in this connection. Timperley says[4]: "After having long sustained the most elevated and rigid tone, (he) suddenly let his alp of ice dissolve in the gentlest thaw that ever occurred in political life. Ambitious he was, but not of martyrdom."

[1] *C.C.C. Oxon. MSS.* CCXCIV, ff. 351–5.

[2] *Sec. Parte*, I, pp. 189, 224–5.

[3] Pierce, *Tracts*, p. 252.

[4] *Dictionary of Printers* (1839), p. 403.

Now no wise man seeks martyrdom for its own sake. Cartwright constantly sought to presbyterianise the Church of England and as constantly opposed Separatism with its implications. On these points he maintained his convictions from the beginning to the end of his stormy career. He did not share the fate of men like Barrow, Greenwood, and Penry, not because he was afraid to die for his principles, but because he never believed in the Separatist opinions which, if not technically, really brought these men to their doom.

Apart from the charge of cowardice that of inconsistency has been made against Cartwright because he tried to be a conformist and nonconformist at the same time and did not follow his premises to what in the opinion of his critics was their logical conclusion, namely, Separatism[1]. Hooker[2] pointed out that one of the dangers of Puritanism was its liability to degenerate or change into secession. Seceders like Barrow and Greenwood acknowledged their debt to such men as Cartwright and were convinced that they were obliged by his principles to separate from the English Church[3]. Certainly Separatism was one way in which to realise some of the anti-episcopal views of the Cartwrightians, but it was not the only way. The Church of Scotland embodied Cartwright's tenets in another way. It became a National Presbyterian Church in alliance with the State. The peculiar nature of the English Reformation made it difficult for Cartwright and his school to convert the Church of England into a Church like that of Scotland, but it was their aim to do so, and they believed that their best method of attaining their goal was by seeking reform from within.

[1] Before the end of the century the question of liberty of conscience was coming to be more fully understood. An anonymous pamphlet published (by Schilders?) in 1599 and entitled *A Triall of Subscription* pleads for the toleration of a peaceable nonconformity and laments that the practice of Puritan conformity, regarded by the writer as a sin, is responsible for a diminution in the number of those who are zealous for a thorough reformation. It enunciates principles that break with Elizabethan notions of uniformity and foreshadows the more modern recognition of the rights of an uncompellable conscience, but it is not a typical pronouncement of sixteenth century Puritanism.

[2] *Pref. to Eccl. Pol.* VIII, § 1.

[3] *v.* F. J. Powicke, *Henry Barrow, Separatist* (1900), p. 153.

About 1590 there was published *A Collection of certaine sclaunderous Articles....Also the Some of Certaine Conferences had in the Fleete, according to the Bisshops bloudie mandate, with two prisoners there.* One section of this publication[1] contains eleven arguments drawn up by Barrow and Greenwood or one of them in favour of Separation. The true Church of Christ is first defined as "a companie of faithfull people, seperated from the unbelevers and heathen of the land," etc. The parish assemblies of England are then measured by this rule and found wanting in eleven distinct respects. They consist of profane members, they do not have true pastors, teachers, elders and deacons, they do not exercise the power Christ has given to His Church, but are in bondage to the Canon Law, antichristian officials and courts, etc., therefore they cannot be true Churches of Christ. Accordingly Separation is necessary. At the end of this list of arguments it is recorded that "These Arguments were more then a yeare & an half since delivered to Mr Cartwright, Mr Travers, Mr Charke and Mr Floyde, which still remaine upon them unanswered." It appears that the above-mentioned *Reproofe* constitutes an answer to this and other similar writings, but whether composed by Cartwright or not, it is difficult to ascertain. It is certainly in accord with his usual line of reasoning against Separation. Burrage, who has printed the *Reproofe* (1907) tries to make out a case for its being the work of the renegade leader of the Brownists and entitles it *The Retractation of Robert Browne*, but it is possible that he has unwittingly published for the first time a writing ascribed, not without reason, by Brook and others to Cartwright.

We have spoken of Leicester's death in 1588 as a great blow to Puritanism. It was a cause of misfortune to Cartwright personally. It brought him and the Hospital into financial troubles, which were complicated by the death of the Earl's brother, Ambrose, the Earl of Warwick, in 1589. On the 23rd of June, 1590, when in London, Cartwright wrote to Burghley, "being (as I am infourmed) thonely person by whose mean relief may be obteyned."[2] He explains

[1] IV, 67.

[2] App. XIX.

that the income of the Hospital—£200, of which £150 was to be divided among the twelve poor brethren, and £50 was allocated to the Master—is drawn from certain lands in Warwickshire and Lancashire, which Leicester had conveyed by deed in 1585. The conveyance was not enrolled within a year and became in the eyes of the law invalid. By letters patent Cartwright received an annuity of £50 from the Earl for life, but this, too, is in danger because Cartwright did not conform in time to a certain legal requirement regarding a writ of annuity. "Now it is said constantly, that her maiesties extent shall goe forth upon all the lands that th'earll of Lecester was seased of" and Cartwright fears that his stipend will be lost and that the brethren will be beggared. Meanwhile the Hospital cannot procure a whit of a legacy of £200 from the Countess of Leicester. Moreover Ugnoll, a rich citizen of London, has defrauded the Hospital of its income to the extent of £20. Cartwright accordingly is obliged to meet the expenses of the foundation out of his own pocket. Since Leicester's death he has had heavy outlays in connection with the very effort to secure the Hospital's rights, *e.g.* "to give attendance here at London in the term tymes." While he thus enumerates his financial embarrassments Cartwright incidentally mentions that Leicester took him from a post, viz., that at Middelburg, which "was (for profit) much better in regard of the charges that this place casteth upon me which th'other did not." "Thus nakdly" Cartwright lays his case before the Lord High Treasurer and humbly prays for redress. That Burghley took the matter in hand we learn from a letter written by Cartwright from Warwick on the 5th of August[1] to his old friend, Michael Hicks, now one of Burghley's secretaries. He thanks Hicks for what he has done, and encloses a letter to Burghley and also a copy of his answer to the Preface of the Rhemish Testament, which his Lordship had requested. He is still unable to enjoy his annuity "only because I never brought a writ of Anuitie against the Earles that are deceassed." He is grateful to Burghley for having "given order that although the hospitall lands be found, yet

[1] App. xx.

they should not be seased upon, but left to such uses of the mayntenance of the poore as my L. of Lecester granted them for," nevertheless, he thinks that the special commission has been so speedy that certain things have been omitted, with which he deals more particularly in his enclosed letter to Burghley thus: "Her Majesties extent upon my Lords lands, which threatned th' overthrow of the hospitall: through her princely hand, and your Lordships singuler favour, is so far frome hurting us that yt might have bene of singuler help unto us, towching xx^{li} goeing out of Crifeild, withholden by Mr Ugnall, and the manner of Shilton which Mr Eglombie now maketh claym unto: yf the return of the commission had not bene so speedy, but that we might have had tyme to produce witnesse that my lord was seased of them boeth. Wherein yf your most honorable place may yeild us anie further help, that the poor hospitall be not driven to consume yt self, in recovering, and houlding that yt is indowed with. As we most humblie thanke your h. for the favour already shewed, so I am an humble suter in the behalf of the poor hospitall, that from that good hand, whereby it standeth now, we may receyve the further benefite both of continuance and of the peaceable state thereof: remembring that yt wilbe no unlike good work before god and prayse before men unto your L. to continew and uphold a good work: then for our deceased Lord and founder to have founded and begunne yt. As towching myne own particuler sute, of the continuance of my annuitie of 50^{li}: I would be glad that to my common bond for your h. favour to the hospitall I might have also this specially to bind me unto you. Although I confesse that the benefits alredy receyved from your L. binde me faster, then I am hable to unlose, by anie dutie which I can perform agayn. Thus with my most dutifull remembrance of your L. I recommend the same with all your waightie affayres and whole family to the gratious keeping and blessing of god in Jesus Christ: whom I most humbly beseech long to praeserve you with all increase of pietie and honour."[1] The case of the

[1] *Lansd. MSS.* LXIV, No. 17. The first portion of this letter dealing with the *Confutation* has already been given (*supra* p. 205). It is subscribed "Warw. vth of August. 90."

Hospital endowments was dealt with by Parliament in 1597–8. "The Bill for confirmation and better assurance and conveyance of certain Mannors, Lands, Tenements and Hereditaments given and intended to an Hospital or Meason de Dieu in Warwick, founded and established by the Earl of Leicester" came before the House of Commons in January, 1597–8[1], and was thereafter carried to the House of Lords, where "The Councel Learned on part of George Ognell, and on the behalf of the Hospital" were openly heard[2]. Sutcliffe afterwards included among his many defamatory accusations against Cartwright the charge that he misappropriated the Hospital funds for his own selfish aggrandisement[3].

For five months Cartwright lived in constant apprehension of imprisonment before he was actually committed to the Fleet. On the 20th of May, 1590, he told Puckering that he had already been sent for by a pursuivant: "being sent for by a Poursuivant I was loeth to be attached before I had made my appearance without attachement."[4] He expected then to be removed from Warwick at any time. He had already made up his mind not to take the oath *ex officio mero* and feared that for his refusal he was sure to be committed. His suspense, however, was prolonged till autumn. On the 30th of August he was still in Warwick, but knew that his day of trouble was near at hand[5]. On Sunday, the 4th of October, he implores Burghley to come to the rescue[6]. After expressing his great grief that Elizabeth regards him with heavy displeasure, he intimates that he now stands "under th'arrest of her high commission in causes Ecclesiasticall for appearance upon thursday next" (8th Oct.). He is not yet cognisant of the matters that will be brought up against him, but assures the Lord High Treasurer that since 1577 he has not written any book "which might be in any sort offensive to her majestie or the state." He protests that he had no finger in the Marprelate Tracts, which from the day of their appearance till now he has consistently condemned. He also defends his ministry in Warwick, which he has exercised for almost

[1] D'Ewes, pp. 579, 581. [2] 23 Jan.; *ibid.* pp. 538, 541.
[3] *v. infra* pp. 364 ff. [4] *v.* App. XVIII. [5] *v. supra* p. 308.
[6] *v.* App. XXI.

five years since his return from the Low Countries and points out that during that period, in spite of provocation, he has but "sparingly spoken of any matter in controversy" between the Puritans and their opponents. "Wherefore," he concludes, "my moest humble sute unto your Lordsh: is that yt would please yow...to relieve me against the troubles that are coming upon me: especially against her majesties heavie displeasure." In a later epistle, written from London on the 12th of October[1], Cartwright incidentally mentions that he has not yet been imprisoned. But his chief concern is to appease the royal wrath and to this end he appeals to Burghley to intercede for him. He is anxious that the Queen should discredit the slanderous reports she has received from his calumniators and regard him as a loyal and dutiful subject. Burghley has told him that his tenure of office in the Hospital is offensive to her Majesty. Now he states that, although his income from the Mastership is the chief means of support for his wife and five small children, he is willing to resign his charge: "Rather then I would remain with her gracis offence, I will be well content to surrender yt, to be bestowed upon whome yt shall best please her highnesse, and to goe into what corner of her majesties dominions soever she shall command me."

It was apparently in the month of October, 1590, that the Puritans held a special Conference in London to consider "whether it were fit or convenient, that the said master Cartwright (after his commitment to prison) should discover or reveale, all or any the matters, which passed in conference and disputation, in any of their former assemblies, or not."[2] The meeting was held at Gardiner's house and those present were Cartwright, Charke, Travers, Egerton, Gardiner, Barebon, Barber, Oxenbridge, Gellibrand, Culverwell, Stone, etc.[3] The result of their discussion is not definitely known, but, as Bancroft suggests, we can deduce from Cartwright's future conduct what conclusion was arrived at. When the interrogatories were put to him he either gave noncommittal answers or did not answer at all. We do not know the precise

[1] App. XXII. [2] *D.P.* p. 94. [3] *ibid.* p. 93.

date of Cartwright's incarceration. It must, however, have been after the 12th of October and before the 4th of November. From his letter endorsed the 5th of March, 1590–1, in which he states that he has been eighteen weeks in prison, we deduce that he was committed towards the end of October.

On the 14th of October Burghley writes to Whitgift advising him not to take his place among the Ecclesiastical Commissioners who were examining Cartwright, lest he might seem to be seeking personal revenge against his old rival and opponent. The old controversy should not be revived especially seeing Cartwright has made some amends and now constantly affirms that he has kept himself free from it. Burghley would like to see greater care taken to win and reclaim such precisians as Cartwright. He writes not only as a patron of the Puritan but also as the advocate of a wise moderation[1]. Shortly afterwards (4 Nov. 1590) Cartwright sends a report from the Fleet to Burghley, as his Lordship had requested, of the proceedings taken by the High Commission against him[2]. After thanking Burghley for writing to the Archbishop in his behalf he briefly relates his experience at the hands of the Commissioners "at boeth their sittinges." "Being offred," he writes, "the generall and indefinite oath to answer to whatsoever I should be demanded touching articles to be objected against me, I returned, that I estemed it contrarie boeth to the lawes of god and of the land, to require such an oath, especiallie of a minister." Eventually his examiners read over "the heads and generalls" of a long series of articles containing charges against him. He noticed that some of these charges were of such a nature "as namely that I had given over my ministerie and taken an other, that I had ordeined ministers, held conventicles and called Synodes" that he desired to free himself "from the suspicion and jelousie of the magistrate, her majestie especially." He was willing to answer such particular articles on oath, provided they were given to him for perusal beforehand. "If," he now says, "there were anie article that I refused to answer upon my oath: I offer to give reason thereof:

[1] *Lansd. MSS.* CIII, No. 71; St. *Whit.* II, p. 25.

[2] App. XXIII.

which if it doe not satisfy them, I will submitt my self to the punishment they shall award."

Bancroft informs us[1] that Cartwright was "moved in the consistory of Paules" by the Bishop of London, the two Lord Chief Justices, Justice Gawdy, Sergeant Puckering, Attorney General Popham and other Commissioners to take the oath and answer certain articles "yet notwithstanding that the cheife points of them were then delivered in generall tearmes unto him & that the said both honourable and grave persons did (every man) severally assure him upon their credits, that by the lawes of the Realme he was bound to take his oath & thereupon to answere, as he was required: he desired to be borne withall, and said that hee thought he was not bound by the lawes of God so to doe." A copy of the articles found in the study of Travers after his death was communicated to Fuller, who printed them in full in his *Church History*[2]. Fuller gives the impression that the articles were presented to Cartwright on the 1st of September, but as we have seen, the Puritan was not called upon to answer them till October. We have already dealt with the various charges contained in the articles as occasion arose during the progress of our study, but at this point we may briefly summarise their contents. In the first five Cartwright is charged with having renounced his episcopal ordination and with having been ordained at Antwerp or Middelburg or elsewhere by imposition of hands. It is implied that he received Presbyterian ordination. Further, he had been instrumental in establishing a Presbyterian Church among the English merchants at Antwerp and Middelburg. Certain English subjects, *e.g.* Travers, had been ordained to the ministry there and others already ordained ministers of the Church of England, *e.g.* Fenner, "were so called." Cartwright had been chief in this Church, where ecclesiastical discipline had been exercised and the Presbyterian forms of worship observed. The next seventeen articles are concerned with his ministry in Warwick. He had promised before his settlement there that, if granted a licence to preach, he would

[1] *D.P.* p. 94.

[2] bk IX, sect. vii, § 27.

respect the laws and usages of the Church as established. Such a licence had not been granted, but nevertheless he had preached at Warwick and in the neighbourhood. Frequently in public and private he had criticised the Church and persuaded his hearers to practise nonconformity. He had condemned Bishops, the Book of Common Prayer, etc. A specific instance is given of his utterance against Bishops, when he preached at Banbury "about a year since." The charges connected with Cartwright's doings in or near Warwick are considered above[1]. The 23rd and 24th articles charge him with having knowledge of the authors, printers, and dispersers of the Marprelate Tracts and Udall's books, before the authorities knew, with having withheld the desirable information, and with having commended the said books. It is likely that Cartwright knew who composed the *Demonstration* and *Diotrephes*, but unlikely that he ever knew who Martin was. There is no doubt at all that he thought highly of writings such as Udall's, for they were in harmony with the arguments and assertions contained in his own productions. He frankly acknowledges to Burghley[2] that he regards some of the so-called libels as "dutifully and learnedlie written," but he is careful to quality his appreciation with the words "Martin set apart." The last seven articles are concerned with Cartwright's complicity in the Conference movement of the 'eighties. He is charged with having penned, or having procured to be penned, all, or some part, of the Book of Discipline. The Commissioners were not sure who the author of it was, if there was indeed a sole author. Cartwright, however, is said to have had to do with the little book, and the securing of subscription to it. The establishment of the Presbyterian scheme expounded in it has been the goal of the Puritans who have met in Conferences and Synods, chiefly in the Midland and South Eastern counties[3]. Cartwright is stated to have taken an active part, since his

[1] pp. 300–1.

[2] 4 Nov. 1590; *v.* App. XXIII.

[3] The shires and towns are: Warwick, Northampton, Rutland, Leicester, Norfolk, Suffolk, Essex, Cambridge and Oxford, and the times: "At London, at terms and parliament times; in Oxford at the Act; in Cambridge at the times of Commencement and Stourbridge Fair."

return from the Continent, in these meetings, further particulars of which are set forth. Gladly would the High Commission have received accurate information regarding these assemblies, but Cartwright, loyal to his comrades' desire that he should reveal nothing discussed in them[1], was unwilling to throw any light upon them. As we have noticed many of the above charges contain inaccuracies and misrepresentations. If Cartwright had been allowed to reply to some of them, as he was willing to do, several of these would have been corrected. But he refused the oath and the Commissioners obtained no illumination at all from him.

The imprisonment of Cartwright was in itself a staggering blow to the Presbyterian cause. It was thought that the event might stir up his followers to make a demonstration in his favour. Bancroft entitles one of his chapters[2]: "Upon Cartwrights committing to prison, some strange attempts were looked (for)" and quotes a letter from Giles Wigginton to Porter (6 Nov. 1590), which shows the consternation and apprehension of violence that now moved the Puritans[3]: "Master Cartwright is in the Fleete for refusall of the oath (as I heare) and Master Knewstubs is sent for, and sundry worthy Ministers are disquieted, who have beene spared long. So that we look for some bickering ere long, and then a battell, which cannot long endure."

The only notable effort in the way of a demonstration was undertaken by three infatuated extremists, Copinger, Arthington and Hacket. Their object was to overthrow the existing Church government, bring to repentance and judgment the Queen and her counsellors, deliver the zealous preachers who were then imprisoned, Cartwright among them, etc. Their conspiracy reached a height on the 16th of July, 1591, when in Cheapside they proclaimed Hacket Messiah redivivus and the advent of his reign of judgment. The trio were arrested. Hacket was executed in Cheapside on the 28th of July; Copinger died in prison the next day; Arthington was ultimately liberated and published in 1592 a penitent retraction. Cosin, Sutcliffe and Bancroft made much of the

[1] *Harl. MSS.* 6849, f. 254. [2] *D.P.* p. 141. [3] *ibid.* p. 143.

conspiracy. Bancroft at great length seeks to prove that the Puritan leaders aided and abetted or at least connived at the proceedings of the fanatics[1]. The section of *Dangerous Positions*, which deals with the affair, is entitled "English Scottizing for Discipline by force," for Bancroft's aim was to prove that the English Presbyterians were inspired by the example of the Scottish reformers, and would have applauded and approved of any violence committed by Hacket, etc., just as their brethren in the North had exulted over the murder of Cardinal Beaton. The facts, however, do not bear out Bancroft's contentions. The three victims of a kind of delusional insanity never secured a following. They were avowed supporters of the Holy Discipline, and admirers of its exponents and of Cartwright in particular, but the one leading Puritan, who seems to have had any great sympathy with them and their crazy scheme, was Wigginton, then a prisoner in the Counter. It is certain that Cartwright was innocent of the slightest complicity in the affair. This is made clear in his *Apologie* (1596) and in Throkmorton's *Defence* (1594).

That there were points of contact between Cartwright and the conspiracy is apparent after a brief examination of it. Copinger became possessed of the notion that he had received an extraordinary calling. One of his earliest revelations took place on a Saturday night at the end of December, 1590, when he and Arthington were holding a fast in Shoe Lane, at the house of a schoolmaster named Thomas Lancaster. Impressed with the importance of his divine mission he proceeded to enlist the sympathy and interest of English and Scottish Puritans, *e.g.* Wentworth, Wigginton, Charke, Travers, Egerton, Cartwright, Gibson (minister of Pencaitland, Scotland), etc. Bancroft quotes extracts from many of Copinger's letters, some of which, dated February, 1590–1, are definitely addressed to Cartwright, and seeks to make out that Cartwright and Copinger were for a time in correspondence. Cartwright, on the other hand, carefully explains his connection with the visionary in his *Apologie*[2]. Some three

[1] *D.P.* pp. 143 ff. [2] sig. B 2 ff.

or four years before the lewd practices began, business connected with the Warwick Hospital brought him to the house of the Earl of Warwick's agent, Ambrose Copinger, where he met the afterwards notorious Edmund. Cartwright avers, however, that he never in any degree countenanced the advances of the latter after the conspiracy commenced to brew. A certain Ralph Hockenhull[1] visited Cartwright in the Fleet on several occasions. During one visit he propounded some questions dealing with extraordinary calling, in behalf of an acquaintance, who turned out to be Edmund Copinger. Cartwright advised Hockenhull to dissuade Copinger from his "frantike opinions," which Hockenhull tried to do. Copinger, using Hockenhull as an intermediary, sought to arrange an interview with Cartwright in the Fleet, but Cartwright, "knowing the broken witte of the man," firmly refused to see him and even declined to read a letter brought from the fanatic. In short, Cartwright denies that he ever conferred, as Bancroft and Sutcliffe alleged, with Copinger, whom, as a matter of fact, he had taken pains to expose, *e.g.* to the Countess of Warwick. At the beginning of March William Hacket came upon the scene. About Easter he visited his old friend Wigginton, by whom he was introduced to Copinger. Arthington met Hacket at Mrs Lawson's house. Job Throkmorton, being then in London, conferred with the three visionaries, but not as an accomplice. Hacket returned to his home in Oundle, but on the 17th of May Copinger begged him to come back to London. "In the same letter hee sendeth Hacket this newes: The zealous Preachers are to be in the Star-chamber tomorrow....My selfe, if I can get in, am moved to be there: and I feare, if sentence with severity shall be given, I shall be forced in the name of the great and fearefull God of heaven and earth, to protest against it."[2] On the 4th of June Hacket arrived in the city and a few days after sought an interview with Cartwright in prison, "but missing of his purpose, hee left his message with the porter, viz., that Master Cartwright should deale

[1] Probably of Chalfont St Peter, Bucks; *v. Black Book*, p. 361.
[2] *D.P.* p. 156.

faithfully in the Lords businesse, etc."[1] Cartwright states in his *Apologie* that he never met Hacket in all his life, and that he never saw Arthington until the latter was released from prison. In the same writing Cartwright points out that the question of his complicity was thrashed out by the High Commissioners and that they could find nothing involving him. Throkmorton in his *Defence*, while meeting Sutcliffe's charge that he, along with Cartwright, Egerton, Udall, Wigginton and others, was in league with the conspirators, incidentally clears his great friend of complicity[2]. He met Copinger for the first time in London on a Sabbath in Hilary term in the "snowie and frostie season" and contracted an ague as the result of Copinger's long and fervent praying with him. "Not long after this," writes Throkmorton[3], "when I had something recovered my selfe, I went to visite Maister Cart. in the Fleete, unto whom I signified what had passed betwixt Maister Copinger and me, and of the newe acquaintance that he would needes fasten and enforce upon me. But he bade me in any wise beware and take heed of him, for he feared him greatlie that certeinlie all was not well with him, and that he had *laesum principium* (*margin*—That is, some crazing of the brain) at the least, telling me howe faine he would have propounded and fastened some of his fooleries and phantasticall revelations upon him. But (sayeth he) I have returned him such an answere, as I beleeve he will not greatlie like of, neither seeke to me in haste againe for resolution." Copinger visited Throkmorton, showed him copies of letters to Cartwright, Udall, etc., told him of his revelations and complained that Cartwright, Egerton and others did not believe in them. Under the influence of Cartwright's advice Throkmorton now called Copinger's visions "illusions of the devil" and refrained from giving the dreamer and his associates any sympathy or support. It is obvious that the authorities should not have treated the offenders as political conspirators so much as fit subjects for the alienist. The plot was, at best, a side-issue of Puritanism, but it was

[1] *D.P.* p. 160. [2] *v.* Sutcliffe, *Ans. to a Pet.* pp. 63, 71, 140, 197, 202.
[3] sig. A iii.

planned by lunatics and brought Cartwright and others under a temporary cloud, whose shadow they neither needed nor deserved[1].

There are extant certain important letters belonging to March, 1590–1, which show that Bancroft and Cartwright carried on at this time an interesting discussion concerning the existence of Presbyterianism in the early Church. "Mr Penry," writes Bancroft to Cartwright from Ely House[2], "writing against a sermon of myne, which was after printed, doth take upon hym to justify your opinion of Constantynes tyme upon your citying of Eusebius etc.[3] Now you knowe that thinking in my conscience you are bothe deceaved, I am bound to cleare that point, which I preached" and he presses Cartwright to prove that the Presbyterian system has the alleged support of antiquity, or to confess that he was mistaken when he asserted in one of his Replies to Whitgift that the eldership was most flourishing in Constantine's time and that the elders mentioned by Eusebius as attending the Council of Nice were not ministers but ruling elders. Bancroft is glad "of my smale acquayntance with you...but especially in respect of the conference had with you already." He is sincerely anxious that "that pointe of my sermon may be maynteyned, which note I sayd is challenged & empeached." He would have come to the Fleet to discuss the matter personally but he has a cold "which might increase by going abroad." On the 18th of March Cartwright replies[4]. "The time," he says, "is verie inconvenient and unholesome for study, and the place much more: where the cause being weightie, requireth great and earnest study. Further I want my *Adversaria* & Ἀπομνημόνευματα, which would be needfull

[1] Soames (p. 398) and Paget (p. 322) give good accounts of the plot. See also *Kenyon MSS.* (*Hist. MSS. Comm. Report*, XIV, App. Pt IV) for memorandum of Hacket's arraignment. This memo. tells of "a solemne meetinge in a woode, where great consultation was had concerninge the deliverye of ther restrained bretheren." *v. Acts P.C.* XXI, pp. 297, 299, 300, 325.

[2] *Add. MSS.* 32092, ff. 123–4.

[3] Bancroft's reference is to Penry's *Briefe Discovery* (1590); *v.* Pierce, *John Penry*, p. 268.

[4] *Add. MSS.* 32092, f. 125.

for me to have in such a case." Besides, his health is greatly impaired. He therefore desires Bancroft to forbear until he is at home again. Meanwhile he does not doubt that he has clearly shown in his Replies that there were elders, who were not ministers, in Augustine's time. He is willing to confess error if it is pointed out. It is, however, a mistake to think that he holds "a Bishop and a minister of the word all one in the times of the Nicene Councell." That is his opinion regarding Apostolic times, but he is aware of the distinction that was developed long before the said Council. But he will not enter into the niceties of the question at issue. Realising that the Fleet was not the best place for the pursuit of historical research, we can understand the handicap under which Cartwright laboured and his reluctance to carry on the discussion. The correspondence, however, is of the greatest interest. It shows that the Bancroftian school, now rising into prominence, was determined to prove with meticulous accuracy that the Church of England was an institution whose Catholic foundations were firmly based on the warrants of antiquity, and whose continuity with the early Church was not broken by any residuum or outcrop of Presbyterianism in the days of Augustine.

At the moment Cartwright was preoccupied with the question of his own release. He applied to the Ecclesiastical Commissioners through one of their members for his discharge on bail. He also wrote in similar terms to the Lord Chief Justices. He was specially anxious to return home as one of his five children had recently died. If, however, he should not be allowed to do so, he begged that he might be placed in honourable detention in the house of a friend in or near London. Those to whom he wrote replied that they were willing to comply with his request provided that the consent of certain members of the Privy Council were first obtained. Now he writes (5 March, 1590–1) to Burghley acquainting him with the result of his petitions[1]. He entreats Burghley to further his humble suit and asks whether he should send a supplication to the whole board of the Council.

[1] App. XXIV.

Besides craving his Lordship's advice and support Cartwright informs him that he has already lain four and a half months in prison and that he sees no prospect of a decision before the next term. Further, his health is greatly impaired by the long confinement. Cartwright complains, in particular, of gout and stone "besides age a disease of yt self."

Cartwright could not suffer restraint without complaining. His life is marked by a series of petitions, which at first sight create an unfavourable impression upon the student. One of his constant pleas is that his health is breaking down. This was his plaint when he sought permission to return from exile. It is repeated when he is imprisoned in the Fleet. There is, however, no reason to suspect him of malingering or exaggeration. The prisons of his time were by no means wholesome abodes. He was now, as he frequently pointed out, an old man, and although he was only about fifty years old, we have to bear in mind that in the time of Elizabeth the average length of life was considerably shorter than it is to-day. Besides, his diligent studies, the rigours of exile, and the atmosphere of controversy, worry and animosity, in which he spent the last twenty years, were sufficiently trying to undermine a more robust man. In his petition to the Council, which he evidently sent after the last mentioned letter to Burghley, he sought to enlist interest in his appeal for liberty by enlarging upon his bodily ailments, and was subsequently reprimanded by Bishop Aylmer for abusing the Council "by infourming them of diseases wherewith he was not trobled."[1] That he was not merely a querulous valetudinarian, who cunningly tried to play upon the feelings of those in authority by abject reference to imaginary physical disabilities, is made apparent by the self-defence made by Cartwright in his letter (13 Aug. 1591) to Lady Russell[2].

At a meeting of the Commissioners in May, 1591[3], it was stated that Cartwright "with others in a Supplication had abused her maiestie in suggesting that th'othe which was tendred was not according to law." Cartwright apparently refers to the same joint petition in his letter to

[1] *v.* App. XXV. [2] *v.* App. XXIX. [3] *v.* App. XXV.

Lord Gray[1], when he says that his doctrine of excommunication is not disloyal, but "the same which the universall church of god and particulerly this our own church of England boeth now houldeth and alwaies heretofore: as in our moest humble supplication praesented to her Majestie in all our behalves is more fully declared." The only supplication known to us to which these references seem to apply is contained in the *Lansdowne MSS.*[2] This document is not dated by the suppliants, but it is endorsed "Ap. 1592." If, as appears likely, it is the supplication referred to, the endorsement is a year too late. It represents the oath as the chief cause of the prisoners' trouble. They refuse the oath because it is not sanctioned by Scripture, is without limitation, requires an answer concerning private speeches to friends, and the furnishing of matter of accusation and evidence against themselves, and disregards the law that demands proper presentation of charges with witnesses. The petitioners deny that they are schismatics or rebels. They believe that the Church of England is a true visible Church in need of further reformation. They have all been ministers of the Church and desire to continue their ministry. They deem it unlawful to seek reform by rebellious or other violent means and protest that they have always used constitutional means for the furtherance of their cause. They have never impeached the Queen's supremacy and have never refused the oath regarding the same. On the question of excommunication they hold by the teaching and practice of the Reformed Churches and the doctrine laid down in the Articles of Religion and the Book of Homilies. They regard excommunication as deprivation only of spiritual comforts and detest the Pope's assumption of power to depose sovereigns and discharge subjects from their allegiance. They declare that they have met in Conferences because they thought it lawful to do so. Their objects were mutual edification, the erection of a bulwark against Romanists and schismatics, and the preparation of a uniform programme of further

[1] 15 Jan. 1591–2; *v.* App. XXXI.
[2] LXXII, No. 49, ff. 137–8; printed in St. *Ann.* VII, App. LX.

reformation. They deny that they ever exercised jurisdiction in their meetings, *e.g.* in appointing ministers, administering censures or ordaining constitutions. Further, their meetings were attended only by ministers, generally six or seven in a Conference, except in a few instances where two or three schoolmasters desirous of training for the ministry joined them. They repudiate the charge of singularity inasmuch as their desire was to establish the discipline of the primitive Church, which the Book of Common Prayer itself calls a godly discipline. All the reforms urged by them were in accordance with Scripture. Accordingly their suit is that the Queen may favour them and grant them their liberty.

Objection was taken by Aylmer to Cartwright's appeal to the Council and the joint petition of the Puritan prisoners to the Queen. Both, urged the Bishop, contained flagrant misrepresentations. This he pointed out at a meeting of six members of the High Commission, who assembled in private one Saturday afternoon in May (1st or 8th?) to examine Cartwright alone. The document, which furnishes a detailed and graphic account of the examination[1], shows that the question of the oath was now the main point of debate between the Commission and the Puritans. The stubborn refusal of the latter to take the oath was bringing the proceedings of the Commissioners to a complete standstill. Accordingly at this private session a determined attempt was made to break the Puritan opposition by persuading the leader of it, Cartwright, to take the oath and thus enable the Commissioners to institute their legal process. Without his compliance he could not be legally tried or convicted. The examination represents a critical juncture in the trial of Puritanism and, accordingly, we give the contemporary report of it in full[2].

The appearance of Cartwright before the High Commission reveals the inefficiency of that Court. Its inability to enforce the oath *ex officio* was the crux of the whole situation. Eminent Puritan lawyers (*e.g.* Morrice) denied the legality of the oath and Cartwright accepted their verdict, but it should be observed that when the Attorney General declared the oath

[1] *Lansd. MSS.* LXVIII, No. 50. [2] App. XXV.

legal he remarked upon the division of opinion on the question and "layd the cheif strenght of his refusall upon the law of god." Cartwright was of opinion that the oath had not always been employed by the High Commission and Bancroft, much to the annoyance of Aylmer, agreed with him. During Whitgift's primacy, however, it came to be insisted on as a necessary preliminary of a trial. Cartwright condemned the procedure as an infringement of the liberty of the subject. To swear on oath to answer certain articles, particulars of which were not known, and that without counsel, "without anie to accuse, without all limitacion, and without reasonable time of deliberacion and advise what to answer," constituted an injustice to an accused person and made him liable to compromise others. It was not a question of refusal to answer, but of refusing to answer in a certain objectionable fashion. Cartwright himself had willingly taken an oath on particular occasions when the matters concerned were definitely prescribed. Cartwright's view of the arbitrary and inquisitorial processes of the High Commission has been fully justified by the events of history[1]. His courageous and triumphant stand in behalf of his conscientious convictions and the beneficial results that flowed from it, furnish an instance of the influence of Puritanism on civil as well as religious freedom.

Bancroft's insinuation[2] that the Presbyterians were impelled by revolutionary motives and the doctrines of disobedience promulgated by Christopher Goodman was part of his favourite hypothesis, which he termed "Genevating" and "Scottizing" for discipline. But his reading of Genevan and Scottish history was not impartial and he misconstrued the mainspring of the Puritan "drift." Lewin's representation[3] of the oath as derived from the authority of the sovereign and his attempt to make the repudiation of it equivalent to disobedience to the Queen may be regarded as a quibble. At any rate Cartwright and his fellow Puritans cherished no disloyal sentiments and resented the imputation of any "lewd" intentions.

[1] *v.* R. G. Usher, *Rise and Fall of the High Commission* (1913).
[2] *v.* App. xxv. [3] *v. ibid.*

The immediate results of Cartwright's refusal to take the oath were important. The High Commission refused to hear his answers. The trial was blocked and the legal process could not be commenced. The court could have decided to fine him or imprison him for the rest of his life, but they could not convict him. In later years in order that such an *impasse* might not hinder the activities of the High Commission it was legally affirmed that refusal to take the oath was a sign of guilt and the recusant declared *pro confesso*[1]; but in 1591 the Ecclesiastical Commissioners sought a way out of their difficulties by handing Cartwright and the other Puritans over to the Court of the Star Chamber for trial. For this Court they furnished evidence, but, as we shall see, the Puritans again emerged triumphant[2].

Before dealing with the trial in the Star Chamber we may touch upon an incident of interest that occurred in May. Brook[3] says that Christopher Hatton wrote to Burghley recommending that Whitgift should appoint the Dean of St Paul's and Dr Andrews to confer with Cartwright and his fellow-prisoners "but whether this measure was adopted, or what was the result, we have not found on record." This is a misreading of the manuscript from which Brook ostensibly quotes. Hatton was not at all desirous of appointing a special conference with Cartwright; indeed, his resolute refusal to take the oath made it futile to attempt any such measure. His fate now lay in the lap of the Star Chamber. But the day of reckoning for Udall (late minister at Kingston), Newman and Hodgkin (the distributor and printer of the Marprelate Tracts) was drawing near, and it was for the purpose of persuading these men to an acknowledgment of their guilt that Hatton was anxious to have the said conference. He therefore wrote on the 17th of May, 1591, to Burghley as follows[4]: "My verie good Lorde, I sent back to your Lo. yeasterday to putt you in mind of a Lr̃e to be written

[1] Usher, *op. cit.* p. 248.

[2] For excellent discussions of the High Commission and the oath, *v.* Usher, *op. cit.*; St. *Whit.* II, p. 28; Soames, pp. 402 ff.; Frere, *Hist.* pp. 279 ff.

[3] *Mem.* p. 353.

[4] *Lansd. MSS.* LXVIII, No. 5.

to my L. of Canterbury. This morning such a Lr̄e came to my handes, but it was not to that purpose which (to my remembrance) we agreed uppon yeasterday in Counsayle. ffor this is, that my L. Grace should appoint the Deane of Paules and Doctor Andrewes to conferre with Cartewright and the rest in the ffleet who are informed against in the Starre chamber; but that which I meant, was for Udall, Newman, Hodgeskis, and those who are condemned of ffelony: bycawse the tyme of their execution, as it standeth now appointed draweth neare, therefore I thought it best that some expedition were used in conference with them; but for the other, there may well be more leysure and advisement taken. Wherefore prayeng your Lo. to geve direction for the speedie drawing of this Lr̄e for Udall and the rest, to the purpose that Mr Deane of Poules, and Doctor Andrewes may conferre with them, and that yf they can by good perswasions draw them to an acknowledgement of their fault, to be sett downe in such a submission, as my L. Anderson shall thinke fitt then the Q. Maties mercie to be extended towardes them: otherwise that they may repaire, by the execution of iustice on them, that harme which they have done in sowing sedition."[1]

The trial in the Star Chamber had now begun[2]. The Bill of Information against the Puritan prisoners was exhibited in May, Bancroft furnishing much of the material for the charges preferred. An exhaustive study of the trial would require a volume for itself. We can therefore only undertake an examination of a selection of the documents that bear upon the proceedings, and particularly those pertaining to Cartwright. On the 2nd of June, 1591, in a letter to Burghley[3] Cartwright protests against the measures now taken, beseeches him to appease the Queen, and procure relief from the hard course with which the Puritans are threatened. In order to give his Lordship a brief and adequate account of the charges and answers he encloses an abstract of the

[1] *v.* letter to Whitgift *sub* 16 May, 1591; *Acts P.C.* XXI, p. 130.

[2] *v.* Knollys' report of the appearance of the Puritans in the Star Chamber on 13 May; *Lansd. MSS.* LXVIII, No. 84.

[3] App. XXVIII.

accusations contained in the Bill and of the prisoners' replies in parallel columns[1].

Some of the original documents connected with the trial are still in the Public Record Office. One bundle[2] contains a parchment membrane with 33 interrogatories to be administered in behalf of the Queen to certain witnesses, and the depositions of the latter. These depositions were taken on dates ranging from the 28th of July to the 30th of October, 1591, and occupy 136 pages. The witnesses are Thomas Stone (Warkton, co. Northampton), Henry Alvey (St John's, Cambridge), William Perkins (Christ's College, Cambridge), Thomas Barber (St Botolph's, Bishopgate), Edmund Littleton (Deane, co. Bedford), Anthony Nutter (Fenny Drayton, co. Leicester), Hercules Cleveley (Wroxall, co. Warwick), Thomas Edmundes (All Saints, Bread St), and John Johnson (late preacher of Northampton). In bundle 49, No. 34, there is a parchment with 18 interrogatories to be administered to some of the above witnesses in behalf of the defendants. The depositions of these—Nutter, Cleveley, Barber, Stone—were taken between the 28th of September and the 13th of October. But the most important for our purpose is bundle A 56, No. 1, which contains a long parchment membrane with 43 interrogatories and 142 folio pages of depositions taken in June. The deponents are Cartwright, prisoner in the Fleet; Daniel Wight (late preacher of Stretton, co. Warwick), Humphrey Fen (late preacher of Coventry), Andrew King (late preacher of Coleworth, co. Northampton), John Payne (late preacher of Hanbury, co. Stafford), all four in the Clink; Edmund Snape (late preacher of Northampton), William Proudlove (late preacher of Weedon, co. Northampton), Melanchton Jewell (late preacher of Thornebury, co. Devon), all three prisoners in "the Bailiffs house of St Catherines"; Edward Lord (late preacher of Wolston, co. Warwick), prisoner in the White Lion, Southwark. All the above depositions are attested by the signatures of the defendants.

Cartwright was examined in the Star Chamber on the 12th

[1] St. *Whit.* III, pp. 242 ff.

[2] *Star Chamber Proceedings*, 33 Eliz. 39, No. 23.

of June, 1591. His answers to forty-three interrogatories are singularly meagre[1]. They are deliberately noncommittal. To most of the questions he refuses to answer at all, as in his opinion they are impertinent to any matter of offence wherewith he is charged. To others he gives a flat denial. In answer to the first interrogatory he denies that he has taught that there ought to be Ephori or other officers in the State, who have power to depose the sovereign. He says that he has not advocated the establishment of the discipline without permission of the civil magistrate. He admits that he has seen the Book of Discipline, but refuses to tell who composed it and points out that the first offence with which he is charged is alleged to have been committed after the said book was set down. He acknowledges that he and others have met since the 30th of September, 1586, to discuss the said book but considers himself not bound to say where and when. He confesses that since the said date he has subscribed to the articles approving of the Book of Discipline, but remarks upon the conditional nature of these articles. He says that he has put in practice only the two points mentioned in the articles: "However, the rather to testify their freedom in the use of the said two points, he saith they varied from the orders contained in the chapters thereof, and that in those things which they might very conveniently have performed. He hath no otherwise performed the order of meeting than as the affair did permit. It is known that it was set down in the said book of discipline that none should give voices in their assemblies but such as had first subscribed to the said discipline, which he saith was set down as a matter of their judgment only, and that the publishing thereof was to be referred to the authority of her Majesty and the parliament, for confirmation whereof he saith that the greater number of those that gave voices in the said meetings did to his knowledge never subscribe to the said discipline. And also saith that there have never been any appeal or appeals made...from any less assembly to a greater." He denies that the censures prescribed in the Book of Discipline have been administered,

[1] *Star Chamber Proceedings*, 33 Eliz. A 56, No. 1.

that any ministers have been ordained in accordance with it, or that any eldership or "presbytery" has been erected. Throughout his deposition Cartwright thus maintains that the Book was not put in operation. It merely contained the scheme that he and his fellows wished to see realised. When asked whether he used the order and form described in the chapter *De ratione liturgie* he answers, "there is not any form of prayer prescribed or put down, but only certain heads, or matter whereof to form prayer, which be not, to his knowledge, repugnant to the laws of the land or the prayers comprised in the Book of Common Prayer....He hath immediately before his sermons at several times used a prayer wherein was mentioned the confession of sins and a petition of a fruitful reciting and delivering of the Word, and after his sermons hath always used a general prayer for all estates of the land, and particularly for the Queen's most excellent Majesty and for her most honourable Privy Council and generally for all the ministry of the land." Cartwright denies that since his first ordination by the Archbishop of the land he has ever been reordained. Although questioned at great length regarding the Conferences alleged to have been held at Cambridge (1587) and Warwick (1588) he refuses to shed any light on these assemblies. When re-examined in the Star Chamber on the 19th of June, Cartwright maintained the noncommittal policy that marked his appearance on the previous Saturday and gave his examiners no illumination or satisfaction.

Cartwright was taken to task for his reply to the first interrogatory by Sutcliffe, who asked[1] "whether M. Cartwright swore truely in the Starre-chamber, when he affirmed on his oth, that he never affirmed or allowed that in every monarchy there ought to be certain magistrates like to the Spartaine Ephori, with authoritie to controll and depose the king, and to proceed further against him, seeing he called M. Fenners booke wherein these points are expresly set downe, the principles and grounds of heavenly Canaan." In his *Apologie*, 1596[2], Cartwright answered Sutcliffe's criticism, in

[1] *Ans. to a Pet.* Qu. 57; *Exam.* sig. C 4 *verso*. [2] sig. C.

our opinion satisfactorily, thus: "I take it Mr Fenner giveth no such authoritie, but only where the lawes of the lande doo establish such an authoritie as the Ephori in Lacedaemonia had. And if Mr Fenner did, yet how doth my Epistle commendatorie set before his booke make me of his iudgement, as if he that commendeth a book iustifieth what soever is in the booke, or as if, notwithstanding Mr Fenners singular learning (which for his age many, I doubt not, both at home and abroade doo esteeme) I might not or doo not differ from him in some things conteined in his booke: besides he [*Sutcliffe*] him selfe confessing, that by oth in the starre Chamber I have disavowed th' alowance of any such opinion which he fathereth of Mr Fenner, let it be considered with what minde he so often rubbeth uppon this point. And both for this and the former charge [*regarding Cartwright's refusal to answer concerning the royal supremacy*] I leave it to bee considered with what Christian modestie Mr Sutcliffe may now the second and the third time (and that in print) moove question of those thinges to our discredite, which her Maiesties most honorable Counsell was pleased should be no further proceeded in, and that he is not contented with that imprisonment we endured, which their Honors are satisfied with. Lastly, my iudgement in sundry matters of the Discipline excepted, where in differing from sundry learned men of our Church I have the consent of many worthie Churches and godly learned both of this and other ages, I would bee ashamed for that singular mercy God hath shewed me by her Maiesties most gratious gouvernment to come behinde Mr Sutcliffe in anie duetie that my poore hand is able to reach unto."

The suspicion that Cartwright did not give a definite answer to the interrogatory concerning the royal supremacy because he refused to recognise the same is unwarranted. Cartwright was silent on the point because the interrogatory went beyond the charge exhibited against him in the Information. He merely stood upon his legal rights. His silence did not mean, as Sutcliffe says[1], that he was unable to clear

[1] *Exam.* sig. D 2.

himself of the matters objected. Afterwards at the command of the Privy Council he definitely answered the question to their satisfaction in writing. His own words[1] are sufficient to explain his silence and to prove his unqualified loyalty to Elizabeth: "I refused it as esteeming it impertinent unto that cause, not otherwise, unto which afterward, upon commandement I gave answere in writing unto her Maiesties most honorable Counsell. And to her Maiesties supremacie I have bene sworne (at the least) five or sixe times, and if there be doubt of any change of my judgement, I am ready to take th'oth againe."[2]

If the answers of Cartwright were disappointing to his examiners they are equally so to the historical student. The excess of care used by him to safeguard himself and his associates makes his utterances in the Star Chamber but shallow sources of information. When supplemented, however, by the depositions of the others who were examined they throw some light upon the Presbyterian movement, which had recently come to an end. The Puritan prisoners, except Jewell and Payne, acknowledged that they met in Conferences. They explained their motives. They assembled as students and as ministers for mutual edification. They thought that in face of the Jesuit invasion and the increase of schismatics there was need of such meetings. The controversies and dangers of the Church required consideration in them. The chief object was to discuss and prepare for the establishment of a National Presbyterian Church. Those who thus met were, with two or three exceptions, exclusively ministers. The membership of the most frequent meetings (*classes*) did not, as a rule, exceed seven and that of the largest (*conventus*) twelve. The meetings were held chiefly in the Midland and South Eastern counties and at times, *e.g.* at the time of Stourbridge Fair, when a large concourse of people would help to preserve the secrecy of the Puritan activity. No provincial Synod was ever attended by delegates from all

[1] *Apologie*, sig. C.

[2] For the form and substance of the oath of supremacy taken by Cartwright at the University, *v.* Cooper, *Ann.* II, p. 148.

the shires in the province represented, and the province of York had never had even the semblance of a provincial assembly. In these meetings the Presbyterians discussed the Book of Discipline and some of them subscribed it. Cartwright, Lord, Fen, Wight and King confessed that they had done so. Cartwright pointed out that most of the ministers who attended the Conferences did not subscribe at all. Thus Neal's computation that there were 500 subscribers is a gross exaggeration. The reasons for subscription are given. The Puritans were charged with being at variance with one another as to the reformation they desired, and as Presbyterians they sought to manifest their unanimity. This they did in a manner that was customary among lawyers, physicians, etc., by subscribing their judgment. Besides, the Discipline to which they appended their signatures was worthy of allegiance, being agreeable to Scripture, the judgment of learned divines past and present, and the practice of many churches ancient and modern. As Soames says[1], the demand for subscription was reasonable, inasmuch as "no society can exist without terms of conformity." If carried out it would have made the Puritan party a league of Covenanters. Care was taken to show the actual nature of the articles of subscription. Those of a declaratory character were meant to express judgment on the scheme of ecclesiastical government presented in the Book of Discipline, *i.e.*, the subscribers indicated that they approved of Presbyterianism, but as the deponents emphatically asserted, they intended to seek the establishment of their favourite form of church polity by constitutional means. They were not revolutionaries, but had decided to tarry for the magistrate. The articles in which the subscribers promise to put certain portions of the Book of Discipline into practice pertained to a course of action legally permissible, and were conditional, *i.e.*, to be carried out only so far as the laws of the land and the peace of the Church allowed. As a matter of fact, however, the promises had not been fulfilled, *e.g.* the system of meetings prescribed in the Book of Discipline had never been put into effect. The opponents of the Puritans

[1] p. 384 n.

were of opinion that the Presbyterians had adopted and put into practice a service book, in place of the Book of Common Prayer, and that the use of this nonconformist Prayer Book was enjoined by the Book of Discipline in the chapters *De ratione liturgie* and *De reliquis liturgie officiis*. Undoubtedly, it was the desire and aim of the accused to use a modified Genevan liturgy. They had presented such a book to Parliament, but that they used it is not substantiated by facts. Cartwright showed that the Book of Discipline did not prescribe a form of divine service but merely furnished a compendious directory. Although he and maybe others slightly modified their conduct of public worship in a Genevan direction it is stated that none of them administered the Sacraments in an unauthorised manner. Although the Book of Discipline prescribed that none should be admitted to Communion or to the Puritan meetings unless they first subscribed the Book it was made clear that the prescription was only a matter of judgment and had never been realised. If some of the Puritans had in corners dared to exercise jurisdiction over their followers, those in the Star Chamber cordially denied that they had ever done so, *e.g.* that they had administered the censures of the Discipline Book, elected and ordained ministers, or erected a Presbytery according to its regulations. In short, the Presbyterian movement of the 'eighties appears as an unfinished fabric; its focal point was the Book of Discipline, on some parts of which the Puritans were never agreed; its chief agencies were the Conferences, which were ministerial gatherings and never came into vital contact with the people; its most important assembly was that which met in London, and generally had as its moderator Cartwright, Travers or Egerton; and its most prominent leader was Thomas Cartwright, whose main life-work was the pursuit of an apparently lost cause[1].

There were many who sympathised with Cartwright and his brethren as they continued to suffer the rigours of the

[1] *v. Harl. MSS.* 7042, ff. 1–118; *Add. MSS.* 32092, ff. 126 ff.; *Lansd. MSS.* LXVIII, Nos. 43, 44, 53, 60, 62; *S.P. Dom. Eliz.* 238, No. 102; St. *Whit.* III, pp. 242 ff.; Fuller, *C.H.* bk IX, sect. vii.

Star Chamber and of prison. Among their well-wishers none were more sincere than the ministers of the Church of Scotland. Heylyn suggests that the English Presbyterians "held intelligence with their Brethren in the Kirk of Scotland by means of Penry here and of Gibson there,"[1] and quotes the extract given by Bancroft[2] from a letter written by Gibson to Copinger, which tells of the sympathy of the Scottish Churchmen with the afflicted Puritans of the south. James Gibson, minister of Pencaitland, an ardent opponent of Episcopacy, was an extremist, who for his outspoken opinion of the King as a persecutor of the Church of Scotland, incurred the odium of James and was frequently dealt with by the Scottish Privy Council and General Assembly[3]. He had been in England and held strong views on the tyranny of the Bishops[4]. But he was not the only or the most important intermediary between the two sets of reformers. Melville and others had gone south when Scottish Presbyterianism was in abeyance, found refuge among the Puritans and become intimately acquainted with their leaders. English nonconformists likewise were befriended in Scotland when they fled from their episcopal enemies. Sectarians like Browne, however, did not receive a warm welcome among the northern Presbyterians. The latter cherished the same antipathy to Brownism as the English Puritans did. During his Scottish tour Browne was placed in ward for a night or two before his doctrines were tried. His teaching was found wanting and he was looked upon by the Scottish ministers as a schismatic and malcontent[5]. John Udall, a true Presbyterian, was treated differently. During his abode in Newcastle, where through the influence of the Earl of Huntingdon he had received an appointment, he came to Edinburgh and enjoyed the high honour of preaching before King James while the General Assembly was in session[6]. Penry and Waldegrave, accomplices in the Marprelate affair, were also given a harbourage in

[1] *A.R.* lib. IX, § 18. [2] *D.P.* p. 6. [3] Calderwood, IV, V.
[4] *ibid.* IV, p. 484. Is it Gibson's initials that appear on the last page of *M. Some laid open in his coulers*? *v.* Pierce, *Hist. Introd.* p. 234.
[5] Calderwood, V, p. 6. [6] 20 June, 1589; *ibid.* V, p. 58.

Scotland. Personal intercourse with Puritan refugees would keep the Scottish ministers in touch with the movement in England and the knowledge of the sufferings of their English brethren would readily elicit the warm sympathy of men who had themselves suffered for their opposition to Episcopacy.

Their common adherence to Presbyterian principles knit the two parties together. The Church of Scotland indeed represented the ideal of the struggling Presbyterians of the south. Not only however were the Scottish Churchmen theoretically at one with the Puritans and opposed to their persecutors, but they were also estranged from the English Bishops by the intrigues carried on between these prelates and Scottish favourers of an Episcopate. Patrick Adamson confessed when Presbyterianism was again triumphant in Scotland that he had conspired with the Bishops of the English Church. "I grant," he said in his recantation (8 April, 1591), "I was more bussie with some bishops of England, in prejudice of the discipline of our kirk, partlie when I was there, and partlie by our mutuall intelligence sensyne, than became a good Christian."[1] The estrangement between the two National Churches was deepened by Bancroft's notorious sermon of February, 1588–9, the effects of which did not pass away for many years. In that discourse Bancroft delivered a virulent attack on Presbyterianism and particularly its anti-monarchical character[2]. He hurled his adverse criticism at Knox and the Church of Scotland. Strangely enough he used as a source of information two writings of Robert Browne, one a treatise against Barrow and the other a letter sent by Browne to his uncle Flower (Francis Flower, J.P.?), dated 31 December, 1588[3]. In this letter Browne writes scathingly of the Scottish and other Presbyterians and holds that if their system were adopted in England "then in stead of one Pope we should have a thousand & of some Lord byshops in name, a thousand Lordly Tyrants in deed, which

[1] Calderwood, v, p. 121.

[2] For criticisms of the support given by Bancroft in his sermon to the superiority of diocesan Bishops *jure divino* by Reynolds and Knollys, *v. Informations* (1608), pp. 73, 88.

[3] Edited under the title *A New Years Guift* by C. Burrage (1904).

now do disdaine the name." "This," he continues, "have I found by experience to be trewe, both in forreine contries and in myne owne Contrie. I can testifie by trial of Scotland, which have traveled it over in their best reformed places, as in Donde, Sct Andrewes, Edenborowe & sundrie other Townes. And have knowne the king in great daunger & feare of his life by their Lordlie Discipline, the nobles & people at great discord and much distracted, & yet all men made slaves to the preachers & their fellowe elders. So that myne owne ears have hard the king by name to be verie spitefully abused by their preachers in pulpitt, his doings & commaundements called in, revoked, or repealed, or els established & performed as he durst or could do for feare or daunger of them. Also in everie Towne I found the cheife Magistrate in awe of them....Further I have sene all manner of wickednes to abound much more in their best places in Scotland, then in our worser places here in England. And to conclude when I came away all the whole land was in a manner wholie divided into parts, much people in armes & redie to ioine battel, some with the king, & some against him, & all about the preachers discipline. In England also I have found much more wronge done me by the preachers of discipline, then by anie the Byshops...before my first voiag beyond sea, & sence my last retourne, I have bene in more then twentie prisons. And for once imprisonment by the byshops, I have bene more then thrise imprisoned by the preachers or their procurings."

Such scraps of embittered Brownist autobiography were eagerly devoured by Bancroft, who utilised and elaborated them. They confirmed him in his conviction that the English Puritans were following in the wake of the Scottish reformers and he spared neither. His attack was much resented by the ministers of the Church of Scotland. His friendly entertainment of "Diotrephes, apostat of St Andrewes" (Adamson), when he was in England, had been most distasteful to them; now they regarded him as a firebrand who was acting as the spokesman of Elizabeth's ecclesiastical dignitaries[1].

[1] Calderwood, v, p. 72.

John Davidson took up the pen and wrote *Doctor Bancrofts Rashenesse in railing against the Church of Scotland*, which Waldegrave printed, much to the King's annoyance, in 1590[1]. Bancroft's subsequent publications, *Dangerous Positions* and *A Survay*, show that he did not abandon his attitude of scorn and hostility. Melville's encounter with the author at a later date, when he said, "If you are the author of the book called *English Scottizing for Geneva Discipline* (*i.e. Dangerous Positions*), then I regard you as the capital enemy of all the Reformed Churches in Europe, and as such I will profess myself an enemy to you and to your proceedings to the effusion of the last drop of my blood,"[2] shows the unfavourable impression created in the minds of representative Scottish Presbyterians by the utterances of their arch-critic.

The fact also that Bancroft maintained a close correspondence with friends and agents in Scotland came to the knowledge of the Scottish ministers. They knew that Adamson and he had exchanged letters, and they were specially incensed when they unearthed one of his secret emissaries, John Norton, at the beginning of 1590. They examined the latter on the 12th of February, 1589–90, "upon suspicion of secreit intelligence with Bancroft to the prejudice of our kirk" and discovered that he had been furnished with a questionnaire, designed to yield accurate information concerning the constitution, practices and deficiencies of the Church of Scotland. The drift and scope of Bancroft's investigations may be seen in the following samples of his questions: "Considering the king's edict, 1584, how came it to passe, that the bishops were so soone overthrowne again? Whether have they in their consistories anie sett jurisdictioun? Whether the king be exempted from their censures? Whether have they anie sett assemblies termed Conferences? And how manie presbytereis (*i.e.* Kirk Sessions) doe apperteane to everie suche Conference? Whether is Buchanan's treatise *De Jure Regni apud Scotos* approved there by the consis-

[1] Dated by J. D. 18 Sept.; Calderwood, v, pp. 6, 112.
[2] McCrie, p. 265.

torians? How have the ministers dealt with the king from tyme to tyme?"[1]

The dominant party in the Church of Scotland plainly and officially revealed their sympathies with the English Puritans in an Act of the General Assembly (3 March, 1589–90), which ordained "that the brethren recommend to God in their publick and privie supplications, the afflicted brethren in England for the confession of the purity of the religion."[2] The attitude and behaviour of the Scottish Church were a source of irritation to Elizabeth, who expressed her displeasure to James in a letter dated the 6th of July, 1590[3]. She warned the King against the danger to monarchy, which she thought was inherent in the Presbyterianism rampant in both realms, and in allusion to the Act of Assembly abovementioned hoped that he would silence the ministers who dared to pray in public for the English Puritans. "Ther is risen," she wrote, "bothe in your realme and myne, a secte of perilous consequence, suche as wold have no kings but a presbitrye, and take our place while the inioy our privilege, with a shade of Godes word, wiche non is juged to folow right without by ther censure the be so demed. Yea, looke we wel unto them. Whan the have made in our peoples hartz a doubt of our religion, and that we erre if the say so, what perilous issue this may make I rather thinke than mynde to write. *Sapienti pauca.* I pray you stap the mouthes, or make shortar the toungz, of suche ministars as dare presume to make oraison in ther pulpitz for the persecuted in Ingland for the gospel. Suppose you, my deare brother, that I can tollerat suche scandalz of my sincere governement? No. I hope, howsoever you be pleased to beare with ther audacitie towards your selfe, yet you wil not suffar a strange king receave that indignitie at suche caterpilars hand, that, instede of fruit, I am affraid wil stuf your realme with venom. Of this I have particularised more to this bearar, togither with other answers to his charge, besiching you to heare them, and

[1] Calderwood, v, pp. 77 ff.

[2] *B.U.K.* II, p. 749; Calderwood, v, p. 88.

[3] *Letters of Queen Eliz. and King James*, *Camd. Soc.* XLVI (1849), p. 63.

not to give more harbor-rome to vacabond traitors and seditious inventors, but to returne them to me, or banische them your land."

The chief nonconformists, whose extradition she craved, were John Penry and Robert Waldegrave. Bowes, the English ambassador, complained (16 May, 1590) of Penry's being allowed to reside in Edinburgh. The Scottish Council in the beginning of August issued a writ of banishment against Penry. In December James assured Bowes on good authority that he had now departed[1], but a considerable time elapsed before he took up residence in England again[2]. The complaint that Waldegrave was harboured in Scotland and allowed to print books against his own country had a different issue. In March he was authorised by the Scottish Council to print official documents, *e.g.* an Act of the Council and the Confession of Faith and in December James told Bowes that he had appointed the Puritan his own printer[3].

In 1591 the Church of Scotland was on the eve of obtaining its Magna Charta. The Presbyterian ministers were now in the ascendant and it was doubtless at their instigation that the King addressed a letter, dated from Holyrood, the 11th of June, to Elizabeth in behalf of their imprisoned coreligionists, Udall, Cartwright and others. Calderwood informs us that Lord Lindsay and Robert Bruce procured the letter from James and that it was written by George Young[4]. Heylyn and Fuller say that the epistle was presented to the Queen by Johnson, a Scottish merchant then in London. Calderwood omits Cartwright's name from his transcript and dates it in error the 12th of June[5]. The letter is given in an Appendix[6].

In the Dedication of his book on *Ecclesiastes* (1604) Cartwright expresses his gratitude to King James for his intervention: *literas de me & Udalo, captivate, qua propter sanctioris disciplinae in ecclesia nostra instauranda studium tenebamur, eximendis scribere...dignatus es* and attributes it

[1] *Reg. P.C. Scot.* IV, pp. 517–8; *S.P. Scot. Eliz.* XLV, No. 44, XLVI, Nos. 22, 64, 73. [2] *v.* Pierce, *John Penry*.

[3] *S. P. Scot. Eliz.* XLVI, Nos. 64, 73; Pierce, *Hist. Introd.* p. 320.

[4] Calderwood, V, p. 131. [5] *ibid.* V, p. 132. [6] XXVI.

to the rare and incomparable royal benevolence: *rarae item cujusdam & incomparabilis humanitatis fuit....* James's letter, however, had no apparent effect, "nor do I find that the King of Scotland was discontented thereat," says Fuller[1], who proceeds to suggest that his interposition was dictated by politic motives "as granted merely for quietness' sake, to satisfy the importunity of others." The importunity was that of the Scottish Presbyterians, but their anxious sympathy was insufficient to bring succour to the Puritan prisoners and the trial in the Star Chamber went on.

Meanwhile Cartwright was not without influential friends in England. We learn from a letter of his[2] that Burghley's sister-in-law, Lady Russell, had offered to use her influence in his behalf. She was one of the notable daughters of the late Sir Anthony Cooke. Mildred, Anne, Katherine and Margaret married Lord Burghley, Sir Nicholas Bacon, Sir Henry Killigrew and Sir Ralph Rowlet respectively; Elizabeth was married first to Sir Thomas Hoby and then to Lord John Russell[3]. Many members of this distinguished connection were zealous supporters of the Puritan cause. We have already noticed Killigrew's interest in the Church at Antwerp. Lady Anne Bacon was a woman of eminent piety, who acted as a sincere and generous patroness to the Puritan ministers[4]. It has been suggested that she helped to finance the publication of the first part of their Register[5]. Her step-son, Nathaniel, was also a favourer of the zealous preachers[6]. Cartwright was personally acquainted with most of this influential circle. On the 23rd of May, 1591, he wrote an intimate letter[7] to Lady Anne's son, Anthony, who after a long sojourn abroad had recently returned to England. It appears that her Ladyship had discussed her son's private affairs, his extravagance, choice of undesirable servants, etc., with Cartwright and now the latter offers counsel. The letter contains an interesting reference to Cartwright's acquaintance

[1] *C.H.* bk IX, sect. vii, § 30.
[2] *v. infra* p. 346.
[3] *v.* J. Anderson, *Ladies of the Reformation* (1855–7), I, pp. 461 ff.
[4] *v.* W. Urwick, *Nonconformity in Herts* (1884), p. 86.
[5] *Sec. Parte*, I, p. 13.
[6] *v. Stiffkey Papers*, *Camd. Soc.* (1915).
[7] App. XXVII.

with Anthony's brother, the illustrious Francis. On the 13th of August Cartwright wrote to Lady Russell[1]. He had received kind treatment at her hands and refers to the time when she presented him to her two daughters and commended him to them as a man "whom for good respects" she favoured. His letter shows that the Puritan prisoners are now at a loss as to what means they should adopt to seek deliverance. Lady Russell has offered her services as mediator. Cartwright points out that her brother-in-law, Burghley, is fully acquainted with the case already. The ministers' suit for bail having been refused, he does not know what further appeal can now be made, especially seeing that "we are not easilie suffred to come to her Majestie by our most humble supplicacion." The best he can do is to state his own desperate plight. He is treated with greater severity than the other prisoners. Their friends are allowed to visit them, but by a special warrant of the High Commission, none are permitted to visit him, except his wife and those who have necessary business with him. He thinks that this warrant has been issued to prevent such a resort of multitudes to his prison as happened when he was committed before (1585). The warden of the prison, either to gratify the Bishops and other enemies of Cartwright, or because of his own hard character, is very exact in his interpretation of the prohibition and cuts Cartwright off from the world as much as possible. The latter does not wish to complain lest the Bishops restrain his fellow-prisoners "also of th'accesse of their friends." The deprivation is a small matter, which he can easily bear, but his bodily ill-health is a more serious affair. Then he expatiates on his physical condition. After laying his case before Lady Russell he leaves her to use her own discretion as to what she should say in her promised suit to Burghley. She, evidently deeming it best to let Burghley read the whole of Cartwright's statement, sent the letter to him and appended her request on the back of it in these words: "Good my Lord, rede this thorow and do what good yow can to ye poore man." Burghley, although sympathetically interested in Cartwright,

[1] App. XXIX.

as the latter believed, "making no dout but that his h. standeth favorablie inclined towards me," did not procure the Puritan's release, and "ye poore man" continued to suffer in the Fleet.

Cartwright, Fen, King, Wight, Payne, Lord, Snape, Proudlove and Jewell, after having been more than a year in prison, resolved to send a joint petition for bail to the Privy Council. On the 4th of December, 1591[1], they make Burghley acquainted with their purpose and beseech him to further their request. They plead that prison life is very hard on men of their upbringing and profession. They think it unfair that imprisoned Papists have received better treatment. They protest that all of them have been sworn to the royal supremacy and are willing to take the same oath again. Some of their opponents condemn them for the interpretation they put upon the supremacy. The signatories assure Burghley that their interpretation is that of all the Reformed Churches and is in harmony with the Queen's own admonition at the end of her Injunctions and the 37th Article of the Convocation, and that in this matter they hold the view commonly held and approved by "the most autentike and classical writers of this Church." They are convinced that Burghley regards them with compassion and that he will do his utmost to deal out impartial justice to them.

Burghley was in close touch with the Attorney General, Sir John Popham, and evidently requested him to furnish an expert verdict on the case in question. Popham's summing up is contained in a letter addressed to Burghley on the 11th of December[2], and being the opinion of the Crown prosecutor is of the utmost importance. "Touchyng the matter off Mr Cartwryght and the rest," writes Popham, "the Books are very long and yet I had alredy redd them through almost all and do ffynd that they hadd a ffull resolucyne to have used means to have had that fform of dyscyplyn consydered off by there selves to have bene generally exercysed

[1] *v.* App. XXX.

[2] *Lansd. MSS.* LXVIII, No. 18, ff. 43–4; Brook (*Mem.* p. 380) summarises St. *Whit.* II, p. 83.

but as most off them say, so farre forth as the same myght be done with the peace off the Churche and lawes off the lande, but yt ys proved that in some off their assemblies yt was thought good and so by them affirmed that sythens it cold not be gotten to be establyshed by humble sute to her Majestie and the parliament yet it shold be brought to take effect and that by this means, that ys, that the mynysters affected as they were (in) the severall parts of the Realm shold wyne as many other mynysters as they cold to Imbrase that fform off dysyplyne and then to wyne the people to have a lykyng thereof, and that done to have yt putt in practyse, which as I gather by the proff was the peasable means wherby it myght be brought in, but thys ones done yt appeareth they were resolved not to geve alowans off eyther Arch B. or Busshoppes to be in the Churche, besydes sondry other partyculers which I omytt to putt down heir, all dependyng upon the establyshyng off their devysed fform of dyscyplyn." The Attorney General recognised that the Puritans intended to establish Presbyterianism only so far as the laws of the land and the peace of the Church permitted. But he regarded it as proven that in some of the assemblies it was affirmed, that, since the Queen and Parliament would not give effect to this aim, the ministers should seek to persuade other ministers, and then the people, to adopt Presbyterian principles. It is true that one small section of the Puritans were inclined to this position, but not the large body of the Puritans represented by Cartwright and his fellow-prisoners. Certainly if Presbyterianism, the ideal of moderate and extreme Puritans, were established the Episcopate would, as Popham feared, be overthrown, but there is nothing in his verdict which makes it clear that Cartwright and the Puritans who followed him had committed any legal offence. They had believed in and hankered after Presbyterianism but had not practised it. The Episcopal fears, it may be granted, were well founded and for the sake of their own interests the Bishops and even the Queen would have been justified in suppressing the Presbyterian movement, but they were not legally or justly entitled to punish, as they did, the moderate leaders such as Cartwright. Besides, the procedure adopted for the trial of the Puritans was unwarranted, and unnecessarily harsh. For lack of witnesses Lord Chancellor Hatton ordered that Whitgift should appoint a D.D. and a D.C.L. to join Popham for his better instruction[1]. But even so, no proof was obtained of seditious practices by Cartwright and his friends. Eventually the Lord Chief Justice persuaded Hatton and the rest of the court of the Star Chamber that they should not deal further in the case until they could prove seditious conduct *de facto*; and yet even after this statement Cartwright and the others were kept in prison without any definite proceedings being taken. Their case had fallen. The charge against them was unproven and yet they remained prisoners[2].

The manifestly unsatisfactory nature of the trial enlisted champions for the Puritan side. Knollys, requested by some of the prisoners to act as mediator, wrote to Burghley expressing his amazement that the Puritans were thought to be as dangerous as the Papists[3]. They could not, and did not try to set up Presbyterianism without the consent of the Queen and Parliament. If they had been proved to be seditious Cartwright and his fellow prisoners would have been punished long ago. Knollys had already protested against the tyranny of the Bishops' methods of dealing with their opponents in the enforcing of the Whitgiftian articles[4]. Now he pleads for the application not of mercy but of justice to men, whose alleged guilt is not proven.

Cartwright and other eight prisoners thank Knollys for his mediation[5]. They tell him that they are advised to make suit to the whole Council, and point out that the time is propitious, the weather being so extreme. Evidently Knollys approved of their proposal, for the prisoners now approach the Council, in a joint appeal[6]. They acknowledge their meetings, which they had deemed inoffensive. They are heartily sorry, however, that they have by these assemblies

[1] St. *Whit.* II, p. 84. [2] *v.* Soames, pp. 402–4.
[3] 9 Jan. 1591–2; *Lansd. MSS.* LXVI, No. 52; Brook, *Mem.* p. 373.
[4] *Lansd. MSS.* LXIV, No. 32.
[5] *ibid.* CIX, No. 9, f. 25. n.d. [6] *ibid.* CIX, No. 11, f. 31. n.d.

incurred the displeasure of the Queen and her Council. They are anxious to give the Council the utmost satisfaction. They would have offered their humble submission sooner had they not been hindered by special interrogatories sent to them by Whitgift. They have answers to these in readiness if the Council requires them to be delivered. All of them, except one, have been deprived or degraded. Their wives have greatly suffered in health, and some of their children have died. The severity of the season is also made to count in their petition for liberty.

The new interrogatories of Whitgift do not call for special consideration. They are almost the same as those administered in the Star Chamber[1]. In one the accused are asked to confess their fault in subscribing the Book of Discipline and putting the same into practice. Cartwright, in reply to this, refers to the humble petition, which he and the rest sent to the Council, as all the acknowledgement he could conscientiously make. If that does not satisfy he will submit himself to the punishment the authorities see fit to inflict. Fen, Lord, King and Wight made a similar answer. Proudlove said he had not subscribed the Book, but was willing to refrain from attending the meetings in the future. Snape answered that he had not subscribed the Book and also referred to the terms of the joint petition to the Council.

In the middle of January Cartwright informs Lord Gray that Whitgift has relieved some of his fellow-prisoners[2]. Those in the Clink (Fen, King, Wight and Payne) and the White Lion (Lord) are allowed on a bond of £40 to leave prison for short intervals, being obliged to return at night. They are also permitted to go to Church on Sunday. But Cartwright and the rest remain in close confinement. Cartwright complains that his enemies have spread the slander that he holds disloyal views of excommunication concerning the Queen and that he is implicated in a plot to put these into practice. He flatly denies the charge and hopes it may be duly examined, for he never applied the question of ex-

[1] *Lansd. MSS.* LXVIII, No. 62, ff. 139–41; St. *Whit.* II, pp. 85 ff.

[2] App. XXXI.

communication "to the person of a Prince generally much les praecisely to her Majesties roiall person." It is as false as the report that he gave up his Anglican orders or that he had a hand in the Marprelate Tracts. His views regarding excommunication are those of the Universal Church and of the Church of England in particular, and they are fully set forth in the supplication which he and the other Puritan prisoners have sent to Elizabeth. The only difference between himself and Whitgift on this point is that while the Archbishop maintains that the Emperor Theodosius was justifiably excommunicated by Ambrose, Cartwright believes that it was not done and ought not to have been done by one man. So he requests Lord Gray to use his influence to procure his liberty or at least bail. He has important business to look after, especially the affairs of the Warwick Hospital, of which he still has charge.

It was now fully apparent that the most hopeful course for Cartwright and his fellow-prisoners was to seek the favour of the Archbishop. He exercised supreme authority. His judgment expressed that of Elizabeth. To satisfy him was to satisfy the Queen. Cartwright's fate thus lay in the hands of his old enemy. The Puritan, however, scrupled to send a humble suit to his Grace, and on the 25th of January, 1591–2 he explained the ground of his unwillingness to Burghley, "namely for that (in my Lo. Chancellors life)[1] he denied me that favour, which he graunted unto other of my fellowes in the same case."[2] However, he has a petition to Whitgift prepared, and is ready to forward it should Burghley advise him to do so.

Not only did Burghley approve the sending of such a petition, but he evidently persuaded Whitgift to give it a favourable reception. This we learn from a letter to the Lord High Treasurer, written on the 31st of January, 1591–2[3], in which Cartwright tells that his wife has taken his appeal to the Archbishop and that the latter, doubtless due to Burghley's mediation, has already granted some relief, and holds out the prospect of more, probably of full freedom.

[1] Hatton died 20 Nov. 1591. [2] App. XXXII. [3] App. XXXIII.

"Through your Lo. honorable word praeparing his Grace aforehand," he writes, "I obteyned the same time for myne own affayres and the Hospitalls, which other my fellowes have for their own alone, that is one day in a weeke, beside the Sabboath; yet is it with limitacion of the Term time, theirs being not bounded at all. Howbeit it pleased his Grace to give my wife so good words, as might seeme to raise me up unto some hope, ether of a quite discharge, or of an easie renewing of this or like releif, if I remayne here, in this toedious and pitifull estate."

Unfortunately at this juncture Cartwright was perturbed by news, which he received on the 29th of January, to the effect that a complaint had been sent to the Council about the undutiful speeches made in Warwick by the man who was conducting prayers with the brethren in the Hospital. He was said to have spoken against the Council, magistrates and judges, probably out of sympathy with the Master, who seemed then to be their victim. Cartwright reports the matter to Burghley in the last mentioned letter. Having no high opinion of the man's intelligence or discretion, Cartwright is ready to believe the complaint. He thinks, however, that his offence should have been dealt with in the town or county courts, and suspects that behind the referring of the affair to the Council there lies a sinister purpose, viz., to bring discredit upon himself through his unworthy representative in the Hospital, and thus make room for the appointment of Mr Bourdman, the Vicar of St Mary's, Warwick, as Master. Already a double-beneficed minister (receiving £100 from Achurch and £20 from St Mary's), Bourdman was supported in his desire to secure the Mastership of the Hospital "by some of note." Cartwright, however, dissociates himself entirely from the conduct of his representative. Two or three times daily for six years he had conducted family worship in the Hospital, "yet shall I be hable to proove that in all that time, nether he nor anie other could ever learn anie such example in me." The man in question had married a maid, who had been in Cartwright's service for twelve years. Mrs Cartwright, when she came up to London, installed her as housekeeper, and her husband was requested by Mrs Cartwright to say the daily prayers. He had already displeased Cartwright by his undue prolonging of the prayers; at times the poor brethren had been prevented from being in time for Church. So he had been warned that if he did not amend his ways he would be dismissed. Cartwright having heard of the present complaint has already sent a letter forbidding him to read the prayers or have anything to do with the government of the Hospital. The Puritan is deeply grieved that his enemies seek thus to do him hurt.

If Cartwright was continually harassed by his enemies he was as constantly blessed by a multitude of well-wishers, many of whom occupied posts of authority and influence. One of these was the trusty Michael Hicks, who had befriended him nearly twenty years before. As one of Burghley's secretaries Hicks had an excellent opportunity of keeping Cartwright's case prominently before his master. On the 2nd of February, 1591–2, Cartwright writes to Hicks imploring him to lay his suit for liberty before Burghley[1]. He is sure that Burghley is doing his utmost for him, but he desires Hicks "to be a remembrance unto his L." He sums up the chief reasons why his suit should move Hicks to solicitude and the Lord High Treasurer to commiseration. First, there is his long and tedious imprisonment, which he has endured "now well towardes a year and a half." This is an overstatement by about two and a half months! Then there is the excessive expenditure incurred by the prisoners, *e.g.* the cost of copies of depositions, which, if the clerks had not been lenient would have amounted to £30, and their Counsel's fees, etc. Further, the prisoners' families are destitute, uninstructed and ungoverned. The health of the prisoners themselves is bad. The spring weather has caused them to suffer much. Cartwright especially has been very ill. The taking of physic has been counteracted by the "evill ayre" of the Fleet and the physicians refuse to administer any more medicine as long as he is in prison. To make sure of the desired mediation Cartwright invokes the affectionate

[1] App. XXXIV.

bond that existed between his deceased brother-in-law, Stubbe, and Hicks: "Now where my suite unto yow overweigheth my acquaintance, or any other cause in my self, let me be not evill thought of, if I seek the supply and counterpoise thereof in the love yow bare to my brother Stubbe, which would have poured all the ointment of the interest of his friendship with yow upon my head, if he had lived."[1] Eight months before Cartwright had sent Burghley an abstract of the charges against the Puritans and their answers to the same. Now he sends another "brief of our whole cause" with a fourth column added and asks Hicks to deliver it to Burghley.

In Cambridge University there were active sympathisers with the afflicted Puritans. Several scholars of that University sent a joint petition to their Chancellor on the 27th of February[2]. The signatories—Roger Goad, Wm Whitaker, Edmund Barwel and Laurence Chaderton—deprecated the hard severity meted out to the true friends and lovers of the Gospel, while Popish recusants were leniently dealt with, and pleaded with Burghley to procure equal justice and relief for the former.

In February the prisoners humbly approached their chief antagonist, Archbishop Whitgift. They had for some time been buoyed up by "the comfortable answer of deliverance" received from the Council in reply to their petition to that honourable Board. Whitgift himself had given them cause to expect relief. After long waiting they, distressed in body and spirit, were constrained to renew their suit for bail to his Grace[3]. They acknowledged that they were of different judgment from him in some controversial points but they assured him of their affectionate devotion to the Church of England. They sent their petition to Whitgift at the hands of their wives, who were directed by him to Attorney General

[1] Brook's garbled version of this passage is a good instance of his misuse of original documents (*Mem.* p. 398): "Though his suit overbalanced any acquaintance, or any other cause in himself, yet, not wishing to be evil thought of, he sought that assistance and redress in the love he bore to him, which would prove of greatest interest unto his lordship."

[2] St. *Whit.* III, p. 265. [3] *ibid.* II, p. 88.

Popham from whom they would receive the terms of submission required from the prisoners before they could be delivered. The Puritans were grieved by the news of the requisite submission. However, they sent their wives to Popham but he was out of London and not likely to return "before the next Sabboath." Accordingly eight of the afflicted petitioners turn again to Burghley to help them in their perplexity. Their joint appeal to him (endorsed 1st March, 1591–2) is based upon the knowledge that he is anxious to set them free from their long and tedious imprisonment[1]. They enclose a copy of the petition their wives had taken to Whitgift. They are distressed at being required to sign a submission, which, they fear, means a confession of guilt, whereas they feel that they cannot conscientiously make such an acknowledgement. They have shown already by their refusal of the oath that they will not be forced to act against their conscience. Their petition to Burghley is indeed one of the most elevated of their utterances and alone would mark them as heroic advocates of liberty of conscience. They had taken special care in their meetings to be law-abiding and if in the eye of the law they have transgressed they have done so in ignorance. However, even if they had been palpable and wilful transgressors of the law, have they not been punished sufficiently already? Since their committal to prison several Papists, known enemies of the Church and State, have been set at liberty without revocation of any error. Roman Catholic recusants and other schismatics may enjoy their liberty merely by promising to come to Church. The Puritan prisoners not only are willing to go to Church but are anxious to strengthen and defend it. Why then should they be compelled to subscribe a confession or submission against their conscience before they can secure their freedom? They are sure that Burghley understands and sympathises with their plight, and plead with him to secure at least their deliverance on bail. Recently four or five of them have fallen dangerously ill and if only for the sake of their health it is imperative

[1] App. xxxv.

that they should be released. The petition is signed by Cartwright, Fen, Wight, Lord, Jewell, Proudlove, Snape, and King[1].

Their apprehensions regarding the nature of the submission were justified. The form which they were required to subscribe[2] was probably drawn up by Popham. It constitutes an express acknowledgement of the full ecclesiastical supremacy of the Queen, a declaration that assemblies, synods, etc., attempting to alter or subvert existing ecclesiastical laws or usages without her Majesty's assent are seditious and unlawful, and that the present ecclesiastical government is lawful and allowable by the Word of God, and a repudiation of the Presbyterian system of government as both unlawful and dangerous. The Puritans are expressly required to acknowledge that it is seditious and ungodly to teach that any Presbyterian officer or court has or ought to have the power to excommunicate her Majesty or to command her subjects to withdraw their obedience from her; and, further, to acknowledge the Church of England as established a true member of the Church of Christ, whose sacraments are godly and rightly ministered, whose whole order of public prayer and ceremonies is such that no man ought therefore to make any schism or contention in the Church or withdraw himself from the same.

Cartwright and his associates could not honourably give their adherence to this document. By signing it they would brand as dangerous and seditious the reformation they hankered after, and believed in, and recant the principles which they conscientiously cherished. Their signatures would have been lies extorted by despotism from cowardice, signatures of the pen that contradicted the convictions of their minds. They preferred liberty of conscience to liberty of body and so refused to subscribe. It would be easy to denounce the attempt, inspired doubtless by Whitgift, to coerce the conscience of Cartwright and his fellow sufferers, but in these "spacious" Elizabethan days Whitgift and his party were of opinion that they were performing their con-

[1] Cf. *Lansd. MSS.* LXXII, No. 50, f. 141. [2] St. *Whit.* III, p. 261.

scientious duty for the sake of the Queen and the National Religion, and their victims, if in authority, would have shown a like intolerance, for neither side then understood the virtue of true toleration. Nevertheless it was the brave stand of the victims that paved the way for the recognition of the rights of conscience. The refusal of Cartwright and the others to sign the form of submission delayed their deliverance, but not for long.

Reading between the lines of the meagre materials dealing with the few months preceding Cartwright's release we are inclined to conjecture that the breakdown in health of the Puritan prisoners accelerated their deliverance. Even after he came out of the noisome Fleet, Cartwright was under the care of a physician. Some time before the 21st of May, 1592, he was delivered from prison, and took up residence at Hackney, whence on that date he sent a brief letter of thanks to Burghley for the part the latter had taken in procuring his freedom[1]. "Havinge felt of your Lo. honourable favour before in prison," he wrote, "and nowe much more in some libertie which I enjoy: I thought it my part assone as I gott out of the Phisicons handes (as out of a seconde prison) to have testified unto your L. my dutyfull remembraunce of so great a benefitt, whereof your L. hath bene so singular a meanes." It is to be noted that Cartwright speaks of "some libertie" as if he had not obtained a full discharge. He was apparently liable to be called before the Ecclesiastical Commissioners should they deem it necessary. His fellow prisoners were evidently released about the same time.

Some writers, *e.g.* Paule, have attributed Cartwright's release to the generosity and clemency of Whitgift, while others, *e.g.* Brook, have sought to rob the Archbishop of any share in it. It is questionable whether one individual was responsible for it. Sympathy and love of justice moved Burghley to seek it; the pressure of circumstances made the Queen and Whitgift willing to consent to it; the Privy Council as a body secured and sanctioned it. In his *Apologie*[2] Cartwright says that "upon commandement" he had to satisfy

[1] App. XXXVI.

[2] sig. C, C *verso*.

the Council in writing as to his attitude to the question of royal supremacy, that the Council was pleased that the charges of sedition, disloyalty, etc., which Sutcliffe continued to hurl at Cartwright after the trial, "should be no further proceeded in," and that Sutcliffe is "not contented with that imprisonment we endured, which their Honors are satisfied with."

CHAPTER VII

THE LAST DECADE, 1593 TO 1603

Puritan literature—writings of Sutcliffe, Bancroft, and Hooker—Cartwright's residence in Guernsey (1595–1601)—his labours among the Presbyterians of the Channel Islands—his return to Warwick—his closing years—appreciation of his character, teaching, writings, and influence—his career illustrative of the history of Elizabethan Puritanism.

THE release of Cartwright and his fellows could not revive their cause. It was losing one powerful patron after another; one of the greatest, Walsingham, died in 1591. Parliament was hopelessly unable to redress Puritan grievances as long as Elizabeth muzzled it, as was again apparent in Feb. 1592–3, when Morrice, supported by Knollys, vainly endeavoured to introduce a bill in the House of Commons to remedy the harsh course pursued by the Bishops towards the godly ministers who refused the oath[1]. Morrice's reward for his attempted intervention was imprisonment. The stringent measures[2] passed against Protestant nonconformists and Romish recusants by Parliament in April 1593 made religious dissent more difficult than ever. Conformity and banishment were the only alternatives. The latter was chosen by large numbers of Separatists who proceeded to Holland to worship according to their conscience; the Puritans proper remained at home, giving their wonted allegiance to the Establishment but waiting for a better day in which to renew their effort in favour of Presbyterianism. Nonconformity of the Separatist type was regarded even by the House of Commons as a grave and growing menace. Sir Walter Raleigh was convinced that there were almost 20,000 Brownists in the country[3]. As many of the Separatists openly acknowledged that they owed their conversion to dissent to the teaching of the Puritans, the anti-Separatist campaign would necessarily oblige the latter to observe unusual circumspection and deter them from excesses. The

[1] D'Ewes, p. 474. [2] Gee & Hardy, p. 492. [3] D'Ewes, p. 517.

Presbyterian Puritans were opposed at this period by the forces of the High Commission and the Star Chamber and a series of effective writings issued by the Episcopal party. Among the most notable literary opponents were Sutcliffe, Bancroft and Hooker. Against their heavy artillery only a pistol shot or two was heard on the Puritan side. Throkmorton and Cartwright, when stirred to reply, were more anxious to defend their own characters against slander than the Presbyterian cause against its critics.

The supporters of the hierarchy were stung to retort by several books issued about 1590. Penry in *Reformation no Enemie* condemns the Bishops and their followers not only for their opposition to the Puritans, but particularly because they have encouraged the growth of Romanism during the last twenty years. The increase of Popery is all the more reprehensible seeing the Bishops "have stopped the mouthes of so many faithful teachers within these 6 yeares."[1] The chief person responsible for the corruption of the Church and the persecution of its reformers is "that notable seducer of your people, the Arch. of Cant."[2] Penry does not mince his words when dealing with "this wicked prelate" and regards with special disfavour Whitgift's election to the Council board[3]: "such a detected enemie unto the gospell as he is hath bene promoted unto one of the highest roomes at the counsell table, to the ende, as the maintaining of his proceedings do witnesse, that he might be a scourge unto Gods Church." Bancroft is also condemned in unmeasured terms as "one of ye most shamelesse & most impudent slanderers that are amongst al our adversaries (intending of set purpose to stain the cause and the favorers of reformation with sedition and treason)."[4] Penry advocates the abolition of abuses (dumb and nonresident ministers, Archbishops, Bishops, etc.) and "the placing in everie congregation within England" of preaching pastors, and doctors, governing elders and ministering deacons[5]. He does not proclaim the full Cartwrightian scheme and is already approaching the Barrowist position.

[1] sig. H 4. [2] sig. C 4 *verso*. [3] sig. C 4 *verso*.
[4] sig. B 2. [5] sig. B 3.

An Humble Motion[1], although less pointed is equally antagonistic to the Bishops. The publisher of it[2] is a true Cartwrightian and in his Epistle "To the Reader" commends the best books on Presbyterianism thus: "For if thou desire to have it disputed against a professed and bitter enemy therunto, thou hast the first and second reply of T. C. against D. W. If thou wouldst have it handled in a sweet and pleasant latine style, the Ecclesiastical discipline (*i.e. Explicatio*, 1574) is able to content thee, if thou be unlearned & desire the same course in thy mother tongue, beholde the Learned discourse (whiche D. Bridges assaying to confute hath confirmed), the sermon upon Rom. 12, etc. If thou desire to see it layd open and concluded in scholastical manner, the demonstration doeth that way satisfy thee," and then the *Humble Motion* itself is commended as an exposition of the approved orthodox Presbyterian Puritanism.

An important book, entitled *A Petition directed to her most excellent Maiestie...* was published anonymously about 1590–1. Written probably by a learned lawyer, it lays down a sound defence of Cartwright, Udall and others. It is contended that those who write in favour of further reformation are not guilty of treason and felony. Their attack on the Bishops is justifiable and their doctrine of excommunication does not imply defamation of the sovereign. Bancroft is strongly condemned for his servility and flattery.

Among the anti-Puritanical writings which appeared at this time is *A Remonstrance* (1590). It was registered at Stationers' Hall, 3 July, 1591[3], but the author's name is not given. The preface is addressed "To the Factious and Turbulent T.C. W.T. I.P. and to the Rest of that anarchicall disordered alphabet." Cartwright is called "the Bel-weather of this bande, out of whose forge the Demonstrationer hath taken up almost all his stuffe on trust."[4] The chief object of the book is to reply to Udall's *Demonstration*, but it also condemns the lately discovered Book of Discipline.

[1] Anonymous, 1590.

[2] Bancroft (*D.P.* pp. 51, 52) was of opinion that *A parte of a register*, *Reformation no Enemie* and *An Humble Motion* were all imported from Scotland.

[3] *Transcript*, ed. Arber, II, p. 587.

[4] p. 2.

Now Matthew Sutcliffe, Dean of Exeter, appeared in the rôle of Martin Mar-Presbyter. He could write as a grave Latinist as in his *De Presbyterio* (1591), but his most notable works were written in the style of a carping critic and a scurrilous slanderer. At the beginning of 1591 he completed his *Treatise of Ecclesiasticall Discipline* (the Epistle is dated 1 Jan. 1590–1). It was published when Cartwright was in prison, but to judge from the jibes thrown at his supposed prosperous life in Warwick, it was composed while he was still there. Cartwright, says Sutcliffe, "is too stout hearted to wander any more, or to gather crummes under other mens tables: and like a wise fellowe, hath purchased more in persecution, then any minister in England in so short space in his greatest prosperitie."[1] With malicious joy the Dean points out the variations in the platforms submitted by the Disciplinarians, *e.g.* the Genevans are pleased with one Consistory for seventeen parishes, but the Cartwrightians desire a Consistory in every parish[2]. He charges Cartwright and his followers with change of views: "Th. Cartw. once would have the people to chuse their Minister, and gave out great words that Christ died to purchase that liberty to the people: they of the Admonition likewise favoured the peoples government: now Th. Cartw. hath changed haire, and telleth us, that it is sufficient if the people do consent after election, nay, that it is sufficient if the people dissent not; which is now the practise of Geneva." He accuses Cartwright of inconsistency inasmuch as he holds a Mastership of a Hospital while he teaches that ministers should not meddle with civil offices[3] and tauntingly says that though Cartwright "loose the office of doctor, yet can he live by his owne purchase."[4] "If Th. Cartwr." writes Sutcliffe[5], "were not maister of an hospitall (as Aerius the heretike, who thought an elder and a bishop to be all one, was afore him) they would have maisters of hospitalles removed too: (*i.e. as well as Bishops*, *Deans*, *etc.*) and that so much the rather for that it is a more popish office then any of the other." The Dean makes a very important

[1] Sutcliffe, *Treatise*, sig. B 1.
[2] *ibid.* p. 8.
[3] *ibid.* p. 35.
[4] *ibid.* p. 26.
[5] *ibid.* p. 100.

point when he says[1] that the Puritans did not speak much of Conferences till of late in their Book of Discipline, and notes that they have drawn this and other parts of their synodical discipline from the polity of the French Reformed Church. Sutcliffe holds that if Cartwright's belief that the discipline is part of the Gospel is true then the Church of England cannot be the Church of Christ, and the Separatists carry his premise to a logical conclusion, and he scathingly denounces him for seeking to defend the English Church against the Separatists when he cannot possibly with any show of self-consistency do so: "If their discipline be a part of the Gospell; then are not they the true Church of Christ, that refuse the same: then have the Barrowists iust cause to depart, and separate themselves from us: then is Th. Cartw. defence against Harr. a most weake and childish defence. I marvell with what face he durst take upon him the defence of our cause, handling the same so weakelie and unfaithfullie....if he will heare good counsell, let him laye hand off our cause, which we are by Gods grace able to defend, as well against him, as against the Barrowistes; both which consent together alike, in defacing the Church of England....if the discipline which they strive for, be a part of the Gospel; then is not the Church of England the true Church refusing it: and Th. Cartw. striveth both with his adversarie and himselfe, most ridiculouslie."[2]

Sutcliffe resumes his attack towards the end of 1592 in *An Answere to a Certaine Libel supplicatorie* etc., which is an answer to *A Petition directed* etc., the author of which, he suggests, is "W. St."[3] Sutcliffe dates his Dedicatory Epistle the 20th of December. He condemns the recent Conference movement at the head of which he places Cartwright, as a seditious attempt to advance discipline by force. Without regard for fine distinctions and lacking a judicial mind he blames Cartwright, Udall and others for complicity in the Copinger-Hacket conspiracy. While his chief hypothesis regarding the Marprelate Tracts is that Penry, Udall, Field and Throkmorton all concurred in making them, he also

[1] Sutcliffe, *Treatise*, p. 193.
[2] *ibid.* pp. 228–9.
[3] Sutcliffe, *Ans. to a Pet.* p. 19.

suggests that Cartwright and other Disciplinarians allowed them. He does not spare "the oracle of discipline," viz., Cartwright, who is again held up to reproach as an unscrupulous self-aggrandising hypocrite: "For he hath bestirred himselfe so that what by rewardes, what by availes of his hospitall, and pinching those that are committed to his charge, and what by buying and selling, the man is growen fatte and riche."[1] "Let him purchase and buy at pleasure: I hinder him not, I envie him not. Onely thus much I must tell him, as I did once, that there is no reason, that Tho. Cartwright, a man that hath more Landes of his owne in possession, then any Bishop that I knowe, and that fareth dayntily every day, and feedeth fayre and fatte, and lyeth as soft as any tenderling of that broode, and hath wonne much wealth in shorte time, and will leave more to his posteritie then any Bishop: should crye out eyther of persecution, or of excesse of Bishops livings: whose povertie I might, but I will not disclose. Secondly, that hee is a most happy man, that with selling a cottage and so much ground as would scarse grase three goslings, worth at the uttermost but twentie Nobles yeerely, can purchase two or three hundred markes land: and gladly would I learne that secrete. Thirdly, that seeing hee hath such authoritie with a packe of Sots that follow him, that every word of his should be deemed good lawe: there is no reason, why he should complayne of the superioritie that is in our governours, and yet continue his bitter invectives against the State. As long as he repenteth not himselfe, of the wrong that hee hath offred to the church, nor renounceth his fond conceits of discipline, nor forbeareth to maintaine a confederacie to revel against al such as are well affected to the State; he must looke not onely to bee carped at, but also to be launced, if hee be not otherwise dealt withall. If he keepe himselfe private, and seeke not to advaunce himselfe by pillage of the Church, I for my part will let him alone: neyther shall his Frierlike begging, nor his covetous dealing with his Hospitall, nor his disloyall dealing with his good friendes, nor his Usurie, nor any other matters bee touched or carped at."[2]

[1] Sutcliffe, *Ans. to a Pet.* p. 124. [2] *ibid.* p. 155.

In 1594 appeared *The Defence of Job Throkmorton against the slaunders of Maister Sutcliffe* etc. In this book Throkmorton disavows any guilty connection with Copinger, etc., and affirms that he is willing to swear on oath that he is not Martin and that he never knew him. He defends the Puritans whom Sutcliffe would make fellow-traitors with Copinger and Hacket and says that Hooker in his "late politicke treatise" honours the Puritans[1]. He also upholds Cartwright against other charges made by Sutcliffe, *e.g.* the purchase of manors.

In 1595 Sutcliffe replied in *An Answere unto a certaine calumnious letter published by M. Job Throkmorton* and repeated at length his charges both against Throkmorton and the latter's idol, Cartwright.

In the following year an important work by Cartwright was published, probably by Schilders of Middelburg, who seems also to have printed Throkmorton's *Defence*. It is entitled *A brief Apologie of Thomas Cartwright against all such slaunderous accusations as it pleaseth Mr Sutcliffe in his several pamphlettes most iniuriously to loade him with.* This source of autobiographical information, which we have already frequently utilised, was written by Cartwright before he left Warwick for the Channel Islands but was published after he had settled in Guernsey. It was edited by Throkmorton who supplied an interesting epistle "To the Reader" and various marginal comments. Sutcliffe's charges, *e.g.* that Cartwright was associated with Copinger, that he was supposed to work miracles in Warwick, that he acted as one of Stubbe's executors, etc., have been dealt with as occasion arose. There are two accusations that still call for treatment. One is that Cartwright commended extempore prayers, as being uttered by the Holy Spirit's secret inspiration and would scarcely be induced to "like of a prescript forme of prayer."

Cartwright's answer is: "Where, in my replie, or in the treatise of what matter I remember not, nor Mr Sutcliffe (I believe) shall ever show that Thomas Cartwright hath so

[1] sig. C iii *verso*.

little knowledge as to affirm that the extemporall prayers of anie (how able soever in these daies) are uttered by the holy ghostes secret inspiration. And in what place or time and in whose hearing could I scarcely be induced to like of a prescript forme of praier? The noting of these circumstances, which he doth diligently, yea curiously (where he thinketh they may serve the turne) would easely have bewraied, th'untrueth hereof. My continuall practise in the ministerie witnesseth against it, for in the space of five yeres I preached at Antwerpe and Middelborough, I did every sunday read the praier out of the booke: And all the while I preached at Warwike there were few sermons I ever made there but (to my remembrance) I did shutt up the praier either before or after the sermon with the Lordes praier: Besides that the praier before the sermon ordinarily was a set and accustomed forme of praier howsoever I read it not out of the booke, and likewise was that after the sermon some small part excepted, where in my praier I applied some principal pointes of the doctrine then handled: All which I would not have done, if I had not alowed, yea well liked also a prescript forme of praier."[1] This opinion is in harmony with that expressed by Cartwright in his first *Reply* in which he pointed out that the Admonitioners did not object to a prescribed form of prayer, but to the particular one enjoined by law, viz., the Book of Common Prayer[2]. The latter was condemned by the Puritans because of its Roman Catholic elements, not because it contained prescribed prayers. Cartwright and his followers desired a new Prayer Book, but they wished one that contained certain definite prayers, which they would use not as stereotyped obligatory forms, but as models for the direction of worship. Richard Baxter afterwards[3] commended Cartwright's *via media*, but it is interesting to note that representative divines of New England referred to Cartwright's opinions as an authoritative pronouncement against a fixed liturgy[4].

The other accusation of Sutcliffe which Cartwright now answers in full is that the Puritan purchased three or four

[1] *Apol.* sig. C 2 *verso*.
[2] *W.W.* II, p. 465.
[3] *v. infra* p. 400.
[4] *A Letter of Many Ministers* (1643), p. 2.

good manors with the spoil of the Hospital and the sale of a small cottage of his own, that he has two leases at Wellborn bought from Alexander Morgan and worth 200 marks a year, that his lands in Norfolk, part of which he had from Stubbe, amount to half the sum, and that he also has property in Warwickshire obtained from Hospital leases. "For the purchase of three or four Mannoures," says Cartwright[1], "I never purchased any Mannour in my life but the Mannour of Saxmundeham in Suffolke, wherof I have yet but the moitie, nether shal have these fourtene or fiftene yeres, if one Mr Johnsons lease be availeable, as hitherto he hath enioyed it by me; who have not disturbed his possession. The rent that he yeeldeth for th'one half of the Demaines is but xxx shillings by yeare. The rente of the demeines that I receive (although enhanced as farre as the tennant may live thereof) is yet but xxvi pound by yeare. Th'other rentes for Copieholdes come yearely to a iii pound or thereabouts, as I remember. So that the whole of that I receive cometh to litle above xxx pound by the yeare." He then describes the farm at Whaddon, the sale of which enabled him to buy the Saxmundham property[2]. As to Sutcliffe's charge that he misappropriated Hospital funds Cartwright replies: "neither I nor anie for me purchased one foote of lande since I came to the Hospitall: I soulde an annuitie in fee-simple of xii pound x shillings by yeare since I came thither, as my L. chief Iustice of her Maiesties common pleas doth wel know, before whom I acknowledge a fine: Leases of the Hospitall I never made but one onely, for which the house and not I received thirtie poundes....I have laied out of mine owne purse fourty markes over and above that which I have received or am like to receive unlesse the stocke which is holden from the house be recovered. This partlie may appeare by an Accoumpt I gave up unto her Maiesties Commissioners who had charge (amongest others) to enquire and certifie the whole estate of the poore Hospitall."[3] He proceeds to exculpate himself in connection with the Wellborn leases, which have brought him loss rather than gain, and repudiates the

[1] *Apol.* sig. C 4. [2] *v. supra* pp. 1–2. [3] *Apol.* sig. C 4 *verso.*

aspersions regarding the execution of Stubbe's will. He denies that he has any lands in Warwickshire or Norfolk. Sutcliffe further accused Cartwright of putting his money, of which he had good store, to usury. The Puritan and another are creditors of a Mr Francis Mitchell, who owes them 200 pounds. "When the day of paiement approched," says Cartwright[1], "he [Mitchell] came to me in the Fleete, and offered me interest to forbeare, which I utterly refusing, did notwithstanding at his earnest suite and complaint of his distresse yeeld to forbeare the debte. And gave him a writing of my hand to this effecte, that I was for mine owne part content to forbeare him, with these conditions, first that my graunt should not bee hurtfull to my friend, not then in towne: and secondly, that it should not be preiudiciall to the principall summe of two hundred pound....And we are so farre of from taking Interest of him, that to this day being about five yeares at the least since the money was due, we have not receyved so much as the principall which wee onely demanded of him, although we had sued out the forfeiture of his Recognoizance. And touching the matter of Interest, albeit I have alwaies bene of iudgement for the lawfulnes of it, so it be with such caution as Charitie (the rule of dealing with our neighbour) be not broken: yet in the time of my greatest necessitie, when I was beyond the sea, I receiving assurance only for the bare money I left in the handes of my friends, did never covenant with them for the valew of one penie: But was content with what soever they them selves of their owne accord did alow, whether anie thing or nothing. Which dealing alowed of those which are the most bitter adversaries of Interest, Mr Sutcliffe may thinke with him self how untruly he dealeth with me in his accusation of Double Usance."

Cartwright's manor at Saxmundham must be distinguished from the manors of Hurts and Murkets in the same district. His was Swan's Manor, the history of which is given in W. A. Copinger's *Manors of Suffolk*[2]. It is recorded that a fine was levied of the manor by John Stubbe and others against

[1] *Apol.* sig. D 2.

[2] (1909), V, p. 164.

Edward Glenham and others in 1584. Cartwright's widow is entered as the lady of Swan's Manor in 1609.

Although the recognised leader of the Puritans, Cartwright had refrained in recent years from using his pen in defence of Presbyterianism. This silence is remarkable, and did not escape the notice of Sutcliffe, who attributed it to fear or inability. In his *Apologie* Cartwright explains his silence. Other writers have recently expounded Presbyterianism better than he, in his old age, can do. Fenner and Udall certainly performed this task well. Nevertheless, he would be willing, if allowed, to publish a reply to Sutcliffe's anti-Presbyterian criticism, if there were anything in the Dean's work that has not already been refuted. "And that he dareth me," says Cartwright[1], "not once but sundry times to answere touching these matters of Discipline, I think it not so fitte for me to undertake it there being so many better able thereunto then I, especiallie in this declyning and forgetfull age of mine. And yet if my answere might have either that alowance of print, or passage that his hath, and none other were found: I my self in this weaknesse I am in, would not be behind with answere to anie thing that he hath bene able to alleadge in this behalfe: If there be any thing in his writings, the answere wherof is not already set downe by such as have written in that cause." Cartwright then refers to his successful effort to call in the manuscript portion of his *Confutation*, the publication of which had been prohibited, to show how he is unwilling to flout the laws of the land by surreptitiously printing a work, from which he was on his honour bound to refrain.

In 1596 Sutcliffe followed up Cartwright's *Apologie* with *An Examination of M. Thomas Cartwrights late Apologie*. He twits Cartwright, now supposed to be in Guernsey, on the slenderness of his book, and on the fact that he has maintained his silence regarding the Discipline. He conjectures that "gibing Job" has written the Preface to Cartwright's *Apologie*, and thinks that Cartwright has wronged himself in allowing such "a lewde and foule mouthed proctor to

[1] *Apol.* sig. C *verso.*

plead in commendation of his innocencie and patience." He continues his destructive criticism of the reformer, calling Cartwright's Replies a fardle of fooleries. Cartwright's "ignorance in the Latin tongue," he writes, "is made famous by that Epistle of his, that is set before Fenners booke, which is the onely thing of his, that ever I saw in Latin, and is full of solecismes." He quotes Whitaker's adverse estimate of the *Second Reply*, regards Cartwright as a borrower from Illyricus, Calvin, and Beza, and condemns his style as hard, rough and "stuffed with farre fetched and outstretched metaphors." "I deny not," he says[1], "that M. Cartwright is a man learned, but that hee is excellently learned, and not ignorant in the points wherein I have iustly noted him, that would be proved." It should be noted that Sutcliffe uses much of the material collected by Bancroft.

In 1593 Bancroft published his *Survay* and *Dangerous Positions*, two books that are indispensable for a proper study of Elizabethan Presbyterianism. They contain extracts from the numerous controversial writings of the Puritans, intercepted correspondence, depositions in the Star Chamber, etc., and furnish a quarry of information regarding the movement which Bancroft did so much to put down. The Book of Discipline is discussed at great length. It and Cartwright are looked upon as the foci of the whole cause which Bancroft sought to expose. A rough history of the Book and of the Conferences that discussed it is given. Bancroft is pleased to see that Cartwright "the chiefe man, that began this course in England is drawing homeward." His answer to Harrison is spoken of as a sign that he has departed from his original tenet that discipline is a necessary part of the Gospel but Bancroft is puzzled by his approval of the Book of Discipline in which discipline is declared essential and wonders whether Cartwright has changed his judgment again, but leaves the matter "to be discussed by them that know his unrevealed mind."[2] The peculiar position of Cartwright is thus misunderstood by the parties of the Right and of the Left. Anglicans as well as Brownists and Barrowists think

[1] f. 24.

[2] Bancroft, *Survay*, p. 449.

him inconsistent. He could not make it clear to them that he could consistently defend the English Church no matter how imperfect against Separatists, while he claimed that the adoption of Presbyterianism was necessary to the Church's perfection. Bancroft failed to appreciate Cartwright's aim aright. In his *Dangerous Positions* he sought to illuminate his mass of evidence by working into it the hypothesis that the Puritans were "Genevating" and "Scottizing" for discipline, by railing, by practice, by threatening, and force. In his eyes the "drift" of the Cartwrightians was purely subversive of the Church and State. Nevertheless his writings are invaluable source-books even to those who manipulate and interpret the store of information, which they contain, differently from their biased compiler.

Bancroft's books were followed by those of a man who was not at the mercy of a prejudiced *leitmotiv*, a man who could see the Puritan wood in spite of its serried ranks of trees. Richard Hooker published the first four books of *The Laws of Ecclesiastical Polity* in 1594; the fifth, and the last of the eight that comes under our purview, was issued in 1597. This classic defence of the Church of England is a product by reaction of Cartwrightian Puritanism. In the calm air of the detached philosopher the tenets of "T.C." are analysed, their implications set forth, and the universal principles of Church government expounded. Hooker discusses the broad question of divine revelation, and exposes the narrow view of Scripture held by the Puritans. He argues that an unalterable polity is not laid down in Scripture, that the latter presupposes laws of nature and reason, the legislative power of societies, etc., and that the government and practices of the Church of England are in accordance with Scripture, reason and tradition. While meeting the Puritan objection to a dumb ministry he shows that the value of preaching is exaggerated by the Disciplinarians, and that there are other means which the Church can use for the salvation of souls. *Abusus non tollit usum* is one of the chief principles used by Hooker when he defends the Book of Common Prayer, the observance of holy days, etc. He shows how an Episcopate grew out of the degrees of ministry existing in the Apostolic Church, and discards many of the Puritan proof-texts that were alleged in support of Presbyterianism as irrelevant. Hooker's work is a great and lasting achievement. He certainly discloses the deficiencies of the Puritan conception of revelation and introduces a strong humanist element into theological thought. Although the substance of ecclesiastical polity is contained in Scripture, man must be loyal to the dictates of his reason and the lessons of history as he interprets the Bible and builds up his Church. Although Hooker's criticism of Puritanism is in many points incontrovertible it does not follow that the Church, which he defended so ably, would not have been greater and better if reconstructed on Presbyterian lines as Cartwright desired. Hooker's general principles are not inherently Anglican. They have been cited in support of the Papacy and they have been adopted by Presbyterians. After the publication of his work Elizabethan Presbyterianism could not be the same again, but it could be more firmly based, viz., on a foundation consisting of Cartwright's contentions clarified by Hooker's philosophy. The Puritans recognised the weight of their latest opponent. Their only reply, *A Christian Letter* (1599), is an insipid production that reveals the consciousness of defeat[1].

Hooker takes Cartwright's controversial works as containing a representative exposition of the Puritan position and frequently cites the author of them by his well-known initials. Although he does not mention Cartwright by name he refers to him in a notable passage[2] thus: "Concerning the Defender of which Admonitions, all that I mean to say is this: *there will come a time when three words uttered with charity and meekness shall receive a far more blessed reward than three thousand volumes written with disdainful sharpness of wit.*"

Cartwright's career during the three years after his release from the Fleet are shrouded in darkness. Apparently he returned to Warwick and helped to resuscitate the fortunes of the Hospital, of which he was still Master. Some writers[3]

[1] Bayne, pp. 589 ff.

[2] *Pref. to Eccles. Pol.* II, § 10.

[3] *e.g.* Urwick, *op. cit.* p. 806.

affirm that he retired to Warwick and remained there till his death. This assertion, however, is manifestly incorrect. In 1595 he left Warwick and proceeded to Guernsey, where he lived as Chaplain at Castle Cornet, not till 1598, as the *Dictionary of National Biography* states, but till 1601. Clarke, the *Dictionary of National Biography*, and others, say that he went to the Channel Isles on the invitation of Lord Zouch, Governor of Guernsey, but Sir Thomas Leighton was still Governor when Cartwright went across and it is likely that it was he who was instrumental in bringing Leicester's old protégé to his new sphere of service[1]. During his prolonged absence Cartwright's place at Warwick was occupied by his friend Edward Lord, late of Wolston, to whom, according to Clarke[2], he allowed the greatest part of the profits of the Mastership, while the rest "he caused to be distributed amongst the poore." Now that his beloved cause was hopelessly lost in England Cartwright would eagerly seize the opportunity of taking a share in the work of a Church, which was thoroughly Presbyterian in its constitution. We have already noticed the rise of Presbyterianism in the island of Guernsey[3]. Unhappily the newly organised island Church did not prosper well. The people were not loyal and generous to their ministers. By 1579 there were few ministers left and several of the Churches were closed[4]. The close relationship between the Churches of Jersey and Guernsey also came to a quick and unfortunate end. For thirteen years (1583–1596) there existed an unhappy rupture between the Colloquies of the two islands, during which time no Synods were held[5]. Leighton, who was sincerely interested in the religious welfare of the islanders, was unable to cement their differences[6]. It was not till after the arrival of Cartwright and Snape in 1595 that a reconciliation between

[1] A modern writer repeats the error regarding Lord Zouch so recently as May, 1923 (*Journal of Presb. Hist. Soc. of Eng.* vol. II, No. 4, p. 189), saying that Cartwright "stayed at Castle Cornet as the guest of his great friend Lord Zouch, the Governor of Guernsey."

[2] p. 372.

[3] *supra* pp. 157 ff.

[4] *S.P. Dom. Eliz. Add.* XXVI, No. 30.

[5] Schickler, II, p. 423.

[6] *ibid.* pp. 434, 441.

the two Presbyteries was effected and the united Church consolidated.

Fortunately, the *Actes* of the Guernsey Colloquy from 1585 to 1619 have been preserved, and are now kept in the Guille Allès Library, Guernsey[1]. They have never been published. As they shed a flood of light upon six years of Cartwright's life, they are of supreme interest and will be utilised in detail. The *Actes* show that the chief topic of discussion in the Guernsey Colloquy, particularly during 1586 and 1587, is the question of reconciliation with the Jersey brethren. The Guernsey ministers proposed an informal conference with the latter, at which to consider the Form of Discipline (of 1576), to determine whether annual Synods representing the Churches of all the islands should be held, and above all to deal finally with the charges brought against certain ministers holding office in Guernsey[2]. A joint meeting was held on the 12th of July, 1586, but did not succeed in solving the differences between the ministers of Jersey and those of Guernsey. The former apparently desired an official Synod to settle the matters in dispute; the latter thinking the time not ripe for such a Synod, and deeming it unreasonable that the accused ministers should sit therein as judges of their own doings, were anxious to refer the whole affair to a neutral body of arbiters and suggested the appointment of an arbitration court consisting of nine refugee ministers and eight refugee elders[3]. The brethren of Jersey objected to the holding of such a court in Guernsey, while the ministers of the latter island insisted on its meeting there. Numerous letters passed to and fro between the two Colloquies, but no definite result was achieved and the unsolved problem of reconciliation was shelved[4] till after the coming of Cartwright in 1595.

We have already noticed that Percival Wiburn was Chaplain at Castle Cornet in 1576. It appears that he was not continuously in Guernsey from that year onwards. The only

[1] The present writer is indebted to Major S. Carey Curtis, of St Pierre Port, for the use of his valuable transcript of these *Actes*.

[2] *Actes*, May, June, 1586.

[3] *ibid.* 6 Jan., 7 April, 1587.

[4] *ibid.* 28 Sept. 1587.

reference to him in the above *Actes* occurs in June 1586, when a certain Thomas Dickinson brought before the Colloquy the need and importance of having the Gospel preached at the Castle in English: *à raison de plusieurs personnes de la maison de monseigneur le Gouverneur et autres habitantz de l'Isle qui n'entendent la langue Francoise.* Dickinson offered his own services, but Leighton referred to the coming of *M. Wiborne, Pasteur ordinaire de l'Église du Chasteau.* Wiburn did not serve later than 1591, when (24th Sept.) Cappelain was suggested for the post. During 1594 there is no record in the *Actes* of the attendance of an English Chaplain at the Colloquy, but on the 27th of June, 1595, the Castle is represented by *un ministre et un ancien.* Cartwright is first definitely named as the minister of Castle Cornet in the Colloquy of the 26th September following, but it is probable that he was the unnamed minister mentioned in June, and as the presence of a minister from the Castle is not entered in the minutes of the Colloquy of the 11th April, it is likely that Cartwright came to Guernsey between the last date and the 27th of June. Tupper's statement[1] that Cartwright was in Guernsey in 1591 is without foundation. Throughout that year he was a prisoner in the Fleet. From 1595 onwards he attends the meetings of the Guernsey Colloquy in St Pierre Port with great regularity.

It has been suggested[2] that these *Actes* reveal the arbitrary exercise of power on the part of clerics and provide a warning to the laity against priestly domination. But it should be noticed that the majority of those who took part in the Guernsey Colloquy and were responsible for the harsh measures complained of were laymen. The very first meeting at which Cartwright is mentioned by name (26 Sept. 1595) markedly illustrates the predominance of the lay representatives of the Island Church. It was attended by six ministers and eleven elders. The Puritan Chaplain himself was accompanied by two elders from the Castle.

The first important task which Cartwright undertook was that of reconciling and uniting the Presbyteries of Jersey and

[1] Tupper, p. 350. [2] *ibid.* p. 177.

Guernsey. At the September meeting he reports to his fellow-Presbyters that he has already conferred with Edmund Snape about the long-standing problem, and that they recommend that all old scores should be wiped out and a new era of friendly cooperation inaugurated. Snape was now Wake's successor at the Castle of Mont Orgueil, Jersey. The Colloquy of Jersey received his certificate of character and status from *des Églises de la province de Northampton*, which certificate was inserted in their minute-book (28 March, 1595)[1]. The privileged position enjoyed by the Governors' Chaplains[2] and their deep interest in the extension of the Synodical Discipline, for which they had both suffered much in England, made them natural and fitting intermediaries between the estranged Presbyterian Churches of the islands. The brethren of Guernsey acquiesced in Cartwright's proposals and requested him to send a friendly message through Snape to the ministers of the sister isle. Their minute runs thus (26 Sept. 1595): *Monsieur Cartwrith ministre du Chasteau Cornet a proposé à ceste compaignie comme il est à désirer pour la gloire de Dieu et bien de ces Églises qu'il y ait une bonne réconciliation et saincte union entre les ministres et églises de ces Isles, Requérant qu'on advisast aux moyens qu'on doit tenir pour y parvenir, Assurant ladite compaignie qu'il en a conféré avec Monsr. Snap ministre du Chasteau de l'Isle de Gerzé: et qu'ilz estoyent d'avis que pour ne rien altérer, on ne parlast plus nullement des choses passées, mais qu'on usast d'une oubliance générale d'une part et d'autre. À quoy la compaignie a faict response, qu'elle sera très ayse de ladite réconciliation et union, et qu'elle la désire de tout son cœur, comme elle le fera paroistre par effect, Priant Monsieur Cartwrith d'en escrire à Monsr. Snap et l'assurer que quand les ministres de Gerzé recognoistront les ministres de Dieu et fidèles ministres du St Évangile de Jésus Christ, et qu'ilz ont esté légitemment establis ès églises de ceste Isle desquelles ilz ont charge, et donneront tesmoignage suffisant pour faire paroistre le désir qu'ilz ont que ceste réconciliation se parface les ministres de ceste Isle*

[1] Schickler, II, p. 447.

[2] A. J. Le Cras, *The Constitution of Jersey* (1857), pp. 25, 57.

leur bailleront pareil tesmoignage, pour monstrer la rondeur et intégrité de leur affection.

On the same day Snape was asked by the Jersey Colloquy to write to Cartwright regarding the reconciliation, and five members were appointed to facilitate the same. This committee consisted of MM. Parent, Snape, Masson, Olivier and Bonhomme[1]. On the 7th of November, 1595, the Jersey ministers drew up an important paper called *Advis sur la réunion du Synode des Églises de Jarsé, Guernezé, Sercq et Origny*, in which they declare in favour of annual Synods, revisal of the Form of Discipline (1576), advise a general act of oblivion with regard to bygone differences, and suggest that Cartwright should give a fraternal admonition to the Guernsey ministers requiring it, and that Snape should do likewise in Jersey: *Afin que ce présent accord ne préjudicie l'honneur de Dieu ou le salut du prochain par une dissimulation ou connivature pernicieuse aux vices, le frère M. Cartwright est chargé de donner les advertissements fraternels à ceux de Guernesey qui en auroyent besoin de quelque qualité qu'ils soient, selon sa conscience. Pareille charge est donnée au frère M. Snape pour le regard de ceux de Jarsé*[2]. The Guernsey brethren after demurring to some of their neighbours' suggestions, *e.g.* that the two Chaplains should act as censors, agreed to the main proposals[3]. They decided in their Colloquy of the 15th September, 1596, to send a deputation on the following Monday (20 Sept.) to meet the Jersey ministers in a Synod at St Helier. Cartwright and one of his elders were appointed deputies along with eight others (four ministers and four elders): *Surquoy la compaignie a esté d'avis de faire que ledit Synode soit tenu au plustost que faire se pourra, et pource faire qu'on parte de ceste Isle dès Lundy prochain 20e de ce mois et que M. Cartwrith prenne l'un de ses anciens pour venir avec luy pour le Chasteau*[4]. The long estrangement now had a definite prospect of an end. The record of this Synod was read on the 17th of December, 1596, at the Guernsey Colloquy, which decided to carry out

[1] Schickler, II, p. 448.
[2] *ibid.* II, p. 450.
[3] *ibid.* II, p. 450.
[4] *Actes*, 15 Sept. 1596.

the important proposal therein contained, viz., that the existing Form of Discipline should be revised: *Le Synode dernièrement tenu à Gerzé estant leu, a esté advisé qu'on s'employra de partiquer l'article y contenu touchant la reveue de la discipline*.

A year afterwards the long awaited Synod representing the Churches of the Channel Islands met in Guernsey and revised the Form of Discipline of 1576. The new Form issued by this Synod is entitled: *La Discipline Ecclésiastique, comme elle a esté practiquée depuis la Réformation de l'Église, par les Ministres, Anciens et Diacres des Isles de Guernezé, Jerzé, Serk et Aurigny, arrestée par l'authorité, et en la présence de Messieurs les Gouverneurs desdites Iles, au Synode tenu à Guernezé le 28e jour de Juin l'an* 1576. *Et depuis reveue par lesdits Ministres et Anciens, et confermée par mesdits Seigneurs les Gouverneurs au Synode tenu à Guernezé les* 11, 12, 13, 14, 15, *et* 17 *jours d'Octobre l'an* 1597. The days on which the Synod met were from the 11th to the 17th of October, exclusive of the 16th, which was a Sunday; the place of meeting was in Guernsey, not Jersey, as Heylyn[1] and Neal[2], etc. affirm. We have already noted that Heylyn, Neal and others have also mistaken the year, putting 1577 instead of 1597.

A comparison of the two Forms of Discipline is valuable. The First is diffuse, and is concerned with the establishment of a new regime; the Second is concise, and deals with the remodelling of a Presbyterian organisation already in existence. The First has the marks of the transition from the Roman Catholic era to that of the Reformation, *e.g.* it lays down regulations for the admission of ex-priests. Both are polities of an Established Church which was dependent upon the favour of the civil authorities of the islands, *e.g.* the approval of the Governor was required for the election of office-bearers. The First Form is printed by Schickler[3]; the Second, a copy of which is in the *Harleian MSS.*[4] has been published several times in an English translation[5], and in the

[1] *A.R.* lib. VII, § 8.
[2] I, p. 271.
[3] III, pp. 311 ff.
[4] No. 3998, ff. 203 ff.
[5] 1642; 1656 in Heylyn's *Survey*; 1815 in W. Berry's *History of the Island of Guernsey*.

original French by G. E. Lee, in *Discipline Ecclésiastique des Iles de la Manche* in 1885. The Second Form is divided into XX Chapters, which deal with office-bearers, services, sacraments and courts of the Church in much the same fashion as the Puritan Book of Discipline. The whole document is a compendious directory of Presbyterian Church Government. The statement[1] that it does not refer to Presbyteries is singularly misleading, as it mentions the Colloquies, which correspond to modern Presbyteries, and these, as the present portion of our history shows, played an all-important part in the activities of the Island Churches. A study of the affinities of this Form of Discipline with similar documents drawn up by the English Puritans, the Scottish Reformers, and the Reformed Churches of the Continent, especially the French, is eminently worth while and long overdue[2]. We merely observe that two leading English Puritans, Cartwright and Snape, had a share in its composition and that it represents the ideal which they and their associates had sought to establish in England, but in vain.

Besides taking a share in the reconciliation of the two Colloquies, Cartwright also took a prominent part in the ordinary work of his own Colloquy. On the 2nd of April, 1596, the members discussed, as true Puritans would, the dancing and drinking that prevailed in the island, *les dances et desbauches qui se font ordinairement et de jour et de nuict*, and directed one of the company to beg Cartwright, who was absent from this meeting, to accompany him in an appeal to the Governor to regulate the alleged disorders: *Monsr. Roullées est chargé de prier Monsr. Cartwrith de l'accompaigner, et qu'eux deux le remonstrent à Monseigneur le Gouverneur pour faire commandement à Messieurs de la Justice d'y donner ordre.* Again Cartwright was asked to act as intermediary between the ministers and the Governor at a special conference (11 July, 1597) held by order of Leighton at Castle Cornet to consider the fitness of Jeremiah Valpy for the ministry.

[1] Odgers, p. 23.

[2] A valuable contribution to the above study has been given by Mrs W. W. D. Campbell in her *Discipline or Book of Order of the Reformed Churches of France* (1924).

Cartwright was requested to report the ministers' favourable opinion to the Governor: *Et pourtant la compaignie a prié Monsr. Cartwrith ministre du Chasteau de rapporter l'advis d'icelle a Monseigneur le Gouverneur, pour envoyer ledit frère Valpy proposer la parole de Dieu le Dimanche ensuyvant en la paroisse où il luy plairra l'applasser, pour cognoistre comment il leur sera agréable.* At an extraordinary meeting of the Colloquy (20 July, 1597) Leighton intimated that he had accepted the ministers' verdict regarding Valpy and that he had sent him to preach in the parish du Castel: *Monseigneur le Gouverneur remonstra à toute le compaignie comme suyvant l'advis par luy receu de Monsr. Cartwrith de la part cestedite compaignie touchant la suffisance de M. Jeremie Valpy....*

In 1599 there were evidently not enough ministers to supply the charges in Guernsey, the dearth being caused by the issue of the Edict of Nantes in the previous year, which gave the Protestants of France their long lost liberty, and induced some of the French ministers in the island to return home. The Governor took the matter in hand and expressed his mind to the Colloquy through Cartwright and Arthur Harris, the representative elder from the Castle, whereupon the Colloquy (19 Oct. 1599) decided to appoint certain ministers to the work of two parishes each: *Suivant la proposition declarée par Monsieur Cartwrig et Mr Atur Harris touchant la volonté de Monseigneur le Gouverneur pour l'accommodement et soulagement tant des ministres que des Églises de ceste Isle est advisé par toute ceste Compagnie que désormais Mr Jeremie Valpy exercera son ministère ès deux paroisses du Valle et de St Samson et Mr Jaques Roulée ès deux paroisses du Castel et de St André, et Mr Dominique Sicard ès deux paroisses de la Forest et de St Martin iusques à ce qu'autrement soit pourveu à la Forest.*

At the last meeting of the Colloquy for 1599 (28 Dec.) Cartwright was not present because of illness: *Pour le Chasteau le ministre absent à cause qu'il est malade et pourtant excusé*, but his elder Wm. Taylor, gentleman porter of the Castle, was in attendance, and Cartwright sent to his brethren three items of business which were laid before them by M. Roullée. The first was a suggestion that a Fast should be held in the various Parishes: *Monsieur Roullée au nom de Monsieur Cartqrith a proposé ou remonstré en ceste compaignie trois choses la première qu'il seroit bon qu'on advisast de célébrer un Jeusne par les paroisses les plus comodes èsquelles le peuple se peust plus aisément assembler pour ouyr la prédication de l'évangille et assister aux prières publicques.* It is interesting to note that one of the reasons for the Fast was the troubles in Ireland. The Colloquy agreed to the proposal, and one of the company was appointed to request Cartwright to write to Snape, that through him the Jersey ministers might be asked to participate in the Fast: *Pour le regard de la première proposition à cause des troubles qui se sont derechef eslevées en Irlande, et de la dificulté des temps et saisons où nous sommes maintenant et autres diverses causes Il a esté accordé et arresté en ceste compagnie qu'il se célébrera un Jeusne ès paroisses les plus comodes, le dernier mercredy du prochain mois de Janvier, et attendant Me Cartwright sera prié au nom de ceste compagnie par quelqun d'icelle, que s'il escrit quelques lettres à Monsieur Snap ministre Anglois de l'Isle de Gersay de l'advertir de notre Ste. résolution afin qu'il en face aussi participant les autres frères ministres de la dite Isle pour qu'ils se joignent avec nous faisant au dit jour le mesme exercice.*

The next matter brought by Cartwright before the Colloquy was the offer of two Jersey ministers (Effard and Milet) to let their sons, if God willed, enter the ministry and take charges in Guernsey, if the ministers of the latter island would undertake to maintain the boys and provide for their education. The Colloquy, which had already under its care several young men (among them Jean de la Place, who lived with Cartwright), who intended to become ministers, willingly acceded to the request and enjoined the elders to make the necessary practical arrangements.

Cartwright's third "proposition" related to an Englishman called Sexton. The Chaplain, having heard that Sexton was guilty of immorality, asked the Colloquy whether he should admit him to Communion. The Colloquy ordered investigations to be made in the parishes where Sexton previously resided and in that of St Pierre Port where he was now living. Subsequent *Actes* (14 March, 27 June, 1600) show that Sexton was found guilty and was obliged to confess his sin publicly. Not only did these Guernsey Presbyterians take a deep interest in the education of youth; they also dealt with moral offences with the utmost zeal and rigour.

At the March meeting of the Colloquy in the next year Cartwright again consulted his brethren about an English defaulter. They decreed that the offender, named Hughes, should confess his fault and deliver his credentials, which he said he had from the Bishop of Hereford, to the Consistory of the Church of the Castle for their examination.

The surveillance of the Island Presbyterians over all the doings of those within their bounds is again illustrated by the case of two Englishmen, which Cartwright brought before the Colloquy on the 3rd of April, 1601. Both of them had belonged to his Church. One, "Jean Start Davide," had not attended the services there for more than two years; Cartwright had not seen the other for several months. During their absence they had not taken Communion. He had told them that they must appear before the Colloquy and explain their behaviour. This they did and were exhorted to attach themselves to a Church, which they submissively promised to do. But because of their failure to attend Church the Colloquy enjoined them to make confession of their fault to the kirk-session or Consistory of Castle Cornet, and because their offensive non-churchgoing was well known it was decreed that their confession should be publicly announced. This instance of the exercise of disciplinary power furnishes an example of the absolutism that characterised the Presbyterianism, which Cartwright advocated and with which he was now associated, and reveals what in our days of liberty is considered one of the blemishes of his system. It illustrates the desire of the Puritans to keep the Church of Christ pure, and their dependence upon Geneva for the machinery, which they thought was adapted to this purpose. The full particulars of the case are as follows: *Sur la proposition faite par Monsieur Cartwrigth asçavoir qu'il y a deux hommes qui se sont départis de son église, et qu'il y en a un qui n'est point allé au presche anglois qui se fait au Chasteau il y a plus de deux ans* (Margin: Jean Start Davide) *et quant à l'autre qui ne luy a point veu l'espace d'un cart d'an, et qu'iceux n'ont point aussi durant ce temps là, fait la Cêne, et qu'à cause de cela, il les a advertis qu'ils ayent à leur trouver en ceste compagnie pour rendre raison de ce qui les a empeschés de continuer ès susdits exercices. Iceux selon l'advertissement qu'ils avoyent eu s'y sont trouvés, et après les avoir ouys, ont esté exorté de se renger à quelque église, à quoy ils se sont submis, l'un a promis de se renger à l'église de ceste Ville, et l'autre que derechef il retournera à celle du Chasteau, et qu'il y continuera le temps qu'il sera en ceste Isle, mais à cause de la faute qu'ils ont faite, de s'estre sy long temps absentes des presches, ceste compagnie est d'advis qu'ils feront tant l'un que l'autre recognoissance de leur faute au Consistoire du Chasteau, et pource que leur faute est cognue entre ceux de l'église, leur susdite recognoissance faite au lieu susdit sera aussi par après publiée à l'église.*

Besides the above-noted references to Cartwright's labours as a member of the Guernsey Colloquy, there are several other available items of interest connected with his sojourn at Castle Cornet. The allusions to his family are few, but there is mention of his son Samuel in the narrative, given in full by Tupper[1], of the tragic drowning accident that took place on the 18th of August, 1597. Samuel with three other young gentlemen, Thomas Leighton, Peter Carey, Walter St John, and their tutor, Isaac Daubeney, accompanied the Governor and his party on a deer-hunting expedition to the island of Herm, and it was on this occasion that Daubeney and St John were drowned while bathing. We learn from one of the *Actes* (10 Nov. 1598), that Cartwright had in his house a student intending to enter the ministry named Jean de la Place. Cartwright still kept in touch with some of his old friends in England. One of his letters of this period is addressed to Michael Hicks[2]. It is a reply to a request of Hicks for a form of prayer, apparently for private use. Cartwright accedes to the request and along with his letter sends the prayer desired.

[1] p. 173. [2] 20 Sept. 1895; App. XXXVII.

He modestly depreciates his own composition, is sure that there are sufficient excellent prayers already in print, but commends Burghley's secretary for his pious interest.

Other letters of this time are known to us through the use made of them by Clarke. From these we gather that Cartwright was requested by Leighton, who desired a tutor for his children, evidently as a successor to Daubeney, to write to Laurence Chaderton to send a suitable person and that William Bradshaw was sent. Bradshaw developed a close friendship with Cartwright at Castle Cornet, and maintained a correspondence with the Puritan till the latter's death[1]. On the 5th of September, 1598, Cartwright in a letter to Sir Francis Hastings commended the tutor's splendid character and conversation[2]. Bradshaw did not stay long in Guernsey; he accepted the tutorship as an interim post, and was waiting for the completion of the building of Sidney College, of which he had been appointed a Fellow. On the 5th of December, 1598, when Bradshaw returned to England, Cartwright wrote to Chaderton thanking him in behalf of Sir Thomas and Lady Leighton for the loan of the tutor, who had given eminent satisfaction. On the same day he wrote in similar terms to Montague, the Master of Sidney College[3]. Early in the following year Cartwright wrote to Bradshaw congratulating him on his escape from drowning[4]. These letters of Cartwright are quoted by Clarke in his *Life of Bradshaw*, in which it is stated that Bradshaw used at divine service a form of prayer, which he modified to suit special occasions, "which he affirmed also to have been Master Cartwright's practice."[5]

Among the *Cecil MSS*. at Hatfield House there is a letter sent by Cartwright from Castle Cornet in September, 1598, to the Earl of Essex[6]. It is apparently but one of a series of letters sent by the Puritan to his Lordship. "In experience," he writes, "of miscariadg of letters through Sir Thomas his absenc from hence, who had alwaies given safeconduit of that I wrote unto your right honorable lordship: I have forborn to write." He now breaks the silence in order to

[1] Clarke, pp. 93, 96.
[2] *ibid*. p. 97.
[3] *ibid*. p. 97.
[4] *ibid*. p. 98.
[5] *ibid*. p. 130.
[6] *Cecil MSS*. LXIV, 69.

congratulate Essex on his appointment to the Chancellorship of Cambridge University and exhorts him to use his gifts and opportunities for the glory of God, Who has made him "in sondry respects of honor and office, a father of his people." "Let the Chronicles of our land be perused," says Cartwright, "and I thinck it will hardly be found, that there hath bene any subject especially of those yeares your L. is yet come unto, clothed with so much honor, and girded with so much authoritie, as yow are." This distinction is due to God, Who "hath put into the hart of our graciouse Queen to exalt your head in honor, as far above other her subjects as Saull was in stature of bodie hygher then all the rest of the men of the land." Essex ought to strive to excel in service even as he excels in honour. Cartwright urges him to give such obedience to God as corresponds with God's "incomparable and peerles munificence," and beseeches him to bear in mind the life to come and its rewards, compared with which the privileges of this life are but as a rattle parents give their children to play with. Cartwright thanks the Earl for his "honorable assistance of the poor Hospitall of Warwick in the last Parlament" and asks him to continue his favour to this institution "now (as I hear) in danger to be utterly spoyled, and that by meanes of some, that should have bene the pillars to uphould it." He points out that "yt is a place for the sutes whereof (it having bene alwaies litigiouse sithence the death of our moest noble Founder) I have spent whole yeares in an utter vacation from all studie." "I have consumed," he continues, "of myne own stock to the valew of 100 li. or thereabout, which the hospitall upon the Audit of certen Gentlemen them selves and I chose, have bene constrayned to confesse, although my expences have bene much greater, as I am hable to make good proof which in respect of the extreme povertie of the house I pursued not knowing nothing, when or how I shall be satisfied of that they have yeelded to pay, not to speak of that I have consumed myself in part, having gotten in the folowing the busynes thereof deseases I shall (in all likelihood) carie to my grave. Therefore it would greive me much to see the worthy remembrance of our noble Founder (beside my own poor travails) to be not onely (touching that monument) blotted out, but made a skorn to his enemies, who by this means will insult upon the dead, as having bestowed in almes that ether was not his, or which he never ment should be enjoyed of the poor. Some of thinjurie will redound to her excellent Matie: there being very few of the poor of that house, which are not of her Gracis preesentment and placing there. And if there shall be found any qualified according to the statute of the howse, in whose hand the cause of the poor Hospitall may fynde further frendship then in myne: to such a one will I willinglie resign albeit it be the best stay of my living, when I depart from hence; where my abode (as your L. may easely know) is uncertain." Cartwright then informs Essex that during his absence he has entrusted "a godly learned minister one Mr Lord" with the charge of the Hospital and commends his deputy to the Earl's favour and patronage.

Cartwright's residence in Guernsey came to an end in the summer of 1601. His last appearance at the Colloquy is recorded on the 26th of June of that year. At the same meeting Amias de Carteret was present as the Lieutenant of the new Governor, Lord Zouch. At the next Colloquy (21 Sept. 1601) the minister representing the Castle is Daniel Dolbel. For six years the veteran champion of English Puritanism had enjoyed a congenial environment. He lived in a climate which, as Heylyn[1] noted during his visit to Guernsey some years later, "is very healthfull, as may be well seen in the long lives both of men and women," and he carried on the work of an active and leading minister of a Presbyterian Church. He had a flock of his own, that consisted of the Governor, his family and suite, and the soldiers of the garrison, among whom, according to Clarke[2] he performed "some efficacious and gracious work." He acted as moderator of the Castle Cornet Consistory: he served as a Presbyter in a Colloquy and a Synod. He put into practice without let or hindrance the principles for which he had suffered so much and so long in England and, his position as English Chaplain

[1] *Survey*, p. 297. [2] p. 96.

being a privileged one, he had an authority that the ordinary ministers of Guernsey did not enjoy. During his sojourn in Guernsey Cartwright realised in a measure his life-long dream and did much to strengthen and consolidate a Presbyterian Church, which lasted till the Restoration.

Cartwright returned to Warwick, where he spent the last two years of his life as an invalid. "In his old age," says Clarke[1], "he was much troubled with the stone and gout, which much empaired his strength, yet would he not intermit his labours, but continued preaching when many times he could scarce creep up into the pulpit."

It is sometimes said that his closing years were spent in comparative luxury, that he "grew rich and had great maintenance to live upon and was honoured as a patriarch by many of that profession."[2] It is doubtless true that the lord of a manor and the friend of so many influential patrons spent his last days in considerable comfort, but to lay stress on this fact is to follow too much in the wake of Sutcliffe, and may tempt one to ignore the worthiest features of the Puritan's manner of life, for instance, his zealous labours in God's service at a time when his strength was ebbing away.

The allegation that before his decease Cartwright lamented the fact that he had troubled the Church, and wished he could lead his life over again in order "to testify to the world the dislike he had of his own former ways"[3] is a half-truth. He changed the accent of emphasis from the destructive attitude of a revolting critic to that of a loyal, constructive, and friendly reformer. His new policy was doubtless influenced by the views of Heidelberg divines, confirmed by the emergence of Brownism, ineradicably fixed by the excesses of Marprelate, and dictated by his experience of the futility of any other course. His friends recognised his change of policy. Edmund Chapman writing to him about the matter apparently after the Marprelate episode says, "Where may I better begyne than at the cause of your smarte, which was

[1] p. 373.
[2] J. Harrington, *Briefe View* (quoted by *D.N.B.* art. "Cartwright"), p. 8.
[3] Henry Yelverton, Epistle prefixed to Morton's *Episcopacy Justified*.

not any affinity you ever had with that marre matter marten, for I am a witnes beside a thowsand other, what small pleasure you ever tooke in such inventions: but your earnest and open profession of grieff for the wante of perfecte comlines and bewty in this English spouse of your maister, which you desired and laboured according to the best of your skill and power to have made more pure and amiable in his eie." Cartwright had evidently uttered his regret that his endeavours have been vain and misunderstood, and Chapman tries to comfort him with the thought that "the bridegroome will not soe much waighe, what you have done for him as what you mente to doe, nor how your endevors were taken by his other servantes, as how they were to be taken." Cartwright has apparently written to his friend confessing the unwisdom of certain features of his reforming effort and Chapman replies: "And what though now after a second vew of your proceedinge in this great cause of Church goverment, yow find that some thinges are not uniustly found fault withall, yet oughte not that much to afflicte yow, seeing yow are not the first man of fame, lerninge and piety, that have confessed and retracted some error, if the substantiall and mayne pointes of your worke stande...if the worke were to begyne againe yow would mend some peece of the matter or manner of yt" and he assures Cartwright that he has no cause to repent that he took the cause in hand and that by him "as an instrument some good thinges have bene put forwarde, some evell discovered and begon to be reformed."[1] It is true, therefore, that Cartwright modified his tactics, not indeed in the manner of a death-bed penitent, but many years before he died. We have noticed how he dropped the controversial pen, but we have also observed his constant loyalty to Presbyterian ideals. To abandon a method is different from renunciation of the principles it was meant to serve. It is certainly wrong to state that he ultimately returned to the Church[2]. He never left it, and he never forsook his desire to presbyterianise it. There is

[1] *P.M.* p. 77.

[2] H. S. Skeats and C. S. Miall, *History of the Free Churches of England* (1891), p. 19.

abundant reason to believe that Cartwright remained to the end of his days a staunch advocate of Presbyterianism. In the year of his death he allied himself with the Puritan party, whose hopes were revived by the accession of James to the throne and by them he was regarded as a leading representative. On his journey into England in April, 1603, the King was not allowed to forget Cartwright. The ministers of the Synod of Lothian met him near Haddington and among other things petitioned him "for releefe of good brethrein of the ministrie of England." To this request he replied "that he was not mindid at the first to urge anie alteration. As for Mr Cartwright, Mr Travers, and some others, he understood they were at freedome. He would show favour to honest men, but not to Anabaptists."[1] After the arrival of James in England the Puritans attempted to win from him a promise of Church reform. They presented their case in several petitions, the chief of which was the so-called millenary petition[2]. In May the Puritan leaders issued to their associates a manifesto called *Advice tending to Reformation*[3], which recommends that "there must be sundrie petitions of ministers of sundrie partes, and yet but fewe in a petition to avoyde the suspition of conspiracie, and the petitions to varie in woords, but agree in the desire of reformacon to be according to the woord, and all reformed Churches about us: provided they do not expresslie desire the removing of bishops." The letter book of Robert Smart[4] contains several of the petitions that were subsequently drawn up, and among them one which was written by Cartwright himself in pursuance of the directions of the Puritan ministers of Northamptonshire (Barebon, Wight, Smart, Spicer, etc.), who decided (21 July, 1603) that Justice Yelverton should be solicited to draw up a petition, which he and the other gentlemen of the county would sign and present to the King[5].

Cartwright, a personal friend of Yelverton's was asked to approach him and did so in a letter from Warwick on the

[1] Calderwood, VI, p. 222.
[2] Usher, *Reconstr.* p. 290.
[3] *Add. MSS.* 28571, f. 199.
[4] *Sloane MSS.* 271.
[5] *ibid.* 271, f. 20 *b*.

12th of November[1]. He depreciates his fitness as a mediator: "for what am I? or who am I? yt I should mediate this matter more then other?" He commends his brethren for seeking the support of such a suitable man as Yelverton, one who has for many years been sincerely interested "in the trueth." The object of the letter is to move the Knight to "take the paynes to drawe a supplication to his Matie in the behalfe of the Nobilitie and Gentrye of that shire, as for a reformation generally of thinges amisse, so more particularly, for the removeall of th'ignorant, idle & unresident ministerye, etc." Cartwright encloses a survey of abuses, probably one of the schedules distributed for the sake of uniformity in their demands by the Puritan organisers. It is noteworthy that Cartwright does not specify in his enumeration of abuses the existence of the Episcopal system, but that omission does not signify that he had ceased to believe in Presbyterianism, but that he was merely falling into line with the Puritan policy expressed in the above-mentioned *Advice*, which counselled petitioners not to express their desire for "the removing of bishops." The further reformation, which included the abolition of the Episcopate, could not be secured at one fell swoop and it was deemed advisable to seek, as the thin end of the wedge, redress of the most obvious grievances first.

One of the demands put forward by the Puritans was for a Conference. This was one of the requests that James could most readily grant without prejudice to his declared or unexpressed policy. It was arranged that representatives of the Episcopal and Puritan parties should meet in November, but because of an infectious epidemic in London the Conference was postponed till January, when it was held at Hampton Court[2]. It is not generally known that Cartwright was one of the ministers originally selected to represent the Puritan party. Calderwood[3] furnishes a most interesting paragraph regarding his selection, and the cold reception he met with at the hands of the King: "The good professors in England were putt in hope of a good beginning of reforma-

[1] App. XXXVIII. [2] Soames, p. 530. [3] VI, pp. 235–6.

tioun; and so muche was pretended when the conference was appointed, but nothing lesse meant, yea, rather, under colour of conference, to procure farther confirmatioun to the corruptiouns and abuses. Good Mr Cartwright, one of the number that was appointed for the conference, was hardlie taikin up by the King, when he went to him to salute him. The King said, 'What, are yee the man that wrote against the Reverend Father, the Bishop of Canterburie?' The honest man tooke this reproofe verie heavilie; and forseing there was no hope of reformatioun, but rather a confirmatioun of all abuses, departed this life before the holding of the conference. What sinceritie was there meant, when, for the sincere partie, were nominated two that were verie corrupt? Appearandlie, they were nominated onlie to be spyes, and to prevaricat." Cartwright's name also appears in a State Paper[1], which furnishes a list of the Bishops and ministers at first proposed for the Conference. The ministers suggested are as follows:

"1. Doctor Rainolds in Oxfoord.
2. Doctor Spark in Buckinghamshere.
3. Doctor Feild in Hampshire or Mr Hilderschame in Lecestershyre.
4. Mr Cartwright at Varrik.
5. Mr Chattertone in Cambridge.
6. Mr Fenne in Varvickshyre at Coventrie in place of Mr Iretone.
7. Mr Knewstubbis in Suffolk."

In this list Cartwright's name is scored through, for before the Hampton Court Conference met he had died. Four of his comrades, Spark, Reynolds, Knewstub, and Laurence Chaderton, were summoned by the King to represent the Puritans at Hampton Court and there they proved themselves, as Bancroft observed, "Cartwrightes schollers,"[2] and made it apparent to the King that most of the English Puritans were Presbyterians at heart. The King, noting that they regarded Presbyterianism as a panacea for the ills of the

[1] *S.P. Dom. Jac. I*, vi, No. 15 endorsed "ecclesiastical Persons appointed for the Conference."

[2] *Harl. MSS.* 824, f. 32.

Church of England, said that they aimed at a Scottish Presbytery, which, in his opinion "as well agreeth with a Monarchy, as God and the Devil."[1] If James and Bancroft were unjustified in their lighthearted and arrogant treatment of the Puritan delegates, they were correct in their diagnosis of the principles that underlay the ministers' grievances. The tenets of Cartwright had not been sown on unreceptive soil. Although dead, he yet spoke with no uncertain voice.

The best account of Cartwright's last days is given by Clarke[2], who tells us that the aged Puritan preached his last sermon on Christmas Sunday, 1603, on the strangely appropriate text, Eccl. xii. 7, "Then shall the dust return to earth, and the spirit shall return to God who gave it." He died two days afterwards (Tuesday, 27th Dec. 1603). In the morning of the day of his death he spent two hours on his knees in private prayer, "in which (as he told his wife) he found wonderful and unutterable joy and comfort, God giving him a glimpse of heaven before he came to it." A few hours afterwards he peacefully passed away in the sixty-eighth year of his age. His funeral sermon was preached by his friend John Dod[3]. To Dod and Arthur Hildersham Cartwright left his papers "to peruse and publish what they thought fit."[4] As both these friends lived for many years afterwards (Hildersham died in 1632 and Dod in 1645) they would hand down many authentic memories of Cartwright, some of which probably reached and were preserved by their contemporary, Samuel Clarke.

Feeling "through the gowte and the stoane" that he was lying upon his weak, rather than his sick bed, Cartwright made his last will and testament on the 10th of May, 1603[5]. In it he expressed his desire to be buried in the churchyard of the place in which he should die "withoute pompe and superstition used in the Popish Sinagogues in times past." Of his public bequests one is of twenty marks to help poor scholars in Cambridge, who intend to enter the ministry,

[1] W. Barlow, "The Sum and Substance of the Conference...at Hampton Court," printed in *The Phenix*, 1707, p. 169.

[2] p. 373. [3] *ibid.* pp. 373, 404. [4] *ibid.* p. 381.

[5] App. XXXIX.

the Masters of Sidney and Emmanuel Colleges to disburse the money. Scholars of Trinity, St John's and Sidney Colleges are to be preferred to others. A sum of forty shillings is left to the poor of Warwick. An annual grant of forty shillings is also left towards the upkeep of his brother William. Twenty years before Archbishop Parker wrote to Burghley about this brother[1], and described him as a vain young stripling, who was the victim of grandiose delusions, *e.g.* that he was the rightful heir of the lands of the realm. William had been brought by the Dean of Westminster to Parker, who committed him to the Gatehouse, and proposed to have him removed to Bridewell, Bedlam or elsewhere to be kept at the charge of young Martin or other friends of his, until his wits returned. He did not wish to deal hardly with the young man lest the precisians might think that the severe treatment was vindictively meted out to him, because he was the brother of a man whose teaching had greatly troubled the realm. Cartwright now makes provision for this unfortunate kinsman on condition that "he be kepte from wandring and rainginge abroad." He also mentions his brother John, to whom he leaves forty shillings and his best cloak. Cartwright has now two married daughters, Mary and Anne, whose husbands are Andrew Wilmer and William Lockey. An interesting item respecting the latter is given in the Visitations of Hertfordshire[2]: "William Lockey, of Holmes in the Parish of Ridge, co. Hert., ob. 1 April, 1662, by accident = Anne, da. of Thomas Cartwright, of Warwick, Mr of the Erle of Lesters Hospital there." At the date mentioned this couple had four children, the third of whom, Martha, married "Jo. Grabrand, of London, mercer." At the date of his will Cartwright has a daughter named Martha to whom he bequeathes "for her better advauncement in marriage the somme of two hundred pounds." The name of his son Samuel, who is still a minor, also appears in the will. Cartwright is anxious that he should become a minister and to help his education provides a legacy of twenty pounds. The four children are each to be given a ring of the value

[1] *Parker Corresp.* p. 469. [2] *Harl. Soc.* p. 152.

of ten shillings. The residue of the Puritan's estate is left to his loving and faithful wife Alice. Wilmer and Lockey are appointed executors. One of the witnesses, Hercules Cleveley, is apparently to be identified with the Puritan of that name who, as minister of Wroxall, took part in the Warwickshire meetings attended by Cartwright. The will was proved in the prerogative court of Canterbury on the 23rd of February, 1603–4. It should be noted that the version of it hung up in the Chapel of the Leicester Hospital, Warwick, is a greatly abridged copy.

From the will of Cartwright's widow, made 5th Nov. 1614 and proved 11th March 1616–7[1], we gather that she left Warwick and made her new home in Totteridge, Herts, and that her daughter Martha married Robert Woodrof. She appoints her three sons-in-law the executors of her will.

Cartwright, says J. B. Marsden[2], "is one of the few men whose life and personal character still interest posterity...and angry writers have not yet ceased by turns to defend and assail his memory." Not in the spirit of the partisan but of the dispassionate research student we have endeavoured to trace his career. We have unearthed many new facts and have sought to fill up the blanks and disentangle the chronological inaccuracies that occur in the pages of his biographers. In making an estimate of his character and worth it is not so easy to preserve an unbiased attitude. The believer in Puritanism and Presbyterianism is bound to have sympathies with Cartwright, which turn to aversion in the Anglo-Catholic. Neal and Brook, accordingly, present a description of the man that is at variance with the one given by Paule and Heylyn. As a result of our researches we have accumulated a mass of information which helps us to steer between the Scylla of idolatry and the Charybdis of hostility. We also take Clarke as a sympathetic guide, who, although liable to err regarding the sequence of events in Cartwright's life, had an opportunity unrivalled among his biographers, of learning the truth respecting his personal character. He also provides us with an engraved portrait[3], the origin of which is

[1] App. XL. [2] *History of the Early Puritans*, 3rd ed. (1860), p. 71.
[3] *v.* Frontispiece.

unknown[1], which shows us Cartwright as a grave, bearded, typical divine of his age[2].

Sutcliffe tried to stigmatise Cartwright as a self-seeking hypocrite. This blot is wiped out by Clarke, who says[3]: "he was far from seeking after great places or great things in the world, and for riches he sought them not, yea he rejected many opportunities whereby he might have enriched himself; his manner was, when he had good summes of gold sent him, to take only one piece, least he should seem to slight his friends kindnesse, and to send back the rest with a thankfull acknowledgement of their love, and his acceptance of it, professing that for that condition wherein God had set him, he was as well furnished as they for their high and great places." Clarke[4] also gives two illustrations of his superiority to the lure of money: "When the Earle of Leicester offered him the Provostship of Eaton Colledge[5], saying, that it was a hundred pounds a year more then enough, besides the conveniency of the place, Master Cartwright answered, that the hundred pounds more then enough was enough for him," and when in the Fleet "he had thirty pounds sent to him from a noble friend, of which he took but ten shillings, returning the rest with many thanks to the donor." Cartwright's diligence as a student is unquestioned. "He continued," says Clarke[6], "his diligence and assiduity in his studies even in his old age, and his usual manner was to rise at two, three, and foure a clock at the latest, both summer and winter, notwithstanding his bodily infirmities were such, that he was forced to study continually kneeling upon his knees." His piety was that of a sincere and fervent Puritan: "He was frequent in prayer every day, and in his younger years hath risen many times in the night to seek out private places to pray in. And as his labours were very great

[1] *v.* H. Bromley, *A Catalogue of Engraved British Portraits* (1793), p. 34.

[2] A close examination of the painting (G. 6) in Dr Williams's Library obliges us to discredit the tradition that alleged it to be a portrait of Cartwright. It is neither a reproduction of Clarke's nor is his a copy of it. Its subject appears to have flourished in the first part of the seventeenth century.

[3] p. 372.

[4] p. 370.

[5] This offer is questioned, *A. C.* II, 363.

[6] p. 372.

in the work of the ministry, so it pleased the Lord to make them very successful for the conversion and confirmation of many, and for terrour and restraint unto others." That he was not a sour and repellent Puritan is evidenced by the mutual constancy displayed in his numerous friendships, and by the affectionate terms in which Loftus expressly spoke of him we conclude that he was a lovable person. Even Whitgift said "I love the man."[1] That he and Whitgift were on terms of amity in their last years[2] is quite likely, but does not mean any renunciation of his fundamental principles. That he was impulsive, and wanting in the self-command and judgment essential in a leader[3] is not borne out by our investigations. On the other hand, he stands out as one, whose opinion remained substantially the same throughout his life, and whose views on matters ecclesiastical and otherwise were regarded as oracular by a considerable body of Puritans, whom Bancroft[4] calls "a company of Apostles, and Cartwright their Christ." He was looked upon as one who ranked with the world's most illustrious and famous men by foreign exiles in England, *quique non dubitant eum cum iis conferre quorum tam illustris est apud externas nationes et pervagata fama*[5]. He was the highly esteemed friend of many Continental men of learning. His friendship with Beza and his correspondence with Drusius have already been mentioned. We find that in his later years he did not lose touch with Franciscus Junius of Heidelberg[6]. Clarke[7] informs us that "he was sent to from divers eminent Divines beyond the seas, wherein they craved his advice for the direction of young men in the method of their studies, as also in the behalf of the Churches in general, for his counsel in regulating their proceedings in the waitiest affairs." There is no doubt that Cartwright was a man of outstanding personality. From the time when he disputed before Elizabeth to the day of his death he proved himself more than an average Puritan. Froude calls him a genius; he is certainly

[1] *Sec. Parte*, I, p. 216.
[2] Paule, p. 364. Fuller, *C. H.* bk X, sect. i, §§ 8, 9.
[3] *v. D.N.B.*
[4] *Survay*, p. 377.
[5] *v.* App. III.
[6] *v.* Hessels, II, p. 835.
[7] p. 370.

entitled to be called a great man. His brave stand as a Professor, the honoured and influential position held by him in Geneva, Antwerp, Middelburg, and the Channel Islands, the leading rôle played by him as a defender and organiser of Puritanism, the fact that he was singled out by the Queen for special disfavour and by the High Commission for particular examination, all these point to Cartwright's right to be regarded as one of the eminent Elizabethans.

His eminence was due in a large measure to his eloquence, but his more lasting reputation rests upon his writings. His controversial works are only a small portion of his output. By their nature they contain much of ephemeral interest, and by the advent of Hooker and the acceptance on the part of Presbyterians of other than Cartwrightian arguments in favour of their polity, they have lost much of their value. But in their day no pro-Presbyterian writings were regarded as weightier and for long they left their stamp upon Disciplinarian propaganda. The widely accepted and probably correct opinion that Cartwright had an important share in the composition of the Puritan Book of Discipline and the Second Form of Discipline adopted in the Channel Islands, must be taken into account when these documents are considered. A translation of the Book of Discipline entitled *A Directory of Church-government* appeared in 1644–5, at the time when the Westminster Assembly was in session. At that time there was a recrudescence of Cartwrightian ideas and the task of examining the influence of these, of the Directory, and of the Channel Islands Second Form of Discipline, a translation of which was issued in 1642, upon the Presbyterianism then in vogue, and particularly upon the Westminster Directory of Church Government, still calls for fulfilment. The sub-title of the Puritan Directory states that it was "found in the study of the most accomplished Divine, Mr Thomas Cartwright, after his decease, and reserved to be published for such a time as this." Had it been preserved by Cartwright's friend, John Dod, who died in 1645? Professor A. F. Mitchell[1] is far out of the true reckoning when he

[1] *The Westminster Assembly* (1883), p. 52.

says that a copy of it was found in Cartwright's study when he was arrested in 1585. He had no study of his own then, and Travers was at that time engaged in the formulation of the first draft of the Book. The *Directory* was "Published by Authority" and was entered at Stationers' Hall on the 11th of February, 1644–5. The entry runs thus: "Entred, under the hands of Master Cranford and Master Whitaker, warden, a booke called A directory of Church goverm^t practized by the first Nonconformists in the dayes of Queene Elizabeth, written by Mr Tho: Cartwright."[1] The possessors of the book evidently regarded it as the work of Cartwright, but whether they meant that he composed the original or only the translation is not clear. At any rate the publication of the work at a time when Parliament and the Assembly of Divines were busily engaged with the consideration of the establishment of Presbyterianism is extremely significant, and it would be of great interest to discover how far they made use of it[2].

Among the writings of Cartwright his *Confutation* occupies a unique place. It is a storehouse of Protestant learning, the true appreciation of which suffered by its being forestalled by Fulke's work on the same lines. Grosart's opinion[3] that our Protestant Societies have neglected it, may be true, but, although a reproduction of parts of it might be of value, a reissue of the whole bulky volume would not serve any fruitful purpose.

As a commentator Cartwright enjoyed for a long time a niche in the temple of fame[4]. The advance, however, of

[1] *Transcript*, ed. Eyre and Rivington, I, p. 149.

[2] *v.* T. Leishman, *The Westminster Directory* (1901), p. 135.

[3] p. xvii.

[4] His expository works include:

In Librum Salomonis, qui inscribitur Ecclesiastes, cum metaphrasi, Homiliae, quae et iusti Commentarii Loco esse possint. (Lond. 1604; Marburg, 1604; Amsterdam, 1632, 1638, 1647.)

A Commentary upon the Epistle of St Paul written to the Colossians. (Lond. 1612; Edin. 1864.)

Commentarii Succincti et Dilucidi in Proverbia Salomonis. (Lugduni Batavorum. Apud Gulielmum Brewsterum, in vico Chorali, 1617; Amsterdam, 1632, 1638.)

(?) *A Plaine Explanation of the whole Revelation of Saint John....Penned*

Biblical scholarship has deprived his expositions of much of their point and worth. The only one of his commentaries reprinted in modern times, viz. that on the Epistle to the Colossians, has elicited no great interest even among the Puritans of to-day. It consists of a series of notes on the Epistle, taken by a hearer who omitted much of importance, and while expressing many plain practical truths regarding the spiritual life, it never rises above the commonplace. His other expository works are more complete but are likewise unsatisfying when judged by modern standards. In the seventeenth century, however, they held a high place in the estimation of Bible students, particularly in Holland, where many of them were printed. John Polyander, in his Preface to Cartwright's *Commentarii in Proverbia* (1617) calls the author a man *qui singulari sacras literas interpretandi dono a Deo exornatus*, and Ludwig Elzevir in his foreword to an edition of the Puritan's *Harmonia* (1647) pays him the highest tribute of praise: *In hac analysi dexteritatem ingenii, subactumque judicium, mirifica ostendit noster Cartwrightus.... Nullas profecto virtutes in Commentatore & Interprete S. Scripturae expetiveris, quas hic in Cartwrighto non inveneris. In explicando perspicuus est, in docendo solidus, in refutando invictus, in reprehendo severus, in adhortando mansuetus, in consolando plane divinus, in omnibus brevis & simplex.*

The importance attached to Cartwright's writings is exemplified in a striking fashion by Richard Baxter. In his *Christian Directory*[1] in answer to the question, "What books, especially of theology, should one choose, who for want of money or time, can read but few?" Baxter enumerates three lists of books for the poorest, the poorer and "the poor man's library, which yet addeth somewhat to the former,

by a faithfull Preacher, now with God, for more private use, and now published for the further benefit of the people of God. (Lond. 1622. *v.* copy in Congregl Lib. Memorial Hall, Lond. ascribed in ink by seventeenth century hand to Cartwright.)

Harmonia Evangelica, commentario analytico, metaphrastico, practico, illustrata: antehac diversis voluminibus edita, nunc summa industria in unum corpus redacta, summariis aucta, & amendis quibus scatebat, repurgata. (Amsterodami. Apud Ludovicum Elzevirium, 1647. Previous edd. 1627, 1630.)

[1] ed. W. Orme (1830), v, p. 595.

but cometh short of a rich and sumptuous library." In the second class he places Cartwright with Bucer, Beza, Calderwood, Smectymnuus and others as an authoritative critic of diocesan prelacy, and with Bradshaw, Amesius, etc., as one of the best judges of the deficiencies in the liturgy and ceremonies of the English Church. In the third list he expressly names Cartwright along with Erasmus, Luther, Melanchthon and others as one of the standard commentators of the New Testament, making particular note of his *Confutation*[1]. When discussing the question "Whether are set forms of words or free praying without them the better way?" Baxter[2] points out the advantages and disadvantages of both methods and pronounces the verdict that "somewhat of both ways joined together will best obviate the incommodities of both," and supports his judgment by referring to recognised authorities of the ancient and modern Church and also to "the famous nonconformists of England, Cartwright, Hildersham, Greenham, Perkins," etc. Baxter thus highly appreciated Cartwright as a learned and judicious writer, but, delightfully daring, he goes so far as to include him among the saints with whom he hopes after death to commune. "It is no small part of my comfort to consider," he says[3], "that I shall dwell with such as Enoch, and Elias and Abraham," and after enumerating many celebrities of the past he comes to "Cartwright and Hooker and Bayne," etc.

We may deduce from the number of Cartwright's books that were published for the first time after his death that Dod and Hildersham, to whom he left his papers, fulfilled their trust well. They are supposed to have edited an edition of his *Harmonia* (1630) themselves. One of the most interesting of the publications issued under their direction is the second edition of *A Treatise of Christian Religion or The Whole Bodie and substance of Divinitie*[4], to which is appended *The Doctrine of Christian Religion, contracted into a short Catechisme, by the Author himselfe*[5]. This duplex work was "imprinted by Felix Kyngston for Thomas Man" at London

[1] *Christian Directory*. Richard Baxter ed. W. Orme (1830), v, p. 598.
[2] *ibid.* v, p. 427. [3] *ibid.* v, p. 426. [4] 4to. pp. viii + 360. [5] pp. 361–78.

in 1616. One of the reasons for the reprint was that unsatisfactory editions of these writings and other works of Cartwright had been published a few years before. The writer of the Preface of the *Treatise*, "W.B.," evidently Cartwright's friend, William Bradshaw, whom we have seen consorting with him in Guernsey, observes: "Many have bin sorrie to see some writings of this learned and godly Author come forth in publike, since his death, with so many defects and maimes. To give an instance hereof, there is an exposition of the Epistle to the Colossians, published under his name; wherein hee hath had very much wrong done to him: it being nothing else but a bundle of raw and imperfect notes, taken by some unlearned hearer, never perused (or so much as seene) by the Author himselfe. Wherein there is scant any good coherence of matter to be found, or any perfect periods and sentences handsomely knit together, or sutably depending one upon another." Bradshaw entreats the reader to "esteeme nothing to bee his [Cartwright's], but what shall bee published or approved by them, to whom by his last will and Testament hee committed the perusall and examination of his writings," *i.e.* Dod and Hildersham. He also notes that "this Treatise of Religion, now reprinted, was the first, whereof there was much expectation and desire, as of that which would be of more generall use to all sorts of people: in which respect the Author himself was known to make more account of it, and would (if God had prolonged his daies to have perfected the same according to his own wishes) have given fuller satisfaction to his iudicious and impartiall Reader." Cartwright's purpose, says Bradshaw, was "to set downe in most plaine and familiar manner, all the necessarie points of positive Divinity, whereunto God (in a gratious measure) hath inabled him; as may appeare even by the first impression, though it were published with many wants and imperfections." For the correction of the first edition use has been made of Cartwright's little Catechism, "some directions in the best and last copie that he left behind him," and of the editor's own knowledge of Cartwright's plan and method.

The *Treatise*, which is divided into fifty-seven short chapters, is a popular exposition of the main doctrines of the Christian religion. The chief subjects dealt with are the nature of God, the Trinity, the Kingdom of God, the divine Decrees, the Creation, the Fall, the Word of God, the Ten Commandments, Christ's person and Offices, the Sacraments, Ecclesiastical Discipline, Prayer, the Lord's Prayer, Judgment, etc. The book is virtually a Larger Catechism, question and answer following in succession thus: "Q. What is the nature of God? A. An absolutenesse of perfection, infinitely excelling all other things. Consisting in unity of Essence and Trinity of Persons." Each chapter has at its head a synopsis of the argument and illustrative verses from Scripture. The theology is typically Calvinistic and the exposition is throughout determined by a literal interpretation of the Bible, the plenary inspiration of which is not questioned. Although in most points Cartwright follows the rigid scheme of Calvinistic theology he does not altogether sink his individuality and it is worth while to note some of the passages in which he reveals a distinctive message. He does not attempt to define God but says, "Hee must have the Art and Logicke of God himselfe that can give a perfect definition of God, but he may in such sort be described, as hee may bee discerned from all false gods, and all creatures whatsoever"[1] and is content to describe God as "a Spirit, which hath his being of himselfe," Whose attributes are simpleness, infiniteness, life, knowledge, will, power, goodness, justice, etc. In answer to the question "Why are all the Commandements (except two) set downe negatively?" he replies, "Because the Negative bindeth more strongly: for the Negative precept bindeth alwaies, and to all moments of time; the Affirmative bindeth alwaies, but not to all moments of time." It is interesting to note that Cartwright who objected so strongly to kneeling at Communion advocates kneeling at prayer[2], and that he who refused to take the oath *ex officio* directs that when called upon to take an oath we should consider "First, whether the matter be

[1] p. 4. [2] p. 102.

doubtfull whereof we speake. Secondly, whether it be weighty and worthie of an oath."[1] He repeats his wonted conviction that it is the civil magistrate's duty "to see that true Religion bee stablished, reformed and maintained, after the example of David, Salomon, Ezechiah, Iosiah, and other good Kings."[2] He teaches that the sixth commandment is broken when a man "useth not the honest recreation, wherewith his health may bee maintained: for wee must not thinke that there are no more waies to kill a mans selfe but with a knife, etc." or "when women with child, either by misdiet, or straine by reaching, violent exercise, and riding by Coach, or otherwise, and much more by dancing, either hurt the fruit of their wombe, or altogether miscarrie."[3] Some of Cartwright's definitions are of particular interest, *e.g.* Faith is "a persuasion of my heart, that God hath given his Sonne for me, and that he is mine, and I his"[4]; a Sacrament is "a signe & seale of the covenant of grace, or an action of the Church, wherein by outward things done according to the ordinance of God, inward things being betokened, Christ and his benefits are offered to all, and exhibited to the faithfull, for the strengthening of their faith in the eternall Covenant"[5]; Prayer is "a calling upon God alone, in the name of Christ, by the titles wherewith (in the Scripture) he is set forth unto us, as well thereby to doe service and homage unto the Lord, as to obtaine all necessary graces."[6] He also calls Prayer a key to open "the storehouses of all Gods treasures, and (as it were) the onely hooke whereby wee reach all the blessings of God, which otherwise would be out of our reach. So that as the covetousnesse of Popish Priests gave occasion of a reprochfull proverbe: *No pennie, no prayer*: the truth of God on the contrary side, doth teach us, *No prayer, no pennie*."[7] He reaffirms his belief in a set form of prayer thus: "Q. Wherefore is it convenient that there be a set forme of prayer? A. First, for testifying the consent of all true Churches, in the things that concerne the worship and service of God, which may

[1] p. 105. [2] p. 131. [3] p. 136. [4] p. 209.
[5] p. 212. [6] p. 242. [7] p. 243.

appeare by such bookes. Secondly, for direction of the Ministers to keepe in their administration (for substance) like soundnesse in doctrine and prayer. Thirdly, to helpe the weaker and ruder sort of people especially; and yet so, as the set forme make not men sluggish in stirring up the gift of prayer in themselves, according to divers occurrents; it being incident to the children of God to have some gift of prayer in some measure."[1] Throughout this *Treatise* Cartwright rarely misses an opportunity of dealing a blow at the Roman Anti-Christ and frequently he hurls his shaft at Anabaptism, but he levels no direct word of criticism at the Church of England. Nevertheless, although his antagonism to diocesan Episcopacy and his advocacy of Presbyterianism are not conspicuous they are implied and in several instances come near to the surface of his exposition, *e.g.* when he says that ministers "are tied to one flocke," should be able to teach, and must not hold any other office in the commonwealth or when he speaks of the deaconship as being merely "neare to the ministry."[2]

Cartwright's Shorter Catechism summarises in abbreviated, almost attenuated form, the chief points of his *Treatise* or Larger Catechism. It defines a Sacrament as "a mysticall signe, and effectuall instrument, wherby Christ with all his benefits is offered to all in the Church, and received also of those that are faithfull"[3]; Prayer as "a calling upon God in the name of Christ, for the more ample and ful fruition of the good things we have need of"[4]; and the Church as "a companie of those which are in Christ."[5] Neither Catechism deals with the Apostles' Creed. Both occupy an important place among the many Catechisms of the first half of the seventeenth century which popularised Calvinism and propagated Puritanism. With others they were forerunners of the Larger and Shorter Westminster Catechisms, for which they doubtless served as suggestive models[6].

From the list of his known and reputed works given in

[1] p. 256. [2] pp. 305-7. [3] p. 373.
[4] p. 374. [5] p. 377.
[6] *v.* A. F. Mitchell, *Catechisms of the Second Reformation* (1886).

Athenae Cantabrigienses[1] we would, for reasons already given, exclude *A Second Admonition* and *An Examination off M. Doctor Whitgiftes Censures.* The Channel Islands Second Form of Discipline (erroneously dated 1577) is attributed to Cartwright and Snape, but its authorship should be ascribed to the ministers of the Islands as a body, Cartwright having only a share, although an important share, in its composition. *A Christian Letter* (1599) is probably not from his pen at all. Cooper[2] rightly points out that *The Popes deadly wound* (1621) was written by another "T. C.," viz. Thomas Clarke of Sutton Coldfield.

R. G. Usher[3] follows tradition in assigning *A Second Admonition* to Cartwright, but his suggestion that the Puritan was also the author of *The Sacred Discipline* etc., *Disciplina Synodica* etc., and *Necessity of Discipline* (1574), is exceedingly devoid of accuracy and discrimination. The first of these three titles is that of the first part of the *Directory* or translation of the Puritan Book of Discipline issued in 1644, the second is that of the second part of the Latin original of the same work, and the third is the title of the first chapter of *A Full and Plaine Declaration.* The ascription of *An Admonition to the People of England* (1589) to Cartwright is an obvious error[4]. It was written by Bishop Cooper, the "profane T. C."[5]

Whatever our judgment respecting the value of Cartwright's writings may be, we cannot deny that they bear ample testimony to the extraordinary studiousness of the man and the extensiveness of his learning. It is also undeniable that they exercised considerable influence at home and abroad for several generations and won for the Puritan both admirers and followers. Moreover, as the weight and importance of a man may be estimated by the opposition he creates, we may look upon the notorious decree of the University of Oxford (21 July, 1683), which condemned among others the writings of Cartwright[6], and the fact that

[1] II, p. 363. [2] *A.C.* II, p. 365. [3] *P.M.* p. xxxii.
[4] *Bibliotheca Britannica*, art. "Cartwright."
[5] For a list of Cartwright's works consulted by the present writer *v.* Index *sub* Cartwright.
Drysdale, p. 402.

his works were put on the Index by the Roman Church, as testimonies to the worth and influence of his books.

Cartwright's life and teaching are particularly worthy of examination because they reflect the quintessential features of Elizabethan Puritan-Presbyterianism. Like a true Calvinist he laid stress upon the reform of abuses that violated the laws of righteousness. As an anti-Romanist he represented the reaction that came with the Reformation against the practices of the unreformed Church. But behind his moralism and his negative attitude to Rome there lay a positive experience, namely, that immediacy of spiritual knowledge, which is sometimes recognised as the essence of Puritanism. It was exemplified in Cartwright's sincere and earnest practice of God's presence in his private devotions. He was a man of fervent prayer. As a sixteenth century Puritan he was limited and moulded by the spirit of his age. He shared the principles of intolerance that were current in his time[1]. He believed in the unity of Christ's Church and proclaimed the need of conformity to his ideals. Divergence of opinion must be severely dealt with. The death penalty must be exacted for those breaches specified in the Old Testament. The severity underlying this principle was due not to Cartwright's hard-heartedness, but to his sense of duty. A nonconformist by force of circumstances, and a conformist at heart, he aimed at ascendancy for his own beloved system and not liberty of conscience for all. If in power he would have sought to impose upon his fellow-men the practices which in his opinion were divinely appointed. He could not see another way. He stood indeed for liberty of conscience, not because he believed in its intrinsic value, but because he bravely endeavoured to secure it for himself. He suffered for his conscientious convictions and, by showing that honest tenacity of belief and purpose cannot be subverted by external coercion, he unwittingly paved the way for the establishment of civil and religious freedom. He was greater than he knew. His aim was not the abolition of the Church of England[2], but its transformation. He believed in

[1] *v.* A. J. Klein, *Intolerance in the reign of Elizabeth* (1917).
[2] *v.* Wakeman, p. 338.

a State Church with a Presbyterian polity. He recognised the right and duty of the civil magistrate to support and co-operate with the Church, but at the same time upheld the spiritual autonomy of the organisation, whose supreme Head is not an earthly monarch but Christ. He was an ardent anti-Separatist. Unable to impose his system upon the Church of England by a mere fiat he was obliged to adopt a policy, which in the words of Browne was tarrying for the magistrate. This policy was conditioned by Cartwright's nationalism. He desired to be loyal to the English Church, the English Monarchy, and Presbyterianism simultaneously. It was difficult to harmonise his loyalties, and in the eyes of some his attempt to do so has been characterised as inconceivable, inconsistent or cowardly. The Church of Scotland proves that it was not inconceivable. Its inconsistency is more apparent than real. When the Seceder thinks that he should have separated from the Church of England in order to be logical, he should remember that such logicality meant for Cartwright disloyalty to Queen and country and the national Church. Critics like Heylyn, who say that he was afraid of "Penry's Price," believe that Penry by his death paid the price of political treason, one of the last things Cartwright's nationalism would have permitted[1]. He was obliged by his principles and the circumstances of his time to seek his goal, not by revolution or separation, but by constitutional means and gradual reform from within the Church. In all these points he represented the Presbyterians of the Elizabethan age.

Cartwright's quarrel with the English Church was not a theological one. Even adherents of the Bancroftian school acknowledged that the Puritans were in agreement with them on the fundamental points of doctrine[2]. Cartwright's chief goal was the transformation of the Church of England into a Presbyterian State Church. His exposition of Presbyter-

[1] We, of course, do not hold that Penry was guilty of deliberate disloyalty and incline to the view of Pierce rather than that of Burrage on this subject. *v.* C. Burrage, *John Penry the so-called Martyr* (1913) and Pierce, *John Penry*.

[2] T. Rogers, *The Catholic Doctrine of the Church of England*. Parker Soc. 1854, pp. 8, 10.

ianism is contained in his polemical writings and are therefore less methodically set forth by him than they were by some of his associates and disciples, *e.g.* Travers and Udall, and by the Book and Form of Discipline in which with others he had a hand. But, with minor variants, it was Cartwright's scheme that dominated the field and moulded the Puritan-Presbyterian movement. The pyramid of courts from the Consistory or *presbyterium* to the Pan-Presbyterian council was his ideal. The officials who were to do the work of these courts were primarily ministers, elders and deacons. One of the main functions of the ministers and elders was to administer discipline in the narrower sense, *i.e.* apply the censures to delinquents, and maintain discipline in the wider sense, *i.e.* government by Presbyterial office-bearers and assemblies. But Cartwright also emphasised the teaching function of the Church. A dumb minister was a contradiction in terms. Each one should be fit to preach. Hence the Puritan's anxious desire that candidates for the ministry should be properly educated, and examined as to his fitness to teach before being appointed to a charge. The campaign against the reading of homilies, and the importance attached to catechisms arose from the Puritan belief in an enlightened ministry and an enlightened people. Cartwright's animus against Roman vestments, his advocacy of a simplified service, and his attack on the Book of Common Prayer, were all re-echoed and reflected by the members of the movement which he led. One of the most momentous corollaries or implications of his system was the need to overthrow the existing Episcopate with its appurtenances. Cartwright certainly believed in the abolition of diocesan Bishops, but his policy prevented him from refusing to acknowledge them before they were supplanted by Presbyters, and made him refrain from scurrilous abuse of them, and seek and be content with the practical reform of other grievances before the central citadel fell. This was the Puritan policy when James became the King of England. Thus the Puritanism of the period, 1570 to 1590, was thoroughly Presbyterian and upon it was stamped the personality of Thomas Cartwright.

While Cartwright drew his principles from the fount of Scripture, he was influenced by the currents of contemporary thought, the example of the Reformed Churches, and intercourse with other Reformers. Bucer, Calvin, Beza and others promulgated ideas that were incorporated in Elizabethan Presbyterianism. Sandys considered Cartwright as the leader of the movement only *post Bezam*[1]. Cartwright represented the nexus between English Puritanism and the Continental Reformation in his personal experience. Not only did he have friends among those who had been in exile in Calvin's city, but he himself resided in Geneva, Heidelberg and elsewhere overseas, and there entered into close association with exponents of Presbyterianism. The connection between the Puritans and the Scottish Reformers was also intimate. The influence of Knox when in England helped to lay the foundations of the Puritan movement; Goodman, who had served in Scotland, brought his experience into it; both during the vestiarian controversy and at a later date the Scottish ministers expressed their sympathy with their southern brethren; when Melville and his fellow-exiles lived in England they conferred with the Puritans and doubtless stimulated the Conference movement and made suggestions based on their own Second Book of Policy for the Puritan Book of Discipline. It is probable that the idea of subscription to the latter was borrowed from the Scottish Covenanters. Elizabeth complained to James of the sympathetic interest his ministers took in the Puritan movement and Bancroft, aware of Scotland's influence, sought to expose it. The interactions between the Church of Scotland and the Elizabethan Presbyterians would make a most valuable subject for an historical dissertation. Cartwright, the personal friend of Melville, the Professor-designate of a Scottish University, one of the particular Puritans singled out for Scottish intercession, illustrated in his career the reality of the bond that united the northern and southern seekers after a similar goal.

The geography of Puritanism would make another interesting subject for the research student. In the Midland and

[1] *Z.L.* I, Ep. CXXIV.

South-Eastern counties lay the chief Puritan breeding ground. Cartwright's connections in his youth and his age were with districts where nonconformity was strong. He was also true to type in being an alumnus of Cambridge. There from the time of Bucer, Lever, etc., Puritanism throve. There the vestiarian strife waxed hot. There Cartwright himself taught the doctrines that marked a new epoch in Puritan history. "If," says Mullinger[1], "to the Cambridge of Cranmer, Latimer, Ridley and Tyndale, belongs the high honour of having first recognised and promulgated in England the doctrines of the Reformation, to the Cambridge of the Pilkingtons, Beaumont and Cartwright belongs the more equivocal distinction of having educated our earlier Puritanism and given shelter to the principles of Dissent." Further, Cartwright's association as factor and chaplain with the Merchant Adventurers reminds us that many of the pioneers of the Reformation and upholders of Puritanism were naturally found among those who traded with Continental countries and thus became acquainted with the adherents and the writings of Protestantism, and among those whose chief delight was to harry the treasure ships of Spanish Papists[2]. Although Froude, in his *English Seamen*, has shown that Spain suffered greatly at the hands of English sailors, who were inspired by a vindictive Protestantism, there is still room for a dissertation on the part played by the Puritans proper in the campaign of the corsairs that was carried on for years before the Armada came. It appears that Froude, like the Romanists of the Elizabethan age, is inclined to a certain extent to confuse Protestants and Puritans. "By the observation," says the anonymous author of *A Triall of Subscription*[3] "of some Popish [*margin. R. Dolemans conference, lib.* 2. *ca. ult.*] (though politike) there be fewe Protestantes in Englande (besides such as depende upon ecclesiasticall dignities) which are not puritans."

Cartwright's friends and patrons throw light upon the

[1] p. 208.

[2] *v.* A. F. Pollard, *Elizabethans and the Empire* (1923), p. 18.

[3] (1599), p. 12, cf. A. O. Meyer, *England and the Catholic Church under Queen Elizabeth*, pp. 347–8, Eng. trans. (1916).

supporters of Puritanism in general. Again he is the mirror of the movement. He enjoyed the special patronage of statesmen like Leicester, Walsingham, Davison, etc., was regarded with sympathy by Burghley, and counted among his friends many of the leading gentry and parliamentarians of the day, the Bacons, Puckering, Hastings, Tomson, Yelverton, etc. His wellwishers were scholars, ministers, and men of social influence, and it was such who were the mainstay of Puritanism. It was not a popular mass movement. Here and there we meet with congregations, who were wholeheartedly devoted to Puritan ministers, *e.g.* the followers of Udall, who went with him to London to communicate privately there[1], and the parishioners of Aldermary, who petitioned for the restoration of the profitable preacher, John Field[2]. Although many of the numerous lay petitions in favour of Puritans were initiated by ministers, they show that in the South-Eastern counties a considerable number of laymen of all classes were earnestly desirous of a preaching ministry. They indicate a sincere interest among many in the Gospel and probably in the redress of clamant abuses, but not that the Presbyterian principles of the Puritans had any appreciable support among the masses. Some of the writings of the party would reach a wide circle. The *Admonition*, Cartwright's first *Reply*, and the Marprelate Tracts had a comparatively extensive circulation, but withal they could not bring the multitude into the central current of the movement, which they were designed to further. Browne and Harrison could gather congregations of Brownists, for theirs was a people's movement, but Cartwright and Travers could not readily gather congregations of Cartwrightians, for their policy was first of all to prepare their scheme and receive constitutional sanction for its realisation. To advance their project they and their associates developed the Conferences, but these, as we have seen, were attended almost exclusively by ministers. It is doubtful whether the people on the whole were sufficiently aware of the existing ecclesiastical grievances or antagonistic to the established hierarchy to feel the need

[1] *Sec. Parte*, II, p. 45. [2] *ibid.* I, p. 135.

of a further reformation, and whether the rigorous disciplinary system of Geneva appealed to the average Englishman of that time.

The Puritan ministers, if they did not have the masses, had many influential representatives of the upper classes behind them. The list of Puritan patrons is remarkably long[1]. At the hands of these laymen many of the ministers received, like Cartwright, the greatest hospitality, or were appointed by them to private chaplaincies, to special posts like the Mastership of a Hospital, or to peculiar benefices, which carried with them salaries that were frequently higher than the average stipend of the clergy. Such patrons were a source of incalculable strength to Puritanism. Some of them may have been animated by selfish motives, expecting to recompense themselves from the spoils of the Church, which Puritanism was counted upon to overthrow; some of them were sincerely and piously interested, like Lady Anne Bacon, in the progress of true religion, righteously deplored the palpable abuses current in the Church and warmly sympathised with those who suffered for their effort to redress these; others recognised in the Puritan forces a bulwark against Popery and its allied dangers. It is certainly a glaring error on the part of Birt[2] to say that Puritanism up till 1577 was almost wholly confined to the lower orders. The fact that there were so many of its representatives in the House of Commons is sufficient to show that it appealed to many of good social standing.

Nevertheless, in spite of influential supporters, Elizabethan Puritanism failed to achieve its purpose. Again the fate of Cartwright is illustrative. He incurred the displeasure of the Queen; his chief opponent at first was Whitgift; the most prominent of his later critics were Bancroft, Sutcliffe and Hooker; he was charged with complicity in Marprelate's adventure and the Copinger-Hacket plot; he was imprisoned by the High Commissioners.

Elizabeth frustrated the development of English Puritanism. It did not accord with her State policy to allow disharmony

[1] *v.* Usher, *Reconstr.* I, p. 270. [2] p. 464.

in the Church. The prescribed uniformity made Presbyterianism impossible. Indeed, nonconformity of any kind could not flourish at a time when the need of national unity was dictated by circumstances and in the eyes of Elizabeth demanded unity in the Church. When greater issues were at stake she played the opportunist and connived at Puritan irregularities. Personally she was not in favour of an ecclesiastical system that had strong democratic elements in it and proclaimed the spiritual independence of the Church. As she pointed out to James the aims of the Presbyterians were in conflict with her principles of autocratic monarchy, and she would be confirmed in her hostile attitude by her Church dignitaries, who exposed the dangers to her supremacy in the claim of the dissenters to self-government. Cartwright wrote[1]: "That excommunication should not be exercised against Princes I utterly mislike." *Omnes ergo fideles*, said the author of the *Explicatio*[2], *atque adeo principes ipsi atque magistratus Dei verbo et Ecclesiasticae Disciplinae parere debent.* It was natural that Elizabeth should not readily give countenance to the exponents of such views. Whitgift disclosed the revolutionary dangers of Puritanism; he called their proposed polity "a democratical ataxy, yea an ochlocracy."[3] Others saw in the movement a resuscitation of the tenets of Christopher Goodman. Accepting the interpretations of the critics, Elizabeth set her face against the designs of Cartwright, prevented her Parliament from advancing them, and against her opposition Cartwright and his co-religionists could make no headway. Although the enemies of sixteenth century Presbyterianism thought that it involved dangerous political principles, its friends would say that these were only the principles of representative and constitutional government. It is, however, but just to point out that Cartwright and his moderate companions refrained from sinister political designs altogether.

Whitgift's coercive measures, the detective work and writings of Bancroft, the calumnies of Sutcliffe, the argumentation of Hooker, the defeat of the Armada, the death of patrons like Leicester, the rigours of the High Commission

[1] *Rest.* p. 65. [2] (1574) f. 143 b. [3] St. *Whit.* II, p. 159.

and the Star Chamber, are also to be counted among the forces that contributed to the failure of Puritanism. Some of its opponents hurt the cause by misrepresenting its programme, *e.g.* by enlarging upon the alleged plebeian character of what they considered the chief Presbyterian court, viz., the Consistory. Although it was never *de facto* deeply rooted in the hearts of the laity the Presbyterianism of Cartwright was theoretically democratic, "as though" to say with Bancroft[1], "Christs soveraigntie, kingdome, and lordship were nowhere acknowledged, or to be found, but where halfe a dozen artizans, shoomakers, tinkers, and tailors, with their preacher and reader (eight or nine cherubins forsooth) doe rule the whole parish." To judge from Sutcliffe the Puritans proposed to inaugurate the reign of a Presbyterian proletariat: *Eorum enim nonnulli artifices sunt, ut fabri, qui nobis arte Vulcania disciplinam excudunt: coqui etiam aderunt, ut aliquid sit in presbyterio insipido condimenti: sutores ut pugnantes presbyterorum sententias sarciant: sine caementariis arx haec presbyterialis aedificari non potest*[2]. Elizabethan Presbyterianism also suffered at the hands of its friends. Marprelate robbed it of the sympathy of moderate men; Copinger and his mates led the undiscriminating to confuse it with the forces of anarchy. The lack of unanimity among its adherents was another obstacle to success. Their endeavour to establish an unlawful system by lawful means was a Herculean task that required the greatest cohesion. The tendency to divide into extremists and moderates, the need of secrecy, and the failure to agree on some points of their programme prevented the co-operation and uniformity that would have increased their effectiveness.

The vogue of Separatism was a further reason for the decay of Presbyterianism. Leading Separatists owned their debt to such men as Cartwright, and many of their followers were converts from the primary type of Puritanism. At times it was difficult to make a clear distinction. Some nonconformist gatherings partook both of Congregationalism and of Presbyterianism. Some ministers were now identified

[1] *D.P.* p. 44. [2] Sutcliffe, *De Presbyterio* (1591), p. 134.

with the one dissenting current, now with the other. There were several pronounced affinities between Elizabethan Presbyterianism and Separatism. Cartwright himself laid weight upon the prerogatives of congregations in the election of their ministers. There are examples of Congregationalism within the bounds of the Dedham *classis*[1]. Brownists and Puritans both looked to Scripture for guidance; both accepted the rule of elders and deacons; both believed in the severe exercise of discipline; both strove for the purity of the Church. Dexter[2] holds that Browne drew his Congregationalist principles from Scripture, Loofs[3] that he was influenced by the Anabaptists, Burrage[4] that he became a Separatist "more because of pressure put upon him from the Archbishop and Bishops." Contemporaries believed that he deduced his conclusions from Cartwright's premises. There is truth in all these views. But it was the contemporary view that counted most in contributing to the detriment of the Presbyterian cause. For the disloyalty to the Church of England that was inherent in Separatism the Cartwrightians had to suffer obloquy and oppression. In this connection it may be observed that Dexter[5] is prejudiced when he affirms that Cartwright's time required a more scriptural, competent, and inspiring ideal than the Presbyterian one set up by the leader of the Puritans. Dexter writes as a Separatist of the nineteenth century and forgets the Biblical basis, the efficiency, and the inspiring record of such a body as the Church of Scotland, whose history shows the ideal of Cartwright in practice.

The comparative seclusion that characterised the last decade of Cartwright's life is paralleled by the relatively inconspicuous nature of the Puritan movement during the same period. While he in his temporary island home could show with impunity that his Presbyterian convictions were as vigorous as ever, his fellow Puritans on the mainland were obliged to retain their Presbyterian principles in a state of suspended animation. Although, however, English Puri-

[1] *P.M.* pp. 62, 69, 71.
[2] p. 103.
[3] *R.E.*[3] III, p. 426.
[4] *E.E.D.* I, p. 130.
[5] p. 57.

tanism was now but latently Presbyterian it remained a distinctive force. It was not indeed called upon to stand alone in its opposition to the rising tide of anti-Calvinistic theology. Whitgift himself in the Lambeth Articles of 1595 defended the doctrines of Calvin as forcibly and dogmatically as the Puritan body could wish. Expression was given to the Puritan spirit in the Sabbatarianism propounded in the 'nineties, most notably by Nicholas Bound. Bancroft's chaplain, Thomas Rogers[1], was inclined to regard this outburst of doctrinal Puritanism as a wily stratagem designed to revive the hopes shattered by the downfall of Presbyterianism, but we believe that it was merely the sincere and natural expression of the precise mode of interpretation that marked the Puritans and gave them their name. The Puritans were also strongly represented at Cambridge in Emmanuel College and later on in Sidney College, where many of the leaders of the future were imbued with the spirit of Cartwright through such personal friends of his as Chaderton and Montague. Moreover, in the declining years of Elizabeth the Puritans the more readily held their Presbyterianism in abeyance because they were buoyed up with the hope of a better day under a successor hailing from Presbyterian Scotland. While they continued to maintain their identity as a numerically small but distinct body, with a specific outlook and influence of their own, their Presbyterianism remained as a hidden but living undercurrent, ready to assert itself should more favourable circumstances permit.

Although his favourite scheme did not fructify as he desired during his lifetime, Cartwright's work was not without result. For some time he left his mark on the ecclesiastical life of the Channel Islands. In Ireland, through Travers as Provost of Trinity College, Dublin, and others, he doubtless influenced the beginnings of the Irish Presbyterian Church. In Holland his writings were for long in vogue and were used as text-books by the theological students of that country. In Virginia Alexander Whitaker organised a Church that was based on Cartwright's principles[2]. The

[1] *op. cit.* p. 17. [2] Heron, p. 195.

Pilgrim Fathers and their Puritan successors who found a new home in America bore his books as well as his tenets with them[1]. The history of the Church life in America during the seventeenth century shows that in many quarters Cartwrightian Presbyterianism had a strong hold alongside of Congregationalism. John Cotton himself said[2]: "The form of Church-government wherein we walk doth not differ in substance from that which Mr Cartwright pleaded." Cartwright did more than merely influence the beginnings of independent Separation in England[3]. He and his associates by their righteous living, deep piety and learning, by their protest against abuses and injustices, and by their endeavour to express at least their own conscientious convictions in an intolerant age, left an example that inspired posterity to emulate them. The spirit of Cartwright was retained by the Puritan party, which remained, and has always found a place, in the English Church. His influence would be carried far and wide by his friends and admirers, who taught in Cambridge or served in the ministry. Through these men the memory and the teaching of the Master Puritan would be affectionately preserved. His principles were reasserted by Puritan pamphleteers in the reign of James[4] and, as we have seen, they came to life again in the middle of the seventeenth century.

The Presbyterians of that time looked upon Cartwright as an authoritative exponent of their favoured system[5]. They not only used his arguments in favour of their Presbyterianism; they also shared his views regarding Separatism[6]. To illustrate the last point we may quote from the *Dissuasive* (1645) of Robert Baillie of Glasgow in which he pours the vials of his scorn upon the Independents and incidentally furnishes an

[1] T. G. Wright, *Literary Culture in Early New England* (1920), pp. 50, 255–7, 267.

[2] *The Way of Congregational Churches Cleared* (1648), p. 27.

[3] W. A. Shaw, *Eng. Hist. Rev.* III, p. 656.

[4] *e.g.* in *A Treatise of Divine Worship* (1604), *English Puritanisme* (1605), *A Protestation of the Kings Supremacie* (1605).

[5] *v. A Vindication of the Presbyteriall-Government*, published by the Provincial Assembly of 2 Nov. 1649 (1650), p. 16.

[6] *ibid.* p. 117.

important seventeenth century Scottish appreciation of Cartwright's anti-Separatist principles: "When Cartwright, Hildersham, Travers, and many other gracious Divines, by the blessing of God upon their great diligence, had undermined and well-neer overthrown the Episcopal Seas, and all the Cathedral Ceremonies; incontinent the Generation of the Separatists did start up, and put such retardances in the way of that gracious Reformation, as yet remain, and, except by the hand of God, will not be gotten removed. It is true, the malignancy of the Episcopal party, and emulation of the Separatists themselves, would make Cartwright and his friends the old Unconformists, to be the Fathers of that Sect; notwithstanding whoever is acquainted with the Times, or will be at the pains, with any consideration, to confer the Tenents of both Parties, or who will advert the issue and sequele of both ways, cannot but pronounce Cartwright and all his followers the Unconformists, very free from the unhappinesse of procreating this Bastard"[1]. It should also be observed that the Scottish Commissioners to the Westminster Assembly expressly claimed Cartwright as an upholder of the ideal embodied in the Church of Scotland. In their joint work, *Reformation of Church-Government in Scotland*[2], they proudly quote his testimony in favour of their Church. But all testimonials in favour of Cartwright do not belong to the past. To-day he is regarded with esteem and gratitude in many quarters and there exists a vital, generous and much respected body, namely, the Presbyterian Church of England, which, by its very existence as the embodiment in a large measure of the system advocated by Cartwright, and by its reverence for him as one of its founders, keeps the fame of the Elizabethan Puritan ever fresh and fair.

[1] *Dissuasive from the Errours of the Time* (1645), p. 12. [2] (1644), p. 15.

APPENDIX I

CARTWRIGHT'S ORATION IN REPLY TO BYNG'S IN THE PHILOSOPHICAL DISPUTATION HELD ON MONDAY THE 7TH AUGUST, 1564, BEFORE QUEEN ELIZABETH IN CAMBRIDGE, THE SUBJECT BEING "MONARCHIA EST OPTIMUS STATUS REIPUBLICAE"

SI ego is essem (erudite vir) qui tibi potuissem quid laudis adjungere, et tu ille qui mea voce et commendatione eguisses, et cujus jam tandem laus nasceretur, reddidissem ego tibi libenter et pluribus verbis commendationem. Sed cum nullum horum sit, faciam quod est, nostro in instituto conjunctius. Mittam meam, sumam orationem tuam, quam dum ego repetivero, et a capite (quod aiunt) ad calcem, quantum memoria patietur, diduxero, attende (quaeso) et dato veniam, comprehendam pressius, quod intelligam te magnam rerum sylvam in angustum contunsisse locum. Praetergredior omnem illam orationis partem, quae fuit ad augustissimum principem habita; versabor in visceribus causae, atque adeo arcem ac turrem rationum tuarum invadam. Atque primum quidem, quod fuerat orationis tuae caput petam, quod si praescidero, reliquum corpus inanime et cadaverosum, nisi tuo praesidio aliquo nitatur, ad solum decasurum est.

Adfers praestantissimum esse Dei principatum, qui cum Rex sit, et unus sceptra teneat, convenire ut id imperium vocemus in imitationem nostram; quod quam bona cum ratione dicitur, non est difficile judicium. Ut enim Deus sapientissimus, cujus centrum ubique est, circumferentia nusquam interminatus, in omne aetatis aevum duraturus, unice praeficiatur; nos ergo homines, loco circumscripti, caduci, jam-jam morituri, et si cum Deo contendamus stupidissimi, soli rerum potiemur, nec alios in societatem laboris et conciliorum nostrorum arcessimus? Olet hoc insolentiam, olet intolerabilem fastum; et argumentum est, et dialecticè dicam, a majore ad minus affirmativè; quod quantum valeat ipse videas.

Sequutus est naturae locus, cujus solertiam a nobis spectandam esse vix et imitandam; cujus instinctu factum esse ut in singulis rebus, quod simplex, solitarium, et uniusmodi esset principatum inter caetera obtineret, unde effectum esse putas in rebus etiam civilibus hoc fieri oportere. Cedo tandem quam tu Naturam intelligis? Si Deum, prius decantata dicis: Si occultam quandam rebus virtutem inseminatam, pace vel tua, vel ipsius Naturae dixerim, quaerat illa cultores suos, quaerat sequaces; me profecto nunquam habebit imitatorem. Est enim in nos homines parva, prorsus a nostra familia aliena quae tot petulos, nevos, silos, flaccos, frontones, strabones, dentones, capitones, et innumeros alios corpores, depravitate insignes in orbem tamquam in theatrum quoddam protrusit deridendos. Verum faciamus tibi eam esse rectam vitae ducem, quam sequendo nunquam aberrabimus; omnium tamen profecto hanc minime fore putavi rationem, si enim quod est in aliquibus imitanda propterea in omnibus vitae regula et actionum esse debet, locus est continuo omnium rerum communitati. Natura enim omnia sunt communia, privatim nihil nisi pactione, forte; notus est locus, tantum fuit attingendus; aut ergo nullum erit imperium, aut si fit, omnibus communicabitur. Natura enim sunt communia singula. Popularis sane haec oratio et percommoda nobis. Omnes reges erimus, ponamus ergo libros, ponamus insignia haec ordinis nostri, arripiamus sceptra, diademata, et alium regiae magnificentiae splendorem et apparatum, nimis profecto diu labore, vigiliis et lucubrationibus attriti sumus. Satis ergo hoc faxem volui.

A praepotenti Deo ad coelestia corpora video te ordine quodam et gradibus descendisse: vide vero quomodo rationem ad abjecta animalcula apes et pecudum greges apposite deducas; non intelligo; praecipitare hoc quidem est, non descendere; quos enim paulo ante ad coelum extulisti, eos subinde subito commutata oratione ad vilissima animalia abjecisti.

Multorum procurationem in invidiam et contemptionem inducis quae cunctationem quandam, et in rebus gerendis oscitantiam adferat: qua in re videor jam primum Aristotelis vocem audivisse, in cujus depulsione patieris tu non iniquè Aristotelem cum seipso, rationem cum ratione contendere, causam cum causa. Idem enim autor est, perinde fieri in gubernaculo reipublicae ut in coena, quae lautior esse solet, plurimorum collatis symbolis, quam si unius sumptu instructa fuerit.

Ventum est ad tyrannidem, quam cum teterrimam esse omnes confitentur, iidem regiam potestatem esse optimam non possunt non diffiteri. Spinosior fuit haec oratio et aliquantulum pugnatior quam ut facile potest evitari; interius tamen intuenti est ubi vacillet. Ut enim suavitati nostrae non conducant dulcissima, non tamen efficiatur, nostram maxime incolumitatem tueri acerbissimum; sed potius temporale quoddam, quod est ex utrisque modificatum. Sic inter respublicas optimatum potestas mediocritatem habet. Regia potestas est illa amara, quae vero communi nomine respublica dicitur, ubi multis atque adeo infinitis respublica committitur, plus aequo dulcior esse solet.

Extremum fuit Homeri testimonium, οὐκ ἀγαθὸν πολῠκοιρᾰνίη. εἷς κοίρανος ἔστω, εἷς βασιλεύς, quo totam hanc terminari placet controversiam. Verum sinamus poetas ludere, non rerum sed fabularum autores. Quod si fas sit clavum clavo ejicere, est Homericus Diomedes, qui cum ad hostilia castra exploranda emitteretur, petit socium itineris et consiliorum, quod esset duorum quam unius gravius judicium. En vero si ita Homero capiaris, profer mihi Homerum philosophorum Aristotelem. Haec cum dixisses silentium est in hac causa consequutum: et ego ut multus sim, hic sistam.

APPENDIX II

EXTRACT FROM HARTWELL'S *REGINA LITERATA* CONCERNING CARTWRIGHT'S ORATION

Talia dicentem vultu Cartwritus amico
Increpat, et dictis dicta remensus, ait:
"Cartwritus opponens" "Tene ulli, veneranda parens Natura, novercam
Cum bona sis, cum sis omnibus aequa, putem?
En proles numerosa tibi, juvenesque, senesque,
Vir, mulier. Tuus hic partus, et ille tuus.
Eia agnosse tuos; atque oscula fige—quid, unus?
Unus in innumeris oscula matris habet?
Quid reliqui tantum meruere? Amor omni in uno est?
Unus in amplexus ire redire potest?
Unus rex? unus rerum moderatur habenas?
Sceptrum, ex tam multis millibus, unus habet?
Nos populos, spurii, spretique et posthuma proles,
Et fastiditum turba parentis onus?
Siccine, tam multos ut spernas, diligis unum?
Unus materni pondus amoris habet?
Nil contra leges, nil plebiscita? nec ulla
Expugnat ratio, quod ratione caret?"
Hoc telum, Cartwrite, tuum est. Volat acta sagitta,
Errat, et infecto vulnere, fracta cadit.
Nec mirum: quae vis armorum, quaeve Monarchas
Viribus humanis acta sagitta premat?
Et (verum ut fatear) laesuris carpere verbis
Terrenos prohibent fasque piumque deos.
Non hoc, Cartwritus, non quae convellere dictis
Res solet ingentes, ipsa Sophia velit.
Tum Chathertonus....

APPENDIX III

18 CAMBRIDGE SCHOLARS TO CECIL, 3RD JULY, 1570

S.P. Dom. Eliz. LXXI, No. 35.

Magnum sane acerbumque dolorem cepimus, honoratiss. vir, ex eo, quo ad nos pervenit nuper, rumore, de molestiis tuis, et alienata a Cartewrighto nostro voluntate. Nam cum tibi omnes tanquam patrono singulari et Academiae parenti unico devinciamur; Cartwrightum vero singulare literarum ornamentum eximie diligamus: nihil potuit nobis accidere molestius quam ut ad curas et labores tuos a nobis quicquam adderetur; aut ille in discrimen nominis et existimationis suae cuique bono venerit. Putavimus itaque officii nostri esse, et eius, quam tibi debemus observantiae, aegritudinem illam ex falsa tantum opinione contractam levare, et Cartwrightum (si fieri potest) in veterem locum apud te et gratiam reponere. Et quamvis videri possumus parum considerate facere, qui in maximis occupationibus et quibus pene conficeris Reipub. negotiis tibi per literas obstrepere non vereamur: putamus tamen non convenire, ut, cum alii ad accusandum fuerint tam celeres, nos ad defendendum simus tardiores: beneque speramus, quod iustam defensionem, quam falsam accusationem multo libentius auditurus sis. Primum itaque de Cartwrighti nostri moribus non erit necesse nobis multa dicere; putamus neminem esse, qui eum alicuius criminis aut in tota vita maculae foedioris criminetur aut accuset; sed tamen ut honori tuo constet, qualem illi hominem vocant in invidiam: hoc de eo vero affirmamus, quod exemplar sit pietatis et integritatis, et quod quo proprius ad illius vitae consuetudinem et instituta accedimus, eo nos ipsos pluris faciamus et amemus. Religionem scimus sinceram esse, et ab omni labe puram: non enim emersit solum ex vasto et infinito papisticarum haeresium pelago, dulcissimaque Christianae religionis aqua se proluit: sed etiam ad nullam earum opinionum futilium et levium, quae quotidie disseminantur et disperguntur, tanquam ad scopulum impegit. Ad sacram scripturam regulam morum et doctrinae certissimam se astrinxit, neque usquam aut errore lapsus aut novitate seductus, illius limites quod scimus transiluit. Itaque magnum in eo non solum adversus senescentes Romanensium fabulas, a quibus magnopere non metuimus, sed etiam peregrinas vafrorum hominum opiniones, quae graviorem plagam minantur, praesidium ponimus; atque idem de eo tu tibi certo potes promittere. Doctrinam suspicimus et veneramur; vero enim de eo potest dici, quod est alicubi apud poetam: quae liberum hominem aequum est scire solertem dabo. Junxit, quod ille in magna laude posuit, graeca cum latinis; addidit etiam ultra, quod erat non exigui laboris, haebraica, atque ita quidem, ut, etiamsi in singulis pares aliquos, in universis certe superiorem invenias neminem. In ea vero quam profitetur theologia quantum valeat ex eo potest intelligi, quod tanta omnium ordinum multitudo atque frequentia ad eum audiendum quotidie confluat, tam diligenter attendat, in eiusque sententia libenter conquiescat. Neque vero hoc fit propterea, sicuti fortasse quidam tibi in aures insusurrasserunt, quod semper veniat novus, et peregrinis sententiis auditorum aures titillet: sed, quod acutus sit in interpretando, foelix in docendo, denique quod rerum gravitatem atque pondus sententiarum verborumque copia superare videatur. Itaque haec nostra de eo sententia est, quam neque precibus ullis, neque privata amicitia persuasi ad te scripsimus, sed quia virtuti hominis et pietati favemus. Nunc humillime rogamus honorem tuum, ut, si quam de eo pravam opinionem concepisti, deponas, atque nobis potius qui vitae eius et religionis et doctrinae conscii sumus fidem habeas, quam rumori, qui auctorem non habet, aut certe multa non satis candide interpretantem. Conservato cancellarie digniss. academiae tuae virum eum, cuius semper cupientissima fuit, cuiusque postquam nacta est, voce fruitur avidissime: dignissimus est tam celebri academia alumnus, dignissimus tanto patrono cliens. Fuit in omni vita magno ornamento et splendori academiae tuae, sed nunc demum multo quam antehac unquam maiori: non enim solum colitur a nobis domesticis et familiaribus, sed a peregrinis multo magis, quorum exilium lenitur suavitate ingenii eius et doctrinae, quique non dubitant eum cum iis conferre quorum tam illustris est apud externas nationes et pervagata fama. Pauci sumus, qui hoc abs te rogamus, rogamus tamen voce multorum: nemo enim fere omnium est, qui eum non admiretur, non diligat, non omni ratione defendendum putet. Si igitur academiae tuae prodesse vis nihil utilius, si gratificari nil acceptius potes facere, quam si Cartwrightum ei conserves, et quovis in ea honore dignum censueris. Deus opt. max. te Reipub. et nobis quam diutissime servet incolumen. Vale. Cantabrigiae, quinto Nonas Julii. Honori tuo devinctissimi

Guilielmus Pachet
Edmundus Rockrey
Robertus Tower
Rob. Linford
Robertus Soome

Bartholomeus Dodingtonus
Joannes Swone
Osmundus David
Richardus Howland
Simon Bucke

Edmundus Sherbroke	Thomas Aldrich
Georgius Joye	Jo. Still
Richardus Grenham	Gualterus Alen
Alanus Par	Robertus Hollande

Honoratissimo viro domino Gulielmo Cecilio etc.

APPENDIX IV

CARTWRIGHT TO CECIL, 9TH JULY, 1570

S.P. Dom. Eliz. LXXI, No. 40.

Communis totius litteratorum hominum nationis (honoratiss. vir) patronus et propugnator cum sis, in bonam spem venio, ut ipse quoque in aliqua parte curae et solicitudinis tuae maneam. Et cum multi docti viri singularem tuam experti sint, et predicarint humanitatem, patere, quaeso me, hominem non a literis prorsus alienum, illius quoque fieri participem. Video, et quidem meo cum magno malo sentio, quam sit verbum illud verum, nihil esse magis quam calumnia volucre, nihil citius emitti, facilius nihil dilatari, quae si nostris parietibus constitisset calumnia, et aulae, et tui in primis honoratissimi viri aures non pepulisset, multum esset de dolore meo detractum. Mihi autem homuncioni, te virum honoratiss. objici, et tanquam adversarium opponi, id me demum pungit acriter. Hic ego primum εὐθυγλώσσους (ut ille loquitur) desidero, qui si non defuissent nulla apud te purgandi fuit necessitas. Liceat enim mihi apud te, quod vere possum, libere etiam profiteri, me esse a seditione et contentionis studio aversissimum, nihil docuisse quod ex contextu quem tractabam non sponte flueret, oblatam etiam de vestibus occasionem praetereundo dissimulasse. Non nego quin docuerim ministerium nostrum ab avitae et apostolicae ecclesiae ministerio deflexisse: cuius ad puritatem nostrum exigi, et efformari cupiebam. Sed dico hoc a me placide et sedate factum esse, ut in nullius nisi aut ignari aut maligni auditoris, aut calumniarum aucupis, reprehensionem potuisset incurrere, de quibus tamen universis, audio me apud tuam praestantiam insimulari. Queris qui ista confirmem? En fero tibi (honoratiss. vir) plurimorum et incorruptissimorum hominum, qui interfuerunt, testimonium. Parum certe abfuit quin Academiam innocentiae meae testem protulissem. Nam nisi mihi roganti vicecancellarius concionem cogere abnuisset, equidem non dubitarem quin illa, a me, contra quae perhibentur calumnias, sententiam diceret. Non possum omnia, quae ea ipsa lectione, quae istum rumorem pepererit, continebantur, κατὰ λεπτὸν epistola includere, sed me nihil eorum quae proposuerim, tibi roganti inficiari velle polliceor sancte. Et cum meae improbitatis (si quae sit) supplicium non recusaverim, tuum in praesenti causa quod illa justa fuerit imploro patrocinium. Ergo ne patiaris (honoratiss. vir) certorum hominum odio, me imo ipsam veritatem obrui. Nam cum mihi privatim invideant, per honestum et gloriosum pacis et ecclesiae nomen oppugnare volunt. Dominus Jesus tuam in dies spiritu sapientiae et pietatis praestantiam augeat.

9 Julii. A° 1570.

Honoris tui studiosissimus

T. Cartwright.

Honoratissimo viro Domino Gulielmo Cecilio Regiae maiestati a Secretis et Academiae Cantabrig: cancellario clarissimo.

APPENDIX V

TESTIMONIAL IN FAVOUR OF CARTWRIGHT

S.P. Dom. Eliz. LXXI, No. 33.

Percrebuit tuae praestantiae magistrum Cartwrightum hoc esse suspectum nomine, quod in theologicae professionis munere quosdam discordiae igniculos, qui post in incendium creverunt, sparserit, et in controversiis de ministerio et re vestiaria, omnino se immodice jactaverit. Nos vero, quorum nomina adscripta sunt, et qui illis lectionibus interfuimus, ex quibus iste rumor fluxit, testamur nullas quas unquam audire potuimus, unde simultates aut discordias emersisse. de vestibus controversiam ne attigisse quidem. de ministerio proposuisse quaedam quorum ad amussim nostrum hoc formari cupiebat, sed ea et cautione et moderatione quae illum debebant merito tueri, et ab ista quae circumfertur calumnia vindicare.

Thomas Aldrich
Alanus Par
Robertus Tower
Robertus Soome
Simon Bucke
Richard Howlande
Robert Willan
Joannes Swane

Richardus Chambers
Christopherus Kirklande
Thomas Barbar
Laurentius Wasshington
Jo. Still
William Tabor
Joannes More.

Honoratissimo viro Domino Gulielmo Cecilio Academiae Cantabrigiensis Cancellario dignissimo.

APPENDIX VI

22 CAMBRIDGE SCHOLARS TO CECIL, 11TH AUGUST, 1570

S.P. Dom. Eliz. LXXIII, No. 12.

Vix credas, ac ne putes quidem (honoratissime vir) quantum nobis Cantabrigiensibus alumnis tuis nuper gratificatus sis, quantumque abs te beneficium accepisse arbitremur. Num cum avide jam diu expectaremus quid de Cartwrighto nostro futurum esset, multaque pericula animo volveremus, fama non dubia ad nos pervenit, omnia illi apud te foeliciter et ex votis nostris contigisse. Criminationibus enim illis, quibus injuste vexabatur, te eum perhumaniter liberasse: literasque ad praesides nostros, ad eorum animos leniendos, qui te contra eum exacuerant, misisse. Et quod unum laetamur maxime, ad ecclesiam poliendam, et nitori suo restituendam, operam promisisse. Quare non tu solum fecisti, idque merito, Cartwrightum, virtutis pietatisque tuae testem et praeconem, sed nos etiam, quotquot sumus, multoque plures, qui illius studio et doctrina ad religionem instituti, in Christiana Repub. majore cum fructu deinceps versabimur. Sed vide quam nihil sit omni ex parte beatum: intervenit huic voluptati nostrae, quam ex tua in Cartwrightum facilitate percepimus, dolor non mediocris, quod etiamsi nobis per te restitutus sit; vivat tamen in silentio, neque ad solitum docendi munus admittatur.

Hic igitur ad te, Cancellarium nostrum dignissimum, et patronum singularem, iterum confugimus, supplicesque rogamus, ut schola illi pateat, et ne ab eo cursu prohibeatur, in quem ingressus est cum magna laude sua, et utilitate nostra non minore. Est quidem nobis valde jucundum, quod bene tibi de eo persuaderi passus es, cui si hoc etiam addideris, ut illius doctrinam regustemus, qua jamdiu magno cum dolore caruimus; ultra tibi in hoc negotio, nisi quod urgeat vehementius, molesti non erimus.

Antea pro Cartwrighto tantum apud te intercessimus: nunc agimus communem causam: non enim illius tantum, sed nostra etiam interest, ut illi haec facultas permittatur. Atque te quidem ad id scimus satis facilem et propensum esse: quia tamen ii, quibus sub honore tuo gubernacula Reipub. nostrae commissa sunt, hoc recusant facere: concede nobis et Cartwrighto rogantibus, ut majore abs te auctoritate ad id confirmentur. Ita fiet, ut et studiis nostris quam optime consuluisse videaris, et integerrimi hominis existimationi; quam eo usque necesse est, tanquam ad metas haerere, quoad interpretandi munus illi restitutum fuerit. Lites ullas aut controversias non est cur verearis; habes sanctissimi viri fidem, se ne ullius quidem vulneris cicatricem refricaturum. Perge itaque ut cepisti de eo bene sentire, et ab injustis malevolorum calumniis vindicare; atque sic habeto neminem esse, vel propter religionem vel doctrinam, tanti viri patrocinio et tutela digniorem. Deus Opt. Max. honorem tuum quam diutissime incolumem conservet, et instituta fortunet. Vale. Cantabrigiae, tertio idus Augusti. Dignitatis tuae studiosissimi.

Thomas Aldrich
Ruben Sherwood, procurat. acad.
Alanus Par
Rogerus Browne
Edmundus Chapman
Hugo Boothe
Willm Tabor
Gualterus Alen
Robertus Holland
Simon Bucke
Robertus Tower
Edmondus Rockrey
Robertus Soome
Robertus Rhodes
Joannes Moore
Thomas Barbar
Jhon. Knewstub
Thomas Leache
Edmundus Sherbroke
Robertus Willan
Richardus Grenham
Georgius Slater

Honoratissimo viro D. Gulielmo Cecilio etc.

APPENDIX VII

CARTWRIGHT TO CECIL, 18TH AUGUST, 1570

S.P. Dom. Eliz. LXXIII, No. 25.

Cum conarer tuam erga me (honoratissime vir) animo meo perceptam, et indubitatam reddere voluntatem collegi quibus hoc efficerem, non pauca nec parvi (ut mihi videbantur) momenti argumenta. Inter quae primum litteris quae tua ad me praestantia scripsit locum, attribui. Velle enim non solum auctioris reipublic. academicae, sed totius regni moderatorem, si non dignitate, at certa cura et solicitudine summum, tantis in occupationibus, propria manu, ad tantulum homuncionem scribere, ut rarae cujusdam humanitatis, sic benevolentiae judicium satis illustre fuit. Quae quidem voluntas utinam ita se diffunderet, sua ut capacitate vellet causam quoque meam imo totius ecclesiae et ipsius Christi aeterni dei complecti. Et quanquam virorum nemo est cujus vel animum conciliare vel conciliatum retinere malim, quam tuum, tamen si optio daretur, vellem ne me, aut causam, tuo destitui patrocinio, si ambos complecti aut nolles, aut non posses, sane aegre me absque te deseri paterer, sed tamen paterer, si hanc gratiam ac causae propugnationem transferre potuissem. Sed hic vires, et humeros quaereris, qui cum imposito oneri, vix sint ferendo, tantam accessionem merito videntur reformidare. Vetus, et quidem sanctiss: et omnium qui unquam rempub. attigerunt sapientissimi viri mosis quaerela: sed si causa justa sit, si ecclesiae necessaria, si sine ea respublica solvatur et partes ab in vicem dissiliant (quod quidem sine disciplina fieri necessum est) causa digna est, quam recipias, et in quam rarum illud ingenii tui lumen, et divinas animi dotes proferas. Illa te vicissim complectitur, et virum alioqui ornatissimum reddet, quam ante splendidiorem, negociorum infinitate oppressum (polliceor) recreabit, succumbentem quasi subjectis columnis sustentabit. Cogitabis etenim non venire illam incomitatam, quae omnium fere non Anglia solum, sed exteris nationibus piorum hominum assiduis votis, atque adeo ipsius praepotentis dei auxilio, stipata et circumfusa sit. Sed ego homo quorundam sermone, honori tuo *νεωτεροποιός* suspectus, causam istam antiquissimam, et cum Christi et Apostolorum ecclesiis natam, eandem in novitatis suspicionem induco. Non sum, non sum (vir honoratissime) *νεωτεροποιός*, et tamen novitatis invidia, nollem a veritate absterrere, neque spero te eum esse, qui cum illis sentias, quibus olim proverbii loco terebatur, *τὰ ἀκίνητα κινεῖν*, qui voluisset quippiam innovare, neque ignoras cuique illae voces sint, *παλαιοὺς νόμους λίαν ἁπλοῦς καὶ βαρβαρικοὺς* fuisse. Sed cur ego novitati defensionem meditarer, cum causa 1570 fere annos agens, ipsa sit antiquitate veneranda, et ipse tu disertus plane esses, si pro novitate, contra antiquitatem velles dicere. Praefectorum, saltem, magni partis iniquitatem (de qua per litteras apud te quaestus sum) jam experior. Quamvis enim condicionem mihi ab honore tuo delatam, lubens susceperim, legendi tamen potestatem non faciant. Quae meae esse poterint, ex istis quae scripsi, petitiones, tua praestantia potest conjicere, et ego superiore sermone, et litteris satis aperui, febris me urget, et gravissimis occupationibus tuis quantum fieri potest concedendum. Causam ergo deo et te illius majestati commendabo quem assidue precabor ut tuam praestantiam velit et servare diutissime et spiritu sancto cumulatissime augere. Cantabrig. 18 Augusti anno 1570 honoris tui studiosissimus

Thomas Cartwright.

Honoratissimo viro Domino Gulielmo Cecilio etc.

APPENDIX VIII

JOHN WHITGIFT TO ARCHBISHOP PARKER, 21ST SEPTEMBER, 1572

Petyt MSS. 538, XXXVIII, f. 61.

My dutye moste umbly to your grace remembred, I am constrayned sooner to troble you, then I had purposed; so yt ys, that I have pronownsed Mr cartwright to be noo fellow here, by cause contrarye both to the expresse words of hys othe, and a plane statute of this colledge he hath contynued here above hys tyme not beeing full minister; which trewly I dyd nott know untill now of late; for yf I had knowne yt before, I myght have eased my self of much troble, and the colledge of greate contention. Hetherto (I thangk god) yt hath bene as quiet a colledg as any was in all chamb. now yt ys cleane contrarye marvealus troblesome and contentius, which I can ascribe to no cause so much as to Mr cartwrights presens heare. I dowt he wyll make sum frends In the courte to mantayne hym, yea thowgh yt be agaynst statute, and I have some understanding, that he goeth abowte the same. I besech your grace let me have your assistans ether by your letters to my L. burghley or my L. of Leacester or bothe, or by any other meanes you thingk best. there whole purpose ys to make me werye, by cause they take me to be an ennimye to there factiusnes, and lewde Liberty. yf they may triumph over me ones, peradventure the state heare wylbe untollerable: but I dowt nott of your graces full assistans. Mr cartwright ys flatlye perjured, and I am veryly perswaded that yt ys godes Just Judgment, that he showld for not beeing minister be so punished, which hath so greatly defaced the ministery.

I have ended the confutation of the admonition, and the first part of yt, I have written owt fayer, which I mynde to send to your grace very shortly, after I have lett my L. of elye and D. perne, or some other peruse yt. the second part I have not as yet written owt agayne, but yt wylbe done shortly. I beseche your grace Lett Mr toy (one to whom I am greatly bownde) have the pryntyng of yt, and your chaplane Mr grafton the correction of the print, for I know he ys very good In that poynt. I wold gladlye know whether your grace wold have me to dedicate the boke to any or noo, and to whome. my lord of london hath appoynted me to preach at the crosse the second sunday in the terme. I besech your grace move hys L. that yt may be the 4. which ys the seconde day of november, so shall I have better leasure to fynisch all my busines, I besech god long to preserve your grace In health and prosperitye.

from trinitye colledg in chamb. the 21 of septemb. 1572.

your graces to commaunde

Jhon Whitgyfte.

APPENDIX IX

CARTWRIGHT TO BURGHLEY, 17TH OCTOBER, 1572

Lansd. MSS. XII, No. 85, ff. 188–9.

Me non ita pridem (honoratiss. vir) collegio eiectum, quo minus ad patrocinium tuum confugerim, impediebant inter coetera regni, quibus pene confici te existimabam negocia. Quorum cum et ad multitudinem et varietatem tempestates hae gravissimum pondus adiunxissent, verebar ne vel minima interpellatione aut tibi occupatissimo importunior, aut reipublicae, cuius id maxime interesset, ut totum te in se unam conversum habeat, iniquior apparerem, si iustissimam (ut mihi persuadeo) quaerimoniam, datis ad te litteris compraehensam consignassem. Qui metus in me gravius, si in hiis fuisset aliquis, qui immoerentem apud te criminationibus onerarunt, et aures tuas acerbissimis querelis conscelerarunt nae illi a falsis (cum me a iustis cohibuerim) accusationibus abstinuissent. Antea igitur quae non fuit, nunc iusta est, et ut spero concessa oratio: Nec enim puto convenire ut cum illi ad accusandum tam fuerint celeres, ego ut sim ad defendendum tardior: nec praestantiam tuam possum (ut a me sit) ab aequitate ita alienam cogitare, quin multo sit iustam defensionem, quam falsam accusationem libentius auditura. Aio me per iniuriam collegio pulsum esse: Quaeris qui probem? si causam recipis, nihil est quod facilius possim expedire. Atque nisi molestum sit, et per occupationes hoc liceat: ut πάλινδικία retractetur, academiae alumnus a summo cancellario humillime petit. Rem perscripsissem, sed prolixitatem veritus, litteris nolebam, ne nimis excrescerent, includere. Mallem coram agere: id enim et mihi ad brevitatem aptius, et honori tuo ad iudicandum certius existit. Ecce autem hominum iniquissimorum, et qui nulla calamitate mea exanimari possint, novam quandam immanitatem: aqua enim et igne interdictus, cui tantum fere culeus defuit ut tanquam matricida punirer: seditionis etiam, ut audio, et partium studii insimulor. O indignitatem, is ut queratur qui damnum intulit! qui gravissimum vulnus alteri inflixerit, perinde si laesus esset exclamet! Sed homo catus, quum apud te de insigni accepta iniuria, iustam quaerendi materiam esse intelligeret, querela praerepta, et calumniis suis creato praeiudicio omnem mihi deinceps informandae, et insinuendae veritatis viam cupiebat intercipere. At ad contendendum natus, scilicet nunquam quiesco, aliis qui mea voce, tanquam dato ἐνδοσιμω excitati se totos contentionibus irrequiete litigandi facem praefero. Credo quod primum cubiculo, post sodalitio motus placide concesserim, ne digitum quidem sustulerim, nullo nec dicto, nec facto, non modo non ulta, sed ne propulsata, et quod maius est, ne ut aut vindicetur, aut propulsetur attentata illius in me, ante hoc tempus inaudita prorsus iniuria. Quid igitur quaerit, aut quid persequitur? me, ut homini sibi in omnibus obsequenti gratificaretur, cubiculo pepulit, tuli: mea domus mihi clausa, alteri patuit, passus sum: praefecturam (me socio) sibi non satis aut tutam aut honorificam fore existimans: solus, inconsulto senatu, indicta causa expulsionis sententiam protulit: id quoque (quia a litibus, quantum licuit et plus etiam fortasse quam licuit) semper abhorrui, mihi sustinendum esse duxi. Nunc suis omnibus, quibus mihi per se officere potuit, quasi exhaustis copiis, nullum tamen nocendi finem statuit: sed criminibus falso confictis, me apud honorem tuum, in odium et invidiam vocat. Eodem enim, sive per se, sive per suos quosdam emissarios illud faciat, res recidit. Atque vel utroque, vel alter utro horum modo, id ab eo tentatum fuisse, nec dubio, nec obscuro sermone, ad me allatum est. Neque hic lenitatis notam mihi sentio extimescendam, ac si famae temere assensionem praebuissem: praesertim cum nihil hic suspicer, quod non ab illo apud nostros disseminari pulchre mihi constet. Supplicissime igitur a te peto (honoratissime vir) ut ab istis (si quae sint) accusationibus, tantisper assensionem cohibeas, dum quid in illis diluendis efficere possum experiaris: nec enim dubito, ne non vita mea placide, et tranquille acta, contra omnes istiusmodi rumores parum sit valitura. Sed finis sit: vides enim quomodo istorum inhumanitas orationem meam longius provexit. Precor dominum ut te velit ad ecclesiae et reipub. instaurationem quam diutissime conservare. Vale decimo sexto calend. Novembris. Cantabrig.

Tui, qui cum dei gloria coniunctus est,
honoris studiosissimus,
Thomas Cartwrightus.

Honoratissimo viro Domino Burleio Angliae thesaurario, et Academiae Cantabrigiensis Cancellario summo.

(*Endorsed*) 16° Cal. Nov. 15...[*1572*].
17 Octob.
Mr Cartwright of Ca...[*Cambridge*] to my L.
Complaines of his expulsion: and Desires his Lordship to suspend his beleif of ye further accusations yt were to bee brought against him. Against D Whitgift.

Calendar of *Lansd. MSS.* dates this letter in error 27 Oct. 1571.

APPENDIX X

CARTWRIGHT TO MICHAEL HICKS, 9TH DECEMBER, 1573

Lansd. MSS. XVIII, No. 18, f. 35.

Mr Hicks, (*defaced*) it was unreasonable yt upon so smale acquaintance as I had, and no dutie or service at all either past or like to come that I should not onlie be chargeable to yow whilst I was there, butt also when I went, should cary away money with me ffor with many such lodginges I might sone growe to ye Riches of an English Bishope. Butt because yow were so earnest with me, and because yow should perceyve yt I was not unwilling to be further bounde unto yow I receyved it. Now geve me leave also, I beseach yow (good Mr Hicks [*defaced*]) to retorne some parte of it unto yow in a booke, wherin are layd up ye Riches and treasures, which last for ever. The doctryne wherof hath on her righte hand liffe, and on her lefte hand honor and every good thinge mete for all ages, butt especially for youthe, for all estates and orders of men, but singularlie for those yt god hath blessed with some better estate then ye rest. I beseche yow therfore receyve it at my hand, having notwithstanding I assure yow reserved a good portion of yt yow sent unto my self, which I will kepe as yow willed me, as a token to putt me in remembrance of yow, bethought I should be very forgetfull, if I should have forgotten your kindnes, if yt had not bene. And thus with my humble thankes unto yow, I commend yow to ye tuicion of our god whom I beseache to encrease with all manner of his gracious blessinges and especially with that swete knowledg of his sonne Jesus Christe our Lord to your full Comforte and Joye yt can never be taken from yow. 9° December 1573.

yours to commande

Thomas Cartwrighte.

APPENDIX XI

ORDER FOR CARTWRIGHT'S APPREHENSION, 11TH DECEMBER, 1573

S.P. Dom. Eliz. XCIII, No. 4.

Wee doe requier you, and therewith streightlie commaund you and every of you in the Quenes Maties name that you be aidinge and assistinge to the bearer and bearers hereof with all the best meanes you can devise for the apprehenc̄ōn of one Thomas Cartwright student in divinitye wheresoever he be within liberties or withowt within this Realme, and you havinge the possession of his bodie by your good travell and diligence in this behalf, wee doe likewise chardge you (for soe is her ma^{ties} pleisure) that he be brought upp by you to London with a sufficient number for his safe apparaunce before us and other her ma^{ties} Commissioners of Oyer and Terminer in causes Ecclesiasticall for his unlawfull dealinges and other his most daingerous dealinges and demean^{ors} in matters touchinge Religion and thestate of this Realme. And this faile ye not to doe everie one of you with all diligence as ye will awnswere to the contrarie uppon your uttermost perilles.

From London this xjth of December 1573.

Your verie lovinge frendes

To all maiors, Sheriffes, Bailiffes, Cunstables, Hedborowes, and to all others the Quenes Maties Officers unto whome these maie cum or apperteine, and to everie one of them, as well within Liberties as withowte.

John Ryvers mayor
Ed. London
Robt. Catelyn
Gabriell Goodman
Thomas Sekford
Thomas Wylson
G. Gerad

Willyam Cordell
Alex. Nowell
W. Fletewode.

Leonell Duckett
Tho. Bromley.

APPENDIX XII

CARTWRIGHT TO WALTER TRAVERS'S FATHER. FROM GENEVA, 1574

Add. MSS. 33271, ff. 41–2 (cf. copy in *Hopkinson MSS.* XVIII, ff. 125–6 in Bradford City Library).

The grace of our Lord god and the most comfortable assistaunce of God his most hollie Spirit through Jesus Christe oure only mediator be with you and remaine with you for ever. That good and holie will of god which I knowe you desire dayly maye be fulfilled in all thinges, that good will the Lorde hath declared unto your sonne Mr Robert Traverse to be this that he would not have him to be any longer in this unkinde and unthanckefull world, which for that which is both ment and done well recompenseth evill againe, but would drawe him to him self where he might fully enioye the fruite of his labor and godlines. And althoughe I doe not doubt but that good Spirit which teacheath you to desire the will of god maye be done, will teach you also at this time to be content and thanckfull nowe when it is done. Yet I knowe you shall not want enemies that will goe aboute to drive you from that patient contentment that you desire so earnestly to keepe. ffirst yt you have lost your sonne but thankes be to the L. he is not lost whome the L. hath in his Cumpanye neyther have you lost him which is there whether you shall goe and enioye him everlastingly. Therefore Mr Traverse I desire you by the gatheringe togeither and metinge of the Sainctes and by the comminge of our Savior Christe that your sorrowe which your naturall affection will move you unto maye be swallowed upp with the consideracon of that meetinge which the very dume and deaf Creatures doe groane for and which we ought much more to sigh for, whose cause that comminge and metinge shalbe for. yf we desire that metinge of Sainctes and comminge of Christe our Savior howe maye we take to hart that whereby our saviour C: maketh him self waye to that his comminge, and howe doe we desire the metinge of his Sainctes, when we would not have them to be gathered into that place where the can only meete & abide togeither. ffor assuredly they can never meete here in this worlde. Therefore as Davide comforted him self with that that once he should enioye his sonne againe, so the god of Comfort make you to feele and your godly bedfellowe also theis greate mercies of the L. that where he somtimes chuseth the parentes and passeth by the Children, sometime choseth the

Children and passeth by the parentes So that when they once be parted in this world they can never meete againe. The Lordes election hath here so mett both in the Children and in the parentes confirmed with such undoubted Argumentes of the knowledge of god and of unfayned faith that you be assuredly perswaded that his partinge is but for a time, the which thinge more assured you be thereof then David could be of his childe, yet beinge such as no certen knowledge of his election then could appeare so much more cause of mercye have you offered into your handes of the L. then David had. But that will strike you that beinge so toward learninge and godlines and what other thinge might make for commendacōn of a yonge man that godly light that shined so cleare him should almost no soner begune to blase and shewe forth it self then the L. would forth with put it forth. Here againe Mr Traverse you knowe right well that light is increased a Thowsand fould and therefore no grief cometh that waye. But you will saye we have no benefitt of it, we have not indeed that fruite we might have had of him yf the L. anger with us for our sinnes had not taken him awaye. But this lamentacōn doth not appertaine unto you, to me rather that did reape and should furth have reaped of his sweete and lovinge Companye more proffitt then ever you should have taken. Here also all the godly that ever knewe him or ever shall understand of him did ioyne them selves with you and will communicate in this sorrowe, whose partes are as greate in yt as yours. And therefore you shall doe them iniury yf you take that all to your self which of right appertayneth to them, and so lament your sorrowe as thoughe none ells but you were sorrye for him. And if greate lamentacōns were required in the behalf of those that dye in the feare of L. and be with god, your Sonne Mr Gualter hath paide it alreadye so plentifully that yf you should not moderate your sorrowe more then he, you might reconne some incommoditie in this your ould age which you should not so well beare out as beinge yonge, which I rather make mention of that at least in regarde of him, and other your Children you doe not exceede in this sorrowe for the death of your sonne. for I make the Accompte after this sorte that for so muche as his brothers death went so neare him that he coulde hardly be brought to Receive comforte, yf he shoulde heare anye thinge otherwise then well yt would geve him such a deepe wound as would hazerd him also, for you knowe he is of nature very weake and sorrowe will sone kill suche. I wisshed him to come home because his thinne nature will hardly devour and overcome the difficulties of travell but I could not perswade him. Towchinge the maner of your sonnes death you have also to reioyce. ffor when as you see somtime the Children of the iust and the Children themselves also godly to be taken awaye by the secreate iudgement of god by deathes violence of drowninge etc. It pleased the L. to call him awaye by such a death wherein no such token of the wrath of god appeared, for he died in his bed of an Ague, and was there where he wanted no kepinge nor phisicke, for there was never a daye that the Phisic̄on came not twise at the least, and was buried in the Land of Conoran very comlye accompanied with the Studentes and professors in the Universitie. The somme is, Mr Traverse, that as you have good cause of reioysinge in many considerac̄ons to what side so ever you turne your self so to reioyce in the L. and to receave the Comforde that the L. offreth in such wise as you maye be hable to comforte your Bedfellowe and your Children. I must as you see make an end of writinge. But I will praye to the L. to comfort you. And I knowe Mr Gwalter hath written at lardge to you and effectually of this matter. And therefore with my hartie Comendac̄ons both to you and to your Bedfellowe I will committ you both to the mercifull kepinge of the Lord our god who kepe you through Christe. Mr Gualter...very dilligent about him all the tyme of his sicknes.

ffrom Geneva

yours to his power

Thomas Cartwright 1574.

APPENDIX XIII

CARTWRIGHT TO WILLIAM DAVISON, FROM ANTWERP, 2ND JULY, 1580 (?)

S.P. Dom. Eliz. Add. XXIX, No. 125.

When I remember the saying of th'appostle, advouched also for the fuller credit and allouance therof from the moest holy mouth of our Saviour Christ, that yt is a blesseder thing to give then to take: as my povertie shutteth my hand from giving, so the perill of infelicitie, or rather of lesse happinesse, which the scripture setteth in the receyving hand, is often tymes ready to make me close yt that necessitie would sometimes open. In which respect I can not sufficiently marvaill at the maner of those rich and noble men, which in sted that they should send furth their fountaynes and conduites of liberalitie abroad, doe not unwillingly behould the gutters of those that ar far their inferiors to come flouing towards them, unlesse peradventure yt be that, that they must receive of many, to th'end that they may give to many, which, yf yt be doen in measure, and with good choise of boeth the givers and receivers, hath (I graunt) a plentifull defence. And although I have (I thank the lord) otherwise to remedie the blemishe and skare of my receyving, in that I am for the lords cause brought to some more need then otherwise I should have bene, keeping therein company with th'appostle and ye lord hymself, which were mainteined at others charges; yet (me thinkes) in this receit from you, I have met with a speciall disadvantage for in this matter of giving and receyving, with others I have somewhat to exchaunge. I graunt yt is somewhat unequall, when for there weightie gould they receive the light wares of paper and yncke: yet for that the goodnes of gould riseth rather uppon thestimation of men then of any passing vertue in yt self, in that red earth is so highly prised of them, yt cometh sometymes to passe that my letters (hou light soever) are, by acceptation and an overweening of me, laid in the balance with the gould yt self. And the trueth is, when they handle holy thinges, having regard to the matter and not to the handling: they are not a whit deceived considering that no gould nor preciouse stone may be weighed therewith: in such sort that if the veyn thereof were not to be found otherwhere they should (as the marchant in the gospell) rather sell all, then to be without so pretiouse and necessary a marchandeise, without the which we shall not be suffered to arrive at the desyred haven of the heavenly kingdome. Nou therefore the disadvantage at your hand ys, partly that my letters which may be of some use to them, can serve you to small purpose: partly that if they (happely) should provoke you to write again, not onely the hope of recompence, but even thendevor of any shew of recompence ys taken from me. In which cas also in some other respects I left order with my wife, that she should not be lighthanded in receiving that alwayes that might be offered. Howbeit whether yt were by th'instance of your offer, or by her weak refusall: ones she is come over with a gilt cup and cover to yt, which if you will needs have yt so, I humbly thank you for yt. Although nether for my bond to you wards was yt needfull, which for your effectuall love towards the synceritie of trueth, might have before commanded whatsoever was in me, nether for the testifying of your good will towards me, which both by your own speach, and by the letters and talk of this bearer, I knew to be unfeyned, not onely towards me but also others that love the trueth. which love for the trueths sake, with other singuler graces that the lord hath bestowed uppon you: are cause enough without any particuler deserts to make me holly yours. Being therefore yours dubbly, boeth in respect of common duetie, and of particuler interest that you have gotten or pourchased rather in me: you see hou you may use me, if there be wherein I may doe you service. And thus with myn humble commendacions unto you and Mrs Davidson (with whome for the great good report of her I wish I had bene acquainted when I was so nere the place where she was) I commend you boeth with the rest of your familie unto the lord our god: whome I beseche to blesse you with all maner of his graciouse blessings in Jesus Christ our onely Savior. The 2[d] of July from Antwerp. My wife hath her also humbly commended unto you boeth, thanking you in like maner for your great kindenes.

yours to command

Thomas Cartwright.

To the right worshipfull Mr Davidson.

APPENDIX XIV

CARTWRIGHT TO CHRISTOPHER HATTON, *ca.* 1580?

Add. MSS. 15891, ff. 31–2.

Your honors love to the Doctrine of the Gospell, with hatred of forren power and poperie, wherof I have conceaved opinion, by reporte of some persones of righte good crediete, (your sincere proceding wherein I beseeche God may make you truely and perfectly honorable) hath putt my pen in my hande to write unto you, for the obteyninge of some of that grace, of which you have so greate stoore with her ma[tie], to my especiall releif in a cause, the equitie wherof, I leave to your honors iudgement after it shall please you to enforme your self of the same: ffor seinge all Godly trueth, is so nere of kyn, one to the other as no Sisterly bonde, is to bee compared there with, the Doore of your harborough beinge open to the one, I trust shall nott be shutt up agaynst the other. Havinge laide here uppon the principall grounde of my incouragement there came to my mynde, for my further confirmation, therein, that if it be of honorable reporte, to doo good to many, it is muche more that your goodnes should lite uppon those, that are trodden underneath the foote: whiche is so much the more acceptable to God, as he hath more especially commended the care of those, then of any other and so much the more welcome unto men, as everye one hath a neerer sense and greater gladnes, of his change from a troublesome estate into a quyett then frome a quyet, into a more commodious. My trouble, if it like your honor, is not only the restraynte of my libertie, these sixe yeares, butt especially, as that which lyeth muche heavier uppon me, the suspition of Disloyaltie, wherof I stande accused, to her ma[tie]. The matter is this: ffirst I doo with most humble thanckes, cheeffly unto the Lorde our God, and then to her ma[tie], whiche is his good hande towardes us, acknowledge the estimable treasure of the Doctrine of the Gospell, that shyneth amongest us: Then I can not denye, butt that I have written some thinges, which run into the evill speeches of divers, other wise well disposed, the cause wherof, is the clamorous, and unconscionable reportes of certeyne which love them selves to muche, who have learned to well this pointe of husbandrie, to sowe their seede of sclaunderous speaches thicke and threefolde, to the ende that some at the leaste, may take: ffor I am charged with thinges, Which not only I did never write, butt which never entered so much as in to my thoughte. As to geve the attempte of the overthrowe of all good goverment in the Comon wealth to myslike of Magistrates, and especially of Monarkes, to like of equalitie of all estates, and of a hedles rulynge, of the unrulie multitude. In the Churche, to perswade the same disorder of setting no difference betwene the people, and their gouvernors: in their gouvernors, to leave no degrees; To geve to the Ministers in their severall charges, an absolute power of doinge what them liketh best, without controllement of either Civill or Ecclesiasticall authoritie: and for the present estate of our Churche, that I carry suche an opynione of yt, as in the myslike therof, I disswade the Ministers from their Charges, and the people from heering the worde, and receaving the Sacrementes at their handes unles it mighte be in suche sorte, as I my self would have it. All whiche iudgementes, as I utterlye deteste, so for the mayntey̅n̅ce of them, there shall not be founde, withoute open and violent wrestinge, so muche as one sentence in any of my bookes that have been publisshed, whearas to the contrarye, their are divers sentences of that cleernes, that none can denye butt he which will saye, that it is not lighte at none daies; Yf happely your honor will aske after proofe, it can not be more certenly had, then of my bookes written in this behalfe. Yf yt may seeme to longe, lett the triall be, by the ecclesiasticall discipline written in latten, whiche, as it handleth the same matter, so by a preface sett before itt, I have testified my agreament therewith. Yf yet a shorter waye be sought, the prefaces in my several bookes contayning the somme of the matter in demaunde, will aunswere of my dewtifull meanynge in these causes. Yf eny other more reasonable waye may be advised of, I will thereunto most willinglie submytt my self: Only my humble suite is, that I be nott condempned in silence, butt there may be a tyme of tryall, as there hath bene of accusatione. Her ma^tie hath an eare open to her poorest subiectes; I am one of that nomber, in humble submissione with the poorest, in affectioned good will towardes her long Raigne, and heaped felicite, with the richest, as that which I have dailye moost humbly commended unto the lord, from the first tyme that ever I had any feelinge knowledge of the Gospell untill this present. Others have audience at her ma^tie handes, when their goodes are but towched, my name, which is a muche more pretious possessione is rent a sunder: there causes concerne butt them selves, myne reache unto many, and diverse persons, their is in earthlie matters, myne is in heavenly: beynge therefore in duetifull allegeance equall, and in a matter which I complayne my self of, above others, my humble suite is, that in indifferent hearinge and informatione of the cause, I may not be inferiour unto them all. I desire nothinge more, then that the cause it self, so far as it is shalbe proved good, mighte so appere unto her ma^tie: my next desire is, that if I must needes remayne in her highnes suspitione, (the grevous sorrowe wherof, I shall not laye downe butt with my lief) yet that it may be accordinge to that which I have written, and not according to that which I am reported of: So shall I be suer to be eased of the slanderous surmyse of my disloyaltie to her ma^ties estate, and to the common wealthe: likewise of my love to puritanisme, and Churche confusione: the contrary of booth which, I doo most ernestlie protest, with this offer, that if either be proved against me, I will refuse no extreamitie to be practised uppon me. This is my humble suite, where in whatsoever your honor shall bring to passe, for that, youe shall not have me a lone, butt nombers of others, favoringe the trueth, bounde unto you. And thus I humbly commende your honor to the lordes gratious keepinge, whome I beeseche dayly to increase in you, all godlynes, and honor to his glorye.

Your Honors humbly to commaunde

Thomas Cartwryght.

APPENDIX XV

CARTWRIGHT TO BURGHLEY, 17TH APRIL, 1585

Lansd. MSS. XLV, No. 77, ff. 180–1.

Illustriss: Domine: Ad Caesaree nostrae maiestatis sanctionem senatum literas dedi. In quo conventu amplissimo, cum tu, vir honoratissime, bona et magna pars sis: tibi easdem inscriptas esse non ignoras. Communibus tamen illis, has ad te privatim literas visum est adjungere hac animi inductione, quod te et in subveniendi facultate nemini concedere probe nossem, et in me iuvandi voluntate non omnino adversum et alienum esse confiderem. Cuius fiduciae de tua in me nonnulla propensione, si causam forte requiras: liceat mihi meam olim cum illa Academia (cuius tu summus Cancellarius existis) conjunctionem et necessitudinem profiteri. Aves quidem suae pullitiei curam ilico abierunt, simul ac pennis instructae e parentum nido provolant. Tuam vero praestantiam longe secus affectam existimarim, ut quae non illos modo curet, qui collegiorum septis et parietibus inclusi tenentur, sed et reliquos corpore ab Academia avulsos, animo et affectu adhaerescentes et adunatos, cura complectatur. Qua spe fretus, et petitionis quam ad te affero aequitate, in summam spem venio, me quod sequor apud te consequuturum. Quinque iam annos peregre a patria agens, eos prope omnes in ecclesiae Anglicanae, quae in transmarinis partibus haeret, ministerio consumsi. Quo tempore, postquam saepius cum morbo dubio plane et ancipiti vehementer conflictatus essem: multorum malorum concussione et agitatione attritus: tandem in tabem seu (quam vocant) Hectikam incidi. Cui morbo quo facilius resisteretur, ex doctiss. medicorum consilio, ab infesto et inimico aere, ad patrium solum et coelum mihi amicum magis et propitium redii, ubi, sicut in tota peregrinatione, tametsi ea cura et sollicitudine usus sim, ut nullius quantum vis iniquissimi offensionem iure me incurrisse mihi persuadeam: meas tamen aures illae voces assidue circumsonant, quae quoniam spem improbis (maxime pontificiis) timorem bonis afferunt: eas ego non valetudinis tantum, sed vitae prope dispendio redimere paratus sum. Ecquid enim homini suam fidem et observantiam submississimam et subiectissimam, Regineae celsitudini, et aliis, quorum hoc scire maxime interest probare cupienti: gravius aut tristius accidere potest, quam turbulentiae et inquietudinis insimulari: sacrae maiestatis indignationem adversus se jactari. Lictores, seu apparitores, compraehendendis maleficis destinatos, passim emissos esse perhiberi, ut in urbe palam versantem et coetus cum ecclesiasticos, tum civiles (prout usus est) adeuntem, ad carceres et publicam custodiam conquirant. Si quid horum de quibus me in odium et invidiam vocant, admisisse me ulla verisimilitudine probare poterint: ipse mihi dicam scribo, sistoque ad illud tribunal quod severissime in illos statuere solet, qui in ecclesiae aut Reipub: pacem delinquunt. Quod si horum nihil sit, supplicissime ab amplitudine tua con(ten)do, ut sive vera sive vana sint quae de principis in me offensione, et vindicta, ministris ad me compraehendendum hinc inde extensis circumferuntur: tua apud principem gratia, apud coeteros auctoritate id efficias, ut illa nec mihi, nec honestae quam affector existimationi fraudi sint. Quod si feceris me tibi communi et regni civium et Academiae alumnorum officio dud...(? um) devinctum: proprio et arctiore quodam obsequii vinculo, ad omnia in quibus meum in te studium et observantia elucere potest, obligabis. Interea dominum praecor ut te quam diutissime nobis incolumem servans, eundem assiduis sui spiritus incrementis, in dies auctum magis et ornatum esse velit. Quintodecimo Calend. Maij A° 1585.

Tuae amplitudinis studiosiss(imus)

Thomas Cartwright.

Illustrissimo Domino D° de Burghly summo Angliae Thesaurario Domino suo observandissimo.

(*Endorsed*) April 1585. Mr Cartwright to my L. Upon his return from beyond Sea officers were appoynted to apprehend him as a Promoter of Sedition, hee prayes ye intercession of his Lordship with ye Queen.

APPENDIX XVI

CARTWRIGHT TO BURGHLEY, 2ND JUNE, 1585

Lansd. MSS. XLV, ff. 182–3.

Scio (vir honoratissime) ea te gravissimarum occupationum mole premi, quae literis meis aditum apud te interclusissent: nisi amplitudinis tuae in petitoriis literis admittendis facilitatem iam ante expertus, de eadem aequanimitate in his accipiendis, quae animi grati significationem continent, persuasus fuissem. Priores illae quibus (in periculo agens) ad tuam gratiam et autoritatem confugiebam: ita et consultae et utiles fuerunt, ut liberae tamen et nullo necessitatis vinculo illigatae tenerentur. Hae vero quas iam ob acceptum beneficium affero, ita iustae et debitae sunt: ut (illis praeteritis) nec illiberalis, nec ingrati animi labem, declinare me posse intelligam. Quamobrem cum et a certis hominibus, et sermone minime dubio, tuae praestantiae testimonium ad me allatum sit, quod in clarissimo regni senatus consessu de me dixisti: committere non debui, ut illud silentio praeterirem, quod mihi cum ad praesentem e malo liberationem, tum ad ministerii mei transmarini honestam inter omnes existimationem opportunum et conducibile fuit. Quam ad gratitudinem testandam sollicitius incumbo: primum quidem quod ab ingratitudine in homines, proclivis admodum et promta est ad impietatem in deum prolapsio. Deinde ut semen beneficientiae tuae laete pullulans atque proveniens, animum praestantiae tuae addat, aliis afflictis et aerumnosis subveniendi: utcunque enim inter homines abiecti et contempti videantur, tuo tamen patrocinio non indignos existimaveris, quos deus summe misericors et reverendus, paternae curae suae complexu compraehendit. Atque hanc grati animi recordationem paucis profiteri, non tam tibi, quam mihi necesse fuit. Quae vero super sunt officia, cumprimis ut deum pro te et rebus tuis venerer, illa domino omnium καρδιογνώστῃ quotidie innotescent. Quibus in praecibus, deum explicatis manibus, et voce in coelum elata quotidie supplex invocavo (? -cavi or invoco): ut te virum consultissimum vero sui timore imbuere pergat, quo consilio omnia ad sanctissimi verbi κανόνα καὶ βάσανον revocata, et reipub. cui haec opera navantur, et tibi consultori pulchre et ex voto succedant. Deus amplitudinem tuam assiduis sancti spiritus incrementis in dies auctam: cum ad ecclesiae plenam instaurationem, tum ad reipub. piam et honestam pacem in omnem posteritatem firmandam quam diutissime servet.

postridie Calendas Junii 1585

Tuae amplitudinis studiosissimus

Thomas Cartwright.

Illustrissimo Domino D° Burghleio summo Angliae Thesaurario.

(*Endorsed*) Junii 1585. Mr Cartwright to my L.
Returnes his Lordsp thanks for speaking in his behalf in the Parlament. Wherby his peace was obtained.

APPENDIX XVII

CARTWRIGHT BEFORE BISHOP FREAKE

Baker MSS. XXVIII, ff. 443–5.

The Earle of Leycester, in favor of the Puritan Faction setts up Mr Cartwright, about Coventry and Warwick, which was in the Diocese of Worcester. Cartwright invaded the Bishops jurisdiction, more than the honest patience of Bp: Freake could endure. Thereupon Cartwright is summond to appear, and bearing himself upon the power of Leycester, comes attended with such Gentlemen as sided with him. The honest good Bp: thought to have had the assistance of Dr Goldsborough and Dr Lewis two of the Prebendaries of the College of Worcester, but they, whether for fear of Leycesters power, or of y[r]: own Inability shrinked away, under a pretence of being sent for to Hereford, where they were Prebendaries: So the poore Bishop was left alone. But it pleased God, that the very same night that Cartwright came to town, came Dr Longworth also to the College. As soon as he was come, word was sent to the poore Bp:, which so much revived him, that he became as it were, a young man again. He sent for Dr Longworth, and acquainted him with the business that was to be done next morning. The Dr comforted the good old Bp: and bid him not fear; no man, says he, knows this Cartwright better then my self, we were Fellows of St Johns College in Cambr: together, and much about one standing.

The morning being come, the Bp: was attended to the consistory, by his Registrary, his Chaplain, and others. Dr Longworth came, and the Bp: entreated him to sit down by him. Then came Cartwright attended with Gentlemen of his Faction, and being called, answered not untill the third time of his Call; and altho he was a bold man, yet was somewhat abashed when he saw Dr Longworth. The Bp: begun, and told him in a mild and gentle manner, Mr Cartwright, you are here accused of disturbing the peace and quietness of the Church by Innovations, and obtruding fancies and devices of your own, or others. Then spake Cartwright and said, he had the word of God for his warrant, and the example of Reformed Churches for his Guide. Then said Dr Longworth, Mr Cartwright, you and I have been of old acquaintance in the University, and Fellows of one and the same House. I know, that you were ever noted to be of a factious disposition and of a discontented mind, and by your travell you have perfected that humor to the height of perswasion, that now you are come unto. And you have brought over with you the dreggs of Geneva, whereby you would instill into the minds of the Queens subjects, that your Doctrine is the only truth to be embraced and entertained. You had best to take heed, you run not upon the same Rock, the Papists split themselves upon, and draw upon yourself the same Penalty ordained for them that alienate the hearts of the subjects from their Prince and Religion both. You have gone very far in it already, and for my own part, I am a man that would be looth to entrap you, or to bring you into a snare. If you have any thing to propose, that you suspect you shall have no favourable audience here, Sett down your self, what are the points and grounds you will stand unto, make your choice of any University in Christendome, where you will have it disputed of, I myself will upon my own charge, be ready to answere whatsoever you can object. Mr Cartwright had no great stomach to have any thing to do with this our Longworth, but fairly stole out of town, not having so much manners as to take his leave, or excuse himself to the Bp: who lovingly invited him to dine with him that next day. He never came any more, being protected by Leycester from being any further questioned. He dyed a rich man, having so much given him by the Brethren and Holy Sisters. He infected all those parts with his errors, which have overthrown our Church of England, and might happily have been prevented. If the good advice and warning given by Mr Hooker, Bp: Andrews, Sr W. Raleigh, and especially Arch Bp: Bancroft had been timely regarded.

APPENDIX XVIII

CARTWRIGHT TO SERGEANT PUCKERING, 20TH MAY, 1590

Harl. MSS. 7042, f. 58.

To the Right Worshipfull Mr Puckering, one of her Maties Sergeants at law.

That having receyved M^ris^ Puckerings letter upon wedensdaie I came no sooner with yt: the cause hath bene in part a straine of one of my leggs, & in part th'importunitie of my Frends by the waye lying upon me to staie untill I had gotten some habilitie of my legge to travaill with more comoditie. And now that I am come to the Town that I bring not the letter my self: the cause is for that being sent for by a Poursuivant I was loeth to be attached before I had made my appearance without attachement

& that I might be myne own Poursuivant as yt were: & partly also because I was loeth that your favor towards me should any waie appear to any manner of hurt of yours & no good of myne.

And now good S^r^ confessing my self greatly behoulding unto yow in my behalfe & the behalfe of my wife my humble desire is that I may yet further be behoulding unto yow in the behalf of the poor Church of Warwick that likelye enough may be deprived of all manner of tollerable Ministry boeth for the good of your own familie which is great & in regard of other poor Soules there: that if the tymes will not bear us that are there praesent now: yet there may be some suche provided as differing in judgment from us may notwithstanding boeth in some good skill and care proceed in thedification of the Church without bitternes of Spirit against other poore men which are other wise mynded: which I am the boulder to crave at your worsh: hand as I understood (& was glad of) that the Town hath chosen you to the Recordership[1] which may be singular mean of doeing much good unto the Town & amongest others that good that yt pleased yow to talk with me of. This I was bould to write in fear of being severed from doeing any more service there & yet not acknown to my self of any breach of law wherby I may be towched saving onely that I feare to be committed for refuseing thoath ex officio mero. And thus I humbly comend yow to the gracyouse keping & blessing of God in Jesus Christ.

May the 20th A° 90

Yours to command in the Lord

T Cartw.

APPENDIX XIX

CARTWRIGHT TO BURGHLEY, FROM LONDON 23RD JUNE, 1590

Lansd. MSS. LXIV, No. 15, ff. 49, 50.

Right honorable and my singuler good Lord, notwithstanding I make conscience of troubling your L with particuler causes whose strenght of bodie and mynde (for longer continuance amongest us) I could desire were consecrated to the generall and state causes of the whole Realm: yet the cause I bring before yow

[1] Puckering was appointed Recorder of Warwick on Thursday, 30th April, 1590, and took the oath next day. *Black Book*, pp. 383–4.

pressing so greatly and your h. being (as I am infourmed) thonely person by whose mean relief may be obteyned: I am even as yt were constrainedly drawn (in most humble sute) to appear before your h. at this time, first and principally in the behalf of the poor Hospitall at warwick, and after in the second place in mine own behalf. The case (if yt please your L.) is as foloweth: The right honorable Erle of Lecester indwed his hospitall in warwick with two hundreth poundes by year. whereof a cl^{li} are to th'use of xii poor men, and th'other fiftie for the stipend of the master, whome he requireth to be a preacher. for perfourmance whereof, he giveth certen Lands in warwick and Lancastre Shires[1] whose rentes (raised unto the highest) amount unto that sum, and no more. These Lands about a three yeares before his death, he conveyed by deed to the Hospitall. which because yt was not inroulled within the year, according to trust he put in one Mr Sutton of Lincolns Inne, was esteemed (in strict construction of Law) insufficient. whereupon the Hospitall was compelled to take a second graunt of the like honorable Erle of warwick, as of his heir. ffurther th'Erle of Lecester over and above th'ordinary stipend of the master gave me by Letters patentes other 50^{li} during my life: not charged (in deed) out of any certen land, but payable by his and his heires receivers generalli which notwithstanding is agreed by the learned in the lawes of the land, to be good as long as the heir hath assetes, or otherwise, wheresoever the land should become, if I had browght a writ of annuitie at any time before the landes had come into the handes of a straunger. which I might in deed have doen (the rent being one whole year behinde) but that yt was not meet for me a man of so low degree, to call such honorable personages into question of Law: especially being suche as I was so greatly bound unto. now it is said constantly, that her maiesties extent shall goe forth upon all the lands that th'earll of Lecester was seased of, ether at the time of his death, or in the 24th year of her maiesties raign. whereupon not my stipend onelie will fall: but, which is more lamentable, the whole Colledg of the xii poor ould impotent men for the praesent,

[1] Marginal note (in Burghley's hand?) specifies sources of revenue as Shilton (manor), Napton and Hampton parsonages in Warwickshire and tithes from Woolton and Poulton in Lancashire. In 1919 the Master of the Hospital informed the present writer that the Hospital income was then received from

tithes	Warwickshire	Balsall Hampton Knowle	and land—Warwickshire	Napton Harbury Meerend.
	Lancashire	Poulton Woolton		

shalbe contrayned to beg: and for the time to come, shall be in danger to be utterly scattered and overthrowen.

Beside this, considering that the Hospitall can not obtein of the Countesse of Lecester any whit of the legacie of cc[li], which the Erle of Lecester devised by will in the name of a stocke unto yt: the master is constreyned to laie furth the charges of one half year, before he receyve one penny of the rent appointed unto the Hospitals maintenance. All which he should leese, if the extent should lie upon all the Earles landes without exception, before the half yeares rent be due.

Hetherto also belongeth (the rather to move commiseration towards the Hospitall) that of the cc[li] of yearly rent, xx[li] have bene deteined from the death of the Erle of Lecester, by the unjust dealing of one Mr Ugnoll a riche Citizen of London, and one which comparing his great wealth with the extreme povertie of the Hospitall thincketh to defraude the Hospitall of that xx[li] by year for ever.

I speak nothing here of my continuall labors and sutes in the behalf of the Hospitall ever sithence the death of the Erle of Lecester: whereby contrary to my disposition and bringing up, I have been driven to give attendance here at London in the term tymes: and contrary to that my poor estate doeth affourd, I have bene constreyned to be at great charges for the Hospitall, not hable to make me satisfaction again, having no maner of stock. which truely, but for the desire of continuance of so good a work to posteritie, and duetie towardes the deceassed Lord, that the good work he honorablie and faithfully purposed might not be dispourposed, I would never have indured untill this time.

I passe by also that the living my L of Lecester toke me from, to bring me to this, was (for profit) much better in regard of the charges that this place casteth upon me which th'other did not.

Having thus nakdly laid down the case before the eyes of your honorable compassion besides my moest humble sute onely, in the behalf of the poor, and of my self: I mean not to labor your L. affections, with such reasons as the pitifulnes of the cawse will yeeld: as that which might be offensive unto your h. becawse of other your moest weightie affaires, and hinder us also, whilest the reasons by us alledged, should be short of that, which your L. of your own accord will conceyve for us better then we can laie down for our selves. Wherefore with moest humble and thanckfull remembrance of your h. favor, I have receyved before, together with this poor cawse commended humbly unto your h: I will most humbly (according to my duetie) commend your honorable estate boeth at home and abroad, to the graciouse direction and blessing of god in Jesus Christ our Lord. London the xxiiith of June A° dni 90.

your honors humbly to command

Thomas Cartwright.

To the right honorable and my very singuler good lord the Lord Burghley Lord high Threasurer of England.

APPENDIX XX

CARTWRIGHT TO MICHAEL HICKS, FROM WARWICK, 5TH AUGUST, 1590

Lansd. MSS. LXIV, No. 18, ff. 59–60.

Mr Hickes, not knowing of the place his Lordship imployeth you in, such as wherein you may be a good hand to further the releif of many which are distressed, I went to Mr Skinner. To whom as I confesse my self beholding that he directed me unto you: so yf I had known I would have come strait unto your self, not douting, but the equitie of the cawse yt self, especially that of the poor hospitall, would have wonne favor ynough at your hand for anie furtherance you had bine hable to have set yt forward. Beside that I persuade myself that one fellowship in one Universitie, and one colledg, especially accompanied with profession of the same fayth could so have graced anie reasonable sute of myne towards you, as even for that yt should have had one finger more of yours to lift yt up and praeferd yt to that good issue, which ether in aequitie or in my Lords honorable favor yt might receive.

And therefore first I thank you hartelie for your care for me, which although yt may seeme to late, comming so long after your freindship in that behalf: yet yf you have hard that I was first at your chamber, and after at Mr Skinners house, where I thought to have found you at dinner during the solemnity of the marriage, to th'end to have acknowledged your kindnes that way: I fear not that you should now count yt out of season which was readie then to have bene yeilded in such sort as I would not have departed before I had done yt, yf my tariance for that purpose might have bene as pleasurable to you, as yt would have bene hurtfull to me.

Now according to his L. request I have sent my answer of the praeface unto the Remish Testament, which I did as soone as I could both get yt written out, and withall a convenient messinger. The which, and together with my letter here inclosed, I desire you to deliver unto his L. And out of the same persuasion of your redines to doe me good, I further crave at your hand furtherance of that of my sute which yet remayneth. There are two branches of my humble petition unto his h. th'one for the hospitall, and another for the continuance of myne anuity of 50[ll] by yere out of my L. of Lecesters lands in Warwickshire, according to the tenure of my patent which yet by extremitie of law I cannot enjoy, only because I never brought a writ of Anuitie against the Earles that are deceassed, which was a thing unfit for me, both because yt was never denyed me, and if yt had, yet yt would have bene unfit for a man of my poor estate to contend with such noble personages, especially being so greatlie beholden unto them as I was. for the first branch, my L. hath most honorablie given order that although the hospitall lands be found, yet they should not be seased upon, but left to such uses of the mayntenance of the poore as my L. of Lecester granted them for. In such sort as we should have bene helped much by her Majesties extent, yf certayn thinges taken away from us had by the jurie bene found for the Queenes Ma[tie] which I doubt not would have bene, yf the return of the commission had not bene so speedy, but that we might have had time to produce our witnesses, that my L. died seased of them. And in this behalf I have a clawse of petition unto his h. that yf his honorable place may further help us, he would not therein refuse to stretch forth his further comforting hand unto us as he hath in the rest. for myne own particuler sute, beside th'equitie of my cause, which I have laid down in my first letter unto his L. and now in this unto your self. I have divers other thinges to inforce that equitie: which I durst not trouble his L. with the reading of, but have sent them unto you herein inclosed: desiring you that as occasion serveth you would let my lord know them from your mouth, or otherwise as you shall think good. In myne anuitie I shalbe behinde one full yeare at Michaelstide next. And if yt may not please my L. to grant me the whole, yet would I be glad to receyve whatsoever yt would please him to releive me with. Thus you see my boldnes with you, which I would be glad you might use to me ward in any kind of duties, that my short hand might affourd you. And so with my hartie thanks once again for your kindnes towards me, I commend you to the gratious keeping and blessing of god in Jesus Christ.

Warwick vth of August 90.

Yours to commaund in the lord

Thomas Cartwright.

To the worshipfull and his loving freind Mr Hicks at his Chamber near unto my L. Treasurers howse in London.

APPENDIX XXI

CARTWRIGHT TO BURGHLEY, 4TH OCTOBER, 1590

Lansd. MSS. LXIV, No. 20, ff. 63–4.

The bouldnes I have to bring my sutes unto you (right honorable and my singuler good Lord) rather then unto any other of her ma[ties] moest honorable privie counsell: groweth from hence that I was once a member of that universitie whereof your L. was and yet is the moest worthy Chauncelor. for yf the entwenes of affection unto yt have power to incorporate me into the bodie thereof: I would nothing dowt but I might now make the same claim unto your honorable protection which at any tyme I did when I corporally and actually remayned there.

So yt is therefore yf yt please your good L. that with much greef of minde I have understood of her ma[ties] heavy displeasure against me: in whose gracyouse favor (next under god) the comfort of my life and of those that depend upon me doeth consist. whereof yt may be that at this tyme I stand under th'arrest of her high commission in causes Ecclesiasticall for appearance upon thursday next, when what matters may be objected, I know not: But this I well know that from the writing of my last book which was thirten years agoe I never wrote nor procured any thing to be printed which might be in any sort offensive to her ma[tie] or the state: much lesse had anie hand or so much as a finger in the bookes under martins name. And although there have bene divers bookes of Antimartin printed and red of all that list wherein I have not onely bene moest contemtuously derided as unlearned: but my good name moest slanderously rent and torne in peeces: as to be a diser, and to have thrust one through the leg with a knife, also that I love a cup of sack and suger, and other such like (whereof I thanck god there is not the least suspicion): yet am I hable to make good profe, that from the first beginning of martin unto this daie, I have continually upon any occasion testified boeth my mislike and sorow for such kinde of disordered proceding. ffor my ministry also which I have exercised now almoest five yeares sithence my return out of the low countreys, notwithstanding there hath bene directed to the place of my abode twise or thrise men that have made whole sermons invective against me: yet have I as sparingly spoken of any matter in controversie betwene us and our brethren, as any whatsoever in that countrey having the same iudgment which I have.

Wherefore my moest humble sute unto your Lordsh: is that yt would please yow ether by counsell favor or boeth which the lord hath moest plentifully bestowed upon yow: to relieve me against the troubles that are coming upon me: especially against her ma[ties] heavie displeasure, which I would redeeme with anie earthlie commoditie how dear soever yt be unto me. So with moest humble acknowledgment of my duetie to your good L. I commend the same with all that belongeth unto yow unto the graciouse blessing of god for all increase of pietie and long life with honor unto th'end. This sonday morning the 4th of October A° 90.

your h. moest humbly to command

Thomas Cartwright.

To the right honorable and his singuler good L. the L. Burghley L. high Treasurer of England.

APPENDIX XXII

CARTWRIGHT TO BURGHLEY, FROM LONDON, 12TH OCTOBER, 1590

Lansd. MSS. LXIV, No. 21, ff. 65–6.

The want (right honorable) of fiftie poundes by year, which sodenly have fallen from me and that for anie thing I can understand from your h. unlikely to be recovered: striketh sore upon the maintenance of my self and my poor familie. The fear also of my imprisonment, which I am in expectation of: can not but encrease my greef. howbeyt nether th'one nor th'other, nor boeth together, come so neer me, as the sorowfull message I receyved from your L. mouth concerning her ma[ties] heavy displeasure against me: the point whereof entring into my hart, will there remain: untill I be restored to the ordinary favor, which other her poor subjectes doe enjoye. wherein my poor and base estate doeth muche discomfort me: in that yt being such, as the princes anger maie moest easelie sease upon; yt is not suche, as can easely appease the same. for first I want an eye to see the best waie. Secondly if I saw yt, yet have I no foot to approch to so great a praesence.

Seeking therefore what hope remayned unto me, for obteining that wherein standeth so great and necessarie comfort of my life: Job came to my mynde, who clearing him self against th'accusacion of his frendes, in the duetie of his governm^{t}: affirmeth that he was eye to the blinde, and foot to the lame. which being propounded as a patern to be folowed of men of such honorable place as yours is: I dispaired not, but that my case through my own unhabilitie being destitute and forsaken, might in your h. singuler habilitie obtain some relief. And I would (if so were the good will of god) that from the same mouth I receyved the wound, I might also receyve the salve and remedie thereof. Your wisdome knoweth, how the ministery of all other professions, lieth open to the point and pricks of mens tunges. And the same is not ignorant, that my ministery, throwgh dealing in some matters of controversey amongest the learned of this age is yet more subject to the lash of the tung then many others is. And therefore we have need most humbly and instantly to pray the Lord, that her ma^{tie} and other great personages of honor about her royall person, may be sparing in credit of such thinges, as may be offred in accusacion against us: without which it is not possible for us (me especially) to remain in any good opinion of them, whom yt most concerneth us to be well thought of. Your L. hath bene acquainted ere this, with the shamefull surmises of one Nedham against me, and with his subornation by men whose note and profession is best knowen to your L. which had the sifting of that matter. I dout not but yow remember thend, and that beside the forge of his own head, and others as evill disposed as he, there was not so much as a shadow of that he charged upon me; being the man whome (to my knowledg) to this day I never saw. I could speak of other such like practises against me not long sithence, reaching partly at my life, and partly at my good name, which ought to be protected, if not for my self, yet for the gospels sake whereof I am a minister, and have been many yeares. Yf they were trwe which are spoken, yt is no marvaill if her ma^{tie} be highlie displeased, being such as for the which I should be unworthie to live. And if being sought into (which is that I humbly desire) there shall appear not onelie anie spark, but so much as the least smoke of the thinges which are surmised; let me (hardelie) have thuttermoest of that justice can laie upon me. But these men (no dout) take incoragem^{t} of their practises, from that they understanding of the disgrace I stand in towardes her ma^{tie} and others in honorable place about her: thinck they may practise unpunished whatsoever their heades can devise. I am privie to myne own hart, touching my moest dutifull love, and humble obedience unto her ma^{tie}, and those which are sent of her: and would be glad it were sounded to the bottom and (if yt were possible) there were a window for all to look into yt. Albeit that shall not need, when in my dailie actions (as in a glasse) yt is offered to be vewed of all. Where for that I am not fit witnesse in mine own cause, I refuse not the testimonie of those which are best affected unto the praesent estate through the whole Shire: assuring my self that (recusantes excepted, and others apparantly noted to retein some remnantes of popery) there will be found few, of whome I have not, or could not have the witnesse of a duetifull and peaceable cariadge in the coursse of my ministerie.

And as I wrote unto your h: so I write again: that there is no earthly comoditie I enjoye, with the losse whereof I would not willinglie redeme her majesties good and graciouse favor. whereunto if the giving over of my place in the hospitall may help: notwithstanding I have a patent of yt for life; and yt be the greatest means I have for the maintenance of my self, my wife and five small children: yet if my being there should be (as your L. tould me) offensive to her ma[tie], rather then I would remain with her gracis offence, I will be well content to surrender yt, to be bestowed upon whome yt shall best please her highnesse, and to goe into what corner of her ma[ties] dominions soever she shall command me.

And for those cawses I come to your L. as unto a principall magistrate in the land who as yow have the princes eare for much good to the comon wealth in generall, so if I might enjoye the benefite of yt in my particuler; yt should be a new bond to tie me to your h. for all dueties which (possiblie) may come from so poor a man as I am.

Yf not, there remaineth that unto the trouble of ould age, which is burden enough of yt self; I must also goe heavely under the charge of her highnesse displeasure. Thus, with my humble praier unto god for your lordships continuance with increase in all pietie and honor, I make an end boeth of my letter and of my sutes: which being laid down before youe, I see not what more I can doe, but onelie to await what issue yt will please the Lord to give.

London the xiith of October. A[o] 90.

your honors moest humbly to command

Thomas Cartwright.

To the right honorable and his singuler good lord the L. Burghley lord high Treasurer of England.

APPENDIX XXIII

CARTWRIGHT TO BURGHLEY, FROM THE FLEET, 4TH NOVEMBER, 1590

Lansd. MSS. LXIV, No. 22, ff. 67–8.

Seing your L. of your honorable favour yeelded me that, which your great and manifould affaires might have denied me; in that it pleased yow to will me to certifie the proceedings against me: I am bould (with all humble and thanckfull remembrance of your L. letter to the Archbishop in my behalf) to use the same favour it pleased yow to graunt me: to th'end that I might have that relief which your L. in wisdome and equitie should thinck meet; at the least that the trueth being known I maie not (through contrarie reportes) be deeplier charged then my cariadg in this matter doeth deserve. The summe and short (if it please your h^r^) of the whole proceeding in this matter is, that being offred the generall and indefinite oath to answer to whatsoever I should be demanded touching articles to be objected against me, I returned, that I estemed it contrarie boeth to the lawes of god and of the Land, to require such an oath, especiallie of a minister. In thend they reading unto me the heades and generalls (as they called them) of my articles which were manie in number: I answered that albeit I held not my self bound by anie law in this case to take an oath: yet becawse I perceived that some of the thinges objected were truelie criminall, from suspicion wherof I would be willing to free my ministerie, and therein to deliver myself from the suspicion and jelousie of the magistrate, her ma^tie^ especially (as namely that I had given over my ministerie and taken an other, that I had ordeined ministers, held conventicles and called Synodes) I would be content (if no other proof would suffise) to take an oath, for clearing of my self in them and others like unto them, if anie were: so that I might have th'articles before, with deliberacion and counsell, to give up my answer whereunto I would be sworn. Also that they objected of making of libels, although I esteme (martin set apart) some dutifully and learnedlie written, which they or sum of them (perhaps) may judg libels: yet becawse I professed unto your h. that I delt not in them: least it might be suspected that I had laid down anie untrueth in a letter to a person of such autoritie and honor as yow are: I will not refuse to answer even to that also, which otherwise (excepting that profession of mine) I would never be drawn upon oath to answer: least by my answer upon oath in this case, others might be praejudiced which should refuse to answer upon theirs. And if there were anie article that I refused to answer upon my oath: I offer to give reason thereof; which if it doe not satisfie them, I will submitt my self to the punishment they shall award. And this is the sum of that which passed at boeth their sittinges: a more speciall discourse whereof I have in redines, if it shall please your L. to see the matter unfoulded more at large.

The case being thus laid open before the eyes of your h. compassion, not of me alone, but of the poor people of warwick utterlie destitute of anie tollerable ministerie, to the great grief of manie good men, and triumphe of papist, & such as make a skorn of religion: I commend the cause to your h. and your self to the graciouse direction, praeservation, and blessing of god, whom I moest humblie beseche to add (with much honor) manie yeares unto your life, for establyshment to posteritie, of pietie honestie and peace amongest us. from the ffleet the fourth of november A° 90.

Your h. moest humblie to command

Thomas Cartwright.

To the right honorable and his singuler good Lord the L. Burghley, Lord High Threasurer of England.

APPENDIX XXIV

CARTWRIGHT TO BURGHLEY, FROM THE FLEET, 5TH MARCH, 1590–1

Lansd. MSS. LXVI, No. 48, ff. 118–9.

Seing (right honorable) no mans calling how base soever, houldeth out his cause from your honorable hearing: I am persuaded that myne also who have bene a minister of the gospell about thirtie yeares under her Maiesties most gracious raign, shall have a ready way unto the same. And yf they have accesse, for decay in their outward estate: my trust is that I shall not be denied, for my health, greatlie impayred by imprisonment.

May yt please your L. therefore to understand, that for the space of xviii weeks I have in prison wayted th'end the honorable and worshipfull of her maiesties high Commission would make with me. Now seing no end like to be at the soonest before the next term, and feeling (beside age a disease of yt self) the gout and stoan boeth to grow fast upon me: I am constrayned in divers regards, and that praesentlie because of th'opportunitie and season of the year, apt for the use of remedie against the diseases, to seek for some releif.

for which cause, by letter to one of her maiesties high Commission, to be communicated with others of the same autoritie: I craved that yf yt would not please them clearlie to discharge me, yet upon sufficient suretie of appearing when and where yt should please them to appoynt, I might return to my own house; the rather considering yt had pleased god to visite yt, by the late taking away of one of my children. And yf that should not like them, yet to graunt their lawfull favour of being bestowed in some freinds howse in or about the citie, with such reasonable limitacion, as may stand with comfort, as well in th'injoying of the common exercise of religion, as of th'use of that freedome and change of ayre, which may convenientlie fit the infeebled and weak estate of my body. Of whom I receyved answer (as I did from the L. cheif Justices of the Kings and Common Bench to whom I had particularlie written) that they were ready for their parts to yeild to my sute: saving that they could not convenientlie release that, whereunto some of her Maiesties most honorable counsell had bene made privie, without their liking or consent.

Wherefore my most humble sute unto your L. is for your h. favour and furtherance in this my humble sute for bayle, in such sort as to your L. wisedome shall seeme most convenient: and that yf my best way be, by supplication unto the whole board of her maiesties most honorable privie counsell (wherin yf I may be so bould I most humblie crave your L. wise direction) yt would please your h. to suffer me yet further to be bound unto you, for such assistance in this sute: as I felt the last time I had the like before the same most honorable praesence. Thus with my most dutifull remembrance of your L. favour unto me at all times: I commend the same with all your most weightie affayres, unto the gracious direction and blessing of god in Jesus Christ.

Your L. most humblie to command

Thomas Cartwright.

To the right honorable and his singuler good Lord the L. Burghley L. high Treasurer of England.

(*Endorsed*) v Martij 1590(–1)

APPENDIX XXV

CARTWRIGHT BEFORE THE HIGH COMMISSIONERS, MAY, 1591

Lansd. MSS. LXVIII, No. 50, ff. 114–6.

Th'effect of th'answer of Mr Cartwright before certen her maiesties high Commissioners in causes Ecclesiasticall, namely the B. of London, the Atturney generall, Mrs D. Lewin, D. Bancroft, D. Stanhop and another whom I know not, which two last were silent. The place was the B. chamber secretlie kept, least anie that favoured his cause (as seemeth) should come in. The time upon Saturday last in th'after noon, without (as I have heard) anie warning aforehand, which is usually given to prisoners.

The B. in a long speach charged him, first that he had abused the privie Counsell, by infourming them of diseases wherewith he was not trobled. Secondlie that he with others in a Supplication had abused her maiestie in suggesting that th'othe which was tendred was not according to law, and that yt was given generally without limitacion. Thirdlie upon that M.C. had confessed twice or thrice before that time, that a man might be saved in observing th'order of the Church established by the lawes of the land: he charged him with the vanitie and frutelesnes of seeking further reformacion. adding further that in the greatest matters he and others contended for, they were of the same opinion, that the Papists be, as partlie appeared by th'answears of those that were the thursday before at Lambeth: his and other the BB. agreement with the Papists being (said he) only in some small ceremonies, which notwithstanding he affirmed not to be small or indifferent, when they were established but such as being disobeyed purchased condemnacion. But now that he was to take th'othe which had bene before offred him. Then Mr Cartwright beginning to speak, Mr Atturney took the speach from him, and made also a long speach, th'effect whereof was to shew how dangerous a thing yt was, that men should upon the conceits of their own heads, and yet under colour of conscience, refuse the thinges that have bene receyved for lawes of long time, and that this oath that was tendred was according to the lawes of the land which he commended above the lawes of all other lands, yet so that because they were the lawes of men, they caried alwayes some stayn of imperfection. Also that he was now to deal with Mr Cartwright in two poynts, one was the peace of the land which was broken by him and others through unlawfull meetings and making of lawes. Th'other was the justice of the land, which he and others had offended against, in refusing th'othe now tendred, which (as he said) was used in other Courts of the land. Nether was there anie in his conscience, learned in the lawes that did judge yt unlawfull. So exhorting Mr Car. to take th'othe, the rather for that he being aged should have more experience, and with yt more wisedome, then th'others: he made an end of his speach.

After this the B. requiring Mr C. to take th'othe: he desired that ere he came to th'othe, he might be receyved to answer the greivous charges, which were given partlie against him apart, and partlie against him with others, by Mr Atturney, but especially by his L. whereunto the B. answering that he should not answer anie thing but only to th'othe, whether he would take yt to th'articles which he had seen, and Mr Cartwright replying that yt was a hard course to give open charges and the same verie greivous and yet to shut him from all answer of them: the B. willed him first to answer touching th'oath, and then he should be admitted to answer the charges, which had bene made upon him. Mr Cartw. following th'order the B. had appoynted him answered that the articles being the same, that they upon oath would examine him of, which he had seen before: he had already made answer to them, which he drew forth of his bosome, and withall offred to be sworn unto yt: and that he could not make anie further answer. Whereof when they demaunded the reason, his answer was, that he had layd the cheif strenght of his refusall upon the law of god: secondly upon the lawes of the land, which in some mens judgement professing the skill of the lawes, did not warrant such proceeding. But seeing that he heard Mr Atturney affirm as he did, and that he had no eyes to look into the depth and mysteries of the law: that he would most principally relie and stand (at this praesent) upon the law of god.

Then D. Lewin spake and said that he would be glad that Mr C. should understand that he was greatlie deceaved, in that he called this oath, th'oath *ex officio*: wheras yt is by expresse words derived from th'autoritie of the Prince by a deligated power unto them. Wherefore that he had need to take heed least in refusall of this oath, he refused that which the prince autorized. which speach the B. greatlie commending and willing Mr C. to take heede unto yt, least by refusall of this oath he should directlie oppose himself to th'autoritie of the Prince: Mr Cartw. answered first that in calling yt an oath *ex officio* he did yt by warrant of this Court using no other languag therein then the B. himself that so called yt, and another of the high Commission that was not then praesent, who called yt th'othe of inquisition. The B. denyed that he had doen so: but Mr Cartw. appealing therein to the testimonie of those which were praesent, he was silent. Secondlie Mr Ca. alledged that he had seen Commissions from her maiestie wherin there was no mention of proceeding by corporall oath. Then D. Bancroft interrupting him: Mr C. desired that he might make an end of his answer. But D.B. saying that Mr Cartw. might speak yf he would, and that himself would keepe silence: Mr C. answered that he would give him place, and proceede after with his answer if he remembred yt. So D.B. said that the high Commissions had bene altered as occasion of time, persons and other circumstances required, and that yt was true indeede that the former Commissions had not inserted into them the clause of proceeding by oath but that there were some men discontented with the state had sought curiously into these thinges and observed them, and that Mr C. had taken them from them. Hereupon there fell some jarr betwixt the B. and Mr D. Bancroft, the B. affirming that he liked not that saying of the D. and the D. making yt good, and not afrayd to professe yt. But the B. said that he had bene Commissioner this 30 yeares partlie in Lincoln and partlie in London, and had had alwayes that clause of th'othe inserted: his fear being (as seemeth) least they having used th'othe alwayes, and having no Commission but now of late, should be thought to be in the *praemunire* for that they had used yt so many yeares without warrant. Then Mr C. said that he had a third poynt remayning of his answer to D. Lewin and the B. which was that although they might by words of her maiesties Commission proceede by oath: yet yt followed not, that therefore they might proceede by othe, without anie to accuse, without all limitacion, and without reasonable time of deliberacion and advise what to answer. And therefore he which refuseth not simplie to swear, but to swear in such sort as they required was not as is said directlie opposite herein to the Queenes autoritie. Hereof there was some debating of the difference of this oath from th'oaths tendred in other Courts, Mr C. alledging that although in other Courts the words of th'othe were generall yet that indeede yt was restrayned to some particuler matter, which the deponent knew before he took the oath, and that himself in title of the Hospitall land, before certen Commissioners had taken th'oath which is accustomably given in other courts. After, Mr D. Bancroft charged him that he had taken this oath 20 year agoe, asking why it was not as lawfull now as at that time. Whereunto he answered that the case was not like, for that then there was but one only matter for him to be examined of, and the same well known unto him before, also that he had not so spent his time (he thanked god) but in that so long a space he had learned something, as in some other things, so in this. I heard also Mr Cartw. say afterward that had he not bene interrupted, he could further have answered that he took not that oath 20 yeares agoe but with exception to answer so far as might well stand with gods glorie, and the good of his neighbour. finally that by th'example of divers ministers and others, refusing this othe before him: he took occasion to search further, then otherwise he was like to have doen. Then D.B. said that for so much as everie man which had offended another, was bound to confesse his faut and to reconcile himself: that he should much more doe yt to the Prince. Whereunto Mr C. answering that the case here was verie unlike, and that his generall rule did admitt some exception, which seeming strange to Mr D.B. he required of Mr Cartw. an instance. who answered that if he had spoken evill to one of a third man, which never came to the knoledge of yt: yt should not stand well with the rule of charitie to open this matter unto the person whom he had wronged: considering that so he might (likelie) break the knots of love, which without that confession might have continued whole.

Moreover upon the charge which Mr Atturney repeated, that Mr Cartw. and others had holden conferences and made lawes: Mr Cartwright answered that touching that poynt, his answer was before them, which (being required) he would confirme upon his oath: that is that they never held conferences by anie autority, nor ever made anie lawes by anie manner of compulsion, to procure anie obedience unto them. Also that he and others had expressely testified by subscription, that they would not so much as voluntarily and by mutuall agreement one of them with another practise anie advise or agreement that was contrary to anie law in the land. Whereto Mr D Bancroft replied that autoritie they had none and therefore could not use yt, and compulsion needed not seeing everie one receyved to their conferences must subscribe to be obedient to all orders he and others should set down, so far, as yf they should set down the sense or interpretacion of a place of scripture yt should not be lawfull for anie to depart from that, which, said he, is deposed by three or four. But said Mr Cartwright he might have ecclesiasticall jurisdiction of reproofe suspension excommunication degradation as they had bene openly but most untruly charged to have doen, if ether he or others with him had thought yt lawfull for them so to doe. And for th'other poynt of ether requiring subscription to anie that was admitted, much lesse such a subscription as Mr D.B. spake of:

he protested that nether had he so doen, nor anie that he knew, and that he was redy to make that also good upon his oath.

further D. Lewin moved Mr Cartwright to take th'othe, and then assured himself that the company would take at his hand anie reasonable answer. To whom Mr Cartw. answered that he could not conveniently give anie other answer then that which was before them. To whom when the B. replied that then they would tell him where his answear was short, and require further answer: So said Mr Cartw. shall not th'othe make an end of the controversie, which notwithstanding is the proper use of an othe. Against which Mr D. Banc. excepted, saying that an othe tended to make an end of a controversie, and that yt was strange that Mr C. said that yt should end a controversie, albeyt Mr Cartw. therein alledged no interpretacion but the playn text. But (said Mr D. Bancroft) Mr C. thinck you thus to goe away in the clouds, or to have to deal with men of so small judgment, as not to see what is your drift? doe not we knowe from whom you draw your discipline and Church government, doe not we know their judgments and their practise? which is to bring in the further reformacion against the Princes will by force and armes. Yt is well known how one of the English Church at Geneva (*margin* "he ment Mr Goodman") wrote a book to move to take armes against Queen Mary, and Mr Whittinghams praeface before, and who knoweth not that the Church of Geneva allowed yt[1]. Also we have seen the practise in ffrance. Likewise yt is written in the Scottish storie how Mr Knocks moved the nobilitie of Scotland to bring in the gospell with force against the Queene there, and likewise well known that Mr Calvin was bannished Geneva, for that he would have brought in the Discipline against the will of the magistrate. Whereunto Mr Cartw. replied that his meaning was not to hide him self in the clouds touching this matter as one which had made a playn and direct deniall hereof, wherin yf anie thing were doutfull he would make yt as playn as Mr D. could set that down. But that he now perceyved, that yf others were like minded to Mr D. Banc. all purgacion of our selves by oath (which was now required of him and others) should be in vayn: considering that whatsoever they should depose, yet yt might be answered as Mr D. doth, that they knew our drift well ynough. Moreover that he did the reformed Churches great injury which never had ether that judgement or practise he speaketh of for anie thing that ever he red or knew: that he had red the Scottish

[1] *How Superior Powers Oght to be obeyd....* By Christopher Goodman. Printed at Geneva by Iohn Crispin, M.D.LVIII. Whittingham's Preface is dated from Geneva the 1st of January, 1558.

storie, but remembred not that which he spake of. yf some particuler persons had written from Geneva some such thing as he spake of: yet that yt was a hard jugement to charge the Church of Geneva with yt which by an Epistle set forth by Mr Beza a principall minister thereof had utterlie disclamed that judgement. With this the B. took them up and asking Mr Cartwright once agayn whether he would take th'othe: upon his refusall commaunded an act thereof to be entred. Then Mr C. putting the B. in minde of his promise of leave to answer the charges which were given against him: he answered that he had no leasure to hear this answer, and yf he would answer, he should doe yt by a private letter to the Bishop. One thing beside Mr D.B. undertook to affirm there: that her maiestie had read Mr Cartwrights answer to th'articles. which although yt were abruptlie brought in: yet yt was esteemed that his meaning was thereby to signifie that her Maiestie notwithstanding the knoledge of that answer, would have this severe proceeding against him.

(*Endorsed*) May 1591. Mr Cartwrightes aunsweares to ye Commissioners

APPENDIX XXVI

KING JAMES VI OF SCOTLAND TO QUEEN ELIZABETH, 11TH JUNE, 1591

S.P. Scot. Eliz. XLVII, No. 63.

Richt excellent Richt heich and myghtye Princesse our dearest sister & Cousine. In our heartye...we recommend ws unto you. Hearing of the apprehensioun of Maister Udell, Maister Cartwright, and certaine utheris, Ministers of the evangele, within youre realme, of quhais gude eruditioun and fructfull travellis in the Kirk we hear a verye credible commend, howsoevir that their diversitie from the Bischops, and utheris of youre clergie in materis tutching thame in conscience, hes bene a meane be thair dilatioun to work thame youre myslykyng at this present, we can not, weying the dewetye quhilk we aw to sic as ar afflicted for their conscience in that professioun, bot be oure maist affectuous and ernist lettres interpone ws at youre hand, to any harder usaige of thame for that cause. Requeisting yow maist earnistlie, that for oure cause and intercessioun, it may pleas yow to lett thame be relevit of thair present strait, and quhatsumever further accusatioun or persute depending on that ground, Respecting baith thair former merite in the furth setting of the evangell, the simplicitie of thair conscience in this defence, quhilk can not weill be thrallit be compulsioun, and the greit sclander quhilk culd nocht failzie to fall out upoun thair further straiting for any sic occasioun, quhilk we assure ws, youre zeale to Religioun besydis the expectatioun we have of youre guid will to pleasyr ws, will willinglie accord to oure Requeist, having sic pruiffis from tyme to tyme of oure lyke dispositioun to yow in any maters quhilk ye recommend unto ws. And thus Richt excellent richt heich and myghtye Princesse our dearest Sister and Cousine we commit yow to the protectioun of the almyghtye. From oure Palace of Halyrudehous the Elevint day of Junii, 1591. And of oure Reigny the 24th.

Youre most loving & affectionatt brother & cousin

James R.[1]

APPENDIX XXVII

CARTWRIGHT TO ANTHONY BACON, FROM THE FLEET, 23RD MAY, 1591

Add. MSS. 4115, ff. 2 *b*–4.

My Duty humbly remembered unto you: It may please you to understand, that of my Speech with her Ladyship some hour & half this was the Effect; that after signification of your dutiful Regard unto her Ladyship, as in all other things, so in this of not doing any thing therein, that may offend her, with this Addition, that as there is a Duty of yours towards her Ladyship in indifferent things rather to live to her liking then unto your own; so is there Duty of her Ladyship towards you in the same things by so much the more sparingly to use her Authority, as both by Age & by Instruction, especially out of the Word of God I esteemed you able to govern your own ways. Wherein what farther I added, I forbear to write: only my humble Desire unto you is, that (as my Hope is you will) you would stir up your self to answer the good opinion, which your religious & wise Discourse gave me Occasion to conceive, & so far as I might upon so small a time,

[1] The 11th June was a Friday and not a Sunday as Waddington states (*Hist.* p. 67). Baker's transcript of the letter is in *Harl. MSS.* 7033, f. 328. *v.* Fuller, *C.H.* bk IX; *A.R.* lib. IX, § 19.

to make report of unto her Ladyship. I spake something also of that you might be interested in the Want of such Servants, as were acquainted with your Ways, especially in regard of such Employment, as your long Travel had fitted you, for I say, upon signification hereof, & much Speech passing to & fro, the Conclusion was, that touching George, upon his profession of Repentance & sorrow for his Misbehaviour before me (she meant no doubt any other, that might be able to have some good Descretion of a good appearance of his Repentance) she would not be against your receiving him again. But for Mr Lawson, in regard of his suspected Condition of Religion, of his swearings, of his Incontinence, which she had great cause to suspect, & in regard of all things going back with you since his coming unto you, which were before his coming very acceptable to her and to all your Friends, more particularly in regard of your excessive Expences after his coming, & long Abode in the Country, she would never condescend that by her good will you should receive him. Whereunto when I replied, that they were Charges, that I was not able to give answer unto, & therefore for the better tryal of the Truth moved her, that she would be content to hear you & himself, what satisfaction might be given unto her touching these Charges, whereas, if it pleased her, I would not be unwilling to be present, thereunto she yielded first, so it were after some further Recovery of your Health: butt afterwards her aggrieved mind against him, whereby she was so impatient of hearing him, that she could not without her hart think upon him, called that back again; adding, that as thus advised he should never have her consent. And fearing, that that might give you any hope of lingering this sute for him, to say the Truth, she willed me, that I should conceal that from you, which notwithstanding trusting upon your Wisdom if well using of it, I have written unto you, that you might either give over that Sute, that hath so small hope of being obtained; or else if it should so greatly concern you you might think of some stronger & more able stand to work it, than mine is. Thus with my humble thanks unto yourself for keeping open the Door of your acquaintance unto me still, & to Mr Francis for so ready an opening of it unto his, I commend you both with your Affairs into the gracious keeping & blessing of God in Jesus Christ. Fleet the 23d of May 91.

Your Worships to command in the Lord

Tho. Cartwright.

APPENDIX XXVIII

CARTWRIGHT TO BURGHLEY, FROM THE FLEET, 2ND JUNE, 1591

Lansd. MSS. LXVIII, No. 52, ff. 119–20.

Yt is (right honorable) our desire and most humble sute, that your L. might understand the trweth of the things we stand charged with before her maiestie in her moest h. court of the Starr Chamber: to th'end, that as we refuse not to bear the punishment of that we shall be found to have deserved; so if it shall appear unto your h. that in our moest secret meetinges and consultations which we never thought we should have comen to th'examinacion of, we have caried ourselves with all dewtifull regard, not onely to her excellent maiestie, but also to the lawes of the land; we maie by your honorable meanes, first and especially be eased of her maiesties high indignation, which by untrwe informacion hath bene conceyved against us, and then in the second place, maie escape the hard course, which is threatned against us. And becawse your L. manifould affaires will not easelie suffer yow to turn over the long bookes of boeth sides: I am bould to send unto your L. an abstract in parallel wise, th'answer of the right side directlie opposed to thinformacion of the left hand. Thus with moest humble remembrance, and acknowledgment of my speciall bond and deutie to your L. I moest humblie commend the same, to the graciouse protection and blessing of god in Jesus Christ: whome I doe likewise dailie praie unto, that after long life with muche honor, he would give unto yow the crown of glorie, that he hath promised to geve unto all those which love his coming, and strive lawfullie therefore. ffleet the 2d of June 91.

Your h. moest humblie to command

Thomas Cartwright.

To the right honorable his singuler good Lord the Lo. Burghley L. High Treasurer of England.

APPENDIX XXIX

CARTWRIGHT TO LADY RUSSELL, FROM THE FLEET, 13TH AUGUST, 1591

Lansd. MSS. LXVIII, No. 58, ff. 131–2.

I was glad (right honorable) that that which I might trulie doe, I did also agreeable unto your honors liking touching the mention of your worthie father in my letters I wrote unto you. Howbeyt to commend you by your father is ἀπὸ τῆς σκιᾶς ἐπαινεῖν τὸν ἀνδριάντα ἢ ἀπὸ τῶν ὀνύχων τὸν λέοντα, which is a slender prayse when there are better notes then these are. for besides the mark of learning in yourself rare in your sex, that is also worthie commendacion that you favour those which are learned or rather (meaning my self) which desire to be learned. Yet this is not that wherein your praise doeth or ought to consist; as that which although of all other parts of the flower of the grasse tarieth longest, yet fadeth it away, and is no better then a summer flower, not hable to resist the sieth of death, yf by the winter storme of sicknes or of old age it be not before praevented. So that the fame and report which riseth from thence hath no more steddines then the voyce which is committed to the ayr or the writing engraven in the water. Godlines only is that which endureth and maketh to endure such as have gotten possession of yt. for which although I might persuadedlie commend your h. as having heard somewhat of others, and somewhat experienced my self: yet I had rather exhort you to a further encrease therein, then enter into the prayse of that which the Lord hath alredy begunne. for beside that yt wanteth not perill in slacking our course towards the goall of the crown of glorie when we are entred into opinion of some good advancement that way; the prayse of that which is good in us is seldome safe unlesse yt be mingled with the reproffe of that which remayneth still amisse and shall remayne as long as we be compassed with this body of sinne. which latter when yt belongeth not unto me that know not your h. wantes, as I have bene made acquaynted with the good things which the Lord god hath planted in you: I easilie see a law of silence layd upon me in that thing which men (suters especially) doe willinglie pursue. Albeyt here I cannot passe by your singuler and verie rare favour towards me, whom yt pleased to become (after a sort) a suter unto me that your h. might doe me good by preventing through your honorable offer that which partlie my poor estate, and partlie the small meanes of accesse by anie dutie of myne sent before did shut me from. Yet forget I not your honorable and kind usage of me when I was with you some five yeares past, so far as yt pleased you to call in two noble plants your daughters and in my hearing to tell them that I was a man whom for good respects you favoured, and willed them for the same respects as anie occasion might serve to regard. But (alas) good Madame, what encoragement could I take thereby, when looking into my self I see so litle that might bear out that opinion you had conceyved of me. Howbeyt seeing yt pleaseth you in your honorable disposition thus to break upon me and (after a sort) to enforce your honorable assistance towards me: yt were to foolish and rusticall a shamefastnes to refuse so honorable a hand reached forth unto me. Wherefore with verie humble and thanckfull acknoledgement, I lay hold of your honorable favour, which although yt should come alone and unaccompanied: yet is yt that for which I will take my self greatlie beholden unto your honor. Then I lay hold of the fruites of your favour as far forth as the same may be convenient for your estate in your honorable mediation towards such as yow shall thinck good especially toward my singuler good Lord the L. Treasurer. Of whom what to desire I know not. His h. knoweth the pitifull case wherin we stand. I trust also he knoweth how innocent we are of the thinges we stand charged with, if for his great and weightie affayres it hath pleased him to inform himself of the proceeding with us. We thought the sute of ministers upon reasonable bayle to return to their houses (amongst whom some of us have preached the gospell xxx yeares of her Majesties raign) would not have bene refused, being that which often times is yeilded unto fellons, and hath bene often to recusant Papists. We being therefore refused herein, I know not what we should make sute for. Agayn yt astonisheth me that we are not easilie suffred to come to her Majestie by our most humble supplicacion. In the Empire of Rome there was not the vilest servant to whom th'Emperours Image standing in the middest of the market place was not a good sanctuary yf he once laid hold of yt. And with us yt hath alwayes bene far better that by supplicacion the poorest subject might come not to the image of our most gracious Prince, but unto the Prince herself. These thinges make me that (as I said) I know not what to desire. But yf I might understand what were likely to be granted, although yt were never so litle, and wherof yt would please his honor to be an honorable mean: there is no ease so small but we would gladlie and thanckfully embrace. Now beside the common calamitie of us all: mine hath something by itself, for all th'other prisonners for this cause having accesse unto them from all their freinds: the warrant of the high commission restrayneth me from all saving my wife and such as have necessarie buisnes with me, which thing I would be well content with, yf it were afourded me accordinglie. ffor (yf I might) I would not for divers causes have many come unto me. But the Warden whether esteming thereby to gratifie the BB. and others whom he thincketh this will be pleasing to, or of his own hard disposition towardes me construeth yt more strictly agaynst me then the meaning of the High Commission was. for I take that upon experience of the multitudes that visited me the last time I was in prison (as much to my misliking as theirs) they sent the warrant of this restraynt. Yet dare I not complayn of his hard usage of me more then other keepers to their prisonners lest he might use that for a mean to cause the BBs to restrayn them also of th'accesse of their freinds. But yt is a thing which I can (I thanck god) well bear, and therefore will not troble your h. with the sute of so small a matter. Agayn yf I should make sute in regard of my infirmities the gout especially which gayneth on me: yt is like that the Counsell is informed that I complayned of them without a cause. for the B. of London speaking openly that I had therein abused her Majesties privie Counsell, would not (although I humblie beseeched him) suffer me answer one word unto yt. for yf he would I could have alledged the testimonie of the phisicion who had witnessed yt under his hand, which th'Arch Bishop taking from my wife would not restore agayn. I could have brought also good testimonie how having but small comfort from the phisicion that phisick would doe me good in prison (as that which the ayr yt self would give the check unto) yet was I fayn to take divers strong purgacions one within three or four dayes of another, to such a pulling down of my body as I was scarce hable to bear myne own cloathes. Now to doe all this without cause of disease I thinck might be rather judged frenzie then hipocrasie. And surely I was so far from being ambitious in laying down my infirmities before the bourd of her Majesties most honorable privie Counsell, that I did not once make mention of the Schiatica, wherewith notwithstanding I have bene exercised manie yeares. But I perceyve I have to much given the raignes to the greif of my minde out of the which my penne hath bene verie liberall to utter my complayntes unto your h. Wherefore I will make an end leaving all to your honorable consideracion what to keepe to your self and what to communicate to his Lo. what to ask or what to leave unasked: that is to say what you thinck his L. can convenientlie and with his good liking effect, making no dout but that his h. standeth favorablie inclined towards me. Yf I obteyn nothing els yet I most humblie pray his L. that I may remayn still in his good opinion that he hath conceyved of me at least so far as to be free from those misdemeanres, which the LBB. doe surmise. And thus with verie humble thanckes for all your honorable favor and care of me: I commend your h. with your whole houshold and children especially unto the gracious keeping and blessing of god in Jesus Christ.

ffleet xiiith of August. Ano 91.

your h. humblie to commaund

Thomas Cartwright.

To the right honorable his verie good Lady the La. Russell.

Endorsed by Lady Russell, who sent the letter to Burghley: Good my Lord rede this thorow and do what good yow can to ye poore man.

APPENDIX XXX

PURITAN PRISONERS (CARTWRIGHT, FEN, ETC.) TO BURGHLEY, 4TH DECEMBER, 1591

Lansd. MSS. LXVIII, No. 60, ff. 135–6.

To the right honorable and their singuler good Lord the Lo. Burghley L. High Treasurer of England.

Having a purpose (right honorable) by most humble peticion, to come unto the LL. of Her Majesties most honorable privie Counsell, for bayle (agreeable unto law as we are informed) untill their LLs shall please to call us to further triall of our innocency in that we are charged with: we thought good, beside our peticion to their LLs. to addresse our most humble sute particulerlie unto your Lo. not only as Def(endan)tes to a principall judge of the Court where our cause dependeth, but also as children of the Land to a cheif father of the same, which taketh no pleasure in this our afflicted estate, but will (as we are perswaded) tenderlie way it, so far as anie aequall course of justice may releive it: for we nothing dout, but your h. in discourse of reason, and in experience of the state of studentes can easilie discern that a yeares imprisonment (which we all with a surcrease have suffred) will strike deeper into our healthes, having regard to our bringing up, then some number of yeares of others, whose bringing up hath bene other, and which have followed otheir trades of life. It is well known that divers Papistes, not only denying her Majesties lawfull autority, but giving the same to a stranger, yea to the sworn enemy of ours and of all Christian Princes: have yet receyved favor of freedome from their imprisonment. There is never a one of us, but hath bene sworn to her Majesties Supremacie, and some of us (upon occasions) divers times. And if we be douted how we stand affected this time, notwithstanding we have given no cause (as we are persuaded) of that suspicion: yet to satisfie th'autority under which we live, we wilbe ready to take th'othe agayn. And notwithstanding some (not so well affected towards us, as we are towards them) doe suggest that we carrie some other interpretacion with us, then the meaning of the law is: yet have we verely no other, then all the reformed Churches have, in the dutifull acknoledgement of th'authority of their severall Magistrates, none other then her Majesties own admonicion in th'end of her injunctions, and the xxxviith article of the Convocacion, and especially the most autentike and classicall writers of this Church, both Bishops, Deanes and other men of note, [who] with priviledge with allowance with oversight of the BB. themselves, and finally with great commendacion of all, have written of that poynt. ffinally we may affirme and that with trueth to be justified, that we hold no other, then that some of the cheifest of them whose hand is against us in this cause of further reformacion, have set down, when they ether quietlie have written of this poynt, or have buckled with the Papistes, which most falsely and slanderously surmise th'enriching and adorning of our most gracious Soveraign with the spoyle of Almightie God, and of Christ his sonne: howsoever writing ἀγωνιστικῶς against us, and put on by mislike of the persons against whom they write, they have crossed and contraried their own judgement. And thus craving pardon of our boldnes in deteyning you from your so weightie affayres of watching continually for the good of this commonwealth, and expecting that favor from your L. which ether equitie, or a regardfull consideracion of our afflicted estate may require: according to our most bounden dutie (wherin we take our selves to be specially tide to your L.) we will not cease daylie to commend your most honorable estate unto almightie god for long continuance amongst us, with great increase of pietie and honor joyned thereunto.

Your L. most humblie to commaund

Prisoners in sundrie prisons, in and about the City

Thomas Cartwryght
Humfrey Fen
Andrew King
Daniel Wyght

John Payne
Edward Lord
Edmund Snape
Willm Proudlove
Melancthon Jewell

APPENDIX XXXI

CARTWRIGHT TO LORD GRAY, FROM THE FLEET, 15TH JANUARY, 1591–2

Lansd. MSS. LXIX, No. 40, ff. 93–4.

Whereas I have bene and continwe an humble suter to your good L. that by your h. mediation I may obtein some relief of my long and toediouse imprisonment: yt may please your L. (for better furtherance of it) to understand that my fellow prisoners in the Clinck and White Lion have all from his Grace this degree of libertie graunted upon their own bond of 40 li onely upon this condition alone to return to their prison at night; that they may goe to church upon the Sabboth daie and to such as alledged speciall cause of busines for it any one other daie in the week; namely to Mr ffenne and Mr King.

ffurther also it may please your L. to be informed concerning the rest of the defs, my self and the Deponentes in our cause according to the note which I have heer inclosed. Moreover where I hear that some misinform against me, that I should boeth write something undutifully touching thexcommunicating of her Majestie, and also be in a plot for thexecution of the same: I beseche your L. to hear my trwe answer to as an (*sic*) unjust an accusation as ever was devised against any. for I unfainedly protest to your L. in the praesence of almightie god the searcher of the heartes, that I am so far from being any partie or privy to any such execution, as that suche a thing never entred once so much as into my thought. As for the rest, how meanly soever they that have so informed, esteme of my discretion: yet I assure my self, it shall never be proved by trwe note of my writing or speeche, that I have undutifully and in unseemly maner treated at any time of excommunication or ever applied it to the person of a Prince generally much les praecisely to her Majesties roiall person. Wherefore I assure my self that when this privie surmise shall be examined (which I moest humblie desire it maie be to the uttermost) it will fall out to have no more trueth then the publick accusation that I had given over my ministerie and taken a nwe, and that my hand was in martins libels: where I of the clean contrary part boeth mainteined my ministrey against some excepting unto it as no ministery, and was ever an enemy to martins disordered course.

Such doctrin also as I taught of excommunication, ether by writing many yeares agoe or sithence by preaching, is no singuler opinion, but the same which the universall church of god and particulerly this our own church of England boeth now houldeth and alwaies heretofore: as in our moest humble supplication praesented to her Majestie in all our behalves is more fully declared. Except it be in the excommunication of the Emperor Theodosius where I maintein that it was nether doen nor to be doen by any one man, Ambrose or other, but by Synod or Councell. And his grace affirmeth it to have bene doen by Ambrose onely; yea and setteth furth the commendacion of the same, as may appear in our bookes. Other difference I know none.

Which being so I humblie beseche your L. as to your wisdome shall seem convenient, to use your honorable meanes for my libertie or baile, as it may be obteyned for ease of this heavy affliction and for dealing in such busines as I have to doe, which greatly import boeth my own estate and some of my frendes, and especially the hospitall whereof I have charge, and which is diversly defrauded by men that pull from it. Thus I moest humblie commend your L. and the rest of your h. house to the graciouse keping and blessing of god in Jesus Christ. ffleet the xvth of January. 91.

Your L. humblie to command

Thomas Cartwright.

To the right honorable and his verie good Lord the Lo. Gray.

APPENDIX XXXII

CARTWRIGHT TO BURGHLEY, FROM THE FLEET, 25 JANUARY, 1591–2

Lansd. MSS. LXIX, No. 41, ff. 95–6.

My dutie most humblie and thanckfully remembred unto your Lo. trusting upon your wisedome which is not ignorant of the hart of a Prisoner: I am bold once agayn to desire your honorable favour for the releif, which may seeme good to your Lo. in regard of the causes I laid down in my last lettre. I made known unto your Lo. the cawse, why hetherto I forbare to make sute unto his Grace, namely for that (in my Lo. Chancellors life) he denied me that favour, which he graunted unto other of my fellowes in the same case. Howbeit if your Lo. shall thinck my sute unto him to be my way: I have praepared my peticion, which I will ether praefer or forbear, as I may anie way understand your Lo.

pleasure therein. Thus with acknoledgment of my bound dutie, for your honorable favour from time to time, and most humble desire of continuance of the same: I moest dutifullie commend your Lo. for increase of all pietie and honor, unto the gracious keeping and blessing of god in Jesus Christ.

from the ffleete xxvth of January. 91.

Your Lo. most humblie to commaund

Thomas Cartwright.

To the right honorable and his singuler good Lord, the Lo. Burghley Lo. High Treasurer of England.

APPENDIX XXXIII

CARTWRIGHT TO BURGHLEY, FROM THE FLEET, 31ST JANUARY, 1591–2

Lansd. MSS. LXIX, No. 42, ff. 97–8.

Seing (right honorable) my thanckfull dutie to your Lo. (through my poor estate) consisteth in words alone, the same being of no use in lettres, but of hinderance to your waightier affayres: I mean to spend them rather in daylie prayers unto almightie god, for that return and recompence of his gracious blessings, which may best sort with your honorable estate, especially which may praepare you to a comfortable appearance and account of your great stewardship before the sonne of god, the Judge of all the world.

Through your Lo. honorable word praeparing his Grace afore-hand, I obteyned the same time for myne own affayres and the Hospitalls, which other my fellowes have for their own alone, that is one day in a weeke, beside the Sabboath: yet is it with limitacion of the Term time, theirs being not bounded at all. Howbeit it pleased his Grace to give my wife so good words, as might seeme to raise me up unto some hope, ether of a quite discharge, or of an easie renewing of this or like releif, if I remayne here, in this toedious and pitifull estate. Now to hinder what-soever I might have looked for that way, there is (as I have bene given to understand) a greivous complaynt come to the Board of her Majesties most honorable Privie Councell, of one which in his prayers before the poor men of the Hospitall, should utter undutifull speaches, against the Councell, the Magistrates and Judges of the Realme. The trueth is, that knowing what judgement he hath in these causes in controversie, and withall the small witt to guide himself in the same: I can easilie thinck that there may slip from him some indiscreet speech. But I leave it unto your Lo. grave consideracion, whether this matter might not have bene ended in the Town or Countrie, without bringing it to so great a praesence, had not there bene a purpose, by his side to have thrust at me, rather than at him, and by my stroke to have placed one Mr Bourdman, who having a benefice for which he receyveth a cli at Allchurch by year, hath joyned thereto the Vickaridge of Warwick, which is but xxli yerely, where he yet resideth, being put in hope by some of note (as I hear) that unto those two benefices, the Hospitall also shalbe united. And where they would cast th'envie and displeasure of it upon me (as in a thing supposed to be doen by a man of mine, and one which hath learned it of me): may it please your Lo. to understand, whatsoever he hath said in that kind, it is not with anie allowance of myne, which may therby appear in that having daily for the space of six yeares used to pray with the familie, twice or thrise in the day: yet shall I be hable to proove, that in all that time, nether he nor anie other could ever learn anie such example in me. My man also he is not, but because he maried a poor maide out of my howse, who served me above a dosen yeares, my wife when she came up, placed her to look unto the howse, with the guidance whereof she had bene best acquaynted. And because he was to lodg in the howse with his wife, she desired him to say daylie prayers for the houshold. Moreover after I heard, that he would continew prayers in such lenght or unseasonable time, as that the old men could not goe to the service in the Church, I gave him warning that ether he should amend his faut or I would dismisse him. Touching this praesent case, I hearing of it but two dayes agoe have alredy sent my letter to discharge him, that he deal no more in the prayers or other goverment of the Howse. I had purposed in the beginning to have complayned of the strange practises, which are and have bene used to bring me into hatred: but my necessarie answer to this praesent matter hath made me so long, that I dare enter no further. Wherefore most humblie craving the continuance of your Lo. lawfull favors: I commend the same to the gracious keeping and blessing of god in Jesus Christ.

ffleete the xxxith of January: 91.

Your Lo. most humblie to commaund

Thomas Cartwright.

To the right honorable and his singuler good Lord the Lo. Burghley Lo. High Treasurer of England.

APPENDIX XXXIV

CARTWRIGHT TO MICHAEL HICKS, FROM THE FLEET, 2ND FEBRUARY, 1591–2

Lansd. MSS. LXIX, No. 44, ff. 101–2.

Mr Hickes, upon some small acquaintance with yow in Trinitie Colledg in Cambridg I am bould to make a great sute for my Lo. honorable favor touching my enlargment. I have good proof already of his honorable disposition, and mediation also that waie. Onely I would desire yow to take the best opportunitie of time to be a remembrance unto his L. in that behalf. The cawses which may move yow to sollicite my case are the same which (I dout not) move his L. to commiseration towardes me: the long and tediouse imprisonment I have endured growing now well towardes a year and a half: the excessive charges thereof rising by th'imprisonment and by the charges of the copies of our depositions which (without the favor of the Clarkes and writers of the court) would have come to xxxli, beside the charges of fees to our Counsell, which we cannot but in duetie have regard of, and make offer of: the desolate estate of our families uninstructed and ungoverned by this mean: not to speak of the necessitie that divers of us have of taking physick this spring of the year, my self especially, in regard of divers infirmities, the remedy whereof, having bene attempted in prison, hath bene so checked by the evill ayre of the same that the physicians refuse to administer any more during this restraint. Now where my sute unto yow overweigheth my acquaintance, or any other cause in my self, let me be not evill thought of, if I seek the supply and counterpoise thereof in the love yow bare to my brother Stubbe, which would have poured all the ointment of the interest of his friendship with yow upon my head, if he had lived. Thus with my dutifull remembrance of yow ceassing any further to trowble yow: I commend yow to the graciouse keping & blessinge of god in Jesus Christ. ffleet ffebr. 2. 91.

Yours to command in the Lord.

Th. Cartwright.

having sent his L. a brief of all our whole cause I am bould to praesent his L. with another, wherin there is a fourth column added, conteyning an answer of all those thinges, that are of any moment against us in this cawse, desiring your hand to deliver it, yf it seem good unto yow.

To the Woorshipfull and his loving freind Mr Hickes one of the Secretaries to the right honorable the Lo. Treasurer.

APPENDIX XXXV

PURITAN PRISONERS (CARTWRIGHT, FEN, ETC.) TO BURGHLEY, 1st MARCH, 1591–2

Lansd. MSS. LXIX, No. 45, ff. 103–4.

Knowing (right honorable and our singuler good Lord) your favorable inclinacion to our freedome from this long and toediouse imprisonment: We were bold in the time of your Lo. sicknes, which we have in divers respects great cause to be sorie for, by our wives to send our peticion to his Grace of Canterbury the copie wherof we have here inclosed. By him we were directed to Mr Attorney generall as to one of whom we were to receyve the cautions and condicions of our deliverance, which it pleased his G. to terme by the name of our submission. Which message was greivous unto us, as that which seemed to impose upon us a confession of guilt in the thinges we are charged with, whereof hetherto we are nether acknown unto ourselves nor can learn by others, whom we have earnestlie intreated to tell us their knoledge in that behalf: Yet to understand the trueth thereof, we sent our wives to Mr Attorney, but found him out of Town, without hope of return before the next Sabboath. Now therefore we come in most humble sute unto your Lo. that it would please you as hethertowards, so now in the shutting up of the matter to stand our good Lo. that we may have Bayle, without further drawing us upon such condicions, as his G. answer giveth us cause to suspect untill such time as it shall please their honors to call for us. for if our libertie be tyed to such condicions, as we cannot undergoe, unles we would say otherwise then is trueth, and burden our own consciences before the Lord: your Lo. may easilie see, in th'experience of our refusall of th'othe ex officio, for which we have indured so long and so heavie imprisonment, that we shalbe so far from the peace, into the hope wherof we are by your Lo. honorable meanes and most comfortable answer given unto our wives latelie brought, that our bonds therby will grow more heavie and hard then before, in such sort that if it were not for conscience towards god, which causeth us rather to desire to be guiltles, then to have libertie: it were better for us (in worldlie respect) to be acknown unto our selves of some crime committed in this behalf, that by a free confession, our deliverance from imprisonment might be more readie and open unto us. If we had transgressed some of the lawes of the land, wherof our consciences set in the praesence of god doe not accuse us: yet seeing it playnelie appeareth by our own answer upon oath, and by the deposicions of witnesses both on her Majesties and our behalf, that we had speciall care in our meetings to keepe our selves within obedience of the lawes, our transgression therein being of ignorance, may in honorable equitie finde th'easier pardon. And although our transgression had bene more greivous: we leave unto your Lo. honorable consideracion whether our so long and heavie imprisonment, being laid in ballance with our faut may not seeme proportionable thereunto. There have bene sithence we came to prison divers Papistes known enemies of the state of this Church and commonwealth, delivered without revocacion of anie error of theirs. And it is universally granted to anie ether papist or scismaticke, that upon promise of coming unto the Church, they may injoy the same freedome that other of her Majesties subjects doe. Our hope is therefore that we which not only our selves come to Church, but labour to th'utmost, boeth to intertayn men in the fellowship of the Church, and to reduce others estranged from it: shall not be more hardlie delt with then they, by enforcing anie confessions or submissions, not standing with the testimonie of our consciences. But this unto your Lo. is (as in proverbe) γλαῦκες εἰς 'Αθήνας, which is hable to speak more for us in this behalf, then we for our selves. Yet is there fallen out of late which maketh us the bolder to importune your L. for it hath pleased th'allmightie to visite some 4 or 5 of us, by reason of our long imprisonment, and lack of convenient ayre, wherof some are both sore and dangerously sick. Nether can the rest looke for better, unles by speedie deliverance we meete with that mischeif through the remedy which this time of the year especially offereth. Wherefore with our most thanckfull remembrance of your Lo. honorable favors towardes us: we commend the same with all your weightie affayres to the gracious direction and blessing of God in Jesus Christ.

Your Lo. most humblie to commaund

Thomas Cartwright	Edward Lord	Edm. Snape
Humfrey Fen	Melancthon Jewell	And. King
Daniel Wyght	Willm Proudlove.	

To the right honorable and their singuler good Lord the Lo. Burghley Lo. High Treasurer of England.

(*Endorsed*) 1 Martij 1591.

APPENDIX XXXVI

CARTWRIGHT TO BURGHLEY, FROM HACKNEY, 21ST MAY, 1592

Lansd. MSS. LXXII, No. 51, ff. 142–3.

The Persians (right honorable) as Xenophon writeth punish an unthanckfull man as a criminous person, which sinne if it were so amongst the heathen, it ought much more to be of evill report amongst christians, taught in a far better school of thankfullnes then they were. But amongst all other it woolde be of the fowlest and blackest note in the ministers of the woord: who teaching thankfullnes to others, shoolde (in beinge unmindfull) receive against them selves a deepe condemnation. Wherefore havinge felt of your Lo. honorable favour before in prison and nowe much more in some libertie which I enioy: I thought it my part assone as I gott out of the Phisicons handes (as out of a seconde prison) to have testified unto your L. my dutyfull remembraunce of so great a benefitt, whereof your L. hath bene so singuler a meanes. Which thinge havinge touched, least in desire of endevoringe some duty, I shoolde be founde trooblesome unto your Lordship, and iniurious to others, which by your honorable travailes inioy their quiet: that which remayneth I will supplie with my dayly prayers unto almighty god; that together with longe lyfe he woolde dayly blesse your Lordship with encrease of all other his heavenly blessinges, which in his infinite wisdome he knoweth best to agree with your honorable callinge.

ffrom Hackney. 21 of May 92.

Your L. most humble to commaund

Thomas Cartwright.

To the right honorable and his singuler good Lord the Lorde Burghley Lord Highe Treasurer of Englande.

APPENDIX XXXVII

CARTWRIGHT TO MICHAEL HICKS, FROM GUERNSEY, 20TH SEPTEMBER, 1595

Lansd. MSS. LXXIX, No. 71, ff. 174–5.

Praier being as it were a bunch of keyes whereby to goe to all the treasures and storehouses of the Lord, his buttries, his pantries, his sellers, his wardrops and whatsoever is needfull ether for this or for the life to come: it was a Christian wisdome in yow to enquire after the skill and knowledg of it: and giveth yow some comfort of being led by the same spirit th'apostles of our Sav. Christ were, when they desired him to teach them how to pray. Houbeit you held not the same tenor of wisdome in addressing your self to me for instruction and direction in it: as to one that findeth no contentment in mine own praiers and therfore unhable to give satisfaction to others: especially unto yow, which having so many formes of excellent praiers printed before yow, seek some further help then those worthy praiers will afourd yow. Therefore I know not whether it were my fault (notwithstanding my det of a greater duetie then this unto yow) so easely to yeeld unto your request in this behalf. But having yeelded I nothing dout but the perfourmance of it lieth so hard and heavy upon me, as without it the charge not onely of unthanckfulnes, but also of lightnes and vanitie will cleave unto me. Wherefore if it be short of that yow looked for, there is cawse yow should laie some blame upon yourself that made no better choise: I had purpose (reserving the same heads) to have drawn yow a shorter form to have used, when the suddenes of your affaires would not suffer yow to be so large. Howbeit it is a thing that your self may easely doe and the praesent time, which was short, would not suffer me to doe. Thus being ready ether in this or any other thing which lieth in me to shew forth my thanckfull remembrance of yow: I commend yow to the graciouse keeping and blessing of god in Jesus Christ.

Guerensey the xxth of Septem^r^ 95.

Yours to command in the Lord

Thomas Cartwright.

To ye worshipfull his loving frend Mr Hickes one of the Secretaries of the right honorable the Lord Threasurer of England.

(*Endorsed*) 20 Sept 1595. Mr Cartwright to me With a Form of Prayer, sent to him according to his desire.

APPENDIX XXXVIII

CARTWRIGHT TO CHRISTOPHER YELVERTON, FROM WARWICK, 12TH NOVEMBER, 1603

Sloane MSS. 271, ff. 21 *b*, 22.

I have beene (right Woorship[ll]) intreated by those (I confesse) I owe much duetie unto, I would become petitioner unto you, for your good and helpfull hand in the common cause of the Church. In which request to me, as I can easly see their care and zeale for reformation of thinges amisse, also their good and sounde Judgment in discerninge wisely of your woorships sufficiencye everye way to forwarde the cause we labour about: so I cannot but impute some oversight in them, that they seeke ffarre of, for that they might have had nearer home. for what am I? or who am I? yt I should mediate this matter more then other? Yf he were fitter for it which is more beholden unto you, & hath received sundrye kindnesses at your hande, I should in that respect (happely) be more fitt then other, & farther fittnes then this I nether knowe nor doe acknowledge. Neverthelesse because I knowe the suite is good, and I am intreated by thos I could beare to be commanded by in such a cause, I humblye praye you, I may without your offence, or brande of selfe conceipt, desire you that in the love you have these many yeeres borne to the trueth, you would take the paynes to drawe a supplication to his Ma[tie] in the behalfe of the Nobilitie and Gentrye of that shire, as for a reformation generally of thinges amisse, so more particularly, for the removeall of th'ignorant, idle & unresident ministerye, and consequently the pluralities, the subscription other then the statute requires, the burthen of Ceremonies, the abuse of the spirituall Courtes, especially in the censures of suspention & excommunication, & the oeath ex officio & such other of that kinde, your worship understandeth to be contrarye to the Lawes of the lande, for which cause I have sent here inclosed a short survey of sundrye the abuses, of the spirituall Courtes, that by confrontinge them with the lawes of the lande, you might the better understande, the Lamentable servitude the Church is in to these harde lords. And yf the lord would enlarge your christian heart so farre, as in subscribinge the same supplication as the principall weather of the flocke, to goe before the rest: as I am perswaded the rest would followe with great chearefulness: so we alreadye bounde unto you for the good dueties you doe to the church, & common wealth of our lande shall yet have a straighter bande dayly in our prayers to remember you, & yours before the lord, for all manner his gracious blessinges, especially those of a better life, he knoweth you have neede of. Thus after myne & my wives humble & thankfull remembrance of yours and my good Ladyes kindnes unto us, I commende you boeth and yours those especially which doe more neerely concerne you, to the gracious keepinge and blessinge of god in Jesus Christ.

Warwicke the 12 of November 1603.

Yours humbley to commaunde

Thomas Cartwright.

To the right Woorship[ll] Sr Christopher Elverton knight one of his Ma[ties] Justices of the Kinges bench.

APPENDIX XXXIX

CARTWRIGHT'S LAST WILL AND TESTAMENT, 10TH MAY, 1603. PROVED 23RD FEBRUARY, 1603–4

Somerset House, Bk. Harte, fol. 26.

In the name of God Amen. I, Thomas Cartwright, maister of the Hospitall of the Earle of Leicester in Warwick through the gowte and the stoane lieing rather uppon my weake, than my sick bed, make this my last will and testament in manner and forme following, first I bequeath my sowle into the hands of Almightie God who hath redeemed me with the moste pretiouse bloud of his owne and onely sonne Jesus Christe my Saviour and redeemer from all my sinnes, And my bodie to be layed up in the church-yard of the place where at it shall please the Lorde to call me out of this life withoute pompe and superstition used in the Popish Sinagogues in times past, to the uttermost of that the same maie be doen with the peace of the church, where it shall please the Lorde I shall be buried, Item I give to the use of poore schollers in Cambridge that shall imploy them selves to serve the Lorde in the Ministery of the gospell the somme of twentie marks of good and lawfull money of England, to be distributed by the advice of maister doctor Mountague and maister Lawrence Chaderton, if they be then residing in the Universitie, or else by such, as my wife shall make choice of with the advice of my sonnes maister Lockey and maister Wilmer, which money shall be distributed within one haulf yeare next after my departure, Provided such as are of Trinitie, Saint Johns, and Sidney College shall be preferred, if in povertie and likelines of being serviceable unto the church, they equall others, Item I give to the poore of Warwick to be distributed within the tearme aforesaid the somme of fortie shillings of lawfull money of England, Item towards the orderly and honest finding of my brother William Cartwright during his naturall life fourtie shillings to be paid yerely by even porcons at the ffeaste of the annunciation of the blessed Virgin, and Saint Michaell The Archangell, orderly and honest I meane that he be kepte from wandring and rainginge abroad from place to place, without which honest and orderly keeping of himself I give nothinge, Item I give to my sonne Samuell towards his maintenance yerely in all good learning that espetiallie that may best fitt him to the Ministerie of the worde whereunto it mai please the Lord to call him twentie pounds of good and lawfull money of England, And if my executors shall recover the debts due by obligacon from Masters Hunte Nevell and Pointer, And also if it fall out that my wief marrie againe, Then I will that my Executors shall paie to my sonne Samuell the somme of one hundreth pounds to be delivered into his hands if he be one and twentie yeres of age or above, or else to be left in the hands of my sonnes Wilmer and Lockey to his use, Item I give to my daughter Martha for her better advauncement in marriage the somme of two hundred pounds or above, that my Executors shall think meete to be paied within two yeres next after marriage: soe that she be married by the advice of her mother or of my sonnes Lockey and Wilmer, if my wife die before assuraunce. Item I give to my sonnes and daughters in token of love towards everie of them a ringe of the value of tenn shillings. To my brother John togeather with my best cloake fourtie shillings of good and lawfull money of England, To every of my servaunts over and above their wages five shillings. The rest of all my goods, debts and chattells undevised I give to my loving and faithfull wife Alice Cartwright, And of this my last will and Testament appoint the executors my sonnes Master Wilmer and Master Lockey. Written the tenth of May in the yeare of our Lorde 1603. Thomas Cartwright. Sealed and subscribed in the presence of us Hercules Cleveley, William Maycock, Richard Gibbard.

APPENDIX XL

LAST WILL AND TESTAMENT OF ALICE CARTWRIGHT, 5TH NOVEMBER, 1614. PROVED 11TH MARCH, 1616–7

Somerset House, Bk. Weldon, fol. 25.

In the name of God Amen. I, Alice Cartwright of Totteridge in the countie of Hertforde Widdowe being weake in bodie but of whole and sounde memorie I give therefore prayse to God doe make and ordeine this my last will and testament this fifte daye of November in the yeare of our Lorde one thousand six hundreth and ffowerteenth in manner and forme followinge, ffirst of all most humblie comendinge my soule into the handes of my God whoe hath redeemed me by the most precious bloud of his onelye Sonne my Lorde and Saviour Jesus Christe from all my sinnes and from all the most righteous judgements due to me for the same, And my bodie to be buried by the discretion of the executors and overseer of this my last will in an assured hope of a most joyfull and blessed resurrection to life eternall at the last daye. As touchinge my worldlie goods wher with God hath blessed me, my will is that within one month next after my buriall the somme of ffortie shillings shall be distributed amonge poore people of good reporte for religion and honest conversation by the good discretion of myne Executors. Also I doe give unto my brother Master Francis Stubbe for a token of my love and remembrance of him halfe a duccatt. Also I doe give unto my Nephewe Samuell Wilmer my broad Silver boule and to my Nephewe John Lockey a dozen of my Silver Spoones. And to my nephewe Robert Woodrof my guilt Silver Salt Seller. And of this my last will I doe ordaine and make my three sonns in lawe Andrewe Wilmer, William Lockey and Nicholas Woodrof Executors. And I doe give unto my said sonne Wilmer and to my daughter Marie his wife my downe Bedd and bolster and such other Bedds bolsters, pillowes, coverletts Ruggs, doun Canapies and blanketts which I have remayninge in his howses custodie or possession And all those darnix hangings which I have heretofore delivered unto him. And as for all the rest and residue of my houshold stuffe linnen and apparrell which are in the houses custodie or possession of my said sonne Wilmer And also my great chest remayninge in the house custodie or possession of my saide sonne Lockey and all the goods which are locked or conteyned in the said chest I will that they be equallie parted betweene my said sonns Lockey and Woodrof and my daughters Anne and Martha their wives. And as for such beddinge household stuffe and other goods which I have heretofore delivered unto my daughter Woodrof and which are remayninge in the house custodie or possession of my said sonne Woodrof my will is that they shall soe rest and continue unto my said daughter Woodrof at her disposinge. And as for such beddinge houshold stuffe and other goodes which I have heretofore delivered unto my daughter Lockey and which are remayninge in the house, custodie or possession of my said sonne Lockey my will is that they shall soe rest and continue unto my said daughter Lockey at her disposinge. And I doe appointe and make my nephew John Shardelowe of Shimplinge in the countie of Norffolke gent Supervisor of this my last will, And I doe give to him for a token of my love and rememberance of him halfe a duccatt. In witnes whereof I have signed, sealed and published this my last will and testament the day and yeare first above written revokinge and renouncinge all former wills by me here before made. In the presence of these whose names are heare subscribed. Alice Cartwrighte. Signed sealed and published the fifte daye of November above written after the blottinge out of the word (October) and interlining over yt the worde November over the fourth lyne of this last will and testament in the presence of us, Roger Hodsden, the marke of Roberte Page, Robert Northe.

INDEX

Items appearing in the list of references and abbreviations are marked with an asterisk.

PRINTED BY W. LEWIS AT THE CAMBRIDGE UNIVERSITY PRESS